Postwar

Foreign Policy

Preparation

1939–1945

GREENWOOD PRESS, PUBLISHERS
WESTPORT, CONNECTICUT

67011

Library of Congress Cataloging in Publication Data

Notter, Harley.
  Postwar foreign policy preparation, 1939-1945.

  Reprint of the 1949 ed. published by the Dept. of
State, Washington, which was issued as its Publica-
tion 3580, and as its General foreign policy series 15.
  Includes indexes.
  1. United States--Foreign relations--1945-1953.
2. United States--Foreign relations--1933-1945. I. Ti-
tle. II. Series: United States. Dept. of State.
Publication ; 3580. III. Series: United States.
Dept. of State. General foreign policy series ; 15.
[JX1417.N65 1975]   327.73   75-16854
ISBN 0-8371-8276-X

DEPARTMENT OF STATE

Publication 3580

General Foreign Policy Series 15

Originally published in 1949 by the Department of State,
Washington, D.C.

Reprinted in 1975 by Greenwood Press,
a division of Williamhouse-Regency Inc.

Library of Congress Catalog Card Number 75-16854

ISBN 0-8371-8276-X

Printed in the United States of America

Contents

PART III
Advanced Preparation
Mid-Summer 1943–Autumn 1944

PART IV
The Unfinished Business Winter, 1944–Spring 1945

APPENDIXES

Postwar Foreign Policy Preparation, 1939-1945

Department of State publication 3580

ERRATA

p. 263: 3d line: date should be March 22 instead of March 24.

p. 316: Footnote 16, line 3: first page number should be 225 instead of 22

p. 335: Footnote 31, line 3: volume number after book title should be II.

p. 360: Last line: replace footnote 18 with "[16] *Ibid.*, XII, 531–33.

p. 440: Footnote 48, line 5: the first half of the line should read "republics, of Argentina, and of Poland."

p. 717: "Dumansky, Constantin, 43" should be "Oumansky, Constantin, 43"

Introduction

THE PRESENT volume originated in the desire expressed on April 19, 1946, by President Harry S. Truman that a record be written of the structure and conduct of the extraordinary preparation of our postwar foreign policy as made in the Department of State during World War II. At the direction of Acting Secretary Dean Acheson, now Secretary of State, this request was carried out as rapidly as circumstances permitted. With the President's consent and approval, this record is now published for the information of the American public.

The preparation spanned the years from the beginning of the second World War in 1939 until the United Nations Conference on International Organization had convened at San Francisco in 1945. Its broad objective was to enable the United States to participate effectively in the solution of the vast and complicated problems of international relations that would confront the world after the defeat of the enemy. It was an effort, first, to determine, during the emergency of war, sound bases for future United States foreign policy designed to safeguard and advance our vital national interests as a great power. This determination involved searching analysis of our interests in regard to every aspect of international relations, in all areas of the world, under the circumstances probable or possible at the end of the war. It was an effort, second, to develop on these bases, and after thorough examination of the nature of relations among nations and the forces at work within and between them, the most desirable policies to adopt toward all the foreseeable problems on which the United States might or would have to take a position. This work as a whole required consideration of the political, territorial, military, economic, and social conditions essential to enduring peace and to human progress in an era when the philosophies and desires of peoples, the relationships and power positions of states, and the scope of United States concern in international cooperation had all become subject to profound change.

The process of preparation on a problem passed through a series of stages before final decisions were made. Although some variation occurred in the different fields, there were in general four stages and in a number of important instances, five. The first was determination and analytical examination of the problems engaging United States interests so far as these could be anticipated. The second was con-

1

sideration of alternative solutions for these problems, weighed in terms of how well each solution would accord with all United States immediate and long-range interests. The selection of the preferred alternative solution and its formulation as a policy recommendation followed. In the next—the fourth—stage, decision on the policy recommendation was reached, constituting the position to be taken by the United States in international negotiations on the problem.

Where the formulation of joint policy proposals among the major powers was involved, as occurred in several fields, the preparatory work as such was completed only in a fifth stage, which comprised the negotiations among those powers. In such negotiations, initial policy was refined and developed in the light of the positions taken by other governments. These negotiations, from the standpoint of the preparation, were a part of the process of reaching an agreed position in which United States policy was expressed jointly with that of other major powers. This volume describes such negotiations to the extent that they were integral to the process of preparation. Negotiations for final international agreement, and the subsequent process of national decision on the agreement reached, were otherwise steps outside the scope of this study. These other steps, like those by which policy decisions were made and applied in specific current and day-to-day situations, constituted operations and were a part of the usual processes of government. The preparation described here took full account of such current developments as they would or might affect the situation to be faced after the war, but it was on this postwar situation and its problems that the preparation was concentrated.

This volume primarily answers the question: How was postwar foreign policy formulated? It is a record of the special structures, methods, working relationships, and other germane aspects of the extraordinary process instituted by the Department of State and the President during the war for the specific purpose of preparing for the peace. The presentation of the substantive ideas and views on foreign policy thus developed has not been attempted except where these are essential to an understanding of the various stages through which the preparation as a whole passed. Furthermore, this volume, while it reflects to some extent both the conduct of United States foreign relations during the war and the events with which the preparation was in some ways interwoven, is neither a study of such relations nor a history of the period. It includes an account of the many interdepartmental activities of importance in the preparation, though without attempting to portray the individual postwar efforts of the several other Departments and agencies of the Government, or the relationships between domestic and foreign policies in such work. Similarly, it does not attempt to cover in detail the consideration of future policy undertaken in the Department of State itself as a normal part of the operating responsibilities of its regular divisions and offices.

Since the extraordinary preparation was extensive and inherently complex, the record is set forth in narrative form. It is written on the basis of the relevant documents—thousands of minutes of meetings, memoranda, reports, telegrams, drafts and revisions of studies, notes on personal ideas and suggestions, as well as matured papers containing recommendations and proposals—and does not constitute an edition of the documents themselves. So far as documents publicly available are quoted, they are cited in footnotes; citation of unpublished documentary materials has been considered impractical. Obviously in some instances documents of such recent date continue to be within the scope of current international relations and of peace settlement negotiations not yet completed, and their publication is therefore precluded. Illustrative and other selected papers emanating from the preparation, or bearing directly on it, appear however as appendixes to the text.

The first effort of preparation for the postwar period was begun during the late autumn of 1939 in the realization that the war would profoundly affect the fundamental interests of the United States. This preliminary preparation, described in Part I, was conducted largely by operating officials of the Department of State working as an Advisory Committee on Problems of Foreign Relations. After the attack on Pearl Harbor and the entry of the United States into the war, special arrangements both as regards personnel and organization were decided upon for intensive exploration of the problems that would have to be dealt with at the conclusion of hostilities. The new instrumentality for this basic preparation was the Advisory Committee on Post-War Foreign Policy, established by direction of President Franklin D. Roosevelt with Secretary of State Cordell Hull as Chairman. The Advisory Committee was composed of members drawn from private life, the Congress, the Department of State, and other Departments and agencies of the Government, and was assisted by a specially constituted research staff. The Advisory Committee's work constituted a unique national endeavor directed toward the determination of the future course of the United States in world affairs. Its influence and many of its methods continued throughout the remainder of the preparation. The main period of its activity, 1942–summer 1943, is described in Part II. The multiple processes used for advanced preparation and its progress between the summer of 1943 and the autumn of 1944 are described in Part III. The completion of the unfinished business of the preparation in the closing months of the war is described in Part IV.

Because of the informality and flexibility of the preparatory effort during most of its course, unusual measures have been taken to assure the inclusiveness and accuracy of this record through its review by a large number of the superior officials, private citizens, and staff members who took part in the effort itself. Aside from present officials of the Department of State, these reviewers included former Secretary of State Cordell Hull, Ambassador Myron C. Taylor, Isaiah Bowman, Leo Pasvolsky, Hamilton Fish Armstrong, Ambassador James Clement Dunn, Judge Green H. Hackworth, Stanley K. Hornbeck, Benjamin V. Cohen, and from the former research staff for the preparation, George H. Blakeslee, William Adams Brown, Jr., Bernard F. Haley, and David Harris. Copies of the manuscript were also sent to former Secretary Edward R. Stettinius, Jr., and to former Under Secretary Sumner Welles, whose health, however, did not permit them to undertake detailed review.

The book was written by Harley A. Notter, Adviser to the Assistant Secretary for United Nations Affairs. Research and editorial assistance was given by a small staff comprised of Mrs. Virginia Fox Hartley of the same Office, Denys P. Myers of the Office of the Legal Adviser, and George Verne Blue of the Division of Historical Policy Research. Miss Edna R. Fluegel, Mrs. Alice M. McDiarmid, and William Diebold, Jr., also assisted in the early research. All of these had previously participated in the extraordinary preparation itself. Further research aid in selected fields was contributed by cooperating officers in various parts of the Department, particularly by Daniel M. Braddock of the Foreign Service, J. M. Colton Hand of the Division of Commercial Policy, John Parke Young of the Office of Financial and Development Policy, and Mrs. Esther C. Brunauer of the United Nations Educational, Scientific and Cultural Relations Staff of the Department of State.

June 26, 1949.

Part I

THE BEGINNING OF PREPARATION
1939–1941

࿇

" . . . If the warfare now in progress on other continents becomes intensified, its effects will fall more and more heavily upon us, as well as upon those directly engaged. If peace should come, we shall be confronted, in our own best interest, with the vital need of throwing the weight of our country's moral and material influence in the direction of creating a stable and enduring world order under law, lest the relations among nations again assume such a character as to make of them a breeding ground of economic conflict, social insecurity, and, again, war.

"It is a comforting thought that since the outbreak of hostilities in Europe, our people have shown a remarkable degree of unity in meeting the vast complexity of problems thrust upon us by that catastrophe. Only thus can we keep strong within, insure the safety and security of our own Nation, and make our appropriate contribution toward helping the world as a whole to seek and find the road of peace and progress. Never before was there greater need in this country for resoluteness of spirit, clear thinking, breadth of vision, and willingness to deal with the grave problems before us in the light of those basic and crucial considerations which affect the lives of each and every one of us today, and which will be decisive in shaping our Nation's future."

——Excerpt from statement by Cordell Hull,
Secretary of State, January 1, 1940,
Department of State Bulletin, II, 11.

CHAPTER I

Initial Effort Toward Preparation
December 1939

THE OUTBREAK of war in Europe on September 3, 1939, had been foreshadowed by a succession of crises, each more acute than the one before. It was met by the United States Government with measures of neutrality instituted swiftly, and almost automatically. These measures flowed from the laws then in force. Despite the evident fact that neutrality of thought could not be asked again as in Woodrow Wilson's day, these measures were supported by the determination, alike of officials and private citizens, that our country should remain a neutral nation—and, however uneasily, at peace.

There were no solutions ready to hand, however, for the basic problems of future United States foreign policy raised by a major European war. Serious dislocations in established prewar international relationships would be the outcome in any event. Responsible officials of our Government, looking back over the eight years of mounting tensions that culminated in the invasion of Poland on September 1, 1939, and looking ahead to the war's consequences, were undecided on the course to pursue.

American preparation for the postwar period grew out of the history and foreign relations of the American people; it also grew directly out of the experiences of the interwar years and out of the experiences of the war itself. A largely new and evolving policy was required, not a set of fixed dogmas or a hurried improvisation of plans at the close of the war. Continuous re-evaluation of the issues and revision of thought as events unfolded became essential.

AMERICAN EFFORTS TOWARD PEACE

UNDERLYING the German aggression upon Poland, to which the British and French responded with declarations of war, was a grave deterioration in international relations. This extended even to deception in the making of formal treaties on vital matters and a disregard of these

7

treaties after they were made, thus destroying confidence and challenging the very bases of international order.

The twenty-one years between the Armistice signed at Compiègne in 1918 and the invasion of Poland in 1939 can be divided roughly into halves, the first seemingly hopeful for the cause of peace, the second increasingly hopeless.

In the first eleven years, the apparent trend toward the realization of mankind's quest for peace had been signalized by various constructive developments. Economic improvement seemed in process. The Washington Conference on the Limitation of Armament, November 12, 1921–February 6, 1922, appeared to constitute a successful prelude to general disarmament. The Locarno Pact, initialed October 16, 1925, appeared to bulwark peace in Western Europe. The obligation of the Kellogg-Briand Pact, signed August 27, 1928, to settle disputes by none but pacific means had been accepted almost universally. Further efforts toward disarmament were underway: A Preparatory Commission for Reduction and Limitation of Armaments to formulate proposals for a future general conference began work, with United States participation, in 1926. A naval conference was held by the United States, Great Britain, and Japan during the summer of 1927. Then the London Naval Conference of the same three powers, France, and Italy convened in January 1930, and a treaty among the first three was successfully negotiated. These in large measure constituted direct efforts among states to strengthen the bases of peace.

The principal international effort to establish peace and to maintain it after World War I was centered in the League of Nations, and the League in the twenties appeared strong enough to survive the difficulties it might confront, though it had been designed to function with the United States as a member and that membership had been declined. Nevertheless, the United States gradually undertook to cooperate with the League in the economic and social fields of its work, and increasingly also in the disarmament field.

To an extent not yet fully calculable, however, the outworking of counter influences also marked this first period. The war itself had had revolutionary implications both within and among nations—manifested not alone in the tendencies toward violence that cropped up in various parts of the world and not alone in communism with its disruptive methods and its revolutionary outlook. A growing cynicism toward the accepted order in many states manifested itself in questioning, denial, or contempt of the precepts of Christianity and democracy. Certainty, loyalty, and unity in regard to moral principles applicable in relations among states and between the state and the individual were widely shaken. Insecurity had grown in the presence of increasing economic and political nationalism, of critical problems left by the war, and of underlying stresses produced over decades by the lag between national and international economic, social, and political policy on one hand and swift technological development and desires for a higher standard of living on the other. No program of constructive economic and social action agreed upon among all the victor powers of 1918 had come into being. Fascism had emerged and dictatorships had come into power in a number of states. Suicidal national economic policies were widely practiced. Tariffs and some of the international loans of the period, particularly those of large powers including the United States, worked away from, rather than toward, stabilization of international conditions. The policies of isolation pursued, for different reasons, by the Soviet Union and by the United States of America were among the other counter influences that prevailed.

These counter influences became dominant late in the decade, and the apparently hopeful trend of the twenties was reversed. The change came as the great economic depression and its consequences settled down over the lives of men and of states, as the militant resurgence of Germany and militarist expansionism in Japan gathered momentum, and as tensions sharply mounted from the revolt launched against the established international order by powers restricted by it.

The decade of the thirties was destined to see in the weakness of many peaceful countries the expression of their fear of war. The forces of aggression with their erosive ideology pitted their growing military strength, move by move, against the weakly armed and disunited forces seeking to keep the peace.

Japan attacked Manchuria September 18, 1931, and, though not decisively checked by the League of Nations, gave notice on March 27, 1933, of its intention to withdraw from that organization. Germany's resignation from the League over the question of armaments followed (October 14, 1933). Italy conquered Ethiopia between October 3, 1935, and May 5, 1936. Germany occupied the demilitarized Rhineland March 7, 1936. The Spanish Civil War, which opened July 17, was to provide a three-year battle-training course for the aggressor powers. Germany joined with Italy to form the Rome-Berlin Axis on October 25, 1936. One month later Germany joined with Japan in an Anti-Comintern Pact.

The intervals between aggressions thereafter shortened. Japan intensified its undeclared war on China with the incident of the Marco Polo Bridge near Peiping July 7, 1937. Italy signed the Anti-Comintern Pact November 6 and left the League December 11. Germany occupied Austria on March 11–13, 1938. The Munich Pact between France, Germany, Italy, and Great Britain and the consequent cession of the Sudetenland by Czechoslovakia to Germany came on

September 29. Full German occupation of Czechoslovakia was effected March 14–16, 1939. Albania was invaded by Italy April 7. Germany made public demands affecting Danzig and the Polish Corridor, April 28, and sought assurance of conditions for a safe move on Poland by a treaty of nonaggression with the Soviet Union August 23, 1939.

In this span of eight years from 1931–1939 the American Government attempted to strengthen peace in every feasible way short of involvements that might prejudice United States detachment. Apart from specific efforts directed toward individual countries such as those made by Secretary of State Henry L. Stimson in the case of Japan in 1931–32, repeated approaches were made to the basic problems involved in the maintenance of peace.

The first was in the field of disarmament and took the form of proposals presented to the General Disarmament Conference at Geneva which convened several times during the years February 2, 1932–April 13, 1935. When the Geneva Conference failed in 1933 to produce a general disarmament agreement, this Government in 1934 proposed a separate treaty dealing with the manufacture of and international traffic in arms. When that failed and when failure to reach any general agreement continued at the London Naval Conference December 9, 1935–March 25, 1936, this Government concluded with Britain and France on the latter date a conditional treaty of qualitative limitation of armaments. This treaty, however, was futile from the standpoint of general disarmament. It had become clear during the course of these efforts, when forms of aggression were multiplying and becoming more complex and insidious, that general limitation of armament would be possible only if political and economic conditions essential to international peace existed.

American participation in the economic activities of the League of Nations was increased during this period, and the United States became an active member of the International Labor Organization. The Export-Import Bank was established in this country to facilitate foreign trade, and a particular effort was made in these years toward the elimination of discriminatory trading practices, which acted as a barrier to world trade. At the International Monetary and Economic Conference in London June 12–July 27, 1933, the economic disintegration wrought by the depression in the United States and abroad operated to preclude any substantial progress toward this end. There was fundamental disagreement on certain basic issues involved; for example, on whether or not exchange stabilization should precede efforts to reverse the downward trend of prices. Yet in the Trade Agreements Act of 1934, the United States took a step that gave promise of improving economic conditions and therefore of contributing toward peace. That promise began to be realized as numerous reciprocal trade agreements were made, involving acceptance of the principle of nondiscrimination as the basis of trading relations and reducing the effects of discriminatory bilateral trade arrangements, which were increasing in number and scope on a scale hitherto unknown. Fundamental as this program was, however, the most important of the trade agreements, that with the United Kingdom, was not concluded until November 17, 1938. The critical state of international relations by that time, with the outbreak of war less than a year distant, gave little opportunity to test the effects of this agreement, or the impact of the program as a whole on the state trading systems of Germany, the Soviet Union, and Italy.

These efforts were paralleled by attempts on the part of the United States to exert its influence toward preventing hostilities through the example of its peace program in the Western Hemisphere, through its neutrality legislation, and through diplomatic approaches and official statements as threatening situations emerged.

The United States peace program for the Western Hemisphere was initiated at the Seventh International Conference of American States at Montevideo, December 3-26, 1933, and was further developed at the Inter-American Conference for the Maintenance of Peace, Buenos Aires, December 1-23, 1936. It was designed to implement the Good Neighbor Policy enunciated by President Roosevelt, and consisted of a series of agreements and arrangements for political and economic collaboration among the twenty-one American republics on the basis of accepted principles of peaceful conduct. The elaboration and implementation of this program was carried out at subsequent inter-American conferences as the world situation grew more threatening to the peace of this Hemisphere.

The Neutrality Acts of 1935, 1936, and 1937 were concrete expressions of American determination to remain at peace in a world where assurance of peace was declining. It was, moreover, the hope of the proponents of this legislation that it might act as a deterrent to war by serving notice on the rest of the world that the resources of the United States would not be readily available to foreign nations should they resort to armed force. Though the President signed these successive acts, disagreement in judgment existed between the executive and legislative branches of the Government on the methods embodied in this legislation to avoid involvement in war.

The neutrality legislation as developed by 1937 sought to preserve this country from war through such measures as an embargo on arms and on loans to belligerents, "cash-and-carry" provisions in the case of trade with belligerents, and other restrictions relative to travel on belligerent vessels, arming of American merchant ships, and belligerent use of American ports. The legislation was applicable impartially to victim and aggressor alike and had both mandatory and permissive

features.   It was the inflexibility of action under this legislation regardless of circumstances, and the lack of discrimination in the treatment to be accorded victim and aggressor that were opposed by the
executive branch.[1]
Secretary of State Cordell Hull and President Franklin D. Roosevelt began in 1935 to give emphatic warning to the country that
Americans could not "look without concern on the darkening clouds
around" and that danger confronted the future of mankind as a whole.[2]
In 1936 the President emphasized that the situation facing the
"peace-loving nations" was one of gravity "which has in it many of
the elements that lead to the tragedy of general war." The Secretary stated the view "that the fabric of peace has been worn perilously
thin" and that "the dominant trend" was "full of menace." [3]
In 1937, as international anarchy spread in Europe and the Far
East, Secretary Hull on July 16 issued a statement on the "Fundamental Principles of International Policy", which he communicated to
all other governments in an effort to obtain universal acceptance of
these principles.   In this statement, the Secretary said:

"This country constantly and consistently advocates maintenance
of peace.   We advocate national and international self-restraint.
We advocate abstinence by all nations from use of force in pursuit
of policy and from interference in the internal affairs of other
nations.   We advocate adjustment of problems in international
relations by processes of peaceful negotiation and agreement.   We
advocate faithful observance of international agreements.   Uphold-
ing the principle of the sanctity of treaties, we believe in modification of provisions of treaties, when need therefor arises, by orderly
processes carried out in a spirit of mutual helpfulness and accommodation.   We believe in respect by all nations for the rights of others
and performance by all nations of established obligations.   We
stand for revitalizing and strengthening of international law.   We
advocate steps toward promotion of economic security and stability
the world over.   We advocate lowering or removing of excessive
barriers in international trade.   We seek effective equality of commercial opportunity and we urge upon all nations application of
the principle of equality of treatment.   We believe in limitation and
reduction of armament.   Realizing the necessity for maintaining
armed forces adequate for national security, we are prepared to
reduce or to increase our own armed forces in proportion to reductions or increases made by other countries.   We avoid entering
into alliances or entangling commitments but we believe in cooperative effort by peaceful and practicable means in support of the
principles hereinbefore stated."

[1] *Peace and War: United States Foreign Policy 1931–1941* (Washington, 1943),
Department of State publication 1983, pp. 266–72, 313–14, 355–65.

[2] Addresses by the Secretary of State, June 17, 1935, and by the President,
Nov. 11, 1935, *ibid.*, pp. 259, 289.

[3] The President's address to the Congress, Jan. 3, 1936, and the Secretary's
addresses of Sept. 7 and 15, 1936, *ibid.*, pp. 305–7, 332, 334.

Although sixty nations, including Germany, Italy, and Japan, accepted these principles without reservations, the trend of events was such that Secretary Hull felt obliged to conclude by August 1937 that Japan sought to dominate Eastern Asia and to extend her "control through the Pacific islands to the Dutch East Indies and elsewhere" and that Germany was "equally bent" on dominating Continental Europe.[4] "If those days are not to come to pass—" the President stated in October, "if we are to have a world in which we can breathe freely and live in amity without fear—the peace-loving nations must make a concerted effort to uphold laws and principles on which alone peace can rest secure." He warned that "the peace of the world and the welfare and security of every nation is today being threatened".[5]

Grave concern was being felt whether in coming months the Western Hemisphere could remain free from aggression. In December 1936 foundations for a common neutrality policy among the American republics in the event of war had been laid at the Buenos Aires Conference, where the principle was enunciated that any act susceptible of disturbing the peace of any one American republic affected all the American republics. At the Eighth International Conference of American States at Lima agreements were made on December 24, 1938, to give effect to the continental solidarity of the American republics in defending themselves if necessary and to provide for meetings of their Ministers of Foreign Affairs informally, and if need be, swiftly. Earlier that year, on August 18, President Roosevelt had assured Canada that "the people of the United States will not stand idly by if domination of Canadian soil is threatened by any other empire." [6]

The ability of nations desiring peace to protect themselves against attack was also put in question. In the United States, a building program to bring the American Navy up to treaty strength had been begun in 1933, and furthered by the passage of the Vinson naval bill in 1934. A slight expansion of the Army was authorized in 1935. Germany, however, was rearming feverishly; Italo-German ties were being strengthened; and at the end of 1934, to be effective in two years, Japan had denounced the Washington and London naval treaties. After Japan's refusal at the Brussels Conference in November 1937 to cooperate in finding a satisfactory peaceful settlement for the conflict in the Far East and after the sinking of the United States gunboat *Panay* on December 12, concern over the adequacy of the American capacity for defense led in 1938 to further strengthening of the armed forces. This was only a minimum program, however, which did not

---

[4] *Ibid.*, doc. 111, p. 424.

[5] Address Oct. 5, 1937, *ibid.*, pp. 383–84, 387; cf. also statement by Secretary Hull, July 16, 1937, *ibid.*, pp. 370–71.

[6] Address at Kingston, Ontario, Department of State *Press Releases* (Aug. 20, 1938), XIX, 124.

keep pace with mounting needs as crisis ominously piled on crisis abroad.

The crisis occasioned by the German occupation of Austria in March 1938 was followed by the Munich crisis in September, when the weakness of peaceful efforts toward just settlements in the face of determined aggression was unmistakably demonstrated. Appeal after appeal was made at that time by this Government to Germany but without result. Tension between the United States and Germany was further heightened by the expression, through the recall of Ambassador Hugh R. Wilson in November, of American moral condemnation of the anti-Jewish program of Nazi Germany. In the Far East, where the Sino-Japanese conflict continued, Japanese interference with American rights and interests increased. As the last year of the period between the wars approached, it appeared to the United States Government that the world stood "at a crossroads" but with *"its power of choice . . . not lost."* [7]

By the opening of 1939, it became clear to the President that, in view of the prevailing undeclared wars, the threats of new aggression, and the inroads being made on the basic institutions of religion, democracy, and international good faith, greater measures of defense were vital to the United States. Such measures, as seen by the President and other responsible officials concerned, included a further strengthening of the armed forces, the building of reserves of strategic raw materials, the preparation for increased industrial production to meet defense needs, and the modification of the neutrality legislation. Both the President and the Secretary of State informed the Congress that experience had shown that the rigid arms embargo provisions of the neutrality legislation, concerning which they had long expressed their doubts, encouraged a general state of war by operating to the advantage of aggressors and to the weakening of the victims, and that changes in the act, especially to eliminate the arms embargo, were urgently needed. [8] Legislative opinion, nevertheless, remained unfavorable in the spring and summer of 1939 to amendment of the neutrality legislation, though steps were taken by Congress to meet American needs with respect to the armed forces, strategic raw materials, and defense production.

Concurrently in Europe the spirit of resistance began to revive, despite the *Blitzkrieg* that threatened as the price of resistance. The last uncontested aggressions were in March 1939, when all of Czechoslovakia and Memel were occupied by Germany, and in April, when

[7] Address by the Secretary of State, Nov. 1, 1938, *Peace and War*, p. 435.

[8] Messages to the Congress, Jan. 4 and 12, 1939; letter from the Secretary of State to the President, Oct. 12, 1938; letter from the Secretary of State to the Chairman of the Senate Committee on Foreign Relations, May 27, 1939; *ibid.*, pp. 62–63, 431–32, 447–54, 461–64.

Albania was invaded by Italy. The tolerable limits of retreat without resort to armed defense were being reached. On March 31, 1939, Prime Minister Chamberlain announced that Great Britain and France had given a military guaranty to Poland, the next probable victim of the Nazis.

On April 14 the President, seeking reciprocal pledges of nonaggression, asked Germany and Italy for assurances that no additional attacks on the remaining independent states of Europe and the Near East were contemplated. In the same message he invited the German and Italian Governments to international discussions that would be promptly held with these thirty-one states, and with United States participation, to "attain progressive relief from the crushing burden of armament" and to open "avenues of international trade." [9] This message was not answered except in a radio speech of April 28 by Hitler rejecting the proposal.

On this same occasion, Hitler denounced the German-Polish nonaggression declaration dated January 26, 1934, and referred to German claims affecting Danzig and the Polish Corridor, which were to be pressed in succeeding months with the support of the now usual "war of nerves" and "fifth-column" activity. Germany's reply to the President's appeals in behalf of peace made late in August 1939 came on September 1, after the German land and air forces had crossed the frontier of Poland, seized Danzig, and bombed Warsaw. By noon of September 3, Great Britain and France had declared that a state of war with Germany existed. By that night, India, Australia, and New Zealand had declared war. The Union of South Africa entered the war September 6, and Canada, September 10. The general war had come as the culmination of an Axis policy of planned aggression.

At that crucial juncture, the facts and the lessons of experience with insecurity between the wars had been but partly assessed by the American people and the rest of mankind. One instant meaning of the war, however, was clear: American efforts, the League's efforts, and all other efforts to prevent it had utterly failed. To think out the lessons of that experience and to conceive a way to restore and keep international peace were vital future tasks. The immediate compelling need in America was to formulate the program of action for a neutral people whose own peace was endangered.

IMPLEMENTATION OF NEUTRALITY, SEPTEMBER 1939

UNITED States neutrality was proclaimed by President Roosevelt September 5. The provisions of the Neutrality Act were at once applied. The arms embargo became effective with regard to all bellig-

---

[9] *Ibid.*, pp. 457–58, 477.

erents, and their use of the Panama Canal was regulated. On that same first day of adjustment to neutral status, September 5, the United States joined with seven other American republics in requesting all the twenty-one American republics to consult at Panama on measures to protect the peace of the Western Hemisphere. On the 8th, the President proclaimed a national emergency—limited to the extent necessary for enforcing neutrality and strengthening national defense.

These were but the initial broad actions as, with public opinion still divided on policy, the nation confronted the problems resulting from declared war in Europe, undeclared war in the Far East, hostilities on the great seas, and the manifold penetrations of foreign espionage and subversive activities in the Western Hemisphere. As the President stated to the Congress in special session: ". . . we find ourselves affected to the core; our currents of commerce are changing, our minds are filled with new problems, our position in world affairs has already been altered." [10]

Within two months, basic steps to preserve national safety had been taken. The necessity for these steps stemmed from the corollary: "When peace has been broken anywhere, peace of all countries everywhere is in danger." [11] The President ordered increases of the Army, Navy, and Marine Corps within the statutory limitations. And, since in the judgment of the President and a majority of the Congress the neutrality act of 1937 was visibly operating in ways dangerous to American security and peace, the act was revised on November 4, 1939. This terminated the arms embargo in favor of "cash-and-carry" purchases, which permitted Great Britain, France, and their allies access to American supplies and, among other provisions, sought to prevent the involvement of American citizens or ships in defined combat zones.

The basic steps taken by this Government in the first two months of the war were also designed to preserve inter-American safety and stemmed from the strategic fact that United States safety "is and will be bound up with the safety of the Western Hemisphere and of the seas adjacent thereto." [12]

Since April 26, 1938, a Liaison Committee, composed of the Under Secretary of State (Chairman), the Chief of Staff, and the Chief of Naval Operations, had been meeting on call for coordination of policy of common concern to the Departments of State, War, and Navy. The Committee in the autumn of 1939 was composed of Sumner Welles, General George C. Marshall, and Admiral Harold R. Stark. The establishment under Mr. Welles of an office of Under Secretary–Liaison

---

[10] Sept. 21, 1939, *ibid.*, p. 488.

[11] Radio address by President Roosevelt, Sept. 3, 1939, *ibid.*, pp. 484–85.

[12] *Idem.*

in the Department of State on October 12, 1939, pursuant to a directive of the President on the same day, was primarily for the purpose of expediting transmission of defense information and views among the three Departments, but the Office also provided regular assistance to the Liaison Committee. The new secretariat was headed by two officers in the Department of State on a full-time basis, with counterpart officers in the other Departments concerned.[13]

Related problems of assuring the safety of the Panama Canal with respect to aviation were being concurrently considered by an *ad hoc* Western Hemisphere Aviation Committee representing the same Departments and also the Civil Aeronautics Authority. These were the first effective steps toward the fruitful working relationships subsequently expanded and consolidated at both policy and operational levels among the three Departments having individually, and together, primary responsibility under the President for the national security and peace.

At the same time, cooperative bilateral arrangements for strengthening the defense forces of the other American republics were being made under standing legislation authorizing, on request by the government of any such republic, provision of United States military, naval, and air missions, training of its student officers in United States service schools, and civilian assistance and training. Furthermore, at the consultative meeting of the Foreign Ministers of the twenty-one American republics, at Panama City September 23 to October 3, 1939, far-reaching multilateral measures were agreed upon to maintain neutrality and to facilitate adjustment to the abnormal conditions imposed by the war upon American neutrals. These measures were designed to provide protection against economic dislocation and to assist industrial, agricultural, and commercial development in the American republics. They also provided for the coordination of police and judicial action against subversive activities. The Conference further expressed opposition to the transfer of the sovereignty of any part of the Americas held by a non-American state to another non-American state, and adopted a declaration defining a continental naval security zone, together with provisions for its patrol.

Subsequent naval actions involving German raiders or other belligerent vessels in Western Hemisphere waters resulted on December 23 in a collective protest to Germany, Great Britain, and France by all the American republics on the grounds that these actions compromised the

---

[13] Members of the secretariat at the outset were Selden Chapin, Liaison Officer, who had been assisting Mr. Welles in the work of the Liaison Committee, and Harley A. Notter, Assisting Liaison Officer of the Department of State on a brief detail from the Division of American Republics; Col. John A. Magruder and Col. Thomas B. Finley, War Department; and Capt. Roscoe E. Schuirmann and Comdr. Arthur D. Struble, Department of the Navy.

aims of continental protection provided for under the Declaration of Panama.

The European war, meanwhile, ran a most confusing course from intense action in the area of hostilities on and near the Baltic to a strange lull in Western Europe, with far-flung naval actions wherever enemy ships encountered each other.   In the Far East, tension resulting from earlier crises but slowly rising under the impact of general war elsewhere marked the situation, though no new major aggression occurred.

In the Baltic area, hostilities had spread to Finland by the end of the year.   The German attack on Poland had been followed on September 17, 1939, by a Soviet invasion from the east, and eleven days later Poland was partitioned between the victors.   The Soviet Union had then moved to strengthen its military position.   During September and October, the Soviet Union obtained, by treaty, bases and other military rights in Estonia, Latvia, and Lithuania, and made territorial and military demands on Finland.   When these demands were not met, the Soviet Union after rejecting a United States offer of good offices, invaded Finland on November 30.   This aggression precipitated the "winter war", which lasted until March 1940 and resulted in Soviet expulsion from the League of Nations on December 14, 1939.

ADVISORY COMMITTEE ON PROBLEMS OF FOREIGN RELATIONS

CONFRONTING these and other developments growing out of the war and with new threats of spreading war and new uncertainties appearing week by week, the Department labored under the urgent necessity of formulating advance policy.   Such policy, in response to the fluid circumstances of those early war months, had then to be adapted to day-by-day developments, and decisions largely made in a matter of hours.   This Government's continuing over-all policy of working for the establishment of a peace on durable, acceptable lines when and as this became possible also made mandatory, however, longer-range policy preparation by the Department that would take into account the uncertainty regarding the outcome and the possible effects of the struggles to the east and west of us.   This over-all policy had been stated at the outset, on September 3, 1939, by the President:

" . . . it seems to me clear, even at the outbreak of this great war, that the influence of America should be consistent in seeking for humanity a final peace which will eliminate, as far as it is possible to do so, the continued use of force between nations."

It was in the interest of this larger, later security, as well as of the immediate tasks of defense, that in the same address to the American people the President made his plea "that partisanship and selfishness be adjourned, and that national unity be the thought that underlies all others." [14]

The necessity of preparing carefully and fully the policy to be pursued in relation to the future peace was being discussed in various American quarters.[15] The Council on Foreign Relations in New York, upon the initiative of Hamilton Fish Armstrong, Editor of *Foreign Affairs*, and Walter H. Mallory, Executive Director, had proposed to Assistant Secretary of State George S. Messersmith as early as September 12 to expand its studies on foreign relations and to make them available for the use of the Department. This offer was accepted after consideration by Secretary Hull and Under Secretary Welles. Various other organizations offered help, including the Federal Council of Churches of Christ in America. The Department did not, however, give directives or special support to any of these groups.

Abroad, Pope Pius XII, in an address delivered November 10, 1939, suggested the need of founding a stable international organization at the end of the war. In the British Foreign Office a group of experts, assisted by the Royal Institute of International Affairs in a semi-official capacity, had been organized directly after the commencement of the war to make preparatory studies for future peace settlements.

Within the Department of State, Secretary Hull on September 16, 1939, appointed Leo Pasvolsky his Special Assistant primarily to work on problems of peace. From time to time thereafter, proposals for organized consideration of these problems were discussed by the Secretary and Mr. Pasvolsky. Similar proposals emphasizing the advisability of such preparation within the Department of State rather than outside, as in the case of The Inquiry under Col. Edward M. House in the Administration of President Woodrow Wilson, were presented to Under Secretary Welles in November and December by Harley Notter, then on detail from the Division of the American Republics to the Office of Under Secretary–Liaison.

The President addressed messages on December 23, 1939, to Pope Pius XII, to the President of the Federal Council of Churches of Christ in America, and to the President of the Jewish Theological

---

[14] *Peace and War*, pp. 483–85.

[15] Among the earliest articles in the American press was that by Mrs. Franklin D. Roosevelt, in her column "My Day," Sept. 11, 1939: "The world must eventually be reorganized for peace, and let us pray that this time we will have strength and foresight enough to plan a more permanent way of peace . . . I should like to see an international group meeting now continuously to plan for future peace." Among discussions and editorial comment was that in the Washington *Post* Nov. 13, dealing with "the question of the kind of a world which is to be ushered in when the guns are stilled . . . It is certainly not too soon to begin thinking about and planning for that new and more orderly world. . . . And nowhere is the necessity . . . greater than in the United States, the greatest of neutrals."

Seminary of America, voicing the belief that while at present no spiritual or civil leader could move forward on a specific plan to build a new order of things "the time for that will surely come." He expressed a desire to "encourage a closer association between those in every part of the world—those in religion and those in government— who have a common purpose." In the letter to the Pope he said that he wished to send "to you my personal representative in order that our parallel endeavors for peace and the alleviation of suffering may be assisted." For this purpose the President appointed Myron C. Taylor as his personal representative to Pope Pius XII, with the rank of ambassador extraordinary.[16]

On December 27 Secretary Hull came to a decision on the organization within the Department of State of preparations on postwar problems. This decision to establish a departmental "committee on problems of peace and reconstruction" was made in a meeting held by the Secretary attended by most of the senior officers on duty at that time: Under Secretary Sumner Welles; Judge R. Walton Moore, Counselor; George S. Messersmith, Assistant Secretary; Adolf A. Berle, Jr., Assistant Secretary; Green H. Hackworth, Legal Adviser; Leo Pasvolsky, Special Assistant to the Secretary; Herbert Feis, Economic Adviser; Henry F. Grady, Assistant Secretary; Stanley K. Hornbeck, Political Adviser; and Jay Pierrepont Moffat, Chief of the Division of European Affairs. The agreed functions of the committee, as projected in the proposal memorandum presented by Mr. Pasvolsky, were

"To survey the basic principles which should underlie a desirable world order to be evolved after the termination of present hostilities, with primary reference to the best interests of the United States;

"In the light of the principles indicated above and of past experience, to determine policies which should be pursued by the United States in furtherance of the establishment of such a world order, both as a basis of our own action and of our attempts to influence other nations;

"In the light of the principles and policies indicated above, to examine proposals and suggestions made from various sources— both official and unofficial—as regards problems of peace and reconstruction."

To provide the necessary assistance to the committee, a further memorandum projected the establishment of a division in the Department for the study of problems of peace and reconstruction, to assemble information and views, and make analyses in regard to international economic relations and related problems, territorial and political problems, armament problems, neutral rights and obligations, and general machinery of international cooperation.[17] As then en-

---

[16] For the exchange of correspondence, see *Department of State Bulletin,* I, 711, and II, 130.

[17] For text of this memorandum, see appendix 1.

visaged, this would have entailed a small staff, gathered from among the existing professional officer personnel of the Department. These officers, however, were already hard-pressed. With the outbreak of war, the Department's routine activities had increased in number and complexity, and new, extraordinary functions had had to be undertaken. As of October 1939, the total professional and clerical staff of the Department, apart from the Foreign Service, was verging on 900—of whom barely 200 were professional officers. This part of the plan of organization therefore was not adopted.[18]

It was determined that the committee would work through three subcommittees considering, respectively, political problems including the organization of peace, limitation and reduction of armaments, and economic problems. Secretary Hull conceived the role of both the committee and its subcommittees to be recommendatory on immediate problems arising out of the war as well as exploratory on longer-range questions. This conception, together with the original idea of organizing a group of departmental officers functioning under the Secretary, caused the committee to be established as advisory to the Secretary of State.

Although the subcommittees began to meet promptly, the name of the committee was not settled until January 8, 1940, when the title "Advisory Committee on Problems of Foreign Relations" was approved. On the same day, in order to obviate possible international and domestic misconceptions if the work and organization of the new group were to become known without clarification of purpose, a public statement was issued, reading:

"*Advisory Committee on Problems of Foreign Relations.* The war has brought about, and is continuing to bring about, a series of measures and policies on the part of both belligerents and neutrals which immediately affect the United States and which may have consequences of an enduring nature upon our country's foreign relations once peace is established.

"Some of the most important and immediate of these measures and policies are in the field of economic activity and relations. The war has absorbed the labor and production of much of the world in armament and military activity. When the war ends, problems of readjustment to peace-time production will be presented, which may gravely affect the United States.

"Accordingly, the Secretary of State has set up in the Department a Committee which will gather data on and study both the immediate and long-range results of overseas war measures and the manner in which the problems arising from them may best be handled so as to avoid shock and to prevent undesirable enduring results.

---

[18] In an effort later to meet the need for technical assistance, the offices and divisions of the Department were requested on Jan. 22, 1940, to render full cooperation.

"Mr. Welles will serve as chairman and Mr. Hugh Wilson [19] as vice chairman of this committee." [20]

The full membership of the Committee finally included, beside the members already named, James C. Dunn, Political Adviser, and Breckinridge Long, Assistant Secretary, Norman H. Davis, former chief delegate to the disarmament conferences in London and Geneva, and George Rublee, then director of the Intergovernmental Committee on Political Refugees. Consequently the Advisory Committee was not only departmental in authorization and in function but was almost entirely departmental in its membership of fifteen.

Its three subcommittees were composed wholly of members of the Committee. George Rublee was chairman of the Subcommittee on Political Problems, the remaining members of which were Messrs. Welles, Berle, Long, Hornbeck, and Hackworth, with the other chairmen also attending its meetings.[21] The Subcommittee on Limitation and Reduction of Armaments was composed of Judge Moore, chairman, and Messrs. Messersmith, Davis, Dunn, and Moffat. The members of the Subcommittee on Economic Problems were Messrs. Pasvolsky, chairman, Berle, Grady, and Feis. Mr. Wilson, as vice chairman of the Advisory Committee, also performed such executive-secretary duties as were required.

Composed of high-ranking officers who were carrying fatiguing burdens of detail as well as of major responsibility in a small Department, dealing with the intricate problems of neutrality and the grave complexities of deteriorating international relations, meeting without agenda or minutes or preparatory studies in the absence of a qualified staff, and subject to hourly interruptions to meet needs for current action, two of the Subcommittees were yet able for a short period, lasting into the spring, to meet with some frequency and to make a degree of progress. Any papers presented were of necessity individual views hurriedly written—sometimes improvised—by one or another member, and not always circulated before meetings. When discussion had developed a general consensus on a matter for early action, a recommendation would be prepared. For the most part, however, the work was exploratory. The Subcommittee on Limitation and Reduction of Armaments met once, but thereafter did not function separately from the Subcommittee on Political Problems.

Under the prevailing circumstances, the Committee itself became primarily an instrument of current policy and, with most of its members active in the two main Subcommittees, met only infrequently. Review of agreed subcommittee views was accomplished through the regular Departmental channels to the Secretary rather than through the Committee as such.

---

[19] At that time Special Assistant to the Secretary of State.

[20] *Department of State Bulletin,* II, 19.

[21] Owing to Mr. Rublee's illness, from the beginning of work Mr. Welles served as Chairman.

CHAPTER II

Program of Preparation, 1940

ORGANIZED preparation for the postwar period began against the background of the President's address to the Congress, January 3, 1940, in which he stated that "we can strive with other nations to encourage the kind of peace that will lighten the troubles of the world. . . ." The President emphasized on this occasion "the leadership which this Nation can take when the time comes for a renewal of world peace," and expressed the hope that all Americans "will work out for themselves the several alternatives which lie before world civilization. . . ."[1] In preparation for this Nation's role in the re-establishment of peace as envisaged by the President, the main purposes of policy consideration by the Advisory Committee on Problems of Foreign Relations were, accordingly, to limit and to end the war if possible, to clarify the requisite bases for a future peaceful world order, and, more immediately, to strengthen the defense of the Western Hemisphere. These purposes were interwoven.

SUBCOMMITTEE WORK AND DIPLOMATIC SOUNDINGS

THE SUBCOMMITTEE on Economic Problems was the first to organize. On January 3 it set out to prepare for possible American participation in some early conference at which economic problems would be dealt with and in the reconstruction efforts that might possibly follow. It was thought that the common interests of nations were more generally recognized in the economic than in the political field. The experiences of the interwar period had focused attention on the effects of economic policies on international relations—both directly as an important source of friction between nations and indirectly as a basic factor contributing to stability or instability within states. Extensive consideration had been given by this Government in the thirties to these effects, so that by 1940 the general goals of our economic policy could be more clearly defined than could our objectives in the political and territorial fields. This Government had already taken steps toward these goals

[1] H. Doc. 528, 76th Cong., 3d sess., serial vol. 10501.

through the Trade Agreements Act and through the various economic policies and arrangements agreed upon with the twenty other American republics. Many of those taking part in the Department's early preparatory work thought that public opinion in this country would go further in support of United States participation in international economic cooperation than in international political arrangements, which the national interest in peace seemed increasingly to require, and that the way might best be paved for the latter through the former. In the light of these considerations it was decided to approach the problem of the restoration of peace first from the economic standpoint.

The Subcommittee on Economic Problems considered on January 3, 1940, a program of work covering the five principal fields of commercial policy and relations, monetary policy and relations, credit and investment relations, production trends, and price trends.[2] The program projected the analysis and appraisal both of interwar economic experience and of current developments affecting the postwar situation, preparatory to an effort to solve the broad problems of postwar economic policy. The lull in the European war, however, appeared to offer an opportunity for the immediate initiation of action, and within two weeks this general program had developed into a more specific proposal of January 15 outlining the bases for an economic settlement, which might serve as a basis for discussion at a conference of neutrals or at a more general economic conference, or at both.[3]

This proposal was discussed immediately by the Subcommittee on Economic Problems and the Subcommittee on Political Problems in terms of a possible conference of neutrals. By January 18 thought was clarifying on the scope of such a conference, which, it was considered, might include economic questions arising from the war, postwar economic desiderata, and cooperation in formulating other foundations for future peace. Further consideration was to eliminate current problems from the scope of the proposed conference, and to limit its terms of reference to postwar economic cooperation and the armaments problem. Papers on suggested procedure, proposed agenda, and the basic questions to be considered in the "formulation of a post-war economic program" were prepared by members of the Economic and Political Subcommittees, and the Political Subcommittee formulated on February 2, 1940, a set of considerations that should be discussed before conversations with the neutrals were initiated.

At the same time that the Subcommittee on Political Problems was occupying itself with the political aspects of the proposed conference of neutrals, first thoughts on the future organization of world order were presented to it by several members. It was appreciated that the problematical course of the war, the many unknown circumstances

---

[2] See appendix 2.

[3] See appendix 3.

ahead, United States neutrality, and the uncertainty of public opinion regarding international political cooperation rendered any such views essentially conditional. Therefore the views presented contained many queries or suggested varying possibilities. Should the United States, apart from cooperation with Europe in matters of economic reconstruction, commit itself to any international cooperation on purely political matters? Perhaps in view of the failure of the League of Nations and the success of the inter-American system, a number of regional leagues—each under an individual, rather than a representative of a government, as president and each having a direct relationship to the others—should be favored. Still another possibility was that the League of Nations might be continued, with modifications, to represent primarily the states of Europe and Africa; a regional group might be formed for Asia; and a collaborating relationship established between these regional arrangements and the inter-American organization. The subcommittee did not, however, reach the point of discussing this subject concretely until several months later.

During this same period memoranda on limitation of armaments and on possible United States mediation in the European war were also drafted for consideration by the subcommittee.

The subcommittee's preparations for the proposed conference of neutrals had progressed so far that Secretary Hull on February 8–10 initiated diplomatic conversations with the governments of forty-seven neutral states.[4] It was envisaged that if feasible the conversations could later be extended to nations engaged in declared or undeclared hostilities. The Secretary proposed on behalf of the President that views should be exchanged concerning "two basic problems" in establishing lasting world peace on a sound foundation: the bases for a sound international economic system and armament limitation and reduction. These exchanges would not involve any of the "present problems" arising in connection with the existing war situation. The intent was to obtain before any peace conference was held a definite understanding and, so far as practicable, commitments with respect to the basic principles of sound and stable international relationships after the war. The only hope of constructive accomplishment, either at the peace conference when held or during the reconstruction period, appeared to lie in such firm prior acceptance of sound policies by as many nations as possible.

[4] The forty-seven neutrals were the 20 other American republics and Belgium, Bulgaria, Luxembourg, Egypt, Saudi Arabia, Afghanistan, Denmark, Greece, Hungary, Iran, Iraq, Ireland, Italy, Estonia, Latvia, Liberia, Lithuania, Netherlands, Norway, Portugal, Rumania, Siam, Spain, Sweden, Switzerland, Turkey, and Yugoslavia.

Replies were favorable without important exceptions, although some were merely sympathetic and some were skeptical of positive accomplishment. Thirty of the forty-three replies received by May 23 explicitly or implicitly showed readiness to give full cooperation. The attitude of others was reserved, particularly as to disarmament, or conditional on specific proposals. One preferred the use of usual diplomatic channels to a conference. Many expressed the desire to see the ideas of the United States set forth as a basis for discussion.

Preparations for the proposed conference were pressed vigorously by the Subcommittees on Economic and Political Problems, taking form particularly in an inclusive memorandum presenting the views of this Government on postwar economic relations and disarmament. Aside from the specific program formulated, which was built on the basic economic policies consistently pressed by Secretary Hull throughout the preceding critical years, this memorandum stressed the necessity for parallel action in the interdependent fields of economic reconstruction, international political stability, and disarmament.

The development of the economic program for the conference of neutrals naturally involved matters of direct interest to other Departments, especially Treasury, Commerce, and Agriculture, and to the Tariff Commission and the Export-Import Bank. The evident scope of the specific implementation that would be required under the broad policies enunciated in the program, and of the conference itself when held, seemed to require organized interdepartmental consultation. A plan for such consultation was prepared February 29, 1940, by the Chairman of the Subcommittee on Economic Problems after discussion with Secretary Hull.[5] It projected a special "Interdepartmental Advisory Committee on Economic Consultations with Neutrals" to work in conjunction with the Executive Committee on Commercial Policy and the Committee on Trade Agreements, which were standing interdepartmental committees. Subcommittees would study individual problems, and technical experts in the various Departments and agencies would prepare materials. Secretary Hull began to confer in March with the Cabinet members concerned. Shortly afterward, however, all these plans were dropped. Although the preparatory papers for the conference of neutrals were completed during April, termination of the lull in the war rendered further action impracticable.

Concurrently with the move for a conference of neutrals, it had been announced by the President on February 9, 1940, that Mr. Welles would undertake conversations with the Governments of the principal belligerents in Europe (Germany, France, Great Britain) and of Italy. The purpose of these conversations was to obtain in

---

[5] See appendix 4.

confidence for the President and the Secretary of State the views of these Governments on the possibilities, in the light of their desires, of establishing a stable and lasting peace. Proposals were not to be offered or committal positions taken.[6] The Under Secretary did not present any papers except for a brief memorandum on the bases of United States foreign economic policy as developed in preliminary form by the Subcommittee on Economic Problems in February and subsequently released for publication.[7]

Upon his return, March 28, Mr. Welles informed the President and Secretary Hull that, important as the territorial, political, and economic problems were, security was the basic problem in Europe. While immediately there was no chance of durable peace if the basis of negotiations was political and territorial adjustment, he believed that there might be a slight chance for restoration of peace if a practical plan of security and disarmament could be proposed by the United States and other neutrals and agreed upon by the great powers of Europe. The only possible source of initiative for such an attempt, he concluded, appeared to be the United States. This report, together with the continuing and deepening impact here of the war abroad, focused attention on security as prerequisite for peace. These findings entered into the Department's preparation of policy thenceforth.

Throughout these early months of 1940 the stagnant period in the war had continued without essential change. A treaty of peace was signed between Finland and the Soviet Union March 12. In the west, hostilities had remained inactive. Suddenly on April 9, without warning, German land, sea, and air forces attacked neutral Norway and Denmark. Denmark was overrun in hours. Norway fell under Nazi control by April 24. To prevent its being used as an Axis base, British troops on May 9 occupied Iceland, which had suspended Danish royal powers on April 10 and initiated direct consular relations with the United States on April 24. Germany attacked the Netherlands, Luxembourg, and Belgium on May 9; all three had fallen before twenty days had passed, and the German forces had pressed into France. On May 10 Winston Churchill became Prime Minister of Great Britain. On May 11 Allied troops landed in the Caribbean possessions of the Netherlands, at Curaçao and Aruba, in order to insure that these areas, with their valuable oil refineries and strategic advantages, did not fall into Axis hands. Meanwhile, in the Far East, Japan expressed concern for the maintenance of the *status quo* of the Netherlands East Indies. Secretary Hull, in diplomatic

---

[6] *Department of State Bulletin*, II, 155. The Soviet Union and Finland, engaged in local hostilities, were not included in either of these developments.

[7] *Ibid.*, II, 461.

conversations and in a public statement on April 17, warned against prejudicing the peace of the South Pacific.[8]

The Government in Washington became preoccupied with trying to limit the extension of the war and with meeting the grave situation created by this widening scope of hostilities. An immediate task was to persuade Italy not to enter the war. The President undertook such action by telegrams to the Premier of Italy, April 29, May 14, May 26, and May 30, sent through the American Ambassador,[9] and by parallel efforts with Pope Pius XII through Myron C. Taylor.[10] Midway in that unsuccessful effort, and again at its end, the President urged the Congress, in view of the possibility of attack on vital American zones, to authorize vast extensions of the nation's air, military, and naval defenses in the light of the lessons so far learned from the actual combat in Europe and to provide selective training of manpower.

Meanwhile, before Mussolini's attitude was known and when a conference of neutrals was not yet patently impossible, the Subcommittee on Political Problems undertook to prepare views on European organization for possible use if events permitted. Its discussions on April 19 and 26 [11] and on May 6 revolved about the establishment of a European "political body" representing both individual states and regional groupings, with which would be associated a permanent court of justice and a series of special advisory and technical bodies. The brief discussion of these ideas led not to conclusions but rather to questions: What minimum attributes must a regional organism in the critical area of central Europe have? What particular structure of organization would be suitable there? How would it work from an economic standpoint? What area should such a regional group include?

Here the discussion of the subject stopped. The war's westward sweep late in May 1940, when the retreat from Dunkirk began, compelled intensive development of American defense and immediate consideration of the economic and political consequences to the United States of a possible German victory.

"CONSEQUENCES TO THE UNITED STATES OF A POSSIBLE GERMAN VICTORY"

CONSIDERATION of the implications of a German victory were well under way in the last week of May. Either of two general economic

---

[8] *Peace and War*, p. 515.

[9] *Ibid.*, pp. 519–22, 526–32, 536–40, 542–44.

[10] *Wartime Correspondence Between President Roosevelt and Pope Pius XII*, with an Introduction and Explanatory Notes by Myron C. Taylor (New York 1947), pp. 5, 27.

[11] See appendix 5.

possibilities became clear. If the German onrush were checked and the war was prolonged, European peoples would face a long period of economic strain and lowered standard of living. If the Allies were defeated, the German system of economic autarky would probably be extended to most of Europe and an effort made to extend it to the colonial possessions of defeated states. The result would again be a lowering of living standards and social deterioration. For our Nation, the basic consequence of a German victory in Europe would be emergence of a "postwar" situation that might confront the United States with "peace-time" problems of greatly different character and portent from those heretofore envisaged.

Accordingly, an inclusive range of economic action might possibly be required of this Government, and consideration of the subject on an interdepartmental basis became essential. The need for such interdepartmental consultations had already been recognized in connection with the proposed conference of neutrals, and the basis for organized consultations had been laid in the plan projected the previous March. An informal group in the Government, of the highest technical competence, was called together on May 27 by the Chairman of the Subcommittee on Economic Problems, which itself never convened again as a separate body. The new group was constituted under the name of the "Interdepartmental Group to Consider Post-War International Economic Problems and Policies," and its establishment was agreed upon in discussions between Secretary Hull and the other Cabinet members concerned. Four Departments were represented initially: State (Leo Pasvolsky, Chairman; Adolf A. Berle, Jr., Lynn R. Edminster, Herbert Feis, Henry F. Grady, and Harry C. Hawkins); Treasury (H. Merle Cochran and Harry D. White); Commerce (Louis Domeratzky, Richard V. Gilbert, and Grosvenor M. Jones); and Agriculture (Mordecai Ezekiel, James L. McCamy, Howard R. Tolley, and Leslie A. Wheeler). In the later meetings, additional representatives from these and other agencies of the Government participated.[12]

---

[12] Additional representatives participated at various subsequent meetings: State Department (Emilio G. Collado, Richard Eldridge, Leroy D. Stinebower, H. Julian Wadleigh, and David Williamson); Executive Office of the President (Lauchlin Currie and James V. Forrestal); Reconstruction Finance Corporation (Clifford J. Durr); Federal Loan Agency (Warren Lee Pierson); Treasury (V. Frank Coe, Simon G. Hanson, and W. L. Ullman); Surplus Commodities Corporation (M. W. McGuire, and Milo Perkins); Commodity Credit Corporation (C. B. Robbins); Tariff Commission (A. Manuel Fox, E. Dana Durand, Oscar B. Ryder, James H. Hibben, Frank A. Waring, and Mark A. Smith); Commerce (P. A. Hayward, E. G. Holt, and W. S. Salant); Interior (Clark Foreman); Agriculture (George B. L. Arner and Arthur W. Palmer); Federal Reserve Board (Walter R. Gardiner, E. A. Goldenweiser, C. P. Kindleberger, Chandler Morse, and Woodlief Thomas); Coordinator of Inter-American Affairs (Nelson A. Rockefeller); War (Maj. Paul F. Logan, Lt. Col. William A. Sadler, Capt. H. R. McKenzie and additional officers); Navy (civilian representative not identified in records).

This Group was to organize, direct, and review studies bearing on the problems of postwar international economic relations, to be made in the individual participating departments and agencies. Its objective was to clarify the possible alternatives of foreign economic policy open to the United States.

The Subcommittee on Political Problems of the Advisory Committee on Problems of Foreign Relations began on May 31 to consider other foreseeable consequences of a possible German victory.

One was the threat that, with the German conquest of countries in Western Europe having possessions in the Western Hemisphere, transfer of those territories to Germany might ensue. Secretary Hull and the President had already approved the draft of a proposed joint resolution regarding this possibility for immediate submission to the Congress. Under this resolution, the United States would refuse to recognize or acquiesce in a transfer of territory in the Western Hemisphere, regarded as including Greenland but not Iceland, from one non-American country to another non-American country. In the event such transfer appeared likely, the United States in addition to other measures would immediately consult with the other American republics to determine upon the steps to be taken.

The phrasing of this resolution was deemed broad enough to cover Canada and the contingency of a removal there of the seat of the British Empire if the British Isles proved unable to withstand attack. The Subcommittee believed that the resolution would have a salutary effect in Europe and a reassuring effect in this Hemisphere. Resolutions along the proposed lines were adopted by the Senate on June 17, 1940, and by the House on June 18.[13]

Another threat envisaged was that, for economic reasons, one or more of the Latin American republics might become politically dependent upon Germany if that state were to organize Europe as an economic union. A third was the possibility that Japan might move into the Dutch East Indies and other Pacific areas. The Subcommittee on Political Problems concluded that all possible preparations should be made to assure the adequate defense of the United States— going beyond measures limited strictly to the Western Hemisphere. Toward this end it was believed necessary to enable the Allies, by changes in existing legislation, to establish credits in this country and to purchase from this Government supplies that could be spared. So great was the danger in the sight of the subcommittee members that the fear was voiced that American opinion might not be ready to act until too late to save the Allies, leaving the United States in a most adverse position as regards the victor or victors.

With the formulation of these views, the Subcommittee on Political

---

[13] S. J. Res. 271, H. J. Res. 556, 76th Cong., 3d sess. The resolutions were not, however, reconciled until Apr. 10, 1941; Public Law 32, 55 Stat. 133.

Problems ceased functioning as a group. Its individual members became engrossed in the urgent tasks arising out of the broad program for bulwarking the national safety.

The outlook rapidly became more menacing. In the first two weeks of June, hostilities spread throughout the Mediterranean and into Africa. On June 10 Italy entered the war against France and Great Britain. Spanish troops then occupied the International Zone of Tangier. The boundaries of defined combat areas were extended by the United States under the neutrality act to this further area of war.

In Eastern Europe, spearheaded in each case by an ultimatum, Soviet troops in succession entered Lithuania, Latvia, and Estonia between June 15 and June 17, and the Soviet Union received Bessarabia and Northern Bukovina from Rumania June 28.

Above all, however, loomed the plight of France and the fearful consequences of French defeat. As Italy struck, the French Premier, M. Paul Reynaud, desperately appealed to the United States for help before it was too late and promised that France would fight if necessary from North Africa and the French possessions in the New World. On the evening of that day, June 10, the President publicly condemned Mussolini's decision and declared that the United States would "extend" to the Allies "the material resources" of the United States. To the French, the President replied that American efforts over the weeks just past to provide airplanes, artillery, and munitions to the Allied Armies would be redoubled, "so long as the Allied governments continued to resist," and he stressed the necessity for the French fleet to continue operations.[14]

The vital role of the French fleet was repeatedly emphasized to the French Government during the next week, with the warning that American friendship with France was at stake, and assurance was received that the French fleet at least would not be surrendered to the enemy. On June 14 German troops entered Paris. The Governments-in-exile of Poland and Belgium moved from there to London, where the Netherlands and Norway had already established their Governments. On June 17 France asked Germany for an armistice, which was signed on June 22. One with Italy was signed on June 24. General Charles de Gaulle called for continued resistance by "Free French" from overseas.[15] While the French fleet did not fall into the hands of the Germans, that part of it remaining in French ports continued to cause anxiety for more than a year.

The capitulation of the Netherlands armed forces and the French request for armistice terms sharply raised the problem of whether

---

[14] *Peace and War*, pp. 545–53.

[15] General de Gaulle was recognized on June 28, 1940, by Great Britain as leader of the Free French. On July 10 Marshal Henri Philippe Pétain was given dictatorial powers within France by the French Parliament.

Germany would obtain their Caribbean possessions and the French islands of St. Pierre and Miquelon off Newfoundland. Secretary Hull on June 17 instructed American diplomatic representatives in Berlin and Rome to inform the Governments of Germany and Italy, respectively, that the United States would not recognize the transfer of, and would not acquiesce in any attempt to transfer, any geographical region of the Western Hemisphere from one non-American power to another non-American power. Germany made a contentious reply which left the matter hanging threateningly.[16]

Meanwhile, in the Far East, Japan expressed further concern lest the political or economic *status quo* of the Netherlands East Indies be affected. This was followed on June 29 with the assertion by the Japanese Foreign Minister that Japan was the stabilizing force for a new order in East Asia and the South Seas, the peoples of which, he believed, were destined to cooperate and to minister to each other's needs for their common well-being and prosperity, united in a single sphere. By July 18, on pressure from the Japanese Government and despite announced American opposition, Great Britain had temporarily stopped the transit of war material and certain other goods to China via the Burma route.

Confronting unprecedented threat to national security within the Western Hemisphere and to American interests throughout the vast combat areas, the President made drastic recommendations to the Congress to augment the national capacity for defense. The defense program became "total." Further naval, military, and aviation expansion was requested July 10 in the amount of over two billion dollars, with more than two and one-half billion dollars additional for contract authorizations.[17] To supplement this huge domestic effort and as a vital part of the defense program, inter-American action was essential both along broad political and specific economic lines.

For such action, political preparations were made within the usual channels of the Department of State, while certain of the required economic preparations were made by the Interdepartmental Group. The economic problems were considered both from the standpoint of current and of postwar policy and primarily on the basis of a possible consolidation of continental Europe under German rule. The German successes signified that the "postwar" period might conceivably arrive in weeks or days, and this in effect reduced "postwar" to "long-term" policy.

A series of ten meetings of the Interdepartmental Group in June and early July was devoted to the formulation of recommendations for strengthening inter-American economic cooperation. The proposals were designed for submission as quickly as possible to a Cabinet

---

[16] *Peace and War*, pp. 555–56, 560–62.
[17] *Cong. Rec.*, vol. 86, pt. 9, pp. 9399–9400.

committee whose views had been requested by the President. This Committee was composed of Secretary of State Cordell Hull, Secretary of the Treasury Henry Morgenthau, Jr., Secretary of Commerce Harry L. Hopkins, and Secretary of Agriculture Henry A. Wallace.

The Group's discussions, of which for the first time minutes of a general character were kept, resulted in two reports. The first was in the form of a letter to the President, presenting an economic plan for the Western Hemisphere in response to a Presidential inquiry of the Cabinet committee on June 15 concerning means of strengthening inter-American economic relations. By June 24 this report had received the approval of the Cabinet committee. Its general purport was determined by the President's desire, of which the Group had been apprised on June 18, to initiate with the other American republics a program for the centralized selling of Western Hemisphere surplus products, including possibly those of Canada, and, since such a program would take time to prepare, to see immediate action taken to give this Government control of these surpluses in the interest of American defense. The second report [18] comprised specific proposals for the implementation of the emergency aspects of this plan and was completed on July 2.

Specific long-range proposals had been considered, but no conclusions had been reached. The Group's recommendations were concerned primarily with the problems of marketing Western Hemisphere surpluses, encouraging diversified and increased production in some American republics, strengthening monetary systems, and providing the necessary mechanisms, national and international, to carry out this program. The discussions of the Group were an indication of the vast difficulties of any attempt to maintain a bargaining relationship between this Hemisphere and Europe, if the European economy were to be organized on lines set by a victorious Nazi Germany, and of the hazards to our own basic tenets of international economic policy, if economic warfare determined the lines of action in peacetime.

The Group recessed after July 2. Its recommendations were immediately given further consideration during the formulation of the definitive United States position to be taken at the Second Meeting of the Ministers of Foreign Affairs of American Republics at Habana, July 21–30, 1940, attended by six members of the Group,[19] and were reflected in the resolution on economic and financial cooperation adopted by that conference. The following month, in line with these same recommendations, an Office for Coordination of Commercial and

---

[18] "Reports to Cabinet Committee on Inter-American Economic Affairs from Inter-Departmental Committee of Experts". The Committee of Experts was the "Group" operating temporarily on a formal basis for this purpose.

[19] Messrs. Berle, Pasvolsky, Jones, Wheeler, White, and Collado.

Cultural Relations between the American Republics was established under Nelson A. Rockefeller; and in September additional economic defense legislation was passed by Congress with particular reference to the development of the resources of the countries of the Western Hemisphere, the stabilization of their economies, and the orderly marketing of their surplus products.

In his address on the second day of the Foreign Ministers Meeting at Habana, Secretary Hull, after declaring that world conditions were then "perhaps graver than they have ever been before" and that the objective of the meeting was to safeguard under these circumstances "the independence, the peace, and the well-being of the American republics," turned first to the economic situation. Describing the disruptive and restrictive effects of the war in Europe on the economic life of the Western Hemisphere, the Secretary said that these difficulties would not only continue so long as the war lasted but that their continuation "for some time after the war ends" had to be anticipated. He emphasized the dependence of general economic rehabilitation after the war on a revival of international commerce conducted in accordance with liberal trade principles, and the self-interest of the American states in resuming "the conduct of trade with the entire world on this basis as rapidly as other nations are willing to do likewise." He further asserted:

"In the meantime, the American nations must and should do everything in their power to strengthen their own economic position, to improve further the trade and other economic relations between and among themselves, and to devise and apply appropriate means of effective action to cope with the difficulties, disadvantages, and dangers of the present disturbed and dislocated world conditions. To accomplish these purposes, the nations of the Western Hemisphere should undertake the fullest measure of economic cooperation, so designed and so conducted as to serve the best interests of each nation and to bring injury to none."

The Secretary then reviewed the steps already taken toward such cooperation within the inter-American system and advocated consideration by the American republics of the following program of immediate action:

"1. Strengthening and expansion of the activities of the Inter-American Financial and Economic Advisory Committee as an instrument for continuing consultation with respect to trade matters, including especially the situation immediately confronting the American republics as a result of the curtailment and changed character of important foreign markets.

"2. Creation of facilities for the temporary handling and orderly marketing of accumulated surpluses of those commodities which are of primary importance to the maintenance of the economic life of the American republics, whenever such action becomes necessary.

"3. Development of commodity agreements with a view to assuring equitable terms of trade for both producers and consumers of the commodities concerned.

"4. Consideration of methods for improving the standard of living of the peoples of the Americas, including public-health measures, nutrition studies, and suitable organizations for the relief distribution of some part of any surplus commodities."

In support of this proposed program, the Secretary described the measures that the United States Government had adopted, and was prepared to adopt, toward these ends.[20]

Resolution XXV on economic and financial cooperation as approved at Habana was based largely on a United States proposal reflecting the discussions of the problem by the Interdepartmental Group. It provided for the expansion recommended by the Secretary of the activities of the recently created Inter-American Financial and Economic Advisory Committee. Under the resolution, that Advisory Committee was directed to consider not only the immediate problems, among them those enumerated by the Secretary, but further "the desirability of a broader system of inter-American cooperative organization in trade and industrial matters." [21]

In his address of July 22 at Habana, Secretary Hull also called for "decisive remedial action" against "fifth column" activities within the American states "to the end that the independence and political integrity of each of the American republics may be fully safeguarded." Finally, he endorsed a proposal for the "establishment of a collective trusteeship, to be exercised in the name of all the American republics" for European possessions in this Hemisphere in the event their existing status was menaced by developments of the war and announced this Government's willingness to cooperate in the execution of this plan should the occasion arise. In so doing, however, the Secretary asserted:

"The establishment of a collective trusteeship for any region must not carry with it any thought of the creation of a special interest by any American republic. The purpose of a collective trusteeship must be to further the interests and security of all the American nations, as well as the interest of the region in question. Moreover, as soon as conditions permit, the region should be restored to its original sovereign or be declared independent when able to establish and maintain stable self-government."

The Habana Meeting, among various far-reaching measures of political defense, agreed upon a formal convention, and an emergency arrangement as well, for placing under provisional inter-American administration any non-American possession in this Hemisphere the

---

[20] For full text, see *Second Meeting of the Ministers of Foreign Affairs of the American Republics, Habana, July 21–30, 1940: Report of the Secretary of State*, Department of State publication 1575, Conference Series 48, pp. 45–55.

[21] For the text of this resolution, see *ibid.*, pp. 80–83.

sovereignty of which was in danger of transfer to another non-American state—such administration to continue until the territory could govern itself or be restored to its former possessor. The meeting also adopted a series of resolutions, one of them based on a United States proposal, designed to provide the "decisive remedial action" called for by the Secretary against activities directed from abroad against domestic institutions. An additional far-reaching resolution directed toward regional defense was also passed, under which, in case aggression was committed or attempted by a non-American state on any American republic, such act or attempt would be considered as an act of aggression against all American republics.

The meeting at Habana had begun just as Hitler offered Great Britain peace and as that offer was rejected. By the date of its close, conditions in Europe were such that the Secretary of War, Henry L. Stimson, voiced the possibility that Great Britain might fall in another thirty days.[22] Though Britain fought on, invasion might come at any moment, and with it a factor long fundamental in American security, the British Fleet, would be in jeopardy.

The scene was one of deep crisis for the United States—and of still widening war. Germany put Britain under "total" blockade August 17. In Eastern Europe, the Baltic republics of Estonia, Latvia, and Lithuania applied for incorporation into the Soviet Union, in each case after elections held under Soviet auspices, and that incorporation was completed in August. The United States publicly condemned on July 23, 1940, the "devious processes" involved.[23] On August 30 and September 7, respectively, Germany and Italy awarded Hungary a part of Transylvania, and Bulgaria the Dobruja, at the expense of Rumania. In the Far East, Japan proclaimed on August 1 the intention of establishing prosperity throughout Greater East Asia—left undefined by boundaries, and by August 30 a Japanese ultimatum had resulted in a right of entry into French Indo-China for Japanese forces. On August 3 Japan protested a United States embargo of July 31, 1940, on the sale of aviation gasoline outside the Western Hemisphere.

To meet the worsening situation, American defense policy developed swiftly. A Permanent Joint Board on Defense was established with Canada August 18, and, to obtain vital bases and to supply Britain with destroyers urgently needed after the losses at Dunkirk, an arrangement was agreed upon September 2 conveying to the United States, under 99-year leases, eight bases, two as gifts in Newfoundland and Bermuda and six in the Caribbean area, and to Great Britain fifty over-age destroyers. At home, selective training and service was

---

[22] *New York Times*, Aug. 1, 1940, p. 13.
[23] *Department of State Bulletin*, III, 48.

approved on September 16. A loan of $25,000,000 was extended to China September 25.

At that juncture, on September 27, 1940, Germany, Italy, and Japan joined in a ten-year military-economic alliance. This tripartite pact, as Secretary Hull immediately observed,[24] did not substantially alter a situation that had existed for many years; nevertheless it formalized the alliance for aggression in Europe and the Far East and hardened the choices before the United States in the future. The Japanese Government publicly mentioned the question of war with the United States October 5, protested on October 7 the prohibition being placed by the United States on further exports of iron and steel scrap to Japan, and on October 13 included the United States in a general invitation to other nations to join the tripartite pact. Repatriation of Americans from the Far East was immediately announced by the United States. In Europe, Italy—joined by Albanian forces—attacked Greece October 28. On November 12, Foreign Commissar Vyacheslav Molotov began consultations with the German Government on subjects then unknown. Hungary and Rumania joined the tripartite pact late in November.

On October 26, 1940, Secretary Hull declared that, in view of the evident aggressive intent of the tripartite pact and of the developing menace to the United States, impregnable defense, established "as speedily and as completely as possible," had become the "first need." He said: "To have peace, we must have security. To have security, we must be strong." [25] Defense, not alone neutrality, had become the guideline of our foreign policy. The national electoral campaign during the autumn, which on November 6 resulted in the re-election of President Roosevelt for a third term, disclosed differences over methods and program in the emergency confronting the Nation rather than partisanship with respect to this fundamental point of view as expressed by the Secretary.

Throughout these autumn months Great Britain, under the heavy bombardment of the blitz, was purchasing supplies under the "cash-and-carry" provisions of the neutrality act. The dwindling possibility of continuing such cash purchases had been formally brought to the attention of this Government in the summer of 1940 upon receipt on July 5 of a British *aide-mémoire* concerning their difficulties. Under the circumstances in which immediate American defense was to a major degree contingent on continued British resistance, this problem was under urgent consideration in Washington by August. It was then that standardization of arms was begun, partly to reduce expenses. And it was then that the possibility of requesting Congress

[24] *Ibid.*, p. 251.
[25] *Ibid.*, pp. 331–36.

to authorize loans for British purchases was rejected by the Cabinet lest such borrowing be on an insufficient scale and lest Allied war debts later impair the peace.[26]

The Secretary in his address of October 26 had declared that any contention that this country should not continue to afford "all feasible facilities for the obtaining of supplies by nations which, while defending themselves against barbaric attack, are checking the spread of violence and are thus reducing the danger to us" was "a denying of the inalienable right of self-defense." This was the principle upon which lend-lease was based. The method to implement it developed in coming weeks. On December 17 the President at a press conference proposed as a solution to the supply problem the lending of the needed materials themselves, rather than the money for their purchase.[27] Following his address on December 29, devoted to the program of making the United States the arsenal of democracy, and stressing the necessity of integrating into our defense activities the war needs of Britain and other free nations resisting aggression, the President on January 6, 1941, requested Congress to pass legislation authorizing lend-lease.

END OF THE FIRST PREPARATORY EFFORT

IN THE CLOSING months of the year 1940 the last seven meetings of the Interdepartmental Group on Post-War International Economic Problems and Policies were held, beginning October 15 and ending December 17. These meetings constituted a second series, distinguished by being devoted for the first time wholly to postwar preparations as originally projected for the Group. The work was done in accord with a program proposed by the Chairman, who stressed, as in the original plan for the entire work of the Advisory Committee on Problems of Foreign Relations, the necessity of basic research as the foundation for policy recommendations.

Under this program, the research would take into account alternative possibilities with respect to the world situation at the end of the war. The postwar political alignments of states and the over-all political and economic policies that would result from such alignments, as yet indeterminable, were of necessity major factors for consideration in any study of postwar economic problems. Widely varying assumptions, therefore, with respect to these factors, including the possibility of a German victory, had to be borne in mind. Furthermore, the unpredictability at that time of the economic effects of the actual fighting and the duration of the war made it necessary

---

[26] See E. R. Stettinius, Jr., *Lend-Lease, Weapon for Victory* (New York, 1944), pp. 55–65.

[27] *Ibid.*, pp. 1, 65.

to assume also wide variations from the prewar data on which the Group's studies had to be based. Consequently, with a view to the eventual utilization of these studies in the formulation of policy, they were to be in a form permitting their rapid adjustment to a developing situation.

The research would be devoted initially to commodity studies on a world basis, which would then be used in studying the economic structures and interrelationships of various regional blocs. It would lead to appraisal of the economic strengths and weaknesses of the major countries and regions and of their trade, productive capacities, and consumption requirements. It would also involve consideration of such questions as the effects of German subjugation on the economies of the various European states and the results, both internally and externally, were continental Europe to become isolated. Alternative possibilities with respect to trade, monetary, and financial policies and relations were to be surveyed, as were shipping and transportation problems. The first item on the program proposed by the Chairman was a survey of the economic aims of Germany, Italy, and Japan, and the last was a survey of possible alternative foreign economic policies for the United States. The basic studies were to be undertaken by various commodity specialists in the Government, working in commodity groups.

To carry out such a program, small sub-groups began to evolve from the start, their purpose being to prepare reports for consideration by the full Group. At the first meeting in the second series on October 15, a sub-group was appointed to study a draft memorandum already prepared on German economic aims. At the second meeting on October 29, it was decided to establish immediately subgroups on cotton, iron ore, and petroleum. By the time of its last meeting, the Group had decided to establish eight commodity groups as follows: (1) foodstuffs, fats and oils; (2) fibers; (3) rubber, hides and skins; (4) coffee, tea, cocoa, spices, tobacco; (5) metals; (6) fuels; (7) lumber, pulp and paper; and (8) chemicals and other nonmetallic mineral raw materials. Their chairmen and members were officials of technical competence in various Departments and agencies of the Government.[28] Four sub-groups on regional studies and one sub-group on commercial policy had also been established. The regional sub-groups were concerned respectively with Germany and the Continent of Europe, Japan and the Far East, the Soviet

---

[28] The sub-groups, in the above-named order, were presided over by representatives from the following Government agencies: (1) and (2) Department of Agriculture; (3) Department of Commerce; (4), (5), and (6) Tariff Commission; (7) Department of Commerce; and (8) Tariff Commission.

Union, and the British Commonwealth.[29]   This sub-group structure as agreed upon December 17 reflected the discussions in the Interdepartmental Group over the previous two months, when the Group had considered such papers as an outline for a typical commodity study and a general statement on the objectives of such studies and had reviewed the experiences of the commodity and regional sub-groups then in operation.   Thereafter, on three occasions beginning December 20, 1940, and ending March 3, 1941, the chairmen of the commodity and regional sub-groups met with Mr. Pasvolsky to consider the research problems being encountered in conducting the two lines of work.

However, the difficulties encountered throughout the first effort to make postwar preparations, arising out of the pressure of current problems, the largely *ad hoc* basis of the preparatory work, and the absence of an organized research staff, were reflected sufficiently even at the technical level of the interdepartmental sub-groups to cause the work rapidly to taper off, albeit without formal action.   Such research as continued from the impetus of the Group practically ceased to be distinguishable from regular governmental operations.   Within the Department of State, the surviving threads of this early pattern were caught up in new efforts made, step by step, to organize the preparation of postwar policy.

---

[29] The chairmen of the first and third of these sub-groups were representatives of the Department of Commerce and of the second and fourth, an officer of the Department of State.   In addition, a regional sub-group on the United States and the Western Hemisphere, three "subject study" sub-groups on monetary and financial policy, transportation, and population movements, and a sub-group on Alternatives of Foreign Economic Policy for the United States, were projected but not established.   See appendix 6.

CHAPTER III

New Measurement and New Organization, 1941

THE YEAR 1941 was decisive for the organization of the preparation of postwar policy. As the year began, organized research was instituted in the Department; as it closed, the decision was made to organize postwar preparation on a new and full-scale basis. The period between was one of spreading war, enunciation of broad long-range policy objectives, and indecision on the question of how to proceed with postwar preparation.

HOW TO PROCEED?

THIS QUESTION had two aspects; one concerned research, the other policy consideration. The efforts so far made toward preparation had shown that the establishment of a staff devoting its full time to research was a basic requirement for effective policy discussion. Such assistance of this character as had been given had been confined to the economic side of the work and was rendered by assignment of papers to junior officers having technical competence, most of them in the Division of Trade Agreements in the Department of State.

Consideration of this matter began in conversations between Under Secretary Welles and Mr. Pasvolsky, who raised the need for organized research in the Department of State in relation to both war and postwar problems. Under then existing circumstances, these two types of problems continued to be inextricably intermingled. A specific proposal was made November 22, 1940, by Mr. Pasvolsky to establish a Division of Special Research "charged with the analysis and appraisal of developments and conditions arising out of present-day disturbed international relations and requiring special study as an aid to formulation of foreign policy." It was also suggested that this Division should collaborate with other interested Departments and agencies of the Government and should have such additional duties as the Secretary of State might assign. A small staff of only eight was contemplated at that time, comprising economists, Foreign

Service officers, and political scientists, with junior research and steno-graphic assistants.[1] The new Division would constitute the secretariat and principal research agency both for the Inter-Departmental Group to Consider Post-War Economic Problems and Policies and, in the political field, the Departmental Advisory Committee on Problems of Foreign Relations when again active. Following approval by Secretary Hull, the Division was established February 3, 1941, as projected.[2] Mr. Pasvolsky was designated its Chief, while continuing to act as Special Assistant to the Secretary. The Departmental Order issued by Secretary Hull was kept confidential in accord with the general policy of secrecy then necessitated in many fields of the Department's work by reason of the tense international situation.

The question of reviving the Advisory Committee on Problems of Foreign Relations had come up in the consideration of the establishment of the research division. However, the same causes that had brought about the Committee's inactivity and the tapering off of the work of the Inter-Departmental Group on Economic Problems and Policies continued to operate. In view of the Committee members' increasing preoccupation with current problems and of the numerous shifts of members to the new defense undertakings, the practical possibility of reviving the Advisory Committee along its old lines appeared doubtful. The difficulty of carrying on work of such a high-policy level on a relatively unorganized basis was also a deterrent factor.

At the same time pressure to arrange for systematic discussion increased. Not only were events during the early months of 1941 enlarging the demands of current problems, but the very consideration accorded these problems was leading to wider bases for American postwar policies. The first wider basis was provided by the President in his annual message to the Congress, January 6, 1941, when in defining the objective of a secure future, he stated:

" . . . we look forward to a world founded upon four essential human freedoms.

"The first is freedom of speech and expression—everywhere in the world.

"The second is freedom of every person to worship God in his own way—everywhere in the world.

"The third is freedom from want—which, translated into world terms, means economic understandings which will secure to every nation a healthy peacetime life for its inhabitants—everywhere in the world.

"The fourth is freedom from fear—which, translated into world

---

[1] The entire Departmental personnel for the fiscal year ending June 1940 totaled but 1,009—only 35 more than the year before. The Foreign Service had risen only 389 in the same period, to a total of 4,119.

[2] See appendix 22.

terms, means a world-wide reduction of armaments to such a point and in such a thorough fashion that no nation will be in a position to commit an act of physical aggression against any neighbor—anywhere in the world.
"That is no vision of a distant millennium. It is a definite basis for a kind of world attainable in our time and generation." [3]

From that time on, human freedoms were fundamental in any consideration of a future world order based on cooperation among free countries.

In the same address the President had requested the passage of legislation authorizing lend-lease. After comprehensive debate on American foreign policy, the desired legislation was approved in Congress by a vote substantially nonpartisan and was signed March 11. While implementation of the act began immediately, negotiation of the necessary international agreements, even in the preliminary form of those with American republics, took place more slowly. These agreements, when made, had significant bearing on postwar policy, particularly on economic policy. That with Great Britain, which had the most decisive effect in this respect and which became the model finally for all agreements, was not completed for almost a year. Responsibility for the Department's work on this matter was vested primarily in the Division of Trade Agreements and related interdepartmental bodies. Although the economic section of the new Division of Special Research took part in this work, it was undertaken chiefly through the usual Department channels and is not, therefore, described in detail here.

The beginning of the year also saw the first evidences of another development that was to have a fundamental effect on postwar policy. The Department received information that Germany intended to attack the Soviet Union. This fact was communicated to the Soviet Government during a series of conversations between Under Secretary Welles and the Soviet Ambassador, Mr. Constantin Oumansky. On January 21, 1941, the Ambassador was informed that this Government had decided to lift the moral embargo applied to the Soviet Union during its war with Finland. [4]

In still other respects, the scene of war was broadening. In February, Germany made military and economic demands on Yugoslavia. Britain mined the waters of Singapore. Japan's Foreign Minister stated that Oceania must be ceded to the Asiatics.

In March, Bulgaria and next Yugoslavia joined the tripartite pact.

---

[3] H. Doc. 1, 77th Cong., 1st sess., serial vol. 10598.
[4] The moral embargo had been imposed as a matter of official policy to curtail exports to the Soviet Union in the absence of any legislative authorization for their prohibition. It took the form of a public request by the Government to exporters to forego certain of their legal rights and thus deprive certain states of supplies as an indication of this country's disapproval of their actions.

The Yugoslav Government taking this action was promptly overthrown by a domestic *coup d'état*. Though still fighting, Italy had failed to defeat Greece. The stage was set for a German thrust into the Balkans. In this month, also, additional information of intended German attack was given to the Soviet Ambassador by the Department.

In April, Germany, Italy, Bulgaria, and soon Hungary attacked Yugoslavia, with which the Soviet Union had just concluded a Treaty of Friendship and Non-Aggression. British troops entered Iraq after a pro-Axis *coup d'état* had occurred there. In Greece organized resistance was broken after German invasion, and British forces there were compelled to withdraw. In the Far East a neutrality pact was signed between Japan and the Soviet Union. The United States sent reenforcements to the Philippines, made an agreement with the Minister of Denmark on the defense of Greenland, and reached a broad arrangement with Canada for production and exchange of defense articles.

In May, Japan undertook to guarantee the new boundaries between French Indochina and Thailand; Rudolph Hess flew on a mysterious errand to Scotland; the Vichy Government in France committed itself to further economic collaboration with Germany; and German troops were advancing in Libya toward the Egyptian border. Sinkings by German naval action, many of which occurred in Western Hemisphere waters, continued at a grave rate. On May 27 President Roosevelt, warning that war was approaching the brink of the Western Hemisphere itself, proclaimed the existence of an unlimited national emergency and announced that American naval patrols had been extended in the Atlantic to assist in safeguarding deliveries to Britain.[5]

As these new expansions of the war occurred, the over-all organization of preparation to meet postwar problems came again, early in April, under consideration in the Department of State. By then all organized postwar efforts at a policy level had come to an end. The main lines of progress were in connection with the organization and staffing of the Division of Special Research. Some economic studies were under way, largely on long-range problems of lend-lease. Political studies had not yet been started. Three staff members, who worked exclusively in the economic field, were on duty: H. Julian Wadleigh and Richard Eldridge, drawn from the Division of Trade Agreements in the Department, and Miss Ruth B. Russell, from the Brookings Institution. It was not until May 19 that an officer in the political field, Harley Notter, was assigned to the new work, and he did not report for duty from the Department's Division of the American Republics until the end of that month.

---

[5] *Department of State Bulletin*, IV, 647, 654.

Meanwhile, on April 11, Mr. Pasvolsky suggested to Mr. Welles that the time was opportune for reviving the Advisory Committee on Problems of Foreign Relations as a single body without division into subcommittees.[6] It would have two principal functions. It would consider the organization of peace, with the Division of Special Research supplying the necessary papers for discussion, and it would review the economic plans worked out by the Interdepartmental Group—to be reorganized—and direct negotiations on economic problems when undertaken. The membership of the reconstituted committee would, as before, be the high-ranking officers of the Department, though some of them might come to meetings only when matters of special interest to them in connection with their individual duties were under discussion. The Committee would continue under Mr. Welles' chairmanship, with a new vice chairman to replace Mr. Wilson who had retired.

This proposal and various substitute plans were discussed over the next several weeks by Mr. Welles with Myron C. Taylor, who had already made a general proposal to the President for a strong study group, and with others. Lack of certainty regarding organizational plans for preparation of postwar policy therefore joined with the burden of current problems in delaying during the spring of 1941 any decision upon a definite course of action with respect to postwar problems. Furthermore, since responsibility for the swiftly expanding international economic aspects of the defense program was scattered among new defense agencies and "old-line" Departments, confusion was beginning to arise over responsibility for formulating postwar policy in regard to various fundamental problems in the economic field. Accordingly, postwar problems were considered in the Department in the spring of 1941 only by the small research staff and by superior officers individually in connection with long-range aspects of current problems. Nevertheless, the preparation, while handicapped and barely in motion, was yet under way, with the question of how better to proceed under consideration on the periphery of the main preoccupations of the period. Secretary Hull, in an address on April 24 in which he stated that the war might last a long time, could report that the Department was at work on "the task of creating ultimate conditions of peace with justice." [7]

That task, which was the subject of growing interest on the part of the public and in many Departments and agencies in Washington, was again stressed by Secretary Hull in a radio address on May 18, 1941:

"   .   .   .   it is none too early to lay down at least some of the principles by which policies must be guided at the conclusion of the

<hr>

[6] For text of proposal memorandum, see appendix 7.
[7] *Department of State Bulletin*, IV, 494.

war, to press for a broad program of world economic reconstruction and to consider tentative plans for the application of those policies.

"The main principles, as proven by experience, are few and simple:

1. Extreme nationalism must not again be permitted to express itself in excessive trade restrictions.
2. Non-discrimination in international commercial relations must be the rule, so that international trade may grow and prosper.
3. Raw-material supplies must be available to all nations without discrimination.
4. International agreements regulating the supply of commodities must be so handled as to protect fully the interests of the consuming countries and their people.
5. The institutions and arrangements of international finance must be so set up that they lend aid to the essential enterprises and the continuous development of all countries, and permit the payment through processes of trade consonant with the welfare of all countries.

"Measures taken to give effect to these principles must be freely open to every nation which desires a peaceful life in a world at peace and is willing to cooperate in maintaining that peace.

.   .   .   .

"In the final reckoning, the problem becomes one of establishing the foundations of an international order in which independent nations cooperate freely with each other for their mutual gain— of a world order, not new but renewed, which liberates rather than enslaves.

"We shall not be able to do this until we have a world free from imminent military danger and clear of malign political intrigue. . . . We can expect no healthy development until the menace of conquest has been brought to an end." [8]

Interest in postwar problems was also increasing in Congress, where a Senate Resolution was introduced by Senator Elbert D. Thomas of Utah to authorize the Committee on Foreign Relations to make a full study of all matters pertaining to the establishment of a lasting peace throughout the world.[9] In this connection, Secretary Hull informed the Chairman of the Committee, Senator Walter F. George of Georgia, on June 7, of the Department's activities in preparation for the future peace. The Secretary wrote:

"Since the outbreak of hostilities in Europe, the Department of State has been, as a matter of course, assembling and analyzing pertinent information bearing on post-war problems of international relations. This includes careful watching of current developments in various parts of the world in their possible bearing on post-war developments; an examination of past experience for whatever light it may throw on the future; and a study of pro-

---

[8] *Ibid.*, IV, 575–76.
[9] S. Res. 110, 77th Cong., 1st sess., *Cong. Rec.*, May 5, 1941, vol. 87, p. 3551.

posals being put forward from various quarters as to ways and means of handling the many and complex problems involved.

"The Department is concerned with defining and formulating the broad objectives of desirable post-war policies, comprising the restoration of order under law in international relations; the elimination of the crushing burden of competitive armaments; and the creation of the kind of international commercial and financial relations which are essential to the preservation of stable peace and to the promotion of economic welfare for the peoples of all nations. The Department is likewise concerned with studying the various alternative methods of moving toward, and eventually attaining, these broad objectives, in order to be able to apply the basic considerations thus developed to specific situations as and when occasion arises for meeting specific problems.

"For the purpose of facilitating this work, there was established, in January, 1940, a departmental Advisory Committee on Problems of Foreign Relations.   More recently, in order to systematize more effectively the assembling and analyzing of the necessary data, there was created in the Department of State a Division of Special Research, which is charged, among other duties, with the conduct of appropriate studies in the field of post-war problems.

"Studies relating to various specialized phases of the subject, especially as regards problems of economic policy, have also been and are under way in several other interested departments and agencies of the Government, notably the Departments of the Treasury, Commerce and Agriculture, the Tariff Commission, and the Federal Reserve Board. The experts of the several departments and agencies working in this field are in contact and consultation with each other, thus making it possible to utilize for the purpose in view the resources of the entire executive branch of the Government."

Concurrently, the events growing out of the war were etching a more portentous picture of national concern. An American ship, the S. S. *Robin Moor* en route to South Africa, was sunk without warning on May 21 by a German submarine. In June, Axis funds in this country were frozen, and the withdrawal of German and Italian consular staffs because of improper activities was requested. Germany and Italy retaliated, asking the withdrawal of American consular staffs from territories under their control. The United States and Canada set up joint economic committees to coordinate defense production and to reduce economic dislocation after the war.

Then, on June 22, 1941, the German Government launched its attack against the Union of Soviet Socialist Republics. The war picture altered swiftly, as the Soviet Union massively defended itself on the Eastern Front, as in the north Soviet-Finnish hostilities were renewed, and as Rumania and Italy entered the struggle in the East. Prime Minister Churchill immediately pledged aid to the Soviet Union. The United States released Soviet credits and promised American aid under its policy of giving assistance to any country fighting aggression. These decisions were basic both to the war and to subsequent Allied policy and, after United States entrance into the war, led to the collaboration of the major powers of the world in defeating the Axis and in creating the international organization of the United Nations after victory. At the moment, it was a matter of question in most quarters, and disbelief in some, whether the Soviet Union could successfully withstand the German attack.

While the Germans pressed ahead in the Soviet Union during July, United States forces, acting pursuant to an exchange of letters between the United States and Iceland July 1, replaced British forces there in order to prevent a possible German occupation of an outpost of fundamental strategic importance to American security. This Government expressed to the Japanese Government its hope that Japan would not attack the Soviet Union and received the reply that no change of policy was then contemplated.[10] A few days later, Japan occupied Indochina. This Japanese action had the immediate effect of removing the basis for continuing the conversations between the United States and Japan that, with exchanges of proposals for a possible general Far Eastern settlement, had been proceeding in Washington during the past several months. Moreover, it threatened essential supplies of American defense materials from the South Pacific. President Roosevelt at once proposed the neutralization of Indochina.[11] While a reply was awaited, the United States froze Japanese assets in this country, July 25, and put petroleum products under embargo with respect to Japan on August 1.[12] The reply of the Japanese Government on August 6 side-stepped the President's proposal. Two days later Ambassador Nomura suggested a meeting of the responsible heads of the two states to discuss means of adjusting the relations of their countries.[13] Exploratory talks concerning that suggestion began later in August.

POSTWAR STEPS BY MAJOR POWERS

In an address at the Norwegian Legation in Washington, July 22, 1941, the Acting Secretary, Mr. Welles, suggested "that the free governments of peace-loving nations everywhere should even now be considering and discussing the way in which they can best prepare for the better day which must come, when the present contest is ended . . ." He emphasized that an "adequate instrumentality must unquestionably be found" to achieve peaceful and equitable international adjustments and advocated international control of armaments with a view to "real disarmament," and establishment in the

---

[10] *Peace and War*, pp. 685, 686–87, 691–92.

[11] *Ibid.*, pp. 699–703.

[12] *Department of State Bulletin*, V, 73, 101.

[13] *Peace and War*, pp. 705–9.

future peace of the right of all peoples to equal economic enjoyment. This address directed attention once again to security as the basic objective in the future.[14]

Two further steps of significance for the postwar preparation were occurring at approximately the same time. The first was the laying of the foundation, during consultations held in London and Moscow by Harry Hopkins as the President's personal representative, for the future system of great power conferences. This took place as the second was being arranged, namely, the cooperative development of postwar policy among the major powers begun by President Roosevelt and Prime Minister Winston Churchill at a conference, held in August off the little coastal settlement of Argentia on the Avalon peninsula, Newfoundland, on the current and prospective problems of joint concern arising out of the war.

Mr. Hopkins, in conversation with Premier Joseph Stalin during July, sought information concerning the Soviet military position in relation to the problem of supplying the aid urgently needed on both fronts in the struggle against Germany. Since planning for a long war was necessary and since the relative strategic weight of each front as well as the interest of each country had to be considered in allocating resources, he unofficially suggested the possibility of a conference of representatives of the United States, United Kingdom, and the Soviet Union at the conclusion of the current battle on the Eastern Front. Premier Stalin replied that, if officially requested, he would issue invitations for such a meeting. Mr. Hopkins then returned to London and accompanied Prime Minister Churchill to the Atlantic Conference, where his report on his Moscow conversations was considered. The President and Prime Minister Churchill agreed on a joint message to Premier Stalin, sent August 15, officially suggesting a meeting on apportionment of joint resources. The meeting, held at Moscow in September, facilitated the early provision of lend-lease aid to the Soviet Union. At the close of this first "Moscow conference," W. Averell Harriman, Chairman of the American Mission, indicated on behalf of all participants that "the conference declares that it is the determination of the three Governments to establish, after the final destruction of Nazi tyranny, a peace which will give all countries an opportunity to live in security on their own territory without knowing either fear or want." [15]

The President and the Prime Minister agreed in their meeting off Argentia upon the issuance of a declaration of common principles on which they based "their hopes for a better future for the world." Agreement was facilitated at the start by the British offer to make available the texts of their wartime agreements and by their assurances

---

[14] *Department of State Bulletin,* V, 75–76.

[15] *Ibid.,* pp. 134, 180, 276, 365–66.

that no secret commitments stood in the way of the contemplated declaration. Recalling the influence of such commitments on the peace that followed the first World War, the President had been particularly desirous of information on this point.

The declaration known as the Atlantic Charter was written, on the basis of a British draft, by the President and the Prime Minister with the assistance, respectively, of Under Secretary Welles and Harry Hopkins and of Sir Alexander Cadogan, Permanent Under Secretary for Foreign Affairs. It was not a formal, signed document, but a statement agreed upon by the two Heads of Government. Two of the "Four Freedoms", freedom from want and freedom from fear, were explicitly included, while freedom of religion and freedom of information were, President Roosevelt subsequently stated, implicit. The Charter, announced August 14, 1941, contained eight points:

"First, their countries seek no aggrandizement, territorial or other;

"Second, they desire to see no territorial changes that do not accord with the freely expressed wishes of the peoples concerned;

"Third, they respect the right of all peoples to choose the form of government under which they will live; and they wish to see sovereign rights and self-government restored to those who have been forcibly deprived of them;

"Fourth, they will endeavor, with due respect for their existing obligations, to further the enjoyment by all States, great or small, victor or vanquished, of access, on equal terms, to the trade and to the raw materials of the world which are needed for their economic prosperity;

"Fifth, they desire to bring about the fullest collaboration between all nations in the economic field with the object of securing, for all, improved labor standards, economic advancement and social security;

"Sixth, after the final destruction of the Nazi tyranny, they hope to see established a peace which will afford to all nations the means of dwelling in safety within their own boundaries, and which will afford assurance that all the men in all the lands may live out their lives in freedom from fear and want;

"Seventh, such a peace should enable all men to traverse the high seas and oceans without hindrance;

"Eighth, they believe that all of the nations of the world, for realistic as well as spiritual reasons, must come to the abandonment of the use of force. Since no future peace can be maintained if land, sea, or air armaments continue to be employed by nations which threaten, or may threaten, aggression outside of their frontiers, they believe, pending the establishment of a wider and permanent system of general security, that the disarmament of such nations is essential. They will likewise aid and encourage all other practicable measures which will lighten for peace-loving peoples the crushing burden of armaments." [16]

---

[16] *Ibid.*, pp. 112, 125.

Although refinements in the text had been made in the process of drafting and redrafting, the substance of the declaration had been readily agreed upon. Only the fourth and eighth points presented difficulty. In the fourth point the clause "with due respect for their existing obligations" was inserted when the Prime Minister stated that, without that clause, the broad postwar economic objectives of the United States draft might conflict with the Ottawa agreements for imperial preference within the British Empire and would have to be submitted to the Commonwealth Governments. The clause was accepted by the United States in order to avoid the delay that would otherwise have been entailed. This discussion reflected the same problem that had been presented earlier and which was to exist for some months thereafter in connection with the drafting of what became Article VII of the Mutual Aid—commonly called Lend-Lease—Agreements. Throughout, the United States insisted on multilateral as opposed to bilateral trade practices and pressed for collaboration in solving postwar world economic problems based on a policy of nondiscriminatory treatment. On the eighth point, the British had preferred in place of "a wider and permanent system of general security," the words "an effective international organization"—a concept about which the President then had some misgivings arising out of the League experience and which he felt might not be fully supported by American public opinion at that time.[17]

The President in his report to the Congress August 21 termed this declaration "a goal." It provided a broader and more definite basis for comprehensive preparation of postwar policy within the United States Government than had existed heretofore, as well as a statement of basic principles and fundamental policies to which international opinion could rally.

The Soviet Government expressed agreement with the principles of the Charter through its Ambassador to Great Britain in a statement to an Inter-Allied Meeting in London on September 24:

"Considering that the practical application of these principles will necessarily adapt itself to the circumstances, needs, and historic peculiarities of particular countries, the Soviet Government can state that a consistent application of these principles will secure the most energetic support on the part of the Government and peoples of the Soviet Union." [18]

This was the second such meeting in London of the Allied Governments. At the first, on June 12, 1941, the Governments of the United Kingdom, Canada, Australia, New Zealand, and South Africa, the

[17] On this point, see Sumner Welles, *Where Are We Heading?* (New York, 1946), pp. 6–17.

[18] World Peace Foundation, *Documents on American Foreign Relations*, IV, 214–16. For the resolution adopted, referred to below, see *ibid.*, p. 219.

Governments-in-exile of Belgium, Czechoslovakia, Greece, Luxembourg, the Netherlands, Norway, Poland, and Yugoslavia, and representatives of General de Gaulle had resolved

> "That the only true basis of enduring peace is the willing cooperation of free peoples in a world in which, relieved of the menace of aggression, all may enjoy economic and social security; and that it is their intention to work together, and with other free peoples, both in war and peace to this end." [19]

These same Governments-in-exile and the representatives of the Free French joined with the Soviet Government at the second Inter-Allied Meeting in a resolution of September 24 adhering to the common principles of policy set forth in the Atlantic Charter and expressing their intention to cooperate in giving them effect. The development of an agreed core of policy to guide international action in the future, as well as during the war, had been begun.

PREPARATORY WORK, AUTUMN 1941

DURING THE remaining months of 1941, consideration of postwar matters intensified, and additional elements of future policy were clarified. The President stated to a "special" conference of the International Labor Organization (ILO) at its final session November 6 at the White House that "this war, like the last war, will produce nothing but destruction unless we prepare for the future now. We plan now for the better world we aim to build." Our object, he said, was "to achieve permanent cures." [20]

This "special" conference, which had convened in New York on October 27, was a substitute for the annual sessions of the ILO interrupted by the war. The conference had adopted a series of resolutions concerned with postwar policy in both the political and economic fields and with the role of the ILO in the preparations for the peace, with particular reference to the problems of relief and reconstruction and to the attainment of the economic and social objectives set forth in the Atlantic Charter, which the conference had endorsed. In his statement to the last session of the conference, the President said with respect to these objectives:

> "In the planning of such international action the ILO with its representation of labor and management, its technical knowledge and experience, will be an invaluable instrument for peace. Your organization will have an essential part to play in building up a stable international system of social justice for all peoples everywhere. As part of you, the people of the United States are determined to respond fully to the opportunity and challenge of this

---

[19] *Ibid.*, III, 444.
[20] *Department of State Bulletin*, V, 357-60.

historic responsibility, so well exemplified at this historic meeting in this historic home of an ancient democracy."

The first impetus toward the development of a general program of international cooperation in the cultural field after the war, which ultimately found expression in the creation of the United Nations Educational, Scientific and Cultural Organization, was given at a meeting on September 18 of the General Advisory Committee appointed by the President on July 31, 1941, to advise the Department of State on this Government's program of cultural relations with the other American republics. At that time, the preparation of a proposal for governmental action "in the Western Hemisphere and elsewhere, in all cultural fields" was projected, and work on this proposal then went forward in the Department, primarily through its Division of Cultural Relations.[21]

The Division of Special Research continued to make headway in its exploratory and other work although handicapped by insufficient personnel, by lack of a superior committee structure to use its research, and by undefined lines of function with respect to postwar matters within the Department. Some increase in staff was made with the addition to the political section of C. Easton Rothwell during the summer and of Mrs. Virginia Fox Hartley late in the year, and during the same period of John W. Evans and Mrs. Margaret H. Potter to the economic staff, and of David Williamson for administration. There were, however, only eleven officers in the Division at the end of 1941. The inadequacy of such a number to carry out the Division's responsibilities—which widened with events and with each stage of thinking, and with the growing realization that the necessary postwar studies would have to be made chiefly through this staff—was recognized by the Department. Nevertheless, expansion was not yet administratively practicable. The eleven officers were for the most part between thirty and forty years of age; most of them had earned degrees in graduate universities; and five had experience in the service of the Department at home or abroad, while two others had experience in other government work. The intention from the start was to create a Division representing, so far as possible, blended experience and constructive capabilities as well as advanced educational qualifications in the relevant general and specific fields of work.

The research officers, under the direction of Mr. Pasvolsky, approached their work variously, though staff meetings for coordination began late in the autumn. In the economic field specific studies continued to be undertaken. Here the lines of wartime and peacetime

---

[21] The Division of Special Research was represented by Mr. Notter in the September meeting of the General Advisory Committee and cooperated in the subsequent follow-through work in the Department.

problems were relatively clear in regard to the basic economic factors involved, and a program of specific studies could be drawn up more readily than in other fields. The interlocking character of commercial, financial, and monetary policies and their basic influence on the postwar economic structure had been recognized by the Subcommittee on Economic Problems in its discussions early in 1940. By the end of 1941 preliminary study of international financial and monetary problems by the economic section of the staff pointed to the possible need for the creation of new international institutions in these fields. The lend-lease negotiations with the British, which had been in progress since June 1941 and for which the Department of State had primary responsibility, had provided an immediate opportunity to obtain acceptance of the fundamental principles of commercial policy regarded by this Government as essential to a sound economic structure after the war.[22] Part of the work of the Division's economic section during this period, therefore, stemmed directly from these negotiations.

Refugees and relief were also major subjects of study. As early as March 1938, President Roosevelt had taken the initiative in proposing an international conference to discuss the problem of refugees from Germany and Austria, forced by Nazis to leave their homes because of their political opinions, religious beliefs, or racial origins. This conference had met at Evian, France, July 6, 1938. Myron C. Taylor, representing the United States and assisted by James G. McDonald and George L. Warren, had been elected Chairman of the Conference. The Intergovernmental Committee on Refugees, established by the Evian Conference, was charged with the responsibility both for refugees outside Germany who had not settled in new locations and for the larger number still within Germany and Austria who for racial, religious, or political reasons found it necessary to seek refuge elsewhere. President Roosevelt's appointment in December 1939 of Myron C. Taylor, Chairman of the Intergovernmental Committee, as his personal representative to Pope Pius XII had been occasioned in part by concern over the future of the millions of persons uprooted by the war.

The problem of postwar relief had been of concern within the Department of State and among many governments. Anglo-American exchanges of view on this subject had been initiated by the British in September 1940, and at the Inter-Allied Meeting in London on September 24, 1941, a resolution, introduced after consultation between

---

[22] Messrs. Acheson, Feis, Pasvolsky, Hawkins, and Hickerson had participated in consultation with the Secretary in the formulation of Article VII of the American draft agreement, in which these basic principles were incorporated. For the text of this draft article as originally communicated to the British and for the final text, see appendix 8.

the British and American Governments, was adopted establishing under British auspices an Inter-Allied Committee on Post-War Requirements. In connection with this resolution, the United States Government declared through Ambassador Winant its readiness "at the appropriate time to consider in what respect it can cooperate in accomplishing the aims in view" and, in the meantime, asked to be kept fully informed of the projected discussions and consulted "regarding any plans that might emerge therefrom." [23] These developments provided the background for the study initiated in September 1941, by the Division of Special Research into the problems of relief, rehabilitation, and displaced persons.

In the political field, basic uncertainties rendered it more difficult to determine the problems that might, or were likely to, confront the Nation at the end of the war. The future circumstances to be dealt with were subject to possibly radical change, since many of the attributes of international life, and even of its basic character, were no longer firmly fixed. It had become necessary to think in terms of questions concerning the conditions or arrangements that would exist, or could or should be brought into existence, at the end of the war: What kind of nations? What kind of international relations? What kind of transitional arrangements? What kind of permanent arrangements? Accordingly, the officers of the political section, aside from such studies as an analysis of the implications of each point of the Atlantic Charter from the standpoint of future policy, undertook to formulate an inclusive program of studies in the light of alternatives with respect to possible future conditions and resulting problems and of such official expressions of policy as had already been enunciated.

The political research studies under way by the fall of 1941 envisaged formulation of an integrated program of policies and action for dealing with postwar problems in three stages or periods of time. The first was the period of transition from war to peace, covering the problems rising immediately after the cessation of hostilities and prior to the conclusion of formal peace arrangements; second, the conclusion of such peace arrangements; and third, the conduct of affairs in the critical period during which such arrangements were being put into effect. These studies took into account from the outset the possibility that a peace settlement with or concerning the enemy states might not be constructed in one step at a formal peace conference and might not entail a peace conference at all. A series of agreements or declarations was regarded as more probable. The possibility that the Soviet Union would share in the postwar decisions was also taken into account practically from the start of research in the late spring of 1941,

---

[23] *Department of State Bulletin,* V, 235.

despite the Nazi military successes on the Eastern Front during the second half of 1941 and in 1942.

The Division, during its pioneer efforts in the summer and autumn, found that the determination of policy in regard to political problems must be given priority since international political stabilization would be a prerequisite for security and for progress in every other field. By the end of the autumn, an inclusive program covering all foreseeable postwar problems except for their technical aspects had been formulated. In order that the basic research might lead into determination of policy, it was proposed to approach these problems so far as feasible from the standpoint of four questions: What does the United States want? What favorable and unfavorable conditions will confront us in achieving these objectives? What course and schedule of action will be required to achieve these objectives? What machinery may be needed in carrying out these objectives when achieved? In the course of this exploratory work it became evident that, to be effective, the research staff must be capable not only of advanced research in the usual sense but also of thinking in the unusual terms of national policy. This was imperative for a staff stemming directly from the office of the Secretary of State through his Special Assistant for postwar matters and charged with doing the research for a superior policy committee when activated.

Research so conceived was policy study, necessarily highly confidential and requiring special arrangements to provide for its needs. One of the early undertakings was the collection and analytical compilation of the views and attitudes of all governments except the Axis on the broad subjects covered in the eight points of the Atlantic Charter.   An information file was established in the autumn to maintain materials, selected from telegrams and despatches reaching the Department, on the facts and trends of developments likely to be needed for the Division's studies. A program for the preparation of new forms and types of maps and related map studies was arranged, to be carried out under the direction of the Geographer of the Department of State, Samuel W. Boggs. Studies made outside the Department were beginning to be available, and their analysis was begun. In particular, the Council of Foreign Relations was preparing valuable studies in its political, armaments, territorial, and economic series, all of which were transmitted to the Division.[24]

Since it was highly debatable in the climate of American public opinion before Pearl Harbor whether, or to what degree, the people of the United States would support active participation in postwar in-

---

[24] From early in 1940 to the end of hostilities, 682 memoranda were transmitted to the Department by the Council on Foreign Relations. These were prepared under grants from the Rockefeller Foundation totaling approximately $300,000.

ternational political, territorial, economic, and social affairs and in an organized world order, studies requiring an immediate assumption, one way or another, concerning United States participation were not stressed. Rather, materials needed in any event for policy consideration were made ready, in anticipation of a decision to establish the necessary superior structure for arriving at policy recommendations.

It was also one of the principal functions of the Division during this initial period to assist in evolving that superior structure. Uncertainty with respect to organizational plans, as well as the urgent problems developing in connection with the war, continued to block all attempts to institute an effective committee structure for consideration of postwar problems. Other nations now began to approach this Government to ascertain the nature of American postwar preparations. On September 25, a despatch was received from our Legation at Canberra enclosing a document on Australian preparations with respect to "reconstruction," with a request for any similar material on United States "Post-Defense Planning." The British Government in October raised the question whether this Government desired to take part in a joint study with the Allied Governments concerning future international juridical organization. To this, only a reply indicating interest in receiving further information was made. Since a position on any one aspect of future policy was impracticable until fundamental questions concerning related aspects were clarified, the need for prepared American views on all major postwar problems was becoming pressing.

Although a reorganization of the former Advisory Committee was contemplated during the early summer, to be effective by September 1941, no action was taken. Questions concerning the scope and feasibility of such a structure were arising especially because of the prospective postwar responsibilities of the new wartime agencies being established under broad executive orders. Until the early autumn the Office of the Coordinator of Information, established July 11, seemed likely to undertake large-scale preparation in the postwar field. The main question regarding the scope of such responsibilities, however, arose in connection with the Economic Defense Board, established July 30 under Vice President Henry A. Wallace, inasmuch as its functions included advising the President on the relationship of defense measures to postwar economic reconstruction and on steps to expedite the establishment of sound, peacetime international economic relationships. In a period when defense preparation had paramount claim on attention in all superior posts of the Government, the extent to which such responsibilities could actually be carried out naturally remained unsettled for some time.

Meantime, the fields that would present postwar problems continued to expand, and the need for an organized committee actively to consider them became more urgent. Various possibilities were explored. One was whether some part of the need could be satisfied by the organization of a group of highly qualified persons outside the Department, who could consult in the Department approximately two days a week. As memoranda prepared in the Division of Special Research pointed out, however, The Inquiry under President Woodrow Wilson had worked as effectively as it did only by overcoming many difficulties that, in considerable degree, were attributable to the lack of regular responsibilities and relationships within the Government by the members of The Inquiry. It was believed in addition that postwar preparations must be carried out within the Department in accord with its constitutional responsibility for the formulation and conduct of foreign policy under the President.

Another possible course was to divide postwar economic preparations within the Government, leaving only political problems for consideration by the Department of State. This solution, however, was highly questionable from the standpoint of effective policy formulation and administration. By September 1941 when many of the agencies of the Government had manifested interest in postwar economic policies, it was evident that, unless some integrative plan could be evolved, the individual agencies might each consider war and postwar policy in intermingled fashion, with postwar policy inevitably subordinated to wartime policy and with confusing and time-wasting results. Complete handling of the problems by a single organization was clearly necessary.

On September 12, Mr. Pasvolsky advanced for the consideration of the Secretary a new proposal, supported by a study of developments prepared by the political research staff.[25] He proposed that the President be requested to authorize the creation of an advisory committee for preparatory work on all phases of postwar foreign policy. The committee would be appointed by the Secretary of State and work under his chairmanship, or alternatively, the President might himself appoint the committee and designate the Secretary of State as Chairman. In either case, its membership would include Vice President Henry A. Wallace, and a number of prominent persons outside the Department as well as a number of officials of the Department. The Under Secretary of State would be Vice Chairman. One of the Department members would be designated its executive officer. Subcommittees were envisaged for political and territorial problems, armament problems, and economic and financial problems. They would

_____
[25] See appendix 9.

be composed partly of members of the main committee and partly of representatives of other interested Departments and agencies of the Government. The Division of Special Research and other appropriate divisions of the Department of State and of other Departments and agencies and cooperating nongovernmental organizations would prepare research studies and draft memoranda. All work would be under the authority of the advisory committee, and its recommendations would be made to the President through its chairman.

This proposal for drawing together the resources of the entire Government and the ability outside the Government constituted the basis of the plan finally adopted. Conversations for the purpose of perfecting a recommendation to the President ensued between the Secretary, the Under Secretary, and Mr. Pasvolsky, whom the Secretary desired to have serve as executive officer of the proposed committee. The main outlines of the plan were readily agreed upon, as was also the suggestion that the Division of Special Research should be the secretariat as well as the principal research agency for the main committee and its subcommittees.

Early in October the Secretary and the Under Secretary took up the proposal with the President orally and in general terms, and shortly thereafter a definitive recommendation covering all principal arrangements was drafted. The necessity of defining more specifically the President's general arrangements for the conduct within the Government of economic defense work having postwar implications remained. At that point, however, the world situation was moving into the final throes of crisis that preceded the Japanese attack on Pearl Harbor, and the Secretary suspended further action on the recommendation.

The crisis was an enveloping one. It heightened during the summer and the autumn simultaneously on sea and land, in the East and in the West. The war was spreading outward from the initial centers of combat. In the Near and Middle East, first Syria and Lebanon and then Iran had become involved in the hostilities. Free French and British forces had invaded the two Levantine states in June in order to prevent their being used, with the acquiescence of the Vichy French, as a base for Axis operations. In August, British and Soviet troops occupied Iran to check Axis infiltration there as the German offensive drove toward the adjacent Soviet oil fields. With the German advance east in Europe and in North Africa and the evident Japanese disposition to move south and west in Asia, the possibility grew of an eventual juncture of these two aggressive powers.

After the U. S. S. *Greer* had been attacked by a German submarine in American defense waters and after several American merchant ships had been sunk, the President announced on September 11, 1941, an order to the U. S. Navy to shoot on sight German and Italian vessels of war entering the waters within the limits of the Western Hemisphere. On October 9 he requested Congressional action to amend the neutrality act so as to permit the arming of American flag ships engaged in foreign commerce, and to permit them to carry cargoes to belligerent ports.[26]   Shortly thereafter, American lives were lost in a submarine attack on the U. S. S. *Kearny*. The "shooting," the President said, "has started. And history has recorded who fired the first shot." [27]   In November the neutrality act was amended as the President and the Secretary of State had recommended, although by a close vote. United States forces, acting upon agreement with the Netherlands and Brazil, occupied Dutch Guiana. Lend-lease aid was extended to the Free French.

In an urgent message to President Roosevelt delivered August 28, Premier Konoye invited the President to meet with him to discuss all important problems between Japan and the United States in the Pacific area and to explore means of saving the situation. The President and Secretary Hull considered that a prior meeting of minds on basic principles was necessary to assure success in such a meeting.[28] Four principles, in particular, were emphasized by the United States throughout the negotiations with Japan as fundamental to good relations among states: inviolability of territorial integrity and sovereignty of all nations; noninterference in the internal affairs of other countries; equality, including equality of commercial opportunity; and reliance upon international cooperation and conciliation for the prevention and pacific settlement of controversies.[29]   In the course of the negotiations that had continued intermittently from the spring of 1941 onward, proposals were exchanged and views were clarified, but the conflicting positions originally asserted by the two participants were not reconciled.

In October 1941 the United States inquired of the Japanese Government its intentions with respect to withdrawal of its troops from China and French Indochina. This point was crucial, but the answer was evasive. On November 7, Secretary Hull warned the Cabinet that relations with Japan were extremely critical. After a Japanese proposal failed to show a clear intent by Japan to pursue a peaceful course, a counterproposal was made by the United States for a broad settlement covering the entire Pacific area. This proposal was considered by the special Japanese emissary, Saburu Kurusu, to

---

[26] *Department of State Bulletin*, V, 193, 257.

[27] Address of Oct. 27, 1941, *ibid.*, p. 341.

[28] *Peace and War*, pp. 720–32.

[29] President Roosevelt's Message to Congress Dec. 15, 1941, *Department of State Bulletin*, V, 533–36.

be tantamount to the end of negotiations, though conversations continued. When reports indicated that Japanese forces were being increased in Indochina, the President on December 2 directed that an inquiry be made concerning the reasons. Following the receipt on December 5 of an unsatisfactory reply, the President in a personal message to the Emperor of Japan, December 6, urged withdrawal of the Japanese troops in Indochina; said that the large increases in Japanese land, sea, and air forces there had created a reasonable doubt of the defensive character of the continuing concentrations; and declared that the United States had no other than a peaceful intent toward Indochina and was prepared to seek the same assurances from other states concerned.

DECISIONS ON WAR AND PEACE

DIPLOMATIC negotiations were continuing when Japan without warning attacked Pearl Harbor, Hawaii, on December 7, at 1:20 p. m., Washington time. Negotiations were formally terminated by Japan fifty-five minutes later.

The following day Congress resolved that "the state of war . . . which has thus been thrust upon the United States is hereby formally declared." Beginning the same day, through other declarations of war or severances of relations by Allied and Axis countries, most of the world became aligned in the decisive struggle. On December 11 Germany and Italy declared war on the United States, and on the same day the existence of a state of war with those countries was recognized by the United States. Further declarations of war or severances of relations followed on both sides. Of the forty-seven neutrals approached by the United States in February 1940 in connection with the proposed conference of neutrals, less than one-half remained disassociated from the war by the end of 1941. After twenty-seven months of uneasy neutrality the United States was committed to world-wide warfare, and the American people immediately attained unity of purpose and action.

The President affirmed to the nation, in an address December 9: "We are going to win the war and we are going to win the peace that follows." [30]

Diplomatic actions toward both objectives were taken at once and almost simultaneously, first to attain victory, second to prepare for the day when victory had been won.

In the week following the attack on Pearl Harbor, this Government initiated a proposal, embodying earlier steps toward Allied unity of view and action, which became the Declaration by United Nations.

[30] *Ibid.*, pp. 476–80.

Decision on a second step in the same direction proposed by the Secretary of State, the creation of a Supreme War Council, was postponed. Instead, the President and the Prime Minister decided immediately to create an Anglo-American Combined Chiefs of Staff and a series of joint boards. Subsequently, unified commands were to be established in the various theaters of military operations.

The Declaration, drafted swiftly in the Department, the White House, and then in negotiation with our Allies, was dated the first day of January 1942. It was signed at the White House by the President, Prime Minister Churchill for the United Kingdom, Ambassador Maxim Litvinov for the Union of Soviet Socialist Republics, and Foreign Minister Tse-ven Soong for China, and at the Department of State by representatives of Australia, Belgium, Canada, Costa Rica, Cuba, Czechoslovakia, Dominican Republic, El Salvador, Greece, Guatemala, Haiti, Honduras, India, Luxembourg, the Netherlands, New Zealand, Nicaragua, Norway, Panama, Poland, Union of South Africa, and Yugoslavia.

Each signatory subscribed to the Atlantic Charter, and each pledged itself "to employ its full resources, military or economic, against those members of the Tripartite Pact and its adherents with which such government is at war" and "to cooperate with the Governments signatory hereto and not to make a separate armistice or peace with the enemies."

The original draft of the Declaration sent by Secretary Hull to the President on December 19 was "a joint declaration by the United States of America, China, Great Britain, the Union of Soviet Socialist Republics and other signatory Governments." The Supreme War Council proposed by the Secretary at the same time was to be composed of representatives of the United States, Great Britain, the Soviet Union, and China, "and possibly the Netherlands." This recognition of the preeminent role of the four major powers in the war and of Allied dependence for victory on their close collaboration was to be carried over from that time forward into our preparations for the peace.

Even before this country's entrance into the war, the Secretary of State on December 5, with the approval of the President, had sent a message to British Foreign Secretary Anthony Eden expressing the view that it would be inadvisable at that time for either the British, Soviet, or American Government to make any commitments with respect to specific terms of settlement after the war. Secretary Eden was then about to leave for Moscow for talks with Premier Stalin on war aims and postwar plans. It was clear from Ambassador Winant's latest reports, in which he gave his opinion that the British would be glad to receive our comments, that territorial and other questions would be raised with Mr. Eden in the talks. The three

Governments, the Secretary pointed out in his telegram, had established a common ground for postwar policies through their acceptance of the principles of the Atlantic Charter.   Discussions would naturally continue between the several governments directed toward the fullest agreement possible on basic policies and toward arrangements that would later be made with full public knowledge at the proper time.   After the war, those nations that had contributed to victory would join together in the restoration of peace and order.   The participation of the Soviet Union in these efforts would be no less than that of the United States and Great Britain. Therefore, the Secretary said, it would be unfortunate if we were hampered at the peace conference by prior commitments to individual countries, which might jeopardize the realization of our common aims with respect to an enduring peace.   Above all, the Secretary emphasized, there must not be any secret agreements.   The extension of the war in the Far East two days later brought China, as the principal military force among the Allies in that area, into the major-power group.

The second decision was to undertake preparation of all aspects of United States postwar foreign policy.   The basis of the decision was the recommendation for an advisory committee, on which no action had been taken since October.

On December 22, 1941, Secretary Hull wrote to the President as follows:

"MY DEAR MR. PRESIDENT:

"In accordance with your desire, recently expressed to me and to the Under Secretary of State, that the Department of State continue and expand its work of preparation for this country's effective participation in the solution of the vast and complicated problems of international relations which will confront us and the world after the final defeat of the forces of aggression and that, for that purpose, a Special Committee be created in the Department under my chairmanship, I am gladly taking appropriate steps to carry out your wishes.

"Enclosed herewith for your approval is a proposed list of members of what is to be known as The Advisory Committee on Post-War Foreign Policy consisting of several officials of the Government and of several prominent persons from outside the Government possessing special qualifications for contributing to the performance of the important task in view.   As the work develops, it may be found advisable to expand the membership of the Committee.

"The Committee will be charged with the conduct of the necessary studies and the preparation of recommendations to be submitted to you.   Its task will be to translate into a program of specific policies and measures the broad principles enunciated in the Atlantic Declaration and in your other pronouncements on post-war policy.   It will, accordingly, work in the inseparably interrelated fields of general security, limitation of armaments, sound international economic relationships, and other phases of international cooperation, the implementation of which is essential to enduring world peace and to economic progress.

"In all these fields, the Committee will establish and maintain close contact with all appropriate Departments and agencies of the Government, and with such non-governmental agencies as may be in a position to contribute to an all-round consideration of the problems involved. It will also establish and maintain close contact with all agencies working in the field of domestic post-emergency problems, in order that due weight may be given to the necessary interrelation of domestic and international policies and measures.

"All this would be for the purpose of making sure that the recommendations submitted to you would adequately take into account all points of view as regards desirable improvements upon, or modifications of, old systems, as well as such wholly new solutions as may be found possible and necessary.

"Since it is your further desire that all recommendations regarding post-war problems of international relations from all Departments and agencies of the Government be submitted to you through the Secretary of State, and that all conversations or negotiations with foreign governments bearing on post-war problems be conducted, under your authority, by or through the Department of State, I should appreciate it if you would cause the heads of the various Departments and agencies concerned to be apprised of your wishes.

"Finally, pursuant to your instructions in the matter, adequate research and other facilities needed for the functioning of the Committee will be set up in the Department of State or under its leadership. For this purpose, an emergency allocation of funds will be necessary, the actual amounts to be worked out by the Department with the Director of the Budget. In view of the urgent need for expanding as soon as possible the Department's existing facilities in this respect, I trust that you will see fit to approve such allocation of funds.

"Faithfully yours,

CORDELL HULL"

(Enclosure)

Tentative List of Members of the Advisory Committee on Post-War Foreign Policy

Mr. Cordell Hull (Secretary of State), *Chairman*

Mr. Sumner Welles (Under Secretary of State), *Vice Chairman*

Mr. Norman H. Davis (President of Council on Foreign Relations and Chairman, American Red Cross)

Mr. Myron C. Taylor

Mr. Dean Acheson (Assistant Secretary of State)

Mr. Hamilton Fish Armstrong (Editor, *Foreign Affairs*)

Mr. Adolf A. Berle, Jr. (Assistant Secretary of State)

Mr. Isaiah Bowman (President, Johns Hopkins University)

Mr. Benjamin V. Cohen (General Counsel, National Power Policy Committee)

Mr. Herbert Feis (Department of State Adviser on International Economic Relations)

Mr. Green H. Hackworth (Department of State Legal Adviser)

Mr. Harry C. Hawkins (Chief of the Department of State Division of Commercial Policy)

Mrs. Anne O'Hare McCormick (Editorial Staff, The New York *Times*)

Mr. Leo Pasvolsky (Special Assistant to the Secretary of State and Chief of the Department's Division of Special Research)

On or about December 28, 1941, the President wrote on this letter: "I heartily approve.   F. D. R."

Part II

THE ADVISORY COMMITTEE
ON POST-WAR FOREIGN POLICY
1942–SUMMER 1943

"The outbreak of war made it clear that problems of crucial importance in the field of foreign relations would confront this country as well as other countries upon the termination of hostilities. It became the obvious duty of the Department of State to give special attention to the study of conditions and developments relating to such problems. As the war spread over the earth, the scope of these studies was extended and work upon them was steadily increased, so far as was compatible with the fullest possible prosecution of the war.

"By direction of the President and with his active interest in the work, the Department of State undertook, through special groups organized for the purpose, to examine the various matters affecting the conclusion of the war, the making of the peace, and preparation for dealing with post-war problems. In doing this work, we have had collaboration of representatives of other interested agencies of the Government and of many national leaders, without regard to their political affiliation, and the assistance of a specially constituted and highly qualified research staff. We have been aided greatly by public discussion of the problems involved on the part of responsible private individuals and groups and by the numerous suggestions and expressions of opinion which we have received from all parts of the country."

—————"Our Foreign Policy in the Framework of Our National Interests," radio address by Cordell Hull, Secretary of State, September 12, 1943, *Department of State Bulletin*, IX, 173–179.

CHAPTER IV

Organization and Meetings of the Full Committee

T HE ADVISORY Committee on Post-War Foreign Policy was a working instrument, national in scope, and composed of specially qualified public officials and individuals from private life. Its purpose was to study world problems of concern to the United States and to submit recommendations for American postwar policy, through the Secretary of State, to the President. It was created in time of grave danger to the country. It was a practical method to clarify the nation's thinking on the problems and issues that lay beyond victory. Victory itself could settle but the first issue, survival. A host of problems, many growing out of the war and others with longer roots in the past, would then have to be faced.

The Advisory Committee carried on its work under circumstances in fundamental contrast to those prevailing during the earlier organization for consideration of postwar problems, described in the preceding Part. The most basic uncertainty about the outcome of the war was gone: victory could be assumed. The nature of American participation in the creation of the international order after hostilities no longer gave rise to questions concerning the influence that a neutral United States could or should exert. We, as a principal power among the victors, would share the heavy responsibility of all the victors in determining the character of the postwar world; we would participate in the war settlements; we would decisively influence the nature of any organization of international peace to follow. The opportunity—in recognition of the imperative need—to build a just and enduring peace would assuredly be forthcoming.

With these fundamentals clear, but with every question of what, how, when, and where unanswered, the necessity to prepare as fully and wisely as humanly possible was unmistakable. Though the war would be long, the preparation for peace would also need much time.

The constantly felt sense of urgency in making the preparation came from a realization of the immensely difficult and basic tasks to be done and of the possibility that postwar policy might have to be implemented in part before hostilities ended. The general national policy of isolation, reflecting the general temper of the country and its viewpoint during the past two decades, had left the nation unready for action on many world problems, especially those of a political character. The fluidity introduced into world affairs by the revolutionary course of events in those decades, by the changing character of thought and action everywhere since the war had begun, and by the anticipation that this process of change would continue after the war, made necessary a thorough study of the entire emerging scene. The future of states as separate and sovereign entities and the character of their rights and relationships were unsettled. The position, nature, and number of great powers were in flux. Beliefs and desires of whole peoples and areas were being shaped anew. The destruction of resources and the disruption of economic life were already so vast because of the war—and were probably to become so critical—that the prospective postwar economic situation gave rise to profound anxiety. Foremost was the cry for security.

Already the Third Meeting of the Ministers of Foreign Affairs of the American Republics, held at Rio de Janeiro, January 15–28, 1942, to permit the consultations projected in resolution XV of the Habana Conference in the event of an act of aggression against any American state by a non-American nation, had adopted a resolution directed specifically toward preparations for the peace. The Rio Meeting asserted in resolution XXV:

"1. World peace must be based on the principles of respect for law, of justice and of cooperation which inspire the Nations of America and which have been expressed at Inter-American Meetings held from 1889 to date;
"2. A new order of peace must be supported by economic principles which will insure equitable and lasting international trade with equal opportunities for all Nations;
"3. Collective security must be founded not only on political institutions but also on just, effective, and liberal economic systems;
"4. It is indispensable to undertake the immediate study of the bases for this new economic and political order. . . ."

The resolution entrusted to the Inter-American Juridical Committee "the formulation of specific recommendations relative to the international organization in the juridical and political fields, and in the field of international security" and to the Inter-American Financial and Economic Advisory Committee a "similar function in the economic field." The resolution further requested the Pan American Union to call an Inter-American Technical Economic Conference "charged with the study of present and postwar economic problems," the necessary preparations for which would be the responsibility of the Inter-American Financial and Economic Advisory Committee.[1]

---

[1] For full text of resolution, see *Department of State Bulletin*, VI, 134–35.

In Europe, moreover, the question of the postwar settlement, particularly with respect to boundaries, had been brought to the fore at the time of Foreign Secretary Eden's visit to Moscow in December 1941. On that occasion Premier Stalin had suggested, in connection with a projected Anglo-Soviet treaty, British recognition in a secret protocol of the Soviet frontiers of June 22, 1941 (the date of the German invasion), with some possible modification in the case of the frontier with Poland. The Premier had also made several other suggestions affecting the postwar settlement, some of them concerned with the treatment of Germany after the war. While Mr. Eden had felt himself unable to make any commitments of this nature without further consultation with his Government and with the United States, the question of the character of the proposed Anglo-Soviet treaty was now a matter of serious concern.[2]

The United States Government continued to adhere, in its reaction to the Soviet claims, to the policy set forth in Secretary Hull's December 5 message to Mr. Eden [3] in opposing any commitments concerning postwar territorial settlements during the war, in the interest of both wartime unity and the achievement of a durable and just peace. The emergence of this question in specific form, however, emphasized the need for the preparation of definite plans and proposals to permit general agreement as soon as possible on the organization of the future peace, to serve as a framework within which specific settlements would be made.

The preparation necessary for effective American participation in the solution of international problems after the defeat of the enemy obviously had to deal with the most fundamental issues of future national policy both of a general nature and of a specific character, and had to cover a vast range of specific problems. For this a united effort by the whole nation was required. The results, though they would have to be adjusted to the needs and circumstances that would mark the immediate scene at the time of decision, must be such as could lead to practical action. It followed that the work must be done directly with the Secretary of State and for the President. The Advisory Committee was constituted accordingly.

MEMBERSHIP

WHEN THE Advisory Committee on Post-War Foreign Policy began its meetings, its composition and its structure of subcommittees were established in principle but not fully elaborated. Its organization was not an action completed on a given day but was rather a process

[2] Cf. *Memoirs of Cordell Hull*, II, 1165–67.
[3] See above, pp. 62–63.

of development. This process continued throughout the Committee's active life, which lasted in most of the political fields of its work until the summer of 1943 and in the economic fields and that of special regional problems until the spring of 1944. This process of growth at all times affected not only the Advisory Committee's membership and structure but the scope and the conduct of its discussions as well. Flexibility of conception, not the rigidity of preconception, characterized every aspect of the Committee and its work. By the spring of 1943 various departmental, interdepartmental, and other mechanisms had begun to grow out of the Committee's activity. In a number of important respects the Committee's powers and functions became the foundation for various later structures through which its work was carried forward, with little interruption but much adaptation, as the periods of advanced preparation and of action arrived in the several fields of work.

Although there was great need to keep the Advisory Committee small, there was greater need to provide the range of competent judgment essential for sound results. Ultimately, specific representation of major points of view among the public and in the Government became a factor that further enlarged the Committee. "Membership" tended for these reasons to be defined strictly but to be widely diversified.

The Advisory Committee proper came to include ten nonofficial members, five Senators and three Representatives, eleven members from the Department of State of whom four were *ex officio*, a member each from the War and Navy Departments and from the Joint Chiefs of Staff as a unit, and one member each from four other Departments, three members from the White House staff, one from the Library of Congress, four from the wartime agencies, and one from among the continuing agencies of the Government. In addition there were other Senators and Representatives, as well as certain individuals from private and public life, who served on the subsidiary bodies of the main committee.

The members drawn from private life were chosen primarily because of their high personal qualifications for policy consideration and because of their capacity broadly to represent informed public opinion and interests. The selection of official members was based both on personal qualifications and on representation of the interested parts of the Government. Emphasis upon "representation" increasingly became a practical objective in building the Committee on effective and influential lines and was reflected in all appointments made after the initial four months of the Committee's activity.

Usually the members from private life and from the Congress were invited by letter from the Secretary of State with the approval of the President. Formal procedure was likewise followed in the case of invitations to members having Cabinet status, who either attended themselves or, while holding direct consultations with Secretary Hull and other officials of the Committee, were represented at meetings by appointees of their own choice. Other members were invited informally, through oral invitations extended by Secretary Hull or with his approval.

The distinction between formal and informal membership was without significance in the actual character of participation. In contrast, however, there were differences in extent of participation between general members, who took part in various aspects of the work, and special members invited to serve in particular problem fields. General members tended to be active in the consideration of political, territorial, and security problems, whereas the special members were active chiefly, though not exclusively, with respect to economic problems.

Five of the persons named in the initial recommendation approved by the President in December 1941 were general members. Of these, three were wholly engaged in nonofficial activities at the time: Isaiah Bowman, President of the Johns Hopkins University, Hamilton Fish Armstrong, editor of *Foreign Affairs*, and Mrs. Anne O'Hare McCormick, foreign-affairs analyst of the *New York Times*. Two were so largely engaged in nonofficial pursuits, though having special official responsibilities, that they also were regarded as representing the public. These were Myron C. Taylor and Norman H. Davis. Mr. Taylor, industrialist and philanthropist, was Personal Representative of the President, with the rank of Ambassador, on the Intergovernmental Committee on Political Refugees and also to Pope Pius XII. Mr. Davis had been in official service for many years, especially in connection with economic and disarmament conferences, and was at the time Chairman of the American Red Cross and President of the Council on Foreign Relations. James Thomson Shotwell, historian and Director of the Division of Economics and History of the Carnegie Endowment for International Peace, was added in June 1942, becoming the sixth member having general and nonofficial status on the Advisory Committee.

Of the special nonofficial members, two were invited in May 1942 to participate in the field of economic problems: Robert J. Watt, International Representative of the American Federation of Labor, and Walter P. Reuther of the Congress of Industrial Organizations. A month later Brooks Emeny, Director of the Council of Foreign Affairs of Cleveland, Ohio, was invited to take part in the same field and in that of legal problems. Early in April 1943 William Green, President of the A. F. of L., and Philip Murray, President of the C. I. O., received invitations formally to represent directly their organizations in the economic field, taking the places held previously on a more personal basis by Mr. Watt and Mr. Reuther.[4] Eric A. Johnston, President of the United States Chamber of Commerce, was likewise invited at the same time directly to represent his organization in the economic field. Two economists, Percy W. Bidwell of the Council on Foreign Relations and Jacob Viner of the University of Chicago, participated in the specialized consideration accorded European regional problems for some months beginning in June 1943.

The membership from the Congress reflected the desire of both Secretary Hull and President Roosevelt to have direct Congressional participation in the preparation on a basis of as nearly equal representation of the two major political parties as practicable. Nonpartisan agreement upon foreign policy and harmony of views between the Executive and the Congress were the objectives. This desire to assure a unified national view on basic foreign policy and so avoid the costly mistakes made at the close of World War I was manifest in the earliest of the invitations, May 27, 1942, and throughout all subsequent developments. Senator Tom Connally of Texas, Democrat, Chairman of the Foreign Relations Committee, and Senator Warren R. Austin of Vermont, Republican, the minority member of that Committee designated after consultation with Republican leaders, were the first Congressional participants.

On January 9, 1943, two Democratic Senators, Walter F. George of Georgia and Elbert D. Thomas of Utah; two Democratic Representatives, Sol Bloom of New York and Luther A. Johnson of Texas; and one Republican Representative, Charles A. Eaton of New Jersey, joined the Committee. Six weeks later, another Republican Senator, Wallace H. White of Maine, also became a member. The Senators named were currently serving on the Committee on Foreign Relations except for Senator George, who after long service as its chairman had recently left that Committee for another important assignment. The Representatives were members of the Committee on Foreign Affairs, Representative Bloom being its Chairman and Representative Eaton its ranking minority member. Participation was undertaken in various capacities by other Republican leaders as political changes occurred and later as international negotiations were undertaken.[5]

In addition to Congressional participation in the Advisory Committee and its initial subcommittees, a number of Members of the Congress later sat on the "special committees" that during 1943, as the main work of the Advisory Committee was drawing to a close, became active in the economic and social fields. Participation in

[4] See pp. 136, 139.
[5] See Parts III and IV.

these bodies did not necessarily involve membership on the Advisory Committee. Invitations were given in such instances by the various "special committee" chairmen directly. The "special committees" included the following Members from the Congress: Senators Scott W. Lucas of Illinois and Claude Pepper of Florida and Representatives Schuyler Otis Bland of Virginia with J. Hardin Peterson of Florida as alternate, and Alfred L. Bulwinkle of North Carolina, Democrats; and Representatives Richard J. Welch of California and Charles A. Wolverton of New Jersey, Republicans.

The number of Department of State officials named as members of the Advisory Committee continued throughout to be severely restricted in order that the Committee might be in fact widely representative of the country. This policy was adhered to strictly in the case of the Committee itself, the President having said, when approving the Committee, that the proposed State Department membership was a little too heavy. The policy was relaxed slightly, however, in the case of the main subcommittees. Membership accordingly was confined largely to officials of the rank of Assistant Secretary or above, with participation of other high officers limited, as a general rule, to attendance on request without membership.

A large proportion of these Departmental officials had taken part in the earlier planning effort. Those having general membership were principally those mentioned in the original letter of recommendation to the President: Secretary Hull, Under Secretary Welles, Assistant Secretaries Berle and Acheson, together with four members of *ex officio* standing. Mr. Pasvolsky was a member *ex officio* on the basis of both his responsibility as Executive Director of the Advisory Committee and his general duties as Special Assistant to the Secretary. The Legal Adviser, Mr. Hackworth, and the Adviser on International Economic Affairs, Mr. Feis, had *ex officio* status based on their regular duties. Assistant Secretary Acheson and Mr. Hawkins, the fourth *ex officio* member as Chief of the Division of Commercial Policy and Agreements, were specialized in their assignments at this time, working wholly in the economic field.

On February 6, 1942, just before the Advisory Committee convened, Assistant Secretary Breckinridge Long and John Van A. MacMurray, who was serving temporarily as Special Assistant to the Secretary, were appointed to take part in a special capacity. Soon thereafter the Chief of the Division of European Affairs, Ray Atherton, was similarly appointed because of his particular personal qualifications for work in connection with political, territorial, and security problems, though he was usually represented in the two latter fields by Cavendish Cannon of the same Division, acting in a personal capacity.

In addition, the four political advisers of the Department—James Clement Dunn for Europe, Stanley K. Hornbeck for the Far East,

Laurence Duggan for the other American Republics, and Wallace S. Murray for the Near East—attended meetings as superior operating officials when political, territorial, and security problems pertaining to the countries and areas of concern to each, respectively, were scheduled for discussion and on such occasions served as special *ex officio* members.   Mr. Hornbeck in August 1942 and Mr. Dunn in March 1943 began regularly to undertake subcommittee duties in connection with international security problems, as did Joseph C. Green, Special Assistant to the Secretary, in the same special *ex officio* capacity beginning June 10, 1943.   The participation undertaken at times in various economic fields by Paul Culbertson, Assistant Chief of the Division of European Affairs, beginning October 9, 1943, and H. F. Arthur Schoenfeld, former Minister to Finland on special duty in the Department, beginning June 23, 1943, did not raise questions of membership.

Three members from the White House staff took part.   Benjamin V. Cohen, who had been named in the original list submitted in December 1941 and who had general duties at the White House in his capacity as Legal Counsel of the Office of War Mobilization and on the basis of his earlier work in the Government, was active in all fields.   David K. Niles, administrative assistant to the President in matters concerning the War Production Board, became a member prior to the convening of the first meeting of the Advisory Committee and concentrated on economic problems.   While serving personally, he spoke in a sense for Harry Hopkins in accord with the wishes of the President.   Subsequently, on April 9, 1943, Lauchlin Currie, also administrative assistant to the President, became a member for work on economic problems.

Archibald MacLeish, Librarian of Congress, joined the Committee on January 2, 1943, taking part especially in the consideration of political problems.

The Secretary of the Navy and the Secretary of War were requested early in the work of the Advisory Committee to designate representatives in connection with problems of international security, and consequently Admiral Arthur J. Hepburn and Maj. Gen. George V. Strong became members at the end of April 1942.   Rear Admiral Harold C. Train began regular attendance as alternate member for the Navy Department in August 1942.   The Joint Chiefs of Staff as an entity was invited in March and April 1943 to be represented.   Its several officers who thereafter attended comprised in fact the Joint Strategic Survey Committee, and they spoke together for the Joint Chiefs of Staff as if they were a single member of the Advisory Committee. They were Vice Admiral Russell Willson of the Navy, Lt. Gen. Stanley D. Embick of the Army, and Maj. Gen. Muir S. Fairchild of the Air Corps.   Shortly thereafter a naval air representative, Capt. George H. DeBaun, was designated to serve with these officers.   Senior representatives of the armed services were assisted throughout by specialists on given problems or by other aides. Among these assisting officers were Brig. Gen. Hayes A. Kroner, Col. Thomas J. Betts, Col. James F. Olive, Jr., Lt. Col. Thomas G. Lanphier, Capt. H. L. Pence and Capt. V. E. Korns, who attended without being members.

Representation of several wartime agencies was rendered highly desirable by the postwar bearings of their emergency functions. Outstanding among these was the Board of Economic Warfare, of which Vice President Henry A. Wallace was Chairman. Since Mr. Wallace himself could not attend, he was represented from the beginning by an appointee of his own choice, Milo Perkins, Executive Director of the Board. Mr. Perkins also was unable personally to attend meetings, and accordingly the further exception was allowed to the general rule against alternates by permitting William T. Stone, Assistant Director of the Board, and also Louis H. Bean, to attend for him, effective with the first meeting on February 12, 1942. Subsequently, on June 6, 1943, Mr. Stone himself was designated as the member for participation in the fields of economic problems of concern to the Board, while Mr. Bean continued thereafter to attend as observer.

Various other emergency agencies were eventually represented. Chester C. Davis, Administrator of the Food Production and Distribution Administration, became a member early in April 1943, though his regular duties shortly proved too heavy to permit his attendance. On April 9, 1943, Marvin Jones, Judge of the United States Court of Claims, was invited to membership, at first personally but subsequently in his capacity as War Food Administrator. Nelson A. Rockefeller, Coordinator of Inter-American Affairs, was invited to membership on April 9, 1943.

It was recognized at the outset that the economic and social problems to be considered by the Advisory Committee would involve at various stages the work of a number of the permanent Departments and agencies of the Government. Preliminary studies in connection with such problems in their respective fields had been begun or projected by a number of the Departments, but, in several instances, time was required to arrange for the representation of these Departments and agencies on the Committee because of the many readjustments of function and responsibility then being undertaken to place the Government on a war footing. Furthermore, there was need of prior exploration by the Committee to clarify the policy problems presented before all the Departments most concerned could be determined.

Harry D. White, Director of Monetary Research and Assistant to the Secretary of the Treasury, was designated April 15, 1942, to represent Henry Morgenthau, Jr., in the case of economic and financial problems. Paul H. Appleby, Under Secretary of Agriculture, was invited to membership on February 9, 1942, representing Claude R.

Wickard, Secretary of Agriculture. The Secretary of Commerce, Jesse Jones, was represented by Wayne C. Taylor, Under Secretary of Commerce, beginning the following July. William L. Clayton, then Assistant Secretary of Commerce, served for a time commencing June 21, 1943, as chairman of a special economic committee, though he did not become a member of the Advisory Committee. Invitations to membership were extended on April 9, 1943, to Miss Frances Perkins, Secretary of Labor, and to Marriner Eccles, Chairman of the Board of Governors of the Federal Reserve System.

Subsequently, officials of other agencies were asked to undertake special responsibilities in the work, though not formally as members of the Advisory Committee. As Oscar B. Ryder, Chairman of the Tariff Commission, could not attend, Lynn R. Edminster of the same Commission participated in his stead beginning June 15, 1943. Leland Olds, Chairman of the Federal Power Commission, and Hugh Cox, Assistant Attorney General, took part in the consideration of economic problems commencing June 4 and July 2, 1943, respectively.

Many other officials in various Departments and agencies of the Government took part in discussions or assisted otherwise in the conduct of the Committee's work. In view of the scope and character of the problems at issue, the number of these officials progressively increased. However, because such participation was pursuant to official duty and accordingly was subject to the frequent changes of personnel or assignment in the Government, the separate identification of all these individuals is not undertaken here. The participation of those active on one or another related committee in the Advisory Committee structure and of those specially placed at the service of the Committee in a professional research capacity is indicated below.

FIRST MEETING AND ORGANIZATION OF SUBCOMMITTEES

The Advisory Committee on Post-War Foreign Policy convened in the Department of State on February 12, 1942, at 3:00 p. m. Secretary Hull being absent for a brief period of rest, the group met in the Under Secretary's office, with Sumner Welles presiding. All its members at that date, except Messrs. Acheson, Berle, and Feis, and the Treasury representative (still to be appointed), were in attendance, namely, Mrs. McCormick and Messrs. Appleby, Armstrong, Bowman, Cohen, Davis, Long, MacMurray, Niles, Stone (for Milo Perkins), Myron C. Taylor, Hackworth, Hawkins, and Pasvolsky (Director). Harley Notter was the Executive Secretary.

Clarification of the Committee's purpose and of its working arrangements were the principal subjects of discussion in this organizing meeting. The acting chairman explained that, by direction of the President, only this Committee and, in a more limited field, the group of officials gathered under Vice President Wallace as Chairman of the Board of Economic Warfare were making authorized preparations concerning postwar foreign policy, and the recommendations of both were to be channeled to the President through the Secretary of State. The President desired to be able later to reach in his basket and to find there whatever he needed in regard to postwar foreign policy and meanwhile wished to devote himself wholly to ways and means of winning the war. It was left to the Committee itself to determine the problems ahead and to provide the information and recommendations needed in dealing with those problems.

The Committee agreed that its work should be approached from the general standpoint of the kind of world that the United States desired after the war. It also took the position that the President, in view of his executive responsibilities, would need to have recommendations for action as well as information on all problems on which a national position would have to be taken or an attitude expressed.

Thought was given to the possibility of informing the public immediately of the establishment and work of the Committee. It was felt that circumstances at the moment, when the United States was being driven back in the Pacific and the United Nations cause was suffering on every front, rendered secrecy imperative until a favorable turn in the war. Publicity on current study of postwar policy might lead to impairment of the war effort by placing in possible question the fact that sustained and prolonged struggle would be required before victory could be won. Accordingly, the Committee's existence and work were kept secret.

The discussions of this matter raised the question of whether the work of the Committee should be confined to the postwar field or should also have to do with current policy and action, in the interest of demonstrating the relationship between wartime developments and the postwar situation and thereby of justifying postwar study at that early and critical time. It was decided by Secretary Hull a few weeks later that, since the Committee's purpose was to advance preparations on the entire range of postwar problems as expeditiously as possible for readiness in case of need, the Committee should devote itself strictly to these problems. Current matters were thus left to the regular operations of the State Department and other parts of the Government. However, because developments of the greatest postwar significance occurred in the form of current decisions and actions and because in many fields action on a postwar problem was begun or carried out before hostilities ceased, the distinction between current and postwar policy remained always a matter of relative definition and degree. The guiding rule was that the Advisory Committee would take day-to-day current policy problems into account in its work, but would not debate them or assume responsibility in connection with them.

On arrangements for the conduct of the work, it was agreed in the opening meeting that the Committee would divide itself for working purposes into subcommittees, three in political fields, two in economic fields, with a sixth to coordinate the work and to provide contact with private organizations actively discussing postwar problems. The Advisory Committee as a whole would deliberate on the recommendations prepared by these subcommittees and would then forward to the President through the Secretary of State the views of the full Committee. The conception was that these subcommittees would constitute the main committee itself meeting in fractions, and would be composed only of members of the Advisory Committee. Subcommittees thus constituted sections of the Committee and not appendages or related autonomous bodies.

At this meeting the chairmanships and the proposed membership of the subcommittees, together with their respective fields of work, were announced, subject to the personal views of the members as considered below in connection with the organizing sessions of the subcommittees. It was felt that on the whole these subcommittees should each meet once weekly, on Fridays and Saturdays, while the full Advisory Committee should meet biweekly or at longer intervals.

It was agreed that each subcommittee would have a research secretary, who would head the staff of specialists being gathered in the Division of Special Research for the respective fields of work and who would supervise the preparation of research studies and policy papers and their circulation to members one or two days in advance of meetings. Summary minutes would be taken by the same officer or an assistant and distributed to members of the subcommittee concerned. Necessary coordination would be provided by the fact that Mr. Pasvolsky served both as Executive Director of the Committee and Chief of the Division of Special Research.

The question arose concerning the discharge of that part of the Committee's general responsibility for encouraging public study of postwar problems by interested American citizens and for taking into consideration the views developed by such private groups, among them specifically the Council on Foreign Relations. The Committee decided to receive these views and studies and accepted the suggestion of the members who were also officers of the Council that the small but selective research staff of the Council be brought into direct contact with the work of the Committee through service in the Division of Special Research.

The subcommittees were requested to lay out their work programs and to establish, subject to review by the Committee, priorities for consideration of problems. For this purpose it was agreed that the subcommittees in the political fields would initially convene together and that the subcommittees in the economic fields would do likewise for their first session. These meetings occurred during the next week.

ORGANIZING MEETINGS OF SUBCOMMITTEES

THE TWO subcommittees in the economic field were the first to meet— on February 20, 1942. Although they were separate bodies meeting under different chairmen, their membership purposely was made largely common. This unusual structure was intended to assure due and coordinated consideration of the ten separate, though related, fields of economic problems, one subcommittee concentrating on short-run and the other on long-range aspects. The more immediate problems that would confront the United States after the war were assigned to the Subcommittee on Economic Reconstruction, whose membership was Mr. Berle, Chairman, Messrs. Acheson, Appleby, Davis, Feis, Hawkins, Niles, Pasvolsky, Myron C. Taylor, and Stone (representing Milo Perkins). Longer-run basic problems were made the responsibility of the Subcommittee on Economic Policy, comprised of Mr. Acheson, Chairman, and Messrs. Appleby, Berle, Cohen, Feis, Hawkins, Pasvolsky, Bean (for Milo Perkins), and a representative of the Treasury (later White). Participation of representatives of labor groups as advisers was broached in this connection and was subsequently arranged. H. Julian Wadleigh was the first research secretary for both subcommittees.

It was agreed that the Reconstruction Subcommittee would consider and make recommendations concerning problems of relief; restoration and reconstruction of production facilities, including nutrition; the immediate aspects of demobilization of persons and movements of populations; labor conditions, social security, and voluntary migration; and transportation and communications, including the economics of aviation and of broadcasting. The longer-range aspects, after reconstruction, of problems in the several latter fields were assigned to the Economic Policy Subcommittee, together with those of commercial policy and relations, monetary relations, credit and investment, commodity agreements and cartels, and international economic sanctions (after their consideration from the political standpoint). Since economic phases of international organization would be studied in conjunction with political phases, there was no need to burden the agenda of this subcommittee with these matters. The interrelation between these international problems and their domestic counterparts was stressed in the discussion.

A detailed exploratory analysis of problems and questions, prepared by the research staff, was accepted as an over-all agenda. The subcommittees arranged to meet thereafter on Fridays, in the morning and in the afternoon, respectively.

The subcommittees in the three fields of international political problems met in Mr. Welles' office on February 21. By this date their projected membership was almost definite.

The Subcommittee on Political Problems consisted of Mr. Welles, Chairman, and Messrs. Armstrong, Berle, Cohen, Hackworth, MacMurray, Myron C. Taylor, Mrs. McCormick, Mr. Pasvolsky, who was an *ex officio* member, and (by decision shortly afterward) the chairmen of the other two subcommittees, Mr. Davis and Mr. Bowman. Mr. Notter was research secretary. At this meeting and usually thereafter, Paul C. Daniels, who at this time served as a personal assistant to Mr. Welles, was also present, though not a participant in discussion. This group undertook to consider the problems of formal reestablishment of peace, national sovereignty, international organization, and pacific settlement of international disputes.

The Subcommittee on Territorial Problems was composed of Mr. Bowman, Chairman, and Messrs. Armstrong, Berle, Feis, and MacMurray, and Mrs. McCormick, with Mr. Pasvolsky as *ex officio* member. Mr. Notter served as research secretary until, after some weeks, Philip E. Mosely joined the staff and assumed this duty. The problems placed before this group included the restoration of independent nations, reestablishment of stable governments, boundaries of independent nations, and dependent areas.

The composition of the Subcommittee on Security Problems at the time of this joint meeting was wholly civilian: Mr. Davis, Chairman, and Messrs. Armstrong, Cohen, Hackworth, Long, and, *ex officio*, Pasvolsky. Representation of the War and Navy Departments was agreed upon on this date, to be arranged as soon as possible. An officer not in the Research Division, Charles W. Yost, was initially appointed as the research secretary on a part-time basis. Mr. Yost soon joined the research staff, and he and later Grayson L. Kirk served regularly in this position.[6] The problems allocated to this subcommittee were those of disarmament of enemy nations, general limitation of armaments, military controls, and freedom of the seas.

An extensive analysis of questions prepared by the research staff, designed to clarify the fundamental problems and possible approaches to their solution as visualized to date, was accepted, subject to additions by members, as the basis for a prompt allocation of definite questions among the three subcommittees and of priorities for discussion. It was also decided that direct representation of various private groups in the work would not be practicable but that their views would be of much benefit and should be studied. The meeting considered that the cooperation of the Council on Foreign Relations

---

[6] For staff provisions and work, see chapter VI.

in establishing and maintaining contact with such private groups, especially groups and persons not of American citizenship, would be helpful to the Committee.

It was decided for the convenience of the out-of-town members that future meetings of each subcommittee would be concentrated on Fridays and Saturdays. Weekly meetings were arranged, except that the Political Subcommittee would not as a rule meet in a week when the Advisory Committee convened. The Security Subcommittee met Friday afternoons, the Political on Saturday mornings, and the Territorial on Saturday afternoons at the outset and subsequently late on Friday afternoons.

The projected Subcommittee on Coordination, with a membership of Mr. Davis, Chairman, Mr. Cohen, Mr. Hackworth, and the Director, Mr. Pasvolsky, with Mr. Notter as Executive Secretary, never convened formally. It was replaced in practice by the more flexible procedure of informal consultations between the Director and research secretaries and the individual committee officers and members.

After a two weeks' interval to allow consideration by the members, each of the subcommittees, except that on Security Problems, convened in its own organizing meeting.

The Subcommittee on Economic Reconstruction met on March 6, 1942, discussing primarily international relief and the need, in this connection, for a special organization. Since the problem of relief policy was already in a preliminary stage of international negotiation,[7] the research staff was directed to make a study of the current status of relief work and to prepare a draft plan for a United Nations relief organization. In a second meeting, on March 20, this subcommittee discussed these same matters.

The Subcommittee on Economic Policy also held its first meeting on March 6 and considered the comparative merits of the bilateral and the multilateral approach to international agreements for the implementation of Article VII of the lend-lease agreements.[8] Under Article VII, the signatories of each agreement were committed to consult together "at an early convenient date" for the purpose of determining the best means of attaining certain specified economic objectives through their own action and that "of other like-minded Governments." These objectives were those set forth in the Atlantic Charter and more specifically, "the expansion . . . of production, employment, and the exchange and consumption of goods . . . the

---

[7] See chapter III, pp. 54–55.

[8] The first of the lend-lease agreements, or mutual-aid agreements, containing Article VII as here described, that with the United Kingdom, had been signed Feb. 23, 1942.

elimination of all forms of discriminatory treatment in international commerce, and   . . .   the reduction of tariffs and other trade barriers." The signatory governments also agreed that "the benefits" to be received by the United States in return for lend-lease aid should include provisions for agreed action directed toward attaining these specific objectives, open to participation by all other governments of like mind. The final settlement should "be such as not to burden commerce" between the signatories "but to promote mutually advantageous economic relations between them and the betterment of worldwide economic relations." In this general connection, the subcommittee also considered the problems of balance of payments and related international machinery and gave directives for necessary initial studies to the research staff.

At the first meeting of the Subcommittee on Political Problems, March 7, 1942, consideration of over-all questions was begun. These included, particularly, whether a general peace settlement should be made promptly at the end of hostilities as in 1919–1920 or delayed until after a period of transition, and whether settlement of certain problems should be attempted during the war through agreements with the governments-in-exile of European countries. Discussion at the subcommittee's second meeting, March 14, was devoted mainly to the broad range of problems to be settled in the armistice period, including the questions of relief organization and relief priorities, but consideration was also begun in general terms of the problems of boundaries and of a possible bill or bills of human rights. At the third meeting, March 21, a "chart" of policy problems covering the entire postwar period was drawn up on the basis of three time stages: armistice, transition, and establishment of international organization.

The first meeting of the Territorial Subcommittee, March 7, was concerned with the definition of its fields of responsibility, the procedure and agenda to be followed, and the research needed. The subcommittee decided to seek "alternative" solutions for the hypothetical problems deemed likely to arise at the end of the war. Its second meeting, March 14, was devoted to the consideration of the principles and procedures to be applied in its study of territorial problems, main American objectives, and the question of timing United States action toward territorial settlements. The subcommittee chose Poland as a "test case" for its general inquiries into these questions, in view of the evident complexity of Polish territorial problems. The typical character of the research generally needed was clarified in terms of such basic studies as population and resources analyses, related boundary alternatives, and internal forces affecting the thought and action of countries. The subcommittee decided to consider first the problems likely to arise in regard to Eastern Europe and to the Near Eastern area.

SECOND, THIRD, AND FINAL MEETINGS OF THE FULL COMMITTEE

On the afternoon of March 21, 1942, the four subcommittees that had organized reported their progress to the second meeting of the Advisory Committee. Mr. Welles presided. At that date the Treasury representative and the War and Navy members had not yet been appointed, and several absences, including that of Secretary Hull, were necessitated by illness or by pressing duties elsewhere.

Mr. Welles reported that the Subcommittee on Political Problems envisaged three stages of action after the conclusion of hostilities by surrender of the enemy: a short stage lasting not more than a year after the armistice, during which an armistice would be signed and action taken on immediate problems connected with the end of the war, then a longer transitional stage of indefinite length leading to the third stage, namely the beginning of definitive permanent peace. The chart of problems thought to fall within these three stages, respectively, was read as follows:

Armistice Period

1. Military and naval requirements of the armistice agreement including some political terms.
2. Agreement as to over-all United Nations authoritative body that should be instituted.
3. Method of organization of provisional government of areas of Europe affected by the war.

(a) For enemy territory conquered.
(b) For friendly territory reconquered in which there is no readily available national authority. In a portion of friendly territory there will be available recognized authority.

4. A code of law or instructions delimiting the functions of the provisional government, giving authority to certain officials, and outlining the division and handling of governmental and military power.
5. A provisional code of justice including therein the right to hear complaints against enemy agents or enemy authorities who have oppressed the local population, and permitting after trial the infliction of penalty.
6. The constitution of authority to undertake relief. Determination of local authorities through which local distribution of relief should be undertaken.
7. Organization of necessary authority to undertake immediate and urgent reconstruction. Determination of shipping and transportation requirements.
8. Determination of financial mechanisms to be utilized in this period.

Transition Period

1. Determination of what should be the individual states of Europe.
2. Constitution of governments of such states.
3. Determination of the regional, political and economic groupings of such states.
4. Continuation of such authorities and activities as are required for the maintenance of order and the restoration of normal life in those areas.

5. Definitive settlement of the boundaries of such states.
6. Transfer of populations and resettlement.
7. Problem of restitution and reparations.
8. Creation of banks and economic institutions to assist in long-range reconstruction, and also including consideration of tariff and monetary arrangements.

Permanent Peace

1. Entering upon full functioning of any definitive international organization that may have been agreed upon beforehand.
2. Conclusion of a definitive peace treaty.

The Committee adopted this division of the postwar period and chart of problems, which became in substance the basic table of time and action for all subcommittees. It was gradually abandoned as thinking developed and as conditions at the close of hostilities became more predictable.

Mr. Bowman in reporting for the Territorial Subcommittee emphasized that its main objective would be to examine the problems of states as they function in terms of other states. It would consider the forces operative upon governments of states, conditions and activities prevailing within states, resources and relative geographic position of states, and problems of boundaries, resettlement, and nationalities. Boundary settlements, it was thought, should not open up new problems through the use of such devices as minority treaties and plebiscites, as had been done in 1919, but rather should be determined in relation to international economic, political, and security decisions, with which all territorial solutions always interlocked. Studies and maps would be essential for every policy decision and in some cases would have to be supplemented by investigations in the field after the fighting was over. Circumstances and conditions created by the war would have heavy effect, and prior policy recommendations on territorial questions would often have to be reached only in tentative terms. The Advisory Committee offered no suggestions with respect to this proposed approach and thereby, under its method, gave it tacit approval. At no time, on any question, did the Advisory Committee take a formal vote.

The report of the Economic Reconstruction Subcommittee, given by Mr. Berle, reflected the thin line between certain current and postwar problems, which was exemplified by the question of relief policy. The necessity to clarify policy on this matter arose immediately from a proposal made on February 3, 1942, by the "Leith-Ross Committee" in London with the support of the British Government, for reorganization of that Committee's work on a wider basis. The Inter-Allied Post-War Requirements Committee under the chairmanship of Sir Frederick Leith-Ross and assisted by a British staff was then engaged in estimating the relief requirements of European countries under enemy occupation. On October 4, 1941, this Government had authorized the presence of a United States observer at the meetings of the Committee, and, after our entry into the war, this observer had been authorized to participate actively in the work of the Committee, with the understanding, however, that any plans developed by the Committee were advisory only and subject to full consideration by the governments concerned. The Soviet Government had proposed in January that the "Leith-Ross Committee" be made more international and given broader functions, and the proposal now made by the Committee involved more explicit and greater responsibilities on the part of the United States than this Government had heretofore assumed.

The views of the Economic Reconstruction Subcommittee were, in brief, that the United States should take the initiative in calling a full meeting of the United Nations; that, in preparation for such a meeting, a group representing the four major powers—the United States, Great Britain, the Soviet Union, and China—should develop a proposal for consideration by the full meeting; and that this four-power body should also act as a steering or executive committee for the United Nations in the relief field. The subcommittee had directed the research staff to prepare for its consideration a project of organization in this field, which might ultimately be submitted to the proposed four-power steering committee. It had further decided that its next task should be to consider the creation of a suitable international organization for resettlement of displaced populations, returning prisoners of war, migration, and related reconstruction problems.

This recommendation for dealing with the problem of organized relief reflected the general thought prevailing among officials of the Department and members of the Political Subcommittee on the role of the major powers in relation to other United Nations in postwar negotiations, organization, and action. It was also a recognition of the need, in keeping with the policy of major-power collaboration, promptly to bring the Soviet Union and China into the exploratory discussions of postwar problems that had already been initiated with the British in the economic field. The Advisory Committee made no effort at this time to formulate views on the recommendation beyond indicating a certain disposition to favor the addition of a representative or representatives of smaller nations to the proposed four-power body. The presentation and consideration of the recommendation, however, was the first concrete manifestation of the concept of major-power collaboration in postwar preparations directed toward the formulation of proposals for consideration by the other United Nations. This concept, which both reflected and to a degree defined the respective relations and roles of the major powers and of the other United Nations as these were being established by the war itself, developed in due course into a fixed policy with respect to the establishment not only of transitional but of permanent international organizations.

Mr. Acheson, giving his report last, stated that the Subcommittee on Economic Policy was considering the agenda for early discussion of long-range economic policy with the British Government, as projected under Article VII of the lend-lease agreement. This would be followed by similar discussions with other governments. Attention was being given to the problem of balances of payment—a major concern to the British and several other Allied governments. The old mechanisms for handling international payments could not work under existing circumstances, and new international mechanisms, it was thought, must be devised to permit continuing operations on a lend-lease basis through commercial channels rather than always through governments. This report was likewise accepted by the Advisory Committee without comment.

The Committee at this meeting agreed to convene every two weeks to keep in closer touch with the work of the subcommittees. The principal organizational question arising by this time was whether the necessary advance drafting and research for the subcommittees could be provided by the extremely limited staff so far available. The projected schedules nevertheless were left unchanged.

At the Advisory Committee's next meeting, April 4, progress was made especially on the far-reaching matter of an over-all United Nations authoritative body for the armistice and transition periods. Mr. Welles gave the views of the Political Subcommittee on this question as developed primarily in its discussion on March 28. Certain of the regional and other fundamental aspects of its plans were to be altered as the result of analyses undertaken a year later, but the thought of the subcommittee at this date was that, in general, an international political organization should be substantially developed during the war itself to provide machinery ready at hand when needed, to prepare the personnel of such an organization through long acquaintance with the problems on which decisions would have to be made, and to provide a mechanism through which agreements could be reached in accord with preliminary decisions prior to the armistice. Representation in the authoritative body would extend beyond the four major powers in order to foster a sense of participation among the smaller United Nations and to strengthen the decision-making organization in handling the "war of ideas" which the subcommittee expected would follow the military war.

More specifically, it was contemplated that a "United Nations Authority" might be created, composed of representatives of all the United Nations. An executive committee of the authority might be instituted, composed of representatives of the four major powers (the United States, Great Britain, the Soviet Union, and China) together with selected representatives from the "regions" of Eastern Europe, the democracies of Western Europe, the other American republics, the Far East, and possibly the Mohammedan peoples. Commissions or committees might be established by the executive committee, some for continuing problems and others for temporary problems, but each containing representation from all the United Nations. It was presumed that the executive committee, possibly to be named "Provisional Armistice Administration," would consult from time to time with the full "United Nations Authority." Opportunity of course would also be provided for group discussion. The projected relationship between the large powers and the small states in this plan led the subcommittee in general to believe that arrangements should be made for some organ or organization to be charged with informing the representatives of small nations of decisions and with encouraging a feeling of recognition and participation on their part. The difficulties of obtaining effective regional representatives on the executive committee had been considered, and, while this problem was not resolved by the subcommittee, the practical necessity of their selection by the four major powers had been suggested as a possibility.

It was contemplated in this report that the United States Government would initiate steps toward creation of the "United Nations Authority" after formulation of recommendations by the subcommittee and after their approval by the Advisory Committee and by the Secretary and the President. This Government would then consult the Governments of Great Britain, the Soviet Union, and China, and subsequently the other United Nations.

In the discussion, it was made clear that, while in the last analysis the four major powers must make the decisions, these powers should act so far as possible in accord with the decisions of all the United Nations, and the executive committee would report to the "United Nations Authority." The concept of an "executive" committee was immediately questioned, but discussion was inconclusive.

Mr. Welles in conclusion reported that at its morning meeting just prior to the convening of the Advisory Committee, the subcommittee had considered the general problem of organizing provisional governments in the areas of Europe affected by the war and had begun to discuss the method of organization in both conquered enemy and liberated friendly territories.

Mr. Bowman reported that the Subcommittee on Territorial Problems on March 28 had considered further the possibility of sending special commissions into various areas to determine the existing facts with respect to political forces, population, and other basic factors at the end of hostilities. It had also selected the major problem areas in order of their priority for study, concluding that most of the territorial questions of greatest concern in Europe lay in the belt of populations and land faced by the Soviet Union, extending from the north of Finland to the Aegean. Priority was therefore being given to the study of this region. In these studies, certain over-all considerations were being held in mind: the degree of certainty with which the existence of a United Nations armed force competent to handle the situation in this area could be anticipated; the possible creation during the war itself of an international organization that might continue as the working machinery of a postwar international association, together with additional international machinery established after the war; and the resettlement possibilities for minorities or displaced groups. In regard to boundaries the subcommittee was proceeding on the basis that exact and rational lines must be drawn between the property of one state and another and that the division line must be defensible. The subcommittee wished next to consider its approach to the solution of dependent area problems and the principles to be applied in such areas.

The third of the subcommittees in the broad political fields, namely that on Security Problems, had no report to offer, but meetings could now begin since Mr. Davis had returned from abroad. With this in view, representation of the War and Navy Departments would be requested at once.

The Subcommittee on Economic Policy had no special report to make. For the Subcommittee on Economic Reconstruction, Mr. Berle offered the recommendation that early action be taken to inaugurate an over-all international relief organization. The form of such organization should fit the pattern proposed by the Political Subcommittee. If an organizational meeting of the "United Nations Authority" were to be delayed, however, the subcommittee believed that some other procedure should be followed. It proposed that an "International Relief Council" composed of representatives of the United Nations should be created and that the council should authorize the establishment of a "Supervisory Relief Committee" composed of representatives of the United States, the United Kingdom, the Soviet Union, and China. At the head of the council should be a director of relief, preferably an American, who should be advised by a personnel committee. Establishment of a financial committee to advise the supervisory committee was being considered. The views of the Advisory Committee were requested on whether the time had come to consult the other United Nations regarding the desirability and practicability of an early meeting of official representatives to gain agreement upon such an organization.

Discussion brought out the preponderant capacity of the United States to provide relief and relief supplies and the need, accordingly, for adequate United States control of relief activities. It was con-

sidered that the steps contemplated for establishing such organization would contribute to the war effort by giving greater official reality to the concept of the United Nations and might serve as an experiment in regard to the organization of the projected "United Nations
Authority." The United States, it was thought, should initiate a
proposal for a meeting of the United Nations on this subject. Also
in support of the proposed plan it was noted that, in accord with the
views of the Political Subcommittee, relief would be handled by a
"continuing" committee and that the various working committees of
the relief organization to be established would provide for participation on the part of all the United Nations. It was accepted that the
necessary consultations among the four major powers for agreement
on policy and procedure would be carried out in the course of the
preparatory work essential to the calling of the proposed international meeting and the decision upon its agenda. Disapproval was
expressed of permitting political purposes to determine relief policy.
It was agreed that for psychological and moral reasons the peoples
of the occupied countries should as soon as feasible be informed
that the United Nations were conferring on how to provide relief
for them.

Although accepting this proposal in principle, the Advisory Committee desired its implementation to be delayed until a detailed plan
had been approved by the Committee and an appropriate directive
given. Some reluctance to proceed with relief organization prior
to action on political international organization, in accord with the
procedure envisaged by the Political Subcommittee, prevailed in the
Committee, and no more definite recommendation was attempted at
this time.

The Economic Reconstruction Subcommittee thought that the
proposed relief administration should handle those problems of
repatriation of displaced persons that would be immediate in character, but before making its report on this question, it wished to have the
guidance of the Political and Territorial Subcommittees on policy and
on the necessary machinery.

A scheduled meeting of the Advisory Committee on April 18 was
canceled to give needed respite to the members and the staff from the
pace of work. The fourth and last meeting of the full Advisory Committee was held on May 2 at 12:50 p. m. Each of the five subcommittees had met at least twice during the interval and the Political and
Territorial Subcommittees four times. By this date, Rear Admiral
Arthur J. Hepburn and Maj. Gen. George V. Strong had begun their
work on the Advisory Committee and on the Subcommittee on Security
Problems.

Secretary Hull convened the Advisory Committee in his office.
Members attending aside from the Secretary were Messrs. Welles,

Acheson, Armstrong, Berle, Bowman, Cohen, Davis, Feis, Hackworth, Hawkins, Long, Niles, Pasvolsky, Stone and Bean (for Milo Perkins), Myron C. Taylor, and White, Admiral Hepburn, and General Strong, together with Messrs. Atherton, Daniels, and Notter.

The Secretary expressed to the members his cordial appreciation of their spirit in undertaking this important work and emphasized that the contribution of all informed and competent groups and persons, both outside and inside the Government, would be needed to build a sound peace and to carry out the construction of a better world order. He expressed anxiety over the interest groups and opposing ideological influences that would inevitably bring their strength to bear against the constructive views on peace settlement and world improvement to be developed by the Committee. Such interest groups and influences constituted perhaps the greatest threat that the work would face; he anticipated that the best document and program that could be devised would be attacked. He was convinced of the necessity of making better preparation for world peace than had been made in the course of the first World War. The chances nevertheless were about one to two or three whether a soundly conceived peace could be carried to fruition. The consequences of the Committee's work were vital, and it was necessary to consider in the work how to help public opinion to educate itself. In his judgment, to have the informed support of American public opinion was of the utmost importance.

The Secretary indicated that arrangements were being made to provide the Committee with more extensive research assistance in studying the implications and the manifold problems of the three periods, into which the work ahead had been divided. He himself wanted to participate so far as possible, and he asked members to call directly on him for any cooperation on matters in which the Department had so far been found wanting. In conclusion, he thanked the chairmen of the subcommittees for their organizational work. He himself felt encouraged regarding the eventual outcome of the effort in which the Committee was engaged. Adjournment followed after various comments on the progress of organizing the work.

No further full meetings were held. The discussion had already involved a number of considerations that it was imperative from the standpoint of future policy and of current war effort alike to keep within strict confidence. This was emphatically the case in the delicate and controversial political fields, and future reliance upon the small subcommittee meetings in these fields was therefore considered desirable. This decision, never formally conveyed to the Committee, did not at the time preclude full meetings later.

That the Committee never met again as a whole was chiefly due to doubt that secrecy on policy recommendations could be assured pending their final review by the Secretary and the President if meetings with such large attendance continued to be held. This, however, was not the sole reason for avoiding such meetings. The plenary meetings had already focused on crucial issues involving major international negotiations during the course of the war itself. Such meetings by nature tended to arrive at immediate recommendations, whereas the postulate basic to the conception of the preparation, insistently maintained by the Secretary of State, was that the use of precious time to mature views and plans outweighed in value the rapid reaching of decisions, which might involve fatal gambles. It was felt that only through adequate analysis and consideration of all the available alternative courses of policy could dangerous error be avoided. Under the impact of events and individual preferences, continued pressure for swifter decision made itself felt from time to time thereafter within the various subcommittees, but the desire to have thorough consideration before arriving at recommendations and final decisions was in the main controlling.

While prevention of unauthorized disclosure was felt to be obligatory, the corollary duty of providing authorized information was also borne in mind. The Secretary of State therefore presented several of the lines of thought developed during the period of full Advisory Committee meetings and by the subcommittees over the next three months in his radio address, "The War and Human Freedom," on July 23, 1942. The writing of this carefully considered address was the object of collaboration for more than two weeks among officials of the Department, several individual members of the Advisory Committee, and the research staff. Its text was approved in advance by the President. It was the first of the series of formal and informal efforts by both Secretary Hull and the President to keep the American public informed of the agreed points of postwar policy as they were evolved in the preparation.

Starting with the assertion that the war was not a war of nation against nation, not a local or regional war or series of such wars, but one war waged against enemies intent on enslaving the entire world, the Secretary discussed the causes of the war and the events leading up to it.[9] Pointing out that war began in 1931 when Japan invaded China and that the United States was an ultimate target of the Tripartite Pact among Axis countries in 1940, he stated that we Americans were "forced to fight because we ignored the simple but fundamental fact that the price of peace and of the preservation of right and freedom among nations is the acceptance of international responsibilities."

The Secretary then discussed postwar matters. "With victory achieved," he said, "our first concern must be for those whose suffer-

---

[9] The full text is contained in the *Department of State Bulletin*, VII, 639–47.

ings have been almost beyond human endurance." Immediate problems of transition from war to peace would confront all countries—problems of conversion of production to peacetime needs, rehabilitation of agriculture, industry, and homes. "During this period of transition the United Nations must continue to act in the spirit of cooperation which now underlies their war effort—to supplement and make more effective the action of countries individually . . . in meeting the manifold problems of readjustment." He said that beyond these problems would "lie before all countries the great constructive task of building human freedom and Christian morality on firmer and broader foundations than ever before." This too would "of necessity call for both national and international action."

The conception of liberty under law as "the only real foundation of political and social stability" and "an essential requirement of progress" was emphasized by the Secretary, who then said:

"Liberty is more than a matter of political rights, indispensable as those rights are. In our own country we have learned from bitter experience that to be truly free, men must have, as well, economic freedom and economic security—the assurance for all alike of an opportunity to work as free men in the company of free men; to obtain through work the material and spiritual means of life; to advance through the exercise of ability, initiative, and enterprise; to make provision against the hazards of human existence. We know that this is true of mankind everywhere. We know that in all countries there has been—and there will be increasingly in the future—demand for a forward movement of social justice. Each of us must be resolved that, once the war is won, this demand shall be met as speedily and as fully as possible.

"All these advances—in political freedom, in economic betterment, in social justice, in spiritual values—can be achieved by each nation primarily through its own work and effort, mainly through its own wise policies and actions. They can be made only where there is acceptance and cultivation of the concepts and the spirit of human rights and human freedom. It is impossible for any nation or group of nations to prescribe the methods or provide the means by which any other nation can accomplish or maintain its own political and economic independence, be strong, prosper, and attain high spiritual goals. It is possible, however, for all nations to give and to receive help."

Following a statement that the pledge of the Atlantic Charter implied an obligation on each state in several essential respects, the Secretary described the effects of the fear of war, under which all nations had lived for decades, upon the world's progress and declared:

" . . . It is plain that some international agency must be created which can—by force, if necessary—keep the peace among nations in the future. There must be international cooperative action to set up the mechanisms which can thus insure peace. This must include eventual adjustment of national armaments in such a manner that the rule of law cannot be successfully challenged and that the burden of armaments may be reduced to a minimum.

"In the creation of such mechanisms there would be a practical and purposeful application of sovereign powers through measures of international cooperation for purposes of safeguarding the peace. Participation by all nations in such measures would be for each its contribution toward its own future security and safety from outside attack.

"Settlement of disputes by peaceful means, and indeed all processes of international cooperation, presuppose respect for law and obligations. It is plain that one of the institutions which must be established and be given vitality is an international court of justice. It is equally clear that, in the process of re-establishing international order, the United Nations must exercise surveillance over aggressor nations until such time as the latter demonstrate their willingness and ability to live at peace with other nations."

The Secretary then turned to the necessity for economic and social betterment. He spoke of problems of employment, rising standards of living, removal of trade barriers, and currency stabilization. He referred to the need for "machinery through which capital may—for the development of the world's resources and for the stabilization of economic activity—move on equitable terms from financially stronger to financially weaker countries" and possibly for "some special trade arrangement and for international agreements" to handle problems of surplus commodities and special economic situations. "These," he said, "are only some of the things that nations can attempt to do. . . . There are bound to be many others."

The Secretary warned: "Neither victory nor any form of postwar settlement will of itself create a millennium." There would be opportunity, rather, to improve world conditions. To use this opportunity, he said, "we must be resolved . . . to find the mechanisms" for most fully and speedily attaining and effectively safeguarding the benefits desired.

". . . There will be need for plans, developed with careful consideration and carried forward boldly and vigorously. The vision, the resolution, and the skill with which the conditions of peace will be established and developed after the war will be as much a measure of man's capacity for freedom and progress as the fervor and determination which men show in winning the victory.

"Without impediment to the fullest prosecution of the war—indeed for its most effective prosecution—the United Nations should from time to time, as they did in adopting the Atlantic Charter, formulate and proclaim their common views regarding fundamental policies which will chart for mankind a wise course based on enduring spiritual values."

For the "support of such policies," the Secretary called for development of "an informed public opinion."

CHAPTER V

The Subcommittees of the Advisory Committee

THE MEETING of the Advisory Committee on April 4, 1942, demarcated the completion of the organizing phase of the Committee. The changes that took place later were adjustments or developments in response to the needs of the work within the main lines determined upon during the period of the full Committee meetings. Effort in the subcommittees now concentrated on their agreed fields of problems.

THE SUBCOMMITTEE ON POLITICAL PROBLEMS

THE STRUCTURE and functioning of the Subcommittee on Political Problems during its lifetime of a year and a half underwent considerable expansion. From the beginning it was regarded as the principal subcommittee, and its judgment, even while the full Advisory Committee met, was sought as essential by the other subcommittees. The political problems in its charge comprised the over-riding issues of the future confronting the United States. By reason of its chairmanship by the Under Secretary of State and later by the Secretary himself, this subcommittee was the only one that could by right assume the active responsibilities, and therefore in large degree the status, of the Advisory Committee itself after the cessation of plenary meetings of that Committee. In addition, this subcommittee contained among its members a greater number of eminent persons from private life and the Congress than other subcommittees and, since most of the chairmen of the other subcommittees were included in its membership, they tended from the outset to report in its meetings.

Mr. Welles continued as the active chairman of the subcommittee from February 21, 1942, until January 23, 1943. During the rare absences of Mr. Welles for all or part of a meeting, Mr. Berle or Mr. Bowman assumed the chair, depending on the subject under discussion. As had been contemplated since mid-October 1942, however, Mr. Hull himself assumed direct charge on January 30, 1943, and, while

Mr. Welles served as acting chairman during the next six weeks, Mr. Hull led all discussions after that of March 13. The last meeting of the subcommittee was held on June 19, 1943: the sixtieth meeting after the joint organizing session of all subcommittees in the political field.

Meetings under Mr. Hull's chairmanship were held in his office. When Mr. Welles presided, meetings were always in his own office adjoining that of the Secretary.

While a number of new members, including particularly Senators Austin and Connally, had been added by mid-July 1942, the largest expansion of the Political Subcommittee's membership came after the completion of the first period of survey and exploration of problems. When intensive and more detailed review of these problems commenced in January 1943, Senators George and Thomas, Representatives Bloom, Eaton, and Johnson, and Mr. MacLeish were asked to take part. Senator White joined the group at the beginning of March.

The full final membership of the subcommittee was Secretary of State Hull, Chairman, Mr. Welles, Vice Chairman, Hamilton Fish Armstrong, Ray Atherton, Senator Warren R. Austin, Adolf A. Berle, Isaiah Bowman, Representative Sol Bloom, Benjamin V. Cohen, Senator Tom Connally, Norman H. Davis, Representative Charles A. Eaton, Senator Walter F. George, Green H. Hackworth, Representative Luther A. Johnson, Archibald MacLeish, John V. A. MacMurray, Mrs. Anne O'Hare McCormick, Leo Pasvolsky, James T. Shotwell, Myron C. Taylor, Senator Elbert D. Thomas, and Senator Wallace H. White, Jr. Its special *ex officio* members were James Clement Dunn, Stanley K. Hornbeck, Wallace S. Murray, and Laurence Duggan. The research secretary throughout was Harley Notter.

Its secretaries to take notes on the discussion in the closing months were C. Easton Rothwell and James Frederick Green, but earlier Paul B. Taylor and Bryce Wood served for short periods. Additional Department officers who attended from time to time included Paul H. Alling, Philip Bonsal, Paul Daniels, Maxwell M. Hamilton, Samuel Reber, and Henry S. Villard of the geographic divisions and Benjamin Gerig, Grayson L. Kirk, Durward V. Sandifer, and Leroy D. Stinebower of the research staff.

The idea of approaching the work in "two rounds" was gradually evolved and adopted in October 1942. The first round was designed to analyze all international political problems likely to require the determination of American policy or attitude, to discuss them in an exploratory way, and to clarify the feasible alternative solutions. This survey terminated December 19, 1942, after which a brief recess was taken over Christmas.

The second round, initiated January 2, 1943, was for the most part under the chairmanship of Secretary Hull. It was designed to lead to recommendations based upon more mature understanding and study of the problems and of the possible solutions as judged in the light of existing facts and prospective circumstances. With the attendance of additional members from the Congress in this round, it became essential to review, in the consideration of any problem, the subcommittee's prior findings with respect to facts and the possible alternative policies. It was still considered advisable to avoid committal decisions until the prospective postwar picture as a whole could be studied. While speed of work was essential, the developments of the war which would determine the conditions of the post-hostilities period were not believed yet to be such as to require final decisions or to preclude careful testing of views in the case of most of the problems at issue.

The fields of major problems, already mentioned, placed within the responsibility of this subcommittee were soon found to be extremely exacting. Accordingly, in order to provide for more detailed examination of certain of the problems, especially of those involving much technical study and precise drafting of proposals, two special subcommittees, composed of members of the Political Subcommittee itself, were instituted. The first, established on June 27, 1942, was in the field of international organization. The other, created August 8, 1942, was in the field of legal problems. These will be described later. It should be noted here, however, that their establishment grew out of the thought that the recommendations of these special groups could be formulated while other subjects before the Political Subcommittee were being discussed, thus permitting the Political Subcommittee simultaneously to consider all the problems in its purview. The belief early expressed that general international organization should be developed during the course of the war itself made such concurrent progress necessary.

There were many instances, practically from the beginning of the subcommittee's work, when members individually or in small groups informally presented their views on the solution of difficult or controversial problems in papers read at the meeting. Such a procedure was followed, for example, at the meeting on May 2, 1942, in considering the question of the unity or fragmentation of Germany.

Ad hoc drafting committees were sometimes named, and occasionally these contained Departmental officers as well as subcommittee members. The first committee of this kind was appointed June 13, 1942, for the purpose of considering the problems of an international bill of rights and of war crimes. It was composed of Messrs. Berle, Armstrong, Cohen, and Hackworth, and was empowered to include in its membership a consultant specialist from outside the Department if necessary. This group was later absorbed into the Special Subcommittee on Legal Problems. An *ad hoc* drafting committee was again resorted to on August 8, 1942, when a group composed of Messrs. Welles, Hackworth, MacMurray, and Hamilton, who was Chief of the Division of Far Eastern Affairs, was constituted to prepare views on organizational problems in the southwestern Pacific and on broad territorial questions relative to Thailand, to be used as a basis of discussion by the subcommittee. This method was also employed in inaugurating consideration of the problem of Palestine, when on August 29, 1942, Messrs. Shotwell, Cohen, and Murray, the Political Adviser on Near Eastern Affairs, were requested to prepare a paper for discussion.

Appointment of committees of members with participation by the research secretary began to develop by December 5, 1942, when a committee was formed to draft on certain aspects of a plan of international trusteeship for dependent peoples and areas. This committee was composed of Messrs. Berle, Hackworth, and Hornbeck, the Political Adviser on Far Eastern Affairs, with Mr. Notter named to assist.

Increasingly, the Political Subcommittee requested specific reports from the other principal subcommittees on problems before it and utilized these reports in commencing or in concluding its discussions. This relationship was initiated with the Subcommittee on Territorial Problems, first on April 11, 1942, in connection with the preparation of maps showing hypothetical solutions of certain territorial problems, and the formulation of views on specific country problems, and then, beginning May 9, 1942, to obtain preliminary examination of the problems that the Political Subcommittee would discuss later the same or the next day. As will be recalled, all members of the Territorial Subcommittee were members of the Political Subcommittee. The intent of this device was to facilitate more advanced and pointed policy consideration in the Political Subcommittee on the basis of a report, usually given orally by Mr. Bowman at the start of its discussion, founded upon as thorough study as staff research and broad specialist discussion by the Territorial Subcommittee could produce. A definition of the precise problem calling for decision, a survey of the main aspects of its background, and an analysis of the factors affecting its disposition, together with preliminary recommendations when possible, would thus be available for consideration at the start rather than near the end of the Political Subcommittee's meeting on the problem concerned.

Although this relationship was at all times closest with the Territorial Subcommittee—extending during the period September 25, 1942, to March 12, 1943, even to efforts to dovetail the respective agendas—the Political Subcommittee frequently requested similar reports from the other subcommittees, beginning with those on Economic Policy and on Economic Reconstruction on May 16, 1942, and with the Subcommittee on Security Problems on June 27, 1942. This relationship, so far as it called for special reports on matters not already scheduled for discussion in these subcommittees, had the effect of rearranging the order and character of their deliberations to fit those of the Political Subcommittee. Otherwise, however, the work of the subcommittees was separate and followed the order of problems each established for itself.

On the whole, the over-all coordination of the work of the Advisory Committee remained unaltered by these developments except for adjustments of schedule; the problems at issue had all to be considered sooner or later. The Director, through his membership on all subcommittees and his consultations with each of the chairmen, sought to coordinate the agendas in their broad lines. The research secretaries concerned undertook, through memoranda and conversations with the Director and with the chairmen prior to meetings, the necessary detailed coordination of the reports, of the specific subjects scheduled for discussion, and of the research studies required each week.[1]

The connection between problems before the Political Subcommittee and developments of the war was peculiarly close, since to an important degree the latter affected and in many cases posed or created the problems at issue in the subcommittee. The Chairman thought it advisable to give the meetings the most recent secret diplomatic information on problems being studied. Much of such information necessarily dealt with the wartime policies of the various governments, and some bore intimately upon war plans. This inter-connection with the war, and the awareness of all members of the chances and sudden changes characteristic of war, tended to heighten their sense not only of urgency but of the necessity to have alternative policy recommendations formulated and ready for quick decision and execution. Naturally this sense of immediacy and need for precautionary hastening of discussion led frequently during the first months of the subcommittee's work to risk of over-concentration on matters of current operation. The system referred to above of having two rounds of consideration was accordingly conceived as the best means of assuring that the subcommittee would systematically undertake basic discussion of all the most important future problems rather than attempt, in the limited perspective of current developments, quickly to formulate its views on some of them.

The subcommittee twice tried to institute two sessions weekly. The first such decision was on June 6, 1942. This caused a shift of the meeting day of the Territorial Subcommittee to Fridays, so that it might discuss related problems prior to the Saturday meetings of the

---

[1] As an illustration, see appendix 10 for schedule of May 10, 1943.

Political Subcommittee. The second decision, on November 21, to become effective with the opening of the second round in January 1943, contemplated meetings once on Friday and once on Saturday, with the earlier meeting devoted wholly to problems of international organization. These decisions were not carried out, largely because of the difficulty of arranging in the crowded last days of the week further meetings that did not conflict with other committee obligations of members, especially those from private life and from the Congress. A subsidiary reason for not doubling the meetings was that provision of the necessary research in the stringently limited time between sessions might prove impracticable for the staff.

The pressure felt by the subcommittee reflected in these decisions arose from its realization of the enormous extent of the problems to be faced in the future and of the profound uncertainties affecting them and influencing their solution. Without discussing the substantive views developed within the Advisory Committee structure, which are outside the concern of this book, some of the general conceptions followed by the Political Subcommittee in its work as a whole may be summarized and the scope of this work indicated here.

The subcommittee from the start sought to clarify for its own guidance the fundamental concepts of American policy that should underlie its approach to the problems and uncertainties of the future. It thought in this regard that the United States should not fix a minimum essential postwar program but rather a maximum program of sound desirable international action. It chose to examine each problem with a view to determining, in as practical terms as were feasible, an ideal settlement which the United States should try to attain within the limits set by international circumstances. The subcommittee not only accepted the principles and policies enunciated in the Atlantic Charter and included in the Declaration by United Nations but also sought to provide for their implementation as completely as possible in a postwar world that, it was anticipated, would be at once both realistic concerning the facts of power and exacting on the highest moral and humanitarian grounds.

Its discussions throughout were founded upon belief in unqualified victory by the United Nations. It predicated, as an absolute prerequisite for world peace, the continuing strength of the United Nations through unbroken cooperation after the war. International security was regarded as the supreme objective, but at the same time the subcommittee held that the attainment of security must square with principles of justice in order to be actual and enduring. Although it was uncertain whether the Congress and the public would approve entering a political international organization, it postulated that the Congress and the people would not only desire but also demand continuing American participation in efforts directed toward the maintenance of international peace and security—military and political as well as economic. A corollary of these views was the general conviction that agreements for organized cooperation to maintain peace and security should be made among the major powers themselves and with other states before the end of hostilities.

That the Soviet Union would probably cooperate in regard to problems concerning ex-enemy countries, at least so far as military occupation was concerned, was a view early adopted. During the next year and a half of its activity, the subcommittee reached the further conclusion that Soviet cooperation on principal international problems would be essential, and as discussion proceeded, the assumption was accepted that such cooperation would be proffered because of the interests of the Soviet Union itself. Nevertheless, these were, of necessity, speculations. By March 1943 the conviction was reached that a definite answer to the basic question whether such cooperation would be forthcoming should be obtained as soon as practicable.

One concrete development during this period supporting the subcommittee's estimates with respect to the Soviet Union had been the signature on May 26, 1942, of the Anglo-Soviet Treaty of Alliance and Mutual Assistance. In this treaty, which omitted any reference to postwar territorial settlements in keeping with the American position on this question, the two signatories expressed their desire "to contribute after the war to the maintenance of peace and to the prevention of further aggression by Germany or the States associated with her in acts of aggression in Europe." They further announced "their intention to collaborate closely with one another as well as with the other United Nations at the peace settlement and during the ensuing period of reconstruction" on the basis of the principles of the Atlantic Charter. In article III of the treaty, they declared their wish "to unite with other like-minded States in adopting proposals for common action to preserve peace and resist aggression in the postwar period," and the treaty itself, it was stipulated, should remain in force until such time as it was "superseded by the adoption of the proposals contemplated in article III," or for twenty years. Under article V the two signatories agreed "to work together in close and friendly collaboration after the reestablishment of peace for the organization of security and economic prosperity in Europe," taking into account "the interests of the United Nations in these objects" and acting "in accordance with the two principles of not seeking territorial aggrandisement for themselves and of non-interference in the internal affairs of other States." [2]

A second development of equal significance from the standpoint of Soviet postwar collaboration in the economic field had been the

---

[2] *Department of State Bulletin*, VII, 781–83.

Soviet signature on June 11, 1942, of the lend-lease agreement with its crucial Article VII.[3]

Among other fundamental concepts of the Political Subcommittee was the view that the postwar world must be so organized as to permit small states to live in independence, peace, and security. Throughout, observing the pervasive and decisive need of international security in connection with nearly every problem, the subcommittee expressed the judgment that a general organization empowered to keep international peace and security by force if and when necessary was absolutely requisite in the interest of every state and people. It was the judgment of the subcommittee, furthermore, that, since many of the problems that would be at issue as the war neared its end and as the postwar period began were matters in which the United States had taken no active part historically, certain of the most significant policy decisions necessitated would require fundamental departures from the traditional American position. The responsibilities of a major power had brought with them such need of international peace, security, and well-being that, in the view of the subcommittee, the policy recommendations must propose new courses of American policy and action where necessary to American vital interests.

As indicated earlier, the subcommittee's attention was devoted initially, during the period while the Advisory Committee was still meeting as a whole, to the preliminary questions encountered in drawing the outlines of the postwar era. These questions raised problems of timing, of assumptions concerning the military situation at the close of war, of the status of governments-in-exile, of the position and policies of the Soviet Union and of the United Kingdom and other countries, and of the national interests of the United States in connection with postwar military, political, and other arrangements, including general international organization.

Thereafter, during its first round, the subcommittee considered in sequence a series of problems: first, the organization of provisional governments and other reconstruction problems in liberated Europe, the treatment to be accorded enemy states in general including problems of armistice and surrender policy, the disposition of each of the enemy states, and immediate post-hostilities problems; next, the situation in the Far East, problems in Eastern Europe, the future of Austria, and problems of the Middle and Near East and Africa; then, international trusteeship for dependent peoples and areas, and questions arising in the Western Hemisphere, including those relating to non-American possessions; and last, policy problems presented by the

---

[3] *Ibid.*, VI, 531–34. China had signed such an agreement with the United States on June 2, and similar agreements were now rapidly concluded with other members of the United Nations. For text of Article VII, consult appendix 8.

Union of Soviet Socialist Republics, by Great Britain and the British Commonwealth, and by France. A number of these problems, especially the more controversial or difficult ones, such as trusteeship, Germany, or Eastern Europe, were considered more than once, not only because of the sheer size and complexity of the issues involved but also because related problems threw these issues into a new focus at successive stages, and because in several cases additional studies had to be prepared before continuation of discussion would be profitable.

The second round, which covered the same main problems and certain additional ones, was not so clearly marked by the reappearance of topics on the agenda from time to time but rather by continuing consideration of basic problems over more than one meeting. Two meetings were devoted principally to Italy; three to Germany; two to Eastern Europe; one to France and the Far East; two to the Near and Middle East; three to international trusteeship and related colonial problems; and nine to problems of general international organization. The issues in the latter case were, on the whole, discussed not on the basis of the draft plans that had been prepared but as matters of basic policy, in the light of which existing drafts would be revised or new proposals drafted. It was primarily in connection with the consideration at the last nine meetings of the fundamental problems of organized international cooperation and relations that Secretary Hull introduced the so-called agenda paper as the primary basis of discussion.[4]

The agenda paper represented a change in method of discussion which was to have an extensive bearing upon the structure for policy consideration that succeeded the subcommittee system, described in Part III. The new method reflected both the experience with the committees and the development of the staff in handling problems of policy. During approximately the first year of the subcommittee's meetings, discussion of given problems normally proceeded on the basis of carefully selected and authoritative solutions or proposals referred, or posed, to the group by the Chairman. With the introduction of the agenda paper in the last months of the subcommittee's activity, discussion then went forward on the basis of a prior determination of the fundamental questions at issue. The paper was prepared in advance in consultation with Secretary Hull and read at the opening of meetings by him—or more frequently, at his request, by Mr. Welles. In this analysis, the issues requiring a policy decision for their solution or disposition were defined as precisely as possible, the relationship of the problems to other problems and essential considerations was briefly stated, and possible alternative solutions were suggested. Use of this method was decided upon because it was thought that it would lead

---

[4] For an example of an agenda paper, see appendix 11.

toward the fullest possible examination of key policy problems in terms of our national interests and responsibilities and of our participation in the international decisions designed to solve these problems. This method would permit the fullest weighing, before a definite preference for any one solution was reached or a concise draft attempted, of the possibilities of successful negotiation and implementation.

In the meetings of this subcommittee there was as much informality in the conduct of discussion as was consonant with the sense of national responsibility shared by all participants and with the fact of chairmanship by the Secretary and Under Secretary of State. There was also conscious avoidance of any assumption that members were necessarily bound either by their expressions of views earlier in the consideration of any problem or by the general consensus of the subcommittee on any problem.

At almost all meetings reference maps were provided, and usually there were special maps or charts showing hypothetical solutions of problems. Innovations in design and coloring had in fact to be made throughout the work in order to portray the needed facts and issues. Such maps were designed by the research staff under the active guidance of the Territorial Subcommittee, especially its Chairman, Mr. Bowman, and with the technical collaboration of the Geographer, Samuel W. Boggs and his assistant, Otto Guthe, and were executed by the cartographic service of the Department and elsewhere in the Government. Special facilities for safeguarding such materials were employed.

From the start, the agenda was supported by policy studies to the full extent permitted by the resources of the research staff. Although special assignment of papers was not infrequently made at the request of members during meetings, the Director and the research secretary assumed the responsibility for anticipating the need for studies and for satisfying these needs so far as possible. The research papers ordinarily received prior consideration in other subcommittees, and often in the interested divisions of the Department, before being presented to the subcommittee. They were for the most part transmitted to the members in their offices, rather than at the meetings, though extracts were at times used during the meetings. Certain highly secret studies of the official views of this and other governments were also prepared; these were transmitted solely to the Chairman to use in meetings as he deemed appropriate. On occasion excerpts from such studies were read to the meetings, and at all times the Chairman had before him a current picture of the status of authoritative views on each problem under discussion. By this means the subcommittee was furnished with as clear insight into the positions of other governments as the facilities of the entire Department of State and Foreign Service made possible. Papers on special developments or problems within a single geographic area were prepared on a number of occasions by the Department's regular geographic divisions in charge of current operations. Several of these took the form of proposals and were presented by the Chairman or by an official invited to attend from the division concerned.

At the same time the views of the American public on the problems under discussion were made available through special studies or through the analyses embodied within the research studies. The views and suggestions received from the many organizations and persons among the public interested in postwar problems were numerous and valuable and were taken into careful consideration. Among these were, for illustration, Judge Manley O. Hudson's studies of the World Court. Periodicals and newspapers were also examined for expressions of opinion on postwar matters. Nonofficial research assistance was never requested, and as a matter of policy no direct guidance of other research programs was ever attempted. The Council on Foreign Relations made many studies, however, which were utilized by the staff and the subcommittee members, and an offer by the Council to make a given study—of the Ruhr—was on one occasion specifically accepted by the subcommittee.

Minutes were always taken, but, to assure a fully free exchange of views, they were in the form of rough, longhand notes. From these a brief summary was written and distributed as "the minutes" to members in their offices in the Department in advance of the next meeting. These minutes stripped the account of the discussion to the essential facts and views useful for further consideration of the same and related problems and avoided attribution of views to any member. This means was adopted from the start in order to assure the freedom of thinking and re-thinking necessary in developing policy on many matters, especially when these were interrelated with problems that often had not yet been wholly shaped by events. The research secretary took the notes during the first few months, but, as research preparations and committee duties increased, this responsibility was delegated, with the consent of the Chairman, to an assistant research officer. Although attendance from the research staff was regularly restricted to this minimum in the case of the Political Subcommittee, the minutes were made available to any officer of the research staff who had clear need of them.

A compilation was made from time to time of the views at which the subcommittee had arrived and of all drafts of concrete plans. Both the views and the drafts were tentative. Even where the term "final" was applied, as on occasion, it connoted only a more advanced stage of maturity and meant that the views still remained subject to change even of a possibly radical nature.

The subcommittee never formally voted on any matter during the period of the Secretary's chairmanship and did so rarely while Mr. Welles was chairman. It did not, as a subcommittee, send views and formal proposals to the President. Although no occasion arose during this first period to give him the subcommittee's prepared views and plans as a whole, he was always kept in touch with its progress. To some extent this took place through the talks that various individual members had with him from time to time in accord with the customary White House practice.[5] The President kept himself abreast of developments in this and other subcommittees principally, however, by conversations with Secretary Hull, frequently and in greater detail with Under Secretary Welles, and commencing in February 1943 with a group composed of the Secretary and Messrs. Welles, Myron C. Taylor, Davis, Bowman, Pasvolsky, and on some occasions Dunn and Hackworth. Mr. Welles at various times conveyed drafts to the President, including particularly a number in the fields of international organization, trusteeship, and the treatment of Germany. The subcommittee was in turn kept informed by him and other individual members of the views expressed by the President in conversations from time to time.

The results of the work of the Subcommittee on Political Problems were reflected in the advice and proposals of the Secretary of State and the Under Secretary of State to the President. The fact that Departmental policy-making officials participated in the subcommittee naturally caused an interflow of influence on thinking, and from the start there was evident effect of the subcommittee's weekly discussions upon Departmental thought. All addresses of Secretary Hull, and those of Under Secretary Welles until March 1943 when the Secretary assumed continuous charge of the work, were based substantially upon the subcommittee's work during this period, and the statements of approved policy contained in them reflected acceptance of its views, matters still in debate being omitted or presented with safeguarding qualifications. Certain of the subjects discussed by the President and Secretary Hull at the first Quebec Conference, August 11–24, 1943, had received prior attention by the subcommittee, and its views had been made available orally and in written papers in advance of the conference. These views were also reflected in the general position taken on organizational and structural questions by the American representatives at the United Nations Conference on Food and Agriculture at Hot Springs, Virginia, May 18–June 3, 1943. Finally, it should be noted that, as in fact the superior subcommittee, its views or the ideas of members developed at its meetings had appreciable influence in all other subcommittees.

---

[5] Such talks were not normally made a matter of formal record in the Department.

Increasingly, as Secretary Hull assumed direct charge in the spring of 1943, the subcommittee became identified as the "Political Committee." At the same time the Secretary developed the practice, both on matters to be raised in meetings of the subcommittee and on the agenda of problems, of informally consulting in advance with a very small group that he invited to his office. These discussions were the origin of the "informal political agenda group" which succeeded the Political Subcommittee and certain other subcommittees. The description of its nature and work is therefore postponed until Part III.

THE SPECIAL SUBCOMMITTEE ON INTERNATIONAL ORGANIZATION

THE INTENTION of the Political Subcommittee in deciding on June 27, 1942, at the suggestion of Mr. Welles, to establish the Special Subcommittee on International Organization was to obtain from a group of its own members draft proposals for an international organization which could then be discussed by the Political Subcommittee itself. The special subcommittee was not expected at that time to constitute a standing part of the Advisory Committee's structure. However, it assumed at once a position of major importance and status not different, except for its delayed establishment, from that of the other subcommittees. It continued in existence as long as the Political Subcommittee itself, holding a total of forty-five meetings, the first on July 17, 1942, the last on June 26, 1943. During the final three months of its work, eight of its meetings were held jointly with the Subcommittee on Security Problems. Its members all continued their work with the Political Subcommittee.

As designated by Mr. Welles and the Director, the Special Subcommittee on International Organization was composed of Messrs. Welles, Chairman, Bowman, Cohen, Hackworth (Acting Chairman when necessary), Shotwell, Pasvolsky, and, for its final meetings, Hamilton Fish Armstrong. Mr. Notter was the research secretary. All meetings after the first one were also attended, practically in the capacity of a member, by Clark M. Eichelberger, Director of the Commission to Study the Organization of Peace,[6] who was consultant to the research staff. At all times an additional member of the research staff was also present in the capacity of an expert. Walter R. Sharp was present in this capacity through a little more than the first half of the special subcommittee's work, and Benjamin Gerig so attended during the latter half. While Mr. Sharp served as secretary for the first four months, Bryce Wood, and subsequently Miss Dorothy Fosdick, assumed this responsibility thereafter.

---

[6] A private organization with headquarters in New York.

The considerable overlapping in membership between this special subcommittee and several other subcommittees was not due solely to the members' special qualifications—though this was the main reason for their selection—but was also designed to assure desirable integration of thinking day by day. While interchange of information with the parent subcommittee was of course automatic, still further integration was necessary, especially with the Security Subcommittee which had to consider certain problems that were likewise before the new special subcommittee. A single agreed position with respect to such problems was essential. This same type of coordination was important in the case of the Special Subcommittee on Legal Problems,[7] which was constituted later and was assigned the drafting of a projected statute for an international court within the structure of the proposals for international organization being worked out by Mr. Welles' special subcommittee. In this case, however, only broad outlines of ideas needed to be held in mind by both special subcommittees, for the integration of specific provisions was not involved during this period.

The work of the Special Subcommittee on International Organization was conducted after the first few meetings almost exclusively on the basis of drafts. At the start each member prepared rough draft sketches of plans. The main task undertaken during the several meetings in July and August 1942 was to examine past experience with international organization. For this, books, treaties, and other similar documentary materials as well as research papers were used directly. This phase of analysis and general examination was concluded with an appraisal, article by article, of the Covenant of the League of Nations in terms of its strength or weakness in international action.

Trusteeship was given attention next. In his address on July 23, 1942, already referred to, Secretary Hull had said with respect to dependent peoples:

"We have always believed—and we believe today—that all peoples, without distinction of race, color, or religion, who are prepared and willing to accept the responsibilities of liberty, are entitled to its enjoyment. We have always sought—and we seek today—to encourage and aid all who aspire to freedom to establish their right to it by preparing themselves to assume its obligations. . . . It has been our purpose in the past—and will remain our purpose in the future—to use the full measure of our influence to support attainment of freedom by all peoples who, by their acts, show themselves worthy of it and ready for it."

Toward the implementation of this purpose, the special subcommittee undertook, beginning in mid-August 1942 and continuing for eight

[7] See pp. 98, 114.

weeks, to draft a proposed system of trusteeship, which was reported to the Political Subcommittee on November 14 and, in revised form, on December 5.

The principal issue to develop on this problem during the "first round" consideration was whether, as in the special subcommittee's drafts, the proposed trusteeship system should cover all dependent territories alike, including those with colonial status, or should differentiate between colonial territories and dependent territories then under mandate or to be detached from the enemy states after the war. As early as November 1942, the latter approach was recommended to the President by Secretary Hull, primarily on grounds of political feasibility; and by March 1943 a draft United Nations Declaration, making a distinction between colonial and other dependent territories, had been drawn up by a special group of Department officers working under the direction of the Secretary, who were at the same time, however, all members of the Political Subcommittee.[8] When the question of international trusteeship came up for discussion in the "second round," the concept developed in the Special Subcommittee on International Organization was first considered, and then the Political Subcommittee turned its attention to a revision of the original proposal, prepared by the research staff in accordance with a Political Subcommittee decision that the proposed trusteeship system should be confined to mandated territories and dependent territories to be detached from Italy and Japan (Germany having lost her dependencies after the first World War).

Concentration upon a draft proposal for general international organization was begun by the special subcommittee on October 23, 1942, and reached a sufficiently finished form by March 26, 1943, to make possible its reference to the Political Subcommittee.[9] As has been seen above, however, Secretary Hull decided upon a new fundamental examination of the principal issues involved with respect to an effective international organization without reference to any specific draft.

Problems not resolved for the purposes of the March 26 draft related chiefly to the international exercise of police power, which affected the use and status of national armed forces. The technical aspects of these problems had been recognized as early as January 15, 1943, which had led to a request to the Security Subcommittee to prepare a draft article for the special subcommittee to consider. For the study of this draft article on international police power, joint meetings were started on April 9, 1943. The various viewpoints on the military and political aspects of this problem, and on timing of

---

[8] For text of draft declaration, see appendix 12.

[9] For the final draft resulting from the work of this special subcommittee, see appendix 13.

action in the armistice and transitional periods, suggested that drafts for two international agreements providing for transitional international action be prepared. One of these envisaged agreement among the major powers only, and the Security Subcommittee was made primarily responsible for this draft. The second envisaged an agreement among all of the United Nations concerning transitional international organization, and chief responsibility for this draft was allocated to the Special Subcommittee on International Organization. The resulting drafts were discussed in further joint meetings, the last being held on June 3.

Being small and having specific drafting responsibilities, the special subcommittee under Mr. Welles undertook at all times to give a more detailed and concentrated type of consideration to the problems before it than could the Political Subcommittee. As regards agenda, minutes, notification of meetings, distribution of papers, and like matters, the conduct of its meetings was the same as that of the Political Subcommittee. Maps were rarely used, although charts were occasionally necessary. Discussion was normally entirely conversational, in which the research secretary and other research officers actively participated. The staff not only put into the form of draft provisions the results of the subcommittee discussion but also customarily itself suggested draft provisions to be considered at the subcommittee meetings. In its suggestions, the staff sought to advance the subcommittee's work along the lines elected by the latter without, as a rule, pressing for fundamental variations. The staff's own views in this field were developed in definite form in the summer of 1943 after discussions by the special subcommittee were suspended.

The special subcommittee on several occasions established small groups or teams to prepare, to revise, or to refine drafts between meetings. These were composed of members solely, though provision was usually made for staff participation. Mixed member-staff groups to prepare drafts on points to be taken up at meetings increasingly became the accepted practice after the first few months. Resort to these methods of drafting was more often spontaneous than formal, being arranged frequently by members on their individual initiative.

In organizing and conducting its work, the special subcommittee had to make certain choices of far-reaching importance. Its judgments on these choices became its working assumptions in drafting, although such assumptions were always subject to rejection or change by the Political Subcommittee and, eventually, to the processes of decision by which all the recommendations arrived at by the Advisory Committee and its component parts would be weighed. These choices were faced not in one meeting but rather whenever the agenda topics raised them. Not all members agreed even for working purposes with the choices made, but all were willing to have preparations proceed along such lines in order to develop a plan, which could later be considered against other plans made on different bases.

A primary choice had to be made at the start on whether a transitional or permanent international organization should be established. The special subcommittee chose to prepare for the former. As between the establishment of the organization through a series of treaties or by a single treaty, a series of steps was deemed preferable at a meeting on August 14, 1942. A further choice presented on this same date was whether to seek to revive the League of Nations and establish general international organization by the process of strengthening the Covenant through amendments. The consensus was that a new international organization should be constructed. A week later, when the principle of trusteeship for dependent peoples and territories was under consideration, a choice had to be made whether this principle should be applied on a universal or on a regional basis. There was general agreement initially to explore the application of the trusteeship principle through regional structures. Another occasion for choice arose at the end of October, when specific drafting of a provisional outline of international organization was beginning, on whether or not to build upon the Kellogg-Briand Pact. It was believed that a completely fresh approach, devoid of rhetorical denunciations of war, was to be preferred.

Many further choices of significance were reflected thereafter in the actual plans evolved by this special subcommittee. Two such choices illustrate the difficult basic problems that this subcommittee confronted concerning the inherent nature of world relations involved in international organization. One was whether general international organization should be founded upon regional organizations of various kinds, with regional representation provided for in its executive organ or organs, or should be wholly or as nearly as possible universal in structure and character. Prime Minister Churchill, early in February and again in May 1943, privately indicated to the President that he favored the organization of the world after the war on a regional basis, and in a public address on March 21, 1943, he projected the establishment of "a Council of Europe and a Council of Asia," functioning "under a world institution embodying or representing the United Nations, and some day all nations." It was thought at this time that the President himself was inclined to favor the regional approach. Opinion in the subcommittee on this controversial question remained divided. The draft developed by the subcommittee was based on regional representation. While all participated in its formulation, it was understood that the exploration, in concrete drafting terms, of this approach was a necessary part of the comprehensive examination essential in the case of a policy problem so fundamental for the United States as the nature of the future international organization to maintain peace and security, and that none was bound against his convictions.

The second such choice was whether membership in the international organization should be held by states or should include other entities, defined at the time as dominions or colonial and other areas nearing complete independence, which might not be wholly identifiable as "states" under the generally accepted concept of sovereignty. The view taken on December 4, 1942, was that states should be members of the international organization. The vitality of the national state was regarded from the outset as of primary importance in the postwar world.

The special subcommittee's work was naturally heavily influenced by prevailing and prospective world and national conditions and by many grave uncertainties with respect to the views of the American public. While strong pressures toward striving for a federalized international organization—or government—were being exerted, there was also at this period a possibility that the dominating American opinion of the years before the war in favor of political isolationism might re-assert itself. Uncertainty regarding Senate consent to ratification of any proposed agreement in this field was ever present. Consequently in several meetings there was discussion of the methods that might be followed in informing the public at large of the issues concerning international organization for peace and security and of the national considerations affecting the question of United States participation. This question, together with that of the desirability of possible Congressional action to dispel doubts concerning the probability of future ratification, was also discussed upon a number of occasions in the parent Political Subcommittee, and in the spring of 1943, Secretary Hull began informal consultations with members of Congress on the matter, to be described in Part III in connection with the Moscow Declaration. For such efforts both in Congress and with the public, prior official clarification of many of the policy problems at issue was of course necessary. These included not only the desirable terms for American participation but the many questions of feasibility of this or that preferred action in the light of the attitude of other states, and the future peace settlements.

Finally, among other uncertainties, two should be emphasized as having given prolonged concern to the special subcommittee. The nature of the profound economic and social changes being wrought by the war was the first. In 1942 the effects of the changes already in process could only be estimated. To strengthen respect for human rights by some common international program was accepted as being imperative, however, as early as October 30, 1942. The second uncertainty concerned armaments and "disarmament". On one hand the relation between armaments and postwar security was clear; on the other hand general demand to curtail expenditures in this field was likely. The regrettable effects of the drain upon budgets in practically all states caused by armaments pointed toward great reduction, but the need had also to be met for the maintenance of armaments at a level that would permit the discharge of international obligations respecting the enforcement of peace and security. The successful aggressions of the enemy against weak neighbors and the attack by Japan upon Pearl Harbor were lessons in the danger of weakness that could not be forgotten if peace and security were not to be imperiled. A minimum level for some states and a maximum for others was envisaged in the tentative views developed.

The results of the special subcommittee's intensive efforts were reported to the Political Subcommittee and were made available to the members of the Security Subcommittee. The Chairman of the special subcommittee personally transmitted the results to the President for his information, June 19, 1943. The definitive policy recommendations later adopted in this vital field were, however, not those formulated by this special subcommittee, and in various respects differed fundamentally, although in other respects the special subcommittee's views entered into the proposals ultimately advanced by this Government. As will be seen in Part III, the final proposals were not made to the President until months after the work of this subcommittee had ended.

THE SPECIAL SUBCOMMITTEE ON LEGAL PROBLEMS

THE SPECIAL Subcommittee on Legal Problems developed from an *ad hoc* drafting group designated by the Political Subcommittee on June 13, 1942, to explore two points on the chart of the armistice period. These points were first, the legal aspects of a code delimiting the functions of provisional governments, and second, a provisional code of justice applicable to persons charged with war crimes. A third task, the preparation of a framework for an international court of justice, was added by reference from the Special Subcommittee on International Organization.

When the Legal Subcommittee was formally constituted on August 8, 1942, it was comprised of Messrs. Hackworth, Chairman, Armstrong, Berle, and Cohen, who originally composed the *ad hoc* group, and in addition, Brooks Emeny and James T. Shotwell. The membership, however, had to be adjusted to other demands on the time of some of those designated. Mr. Pasvolsky, though an *ex officio* member, could not attend the meetings; Mr. Armstrong could not arrange to come at the hours set for meeting; and after the first meeting, Mr. Berle's other duties kept him from attending. Although the post of research secretary was filled by Mr. Notter for the first six meetings, Mr. Sandifer upon joining the staff assumed this duty. This subcommittee, which worked largely on the basis of draft proposals, developed the practice of having for its given fields specialized research secretaries who attended according to the appearance of topics on its agenda. Lawrence Preuss served as the specialist on problems of war crimes; Mrs. Alice McDiarmid on the legal problems relating to human rights, which arose in connection with the projected code for provisional governments and also in connection with general international organization; and Mr. Sandifer on the problems concerning the international court of justice. The necessary secretarial work for the subcommittee was performed in succession by Mr. Sandifer, John W. Halderman, and Mrs. McDiarmid.

This subcommittee held a total of thirty-three meetings from August 21, 1942, to June 25, 1943, inclusive. It met weekly, usually on Thursday afternoon, for about two hours. Being predominantly a mixed technical and policy group, with the closest of relations between the members and the attending staff, its organization, conduct of work, and discussions were like those of the Special Subcommittee on International Organization.

Inasmuch as the Legal Subcommittee functioned as the reference body on legal questions for all other subcommittees, it decided not to initiate the submission of views or requests to other than the parent Political Subcommittee. It first considered the problems of basic human rights, from August 21 through December 10, 1942. Its next field of discussion, until March 11, 1943, concerned war crimes. In this respect participation by the Department of Justice was necessary, and, as a result of conversations between Mr. Welles and the Attorney General, the Assistant Solicitor General, Oscar Cox, was informally designated as a temporary member for these discussions. Mr. Cox did not personally attend, but was represented by Douglas Maggs, Louis Hector, and Benjamin Schwartz. The problems of an international court occupied the remaining meetings from March 18 to June 25, 1943, inclusive.

The approach of the Legal Subcommittee to each of these three fields may be briefly described. The subcommittee assumed that the international recognition and, within each state the guaranty, of basic human rights would be conducive to the development of conditions favorable to the maintenance of international peace. The aim was to formulate the basic rights of individuals that should be universally respected, even if not formally subscribed to by all states, in a brief and forceful statement of general principles. This should include both traditional rights and certain principles of social and economic justice that were beginning to be regarded as basic. Accordingly the subcommittee's work related to personal freedoms, property rights, social rights, political rights, and procedural rights.

The results of its work, including a draft "Bill of Rights" dated December 3, 1942,[10] were held ready for the time when they would be needed, and the papers were not transmitted to superior authority during this period.

In regard to the punishment of war criminals, the subcommittee assumed that the main lines of policy had already been laid down authoritatively for the signatories of the United Nations Declaration in the statements of Prime Minister Churchill and President Roosevelt on October 25, 1941, the Allied Declaration on German War Crimes of January 13, 1942, and the President's statement of August 21, 1942, when the intention to exact retribution for war crimes had been declared. The canalization, in the form of orderly judicial procedures, of the demand everywhere for punitive action against war criminals was regarded as necessary to forestall indiscriminate reprisal. The views developed by the subcommittee in this regard were sent to appropriate authorities directly after their definite formulation, March 11, 1943. They included recommendations for the establishment of a United Nations commission for the prosecution of war criminals at the conclusion of hostilities, and recommendations regarding the United Nations Commission to Investigate War Crimes projected by the British and American Governments in October 1942. The Commission was established in the autumn of 1943.

The subcommittee contemplated the creation of a new international court as an organ of the general international organization and not administratively independent as the World Court had been. Since arrangements for integration of this court with other organs of the international organization were viewed as a responsibility of the Special Subcommittee on International Organization, the Legal Subcommittee addressed itself primarily to such questions as the composition, internal organization, competence, and procedure of the court. Its drafting took the form of remolding the Statute of the Permanent Court of International Justice. The proposals of the Legal Subcommittee for the new court were well developed prior to the suspension of its active work in July 1943, but its views were not submitted for superior consideration.[11] They were taken up by the succeeding preparatory structure described in later pages.

The British had approached this Government again in October 1942, suggesting United States participation in the work of an informal inter-Allied committee being established in London to study the future of the Permanent Court of International Justice. No immediate action was taken on this British proposal because our views on this question had yet to be formulated. It was still considered

---

[10] See appendix 14.
[11] For Legal Subcommittee draft statute, see appendix 15.

preferable, moreover, to postpone the discussion of any single aspect of postwar international organization until this matter could be taken up in its entirety.

THE SUBCOMMITTEE ON TERRITORIAL PROBLEMS

IN PROJECTING the organization of the Advisory Committee, a single group had at one time been envisaged for the consideration of both political and territorial problems because of the interwoven character of such problems. The final decision, however, was for a separate Subcommittee on Territorial Problems composed of a few members who would also be members of the Political Subcommittee.

This, it was believed, would permit specially qualified members to concentrate on a detailed study of all territorial problems and thereby provide a core of sifted views and judgments for subsequent discussion in the Political Subcommittee. Such an arrangement would offer a means to test and re-test views on principal issues of policy regarding countries, which would help to make the ultimate recommendations as free from error as possible. Furthermore, considering the emotionally explosive nature of the territorial problems of countries and peoples, as the peace settlement after World War I had demonstrated and as all historical experience so amply revealed, it was thought advisable to have a thorough study of each foreseeable territorial problem made by a highly restricted body. Such a small group could be kept informed of all relevant current developments without the limitations otherwise necessary to maintain the secrecy obviously imperative in these matters during the war. Since the only assurance of military victory lay in unity and since military actions and old or new conflicting interests in the areas concerned had to be taken into account in the subcommittee's work, even the problems studied had to be kept secret in order to avoid the risk of misunderstanding and of facilitating divisive enemy propaganda.

The original membership of the Territorial Subcommittee was constituted of Messrs. Bowman, Chairman, Armstrong, Berle, Feis, and MacMurray, and Mrs. Anne O'Hare McCormick, with Leo Pasvolsky member *ex officio*. Myron C. Taylor became a member effective August 28, 1942. Cavendish Cannon of the Division of European Affairs represented Ray Atherton in the capacity of a specially designated Departmental participant beginning late in December 1942, and at various times, in accord with the areas being considered, Messrs. Dunn (Europe), Hornbeck (Far East), and Murray (Near East) were invited to take part. Mr. Notter was the research secretary during the first five months of work, following which Philip E. Mosely, who by then had joined the research staff, carried this responsibility. Almost from the outset, this subcommittee also required the assistance of a secretary to take notes on its discussions. This work was undertaken during the first two months also by Mr. Notter and then, in succession, by Mr. Rothwell, Paul B. Taylor, William Koren, Jr., James Frederick Green, John W. Masland, Jr., and Cyril E. Black, all of the research staff.

Since the membership of this subcommittee and those on economic and security problems overlapped, formal requests by the former to the latter were rarely made. Coordination in this regard took place rather on the working level and in the Political Subcommittee itself.

The Territorial Subcommittee met on Saturdays for the first four months, and thereafter on Friday afternoons. Aside from the original joint organizing session with other subcommittees, it held 59 meetings covering the period from March 7, 1942, to December 17, 1943, inclusive. The last eight of these were held after the suspension of the other subcommittees in the political fields of the preparation.

Because of the almost complete dependence in the territorial field of discussion upon research, the subcommittee adopted a proposal made by its Chairman and the Director to alternate its meetings with special or technical meetings devoted to research preparations. This was an effort to expedite the work of the regular meetings through a prior selection and analysis of the problems to be considered. Regular meetings were biweekly while technical meetings were being held. The technical meetings were attended by Mr. Bowman, the Director, the research secretary, and the research specialists on the problems next on the agenda of the subcommittee. When first instituted, April 18, 1942, this procedure was followed only until requests from the Political Subcommittee necessitated regular weekly meetings, starting May 23. The technical meetings were resumed briefly in the early part of September, again being suspended because of the need to dovetail the agenda of the Territorial Subcommittee with that of the Political Subcommittee. However, by March 4, 1943, with various changes in the work of the Political Subcommittee and its subsequent concentration on international organization, the Territorial Subcommittee was free to determine its own agenda, and the practice of holding technical meetings in alternate weeks became fixed. These meetings, apart from the three held in the first period and one in September for which minutes were kept, developed along informal, consultative lines, with only the basic questions selected for definite consideration by the subcommittee and the resulting research assignments recorded. In addition to these meetings, ad hoc informal conversations between the Chairman and various individual specialists occurred throughout the subcommittee's work, becoming an accepted practice after June 1942. Most of these conversations related to the presentation of experts' papers in the subcommittee and to plans for future studies.

In the earliest meetings, the subcommittee's proceedings were exploratory, and did not involve substantial participation by the attending staff specialists on the several problems. As discussion became increasingly specific thereafter and as the staff was expanded and maps and studies became available, attending specialists began to be invited to discuss the points at issue. Further development of methods ensued. Beginning July 31, 1942, discussion was inaugurated with an oral statement by a staff specialist. After September 18, the subcommittee itself undertook to identify the problems it wished studied, often defining the basic issue that had eventually to be faced. Starting December 11, meetings were opened with an introductory exposition of a policy problem, the essential background involved, the alternative solutions or courses possible in the circumstances, and an analytical evaluation of each of these solutions in as strictly objective a spirit as possible. In the subsequent discussion technical questions were put to the specialists, and as a rule their personal opinion was also requested on this or that possible solution.

Participating specialists, although mainly from the staff specially recruited for postwar policy preparation, eventually also included experts from the operating divisions of the Department. Attendance of officers dealing with political, security, economic, and social problems reflected the integration of all substantive lines of thought involved in territorial problems.[12] Close and continuous relationship between research and the subcommittee's discussion thus characterized the work in this field from the outset and deepened progressively. On only one occasion, April 16, 1943, did the subcommittee members convene by themselves alone. That meeting con-

---

[12] In addition to the staff specialists serving the subcommittee as named above, the additional ones who attended as problems in their fields arose were Miss Evelyn M. Acomb, Miss M. Margaret Ball, George H. Blakeslee, Hugh Borton, Ralph H. Bowen, John C. Campbell, Waldo Chamberlin, Norris B. Chipman, Shepard B. Clough, Richard Eldridge, Robert A. Fearey, Holden Furber, Leon W. Fuller, Benjamin Gerig, David Harris, Harry N. Howard, Philip W. Ireland, Grayson L. Kirk, Melvin M. Knight, C. Hawley Oakes, Thomas F. Power, Jr., George L. Ridgeway, and Andreas G. Ronhovde, Miss Julia E. Schairer, Walter R. Sharp, Leroy D. Stinebower, Robert Terrill, Amry Vandenbosch, H. Julian Wadleigh, Wilbur W. White, Jesse Van Wickel, Frank S. Williams, Bryce Wood, and William Yale.

Operating officers attending in the same manner were Charles E. Bohlen, James C. H. Bonbright, W. Percy George, L. Randolph Higgs, J. Wesley Jones, Perry Laukhuff, and Robert B. Stewart of the European Division; Maxwell M. Hamilton, Kenneth P. Landon, Joseph W. Ballantine, H. Merrell Benninghoff of the Far Eastern Division and Alger Hiss of the Office of the Political Adviser on Far Eastern Problems; Lt. Col. Harold B. Hoskins, Foy D. Kohler, Charles W. Lewis, Jr., Henry S. Villard, and Paul H. Alling of the Near Eastern Division; and Samuel W. Boggs and Otto Guthe of the Office of the Geographer.

sidered future plans of work in the light of developments in the Political Subcommittee noted above.

Meetings were held around a table, with papers on it and maps facing it. Studies were concerned with either factual background information or analysis. The former were used for the initial stage of problem exploration on the basis of existing facts so far as they could be ascertained, while the latter papers contained alternative courses of action and were used in considering the solution of given problems. These policy problem papers developed during the autumn of 1942, and out of them, commencing in this field in February 1943, grew finally the most matured research papers used, called policy summaries or handbooks—in the territorial field, called country handbooks.[13] It was only in these "handbook documents" that the views of the subcommittee were embodied, since by a decision made in the interest of security July 31, 1942, the minutes in the form weekly circulated were not permitted to state the views of the subcommittee.

Papers written by the Chairman and other individual members were also employed occasionally as starting points for discussion. These were of a different nature, however, than the handbook documents, being appraisals and proposals concerning principles to be followed or points to be stressed in the work or conclusions of the subcommittee.

The maps were of two principal kinds: reference or data maps and "application" maps. The latter type was used to illuminate specific considerations in connection with a problem and the alternative proposals for its settlement.[14] They were also used to record graphically the various views developed at the meetings.

The scope of the fields of preparation for which the Territorial Subcommittee was responsible required it to consider almost every part of the globe. It began with the Near East and Eastern Europe and covered all the countries of Europe, Asiatic and African problem areas, colonies and mandates throughout the world, territorial settlements in the case of all enemy states, the areas of the Arctic and the Antarctic, and, especially in the autumn of 1943, the future settlement in the Far East and the Pacific. Problems that cut across countries and areas, such as those involving possible transfers of population or resettlement, also were taken up. Various problems were considered time and again as studies were matured or difficult aspects had to be reviewed. Furthermore, the march of events caused some problems to be considered out of planned order. The North African invasion, the Soviet break with the Polish Government-in-exile, the situation in Italy as the American and British forces attacked, all had such effect upon the agenda.

The subcommittee's initial question was: "What do we need to

---

[13] For examples of these three types of papers, see appendixes 16, 17, and 18.

[14] For an example, see appendix 19.

know" about the problems ahead? It concluded that for each foreign country it would need factual studies and analyses of its population; the groups, movements, and leaders in the country; its resources, including the probable effects of the war on major resources and activities; and the probable character of its relations with other nations after the war. It would also need maps and charts portraying boundaries, significant historical changes in and among states, transportation routes, communications, industries, agriculture, ethnic and other groupings, religious factors, resources, and geographical strategic factors. Finally, it would need analyses of the official views on territorial questions held by all governments and of the views of groups within countries.

When the subcommittee came to the problems of dependent areas it adjusted this approach. These areas varied widely in their capacity for self-rule. Hardly a single principle was applicable to all. The required studies were first in terms of questions: What constitutes a dependent area? Which areas are dependent? What is their relative status? Which will require consideration owing to Allied victory? Which have resources needed in the economic activities of great powers and other industrial states? Which have strategic significance for general international security? What are the comparative long-range effects of the several existing and likely colonial policies? What are the relations among the metropolitan countries themselves attributable to their colonial possessions? In addition, the mandates system had to be analyzed in full, and each of the dependent areas had to be studied factually to reveal the nature, availability, and extent of exploitation and conservation of its resources, the status and potentialities of transportation including aviation, the economic development and opportunity for the local inhabitants, political institutions, the degree of direct and indirect rule and local political participation, health and sanitation conditions, and possibilities of settlement.

The subcommittee determined to have its thought prepared on all problems of possible concern up to the point where the policy choices and their consequences with respect to these problems were clear so far as the circumstances of the war permitted. It sought to avoid any attempt to provide encyclopedic studies built on the assumption that the exact nature of postwar political problems could be accurately determined. The subcommittee's endeavor to study problems in terms of alternative policy decisions, with the final choice among these alternatives left to be made in the light of conditions at the time of settlement, was a conscious departure from the practice of The Inquiry twenty-five years earlier.

The subcommittee dealt in tentatives. It felt that every major territorial problem was likely to be affected in one or more fundamental respects by the war and resulting immediate and long-range economic, social, and political developments. Also, territorial solutions hinged in many cases on unresolved questions concerning the nature of the future general international organization and the extent and powers of any regional arrangements that might evolve by the time the war ended. Accordingly the subcommittee believed that its conclusions had necessarily to be almost wholly in conditional terms. Only on such specific questions as boundaries could it attempt concrete recommendations, and even then, often with "ifs". For these reasons it early decided not to offer final recommendations on problems, but rather to reduce their uncertainties and complexities so far as practicable and to formulate the most feasible alternatives of policy from among which a choice could be made or an adjusted solution devised, in the light of conditions obtaining when decisions became necessary.

The term "territorial" was defined in two senses: first, as land with the people on it. As land, it signified property, which must be delimited for tax purposes, administration of law, and national defense. Boundaries therefore could not be ignored. They still meant what they always had, only to a lesser degree. Aviation and other modern developments of a military and economic nature had modified the significance but not entirely removed either the security or the economic implications of boundaries. These boundaries afforded, in particular, a reduced but still strategically vital period of military warning.

Second, the word "territorial" was considered to mean the historical and present economic, social, and political forces and activities at work within any area. The center of emphasis, accordingly, was the individual country and its people, but to understand its problems and conditions one had to see beyond it, always keeping in mind the historical forces at work in and around it. The deliberations of the subcommittee focused in this regard upon the requisite conditions for peace and stability both within and among countries.

The subcommittee assumed from the outset that the United Nations would be victorious, that they would have responsibility for all war settlements, and that the United States would assume its share of this responsibility. It soon arrived at the view also that differences of purpose among the victors must be expected and that preparations should be made in advance to ward against the divisive effects of these differences. Hence an over-all plan of settlement and of reconstruction was held to be the prime objective. It felt that the answer to the question of whether to favor separate settlements or one inclusive peace settlement was contingent upon the state of affairs when victory was attained.

In the subcommittee's judgment the postwar situation would be affected by new ideas and values not yet clearly formed. The peoples in the various parts of the world as never before were developing desires and plans for their future society. The social coherence of states was being affected by such swiftly developing conceptions. New leaders and groups were emerging, and power would accrue to one side or another with consequences not yet foreseeable. With this prospect ahead the subcommittee felt that it could not conclude, in the face of the conflicting and uncertain forces that states confronted, that an ideal solution would be possible. Dilemmas would certainly arise in choosing between the most important principles and less important ones. The extent to which intelligent policies could be carried into effect could not be determined until conditions at the end of the war were known. A fixed conclusion of the subcommittee in this connection was that the vital interests of the United States lay in following a "diplomacy of principle"—of moral disinterestedness instead of power politics—and in continuing to adhere to the policy already enunciated by Secretary Hull that the United States must refrain from undertaking any commitment on territorial settlements until after the conclusion of hostilities.

The views of the Territorial Subcommittee, while never formally presented as a whole to superior authority, reached the Secretary of State and the President selectively and in several ways. Some were reflected rapidly in current policy decisions. Others were taken into account in the Political Subcommittee on the basis of the positions taken there by individual members or the reports of Mr. Bowman in the meetings. Secretary Hull was kept apprised of the Territorial Subcommittee's views orally and through the summaries prepared by the staff, and he utilized them in the preparation of his addresses and other declarations of foreign policy. Likewise, through consultations with the President attended by the Chairman and certain other members, the views of the subcommittee were made known and discussed. Papers on given problems were made available to Secretary Hull and to the President in connection with the first Quebec Conference, and at other times as well.[15] The many specific functions and views of the Territorial Subcommittee and the large capital of research ready for use after its work was done had great effect, however, in the subsequent work of the country committees which formed part of the later structure for policy preparation considered in Part III.

---

[15] For illustration, see appendix 20, letter of May 24, 1943, Mr. Bowman to Mr. Pasvolsky.

THE SUBCOMMITTEE ON SECURITY PROBLEMS

THE FIELDS of the Subcommittee on Security Problems as approved at the initial meeting of the Advisory Committee required professional military judgment on over-all policy and specific arrangements alike. It was clear that agreed recommendations among the Departments of State, War, and the Navy would ultimately be required. The joint organizing meeting of all subcommittees in the political fields on February 21, 1942, accordingly considered that representation of the War and Navy Departments, including an air representative, was desirable, and the Advisory Committee promptly concurred.

As soon as the Subcommittee on Security Problems convened in its first separate meeting, on April 15, 1942, it proposed specifically that if possible, General Strong of the War Department and Admiral Hepburn of the Navy Department, because of their personal qualifications and their unusual experience with international developments relating to security in the years between the two wars, should be named representatives and that the War and Navy Departments should be consulted on an air representative.

Joint study among the three Departments had not existed up to this time, although various policy decisions in the past had been the subject of consultation among the three Secretaries, and a number of decisions in the immediately preceding years had been discussed by the Liaison Committee.[16] The decision of the three Secretaries to accept the subcommittee's proposal accordingly constituted a major development in the coordination of the political and the military and naval aspects of foreign policy, which ultimately grew into an organized system of policy consideration among these Departments on a continuing basis.[17]

The original membership of Messrs. Davis, Chairman, Hackworth, Long (who presided when the Chairman was absent), MacMurray, and Pasvolsky ex officio, was enlarged with the arrival of General Strong and Admiral Hepburn at the second meeting, April 29. Participation from time to time of air advisers was immediately agreed upon. Thereafter, by a process of development lasting almost until the termination of the subcommittee, further extensions of membership occurred. Messrs. Taylor and Shotwell began to attend on July 3 and 10, 1942, respectively. Senators Connally and Austin became members at this time but, apart from Senator Austin's attendance on July 31, were not able to be present because of pressure of duties in the Senate. From the Armed services, Admiral Train began to take part as alternate naval member on August 21, 1942. Cavendish Cannon

[16] See p. 16.
[17] See Part IV, p. 347.

normally attended for Mr. Atherton, Chief of the Division of European Affairs, after mid-January 1943, in a special liaison capacity, and Mr. Dunn, the Political Adviser in that area, also began to attend regularly commencing March 12, 1943, in an *ex officio* capacity.

The membership of the Joint Chiefs of Staff through its Joint Strategic Survey Committee was inaugurated with the arrival of Lieutenant General Embick (Army) and Major General Fairchild (Air Corps) on March 24, 1943, and of Admiral Willson on April 9, 1943. Capt. George H. DeBaun was designated the naval air representative on the subcommittee beginning March 31, 1943. The *ex officio* membership of Joseph C. Green, Special Assistant to the Secretary of State, and the appointment of Mr. Armstrong to membership followed, effective June 10 and 17, 1943, respectively. Also, on the Chairman's standing invitation, Mr. Bowman took part on occasion, and in addition a number of officers attended when matters of special concern in connection with their regular assignments arose, including Mr. Hornbeck, Maxwell M. Hamilton, Col. Thomas J. Betts, Capt. V. E. Korns, Brig. Gen. Hayes Kroner, Lt. Col. Thomas G. Lanphier, Col. James F. Olive, Jr., and Capt. H. L. Pence. Samuel Reber and Stanley Woodward attended when each, for a few weeks, served as personal assistant to Mr. Davis.

The Security Subcommittee met weekly but on fluctuating days and hours in order, primarily, to facilitate the attendance of the military and naval representatives. The fiftieth and final meeting of the subcommittee was held on August 11, 1943. Charles W. Yost for the first seven months, and then Grayson L. Kirk, served as the research secretary. Mr. Yost also took notes on the discussion for the first three months, after which this duty was undertaken in succession by Mr. Kirk, Waldo Chamberlin, Marion W. Boggs, Miss Pauline Reinsch, and Llewellyn Pfankuchen. Except in this secretariat capacity, research staff members were not present at meetings until January 1943, but thereafter the meetings were attended by Mr. Sandifer or alternatively Donald C. Blaisdell, and, when needed, by Philip W. Ireland and Andreas G. Ronhovde. In the closing months Mr. Notter also attended regularly.

The work of this subcommittee centered mainly on measures to maintain international security in relation to ex-enemy states in the period immediately after armed hostilities ceased; general security arrangements, including control of armaments, in the period before an international organization was established to keep peace; and the security provisions to be contained in the basic instrument of that international organization. While not all the problems involved were new to the scope of American interests, the circumstances after the war, in relation to which they would have to be considered, were certain to be different in some fundamental respects. Issues in the security field would plainly be sharper, and their decision more direct in its impact upon the United States than ever before. Conceptions of strategy had broadened profoundly, and the requirements of security were being widened correspondingly. The postwar responsibilities of the United States as a major power would be so different in degree, and presumably in kind, as to make imperative a thorough reappraisal of the world's, and our own, security needs. For sound determination of future lines of action so far as possible, the subcommittee believed it necessary to work on the basis of permanent factors and to consider our own future security policy not only in terms of the American position alone but in terms of the world's requirements for peace. With these our own requirements were merging. The subcommittee had to envisage fluid circumstances while attempting to find a definite foundation for future action by this country on the issues of world security.

The subcommittee, at its first meeting on April 15, 1942, began the process of "thinking through" these circumstances and issues with a preliminary discussion of the practicability of an international police force, of the general nature of security machinery needed in the armistice period, and of the organized means for enforcing international peace that might be effective on a continuing basis. Two weeks later it surveyed various questions concerning armistice terms, the occupation and disarmament of Germany and Japan, and general limitation of armaments among the victors. These subjects, together with the initial framework of action and timing accepted for the postwar period and various ideas expressed in these early meetings with regard to "policing", "armistice", and "great power agreements", derived from the preliminary lines of thought already developed for purposes of initial guidance by the Advisory Committee.

During the next several months, as imponderables and the interrelated complexities of questions emerged with the revolving of topics on its agenda, the subcommittee resorted to the method first of considering the conditions deemed necessary for the achievement of this or that desirable objective and then of formulating general tentative views, which were frequently summarized and re-examined. By late August 1942, consideration was begun of security problems in the Pacific area. Draft surrender terms and occupation policy were discussed in September and October. By November 13, 1942, specific discussions of an international security agreement commenced. Thereafter the subcommittee considered the problems that would be presented in the enemy's evacuation of occupied countries, policy on occupation of enemy countries, security features of an international organization to maintain peace, possible post-victory actions of the Soviet Union and the related question of the attitude it might take toward international cooperation, security aspects of civil aviation, the nature of "aggression", security factors in the peace settlements with Germany, Japan, and Italy, and draft surrender terms for these enemy states.

The problems concerning the enemy states absorbed much of the subcommittee's attention throughout its work. In this field, however, the governing considerations from a security standpoint were clarified without prolonged difficulty. The subcommittee believed that the victory of the United Nations would be conclusive. As between a negotiated cessation of hostilities or armistice on one hand and an imposed unconditional surrender on the other, the subcommittee rapidly reached the consensus that nothing short of unconditional surrender by the principal enemies, Germany and Japan, could be accepted, though negotiation might be possible in the case of Italy. The subcommittee's calculation of the relative advantages of this policy was based in part on historical experience with international conflict, which conferred a degree of concreteness on its conclusions. The President's enunciation of the policy of unconditional surrender at Casablanca on January 26, 1943, reflected no recommendation by the Department; none had been made. He had, however, been apprised informally of the subcommittee's early thinking on this point by its Chairman.

Even in the case of the most difficult of the larger problems of post-hostilities control of the enemy states, the subcommittee could bring some definite facts and historical evidence to bear on this or that alternative course—on whether, for example, the occupation and disarmament of Germany could best be accomplished through zonal control by the victor nations separately or through a central control administration; whether for future peace Germany should be allowed to remain unified or should be partitioned; and whether Italy should be denied any or all colonial outposts. The limitations to be placed on Japan in order to assure peace in the Pacific also came in this category.

In contrast, the attainment of over-all security after the defeat of the enemy posed new and even strange problems, with uncertainty marking the considerations to be taken into account and the political and economic feasibility of courses of action that might seem best on purely military grounds. With all prewar arrangements for the maintenance of international peace and security destroyed by the onset of the second world-wide war of the century and with several states presumably fated for elimination from the roll of major nations after the war, which would result in a profound reallocation of power, the Security Subcommittee had to attempt to sketch the lines of over-all security arrangements in terms mainly of broad choices and assumptions.

First of all, the fundamental choice between seeking security by our own efforts alone or through cooperative action with other powers on an agreed basis had to be made. Viewing our security as something more than our being well-equipped to fight for the maintenance of our national possessions and interests and as existing genuinely only when we were as free as contrivable from the menace of having to fight to protect ourselves, the subcommittee early accepted the need for organized international action to maintain security on the basis of agreements among the United Nations. It assumed that necessary international political and juridical machinery for the settlement of international disputes would be established and that such international organization should have the means of enforcing compliance with its decisions when necessary for the maintenance of peace anywhere in the world. It also assumed that in the transitional period, pending the establishment of a permanent general international security organization, the four major powers would have to accept the principal responsibility, though with the participation of the other United Nations, for the keeping of peace and for the enforcement of compliance with treaty limitations upon armaments. The early association with these four of a revived France was anticipated.

In regard to an armaments treaty, the subcommittee envisaged that the major powers might undertake by an agreement, to be effective as soon as practicable after the war, to fix maximum and minimum limits for their armaments and military forces and that subsequently the stabilization of all armaments might be reached through agreement among the other United Nations. The international organization, when established, should have forces, resources, and facilities made available to it by all members proportionately on the basis of their respective capacities. This should be accomplished by means of a mutual undertaking. The forces should act on behalf of the international organization and in pursuance of its decisions. In this connection, the subcommittee also envisaged cooperative action in the application of economic sanctions when necessary to the maintenance of peace.

Believing that peace and security were dependent not only upon enforcement but on other essential conditions, the subcommittee set down a number of further requirements. It considered that the maintenance of peace could not be guaranteed by any institutional security devices if trade were obstructed after the war by unreasonable barriers. Accordingly, in addition to immediate measures of relief and reconstruction, the subcommittee believed that financial stabilization, reduction or abolition of unreasonable trade barriers, and assurance of such access without discrimination to raw materials as was needed for peaceful purposes were indispensable to postwar security.

Practically from the opening of discussion on over-all security, emphasis was laid upon the necessity, as the most imperative basis for assurance of peace and security after the war, of a firm pact among the chief victor powers agreed upon prior to the conclusion of the war. A corollary of this conviction was that every effort should be made to come to an understanding with the Soviet Union and that a common policy with respect to future postwar settlements should be reached. It was thought that the great powers in the future must recognize and honor their collective security obligations and that the smaller states would tend not only to accept but even to welcome this new assumption of responsibility by the great powers.

Each of these broad assumptions, and almost each related problem, inevitably posed choices and even dilemmas not resolvable by the presentation of tangible facts so much as by hypotheses and reasoning. Would general disarmament make a large international police force unnecessary, or would not disarmament have to be enforced through an international organ having a police force and armaments of considerable size and striking power? Would not these armaments have to come from nations? Should each of the principal victor powers be primarily responsible for authorized enforcement action in a given region, or should all of them acting in conjunction be responsible for maintaining peace throughout the world? Should the forces made available for enforcement constitute an international force, or, instead, should the forces placed under the orders of the general international organization be national? Should the decision with respect to the use of international police forces be reached by a unanimous vote or by less than a unanimous vote? These and many more, including matters relating to bases and other facilities needed for effective enforcement action, raised profound questions concerning sovereignty and equality among the large and small states cooperating for maintenance of peace. These questions could be adjusted only within a new concept of "sovereign equality", which was gradually being clarified in other parts of the Advisory Committee structure.

Coordination between this subcommittee and other subcommittees was accomplished not so much through formal arrangements as through the carrying of thought from one group to another by the civilian members who took part in the work of the other subcommittees and through the research papers and common research staff. The professional views of the armed services on major strategic and other security factors thus found their way into the related discussions of the other subcommittees. Throughout the period from the spring of 1942 to the summer of 1943, members from the armed services were represented only in the Security Subcommittee.

There were, however, formal relations with other subcommittees. The Security Subcommittee decided at the start that the problems relative to the safeguarding of security required it to work closely with the Political Subcommittee, both in suggesting the type of permanent international organization that would best promote security and in devising security mechanisms to implement the proposals developed by the Political Subcommittee.   In its turn, the Political Subcommittee referred several matters to the Security Subcommittee for special consideration.   The first such reference, considered at the sixth meeting of the latter subcommittee on July 3, 1942, consisted of the questions whether certain possible policies regarding the treatment of Germany were desirable from the standpoint of security and what effects could be expected from a division of Germany into three or more zones during the period of military occupation and from the administration of these zones separately or under unified command. The Special Subcommittee on International Organization, as has been observed, also referred to the Security Subcommittee various drafting problems, such as the preliminary drafting of a provision for the exercise of police power, and in April, May, and June 1943, met with the Security Subcommittee to consider jointly the major proposals of mutual concern.   A proposal developed by the Legal Subcommittee for trial and punishment of war criminals was taken as the basis by the Security Subcommittee for a provision on war crimes in its draft surrender terms.

The views of the Security Subcommittee on an international air-police force and on air policy toward ex-enemy countries were transmitted on request to the interdepartmental Special Committee on International Aviation, which operated under the Taylor Committee, described below.   Also, various security papers were made available to the Political Planning Committee of the Department [18] to facilitate its consideration of current policy, to which further reference will also be made later.   Direct, though less extensive, reference of work by the Security Subcommittee similarly obtained.   For example, the economic problems that were foreseen by the Security Subcommittee in connection with inspection and control of armaments were referred to the Economic Subcommittees.

Although various of the problems before it were regularly studied in the War and Navy Departments and by the Joint Chiefs of Staff as a result of the participation of military and naval members in the work of the subcommittee, the first formal request made by the Security Subcommittee to the Joint Chiefs of Staff for examination of a problem was in connection with Pacific security arrangements.   The request arose from the discussion held August 21, 1942, of an inquiry from the Political Subcommittee for an opinion on the general disposition that should be made, on the basis of strategic considerations, of Japanese insular possessions.   The reply of the Joint Chiefs was

[18] See p. 156.

considered in the meeting of September 18, 1942, and was then transmitted to the Political Subcommittee. On November 20 study of possible proposals for maximum and minimum limitation of armaments after the war was requested of the War and Navy Departments. It is noteworthy, as reflecting the conduct of work by this subcommittee, that the views of the members from the War and Navy Departments and the Joint Chiefs of Staff were not usually expressed on the basis of formal instructions but rather as the thinking to date of the superior military authorities.

The subcommittee did not follow a uniform practice with respect to the preparation of drafts and other papers. Papers were drafted in several instances by individual members. A number were written in collaboration by General Strong and Admiral Hepburn. Sometimes, by request, a member and the research secretary together drew up a needed document. On a few occasions papers prepared by the Council on Foreign Relations or articles appearing in generally available publications were introduced. On the whole, however, most of the papers placed before the subcommittee were prepared by the research staff, working on its own initiative or on the basis of assignments. Minutes were taken and frequently were reviewed by the subcommittee, although as in the case of other subcommittees no formal procedure of approval was followed.

On three occasions the subcommittee appointed special subcommittees to handle a particular task. Each was composed of a few members assisted by the research staff and functioned only for one or two weeks. The first instance was on June 17, 1943, when Admiral Hepburn (Chairman), General Strong, and Messrs. Dunn, Joseph C. Green, and Myron C. Taylor were designated to study surrender terms, with particular reference to the urgent consideration of the terms for Italy that had been drafted in the War Department and that were shortly to be presented to the Joint Chiefs of Staff. This group held three meetings with a view to recommending revisions in these terms before their final approval for presentation to the enemy. Its report was approved in meetings of the full subcommittee and sent to the Joint Chiefs on July 8. The second instance was for the purpose of providing Mr. Berle, Chairman of the Special Committee on International Aviation, with comments on the security aspects of the proposals his committee planned to submit to the President. This special subcommittee on international aviation, appointed July 8, consisted of Admiral Hepburn (Chairman), Captain DeBaun, Messrs. Green, Hackworth, and Pasvolsky, and General Strong. It met on July 12 and 19, 1943, and its work was promptly approved and transmitted. The third instance arose on July 23, 1943, in connection with the determination of principles to govern the cessation of hostilities with European members of the Axis, on which a defined position had become necessary in order to reply to an *aide-mémoire* received on July 16 from the British. . This special subcommittee met but once formally and was composed of Messrs. Davis (Chairman), Dunn, Hackworth, Pasvolsky, and Taylor, General Strong, and Admiral Hepburn. Its conclusions were reflected in our discussions with the British at the first Quebec Conference and in the new impetus given just prior to that conference toward the initiation of negotiations on a general international organization.

In addition to these groups, need had been felt by the officials of the Advisory Committee as early as the autumn of 1942 for the establishment of a different type of body to function on a standing basis at a technical level. The Security Subcommittee had increasingly found it impossible to give sufficient attention in its own meetings to security problems concerning individual countries, other than the principal enemy states. It therefore instituted, by a decision December 5, 1942, a Security Technical Committee, working under its general direction, particularly to integrate the high staff-level consideration of country security problems with the work of the Territorial and Political Subcommittees.

The Security Technical Committee was composed of officers of the research staff, of representatives of the War and Navy Departments, and of desk officers from the geographic divisions of the Department. Its regular members were Mr. Kirk of the research staff, Chairman, Mr. Cannon (Liaison Officer for the Geographic Divisions of the Department of State), members of the security unit of the research staff, Messrs. Sandifer and Howard from other units of the research staff, and Captain Pence (Navy) and Colonel Olive (War). The Geographer's Office was usually represented by Otto Guthe, and a large number of other officers of the Department attended at different times as subjects of direct concern to them arose. This committee functioned from December 23, 1942, to July 2, 1943, holding a total of twenty-one meetings. It proceeded systematically with studies of the countries of Europe and then those of the Near East, Africa, the Far East, and the Pacific, giving attention at all times to our national security interests and to related Western Hemisphere factors. Thereby it examined most of the world's strategic problems in considerable detail. Its documentation was utilized directly in the research conducted for the Political and Territorial as well as for the Security Subcommittee.

When the meetings of this technical group had terminated, its military and naval experts and the members of the research staff kept in touch. This association provided a continuing link among the three Departments after August 11, 1943, when the Security Subcommittee completed its work, until a new interdepartmental structure was developed for coordination of views on terms of surrender and the control arrangements for enemy countries.[19] The remaining over-all work of the Security Subcommittee was absorbed, as will be seen, by the group taking responsibility for the consideration of general international organization after the departure from the original structure of the Advisory Committee in the latter half of 1943.

THE TWO ECONOMIC SUBCOMMITTEES AND THE COMMITTEE ON POST-WAR FOREIGN ECONOMIC POLICY

THE SUBCOMMITTEE on Economic Reconstruction and the Subcommittee on Economic Policy differed considerably from the subcommittees in the political field in function, composition, and organizational experience. The principal reasons for this difference were the relatively advanced stage of general economic policy formulation reached before these subcommittees began work and the diffusion of economic activity throughout the old-line and wartime agencies of the Government during the period of the preparation.

General economic foreign policy was in process of elaboration, rather than of exploration and consideration, when the Advisory Committee was instituted. The economic policy statements of the 1930's, the Atlantic Charter, and Article VII of the United States– United Kingdom Mutual Aid Agreement were relatively explicit, and showed a high degree of continuity. The essential elements on which United States economic foreign policy was based were not undergoing shifts and alterations of such major proportions as those determining political policy. The contrast between the functioning of the economic and political subcommittees was apparent in the first subject considered by the former, relief. Arrangements for meeting this problem were already in the early stages of negotiation by the time of the first subcommittee meetings, and the Subcommittee on Economic Reconstruction could immediately agree on the need of a relief organization and proceeded to consider its character.

Likewise, the first long-range subject considered by the Subcommittee on Economic Policy, preparation for Article VII discussions, necessitated essentially only a further development on the basis of policies already formulated.

Certain circumstances tended to cause somewhat uneven consideration of general economic policy problems in the period February 1942– March 1943. In view of the appreciable extent of continuity among the relevant economic considerations extending beyond the war itself into the postwar period, the line between short- and long-range problems

---

[19] The Interdepartmental Working Security Committee established in December 1943, described later, p. 225.

was often indistinct, and any attempt to be guided by it was sometimes justified only for purposes of orderly analysis. Moreover, given the uncertainties in regard to postwar political policy, the economic subcommittees could proceed to detailed preparation only to a limited extent in several most important fields, pending decisions on over-all political policy questions. These and related factors, including the increasingly evident advisability of having high-level governmental coordinating structure to arrive at agreed policy on the problems in this field, were influential in producing fundamental changes in the organization for the economic field after the first year.

The diffusion of the Government's economic postwar work had been reflected in the initial membership of the subcommittees. As Under Secretary Welles explained at the first meeting of the Advisory Committee, the postwar planning function in the economic field was divided between the Board of Economic Warfare and the Department of State, although recommendations to the President from both agencies were to be made through the Secretary of State. Other parts of the Government were directly interested in the subjects under consideration, however, and the interdepartmental character of the two subcommittees was initially and increasingly evident. Representation of official jurisdictions, rather than selection of members on the basis primarily of personal qualifications, consequently determined the composition of the subcommittees in the economic fields more than in the political fields.

As previously noted, the Advisory Committee used the device of two subcommittees and two chairmen to insure due concentration on both short-range and long-range economic problems, but provisions had been made for a large degree of common membership and for freedom of members to attend the meetings of both subcommittees. Similarly, while the short-range problems of relief and of restoration and reconstruction of production facilities were assigned to the Reconstruction Subcommittee and the long-range problems of commercial policy and relations, monetary relations, credit and investment, and international commodity agreements and cartels were assigned to the Economic Policy Subcommittee, certain problems were assigned to both subcommittees. This was done to assure adequate examination first of short-range and then of long-term aspects of these problems. Such common assignments included demobilization of persons and movements of populations; labor conditions, social security, and voluntary migrations; and shipping and land transportation. Aviation, broadcasting, and economic sanctions were also assigned to both, though priority of consideration for these fields was vested in the Security Subcommittee.

The organization as established by the Advisory Committee and amplified at the first joint meeting of the economic subcommittees in February 1942 remained unchanged until July 17, 1942. During that period the following served as members of both subcommittees : Messrs. Acheson (Chairman of the Economic Policy Subcommittee), Berle (Chairman of the Reconstruction Subcommittee), Appleby, Feis, Hawkins, and Pasvolsky. Messrs. Cohen, White, and Bean were members of the Economic Policy Subcommittee only but attended some meetings of the other subcommittee. Conversely, Messrs. Davis, Niles, and Myron C. Taylor were members of the Reconstruction Subcommittee but attended some meetings of the Economic Policy Subcommittee. Mr. Stone was present only at meetings of the Subcommittee on Economic Reconstruction. H. Julian Wadleigh served as secretary to both subcommittees and, until October when Walter A. Radius participated, was the only attending subordinate officer from the research staff.

During the period February 20–July 17, 1942, there were eighteen meetings : two joint meetings, ten meetings of the Reconstruction Subcommittee, and six of the Economic Policy Subcommittee. Although it was intended to have the subcommittees meet on alternate weeks, actually the scheduling of meetings was determined by the urgency for dealing with the subject under consideration. International relief was the subject at the ten meetings [20] of the Reconstruction Subcommittee. The discussions ranged from operational activities in connection with a preliminary exchange of views with the British Government to the drafting of a detailed charter for what became, in the next year, the United Nations Relief and Rehabilitation Administration. In the Economic Policy Subcommittee, a start was also made on preparing for discussions under Article VII of the lend-lease agreements in meetings on March 6 and 27 and April 10 and 24, leading to the initiation of necessary research on the full array of problems encompassed in that article. A significant feature of this initial approach was the emphasis placed on calculating the probable conditions of the postwar economies of various nations and on determining the measures that would be required to restore and to promote their economic health. While the probable status of British balance of payments was first explored, strong emphasis was placed on the need to bring the Soviet Union, the nations of Latin America, and other countries into Article VII discussions.[21] On May 22 and June 26, 1942, consideration of the economic aspects of the several suggestions currently being made for a regional arrangement in Eastern Europe was undertaken at the request of the Political Subcommittee. From the earliest meetings, a general international organization, although outside the province of the economic subcommittees, was regarded as desirable; its precise

---

[20] On Mar. 6, 20, Apr. 3, 17, May 1, 15, June 5, 12, 15, and 19, 1942.

[21] By the end of 1945, twenty-three nations had either signed lend-lease agreements incorporating Article VII or comparable provisions or through other agreements had subscribed to the principles embodied in Article VII.

nature and the relationship of any postwar organization in the economic field to it was, however, to remain for long a major question.

The experience with these initial discussions was reflected in the reallocation of fields of work involved in the first readjustment of the Advisory Committee structure for economic preparations. This change was instituted on July 17, 1942. It was on this occasion, it will be recalled, that Messrs. Emeny, Reuther, and Watt commenced their attendance as members. The readjustment stemmed directly from proposals made on that date at a joint meeting of the economic subcommittees. Mr. Berle proposed that he handle long-range problems and have on his subcommittee Messrs. Bean, Feis, Niles, Pasvolsky, Reuther, Myron C. Taylor, and White, and that Mr. Acheson's subcommittee should handle short-range and transitional problems, and be composed of Messrs. Appleby, Cohen, Davis, Emeny, Hawkins, Pasvolsky, and Watt. These proposals, which included suggestions that the two subcommittees should meet on alternate Fridays and that copies of the agenda and documents of each should be circulated to the other in recognition of the special interests of individual members in particular subjects, were accepted and followed until the next spring. This procedure, which encouraged an intermingling of attendance and discussion, rendered the two bodies in effect one committee with dual chairmanship. Their minutes and documentation were numbered in a single series and the prior records of the subcommittees on reconstruction and economic policy were incorporated into this series.

The combined membership during the period July 1942–March 1943 was Messrs. Berle (Chairman at sixteen meetings), Acheson (Chairman at eight meetings), Appleby, Cohen, Davis, Emeny, Feis, Hawkins, Niles, Pasvolsky, Stone and Bean (for Milo Perkins), Reuther. Myron C. Taylor, Wayne C. Taylor (who joined the committee July 24, 1942), Watt, and White. In January 1943 Mr. Stinebower succeeded Mr. Wadleigh as secretary. During 1943 there was notably active participation by the staff in discusssions and in initiation of work.[22] During this period as a whole, four major problems were considered: relief, European economic organization, shipping, and general commercial policy. The first of these was in a negotiating stage.

---

[22] Additional officers from the research divisions who attended some of the meetings were Allen T. Bonnell, Shepard B. Clough, Mrs. Eleanor L. Dulles, Richard Eldridge, Harold V. Fay, David Harris, Melvin M. Knight, Walter A. Radius, Alexander M. Rosenson, Robert P. Terrill, and John P. Young. Other officers in the Department who attended occasionally were Samuel W. Boggs, Robert Carr, Herbert Cummings, Julian Foster, John S. Hooker, and Eugene Rostow. Occasionally officers from other government Departments, and especially wartime agencies, attended meetings, reflecting the range of specialized contributory interests involved in such problems as relief and shipping.

In June 1942, exploratory conversations had been initiated with the British on the basis of the draft agreement for the establishment of a relief organization as developed in the Reconstruction Subcommittee.[23] On the American side, representatives of the State, Treasury, and Agriculture Departments and the Board of Economic Warfare participated in these discussions, which resulted in the modification of the draft agreement under consideration. Following Secretary Hull's statement concerning postwar relief on July 23, 1942, "Victory must be followed by swift and effective action to meet these pressing human needs," preparations for the administration of relief were expedited. A suggestion made by Mr. Acheson on August 7, 1942, for the establishment of five working committees, on which the Departments of State, Agriculture, Commerce, and Labor, Board of Economic Warfare, War Production Board, Tariff Commission, Public Health Service, and the American Red Cross should be represented, was adopted.[24] Mr. Acheson reported on October 9, 1942, that the President had approved the plan worked out with the British for an international relief organization, but felt that no announcement of the proposal should be made until after a United Nations victory or until the military situation had become stabilized; in the meantime the working committees were to proceed to explore likely postwar relief requirements and possible resources and machinery for meeting them.

The favorable military developments in North Africa soon afterward made the handling of relief an immediate problem. With the establishment in the Department of State in November 1942 of the Office of Foreign Relief and Rehabilitation Operations as a stopgap organization, the stage of operations was entered, and postwar policy preparations began to merge into current policy. This office, on the appointment of former Governor Herbert H. Lehman of New York as Director early in December, took over the five working committees and the studies in this field prepared by the economic subcommittees.

During this same general period, studies were made of the possibilities for economic organization in Eastern and in Western Europe, respectively. The same type of study was also made for Europe as a whole, both apart from, and within, the framework alternatively of an international economic organization or of an inclusive general international organization. This search for ways of solving the serious European economic problems that were anticipated, which had begun

---

[23] For text of this draft, see appendix 21.

[24] The following committees were organized (1) Food Relief, Howard R. Tolley, Agriculture, chairman, (2) Agricultural Rehabilitation, H. R. Tolley, Agriculture, chairman, (3) Clothing Requirements and Supplies, W. A. Graham Clark, Tariff Commission, chairman, (4) Health and Medical Requirements and Supplies, Dr. J. A. Crabtree, U. S. Public Health Service, chairman, (5) Essential Services and Industries, H. D. McCoy, Commerce, chairman.

with the first meetings of the original subcommittees, yielded increasingly firm projections of several of the major specialized agencies established later. The prevailing uncertainties regarding future international political organization, however, hampered definitive economic preparation in this direction. The general conclusion was repeatedly reached that regional economic organization could be fully effective and desirable only within such a larger political framework. Accordingly much of the thought on regional problems was necessarily conditional.

Problems of general commercial policy were considered *per se* at several meetings in September and October. These problems, however, arose in practically all meetings, since they were inseparably involved in all other problems before the subcommittees. Much attention was also given during and beyond the fall of 1942 to Germany's capacity to absorb additional population in a reduced territory and to the economic consequences if Germany, alternatively, were partitioned or left united. The problems of postwar shipping, which were of both current and long-range significance, were discussed on four occasions between December 11, 1942, and February 13, 1943.

The adequacy of the existing structure for preparation of economic policy came under discussion during the closing months of 1942, and plans for reorganization were drafted at that time. The division between short- and long-range economic and social problems was ceasing to have validity. The general exploratory work in most of the economic field had been accomplished more rapidly than in the political. The need for detailed technical consideration was becoming urgent, and this required more representation of other government agencies and greater utilization of the resources of those agencies. The period was one of transition, when economic mobilization for war was still the first consideration but when the problem of future adjustment was coming to be recognized as also of major importance. An intermediate structure, drawing in all interested parts of the Government to assure the needed preparation for postwar foreign economic policy and operations, was believed necessary for the best possible coordination of wartime economic measures and postwar objectives.

The replacement of the economic subcommittees by the Committee on Post-War Foreign Economic Policy was effected April 9, 1943.

The new Committee had representation at a Cabinet level. It was established under the Chairmanship of Secretary of State Cordell Hull, with Myron C. Taylor designated to preside in the absence of the Secretary of State and to direct the work of the Committee and its subcommittees. It accordingly became known informally as the Taylor Committee. The Committee was part of the Advisory Committee structure in conception and status. It was, moreover, the structure that formed the bridge between earlier organized interdepartmental cooperation in the economic field and the Executive Committee for Economic Foreign Policy, established one year later. The ECEFP stemmed directly from the Taylor Committee, absorbed nearly all of its subordinate committees, and still remains the principal interdepartmental structure for economic policy consideration and recommendation in the Government. Three of the subordinate committees under the Taylor Committee were, moreover, the forerunners of the present interdepartmental Air Coordinating Committee, Shipping Coordinating Committee, and Telecommunications Coordinating Committee, which are outside the ECEFP structure.

Besides Mr. Taylor, the following members of the economic subcommittees continued to serve as members of the new Taylor Committee: Messrs. Acheson, Appleby, Berle, Cohen, Emeny, Feis, Hawkins, Niles, Pasvolsky, Milo Perkins, Stone, Wayne C. Taylor, and White.[25] Since membership in this Committee was made representative, Messrs. Reuther and Watt, who had served in a personal capacity, were replaced by the heads of the C. I. O. and A. F. of L., respectively.

The additional members, who participated on invitation from the Secretary with the approval of the President, were Isaiah Bowman, Hugh Cox, Lauchlin Currie, Chester C. Davis, Marriner S. Eccles, William Green, Eric A. Johnston, Marvin Jones, Breckinridge Long (beginning July 2, 1943), Philip Murray, Miss Frances Perkins, and Nelson A. Rockefeller.[26] Under Secretary Welles participated *ex officio* until his resignation from the Department. Mr. Stinebower, now head of the economic research staff, was Executive Secretary of this Committee. Mr. Wadleigh continued for a few months to take minutes. Messrs. Radius and Terrill of the economic, and frequently Mr. Notter of the political, research staff also attended. Reciprocal cooperation between the Committee and the two chiefs of the research staff in initiating work and in considering problems exercised from the outset a new coordinative influence upon all aspects of the work now instituted.

At the first meeting on April 9, 1943, Secretary Hull announced that the time had come to broaden the economic work, and Mr. Taylor presented plans for the prompt establishment of seventeen special committees representing all interested Departments and agencies to deal with particular topics and to prepare materials and recommendations for the Committee. The recommendations would be submitted by the Committee to the Secretary of State and, through him, to the Presi-

---

[25] Mr. Stone represented Milo Perkins until directly named a member on May 6, 1943. Norman H. Davis was unable to continue in this field because of other work. Louis Bean also came to meetings as an observer. David K. Niles did not serve actively in the period of this Committee's meetings.

[26] Chester Davis did not attend the meetings. Mr. Cox did so rarely.

dent. Each special committee would have as chairman an official of the appropriate Department or agency. For general guidance, however, eight special committees would be grouped under Mr. Acheson, eight under Mr. Berle, and certain integrative phases of the work would be put in charge of the remaining committee, under Mr. Pasvolsky.

The special committees were grouped as follows: (1) Under Mr. Berle's general supervision: Monetary and Banking Relations, Long-Term Investment, Labor and Social Security, Migration and Settlement, Aviation, Inland Transport, Power, Communications; (2) Under Mr. Acheson's general supervision: Shipping, Relaxation of Trade Barriers, Commodity Agreements and Methods of Trade, Private Monopolies and Cartels, Food and Agricultural Products, Metals and Heavy Industries, Petroleum, Rubber; (3) Under Mr. Pasvolsky: International Coordination of Anti-Depression Policies.

At the three subsequent meetings of the Taylor Committee on May 7, June 4, and July 2, 1943, reports were received on the initial organization and work of the special committees; on the preparations for and accomplishments of the Food and Agriculture Conference held May 18–June 3 at Hot Springs, Virginia; on the status of the international monetary discussions at a technical level then in progress; and on the renewal of the Trade Agreements Act. The Committee recessed for the summer following the last of these meetings.

The Taylor Committee was inherently transitional. Although it had planned to reconvene after its summer recess, it did not do so, owing chiefly to the heavy schedule of its members in the autumn of 1943 and the necessary delay until the special committees had advanced their work further. To a lesser extent, the plans for the Committee were also affected, through its membership, by the abolition of the Board of Economic Warfare and the simultaneous establishment of the Board of Foreign Economic Warfare, which was superseded later in the autumn by the Foreign Economic Administration. The thought already being given to adjustment of the Advisory Committee structure as a whole and to permanent interdepartmental organization in the economic field was an additional factor contributing to the decision not to reconvene the Taylor Committee.

As matters developed, the twelve special committees that were established continued to function, and it was their activity that was relied upon to meet the need for transitional organization in the economic field during the period when the work of the Advisory Committee was being adapted to the new stage of action.

The organization and work of the special committees constitute a part of the record that falls primarily within the transition period in the structure of postwar policy preparation generally and is accordingly given attention in Part III. Five projected special committees were not established. The proposed Committee on Food and Agricultural Products, to have been under the chairmanship of Judge Marvin Jones of the War Food Administration, never functioned because of a change in the organization of the Government's work in this field that occurred shortly after this committee was projected. The Special Committees on Rubber and on Problems of International Coordination of Anti-Depression Policies, to have been under State Department chairmanship, and on Long-Term Investment, under the chairmanship of the Export-Import Bank, were not established for various operational reasons. The work of the projected Special Committee on Monetary and Banking Relations was taken over by the American Technical Committee on the Stabilization Fund and the Reconstruction and Development Bank, with the Treasury as its focal point.

The organization of the preparatory work in the monetary and banking field was atypical in that it did not develop as part of the Advisory Committee structure, but as a concurrent activity under Treasury leadership having informal ties with the Committee. Preparations in this field stemmed directly from a proposal developed in the Treasury early in 1942 but had their roots in the exploratory work done by both the State and Treasury Departments, 1940-41, and in the discussions, already noted, of the early Interdepartmental Group to Consider International Economic Problems and Policies. While the initiative in the organized preparations was the Treasury's, they had from the beginning been carried forward on an interdepartmental basis.

On May 25, 1942, an informal interdepartmental group, which came to be known as the "Cabinet Committee" and continued until the preparations for the Bretton Woods Conference had been completed, met in Secretary Morgenthau's office to consider, at the suggestion of the President, a Treasury memorandum of March 1942 proposing the establishment of a United Nations stabilization fund and bank for reconstruction and development, and dealing also with various economic problems in the field of commercial policy and commodity agreements.[27] Present at this meeting were Secretary Morgenthau and Daniel W. Bell, Edward A. Foley, Harry D. White, Bernard Bernstein, and Frank A. Southard, Jr., Treasury Department; Leo Pasvolsky and Herbert Feis, State Department; the Secretary of Commerce, Jesse H. Jones; Chairman Marriner S. Eccles and Emanuel A. Goldenweiser of the Board of Governors of the Federal Reserve

---

[27] This Treasury proposal was subsequently narrowed to more strictly financial problems.

System; and Louis Bean and V. Frank Coe, Board of Economic Warfare.

It being agreed that it was desirable for this Government to proceed with its plans for the creation of an international monetary fund and bank, it was decided at this meeting to establish an interdepartmental subcommittee, which would report to the "Cabinet Committee". This subcommittee, known as the American Technical Committee, held its first meeting on May 28, 1942, under the chairmanship of Harry D. White, who was primarily responsible for the Treasury's work in this field. It was this group that developed the United States proposal for an International Stabilization Fund released to the press on April 7, 1943. In May 1943 the subcommittee was established on a formal basis, pursuant to a memorandum from the President to the Secretary of the Treasury requesting Mr. Morgenthau to establish relationships with other relevant agencies to discuss the matters of a stabilization fund and a bank for reconstruction and development. It then became the American Technical Committee on the Stabilization Fund and the Reconstruction and Development Bank, reporting to the Secretary of the Treasury.

Although the interdepartmental structure for consideration of the bank and fund proposals centering in the Treasury Department had no formal relationship with the Advisory Committee structure for postwar preparations in the State Department, there was a significant interlocking of membership in these two groups. Mr. White, chairman of the American Technical Committee, was a member of the Economic Policy Subcommittee and, later, of the Taylor Committee. The State Department was represented on the "Cabinet Committee" at different times by Mr. Acheson, Mr. Berle, and Mr. Pasvolsky, all members of the Taylor Committee, and the latter was also a member of the Technical Committee. Mr. Feis of the Taylor Committee also sometimes attended the "Cabinet Committee" for the Department of State. Mr. Cohen was a member of the Advisory Committee and also of the American Technical Committee. The Department's representation on this latter committee was comprised of officers from both the research staff and the operating divisions, and extensive consideration was given in the Division of Special Research and the subsequent Division of Economic Studies to problems of concern to this committee.[28]

---

[28] Membership on the American Technical Committee varied from time to time, but the principal attendants, in addition to those mentioned above, were Treasury Department, Elting Arnold, Edward M. Bernstein, Henry J. Bittermann, Ansel F. Luxford, and Raymond F. Mikesell; State Department, William Adams Brown, Jr., E. G. Collado, Frederick Livesey and John Parke Young; Commerce Department, W. L. Clayton, Hal B. Lary, and August Maffry; Federal Reserve Board, Alice Bourneuf, Walter Gardner, E. A. Goldenweiser, and Alvin H.

The preparations relating to food and agriculture were also somewhat atypical, though not to the same degree or in exactly the same way. At the first joint meeting of the economic subcommittees on February 20, 1942, the Chairman, Mr. Acheson, had stressed the importance of nutrition problems, but no special consideration was given to these problems at the subsequent meetings. At the second joint meeting on July 17, specific reference was made to the "establishment of international machinery dealing with standards of nutrition and more rational development of food resources" as one of the basic longer-range problems. Again, however, no special consideration was given to this problem by the subcommittees except in connection with the discussions of East European and European economic organization, when the desirability of a regional approach to this problem was questioned.

On the day following a conference with Secretary Hull, Under Secretary Welles, and Messrs. Taylor, Bowman, and Pasvolsky, the President at a press conference on February 23, 1943, revealed that plans were being discussed for a United Nations conference that spring to explore long-range and fundamental postwar food problems. The initiative in this move was the President's. The desirability of such a conference had been raised in the Department only a few days before, on the grounds that there was some public feeling that international discussion of postwar problems was being too long delayed and that food was a relatively noncontroversial subject on which to proceed for the first full United Nations Conference at this still exploratory stage. The President was much interested in the nutrition problem and was aware of the ideas in this connection that had been developed unofficially through informal discussions in Washington principally among Americans, Australians, and Canadians. He favored at this time the establishment of entirely separate functional agencies in the economic field and chose food and agriculture as the subject offering the best chances for immediate success in the first attempt to test the willingness and ability of the United Nations to cooperate on postwar problems. He felt that this test should be made promptly.

The preparations for the projected conference were made outside the formal Advisory Committee structure, but there was, as in the case of the preparations in the investment and monetary field, extensive overlapping of officials and experts involved. Mr. Pasvolsky initiated the telegrams that the Secretary sent on March 8 to start the necessary preliminary discussions with the other three major powers, which led to the issuance before the end of the month to all United

---

Hansen; Securities and Exchange Commission, Walter C. Louchheim; Export-Import Bank, Hawthorne Arey and Warren Lee Pierson; Foreign Economic Administration, James W. Angell, and V. Frank Coe.

Nations, and nations associated with them, of an invitation to a conference on food and agricultural production. A decision was made at this time not to limit the conference to those governments that had actually signed the Declaration by United Nations but to include those American republics that had yet to sign the Declaration but were assisting in the prosecution of the war against the Axis, and also to include certain other states, namely Egypt, Iceland, Iran, and Liberia, that without having declared war were collaborating with United Nations. This decision was to constitute a precedent for the later UNRRA and Bretton Woods Conferences [29] and was to be followed generally, though with some variation, in all subsequent conferences.

Messrs. Emilio Collado (Associate Adviser on International Economic Affairs), Hawkins, and Stinebower were initially charged with responsibility for the preparatory work for the conference. Late in March, Mr. Acheson assumed the active direction of this work, with Mr. Stinebower and Mr. Tolley of the Department of Agriculture serving as his chief deputies. An *ad hoc* working group composed of representatives from the State and Agriculture Departments was set up to prepare a draft agenda for the conference in collaboration with Judge Jones, Under Secretary of Agriculture Appleby, Assistant Secretary of Commerce Clayton, and Dr. Thomas Parran (Surgeon General, United States Public Health Service). The four latter officials were members of the United States Delegation to the conference.[30] Mr. Stinebower served as Adviser and Executive Secretary to the American Delegation at the conference, and another member of the research staff, Benjamin Gerig, was a member of the conference secretariat. As noted above, Mr. Acheson reported to the Taylor Committee both on the preparations for and the results of the conference.

In Mr. Acheson's report to the Taylor Committee on May 7, 1943, he emphasized that no agreements or commitments would be entered into by the delegates to the conference and that their conclusions would take the form of recommendations to their respective governments. The conference was not to consider political questions and was to be primarily of a technical nature. It would have as its purpose to work toward broad objectives and to emphasize the new responsibility of governments to see that their peoples were well fed. This approach, rather than consideration of immediate and specific problems, it was hoped, would avoid the danger of concentration on restrictive commodity schemes.

---

[29] See pp. 203 ff. and 240 ff.

[30] Other members of the Delegation were Murray D. Lincoln, Executive Secretary of the Ohio Farm Bureau Federation, and Miss Josephine Schain. Judge Marvin Jones was Chairman.

In keeping with this general plan, the draft agenda developed by the *ad hoc* working group, which, with very slight modification after consultation with the other participating governments was released as the definitive agenda on April 27, was concerned with the following broad topics: consumption levels and requirements, expansion of production and its adaptation to consumption needs, facilitation and improvement of distribution, and arrangements for continuing and carrying forward the work of the conference. In connection with the last topic, Mr. Acheson explained on May 7 that the conference would consider the problem of establishing a permanent organization to carry out its recommendations and to bring together in one body the dispersed efforts in the agricultural field being made by such agencies as the International Institute of Agriculture at Rome, the League of Nations, and the ILO. He also explained that the question of distribution would be considered in relation to the broad economic problems of stabilization, investment, and trade barriers as well as from a more technical and specialized standpoint. Mr. Acheson's report to the Taylor Committee on the results of the conference was made on June 4. He termed it a success and described its discussions as being of a high level and the work of its technical secretariat outstanding. He noted, in summarizing the conference recommendations, that it was felt that after the war, agricultural policies of an expansionist, as contrasted with a restrictive, character would only be possible if international security were assured, since otherwise efforts to gain self-sufficiency would lead again to restrictions. He also noted that the conference, in addition to projecting a permanent organization in the food and agriculture field, had believed that there should be an international body authorized to initiate or review international commodity agreements.[31]

The conference provided for the establishment of an Interim Commission to continue the progress begun at Hot Springs, including the preparation of a basic plan for a permanent organization in this field. Primary responsibility for maintaining relations with the commission was vested in the Department of Agriculture, but the Department of State continued to be actively interested in various aspects of the work, particularly that relating to the plan for a permanent organization. An interdepartmental advisory group was established to carry forward American participation in this work. This group was composed of Mr. Appleby, who was the only American member of the commission, Mr. Clayton (who had assumed the chairmanship of one of the special committees of the Taylor Committee in June), Dr. Parran, and Mr. Acheson, with Mr. Stinebower acting as his alternate.

---

[31] For the text of the Final Act of the Conference, see *Department of State Bulletin*, VIII, 546–72.

THE SPECIAL SUBCOMMITTEE ON PROBLEMS OF EUROPEAN ORGANIZATION

DURING the first year of the Advisory Committee, a substantial number of ideas were developed by Europeans and projected variously by Americans for regional groupings of European states or at least regional arrangements for economic cooperation. The Greek-Yugoslav Agreement of January 15, 1942, and the Polish-Czechoslovak Committee of Coordination of June 10, 1942, were directed toward this end, as were various statements by responsible leaders of several other governments during 1942 and early 1943. In this period proposals also emerged for a political organization covering Europe as a whole, and as noted above, a regional basis for general international organization was advocated by Prime Minister Churchill in his radio address of March 21, 1943, and privately. These proposals were the subject of much study in and out of the Government, especially by the standing subcommittees. At the same time, the exchanges proceeding in the period February to April 1943 between the Soviet Union and Poland, marked by strong differences of view over Poland's eastern boundaries, raised additional questions affecting the whole matter of regional developments in Europe.

The decision to establish a Special Subcommittee on Problems of European Organization was reached gradually during April and May 1943. This subcommittee was to study the converging territorial and economic questions of regional organization, especially with regard to Europe, in order to clarify the alternative policy choices presented the United States with respect to regional developments in that area. Primary attention was given to economic organization, but the subcommittee from the outset pursued a program of discussion and research designed to explore every major aspect of European regional organizations and related problems.

Preliminary informal meetings between the Chairman, Hamilton Fish Armstrong, and officers of the economic and political research staffs began on May 24. The first task was to determine the feasibility of specific groupings and various types of European regional arrangements that had been, or might be, projected. In addition, it was necessary to analyze the possible economic and political functions of such regional arrangements and to weigh the effects on American interests that would flow from the development of such structures. This period, as will be recalled, was one of uncertainty regarding the further course of the war and the territorial conditions at its conclusion and regarding the course of postwar policy that the American people and the Congress would support. Within the Advisory Committee there was still a great degree of uncertainty on most controversial problems. This was reflected in one of the general contributions expected from this special subcommittee when it was created, namely that it would be able to further the work of the other subcommittees toward determining whether a regional approach might have sufficient merit to fall back upon in the event the plan for United States entrance into a universal international organization failed of fruition.

The new group was formed practically on an *ad hoc* basis. It had the status of a subcommittee of the Political Subcommittee in order to give it the central position necessary for study of problems that touched upon all aspects of the Advisory Committee's inquiries. Its first meeting was held on June 4, 1943. Its sixteenth and last meeting was held March 31, 1944.

The Subcommittee's membership of eleven was drawn largely from the membership of other subcommittees, thus providing an integrated body for the study of one set of questions faced in common by all. Its nine members who served on other subcommittees were Messrs. Armstrong, Atherton (represented after the first meeting by Cannon), Berle, Bowman, Cohen, Feis, Hawkins, Myron C. Taylor, and Pasvolsky *ex officio*. The remaining members, Percy W. Bidwell and Jacob Viner, were drawn from outside the subcommittee structure for reasons of special technical competence. The participation of the research staff in the work of this subcommittee was especially active since it was never possible for more than a small number of the subcommittee members to attend meetings. Ralph H. Bowen from the economic side of the staff was secretary. The continuing nucleus of participating staff members was headed by Messrs. Stinebower and Melvin M. Knight for the economic field and Messrs. Mosely and Harris for the field of political territorial problems, and included particularly Homer P. Balabanis, Shepard B. Clough, Vernon L. Phelps, and Alexander M. Rosenson in the former field and Cyril E. Black, John C. Campbell, Harry N. Howard, and Amry Vandenbosch in the latter.[32] Charles E. Bohlen, Assistant Chief of the Division of European Affairs, Carl F. Norden of the Foreign Service, and William C. Trimble of the Division of Exports and Requirements, also attended on occasion.

The subcommittee confined its considerations to Europe west of the Soviet Union. It began with an examination of over-all European organization, specifically the political and economic functions that could be performed by such a continental structure. While past ex-

---

[32] In addition, a considerable number of the staff took part in individual meetings, especially Miss Elizabeth Armstrong and Donald C. Blaisdell, Waldo Chamberlin, Eugene Chase, Norris B. Chipman, Clyde Eagleton, Richard Eldridge, William Fowler, Merrill C. Gay, Benjamin Gerig, Grayson Kirk, William Koren, Jr., Harley Notter, Durward V. Sandifer, Smith Simpson, Howard Trivers, Harold C. Vedeler, and Arthur P. Whitaker.

perience was drawn upon, reliance was mainly upon new analysis. Discussion was largely in terms of questions, such, for example, as "what aspects of European economic life could benefit from closer collaboration among European countries?"

In discussing the over-all type of European organization, various well-known suggestions of the past were studied, and German plans for the unification of Europe so far as ascertainable were examined. Among the possibilities considered, for illustration, was a full European customs union, which was examined to determine whether it would necessarily be either advantageous or detrimental to the long-run interests of the United States, depending on economic developments within its scope and the type of external commercial policy pursued by such a union. When considering the achievement of closer economic and political collaboration in Europe under a continental regional organization, an effort was made to ascertain from a security standpoint the potentialities of such collaboration toward peace or war depending upon the terms of organization, the type of policy pursued, and the degree of independence that such organization left the participating member states. Unification of technical services such as transport and communications among European countries so far as the countries directly affected deemed feasible was another possibility explored. Such questions as the possible domination by any one country of a regional structure, the relationship between the continental organization and the great powers after the war, and the dependence of Europe on external economic relations were given much attention. Subsequently, bilateral or other smaller regional groupings were taken up, including the possibilities, whether likely or unlikely, of Balkan federation, federation of the Low Countries, and other political and economic associations. The functioning of multinational states such as Yugoslavia and Czechoslovakia was examined in connection with the foreseeable problems involved in such neighborhood groupings. The subcommittee also appraised possible Soviet programs and attitudes with respect to Eastern Europe so far as they were then known or could be conjectured.

The subcommittee made no report at the time of its adjournment. Its thought had largely been introduced by its individual members and the staff into the other meetings they were attending and into the staff papers, which remained available for use as policy needs arose.

This subcommittee was the last subcommittee directly a part of the Advisory Committee structure. It operated almost wholly in the period of transition from this structure to the new Governmental and Departmental machinery by which final decisions were made and operations undertaken. The developments in this regard will be found in Part III.

CHAPTER VI

The Research Staff

THE WORK and structure of the Advisory Committee and its subcommittees were interwoven with the work and structure of
the research staff. All the Committee's discussion was intended to
rest, and in large measure did rest, upon policy studies of postwar
problems by a staff of specially qualified experts. The staff was
engaged solely in research and policy studies. The scope and character of the preparation developed by the Committee accordingly not
only extended the Committee's original structure in the ways described above but likewise affected the composition, organization, and
work of the research staff.

THE INITIAL RESEARCH ORGANIZATION, 1941–1942

THE DIVISION of Special Research continued to be the research staff
for the Advisory Committee during 1942.[1] Throughout the first round
of the policy-level discussions, therefore, the research staff functioned
within the framework originally projected for it, accommodating
itself to the Committee's requirements without major reorganization
for approximately a year.

As the research staff, the first responsibility of this Division was
to analyze and appraise developments and conditions arising out of
the war and requiring special study for the formulation of policy
and to prepare the studies found to be necessary for discussion of post-
war problems. This was in essence a duty to anticipate study needs
and to initiate policy suggestions to superiors regarding postwar
matters. It was this function that had dominated the work prior to
the establishment of the Advisory Committee and that was continuously the prime function thereafter.

The earliest studies of the Division were mainly confined to such
analyses of international developments and their long-range implications and to exploratory studies of the problems that might arise
immediately after the war and at longer range in bringing about

---

[1] See appendix 22.

149

conditions of political stability, sound international economic relations, and enduring peace. The purpose was to obtain as complete a picture as feasible of the conditions that would have to be faced at the time of postwar reconstruction and to state the questions and present the considerations that would have to be taken into account in making policy decisions and in formulating a program of international action. Each question was canvassed from the viewpoint of objectives, of alternative types of machinery or processes appropriate to the attainment of the objective desired, of alternative methods of creating such international machinery as would be needed, of past and current experience, and of the effects of any given policy decision upon related matters.

In anticipation of the convening of the Advisory Committee, a study, which stemmed from the earlier analysis of official views on the principles of the Atlantic Charter, was begun early in 1942 of all public and confidentially expressed official commitments and views concerning the postwar settlement as expressed by the Allied and neutral governments from the outbreak of the war in Europe. The purpose of the study was to show the aspects of postwar settlement thus affected so far as discernible in the reports accessible in Washington. The study of "official commitments" thus begun was maintained on a current basis at all times and was used henceforth in all other research, committee discussions, and international negotiations stemming from the Department's preparatory work. The intent of such study was not unlike that expressed by President Wilson in regard to The Inquiry when on September 2, 1917, he requested Colonel House to "prepare our case with a full knowledge of the position of all the litigants."

As an adjunct to the political memoranda series and the economic memoranda series, into which the research was divided for purposes of orderly presentation and filing, the necessary map construction was carried on simultaneously through the Office of the Geographer. Special maps adapted to policy discussions began to be available in the spring of 1942, although on a critically scant basis. Recruitment of added cartographic staff and the essential research for map construction required time and new arrangements, as in the case of the policy research itself. The pressing proposals of the policy research staff for maps and charts, needed in connection with the new types of postwar policy studies being developed, stimulated a cooperative interdepartmental program and also required various contractual relations with the American Geographic Society and some commercial cartographic companies. The result was that, after the summer of 1942, the map program, which had greatly matured under the direction and advice of the Territorial Subcommittee as noted above, was increasingly able to satisfy the needs of the Advisory Committee.

The fund of research studies made before February 1942 was swiftly exhausted after the Advisory Committee met, and new requirements immediately began to pile up. The necessary studies therefore had to be prepared on a basis of day and night work—a condition which unfortunately prevailed, though to a lessening degree, throughout the war, since qualified experts and assistants could never be recruited fast enough to meet the need.

These early preparations resulted in the determination of basic methods of study which, while they increased the exactions on the professional staff, at least enhanced the direct usability of the resulting papers. The question method was used in approaching every study. This evolved during the autumn of 1942 into a more matured method called "problem papers," which began with a statement of the precise practical issue to be faced so far as it could be defined and then proceeded to an analysis of all alternative solutions that might be considered in choosing a course of policy designed to settle the issue or at least to put it on the way toward settlement, with the foreseeable consequences of each of these possible choices carefully reasoned in every case.[2] Such studies embodied expert judgment of past policies, but they at first avoided explicit judgment on the best course to adopt. However, an indication of the preferred alternative could hardly be avoided and this rapidly became the practice.

The staff at all times sought to consider problems from the standpoint especially of the long-run national interest of the United States: "What does the United States want? What do other states want? How do we obtain what we want?" The question that staff members then posed to themselves was "what do we need to know?" in order to answer these questions. Such questions appeared to offer the most practicable method by which the staff could steer its course in the vast uncertainties that then prevailed regarding the war and the postwar period. At that time, the chief certainties were merely the anticipated fact of victory and the consequent fact that this country—emerging from the victory with tremendous power—would have profound new responsibilities in connection with practically all vital problems of world affairs and would have to state a policy or at least express an attitude on such problems.

The remaining principal responsibility of the Division was to constitute the secretariat of the Advisory Committee and its component subsidiary bodies. This function was exceptional in that the personnel performing the secretariat duties were the professional research officers themselves, by reason of the policy character of the meetings and the preparatory role of the staff. Thus the supplying of agenda and taking of minutes were performed directly by responsible heads

---

[2] For example of "problem paper," see appendix 17.

of the research staff, acting under the supervision of the Special Assistant to the Secretary.

The staff members were officers of the Department at the working level, and it was extraordinary in Departmental practice to that date for them to be present in meetings at a policy level. Attendance was at first restricted to the Assistant Chief of the political section for committees dealing with political matters and to the Assistant Chief of the economic section for committees in that field. Attendance by other economic officers was soon permitted in the latter committees, but it was several months before an additional officer to take minutes was allowed to be present at the meetings in the political field, since the discussions of the political committees involved matters with stringent secrecy requirements.

Attending research officers were called upon to make explanations in connection with any paper or subject coming before a committee and increasingly took part in the discussions, thus linking together the policy discussions and the research studies. Furthermore, the practice gradually developed of discussions before and after meetings between chairmen and the responsible research officers, on the initiative of either, for the purposes of conveying information, exchanging views, and deciding upon plans, research problems, and schedules of discussion. Anticipation of committee needs and the shaping of studies to the likely requirements of policy consideration consequently could better be undertaken by the staff, with full understanding of the developments in and regarding the committees, and with the informed support of the chairman concerned. Gradually also, special additional meetings of chairmen and members with the staff experts developed, especially in the territorial and economic fields.

When the meetings of the Advisory Committee began, the staff was composed of only ten officers, including the chief of the Division, Mr. Pasvolsky. This limited group was called upon to meet the almost unlimited demands of the various committee groups with respect to the vast range of problems that had to be studied, on most of which no papers were ready. Although consultative status on the basis of one day each week had been arranged for the five "research secretaries" employed by the Council on Foreign Relations, effective March 26, no full-time officers could be added to the staff for administrative reasons during the first four months, primarily because of finances. Secrecy had required from the outset the utilization of emergency funds, at first Departmental and then, at the start of 1942, Presidential. Allocation of these funds, however, necessitated approval of specific amounts for staff additions, which was subject to various delays. Meanwhile it was found that rising demand for personnel throughout the Department and the Foreign Service precluded transfer of other officers to this work. There were, futhermore, many unusual difficulties in providing facilities for adequate research of such a new and unaccustomed character, numerous and detailed adjustments being necessary to permit the existing staff to function for the Advisory Committee in the established organization of the Department. Adjustments relating to the receipt of secret telegrams, despatches, and intelligence reports needed for essential information, and even arrangements for quarters and safes, were not completed satisfactorily until much later.

In June 1942, however, the staff began to be expanded by men and women drawn, apart from a few Foreign Service officers, from college and university faculties and research foundations. The inroads of the Selective Service Law by that date made it necessary to protect the continuity of the work by inviting only those relatively certain not to be required in the armed services. This was an unavoidable handicap from which the work was never free. The recruitment of qualified personnel was also handicapped by the competitive attraction offered by the larger salaries and higher positions obtainable in the new wartime agencies engaged in current war operations, which drained heavily upon the limited supply of competent specialists in international fields.

The staff of political scientists, historians, international lawyers, and economists brought together in the Department was built with the fixed aim of obtaining, so far as compatible with the high qualifications set for all personnel, persons from every section of the country. This had the objective of providing automatically in the staff a working knowledge of the points of view in the major sections of the country on or affecting international issues.

Effort was also made to obtain a balance of experience and maturity in persons of sufficiently youthful age to make possible a fresh but well-grounded approach to problems, many of which were new to the United States and some of which were revolutionary in world affairs. It was believed that such a staff, furthermore, would be most adaptable to the conditions of research peculiar to official undertakings. An additional desire was to assure that, since the period of peacemaking might be more protracted than after previous wars and since the postwar position of the United States would require activities more extensive than those of the prewar years, a considerable number of these officers trained to "think through" the emerging problems of United States foreign policy would remain on duty after the period of preparation had passed. These new officers would all have made the transition from their individual work in academic life to the conditions of group research on policy problems, and often group writing, prevailing in the Department. The result of the expansion that occurred on these lines was a staff largely concentrated in the age range 30 to 40, with most of the ranking positions held by men in their early forties, although in notable instances older officers in their fifties and even seventies were among the most effective members.

The realization of the significance of the work outweighed for these men and women the lack of the advantages conferred only by regular rights and status in the Government, which most of them had not secured by the time the postwar period was reached. This realization was strengthened by the statement of Secretary Hull in his radio address of July 23, 1942, on "The War and Human Freedom":

> "The manifold tasks that lie ahead will not be accomplished overnight. There will be need of plans, developed with careful consideration and carried forward boldly and vigorously. The vision, the resolution, and the skill with which the conditions of peace will be established and developed after the war will be as much a measure of man's capacity for freedom and progress as the fervor and determination which men show in winning the victory."

The existence of the Advisory Committee as the authorized superior structure to formulate policy and the fact that the Director of the Committee in the person of Mr. Pasvolsky as Special Assistant to the Secretary of State was the head of the research provided assurance of a prerequisite condition for effective policy studies: their direct and sure use in policy determination. It became possible, accordingly, to have a staff of outstanding qualifications despite the handicaps mentioned above.

Twenty-nine officers and two consultants were added to the Division from outside the Department in the months of June, July, and August 1942, with further increases in the autumn. During the same period, six Departmental and two Foreign Service officers were assigned to the Division. These increases coincided with the establishment of the Subcommittees on International Organization and Legal Problems but were not confined to these fields. By the end of 1942, there were ten officers in the political branch, twenty-four in the territorial, sixteen in the economic, and five in the security and armaments branch of the Division.[3] These numbers approximately reflected the emphasis on types and amount of work at that time.

Under Mr. Pasvolsky as Chief, the organizational lines of the Division by the latter part of 1942 were as follows:

Mr. Notter, Assistant Chief, headed the political work. Serving with him in the political branch, Philip E. Mosely, who was designated an Assistant Chief November 16, 1942, supervised the territorial studies. These were divided into units, with Walter R. Sharp in

---

[3] Six officers, one consultant, and one Foreign Service officer transferred from the Division or left the Department in the year 1942.

charge of studies concerning Western European countries; David Harris, Central European countries; Harry N. Howard, Eastern European countries; and Philip W. Ireland, Near Eastern countries. A Far Eastern unit was still in the process of establishment. Durward V. Sandifer, designated Assistant Chief November 16, 1942, supervised the studies in the fields of international law and security and armaments, set up in units under Lawrence Preuss and Grayson L. Kirk, respectively.[4] Mr. Notter with the assistance of Benjamin Gerig directed the work on international organization and arrangements.

The economic branch, headed by Mr. Wadleigh as Assistant Chief, was not clearly separated into sections or units, its work still being divided between short-range and long-range policy problems and individual officers being assigned specific problems to study.

In addition, there were five units with a total professional personnel of 15 by the end of 1942, that served both the political and economic officers, although for the time being these units remained administratively within the political branch where they originated. The first was the Commitments Unit, under the supervision of Mrs. Virginia Fox Hartley, responsible for collecting and reporting on the public and secret official views and commitments of all governments members of the wartime "United Nations" and of the neutral countries. The Post-War Trends Unit, under the supervision of Joseph M. Jones, analyzed the ideas on postwar organization developing in unofficial circles, as disclosed by statements, articles, books, and letters, both of American and foreign origin. A closely related function was performed by the Public Relations Unit headed by S. Shepard Jones, which had responsibility for relations with private organizations interested in the problems of the future peace and for collecting and analyzing information on public attitudes and trends of opinion here and abroad on postwar problems. The specialized library, with Miss Alice Bartlett in charge, collected basic texts of documents for use at future international conferences and provided professional reference assistance in regard to published materials needed in the staff research. The final service unit was that of Documents and Records which, together with the library, was supervised by Waldo Chamberlin. It maintained a complete file of all research papers prepared in the Division and other relevant official and unofficial materials obtained from a variety of sources, including those that came regularly to the Department from the Foreign Service posts abroad.

---

[4] Messrs. Mosely, Kirk, Sharp, Diebold, and for a time also William P. Maddox, were research secretaries of the Council on Foreign Relations who were at first loaned by the Council to the Department part-time, the first four entering the staff full-time as funds became available.

With the approach late in 1942 of the end of the exploratory "first round" consideration of postwar problems by the subcommittees, to be followed at once by the "second round" for more matured consideration and recommendations by the Advisory Committee, a further expansion of the staff became advisable. Readjustment of the research organization was therefore timely. To a degree this was suggested by the distinct specialization of functions that had existed from the start in the political and economic fields and that had further developed in the differing conduct of work by the two sections. This corresponded with differences in the character of the subcommittees. In addition, widening responsibilities of members of the political and economic staffs in committee work created a need for full divisional status for these two branches, if only to relieve Mr. Pasvolsky of the burden of detailed supervision of the expanding research preparations.

At the same time, developments of other kinds pointed toward a reorganization of the staff work. The need had arisen for the Department's operating divisions to make immediate recommendations on such problems as the treatment of liberated areas, relief and rehabilitation, and relations of leaders and groups in the areas into which American troops were moving. This was precipitated by the invasion of North Africa, and it was obvious that such problems would recur and multiply as the Allied forces advanced. The line between current and postwar policy was thus already beginning to merge where areas liberated from enemy control were concerned. Responsibility for policy work in the field of relief and rehabilitation, which heretofore had been vested in several parts of the Department, including the Division of Special Research and the Advisory Committee, was centralized with the appointment, on December 4, 1942, of Herbert H. Lehman, former Governor of New York, as Director of the recently created Office of Foreign Relief and Rehabilitation Operations in the Department. Responsibility for other occupation policy was vested in the Division of European Affairs late in November. These shifts involved change in the focal point of preparation in these fields and later the transfer of a few members of the research staff.

Furthermore, a departmental Committee on Political Planning composed of operating officials [5] was established on November 2, 1942, charged with the development of plans for consideration by the

---

[5] The four Political Advisers of the Department (Messrs. Dunn, Chairman, Hornbeck, Murray, and Duggan), the Economic Adviser, Mr. Feis, and representatives of the Divisions of Foreign Activity Correlation, Current Information, and World Trade Intelligence, with Selden Chapin of the Foreign Service as Executive Secretary. When reorganized Mar. 20, 1943, the members designated were the four Political Advisers, Assistant Secretary Long, Mr. Feis, the Legal Adviser, Mr. Hackworth, and Mr. Pasvolsky. Mr. Chapin continued to be the Executive Secretary.

Secretary and the Under Secretary in the field of the Department's political functions. While this Committee's work was of a current character, the inevitable conversion eventually of all postwar into current problems raised momentarily the question of the absorption at this early date of the territorial and economic research staffs into the operating divisions of the Department. This course was rejected as premature, but it suggested the need for closer relationship between the research and the operational structures of the Department and, hence, of several adjustments affecting both.

THE DIVISIONS OF POLITICAL STUDIES AND ECONOMIC STUDIES, 1943

REORGANIZATION was effected on January 1, 1943. The political staff was organized as the Division of Political Studies with Harley Notter as Chief, and with Durward Sandifer, Philip Mosely, and S. Shepard Jones as Assistant Chiefs. The economic staff was similarly organized as the Division of Economic Studies with Leroy Stinebower, formerly Assistant Adviser on International Economic Affairs, as Chief, and with H. Julian Wadleigh remaining for a time as Assistant Chief.[6] These Divisions continued under Mr. Pasvolsky's general supervision and were given an expansion of functions in their respective fields regarded as extraordinary in Departmental practice:

". . . responsibility for the conduct of continuing and special research, for the preparation of studies required in the formulation of policies, the planning of integrated programs as a basis for action in the field of foreign political [and economic] relations affecting the interests of the United States, with particular reference to the long-range implications of current policies, actions and developments . . . affecting post-war political [and economic] reconstruction, and for the formulation of appropriate recommendations with respect to the foregoing."[7]

Cooperation and liaison were required between these companion divisions. Each was directed, furthermore, to cooperate fully and to have effective liaison with all other parts of the Department of State and with other Departments and agencies of the Government having joint interest or authority in the field of activity concerned. Other divisions of the Department were likewise directed to cooperate with the new divisions and, in particular, to keep them fully informed of current decisions, activities, and developments, and to invite them to participate in formulating decisions having long-run implications.

---

[6] Mr. Wadleigh resigned Aug. 11, 1943.

[7] The duties of these divisions were stated largely in identic terms. The words in brackets have been inserted above to show the duties of both in Departmental Order 1124. For full list of personnel of the Research Staff in 1943, see appendix 22.

For the purpose of coordination within this broad definition of work and relationships, the reorganizing Order established a Committee on Special Studies under Mr. Pasvolsky's chairmanship, with Mr. Notter and Mr. Stinebower named to membership. While there was provision for other officers to be designated as members by the Secretary of State, no further members were added. This committee constituted the directing group for the research staff, and each of its three members in their *ex officio* capacity attended the meetings of the subcommittees of the Advisory Committee. If all were not present at every meeting, at least one or two were.

The Committee on Special Studies was particularly concerned with the identification of the problems requiring consideration, the determination of the most urgent studies and special papers needed for top-level use, the development of handbooks and policy summaries, and various aspects of the relationship between the staff work and that of other parts of the Department and of the Government as a whole. It also considered the organizational changes almost constantly required by the progressive stages reached in the work of the Advisory Committee's subcommittees and by the growth, so far as this affected the preparatory work, of the Department's functions and personnel, which began in this period to be rapid. Coordination with current policy and operations was provided through the reorganization of the Political Planning Committee on March 20, 1943, which added to its membership the Chairman of the Committee on Special Studies, Mr. Pasvolsky, and two other higher officers active on the Advisory Committee, Mr. Hackworth and Mr. Long. At the same time Mr. Dunn and Mr. Hornbeck, as the senior Political Advisers, became increasingly active in the work of the subcommittees considering postwar political problems.

The structure for the staff work sketched above was maintained throughout 1943, although expansion of staff, best described in connection with the developments recounted in the next Part, occurred within this framework. Here it may be noted that the Division of Economic Studies was rapidly and more effectively organized by the grouping of problems under three assistant chiefs: general economic under Bernard F. Haley, financial under Paul T. Ellsworth, and territorial economic under Melvin M. Knight. The expansion of the Division of Political Studies was greater, corresponding to the proportionate multiplicity and newness of the problems anticipated in its fields of responsibility. C. Easton Rothwell was made Assistant Chief in charge of administration and also, by cooperative arrangement, of the joint services for the staff of both Divisions. To these services was added in the summer a Unit of Biographical Analysis, under Miss Edna R. Fluegel, to study the background of current and emerging leadership in all enemy-occupied countries in Europe. This unit absorbed certain of the work previously undertaken by the Post-War Trends Unit, which had been dissolved and whose remaining functions were being performed by the Public Relations Unit.[8] Study of Central European territorial problems was intensified, and placed under David Harris as Assistant Chief.

This organization spanned roughly the period after the Allied invasion of North Africa and the holding of the Moscow, Cairo, and Tehran conferences, or, in other terms, the final period of work by the original Advisory Committee subcommittee organization and the beginning of the period when definite recommendations began to be formulated. It was during this period that Mr. Welles resigned and Edward R. Stettinius, Jr., became Under Secretary.

The new research structure so instituted in January 1943 increased the number of ranking officers at the divisional level, which at that time was the highest level in the Department below the rank of Political and Economic Adviser, Special Assistant to the Secretary, and Assistant Secretary, and thus inaugurated wider staff participation in policy consideration. It was designed, furthermore, to assure the utilization of all the resources of the Department and the integration of current policy and developing postwar policy so that each would be formulated with due regard for the other. It also reflected a general view that the staff should be made ready, by appropriate organization, for the performance of advisory and secretariat functions at international conferences, the approach of which was now beginning to be discernible. The first such conference to engage the staff directly on the scene was the United Nations Conference on Food and Agriculture. At this Conference, as noted above, members of both new Divisions, particularly the Chief of the Division of Economic Studies commenced the active participation in negotiations that in some fields of work were, as will be seen, integral to the preparation.

This reorganization was, however, only one of the steps in adjustment to new needs and the emerging world situation affecting the nature of postwar policy. The structure for staff work, like that for all other phases of the preparation, was adjusted constantly, more often through the way it functioned than through change by formal order .

---

[8] The public relations work was transferred in the autumn of 1943 elsewhere in the Department.

CHAPTER VII

Suspension of the Advisory Committee

THE DECISIONS of December 1941 to establish the President's Advisory Committee assumed eventual victory. Darker days of catastrophe and dire risk followed—days when the wartime alliance of the United Nations was hard-tested and strained by the conflicting demands on every hand of national versus over-all strategy and aims. The Advisory Committee's main work was carried on in the darkest period of the war.

It had begun when the retreat of United Nations forces both in the East and in the West was the almost daily theme of news. Then came the months of holding, of contesting the enemy's advance, and the beginning of the offensive against the enemy's outposts. The Battle of the Coral Sea, May 4–8, 1942, checked the Japanese advance southward in the Pacific theater, but not until June of 1942 was the threat of an invasion of Australia removed. In Africa, the German thrust reached El Alamein on July 1, 1942, placing the Near East in jeopardy. While the British defense there held and, in combination with the American and British landings, was turned to offense in North Africa on November 7, 1942, to push Axis forces out of Africa, it was not until July 10, 1943, that it became possible to invade Sicily. The tide did not begin to turn on the Eastern Front until, following the fall of Sevastopol and Rostov in July 1942, the capture of Stalingrad was prevented in the autumn, and the Soviet forces mounted an offensive in the Caucasus in December, forced a favorable turn in the area of Leningrad in January 1943, and exacted the surrender of the Nazi armies at Stalingrad on January 31–February 2 of that year. A Soviet general offensive then started, and a seesaw struggle ensued from which the Soviets emerged with sufficient strength to counter with a new offensive on July 12, 1943. By the end of that month, when the Advisory Committee ended its "second round" the tide of battle had turned in Eastern Europe; the Japanese thrust was being contained; North Africa was liberated; Sicily was invaded; and Mussolini had been deposed.

Since, however, the power of the Allies to inflict quick defeat was lacking, the enemy might hope to salvage victory by protracting the war and attempting through friction or inducements to break up the United Nations coalition. On the other hand, rapid collapse of some one or other of the enemy was another possibility that could affect the stability of the United Nations coalition. And the risk was always present that under certain circumstances the national aims of any of the United Nations might adversely affect the general war effort jeopardizing, through alliances, territorial or other claims or *faits accomplis*, cooperative postwar relations as well as victory itself.

While such potentialities were considerations to be weighed, there were actual strains that augmented the difficulties anticipated in establishing a sound peace and which therefore confronted the postwar preparation as outlined above. While the United States and Great Britain were at war with Germany and Italy and with Japan, the Soviet Union was not at war with the latter. This factor in itself made necessary a closer coordination of effort between Great Britain and the United States, reflected, for example, in the establishment of the Combined British-American Boards on Raw Materials, Munitions Assignments and Shipping Adjustment, January 26, 1942; of the Combined Chiefs of Staff, February 6, 1942; and of the Pacific Council, March 30, 1942. It also meant that the United States and Great Britain, but not the Soviet Union, were waging war on a second gigantically difficult front—the Pacific—which Soviet leaders appeared to discount. Geographical location and other imperative military factors dictated that the major German land assault would be borne by the Soviet Union at this stage of the war, and that when the initiative on land was taken in Western Europe, it would be a combined Anglo-American action. A third factor was the uneven course of the war: the tide of battle turned in Africa and the Pacific, while the German offensive on the Eastern Front was still sustained.

These and related conditions, including the doubts and mutual distrust continuing from the prewar years and the developments of 1939–1941 preceding the German attack on the Soviet Union, were prominent among the causes of the "second front" controversy, which had important repercussions on wartime international relations, including those affecting the postwar period.

The measures taken initially to offset the friction engendered by this dispute were in substantial measure economic and diplomatic. Immediately following the signature of the Anglo-Soviet treaty, the problem of Soviet-American relations was discussed May 29–June 4, 1942, by President Roosevelt and Foreign Commissar Molotov. The announcement issued at the conclusion of the conversation specified:

"full understanding was reached with regard to the urgent tasks of creating a second front in Europe in 1942. In addition, the measures for increasing and speeding up the supplies of planes, tanks, and other kinds of war materials from the United States to the Soviet Union were discussed. Also discussed were the fundamental problems of cooperation of the Soviet Union and the United States in safeguarding peace and security to the freedom-loving peoples after the war."[1]

On June 12, the signature the previous day of the lend-lease agreement with the Soviet Union was announced. Shortly thereafter (June 19–26, 1942) Prime Minister Churchill and the President conferred in Washington on "all the major problems of the war," and in July General Marshall, Admiral King, and Mr. Hopkins as personal representatives of the President, went to London for further military discussions. In August, Prime Minister Churchill conferred in Moscow with Premier Stalin. W. Averell Harriman represented the President in these discussions, at which a "number of decisions were reached covering the field of the war against Hitlerite Germany and her associates in Europe."[2] As the German attacks heightened, however, and as the United States and Great Britain concerted moves for the landings in North Africa, the plight of the Soviet Union became more and more serious, and Soviet demands for a second front became more exigent.

On October 4, 1942, Premier Stalin stated that the second front occupied a place of "first-rate importance" in Soviet estimates of the current situation, that Allied aid to Russia had been "little effective" in comparison with the Soviet contribution to the Allies in occupying the German forces, and that "to amplify and improve this aid, only one thing is required: that the Allies fulfill their obligations fully and on time."[3] Three days later a protocol regarding the delivery by the United States and Britain to the Soviet Union of military equipment, munitions, and raw materials was signed in Washington. A month later, November 7, 1942, President Roosevelt, in announcing the landings in North Africa, stated: "In addition, it provides an effective second-front assistance to our heroic allies in Russia."[4]

On January 14–26, 1943, the first of the formal wartime conferences was held at Casablanca, between President Roosevelt and Prime Minister Churchill and their combined staffs. Although Premier Stalin stated that he was unable to attend by reason of the Soviet offensive he was directing, he was kept informed of the military plans evolved by the British and American leaders for "the offensive campaigns

---

[1] *Department of State Bulletin*, VI, 531.

[2] For full text of the joint Anglo-Soviet Communiqué, issued Aug. 17, 1942, see World Peace Foundation, *Documents on American Foreign Relations*, V, 249–50.

[3] *Ibid.*, pp. 250–51.

[4] *Department of State Bulletin*, VII, 891.

of 1943." [5]   A policy of "unconditional surrender" was enunciated at Casablanca, which President Roosevelt said upon his return was an "uncompromising policy" that meant "no harm to the common people of the Axis nations" but did mean "punishment and retribution" for their leaders.[6]   The invasion of North Africa, the plans for 1943, and the policy of "unconditional surrender" were not, however, regarded by the Soviet Union as a satisfactory substitute for a second front in Europe.   Only after complaint in March by the American Ambassador in Moscow, Admiral W. H. Standley, that information on American assistance was being withheld from the Russian people, were several statements recognizing American aid issued by the Soviet Government or its officials.

Stresses of other kinds were also in evidence.   The acrimonious exchanges between the Soviet Union and the Polish Government situated in London beginning in January 1943 over the treatment of "Polish" citizens and conflicting territorial claims led to suspension of relations between the parties on April 25 of that year.   The dissolution of the Comintern was announced in Moscow on May 22, an action which from the standpoint of the preparation did not remove existing and potential difficulties or basic uncertainties but which was officially welcomed for its promotion of "a greater degree of trust" and its contribution to cooperation "for the winning of the war and for successful postwar undertakings." [7]

Taken as a whole, these conditions were indicative in a broad political sense of the costly risks that would be entailed by any lack of preparation and any unnecessary delay in making policy decisions to meet the problems that victory would precipitate upon the victors. By early summer 1943, this realization, felt throughout the Advisory Committee and the various parts of the Department most affected, became a spur toward proceeding as rapidly as practicable into negotiations to convert the wartime United Nations coalition into an international organization for cooperation to preserve peace after the war. The "postwar" had already arrived in North Africa and outlying parts of Italy, and its widening area northward was plainly imminent.

Salient prior questions concerning the intentions of the Great Powers and the prospects of future cooperation among them, however, had as yet been neither asked nor answered.   A major conference among these powers was accordingly believed to be imperative.   This necessity forecast a new stage in the preparation of postwar policy, and

---

[5] *Ibid.*, VIII, 93–94. The President and Prime Minister were also in communication with Generalissimo Chiang Kai-shek, who did not attend the Conference.

[6] *Ibid.*, p. 146.

[7] Statement of the Secretary of State, *ibid.*, p. 473.

the meetings of the subcommittees, with the exceptions already noted, were suspended while the procedure best adapted to the new situation was clarified, the views and possibilities already developed were examined, and the main lines of conference negotiation determined in the light of rapidly unfolding developments. Furthermore, the need for exploratory thinking had largely been satisfied and the next need was for specific recommendation. For these reasons, it was desirable to take bearings on the progress of work done and to determine the points on which to concentrate effort ahead.

Secretary Hull's letter to members suspending meetings of the Advisory Committee and its subcommittees stated:

"Work has reached a point at which it is imperative that the results of our discussions to date be brought together in the form of documents which can serve as a basis of a more specific consideration of policies and proposals. I am therefore adjourning the meetings of the Committee until September 18 in order to enable the technical staff to carry out the work of intensive preparation for a more definitive round of discussion."

The period of advanced preparation of United States postwar foreign policy was to open, in terms of the kind of work undertaken, with the date, July 9, 1943, on which this letter was drafted at the Secretary's instruction. The letter was signed and sent July 12, 1943.

Part III

ADVANCED PREPARATION
MIDSUMMER 1943–AUTUMN 1944

"As I read our history and the temper of our people today, our nation intends to do its part, jointly with the other peace-seeking nations, in helping the war-torn world to heal its wounds. I am sure also that our nation and each of the nations associated today in the greatest cooperative enterprise in history—the winning of this war—intends to do its part, after the victory of the United Nations, in meeting the immense needs of the post-war period. Those needs will embrace the task of taking practical steps to create conditions in which there will be security for every nation; in which each nation will have enhanced opportunities to develop and progress in ways of its own choosing; in which there will be, for each nation, improved facilities to attain, by its own effort and in cooperation with others, an increasing measure of political stability and of economic, social, and cultural welfare."

——"Our Foreign Policy in the Framework of Our National Interests," radio address by Cordell Hull, Secretary of State, September 12, 1943, *Department of State Bulletin*, IX, 176.

CHAPTER VIII

Adaptation of the Structure
for Preparation

ADVANCED preparation of United States postwar foreign policy characterized the period of about a year and a third from the suspension of the Advisory Committee and its subcommittees on July 12, 1943, through the autumn of 1944. As this period began, the invasion of Sicily by the Allies was in progress, an event leading to the signing of the Italian armistice September 3, 1943, effective on the 8th. By August 28, organized resistance of Japanese forces had been broken on New Georgia—at the far point of their thrusts in the Pacific. As the period ended, the combat lines on the Eastern and Western Fronts were drawing in on Germany and the victorious close of hostilities in Europe was coming within grasp. In the Pacific, the war was coming close to the home islands of Japan.

The intense preparatory work in the months between these events—from organized exploration by the Advisory Committee and its subcommittees to the close, in November 1944, of separately organized postwar policy consideration in the Department of State at a superior level—is described in this Part. The extraordinary preparation did not, however, entirely conclude with this work; the "unfinished business" is discussed in Part IV.

Few of the many lines of the extraordinary preparation can be said to have ended at any exact date. Rather, they merged one by one into operations, and the precise moment of passing from the one definitely into the other was often indeterminable. It is the occurrence of such absorption into operations, rarely on a given date or by a specific directive, that best marked the fact of termination. This absorption took place to a degree in all fields before D–day, June 6, 1944, to a slight extent in some, to a greater extent in others, and occurred more rapidly thereafter as hostilities drew toward their close. The distinctive character of the preparation that made it "extraordinary" had for the most part disappeared by December 1944. The preparation as a whole was thus concluded in step with the progress of the war. Its special structures had been determined in considerable measure by administrative decisions reflecting the military developments and by international negotiations which were related to these developments as well as to the preparation directly. Insofar as these structures were not absorbed into continuing operations, they were terminated in response to events as well as by the progress of the preparation itself.

The extraordinary preparation ended before the surrender of the principal enemy powers. Its methods and results were thereafter incorporated into the processes by which policy is always formulated in the normal and unending operations conducted within the Department and other parts of the Government, namely on the basis of specific immediate and emerging problems requiring initiation of action by this Government or determination of official views concerning courses instituted by other governments. Then, the policy that had been "postwar" became "current;" it was in the care of operating officials at home and in missions abroad, many of whom had not taken part in the preparation for the postwar period made during the war years, and was conducted under new superior authorities. Then, also, it was conducted in the light of actual postwar international and national conditions rather than of anticipated circumstances.

The framework of organization through which the advanced—and in some respects final—preparation of postwar policy was carried out during approximately the fifteen months after the subcommittees of the Advisory Committee were suspended is described below. Certain of the broadest policy decisions that were made during this period are also described; they marked significant stages of progress reached from time to time, and each added to the firm basis for subsequent work during the next stage.

This organizational framework was developed pragmatically. Throughout the period of its development there was expectation that the Advisory Committee would resume work. The letter of suspension stated that meetings were adjourned until September 18. Two of the subcommittees in fact did continue to meet for some months.[1] The advent of the Quebec Conference, the decision to proceed with the Moscow and other conferences, and the resultant immediate needs of preparation, together with the persistence of uncertainty regarding the precise character the Advisory Committee should have when it resumed, led, except in the case of two of the subcommittees, however, to prolongation of the suspension. New instrumentalities for the necessary work meanwhile grew up.

One of the new organizational structures emerged while the Advisory Committee was still active. This structure is described below.

---

[1] See pp. 118 and 147.

In other instances they were an outcome of the rapid and uneven maturing of problems and movement of war operations. The chart of these structures was neither symmetrical nor constant. The lines of developing views and events had themselves become especially fluid by the summer of 1943, and the organizational devices employed were, as a practical matter, adapted to the needs of the preparation as they arose. Parts of the organization were flexible, other parts fixed. Certain important aspects of its functioning were formal, others intentionally kept informal.

The relevant developments took form by periods, the initial one starting with the suspension of the Advisory Committee subcommittees on July 12, 1943, and continuing to the end of the year. Beginning with the new year, the organization of the work was affected by the Departmental reorganization of January 1944 and the nature of the work was affected by the results of the great conferences held during the preceding autumn.

THE INFORMAL AGENDA GROUP

THE NEED of a senior group to plan, select, and guide the agenda of discussion, problem by problem, toward a final inclusive pattern of recommended policy had been anticipated at the inauguration of the Advisory Committee in 1942. While the projected subcommittee on coordination had not been established, the expanding and more advanced work that autumn had caused its Director and its Executive Secretary to discuss as early as September 1942 whether the projected subcommittee would continue to be unnecessary.

The proximate beginning of an agenda group coincided with the start of the "second round" on January 4, 1943, when Secretary Hull first assumed the chairmanship of the Subcommittee on Political Problems. He at that time discussed with Sumner Welles, Isaiah Bowman, Norman H. Davis, Myron C. Taylor, and Leo Pasvolsky the plans for future work. He asked them to meet with him privately prior to the usual meeting of the subcommittee on the following Friday morning, the 8th, to discuss the problem of Italy scheduled for consideration and to advise him on the main issues that the subcommittee should be asked to take up and on any points members might be expected to raise. He requested the same group to talk with him on several other occasions during the next two months, while Mr. Welles was acting chairman of the subcommittee.

It was in this interval, moreover, that this group, except for Mr. Davis, first accompanied the Secretary to the White House, on February 22 and March 18, 1943, to report on the status of the preparations and to discuss various questions, including the forthcoming

Food and Agriculture Conference. These White House consultations, however, were temporarily discontinued after March as likely to encourage premature speculations on postwar policy, which had been aroused by the talk on March 18, and the consultations were not resumed until the summer.

Starting in March, the group met with the Secretary weekly, and its individual members were also frequently asked in for further conversations. These pre-meeting talks with the Secretary appreciably influenced the nature of the Political Subcommittee's work and progressively sharpened the basic issues in its discussions, but the activities of the group did not fully satisfy the need for coordinating and steering the work of all subcommittees in the political field and were not suited to meet the increasing need for fuller integration of the work of the Advisory Committee with that of the Department. These lacks were considered informally on May 20, 1943, by Messrs. Pasvolsky, Bowman, Dunn, and Notter, when it was decided to project an agenda for several meetings and to invite additional members to meet each Thursday for similar discussions.

These pragmatic beginnings marked the inauguration of the Informal Agenda Group. The group was never large and worked without announcement or official status of any kind. It was never formally established, and throughout its intensive activities commencing May 20, 1943, and covering more than a year, it functioned solely on the basis of Secretary Hull's confidence and his desire for its assistance.

It was named the Informal Political Agenda Group on December 9, 1943, when the first phase of its work as a steering, advising, and drafting group ended and the second phase, preparing concrete proposals for a general international organization, began. This name for it continued to be used until, on June 14, 1944, it was designated the International Organization Group. The group functioned under this title only until July 10, 1944. It was absorbed at that time into the structure of the American Group, which it had proposed for the conduct of the international negotiations known as the Dumbarton Oaks Conversations and any further negotiations leading to a general international organization. Thus the Agenda Group was, in fact, never disbanded, but ended by becoming the corps of advisers at international conferences leading to the establishment of the United Nations.

The Group had no specified chairman. Its meetings were held in Mr. Pasvolsky's office, and he acted as chairman except on the few occasions when Mr. Davis could be present at meetings considering international security problems and was asked to preside over the discussion of such problems.

Its membership during the first phase of work included four of the five seniors already mentioned, namely, Messrs. Bowman, Davis, Taylor, and Pasvolsky.   Mr. Welles attended the regular consultations in the Secretary's office but none of the drafting meetings. Following his resignation and the appointment of Edward R. Stettinius, Jr., as Under Secretary in September, the latter similarly took part in the Secretary's consultations and on occasion came to the drafting meetings for a few minutes at a time.   Mr. Davis attended irregularly.   Mr. Cohen of the White House staff, Mr. Dunn and Mr. Hornbeck, the ranking Political Advisers of the Department, and Mr. Hackworth, the Legal Adviser, were the remaining members.   Mr. Notter participated throughout as Chief of the Division of Political Studies and its successor Division of International Security and Organization, which constituted the staff of experts in this field.

The members were all active in various parts of the Advisory Committee, as already described.   While the Group functioned originally as an adjunct of the Political Subcommittee, it almost immediately became in effect a general coordinating agency for the Advisory Committee, pulling together the exploratory thinking developed in the subcommittees and focusing the views reached in draft recommendations to be considered for adoption.   The Group, from its first meeting, considered the issues of international security and organization to be of paramount concern in postwar policy and at its meetings in May 1943 began to weigh the merits of a major-power declaration of intentions on this subject.

After the general suspension of the subcommittees and until December 9, 1943, the Group gave most of its attention to the studies that the research staff should have ready for the subcommittees when they reconvened, as was expected, and to the improvements in the structure of the Advisory Committee that should be instituted at the time of reconvening in order to facilitate rapid arrival at formal recommendations.   On July 9, when apprised of the analyses of the functions, powers, machinery, and procedure of permanent international organization being completed in the Division of Political Studies, and of related research plans concerning the type of international organization to be favored from the standpoint of the United States, the Group decided to have such papers submitted to it for review, refinement, and judgment before their transmission to the Special Subcommittee on International Organization when it resumed.

The Group held eight meetings to and including July 9, followed by four meetings prior to December 9, 1943.   Throughout these months, however, members met specially and frequently for intensive drafting in connection with the Quebec and Moscow Conferences and other negotiations of this period and with major policy addresses by the Secretary.   These gatherings were not recorded as meetings since most of the drafting was essentially *ad hoc* for, and with, Secretary Hull.   In completing urgent papers all members met collectively on various occasions with the Secretary, and the Secretary continued to confer with the members individually as well.

The original "senior members" of the Group, with the not infrequent addition of Mr. Dunn and Mr. Hackworth, comprised the "consulting group" that began again in the summer of 1943 to accompany Secretary Hull to the White House. The President himself referred to the Secretary and this group as "my postwar advisers" or "my postwar group." It was not always possible for all the members of the "consulting group" to attend the White House discussions, but the number present was normally four or five. The remaining members of the Informal Agenda Group were always informed of such of these discussions as were pertinent to the work as a whole.

The "consulting group" talks with the President were resumed after the Secretary alone had seen the President twice in the month following July 9 to discuss the problems then before the Agenda Group in connection with the Quebec Conference and Mr. Churchill's visit with the President before that Conference. Messrs. Welles, Bowman, Davis, and Pasvolsky joined the Secretary on August 10 for extended discussion with the President of several problems, including colonial policy, general international organization, and the type of agreement to be sought among the major powers. On the latter, the consensus was that such an agreement should take the form of a declaration. Another extensive discussion at the White House was held before the Moscow Conference, on October 5. The Secretary was accompanied by Messrs. Stettinius, Dunn, Hackworth, and Pasvolsky. In this consultation the same problems and also broad questions relating to Germany and several other individual countries were covered.

When the Informal Agenda Group convened on December 9, 1943, in its first meeting after the negotiation of the Moscow Declaration, it decided to prepare within two weeks basic proposals on a general international organization for recommendation to the Secretary. This decision was made in the light of already clear pressures for a general position on the matter and in anticipation of the wishes of the President, who, on December 21, requested an early recommendation. With this undertaking, the Group entered the second and principal phase of its work, and became the Informal Political Agenda Group. Various experts, never many, from the postwar staff and elsewhere in the Department now began for the first time to attend the meetings of the Group. Thereafter the Group, usually but not always, included specialists in the international organization field.

Before discussing in detail the Group's conduct of this second phase of its work, however, three other developments of related interest in the second half of 1943 will be described. These were the summarization of the views of the Advisory Committee and its subcommittees, adjustments at the expert level for departmental work on the problems of countries, and adjustments for coordination of interdepartmental work on economic problems. All represented efforts to prepare more rapidly for international negotiations. All represented also the onset of heightened specialization in the postwar preparation as it drew closer to negotiations and to the operational activities that would result from them. The period of the last six months of 1943 consequently was a mixture of old and emerging new organization.

POLICY SUMMARIES

WHILE THE two Divisions composing the research staff continued unchanged by the suspension of the subcommittees, the expected resumption of their meetings and the impending negotiations in several fields of postwar problems produced two lines of work.

The first of these lines affected all the staff and involved the preparation of analytical summaries bringing together the results of the deliberations during the past 16 months, in a type of document designed to obtain more specific or formal recommendations. These were called "policy summaries." The staff had begun to make such summaries late in February 1943 in the territorial field. It turned to them intensively after July 9 and, under the guidance of the Committee on Special Studies, developed them in all political fields and then in the economic fields. The general objective was to have a "handbook" for each field, arranged to present in a single series the policy summaries on the problems in that field. Thus, one series presented the security problems, another the territorial, others the economic and social, legal, regional, dependent area, and international organization problems. Each problem was the subject of a separate policy summary, or "H document," which incorporated views upon the problem and its possible alternative solutions as developed by committee discussions and research studies to date.[2] The writing of the policy summaries proved to be the last stage of research before the actual drafting of final recommendations and of accompanying papers for presentation and use in negotiations. In fields where such a final stage had not been entered by the end of the preparation, these summaries represented the ultimate stage reached in policy study prior to absorption into operations.

The policy summaries on the economic problems of countries were organized to present separately the short-run and long-run aspects of problems on which the United States would probably be required to adopt a policy position or at least an attitude or point of view. In the case of Italy, for example, the following were involved: economic aspects of colonial problems, commercial policy, money and prices,

---

[2] For illustrative document, see appendix 18.

reparations, investment, migration and related problems, communications, aviation, shipping, inland transport, power, cartels, raw materials, labor, international organization, and agriculture. On each of these, the views of the Advisory Committee or its subcommittees were given briefly, or if the committee discussion had not yet resulted in the formulation of views, proposals developed by the research staff were stated and the principal documents available to date cited. Finally, suggestions for further study and points of discussion were noted, and the studies in progress or planned were reported. While normally short, especially where territorial economic problems were concerned, the summaries on functional economic problems, such as reparations, were as long as four or five pages and in rare cases, such as trade and commercial policy, eleven pages.

Throughout the political fields, covering the strictly governmental, territorial, security, legal, and international organization problems, all policy summaries sharply defined the problem for decision. The summaries then stated why the problem arose, identified the principal considerations and the significance of the issues involved, including the views of other governments so far as known, and presented the preferred solution and the alternative courses open, with their advantages and disadvantages. The discussions of the Committee and subcommittees were analyzed, the completed studies and drafts and pertinent minutes of discussion listed, and the summaries concluded with a statement of further research needed. Some of the problems were so complex as to require breaking into parts, and such summaries ranged in length up to twenty or even twenty-five pages.

"H documents" in the territorial field frequently required maps—sometimes three or more as in the case of the summary on the Italo-Yugoslav frontier problem. In the case of a large number of problems in this field, the sections on alternative solutions had to report the views of both the Political and the Territorial Subcommittees, which were not always in complete accord. Up to this time, it will be recalled, the final fusion of views had not been attempted, and occasionally a more favorable attitude toward a given alternative was held by one subcommittee than by the other. Summaries on difficult political problems, such as those concerning the future status and organization of Germany and especially its unity or partition, had likewise to include the discussions of more than one subcommittee.

The policy summaries on security were by groups of problems concerning occupation, surrender, disarmament of enemy powers, prevention of rearmament of enemy powers, international security, obligation to enforce security, enforcement of security by military and by economic measures, and control and limitation of armaments transitionally and permanently. These followed the pattern of the political summaries.

The series on international organization was arranged rather differently. It included the same scope of information but went beyond this to develop the findings on the basis of the essential elements of a general international organization, giving the pertinent provisions of the Covenant of the League of Nations and of other international organizations and indicating the nature of past experience. Seven handbooks were written.

The first was on the executive body, and covered the questions of its desirability, form, powers, basis of representation, composition, selection, and voting. The second dealt with technical organizations [3] and included a broad organization for considering international economic and social problems and coordinating the agreed action on such problems, as well as separate organizations for communications and transit, labor, investment and finance, trade, health, cultural relations, and social welfare. The policy summary analyzed in each of these cases the factors of desirability, method and timing of establishment, nature of structure and its relationship to a general international organization, and membership and representation. The third handbook dealt with steps toward a permanent international organization. The fourth analyzed the basic objectives of such organization, especially the maintenance of peace and security, prevention and settlement of disputes, promotion of economic and social welfare, and the safeguarding of human rights. The fifth was devoted to the deliberative body of a general international organization: the basis and nature of its powers, the distribution of powers between it and the executive body, and its composition, representation, and voting. The sixth, on the secretariat, set forth the problems of whether it should have an international or national character, the nature of the office of its secretary general, selection and tenure of its officials, and the centralization or decentralization of its headquarters. The final handbook was on "an international judiciary," although it also covered other problems in the legal field. It was comprised of six summaries devoted to the organs and structure of an international court, establishment and promotion of legal order in the world, separate handling of punishment for war crimes, property settlement after hostilities, the problem of guaranties of minority rights within states, and the development of an international bill of rights. These "seven volumes" were intensively used by the Informal Agenda Group in developing its recommendations concerning international organization.

A full draft constitution of a general international organization representing the views of a staff group in the Division of Political Studies was the remaining new documentation placed before the

---

[3] Later called specialized agencies in the case of such of these as became related to the general organization itself.

Agenda Group in the summer of 1943.[4] The Agenda Group had already before it drafts of occasional articles written by several of its own individual members and the text that had been developed by the Special Subcommittee on International Organization. The staff draft bore the title, "The Charter of the United Nations," and was written between August 4 and 14, 1943, by a drafting group of ten staff officers: Messrs. Gerig, Chairman, Blaisdell, Kirk, Myers, Notter, Padelford, Preuss, Sandifer, Miss Fosdick, and Mrs. McDiarmid. This text, which was less than twelve pages in length, contained a number of provisions later incorporated in the proposals presented by the United States at Dumbarton Oaks the following year. The word "Charter" was first formally employed here in connection with the future general international organization, and the term "United Nations," coined by the President for the wartime coalition, was first used here as the name for the future permanent organization. A "Commentary" on each article of the "Charter" was completed September 7, 1943, written by the same staff members working individually or in small teams.

While this staff work, although more advanced, was accomplished in a manner characteristic of previous work, certain developments were under way that were greatly to affect the staff organization for postwar and also current policy preparation. The concentration on a special field that marked the work on international organization described above also occurred in connection with the territorial and economic preparations. In this process, the over-all aspects of security, after suspension of the Security Subcommittee in July, were absorbed into the complex of problems relating to over-all international organization. The regional aspects of security from an organizational standpoint likewise entered into that complex of problems. Other aspects of security tended to be considered in terms of the postwar territorial problems of specific countries.

INTERDIVISIONAL COUNTRY AND AREA COMMITTEES

PLANS FOR country committees were projected under direction from the Secretary in June 1943 before the suspension of the Advisory Committee in July. The urgency for joint consideration at the expert level by the postwar research staff and by the "desk officers" in the operating geographic and functional divisions had grown considerably since the invasion of North Africa, and the operating divisions had been increasingly represented in the meetings of the Territorial Subcommittee during the spring of 1943. As the action stage was being reached in some areas and approached in others by reason of the progress of the war, the need was to tie the consideration of

---

[4] For text of this draft, see appendix 23.

current and of postwar policy closely together in order to have available, at all times and on all foreseeable problems, policy recommendations that would reflect the combined knowledge and judgment of all interested divisions of the Department. The first practical step in this direction was to provide for the continuing review and supplementation of the policy summaries to take into account the new experience with concrete situations and problems immediately resulting from the war.[5] This need was strongly felt by the Political Planning Committee, as well as by the Divisions of Political Studies and Economic Studies. Arrangements were completed between July 27 and August 4, 1943, to expedite the establishment of country committees. The chairmanship of each of these committees would usually be held by an officer of the Division of Political Studies; the research work for them would be done largely by that Division and by the Division of Economic Studies; and designated officers from the geographic and functional divisions concerned with the given country or countries would participate in this work while carrying on their regular duties.

The Interdivisional Committee on the Balkan-Danubian Countries was the first to be established, on August 12, 1943, with Harry N. Howard as Chairman, and began to function in September. Mr. Howard was also Chairman of the Committee on Greece, which was set up August 17, and of the Committee on Russia and Poland established later in August. By arrangement, the Committee on Greece at first covered Turkey as well, Philip W. Ireland presiding when it considered problems concerning the latter state. A separate committee on Turkey under Mr. Ireland's chairmanship was established the next month. Meetings were held in August by officers working on Germany, and a committee on this country was formally established in September under the chairmanship of David Harris. Other committees beginning in September were those on France (Chairman, Robert K. Gooch), on the Low Countries—Netherlands, Belgium, and Luxembourg—(Chairman, Hugh S. Cumming, Jr., of the European Division), and on Iran (Chairman, Mr. Ireland).

The Committee on Colonial Problems which also began work in September, with Mr. Rothwell and later Mr. Gerig as Chairman, was atypical. It dealt not only with the colonial problems of the states possessing such dependencies but also with the problems of policy toward dependencies as such. These dependencies being scattered over the globe, a need had become apparent for a committee to coordinate work on problems that related to more than than one country. When the problems in the Far East were contemplated in terms of a committee, it was also obvious that an "area" rather than a "country" committee was required. The Committee on the Far East was approved in September.

---

[5] See appendix 24.

Area consideration soon came to be regarded as desirable in the case of all major geographic regions, and a recommendation to institute such "area" committees was made by the Committee on Special Studies, October 20. This was promptly approved by the four Political Advisers, who, it was projected, would themselves head these committees. This plan was largely effectuated. Mr. Hornbeck had designated George H. Blakeslee as his alternate for the chairmanship of the Far East Area Committee. An area committee for Latin America was then established in November with the Adviser, Mr. Duggan, as Chairman. No committee for Europe was established. The area committee on Africa, which started in November, and the "country" committee on the Arab countries, approved by December, over both of which Mr. Ireland presided for the Adviser, Mr. Murray, in effect substituted for the area committee contemplated on the Near East and Africa.

By the close of 1943 there were nine country committees and four area committees. In the course of the next year, other committees were formed, and their development will be noted later in considering the broader arrangements that emerged at that time. The scope of the work of these committees embraced all direct postwar problems of the country or area concerned, and the expert membership composing them was in each case representative of the several divisions of the Department that were charged with research or operations in the field concerned.

Throughout most of the period covered here, no formal organization of these interdivisional committees was undertaken except for the designation of chairmen; no secretaries were appointed; and no minutes were attempted beyond the drafting notes of the officer or officers charged with writing on the problem under discussion. Those taking part did so pursuant to their regular assignments in their respective divisions and offices. The area committees employed the device of instituting subcommittees for specialized consideration, but these were usually of an *ad hoc* character. The committees initially were, in the main, simply authorized groups carrying on their work informally. The usual, more formalized processes, however, began to develop during the winter.

The rapidity with which these committees were established during August and September was due, in part, to the necessity of having papers ready on a number of territorial problems for the Secretary's possible use at the Moscow Conference should the occasion arise. This need could best be met by joint work. A similar need in the case of the Quebec Conference in August had been satisfied by *ad hoc* circulation of drafts for review, and experience on this occasion had suggested a more thoroughgoing collaboration in the prior writing stage. The technical preparations so undertaken were based, wholly at first and to an important degree later, on the discussions by the subcommittees of the Advisory Committee and the studies already made by the research staff. Furthermore, as will be recalled, the Territorial Subcommittee and the Special Subcommittee on European Organization remained active through 1943, and the latter even longer, and they could and did review a number of the papers produced by the new country and area committees. The special committees in the economic field likewise continued, and the results of their work were also available to the new country and area committees.

The demands of the international conferences were heavy, especially since these demands were characterized by extremely close deadlines. They had wide effects on the preparation, each one bringing the exacting process that had been laid down for all postwar preparation closer to fulfillment in the fields of work concerned. The use of papers in immediate negotiations increased the need for definite recommendations and decisions on long-range policy. At the same time, the adopted policy of deferring boundary and related questions until victory, the uncertainties at every turn ahead, and the staggered movements of the war in liberating certain areas, and initiating the postwar period in such areas long before it was possible in other theaters of the war, continued as influential factors in the last half of 1943 as they had been earlier. These complicated conditions were prominently reflected in the work of the country and area committees.

These committees and the additional ones established from time to time served henceforth as the basic Departmental instruments for obtaining interdivisional agreement on views and recommendations. The use of such committees has in large measure survived.

COORDINATION OF SPECIAL ECONOMIC COMMITTEES

THE COMMITTEE on Post-War Foreign Economic Policy, or Taylor Committee, had recessed on July 2, 1943, a week earlier than the subcommittees in the political field. It expected, as already noted, to resume work in the early autumn. Continuing suspension, however, rapidly brought about an interim means of coordinating the activities being carried on by its subordinate special committees, which, like the Taylor Committee, were interdepartmental and representative of most parts of the Executive branch of the Government.[6]

By the date of recess, ten special committees were functioning. In the order of their establishment these, and their chairmen, were International Aviation,[7] Mr. Berle; Labor Standards and Social Security,

---

[6] See appendix 25.

[7] An informal Interdepartmental Committee on Aviation in existence since the preceding January was converted into this Special Committee under the Taylor Committee at its first meeting in April after the latter's decision to institute these committees.

Miss Frances Perkins; Power, Leland Olds; Private Monopolies and Cartels, Mr. Acheson; Relaxation of Trade Barriers, Mr. Hawkins; Commodity Agreements and Methods of Trade, Lynn R. Edminster; Petroleum,[8] Mr. Feis; Communications, Mr. Long; Metals and Heavy Industry, Mr. Feis; and Migration and Settlement, H. F. Arthur Schoenfeld, acting Chairman. The Special Committee on Shipping, with Mr. Long as Chairman, was established a few days later, while the twelfth and last to function, the one on Inland Transport, presided over by Paul T. Culbertson, was organized during the summer and became active in October.

Many of these committees, in turn, created subcommittees of experts on particular aspects of their fields so that within a year a total of thirty-five subcommittees were functioning. The largest structure of this nature obtained in the case of the Committee on Trade Barriers, with eight subcommittees, while the Committee on Inland Transport created no subcommittees. Nine of the twelve chairmanships of the special committees were occupied by officials of the Department of State, but only four of the thirty-five subcommittees had Department members in charge, the practice throughout being to allocate the responsibilities of chairmanship and research service as well to the department or agency having the most direct or largest interest and technical jurisdiction. The expert nature of the subsidiary bodies was further indicated by the fact that one of the chairmen was drawn for the purpose from a university faculty.

The original membership of the special committees ranged from seven to sixteen persons, but in due course became a little larger, in one instance, twenty. There was substantial diversity among these committees. Members from private life were on some, but not on others; as time passed the Special Committee on Labor Standards was composed half of private and half of official members. Cabinet or sub-Cabinet members were chairmen of some; senior technical officers presided over others. Some committees were composed only of experts, while Under Secretaries, Assistant Secretaries, Generals, Admirals, and Congressmen served on others. Invited directly by the committee concerned, rather than solely by the Secretary of State under the hard and fast rule of the Advisory Committee, Senator Claude Pepper of Florida and Representatives Alfred L. Bulwinkle of North Carolina, Democrats, and Charles A. Wolverton of New Jersey, Republican, served on the Special Committee on Communications, and Senator Scott W. Lucas of Illinois and Representatives Schuyler Otis Bland of Virginia, J. Hardin Peterson (alternate) of Florida, Democrats, and Richard J. Welch of California, Republican, were members of the Special Committee on Shipping. Other com-

---

[8] This special committee held only two organizational meetings and never became operative on substance.

mittees did not have representation of the Congress. Representatives from war agencies were included in several instances. Despite insistence upon the general practice of avoiding "alternates" to designated members, some committees regularly permitted attendance of alternates. Some developed elaborate documentation and minutes; a few did not. The committee on aviation once sought the views of a political body, the Subcommittee on Security Problems; all others in this period carried on their work without direct reference to the political committee dealing with related matters. The International Aviation Committee also formally sought the views of private industry; no others did so. Some were representative of all agencies concerned; the representation on others was more limited, at least at the beginning.

The force of the committees' recommendations, under their own usage, also varied. One recommendation by the Migration Committee was implemented by the War Department as a final decision; three committees reported recommendations through their chairmen, who were officials of the State Department, directly to the Secretary of State for action; other committees regarded their recommendations as tentative pending approval by the Taylor Committee.

These were all, in part, normal variations in governmental practice among the components of the Executive branch. They were also, in part, indications of the transitional activity under way in a very large organized effort that had both current and postwar aspects. Besides revealing the risk of gaps in coverage or of overlapping among agendas, except on such broad problems as terms of surrender or peace terms where overlapping was essential in certain respects, the diversity suggested the need for a greater degree of coordination, not so much of methods as of substantive work. A report of the Division of Economic Studies on September 8, 1943, focused chiefly on this need. The fact that the most urgent work of the special committees in the summer of 1943 concerned the impending discussions with the United Kingdom under Article VII of the Lend-Lease Agreement, which opened September 20, added weight to the suggestion. Accordingly, a new coordinating structure emerged in the economic field during the interim between suspension of the meetings of the Taylor Committee and their anticipated but postponed resumption, in much the same way as the Informal Agenda Group developed in the political field.

Commencing shortly after its recess on July 2, a small group of members of the Taylor Committee had been meeting occasionally. These group meetings were presided over by Myron C. Taylor, though sometimes by Secretary Hull, and were attended by Messrs. Berle, Acheson, Long, Pasvolsky, Feis, Stinebower as executive officer, and Haley as secretary. Their purpose was to direct and to review the work proceeding in the special committees and to undertake drafting on economic problems as required by the Secretary and the President.

At the direction of Secretary Hull, the group was formally constituted on September 22, 1943, as the Committee on Coordination of Economic Policy Work. Mr. Hawkins was added at that time to its membership. Mr. Bowman and Mr. Notter attended various of its meetings primarily for coordination with the political side of the preparation. This committee was conceived as a steering and agenda group to serve the Taylor Committee, if and when the main committee reconvened, and otherwise to carry on pending establishment of a more permanent and executive type of interdepartmental organization, which for some weeks had appeared increasingly to be needed.

While regular interdepartmental consideration of current as well as postwar economic problems was essential for adequate integration of foreign economic policy, numerous interdepartmental committees were outside the framework of the Advisory Committee and unattached to any coordinating body. Confusion and divergence of views between agencies operating in the foreign economic field had been illuminated by the Henry Wallace–Jesse Jones exchanges and the letter from the President in that connection published in July 1943. The attempt, however, to resolve this particular difficulty through Executive Order 9361 of July 15, 1943, which established the Office of Economic Warfare, had raised several new questions of jurisdiction and responsibility while resolving several old ones. It was clear that questions of domestic policy were unevenly interwoven with those of current and postwar foreign policy and that there was an overlapping of authority and personnel and a multiplication of operations not easily kept in harmony.[9] A recommendation to create a high-level, interdepartmental-coordinating, and policy-recommending committee was therefore initiated by the Committee on Coordination of Economic Policy Work in the autumn of 1943, cleared through the Department, discussed with other agencies, and ultimately approved by the President the following April.[10]

[9] Coordination of the economic activities of Government departments and wartime agencies dealing with liberated areas and the relating of such operations to United States policies in political and military fields had already been undertaken in the Department, through the establishment on June 24 of an Office of Foreign Economic Coordination in response to a directive from the President dated June 3, 1943. The vast scope of this work, carried on under the direction of Assistant Secretary Acheson, was clear from the representation, subjects, and large interdepartmental committee and subcommittee structure involved in this type of operation. On various important issues, conflicts of view had appeared among the four Departments and three agencies concerned: the State, Treasury, War, and Navy Departments and the Board of Economic Warfare, Office of Lend-Lease Administration, and Office of Foreign Relief and Rehabilitation Operations.

[10] See the Executive Committee on Economic Foreign Policy, p. 218.

While action on the recommendation was going forward, the Coordination Committee cleared the documents of the special committees, resolved conflicts in their terms of reference, approved additional membership, and instituted various studies required by the international negotiations of the period. It ceased functioning in January 1944, when clearance for the reports and recommendations of the special committees was provided for through the new machinery established in the course of the reorganization of the Department.[11]

The Taylor Committee, its special committees, and the Committee on Coordination were essentially transitional instruments. They carried through the difficult year beginning with April 1943, serving as the working machinery for economic preparation and at the same time as the bridge between the Advisory Committee structure and the executive structure that was created for the stage of action during 1944. As a December 1943 report observed, the special committees wrote drafts of operating economic instructions and policy directives to military theater commanders—sometimes limited to the execution of surrender terms, sometimes dealing with longer-range matters; formulated policy recommendations of a short-run character having to do with economic operations of the war period, military occupation, and transition; drafted terms and conditions to be incorporated in the peace settlement; prepared proposals relative to the creation and implementation of organizations for international economic cooperation; prepared long-range policy proposals for adoption by more or less formal agreement among nations; and assembled factual data necessary to negotiations.

AD HOC ECONOMIC GROUPS

THERE WERE, in addition to the special committees, several working groups instituted in the summer and fall of 1943 for *ad hoc* purposes. These groups represented further types of adjustment in the preparation necessitated by participation in international economic negotiations during the period after the recess of the Advisory Committee. The peculiar nature of these adjustments stemmed from the fact that, whereas the technical responsibility for such matters as food and agriculture, labor, and investment and finance lay primarily with other agencies, our international activities in these fields constituted part of United States foreign relations and had no slight impact on foreign political policy. Such interrelationship normally and constantly involves accommodation of views within the government. In the period beginning in 1943, it was particularly important that all steps taken should be within the over-all pattern of postwar

---

[11] See the Post-War Programs Committee, p. 208 ff.

policy being evolved, in which plans for the establishment of a general international organization were predominant. Moreover, the advent of these working groups was another indication of the merging of postwar preparation and current operations already under way.

Following the Hot Springs Conference in the spring of 1943, for example, an Interdivisional Working Group on the projected United Nations Food and Agriculture Organization was informally established in the Department. Its tasks were to formulate the Department's position in regard to the work of the United Nations Interim Commission on Food and Agriculture directed toward the establishment of a permanent organization in this field, and, through the interdepartmental group, referred to above,[12] to advise the American member, Paul H. Appleby of the Department of Agriculture, particularly concerning developments regarding general international organization. This interdivisional group was composed of the following members of the Advisory Committee, research staff, and functional divisions: Assistant Secretary Acheson, Chairman, and Messrs. Stinebower, Deputy Chairman, Pasvolsky, Hawkins, Gerig, Tomlinson, Warren Kelchner (Chief of the Division of International Conferences), and Emilio G. Collado. The recommendations of this group were cleared through usual Departmental channels until, at the beginning of 1944, new superior structure for postwar problems was established. The technical responsibilities in this field rested in the Department of Agriculture and were outside the scope of this group.

An Interdivisional Committee on Finance was established at an expert level in the Department in November 1943 to coordinate and prepare recommendations concerning the Department's position on both long-range and current problems in the international financial field, especially with respect to an international bank and fund. These recommendations would guide the State Department representatives on the interdepartmental American Technical Committee, described above,[13] which reported to the Treasury Department. Mr. Posvolsky was Chairman of the interdivisional committee, and as in the case of the Food and Agriculture Working Group, its remaining membership reflected both research and operations, being composed of Miss Ruth B. Russell, Paul T. Ellsworth, Leroy D. Stinebower, John P. Young, Mrs. Eleanor L. Dulles, William Adams Brown, Jr., Alexander M. Rosenson, and Miss Julia E. Schairer, secretary, from the research staff, and Harry C. Hawkins, Frederick Livesey, John S. Hooker, Dudley M. Phelps, Emilio G. Collado, Jacques J. Reinstein, and Woodbury Willoughby from the interested functional divisions.

The two other special groups established during this period in con-

---

[12] See p. 145.
[13] See p. 141 ff.

nection with international economic negotiations were in the labor field. The Special Committee on Labor Standards and Social Security had undertaken the necessary initial exploration of the issues involved in the question of the future status of the International Labor Organization and had recommended the early convocation of a regular conference of the ILO.   This recommendation had been accepted by both the American and British Governments in the autumn of 1943. Steps had been taken, though without result, to bring about the participation of the Soviet Union, which was not a member of the ILO, and a meeting of the Governing Body of the Organization had been called for December in anticipation of the proposed conference.   To prepare the American position for this preliminary meeting within the framework of the broad postwar policy then being developed, an *ad hoc* Interdepartmental Group on the ILO was established.   This consisted of the following members of the Special Committee on Labor Standards : Assistant Secretary Berle, Carter Goodrich of the ILO, Isador Lubin and A. F. Hinrichs of the Labor Department, and Otis E. Mulliken, then in the Office of the Under Secretary of State.   This *ad hoc* group, in turn, recommended the establishment in the State Department of a working committee to formulate the Department's position on specific problems connected with the forthcoming ILO conference, in order to avoid any steps that might be inconsistent with the projected establishment of an inclusive international organization. In December 1943, therefore, an Interdivisional Committee on the Agenda of the ILO was set up, which is discussed later in connection with the ILO conference of April–May 1944.

CHAPTER IX

Development of International Conferences, Autumn 1943

WITH THE series of international conferences that began at Quebec in August 1943, the Department's work on postwar political problems began to move from the exploratory into the negotiating phase. In the economic field, as has been noted, this development had begun much earlier. The Anglo-American discussions of relief and rehabilitation inaugurated in June 1942 had culminated, following consultation with the Soviet and Chinese Governments, in the publication on June 11, 1943, of a draft of the UNRRA agreement[1] that, after further international exchanges of view, was to be concluded by the United and Associated Nations on November 9 of that year. In August 1942, proposals had been exchanged with the British in the monetary and financial field that resulted, after extensive exploratory discussion with Great Britain and other countries during 1943 and early 1944, in the Bretton Woods Agreement of July 22, 1944, for the establishment of an international bank and monetary fund, as described later. The first United Nations Conference, the meeting at Hot Springs, Virginia, May 18–June 3, 1943, discussed above, had already laid the foundation for a permanent international organization in the field of food and agriculture.

In the political field, however, only one problem had reached the negotiations stage, and this was of a technical character primarily. The United Nations were committed individually and collectively to the general policy of punishment of war criminals, and agreement had already been reached on the establishment of a United Nations Commission for the Investigation of War Crimes, which held its first meeting in London on October 20, 1943. Prior to the Quebec Conference there had also been certain informal exchanges of views with the British, notably between the President and Prime Minister Churchill in February and May 1943 and between the President, Secretary Hull, and Foreign Secretary Eden in March 1943, on the organization of the peace. With one exception, these exchanges had been concerned

---

[1] For text, see *Department of State Bulletin*, VIII, 524–27.

with broad objectives and had not involved the presentation of specific proposals. The one exception had been the draft of a proposed United Nations declaration on dependent peoples, referred to above,[2] which had been given to Mr. Eden at the time of his visit, not as a definitive proposal, but informally to obtain the general British reaction to our developing thought on this problem. This step had been taken after the receipt in February 1943 of a British draft of a corresponding declaration.

Apart from these informal exchanges at Cabinet level and above, exchanges of ideas and, in some fields, of factual research papers had been instituted on British initiative as early as April 1942. Such informal exploratory exchanges were chiefly at an expert level and continued at intervals throughout the war in Washington and, to some extent, in London. There were also many conversations, both of a diplomatic and technical character, between individual American officials and those of other Allied governments on postwar problems. It was in part through such exchanges that the Department gathered the information on the views of other governments essential to its preparations for the conferences that followed.

THE FIRST QUEBEC CONFERENCE

THE MEETING of the President and the Prime Minister at Quebec August 11–24, 1943, provided the first occasion for the presentation by the Department of definite policy recommendations based on the preparatory work done on postwar problems. While this meeting between the two heads of government was concerned in the first instance with military matters, it was also, unlike their conference at Casablanca earlier the same year, concerned with a wide range of political and economic problems, and both Mr. Hull and Mr. Eden were present.

The change in the course of the war was bringing to the fore the question of the postwar world. The Italian surrender appeared imminent. The liberation of French North Africa had intensified the problem of the status of the French Committee of National Liberation.[3] Internal political developments with respect to Greece and Yugoslavia already foreshadowed the difficulties that were to be encountered in reestablishing acceptable governments in these nations upon their liberation. The rising sense of United Nations power to force a victorious conclusion of the war gave urgency to such questions as the treatment to be accorded Germany after her defeat and postwar international economic policy and arrangements. It now appeared imperative that, if United Nations collaboration were to continue after the war, some way be found to ascertain the attitude of

---

[2] See p. 109.
[3] Formerly the French National Committee.

the Soviet Government toward postwar cooperation and to obtain the participation of the Soviet Union in preparations for the peace. Marshal Stalin had been invited to the Quebec Conference but had replied that it was not possible for him to attend.

Following the meeting on August 10 of the Secretary and Messrs. Welles, Bowman, Davis, and Pasvolsky with the President to discuss recommendations for the forthcoming negotiations and to receive the President's views and instructions, the research staff, and members of the Informal Agenda Group, drew together the required policy summaries and supporting papers for the Quebec meeting. These included a redraft of the papers for a Four Power agreement in the form of a declaration, and, for background purposes should these issues arise, a series of problem papers on such questions as future boundaries of Germany and of Italy, the partition or unity of Germany, the future of the Italian colonies, and methods of dealing with the internal political situation in Italy following its surrender. A map of the problem areas of Europe was included,[4] as was also a memorandum outlining Soviet views on postwar problems so far as these views were known. Some of these documents had already been prepared by the research staff, while others were specially drafted.

The communiqué issued at the conclusion of the discussions of the President and Prime Minister Churchill at Quebec referred to the meeting as an "Anglo-American war conference." It stated that, in addition to the necessary military decisions, agreements had been reached "upon the political issues underlying or arising out of the military operations," and specified that consideration had been given to the question of relations with the French Committee of National Liberation. The communiqué specified that the Soviet Government would be informed of decisions reached by the Conference affecting the war against Germany and Italy and also referred to the possibility of a tripartite meeting with the Soviet Union before the end of the year. After the meeting adjourned, President Roosevelt, in an address at Ottawa on August 25, 1943, said: "It is no secret that at Quebec there was much talk of the post-war world."[5]

Secretary Hull had joined the Conference on August 20 and met with Foreign Secretary Eden and with the President and the Prime Minister for the intensive discussions of international political problems commencing the same day. Also present at these discussions were James C. Dunn, Political Adviser and a member of the Informal Agenda Group; the United States Minister to Canada, Ray Atherton; the British Permanent Under Secretary of State for Foreign Affairs, Sir Alexander Cadogan; and on occasions, Harry L. Hop-

---

[4] See appendix 26.
[5] *Department of State Bulletin*, IX, 122–24.

kins. The discussions ranged from exchanges of tentative views on such problems as the treatment to be accorded Germany and the draft United States proposal regarding dependent peoples to the formulation of a draft statement on Allied policy in liberated countries. The United States draft of the Four Power Declaration was introduced and agreed upon as a basis for further negotiation,[6] and the possibility of obtaining Soviet and Chinese participation in future conferences was explored. Most of the discussion of long-range subjects was preliminary and inconclusive, however, and was to be carried further at subsequent meetings.

Following the Conference, on September 12, Secretary Hull delivered a major policy address,[7] which was drafted in a long series of working sessions with him by most of the high officers of the Department, including those taking part in the Agenda Group, with assistance from the research staff. In it the Secretary reported the progress that had been made in our preparations for the peace and discussed the basic objectives of this Government in such conferences among the major powers as that just held at Quebec and the forthcoming one at Moscow, to be described shortly.

Stating that the "foreign policy of any country must be expressive of that country's fundamental national interests," he defined our own as being "the assuring of our national security and the fostering of the economic and social well-being of our people." The maintenance of these interests, he said, required not only that our foreign policy deal with the current situation, where our paramount aim was final victory, but that it "plan for the future in the light of the concepts and beliefs which we, as a nation, accept for ourselves as the guiding lines of our international behavior."

The Secretary pointed out that while there were differences among nations "as regards their respective aims and purposes and as regards the means of attaining them," there were also "immense areas of common interest." By cooperation within these areas, he said, "nations not only can advance more effectively the aims and purposes which they have in common, but can also find increased opportunity to reconcile, by peaceful means and to mutual advantage, such differences as may exist among them." The United Nations had recognized this area of common interest in the Atlantic Charter and in their joint Declaration of January 1, 1942. Therefore, the Secretary declared, it was our task and the task of our Allies "to utilize this common interest to create an effective system of international cooperation for the maintenance of peace."

The Secretary made specific reference to two of the major policies he had discussed at Quebec and toward the furtherance of which his efforts at Moscow were to be directed—"our desire and our settled policy" that collaboration between the United States and the Soviet Union should "steadily increase during and following the war" and recognition of the role of China both in the war and in the "achievement of a stable peace." He expressed his confidence that the United States, as well as the other nations associated with us in the war effort, would "do its part, after the victory of the United Nations, in meeting the immense needs of the post-war period," which he defined as follows:

"Those needs will embrace the task of taking practical steps to create conditions in which there will be security for every nation; in which each nation will have enhanced opportunities to develop and progress in ways of its own choosing; in which there will be, for each nation, improved facilities to attain, by its own effort and in cooperation with others, an increasing measure of political stability and economic, social, and cultural welfare."

Reiterating the position he had first enunciated on July 23 of the previous year, the Secretary declared that "a system of organized international cooperation for the maintenance of peace must be based upon the willingness of the cooperating nations to use force, if necessary, to keep the peace." He then discussed in greater detail than before the functions of an organization for the maintenance of peace, and he again stressed the dependence of such a system of organized international cooperation for its success on conditions of economic and social well-being throughout the world.

The Secretary concluded by referring specifically, for the first time, to the Department's preparations for the peace and to the discussions of postwar problems that had been inaugurated with the British and that were soon to be extended to the Russians. He said, in part:

"The form and functions of the international agencies of the future, the extent to which the existing court of international justice may or may not need to be remodeled, the scope and character of the means for making international action effective in the maintenance of peace, the nature of international economic institutions and arrangements that may be desirable and feasible—all these are among the problems which are receiving attention and which will need to be determined by agreement among governments, subject, of course, to approval by their respective peoples. They are being studied intensively by this Government and by other governments. They are gradually being made subjects of consultation between and among governments. They are being studied and discussed by the people of this country and the peoples of other countries. . . ."

"ARTICLE VII" DISCUSSIONS

In November 1942, this Government had apprised the British that we looked forward to the informal and exploratory talks with them and other powers envisaged in Article VII of the Mutual Aid or Lend-

Lease Agreements, and on August 4, 1943, the British had informed us of their desire to send a delegation of senior officials to Washington in the first half of September to initiate these discussions. In order to insure that the projected exchange of views would be informal in character, the Secretary had raised with Mr. Eden at Quebec the question of the Anglo-American economic discussions to take place shortly in Washington.

Work in preparation for the projected discussions was being carried forward by the special committees established under the Taylor Committee and was subject to the direction and review, following the recess of the main Committee, of the informal group that later became the Committee on Coordination of Economic Policy Work. The British had expressed the view in their *aide-mémoire* of August 4 that conversations should begin on the whole field covered by Article VII, and had specifically referred to the questions of commercial policy, monetary policy, international investment, and the regulation of primary products and related topics. The Department, in its reply, indicated its readiness to discuss commercial policy and the regulation of primary products and related topics but suggested that monetary policy and international investment be handled through the Treasury, where discussions with the British on the first of these questions were already in progress.

The Treasury, in May 1943, had obtained from the President primary authority in this field, and at Quebec the Secretary emphasized to Mr. Eden the desirability of having the financial discussions, to quote the memorandum of conversation, "treated as a continuation of conversations which were already in course with the United States Treasury." He also took the position that the projected discussions with the Department should be directed toward drawing up an agenda of topics to be discussed rather than toward reaching agreement on the topics themselves, on the ground that it would be unfortunate "to give the impression that the United States and Great Britain were coming to previous agreement on these matters before other governments were brought in and acquainted with the progress of the discussions."

The Anglo-American economic conversations that began in Washington on September 17 were in two parts. The American Group in charge of that part of the discussions held in the State Department was drawn primarily from the Advisory Committee, particularly the Taylor Committee and its special committees. There was no need, therefore, for extensive briefing before, or elaborate clearance of policy views during, the conversations. The Group was composed of Myron C. Taylor, Chairman; Messrs. Pasvolsky, Hawkins, Stinebower, and Hickerson of State; Mr. White of the Treasury; Messrs. Clayton and Taylor of Commerce; Messrs. Appleby and Wheeler of Agriculture; and Messrs. Ryder and Edminster of the Tariff Commission. This part of the conversations, which began on September 20 and continued until October 16, covered the general topics of commercial policy, international commodity arrangements, cartels, and coordination of measures to promote employment. The second part was conducted at the Treasury, under the chairmanship of Mr. White and with participation of several members of the Group conducting the State Department phase but with broader interdepartmental representation otherwise. The Treasury part, which opened on September 17 and continued until October 9, was devoted to probing the questions of monetary stabilization and the promotion of international investment.

In keeping with the position taken by the Secretary at Quebec, no effort was made during the conversations to arrive at any definite conclusions "but rather," in the words of a United States memorandum presented shortly thereafter at the Moscow Conference, "to prepare an orderly agenda for further study by each of the respective governments and for possible further informal joint conversations." The Anglo-American conversations, an accompanying memorandum stated, had provided "an opportunity to discover the extent to which there is common ground and the extent to which there are differences of importance in the points of view of those whose expert advice may frequently be utilized in the formulation of policy." [8]

Besides developing various alternative formulas for the reduction of tariffs and examining such problems as quantitative restrictions on imports, export taxes and restrictions, subsidies, and state trading, the conversations in the field of commercial policy had involved extensive consideration of the relative advantages and disadvantages of the multilateral as against the bilateral method of reducing tariffs, on which there was considerable difference between the American and British views. They had also involved extensive consideration of the question of preferences—the same problem that had arisen in the earlier negotiations with the British of Article VII of the Mutual Aid Agreement and in connection with the fourth paragraph of the Atlantic Charter [9] and that was to continue to be a basic issue between the two Governments in the later conversations under Article VII which culminated in the formal Anglo-American discussions in this field in the autumn of 1945.[10]

The conversations in the field of commodity policy had examined the problems of short-term price fluctuations in primary products, periodic slumps in demand and prices in relation to the business cycle,

[8] See appendix 30.
[9] See p. 50.
[10] See p. 361.

and excess capacity arising out of past stimulation of high-cost production and because of the war. They had also examined such methods of meeting these problems as the maintenance of buffer stocks, quantitative regulations, and subsidies, and considered the possibility of setting forth principles to govern arrangements in this field, together with the possible relation of such arrangements to the international economic system generally. There was agreement that international commodity arrangements should be in harmony with the general developmental or "expansionist" economic policy that it was hoped would be adopted by the nations after the war.

The conversations with respect to the problems of cartels and employment were of a less extensive and specific character. The British were not prepared to discuss the former in any detail, while the latter, being subject to the influence of a complex of economic policies, both national and international, was therefore approached primarily from the standpoint of the coordination of these other policies.

The agenda resulting from these exploratory conversations projected the possible establishment of an international commercial-policy organization, an international commodity-policy organization, and an "Advisory Economic Staff" to study international economic questions, particularly the coordination of international measures for the maintenance of high levels of employment. The discussions of this latter problem had pointed to the need for coordinating economic policy generally, with particular reference to the separate international organizations existing or projected in specialized fields. To meet this need the creation of some over-all economic body, possibly within the framework of a general political organization, had been suggested.

The documentation embodying the thought developed in these conversations was to prove fundamental in the continuing consideration given to these problems by the United States Government in the following two years.

Further conversations under Article VII, this time with the Canadians, were held in Washington, January 3–7, and in New York, February 12–13, 1944. These conversations followed the pattern of the earlier Anglo-American discussions except that they did not include consideration of monetary and international investment policy and were conducted by the State Department alone. The President, on December 20, 1943, approved the use in the projected conversations with the Canadians of the same group, under the chairmanship of Myron C. Taylor, that had been in charge of the State Department phase of the Anglo-American discussions. At the same time he approved this group for subsequent conversations with other countries.

It eventuated that this series of exploratory economic discussions ended with the Canadian conversations. Both the Soviet Union and China had been apprised on September 3, 1943, of our readiness to undertake similar conversations with them, and discussions had originally been projected with additional countries if satisfactory progress was made in the initial exchanges of views. No further bilateral conversations could be arranged, however, before developments in related fields called for a change in approach. The further discussions of the questions arising under Article VII took place, as will be seen in the following pages, on a multilateral basis at the Bretton Woods Conference, at the Dumbarton Oaks Conversations later in 1944, at the San Francisco Conference, and at conferences held after the end of hostilities.

THE MOSCOW CONFERENCE

ON AUGUST 24, 1943, Marshal Stalin had replied favorably to Anglo-American overtures looking toward an early meeting of the Foreign Ministers of the three major powers, and on September 11, the President agreed to the Soviet suggestion that this meeting should take place at Moscow in October. The meeting was to go beyond an exploratory exchange of views and lay the ground for definitive Three Power decisions. The agenda included military, political, and economic topics, those of its points attributable to United States initiative having postwar significance primarily.

The preparations for the Moscow Conference were begun in the Department immediately upon the Secretary's return from Quebec. The scope of the problem papers drawn together for use in negotiation or as background material at Quebec was enlarged, and, in the case of Germany, the papers were supplemented by definite recommendations arrived at in the newly created interdivisional committee on Germany.[11] Also a comprehensive memorandum on the "Bases of Our Program for International Economic Collaboration," reflecting the experience of the Anglo-American economic conversations then in progress, was written. The appropriate operating divisions and the relevant postwar groups and staff worked jointly in readying these materials, although for papers dealing with current issues the geographic divisions and advisers exercised the paramount responsibility. The materials bearing upon the proposed Four Nation Declaration were reviewed and amended by the Agenda Group. In addition, thorough consideration was given in the Department to the topics proposed by the Soviet and British Governments for inclusion on the agenda of the conference and to our own proposals, which were the draft Four Nation Declaration previously presented at Quebec, the treatment of Germany and other European enemy states, economic reconstruction, and methods of dealing with current political and

---

[11] For example of papers on Germany, see appendixes 28 and 29.

economic issues and those arising as the war progressed.   Just prior to his departure for Moscow, the Secretary, on October 5, as noted above, accompanied by Under Secretary Stettinius and Messrs. Pasvolsky, Dunn, Hackworth, and Matthews visited the White House to obtain the President's directives and views on questions that had been, or might be, raised in connection with the forthcoming conference.

The further aspect of preparation for the Conference concerned American support of a world security organization.   Thought had been given to this matter by the Political Subcommittee.   The Secretary gave attention to it in his address of September 12 [12] and it was the object of the Fulbright resolution passed on September 21, 1943.[13]   In outlining to the Nation our objectives in the consultations with other governments on postwar problems and arrangements that had begun at Quebec, the Secretary said in that address, "In the final analysis, it is the will of the peoples of the world that decides the all-embracing issues of peace and of human welfare."

He then commented:

"We have now reached a stage at which it becomes possible to discuss in greater detail some of the basic problems outlined in this address and in my previous statements.   I hope to be able to undertake this from time to time in the early future.

"The supreme importance of these problems should lift them far above the realm of partisan considerations or party politics. It is gratifying that both in the Congress and elsewhere great numbers of thoughtful men have so approached them.   A heavy responsibility rests upon all of us to consider these all-important post-war problems and to contribute to their solution in a wholly non-partisan spirit."

The subcommittee discussions had early taken into account the fact that one of the principal elements of uncertainty in our preparations for the peace was the question of how far public opinion in this country would be willing to go in international cooperation after the war.   The experience of 1919–20 with the Treaty of Versailles and especially the League of Nations was much in mind.   United States participation in any postwar system of organized international cooperation was dependent on congressional approval, which would be jeopardized by an antagonistic, or even an apathetic, public reaction to such a policy.   It was thought that the position of our Allies on postwar problems, particularly that of security, was strongly influenced by their doubts that this country would assume a responsibility for the maintenance of peace after the war commensurate with its position as

[12] *Department of State Bulletin*, IX, 173–79.

[13] H. Con. Res. 25, 78th Cong., 1st sess., *Cong. Rec.*, vol. 89, p. 7729; H. Rept. 553, serial vol. 10762.   The Senate acted upon S. Res. 192 (the Connally resolution), Nov. 5, 1943, 78th Cong., 1st sess., *Cong. Rec.*, vol. 89, p. 9222; S. Rept. 478, serial vol. 10757.

a great power. It was further recognized that our own negotiating position in any discussions with our Allies was weakened by their fear that our proposals, even if accepted by them, might later fail to obtain the endorsement of the American people and the Congress.

It was therefore considered essential, both to insure that the United States would accept its full responsibilities for the maintenance of the future peace and to facilitate acceptance by our Allies of this Government's views on the organization of that peace, that widespread understanding and support of our objectives for the future and of our plans to achieve these objectives be obtained both in the Congress and among the American people. A mounting public interest in our preparations for the peace was noted, and it was thought that sentiment favorable to United States participation in postwar international arrangements was growing throughout the country. At the same time, it was realized that excessive public discussion of our plans while they were still in the formative stage might lead to their premature crystallization and might arouse friction and animosities, both at home and abroad, harmful to the war effort.

These were the aspects of the problem discussed at two meetings of the Political Subcommittee in February 1943, and at greater length when the subcommittee, late in April under the chairmanship of Secretary Hull, began its analytical consideration of the problems of international organization. In this connection, the desirability of a congressional resolution in support of United States participation in postwar international arrangements for the maintenance of peace was favorably studied by the subcommittee at meetings in which members of Congress from both parties took part. A number of resolutions had already been introduced in Congress toward this end, and the Secretary throughout the spring and summer of that year held informal consultations with members of Congress from both parties on these resolutions. He also conferred with the President and other political leaders.[14]

Preliminary to his consultations with members of Congress, the Secretary of State asked his advisers for information concerning public and official attitudes during the years from the outbreak of war in 1914 until 1941. The research staff with the cooperation of several officers in other parts of the Department made a series of analytical studies, between January 12 and March 2, 1943, of party platforms, various phases of isolationism, the activities and effects of pressure groups, and public opinion in relation to the policies of the interwar period.

On September 7, 1943, a conference of Republican leaders at Mackinac Island, Michigan, endorsed United States participation in a post-

---

[14] Cf. *Memoirs of Cordell Hull*, II, 1258–63.

war international organization. Two weeks later the House passed the Fulbright resolution "favoring the creation of appropriate international machinery with power adequate to establish and to maintain a just and lasting peace, among the nations of the world, and as favoring participation by the United States therein." Similar Senate action had been under contemplation during this period, although it was not until November 5, 1943, that a comparable resolution, introduced by Senator Connally, was passed by the Senate. Nonpartisan support for this Government's advocacy of organized international cooperation after the war in which the United States would take part had, therefore, been strongly and unmistakably evidenced prior to the Secretary's departure for the Moscow conference, and, in his address of September 12, the Secretary had laid the public basis for the Four Power Declaration that he was to present there.

The Conference met at Moscow October 19–30, 1943. It was the first meeting of the Foreign Ministers of the United States, United Kingdom, and the Soviet Union, and was designed primarily to prepare the ground for a meeting of the heads of government of these three states. Its major substantive objective from the standpoint of the United States was to determine the Soviet position on postwar cooperation with a view to holding the three powers and China together after victory in policy and action on matters concerning international peace and security.

Secretary Hull was accompanied to the Conference by a number of political and technical advisers, among whom were two Department officials who had participated in the Political Subcommittee and the informal Agenda Group, Mr. Hackworth and Mr. Dunn, and one member of the research staff, Philip E. Mosely, senior assistant chief for studies in the territorial field. The Foreign Ministers met daily in regular session, at which Ambassador W. Averell Harriman, Maj. Gen. John R. Deane, and Messrs. Hackworth and Dunn were also present for the United States, with Charles E. Bohlen acting as interpreter. In addition, the Conference provided opportunity for the Secretary to have informal discussions with Mr. Molotov and Mr. Eden and, on two occasions, with Marshal Stalin.

The deliberations of the conference covered many problems. The discussions were often inconclusive, sometimes involving no more than an exchange of views, as in the case of the question of Soviet-Polish relations, or reference of the problem elsewhere for further consideration, as in the case of a proposed resolution on Iran. In certain instances, however, fundamental decisions of primary importance were taken. Those that were to have determinative influence on the Department's future work in preparation for the peace were (1) the adoption, with minor amendment, of the United States draft of the Four Nation Declaration on General Security with China as one of the signatories of the Declaration as released; (2) the decision to create the European Advisory Commission to consider European questions connected with the termination of hostilities; and (3) the agreement on the basic policies set forth in the Declaration Regarding Italy, the Declaration on Austria, and the Declaration on German Atrocities.

The Secretary pressed for action at the Conference on only one United States proposal—the draft Four Nation Declaration, on which there had been some prior negotiation by cable with the Kremlin since the Quebec Conference. He circulated the United States proposal concerning dependent peoples previously discussed with the British, but this question was not included on the agenda. He also circulated papers on two other subjects to show the trend of our thinking on these matters but not as concrete proposals requiring decision. One paper was on the treatment of Germany after the war, which reflected the recommendations of the newly created interdivisional committee on Germany and was referred by the Conference to the European Advisory Commission for consideration. The others were four economic documents considering, respectively, cooperation in the rehabilitation of war damage in the Soviet Union, joint action for assistance to other countries in the long-range work of reconstruction and rehabilitation, the bases of our program for international economic cooperation, and reparations.

The paper on economic cooperation included a supporting memorandum on the recent Anglo-American economic conversations in Washington and expressed the "earnest hope," reiterated by the Secretary personally, that the Soviet Union would "find it possible to arrange for such an interchange of views in the near future." It also referred to the obvious "need for organized discussions among the United Nations, both informal and in formal conferences," of basic international economic problems, and suggested the establishment of a Commission comprised of technical economic experts from the principal United Nations and possibly certain others to plan the best procedures toward obtaining international economic collaboration after the war.[15]

A Civil Affairs Agreement for France, jointly presented to the Conference by the United States and the United Kingdom, was referred to the European Advisory Commission for further examination.

Upon his return from Moscow, the Secretary addressed a joint session of Congress on November 18 to report on the Conference. Stressing the necessity, if the fruits of victory were not to be lost, of agreement among the major powers and other United Nations on "those basic principles and policies which will render impossible a repetition of our present tragedy" and of the prompt creation of the

---

[15] For text of this memorandum, see appendix 30.

"machinery of action necessary to carry out these principles and policies," the Secretary stated:

"The attention of the Conference was centered upon the task of making sure that the nations upon whose armed forces and civilian efforts rests the main responsibility for defeating the enemy will, along with other peacefully minded nations, continue to perform their full part in solving the numerous and vexatious problems of the future. From the outset, the dominant thought at the Conference was that, after the attainment of victory, cooperation among peace-loving nations in support of certain paramount mutual interests will be almost as compelling in importance and necessity as it is today in support of the war effort.

"At the end of the war, each of the United Nations and each of the nations associated with them will have the same common interest in national security, in world order under law, in peace, in the full promotion of the political, economic, and social welfare of their respective peoples—in the principles and spirit of the Atlantic Charter and the Declaration by United Nations. The future of these indispensable common interests depends absolutely upon international cooperation. Hence, each nation's own primary interest requires it to cooperate with the others."

After discussing in detail the various achievements of the conference, beginning with the Four-Nation Declaration, the Secretary defined its significance as follows:

"Of supreme importance is the fact that at the Conference the whole spirit of international cooperation, now and after the war, was revitalized and given practical expression. The Conference thus launched a forward movement which, I am firmly convinced, will steadily extend in scope and effectiveness. Within the framework of that movement, in the atmosphere of mutual understanding and confidence which made possible its beginning in Moscow, many of the problems which are difficult today will as time goes on undoubtedly become more possible of satisfactory solution through frank and friendly discussion." [16]

THE TEHRAN AND THE TWO CAIRO CONFERENCES

At Moscow, the Secretary obtained Marshal Stalin's [16a] assent to the projected meeting with the President and Prime Minister Churchill, which it was subsequently agreed among the three heads of government should take place at Tehran. This Government had first proposed a meeting between the President and Marshal Stalin shortly after American involvement in the war. When Ambassador Standley, Mr. Harriman's predecessor, arrived in Moscow in April 1942, he had instructions to inform the Marshal of the President's desire to meet with him in order to coordinate Soviet-American efforts in

---

[16] For full text, see *Department of State Bulletin*, IX, 341–45.

[16a] He was Premier Stalin at that time; he received the title "Marshal" in March 1943.

bringing about the collapse of Germany. The Ambassador had delivered this message on April 23, but neither this nor subsequent approaches had been successful. Marshal Stalin had indicated that he regarded the military situation on the eastern front as too critical to permit his attendance at either the Casablanca Conference or the Quebec Conference. The conference that met at Tehran, November 28–December 1, 1943, was the first meeting between the President and Marshal Stalin. It was also the first of the two meetings of the heads of government of the three major powers before the German surrender.

The Tehran Conference had no such immediate effect as the Moscow Conference on the Department's preparations for the peace, nor was the influence of the work already done in this field so clearly discernible. Although at the request of the President, who wished to discuss the matter with Prime Minister Churchill, a memorandum was prepared early in November by officers from the Division of Political Studies, the two geographic divisions concerned with Europe and with the Far East, and the Geographer's Office on the question of trusteeship for certain islands in the Pacific, no other special preparations for the forthcoming discussions were made by the research staff. The Department was not represented among the advisers, most of whom were military, taken by the President to Tehran. The Secretary, however, had conferred with the President upon his return from Moscow, and en route to Tehran, the President was joined at Cairo by Ambassador Harriman and Mr. Bohlen, as interpreter, both of whom had been present at the Moscow Conference. Furthermore, as already noted, the President had been kept currently informed of the trend of the Department's thinking on postwar problems from the inception of its preparatory work.

The three heads of government explored a wide range of political and military questions in their conversations at Tehran. These discussions resulted in certain concrete military commitments, notably that to launch the Normandy invasion in May 1944, and other military offensives relating to that invasion. Marshal Stalin on his own initiative reaffirmed at this conference his intention, which he had already asked Secretary Hull at Moscow to convey to the President, that when Germany was finally defeated the Soviet Union would join in the effort against the Japanese.[17] The Marshal placed no conditions on this intention, and the fragmentary discussion of this matter was confined to mention of the possibilities of preliminary military planning.

The discussion of political questions was essentially introductory and exploratory. The three heads of government reaffirmed the principle set forth in the Four Nation Declaration of continued collabora-

[17] Cf. *Memoirs of Cordell Hull*, II, 1309.

tion among the major powers after the war. The Declaration of the Three Powers issued December 1, 1943, stated in part:

"We express our determination that our nations shall work together in war and in the peace that will follow.

.　　.　　.　　.　　.　　.　　.

"And as to peace—we are sure that our concord will win an enduring Peace. We recognize fully the supreme responsibility resting upon us and all the United Nations to make a peace which will command the goodwill of the overwhelming mass of the peoples of the world and banish the scourge and terror of war for many generations.

"With our Diplomatic advisors we have surveyed the problems of the future. We shall seek the cooperation and active participation of all nations, large and small, whose peoples in heart and mind are dedicated, as are our own peoples, to the elimination of tyranny and slavery, oppression and intolerance. We will welcome them, as they may choose to come, into a world family of Democratic Nations." [18]

The structure and character of the general international organization projected in the Four Nation Declaration was discussed in broad terms, the President stressing the desirability of a world-wide rather than a regional approach, particularly from the standpoint of American participation. The President also referred favorably on several occasions to the concept of international trusteeship already presented by Secretary Hull at the Moscow Conference. Other problems such as strategic bases, the treatment of postwar Germany, the future boundaries of Poland, and the traditional Russian desire for warm water ports were explored. These discussions were significant in that they threw light on the individual objectives of each of the participating powers and on the policies that each might be disposed to pursue, but with one exception they involved no commitments. The exception was the Declaration Regarding Iran, in which the three major powers asserted "their desire for the maintenance of the independence, sovereignty and territorial integrity of Iran" and agreed that Iran's economic problems should receive full consideration both during and after the war—concluding thus the discussion of this question that had been begun at Moscow.[19]

Before their meeting at Tehran with Marshal Stalin, the President and the Prime Minister had conferred in Cairo, November 22–26, with Generalissimo Chiang Kai-shek, and after the Tehran Conference, they returned to Cairo for discussions with President Inönü of Turkey.[20] The second of these meetings, December 4–6, involved

---

[18] *Department of State Bulletin*, IX, 409.

[19] *Ibid.*

[20] There was no representation of the Department of State as such at these Cairo meetings. Willys Peck of the Foreign Service was on the American staff as a Chinese language expert at the first.

no developments of significance to postwar problems except insofar as the conversations, in the words of the communiqué issued at their conclusion, were "most useful and most fruitful for the future of the relations" between Turkey and the United States, the United Kingdom, and the Soviet Union. The latter had joined in the invitation to hold the Conference.

The meeting with Generalissimo Chiang Kai-shek, however, which followed by almost a year the British and the American relinquishment, on January 11, 1943, of their extraterritorial rights in China, produced the agreement on war aims in the Far East announced in the tripartite statement issued on December 1, 1943. At Tehran, Marshal Stalin, on November 30, had given this statement his unqualified endorsement, although he said he could make no commitment. The definition of Anglo-Sino-American policy in the statement of December 1, which strongly influenced the Department's subsequent work on the Far Eastern peace, declared:

> "The Three Great Allies are fighting this war to restrain and punish the aggression of Japan. They covet no gain for themselves and have no thought of territorial expansion. It is their purpose that Japan shall be stripped of all the islands in the Pacific which she has seized or occupied since the beginning of the first World War in 1914, and that all the territories Japan has stolen from the Chinese, such as Manchuria, Formosa, and the Pescadores, shall be restored to the Republic of China. Japan will also be expelled from all other territories which she has taken by violence and greed. The aforesaid three great powers, mindful of the enslavement of the people of Korea, are determined that in due course Korea shall become free and independent." [21]

On his return, the President, in a radio address on December 24, emphasized the need for unity among the four major powers and their cooperation with "all the freedom-loving peoples" after the war.[22] In his annual message to Congress on January 11, 1944, he summarized the objectives and accomplishments of his recent conversations with the heads of government of the three other major Allied powers as follows:

> "When Mr. Hull went to Moscow in October, and when I went to Cairo and Tehran in November, we knew that we were in agreement with our Allies in our common determination to fight and win this war. But there were many vital questions concerning the future peace, and they were discussed in an atmosphere of complete candor and harmony.
> "In the last war such discussions, such meetings, did not even begin until the shooting had stopped and the delegates began to assemble at the peace table. There had been no previous opportunities for

---

[21] *Department of State Bulletin*, IX, 393.
[22] *Ibid.*, X, 3–7.

man-to-man discussions which lead to meetings of minds. The result was a peace which was not a peace.

"That was a mistake which we are not repeating in this war.

. . . .

"The one supreme objective for the future, which we discussed for each nation individually, and for all the United Nations, can be summed up in one word: Security.

"And that means not only physical security which provides safety from attacks by aggressors. It means also economic security, social security, moral security—in a family of nations.

"In the plain down-to-earth talks that I had with the Generalissimo and Marshal Stalin and Prime Minister Churchill, it was abundantly clear that they are all most deeply interested in the resumption of peaceful progress by their own peoples—progress toward a better life. All our Allies want freedom to develop their lands and resources, to build up industry, to increase education and individual opportunity, and to raise standards of living.

"All our Allies have learned by bitter experience that real development will not be possible if they are to be diverted from their purpose by repeated wars—or even threats of war.

"China and Russia are truly united with Britain and America in recognition of this essential fact:

"The best interests of each nation, large and small, demand that all freedom-loving nations shall join together in a just and durable system of peace. In the present world situation, evidenced by the actions of Germany, Italy and Japan, unquestioned military control over disturbers of the peace is as necessary among nations as it is among citizens in a community. And an equally basic essential to peace is a decent standard of living for all individual men and women and children in all nations. Freedom from fear is eternally linked with freedom from want." [23]

THE FIRST SESSION OF THE UNRRA COUNCIL

THE AGREEMENT for United Nations Relief and Rehabilitation Administration signed at the White House on November 9, 1943, was a product of thorough discussion both within the United States Government, including informal consultations between the Department and the Congress, and among the forty-four United and Associated Nations that eventually became the signatories of the Agreement.[24] These consultations had resulted in the modification of the draft agreement published on June 11, 1943, primarily to relieve the apprehensions of the smaller states that the organization would be dominated by the four major powers and to meet congressional de-

[23] H. Doc. 377, 78th Cong., 2d sess., serial vol. 10878.

[24] For text of this Agreement, see *First Session of the Council of the United Nations Relief and Rehabilitation Administration*, Selected Documents, Atlantic City, N. J., Nov. 10–Dec. 1, 1943, Department of State publication 2040, Conference Series 53, pp. 7–15.

sires to have provided a means of withdrawal for member states and to have assurance that the financial contributions of these states to the organization would be subject to their respective constitutional procedures.

These consultations had also resulted in a decision that both the life and the scope of the organization should be limited. There had been two definite schools of thought in the United States Government on this question throughout the period of preliminary discussion and negotiation, but the Agreement signed on November 9 made it clear that UNRRA was designed to be an emergency organization and that it would not function in the field of postwar reconstruction as such. The view that prevailed was that the problem of reconstruction should be considered in relation to the broad and long-range problems of postwar economic policy generally rather than to the more immediate and narrower problems of relief and rehabilitation. Moreover, the difficulties of obtaining appropriations on a scale and over a period that would permit an effective handling of the problem of reconstruction were recognized.

This limitation on the scope of UNRRA and its emergency character were stressed by the President in requesting, on November 15, 1943, congressional authorization of funds to permit United States participation in UNRRA.[25] The President defined the purpose of the organization as "to give first aid in the liberated areas," and its task as "to assist in furnishing the medicine, food, clothing, and other basic necessities and essential services which are required to restore the strength of the liberated peoples." The President then stated:

"UNRRA will not, of course, be expected to solve the long-range problems of reconstruction. Other machinery and other measures will be necessary for this purpose. What UNRRA can do is to lay the necessary foundation for these later tasks of reconstruction."

Secretary Hull in a letter on December 7, 1943,[26] to Chairman Bloom of the House Foreign Affairs Committee, endorsing a resolution introduced by Mr. Bloom in accordance with the President's request, recalled that the "UNRRA Agreement itself was carefully worked out after consultations with members of Congress, and especially with the Foreign Affairs and Foreign Relations Committees." He further said:

"The broad plans growing out of the Moscow Conference, which Congress has so warmly endorsed, will need the work of this great organization to ensure, in the words of the Four Nation Declaration, 'a rapid and orderly transition from war to peace' so that we may proceed to our announced purpose of 'maintaining international

---

[25] *Department of State Bulletin*, IX, 372–73.

[26] *Ibid.*, p. 416.

peace and security with the least diversion of the world's human and economic resources for armaments.'

"It is as essential to be prepared for the emergency which will follow the end of the war as it is to be prepared for the great operations which will bring the victorious peace. . . ."

The day after the UNRRA Agreement was signed, the Council provided for in the agreement convened at Atlantic City for its first session, which lasted until December 1, 1943. The preparatory work for this meeting as well as that leading to the conclusion of the agreement itself, had been primarily the responsibility of the Department of State operating through the Office of Foreign Relief and Rehabilitation Operations under Governor Lehman [27] and through an informal group under Assistant Secretary Acheson. The Division of Economic Studies had participated in this work through its chief, Mr. Stinebower, who was a member of Mr. Acheson's group and later one of the United States advisers at the Atlantic City Conference.[28] The United States was represented at the first Council meeting by Mr. Acheson, with Francis B. Sayre, Special Assistant to the Secretary of State, as alternate.

At its first session the Council, under the chairmanship of Mr. Acheson, elected Governor Lehman Director General of the new organization and provided, through a series of resolutions, for the actual establishment of the Relief and Rehabilitation Administration and laid down the broad policies and procedures to be followed in its operations. One of these resolutions (no. 12) further defined the scope of UNRRA as follows: [29]

"The task of rehabilitation must not be considered as the beginning of reconstruction—it is coterminous with relief. No new construction or reconstruction work is contemplated, but only rehabilitation as defined in the preamble of the Agreement. Problems, such as unemployment, are important, but not determining factors. They are consequences and, at the same time, motives of action. The Administration cannot be called upon to help restore continuous employment in the world."

[27] See pp. 137 and 156. By Executive Order 9380 of Sept. 25, 1943, OFRRO was absorbed into the newly established Foreign Economic Administration.

[28] The other advisers were: Mrs. Elizabeth Conkey, Commissioner of Public Welfare, Cook County, Illinois; Max Gardner, former Governor of North Carolina (who did not attend); Harold Glasser, Assistant Director of the Division of Monetary Research, Treasury Department; Roy Hendrickson, Director, Food Distribution Administration; Murray Latimer, Chairman of the Railroad Retirement Board, Assistant Director, Liberated Areas Branch of Foreign Economic Administration; Abbot Low Moffat, State Department; Dr. Thomas Parran, Surgeon General, U. S. Public Health Service; Herman Wells, State Department; Mrs. Ellen S. Woodward, Member, Social Security Board.

[29] For the text of these resolutions, see *First Session of the Council of the United Nations Relief and Rehabilitation Administration*, Department of State publication 2040, Conference Series 53, pp. 27–81.

The Congress in its joint resolution making possible United States participation in UNRRA specifically approved this statement and incorporated in the joint resolution four reservations. These related to the interpretation of "rehabilitation," UNRRA's power to incur obligations, amendment of the agreement of November 9, and the determination by the Congress of the United States contribution. The Congress limited its authorization of appropriation to June 30, 1946. The Council of UNRRA at its second session in Montreal, September 15–27, 1944, accepted the reservations laid down by the Congress.[30]

---

[30] H. J. Res. 192, 78th Cong., 2d sess., approved Mar. 28, 1944 ; 58 Stat. 122. The action taken by UNRRA was naturally silent on the time limit of June 30, 1946, this date being a matter wholly within American determination.

CHAPTER X

Organization for Advanced Preparation
January–July 1944

T HE ALLIES were moving toward victory as 1943 closed. In southern Europe, the new Government of Italy, after the signature of surrender terms early in September 1943, had entered the war against Germany on October 13. On the Eastern Front, Russian forces had advanced to the Dnieper in September and had retaken Dnepropetrovsk in October and Kiev early in November. In the Pacific some gain had been registered, in the Ellice Islands in September and in the Gilberts in November. The coming January was to find the Russians driving into prewar Poland, the Western Allies landing on the Anzio Beach in Italy, and a further victory won against the Japanese at Rabaul.

The Three Power conferences in the autumn of 1943 had resulted in two far-reaching developments. The strategic coordination of future major offensives against Germany was accomplished;[1] and a general basis of agreed objectives upon which the preparation of postwar policy could proceed toward definite recommendations was achieved. The most notable of these agreed objectives was the future establishment of a general organization for international peace and security, but international discussion had also been started on the treatment of enemy states, fundamental economic problems, and other aspects of postwar international relations. In addition, machinery for further joint consideration of some postwar problems had been agreed upon—the European Advisory Commission and the Advisory Council for Italy agreed upon at the Moscow Conference—and the practice of Great Power discussions and meetings was established.

The changing situation suggested by these developments was reflected in the Department's preparation for the peace, which had passed in this period from the exploration and analysis of postwar problems into an intermediate stage in which main lines of action were clarified and major negotiations undertaken along some of these lines. By the end of 1943, the preparation was no longer confined largely to

---

[1] Department of State press release 240, Mar. 24, 1947.

the Advisory Committee and the research staff. It had become an effort involving many operating units of the Department, interdepartmental collaboration, consultations with the Congress and the President, increased public discussion, negotiations among the major powers, and exchanges of view with other United Nations looking toward the establishment of international agencies of both a transitional and permanent character in various specialized fields.

These developments pointed in the main, despite the varying rates of progress possible or desirable in the case of the different problems concerned, to the imminent arrival of the stage of final recommendations, decision, and action. The need for adjustments to meet the requirements of this stage of advanced preparation was influential among the reasons for the Departmental reorganization put into effect by Secretary Hull on January 15, 1944, better to adapt "the administrative framework of the Department to meet the constantly changing war situation and the foreseeable postwar demands upon our foreign policy." [2] The reorganization marked the close of the two-year period during which the postwar preparation had rested structurally on the Advisory Committee and had depended for its financial support almost wholly upon the President's Emergency Fund. Much that had distinguished the approach, method, and structure of that Committee and its subcommittees and research staff now entered into the "regular" organization of the Department.

THE POLICY AND POST-WAR PROGRAMS COMMITTEES

Two HIGH-LEVEL policy committees were established under the reorganization, distinguished not by superiority of one over the other but by their different purposes. The Policy Committee was to assist the Secretary of State in considering major questions of foreign policy and was therefore to concentrate on current questions. The Post-War Programs Committee was to give him assistance in formulating postwar policies and in making the appropriate international arrangements for their execution.

Secretary Hull was Chairman, and Under Secretary Stettinius Vice Chairman of both Committees. In their absence, Assistant Secretary Berle or one of the other Assistant Secretaries presided, in order of precedence. To a substantial extent, the two Committees had a common membership: the Assistant Secretaries, the Legal Adviser, the Special Assistants to the Secretary, and *ex officio*, the Directors of the twelve Offices that were created on January 15. Isaiah Bowman, Norman H. Davis, and Myron C. Taylor of the Informal Political Agenda

---

[2] Departmental Order 1218, *Department of State Bulletin*, X, 45–67. This reorganization is not to be confused with that brought about by Mr. Stettinius at the close of 1944.

Group and the Secretary's "consulting group" were members of the Post-War Programs Committee, and not infrequently also attended Policy Committee meetings, particularly when these meetings were held immediately before those of the Post-War Programs Committee. Limited attendance of alternates to the Directors of the twelve Offices was permitted from the start in the Post-War Programs Committee, and from the third meeting in the case of the Policy Committee. Directors who had originally attended continued in certain instances to participate after transferring to some other position. One or more specialists from the Divisions interested in the problems under consideration customarily briefed the Committee on behalf of the country, area, economic, or other interdivisional committee that had prepared the papers being discussed and took part in that discussion as experts. A total of approximately seventy officers thus appeared at one or more meetings of each Committee.

The Policy Committee held ninety-one meetings, January 19–November 29, 1944, inclusive. It met Monday and Wednesday, 9 to 10 a. m., and Friday 9 to 9 : 15 a. m. before the meeting of the Post-War Programs Committee. Visiting ambassadors or Foreign Service officers back from their field posts often joined in these meetings.[3] The Executive Secretary was Charles W. Yost, who was assisted by a small secretariat to maintain minutes, distribute documents, send summaries to United States Missions abroad, and in some matters follow up the decisions taken.

The Post-War Programs Committee held sixty-six meetings, ending November 17, 1944, for sixty of which minutes were issued.[4] It was

---

[3] The membership and attendance of the Policy Committee, aside from visiting ambassadors and invited experts, were Secretary Hull (14) ; Under Secretary Stettinius (64) ; Assistant Secretaries Berle (71), Long (78), Acheson (70), and Shaw (69) ; Legal Adviser Hackworth (71) ; Special Assistant Pasvolsky (63) ; Special Assistant Joseph C. Green (49) ; Special Assistant Maxwell M. Hamilton (6) ; Assistant to the Secretary Charles E. Bohlen (8) ; and Office Directors *ex officio* : John Dickey (63) ; Laurence Duggan (50) succeeded by Norman Armour (17), Philip Bonsal, alternate (5), Joseph McGurk, alternate (6) ; James C. Dunn (64), H. Freeman Matthews, alternate (10), John D. Hickerson, alternate (5) ; Stanley K. Hornbeck (82), and later Joseph C. Grew (45), Joseph Ballantine, alternate (7) ; Wallace Murray (61), Paul Alling, alternate (27) ; John G. Erhardt (25) ; Harry C. Hawkins (49) and later Bernard F. Haley (16), Leroy D. Stinebower, alternate for each (34) ; John C. Ross (15) ; Charles P. Taft (85) ; Edwin C. Wilson (21), alternate Harley Notter (20) and later Alger Hiss (17) ; and General Consultant Carlton Savage (51). Experts frequently attending included Cavendish W. Cannon (8), Durward V. Sandifer (12), and George L. Warren (14).

Isaiah Bowman participated in eight meetings, Norman H. Davis in three, and Myron C. Taylor in eleven.

[4] One organizing and sixty-six substantive meetings were noted in the record, but the 11th was combined with that of the Policy Committee, the 13th was canceled, and minutes were not distributed for five meetings.

constituted of the following, the number of these sixty meetings attended being indicated after each name: Secretary Hull (15) ; Under Secretary Stettinius (31) ; Myron C. Taylor (16) ; Isaiah Bowman (18) ; Norman H. Davis (1) ; Assistant Secretaries Berle (41), Long (55), Acheson (44), Shaw (40) ; Legal Adviser Hackworth (44) ; Special Assistant and Executive Director of the Committee Pasvolsky (48) ; Special Assistant Joseph C. Green (45) ; Special Assistant Maxwell M. Hamilton (2) ; Special Assistant Michael J. McDermott (40) ; Assistant to the Secretary Charles E. Bohlen (2) ; and Office Directors: John S. Dickey (33) ; Laurence Duggan (34) succeeded by Norman Armour (3), Philip Bonsal, alternate (1), Joseph McGurk, alternate (5) ; James C. Dunn (37), H. Freeman Matthews, alternate (7), John D. Hickerson, alternate (8) ; Wallace Murray (22), Paul H. Alling, alternate (21), George V. Allen, alternate (5) ; John G. Erhardt (7), Nathaniel P. Davis, alternate (1) ; Harry C. Hawkins (32), Bernard F. Haley (7) and Leroy D. Stinebower, alternate for each (43) ; Stanley K. Hornbeck (58), Joseph C. Grew (30), and Joseph Ballantine, alternate for each (36) ; John C. Ross (4), Robert E. Ward, alternate (1), Robert J. Ryan, alternate (1) ; Charles P. Taft (52) ; Edwin C. Wilson (7), Harley Notter, alternate (33) and Alger Hiss, alternate (16) ; and General Consultant Carlton Savage (47). The experts from the research staff most frequently attending included George H. Blakeslee (9), David Harris (20), Philip E. Mosely (28), and Durward V. Sandifer (15), with many others attending a few times. Experts from operating Divisions frequently attended one or more meetings on subjects in their fields.

The Post-War Programs Committee convened February 1, having delayed its first meeting until a small professional secretariat could be assembled and a long-range agenda and special documentation for the early meetings prepared. This agenda of twenty-six problem fields was endorsed by the President.[5] The Committee suspended meetings during the period of the Dumbarton Oaks Conversations, but otherwise it averaged over its ten active months approximately two meetings a week, Friday at 9 :15 a. m. and Thursday at 9 a. m., with some meetings on other mornings. The meetings lasted up to two hours and occasionally longer.

The secretariat of the Post-War Programs Committee, unlike that of the Policy Committee, was by intention entirely a professional body, with initiatory as well as executive duties similar to those of the research staff in its comparable work under the previous preparatory structure. The institution of a central or executive secretariat, which hereafter became a fixed part of subsequent Departmental or-

---

[5] For the list of fields, see appendix 31.

ganization, was thus derived structurally from the type of secretariat functions developed by the research staff of the Advisory Committee.

The Executive Director of the Post-War Programs Committee, Mr. Pasvolsky, was vested with "full authority under the Secretary to organize the Committee's work and to call upon the various Offices and Divisions of the Department for such assistance as may be required in carrying out the Committee's responsibilities." Serving under Mr. Pasvolsky were two executive secretaries: Mr. Rothwell in the political field and John H. Fuqua in the economic field. They were assisted by William A. Brown, Jr., Robert W. Hartley, Miss Ruth Russell, Wells Stabler, Miss Carmel Sullivan, and later Miss Edna Fluegel. All but two of these officers had been members of the research staff or had previously been assigned to Mr. Pasvolsky's office. Moreover, in the work of both the Post-War Programs Committee and the Policy Committee, the techniques already developed by the research staff of the Advisory Committee were carried over and further elaborated. The use of background papers, problem analyses, and policy summaries as developed by the research staff became widely disseminated throughout the Department beginning with this absorption into Departmental organization of the Advisory Committee and its procedures.

The two superior Committees undertook to provide central coordination of all postwar preparation, the refinement and approval of recommendations, and the rendering of decisions within the jurisdiction of their highest officials. They were the principal instrumentalities under the Secretary for formulating foreign policy to meet the problems that pressed for decision in 1944 as the war effort drove month by month nearer victory. They represented also a new basis of organization for the Department, evolved in the light of its expanding responsibilities as the range of international relations of probable concern to the United States as a world power widened.

Although the work of the Post-War Programs Committee was longer-range than that of the Policy Committee, the former Committee, in practice, functioned under a no less urgent demand for decision than the latter, since many postwar problems were swiftly becoming current problems either for negotiation or for action in areas already or about to be liberated by the Allies. That the current and postwar aspects of foreign policy were converging could be seen in the early request of the Policy Committee for an analysis and statement of the principles and concepts governing the present war aims and probable future objectives of each of the Great Powers, and in the early decision of the Post-War Programs Committee to give priority to policies and programs affecting current operations. On occasion, consequently, the separateness of the two Committees became indistinct. As time passed and urgency increased, the two Committees frequently convened as one, devoting the first few minutes of their meeting to immediate matters that were pressing. Whether or not the two convened together, however, meetings began with a briefing by the Chairman and sometimes by additional members on current developments in international relations and the progress of the war in all theaters.

The recommendations and principal instructions to the United States representative on the European Advisory Commission were cleared by the Post-War Programs Committee. This Committee also formulated in final form the policy instructions for United States representatives at the growing number of international conferences and discussions being held or projected in special fields and for the State Department representatives on interdepartmental committees. *Ad hoc* decisions sometimes appeared necessary in some foreign-policy fields before consideration of general policy could be completed, such decisions being taken by the Post-War Programs Committee and elsewhere in the Department of State, and also, where military and naval operations were concerned, by the Departments of War and the Navy, all working against time. These *ad hoc* decisions added to the complexities inherent in the problems faced and to the urgency for consideration of all the Committee's twenty-six fields of work.

By July 27, 1944, the Post-War Programs Committee had considered policy papers in each of the twenty-six fields, and policy had been tentatively formulated in each. In addition, general policy papers on territorial settlements and detailed policy papers on military government for Japan and on displaced persons of foreign nationality in Germany were under study. Negotiating documents had been approved in several fields, including those to be used in the Dumbarton Oaks Conversations on general international organization. Two hundred and seventy documents, of which one hundred and eighty-nine were major policy papers, had been acted upon. The entire policy-formulating and policy-reviewing machinery of the Government had been brought into play at one stage or another. The preparatory work for this Committee engaged ten of the twelve Offices, twenty-four Divisions, the interdivisional country and area committees, an interdepartmental working committee on security, the economic committees, the committee and staff on international organization and security, and interdepartmental consultation on many aspects of the problems involved.

During the period of the Dumbarton Oaks Conversations, the secretariat of the Post-War Programs Committee prepared, in the form of a report to the Secretary of State, a complete record of American postwar policy thus formulated and of the status of the relevant negotiations. The Secretary's "black book" of current foreign policy has been compiled periodically ever since as a standing practice in the Department.

AN "ADVISORY COUNCIL ON POST-WAR FOREIGN POLICY"

AN ADVISORY group in connection with the foregoing superior Committees was contemplated at the time of the reorganization as a related part of the new policy structure. An "Advisory Council on Post-War Foreign Policy" was projected to succeed the Advisory Committee—which was still suspended, not abolished. Much thought had been given this matter in the autumn of 1943 by the Informal Agenda Group; a decision to establish it was made by January 15, 1944; and further attention was at once given it by the Post-War Programs Committee at its earliest meetings in February 1944.

The proposed "Advisory Council" was initially envisaged as a large nonpartisan group to be consulted on major questions of postwar foreign policy. It was to be composed of a number of representatives of influential public organizations, Members of Congress and the Cabinet, ranking officials of the Department, and certain additional highly qualified citizens. Subsequently, particular thought was given to having its congressional and noncongressional members meet separately, since their responsibilities were different and there would be special need for consultation with the congressional members on a more specific basis as plans and events developed. It was thought that the group would not be asked in its meetings, to be held once or twice a month, to make formal recommendations or decisions, but rather that it would be informed on problems through the Department's explanation of developments and invited to give the Secretary of State the benefit of its discussion and advice. The group would, in turn, keep the organizations represented informed on these problems, except where secrecy was for the time being necessary.

The conception of the new body projected at this advanced stage of the preparation thus differed from that underlying the Advisory Committee in several respects. The Council was to be a related part of a large policy-formulating structure within the Department and between Departments and not itself the superior organization. It was to advise on the basis of papers and policies placed before it for consideration and advice, not to originate its own agenda and proposals. Its members, except those from Congress and Departmental officials, were to be primarily representative of particular public organizations, rather than persons invited from the general public to participate on the basis principally of their personal experience and other special qualifications. Representativeness was already tending, as has been observed above, to become the basis for participation in the Advisory Committee as its work developed, shown not only in the congressional membership of this Committee but, especially during 1943, in the composition of the Taylor Committee and its special committees.   Since, in the new final stage of preparation, competence to interpret and to inform public opinion and to enlist public cooperation in the guidance of postwar policy had become a major need, representation in the proposed new Council of the organizations active in American public life appeared best adapted to meet this need.   This need was not to be preclusive; there was to be some membership not of representative character.

The decision to institute the Advisory Council had been made in connection with the Departmental reorganization, and it also was announced on January 15, 1944.[6] This was before the completion of detailed plans for the Council's membership and functioning. The announcement stated:

> "The Secretary of State has also established an Advisory Council on Post War Foreign Policy and so far has designated Mr. Norman H. Davis, Mr. Myron C. Taylor, and Dr. Isaiah Bowman as Vice Chairmen of this new Council, which will be under his Chairmanship with the Under Secretary as his deputy. The Secretary has asked Mr. Davis, Mr. Taylor and Dr. Bowman, who with others have been associated with him in this field for the past two years, to assist him in organizing and carrying forward the work of this Council which will bring together outstanding and representative national leaders to advise the Secretary on post-war foreign-policy matters of major importance." [7]

It was expected that the list of other participants would also be published, which demanded that the greatest care be used in selecting the organizations to be represented in order to avoid giving justified offense to those omitted. The difficulties of arranging truly "representative" membership for the large Council envisaged and the harassing pressure of the daily demands upon the Secretary personally and on the Department as a whole hampered the conclusion of the remaining plans. Nevertheless, a tentative plan for the public membership was completed on February 11 and submitted to the President. It was reported on February 18 that, thinking revision necessary, the President would present to the Department an amended list of the proposed members. When this was received, it appeared that extensive changes and enlargement of the membership would be involved. Although further steps in the matter were repeatedly discussed in the Department, with particular reference to the shortening of the long membership list in the interest of effective participation by the members, the project continued in abeyance for some weeks.

---

[6] *Department of State Bulletin*, X, 43.

[7] Subsequently Mr. Pasvolsky and Robert W. Hartley were designated within the Department to be its Director and Executive Secretary, respectively.

As time passed and the rapidity of developments increased during the spring, further effort in the direction of an "Advisory Council" was regarded as less and less timely. The project was abandoned May 22, 1944. However, the abandonment was of the form rather than of the substance. As will be seen, the projected congressional consultations were inaugurated by Secretary Hull informally during March 1944. Consultations between the Secretary and leaders of various national organizations in that summer and autumn, and the off-the-record discussions undertaken throughout the country in the closing months of the year, to a degree carried out the original aim of the project to inform the public and to obtain its thought, primarily but not exclusively, on the problems of postwar general international organization. Furthermore, the Department's thinking on the entire matter and the several suggested lists of participants in the projected Council were used during the following year when forty-two national organizations were invited by the Secretary of State to serve as consultants to the American Delegation at the San Francisco Conference.[8]

REORGANIZATION OF THE STAFF

THE REORGANIZATION of the staff on January 15, 1944, reflected similarly the course of events and the resulting rapid movement of the preparation of postwar policy toward final recommendations, negotiations, and subsequent operations. In most of the fields of research, the stage of concentration upon "studies" had passed; in the remainder, it was passing, giving way to the drafting of proposals and recommendations. Consequently, when the Departmental reorganization introduced the new structural unit of operational "Offices," within which all divisions would be grouped, a major adjustment in the organization of the staff was required. This adjustment was not completed at one step, however, because the original concept of a "research staff" no longer applied equally in the political and economic fields, and within the political it remained more applicable to the territorial than to the international security and organization aspects of the work.[9]

The political work was organized within a new Office of Special Political Affairs, created as one of the five new Offices charged with responsibility for political foreign policy and relations under the high-ranking officials of the Department. James C. Dunn was its

---

[8] Members of public organizations in fields of labor, business, and farming were among the advisers on the Delegation to the Inter-American Conference on Problems of War and Peace, at Mexico City, Feb. 21–Mar. 8, 1945, but this was not unique in American practice and, though influenced by it, did not stem primarily from the above project.

[9] For listing and assignment of staff under the reorganization, see appendix 32.

Acting Director [10] until Ambassador Edwin C. Wilson assumed the directorship on May 8, 1944. Alger Hiss was appointed Special Assistant to the Director late in April. The new Office contained two divisions, created out of the Division of Political Studies, which was abolished. These units were all of "regular" Departmental status, functioning from this time forward wholly within the Department's budget.

The Division of International Security and Organization was established to initiate and coordinate policy and action pertaining to "general and regional international peace and security arrangements and other arrangements for organized international cooperation," liaison with international organizations on these matters, and "liaison within the scope of its responsibility with the War and Navy Departments" and other Departments concerned. Studies were of course continued under this mandate, but they were now amalgamated with new operational functions. Mr. Notter was named Chief of this Division and Messrs. Sandifer, Rothwell,[11] and Gerig, Assistant Chiefs. All of these were members of the former research staff. The work of this Division was to develop through subsequent years and further organizational adjustments.

In the case of the second of the two divisions, the Division of Territorial Studies, the concept of the "research staff" was maintained, but on an obviously temporary basis although not expressly so stipulated. This Division was charged with analyzing and appraising developments and conditions in foreign countries "arising out of the war and relating to post-war settlements of interest to the United States;" with formulating "policy recommendations in regard to these matters in collaboration with other divisions in the department;" and with maintaining liaison with other Departments and agencies of the Government. Its Chief, Mr. Philip Mosely, and Assistant Chiefs, Mr. Harris and Mr. Ireland, were likewise from the preceding Division of Political Studies.

These two Divisions reported to the Office of Special Political Affairs which in turn reported to Under Secretary Stettinius and Secretary Hull. However, Mr. Pasvolsky, as Special Assistant to the Secretary of State, continued in charge of the substantive preparation with regard to international organization and security, on which his work was concentrated at the Secretary's request. He also, as Executive Director of the Post-War Programs Committee, super-

---

[10] Mr. Dunn was Director of the Office of European Affairs.

[11] Mr. Rothwell served only briefly in this capacity, since he was almost immediately designated one of the two executive secretaries of the Post-War Programs Committee.

vised the arrangements for the further preparation made on territorial problems until completion of their consideration by that Committee during 1944. Responsibility for substantive preparation on these latter problems was vested in the Directors of the four geographic Offices, Mr. Dunn being the senior among them.

It was the economic research staff that was most fully absorbed into Departmental operations by the reorganization. The Division of Economic Studies was abolished, and most of its personnel were transferred either to the new Office of Economic Affairs and its several divisions, the new Office of Transportation and Communications, or to the divisions of the Office of Wartime Economic Affairs, where such further research as was required was geared to current or developing operations. These Offices were organized on the basis of the same distinction between long-run and short-run problems that had determined the structure for the previous economic preparation both in the Committees and the research. The remaining personnel of the economic staff were placed in the Division of Territorial Studies, which now undertook combined political and economic research.

Certain former joint services developed by the research staff as essential to its work and not provided elsewhere in the Department between 1942 and 1944 became the nucleus of new divisions and offices created for wider Departmental use or were absorbed in expanding established lines of work. Some of the committee service and documentary work was transferred to the secretariat of the Post-War Programs Committee. Transfer of the biographic analysis work concerned with foreign groups began, but was not concluded at this time. Remaining services were continued in the Office of Special Political Affairs.

These structural changes in regard to the research staff that had served the Advisory Committee and the Department in the initial years of the preparation were but a part of the reorganization, which as a whole constituted a Department-wide adjustment to new conditions and was necessitated by the expanding scope of foreign policy and the increasing participation of the United States in world affairs. The establishment of such Divisions as, for example, those on Labor Relations, Liberated Areas, and Supply and Resources indicated the effects by the start of 1944 of this broad development.

Two further organizational adjustments in the early months of 1944 were of particular significance to the preparation. The first concerned interdepartmental structures in the economic field; the second involved a new process of arriving at integrated recommendation within the adjusted structure for final preparation.

EXECUTIVE COMMITTEE ON ECONOMIC FOREIGN POLICY

AFTER THE Departmental reorganization of January 15, 1944, recommendations from the twelve special interdepartmental economic committees came before the new Policy and Post-War Programs Committees for a period of approximately four months. Simultaneously, a proposal for a superior permanent interdepartmental economic committee was being considered by both Committees. This consideration, it will be recalled, had been begun the previous autumn in the economic coordination committee headed by Myron C. Taylor. The specific proposal from which action resulted took the form of a draft letter for the President's approval and signature, to be addressed by him to the Secretary of State.

This draft was circulated in the Post-War Programs Committee on February 4, and the proposal it advanced, after several revisions and refinement through consultations within the Government, was approved by the President. The following letter was then sent to Secretary Hull under the date of April 5, 1944, similar letters being sent to the heads of the other Departments and agencies of the Government named therein:

"MY DEAR MR. SECRETARY:

"As the final military victory of the United Nations draws closer, the United States is increasingly faced with difficult and complex problems in the foreign economic field. In day to day operations we are of necessity making decisions which importantly affect future foreign relations. We should, therefore, be formulating adequate policies for the period ahead in order that our daily decisions may be consistent with long range objectives.

"The principal responsibility in the Executive branch for the determination of policy in relation to international problems devolves, of course, upon the Department of State. Yet the subject matter of specific policies is frequently of proper concern to other Departments as they administer laws in their respective fields. Moreover, many departmental policies although conceived in terms of domestic needs inevitably affect our foreign relations. Consequently, economic foreign policy should be developed with the assistance of other departments.

"Much interdepartmental work is already being carried on in certain areas of economic foreign policy but it seems to me that it is desirable to have an interdepartmental committee properly to relate the many segments.

"I am therefore asking the following agencies to designate a member for an Executive Committee on Economic Foreign Policy: the Department of State, the Department of the Treasury, the Department of Agriculture, the Department of Commerce, the Department of Labor, the United States Tariff Commission, and the Foreign Economic Administration. The Chairman will be appointed by the Secretary of State. From time to time representatives of other departments and agencies should be invited to participate on the Committee, or its subcommittees when matters of special interest to them are under consideration. The members should be in a position to ascertain and express the views of their respective departments and agencies and they should be able to give adequate attention to this important work.

"The function of the Executive Committee on Economic Foreign Policy will be to examine problems and developments affecting the economic foreign policy of the United States and to formulate recommendations in regard thereto for the consideration of the Secretary of State, and, in appropriate cases, of the President.

"It is my expectation that major interdepartmental committees concerned with foreign economic affairs including those established in the Department of State will be appropriately geared into this Committee.

"I attach the utmost importance to this committee and I trust that you will forthwith call its members together in order that its work may begin without delay.

"Sincerely yours,

FRANKLIN D. ROOSEVELT"

The new committee convened on April 18, 1944, and still functions. With its establishment, the work in the economic field of the Advisory Committee on Post-War Foreign Policy, which had been instituted on February 12, 1942, was merged into regular operations. An extraordinary mechanism in this field thus became a continuing structure within the Government.

The initial membership of the Executive Committee on Economic Foreign Policy was Messrs. Acheson, Chairman, and Hawkins, Vice Chairman,[12] State Department; White, Treasury Department; Wheeler, Department of Agriculture; Amos E. Taylor, Commerce Department; Oscar B. Ryder, Tariff Commission; Lauchlin Currie, Foreign Economic Administration; and A. F. Hinrichs, Labor Department. The original secretariat, provided by the State Department, included Robert M. Carr, Executive Secretary; Miss Eleanor E. Dennison, research secretary; James Q. Reber, recording secretary; and Miss Amelia D. Stone, administrative secretary.

This Committee undertook in its weekly meetings to develop subordinate machinery for its work and to establish the requisite relationships with existing committees in the economic field. In so doing, it altered or abolished certain of the special committees and converted several of the surviving ones into subcommittees of itself. The special committees on shipping, aviation, and telecommunications, however, retained for certain organizational reasons the relatively independent status that in fact they had under the Taylor Committee, maintaining liaison primarily by the exchange of documentation through their separate secretaries.

The Executive Committee on Economic Foreign Policy did not

---

[12] Later succeeded by Bernard F. Haley of the Department.

directly contribute to the preparatory work for general international organization, which was continuing in the State Department during the spring and summer of 1944 and which included provision for international economic cooperation and organization. It became actively concerned in this matter, however, and particularly with specialized international economic and social organization, late in 1944 following the Dumbarton Oaks Conversations, as will be described in due course.

PROCESSES OF INTEGRATED RECOMMENDATION

THE RECOMMENDATIONS on postwar problems placed before the Post-War Programs Committee and, where appropriate, the Policy Committee and the Executive Committee on Economic Foreign Policy were produced within the framework of the Departmental and interdepartmental structure at the working level already described, supplemented by new organized relationships between the Departments of State, War, and the Navy and by new committees and groups within the State Department. The processes of arriving at integrated recommendation varied in the several fields.

Territorial Problems

In the field of territorial problems, the interdivisional country and area committees provided the mechanism through which the recommended policies or positions were formulated. The charge laid upon the Division of Territorial Studies in the reorganization—to formulate recommendations on these problems in collaboration with other divisions—placed the initiatory and drafting responsibilities upon it. Accordingly, the substantive views advanced were worked out in cooperation with the interested divisions, including the geographic and economic divisions and, in many instances, the Division of International Security and Organization. This process was accomplished chiefly through the existing interdivisional committees and others created as necessary, with additional direct consultation between the officers especially concerned on given problems. Coordination of views between committees was frequently necessary. Sometimes this involved formal requests for an opinion, but usually it was accomplished through the circulation of papers and direct consultation among the interested officers, the Post-War Programs Committee secretariat making sure that the necessary coordination was undertaken.

Such work was entirely at an expert level, and was relatively little affected by the Departmental reorganization. In the case of the Division of Territorial Studies, the reorganization had basically meant only that the territorial branch of the former Division of Political Studies had acquired divisional status. It had retained most of its officers, and the additions to its staff came mostly from the associated former Division of Economic Studies. Similar development of branches into divisions had occurred in the related geographic and economic offices that were established.

To the existing country and area committees, there were added early in 1944 two country committees, one on Burma with Mr. Ireland as Chairman, and one on Finland with Mr. Howard as Chairman, and two area committees, on Scandinavia and on the British Commonwealth, with Robert K. Gooch serving as Chairman of both. These were followed in May by the inauguration of a Country Committee on Italy with Mr. Harris as Chairman. In September a Near East Area Committee replaced the Committee on the Arab Countries, Mr. Ireland continuing to serve as Chairman. These committees utilized *ad hoc* subsidiary drafting groups or subcommittees, but as a rule did not set up formal subcommittees. The principal exceptions to this rule were two: the Latin American Area Committee, which had a subcommittee on countries with Arthur Whitaker as Chairman and another on international security and organization with John M. Cabot, an officer of the Office of American Republic Affairs, as Chairman; and the older Committee on Problems of Dependent Areas, which for a time had nine subcommittees dealing with such phases of its work as regional commissions, trusteeship, a declaration of principles, and questions arising out of existing treaties. Like those established earlier, the new committees were authorized groupings of divisional experts, with their chairmen and secretaries drawn mainly from the Division of Territorial Studies and their drafting duties entrusted mainly to its experts. The frequency of meetings varied among these committees, the Far East Area Committee meeting most often: 221 times before the close of hostilities with Japan.

A report compiled in April 1944 showed that 264 papers had been cleared by the area and country committees, ranging from one submitted by the Committee on Finland to seventy submitted by the Committee on Germany. These figures reflected both the backlog of documents ready when the Post-War Programs and Policy Committees were established and the intense work entailed when these Committees were each meeting twice a week, and sometimes more often, in order to arrive at definite recommendations and decisions so far as international circumstances required or permitted. The papers produced were by no means all presented to the Post-War Programs Committee or to the Policy Committee during their period of activity. Papers not submitted were naturally those involving matters not yet urgently in need of decision, or of a background character, and repre-

sented work initiated by the experts as possibly required or desirable
for the completion of the preparation.

Economic Problems

The process of arriving at integrated recommendations was most
complex in the case of economic foreign policy problems. These, with
two principal exceptions, were considered on an interdepartmental
basis, primary authority for policy decision, however, remaining in
the Department of State.

One exception concerned economic territorial problems, which were
handled by the country and area committees within the Department.
Economists, as already noted, took part in these committees. The
other involved the problems of over-all economic organization, to consider which an interdivisional committee at the expert level was
established in March 1944. This committee was composed of Messrs.
Pasvolsky, Chairman; Charles P. Taft, Director of the Office of Wartime Economic Affairs; Harry C. Hawkins, who had become Director
of the Office of Economic Affairs; Leroy D. Stinebower, Adviser in
the latter Office; Bernard F. Haley, Chief of the newly established
Commodities Division; Warren Kelchner; Harley Notter; Benjamin
Gerig; John Fuqua; and Miss Ruth Russell. This committee functioned during the spring of 1944 within the Department's preparatory
structure, its work being absorbed in June by the Group preparing for
the Dumbarton Oaks Conversations. The new committee was specifically concerned with preparations for the possible establishment of
the international commission of technical experts in the economic field
proposed by Secretary Hull at the Moscow Conference and for a possible general economic conference to be held at an early date. It was also
concerned with the formulation of proposals for permanent economic
organization to accompany those being developed in the political field
for the maintenance of peace and security.

In certain other lines of activity, both interdepartmental and intradepartmental arrangements prevailed as exceptions to the rule in this
field during 1944. The handling of problems arising in connection
with the work of the Interim Commission on Food and Agriculture
and with the preparations for the scheduled ILO conference was such
an instance. This work was interdepartmental, but the Department's
position on certain aspects of these problems, particularly on questions
of organization, was being defined through the two *ad hoc* interdivisional groups described earlier.[13] The interdivisional Committee
on Reparation, Restitution, and Property Rights constituted a
further exception; it was wholly intradepartmental and reported to
the Post-War Programs Committee. The results of its work, how-

---

[13] See pp. 184–85.

ever, were ultimately submitted to the Executive Committee on Economic Foreign Policy for review. This interdivisional committee, under the chairmanship of Paul T. Ellsworth from the Division of Economic Studies (later of the Division of Financial and Monetary Affairs), was established in November 1943 and continued throughout 1944. It had six subcommittees considering, respectively, reparations as related to the preservation of peace, compensation for losses, a viable plan for postwar Germany, the peace settlement and development of a system of international economic relations, the liability of Germany, and restitution and replacement of property. It was kept apprised of all interdepartmental work of related concern and informed of the views of interested Departments and agencies. Much of its work was designed to meet the needs of American participation on the European Advisory Commission.

All of the interdivisional committees mentioned above were small, the last being the largest. The representation on these committees was mainly on a technical level and their recommendations were submitted for the review and concurrence of the chiefs of those divisions whose officers participated and by them on the most important matters to their office directors. In frequent practice, however, authority was delegated to the members of the committees to speak finally for their divisions or offices at their own discretion. In such instances, prior consultation with their superiors on the issues involved, with referral to them only if the committee recommendations varied from views strongly held by the superiors, was undertaken by the attending members. Thus, in general practice, interdivisional committee recommendations passed directly from such committees of experts to the Post-War Programs Committee or to the Policy Committee, depending on whether the problem concerned had reached the action stage.

Decisions on follow-up recommendations in connection with matters on which basic policy had already been decided were made by operating officials if no question of important change in policy was involved. Finally, an interdivisional committee, after being apprised of a policy decision, completed any additional preparation necessitated by the decision, and then submitted its further recommendations, proceeding in this manner progressively to cover its entire field. Requests for papers were also occasionally addressed to such groups by one or the other of the two superior Committees, and these papers passed directly to the superior Committee concerned. The participating experts formed the corps from which, at the negotiating stage, advisers or technical experts were selected to assist the United States delegates or representatives.

The interdepartmental economic committees concerned in the preparation were of two types. The first was comprised of the subcommittees of the Executive Committee on Economic Foreign Policy

(ECEFP). On September 25, 1944, these numbered seven, most of which were partly and some of which were wholly concerned with post-war policy. These subcommittees, with their chairmen, were Relaxation of Trade Barriers, William A. Fowler (State) ; Private Monopolies and Cartels, Edward S. Mason (Office of Strategic Services) ; Commodity Agreements and Methods of Trade, Lynn R. Edminster (Tariff Commission) ; Inter-American Economic Development, Arthur Paul (Foreign Economic Administration) ; Wartime Trade Controls, Courtney C. Brown (State) ; Wool, Leslie A. Wheeler (Agriculture) ; and the Recommendations of the West Indian Conference, Otis Mulliken (State). The second type of interdepartmental committee was comprised of the continuing special committees and other specialized bodies, all maintaining liaison with ECEFP. As of the same date, these, with their chairmen, were the Committees on Shipping, Aviation, Communications, Mr. Berle being Chairman of each; Trade Agreements, Mr. Fowler (State) ; Labor Standards and Social Security, Miss Frances Perkins (Labor) ; Inter-American Post-War Economic Policy, Frank A. Waring (Office of Coordinator of Inter-American Affairs) ; Migration and Resettlement, H. F. Arthur Schoenfeld (State) ; Liberated Areas, Dean Acheson (State) ; and the Stabilization Fund and the Reconstruction and Development Bank, Harry D. White (Treasury).

The recommendations of the interdepartmental committees responsible to the Executive Committee on Economic Foreign Policy were submitted to it for review and approval, the views of the State Department being conveyed through its experts on the committees formulating the recommendations and, at the policy level, through the chairman of the Executive Committee. The decisions were then communicated to the participating Departments and agencies and, depending on the magnitude of the problem, the degree of agreement on a recommendation, or its relation to other major matters pending decision, were also on occasion referred for decision at a Cabinet level or directly to the President. The recommendations of the other interdepartmental committees were referred either to the ECEFP or to the heads of the participating Departments or agencies, with the same process of referral when necessary for decision at the highest levels, depending again on the problem and its relationship to other matters pending. Officers representing the State Department on these committees normally obtained guidance or instructions, both in regard to long-range and to current recommendations being formulated in the committees, from the Post-War Programs or Policy Committees, and otherwise from the Secretary or Under Secretary.

Problems of Security

The consideration of international security problems tended after the Moscow Conference to separate along three lines. One related to the security aspects of territorial problems. The intensive preparation already made in this field under the Advisory Committee and its subcommittees provided the basic policy views to guide the interdivisional committees. On further studies and development of views, there was direct consultation between experts in the Department and the corresponding experts in the War and Navy Departments. There was no special instrumentality established for this phase of the substantive work.

The second line was the preparation required in connection with the functions of the United States representative on the European Advisory Commission, sitting in London to consider problems relating to the termination of hostilities in Europe. To meet this need, a Working Security Committee was established on December 21, 1943, for interdepartmental formulation and clearance of instructions to the United States representative. The membership of this interdepartmental committee reflected, at an expert level, the responsibilities of the Department of State for territorial, economic, and political questions of foreign policy and the multiple responsibilities of the War and Navy Departments in connection with the administration of occupied enemy territories and related military problems affecting foreign policy.

In this instance, representation was again on the basis of interested divisions and offices. Alternates to the persons actually named as members were frequently the participants in the meetings held. This practice was followed for prolonged periods in some cases, since 1944 was a year in which certain officials were under extreme pressure of work. Thus it was not usually possible for Mr. Dunn to serve as Chairman, and his alternate, James Riddleberger, Chief of the Division of Central European Affairs, presided at most meetings. Donald Blaisdell usually attended in place of Mr. Notter, and Mr. Harris in place of Mr. Mosely. Though there were other instances of alternates, they were less regularly the participants. The further members of the committee were Mr. Stinebower, Office of Economic Affairs; Henry P. Leverich, Division of Central European Affairs; William Adams Brown, Jr., Post-War Programs Committee secretariat; Lt. Col. Edgar Allen, Civil Affairs Division, War Department; Commander Curtis C. Shears, Office of the Chief of Naval Operations, who was succeeded by Capt. Oswald S. Colclough, Director of the Central Division in the Office of the Chief of Naval Operations; and Lt. Ross Cissell of the same Office, later assigned to the Occupied Area Section and then to the Military Government

Section. Sydney Mellen of the Liberated Areas Division, State Department, attended as observer. Additional experts took part as needed. The recommendations of this committee were submitted to the Post-War Programs Committee, but the Office of European Affairs was primarily responsible for this work, much of which was essentially of an operational character in that it was directly related to the current negotiations then in progress in London.

As previously noted, by the time of the establishment of the Working Security Committee in December 1943, the former Subcommittee on Security Problems under Norman Davis, and even its Technical Security Subcommittee, had been inactive for some months. There was, therefore, in existence no high-level committee for joint postwar preparation among the State, War, and Navy Departments. This lack was filled largely through numerous *ad hoc* consultations by Mr. Dunn personally, or at his direction, to supplement those ordinarily held among the Secretaries of the three Departments. It was, however, the new Working Security Committee that, though not originally so designed, in effect constituted the substitute and transitional structure, which during 1944 furthered the development of those organized arrangements for joint consultation among the three Departments that culminated at the end of the year, as will be seen, in the establishment of what became a continuing high-level coordinating committee. This same development, however, was equally furthered during 1944, both at the expert and at the policy level, by the interdepartmental representation provided in connection with the arrangements for the final preparation in the fundamental field of general international organization.

It was this latter preparation that determined the third dividing line in the arrangements for the consideration of international security ' problems. As noted above, the drafting of policy recommendations on general international organization was carried out by the Informal Political Agenda Group. The resulting views and proposals at the several stages of their development were reviewed and approved by the Post-War Programs Committee, which included nearly all members of the Group. The process of arriving at complete and final proposals in this field did not, however, stop here, and differed in several respects from the processes already described for arriving at integrated recommendation in other fields. In the international organization field, the formulation was concentrated in a Group that, though incidentally interdivisional, or more accurately, interoffice, was constituted on the basis of special qualification and responsibility vested in it by the Secretary of State, and included, as will be recalled, several persons from private life and a member of the White House staff. The senior members of the Group not only participated in the formulation of proposals but also served as advisers to the Secretary of State and the President on the final decisions. Interdepartmental consideration was also a part of the process of formulation, accomplished through participation in the preparation by representatives of the War and Navy Departments and the Joint Chiefs of Staff, who attended the meetings of the Group on all security aspects of the proposals, and through review of the proposals by the highest officials of those Departments and of the Joint Chiefs of Staff.

The initial exploration of the problems in this field had been made under the Advisory Committee, with the participation of especially qualified persons from private life. Extraordinary consultation on a nonpartisan basis with Members of Congress and with a number of distinguished private citizens was throughout an important part of the process of formulating the proposals on general international organization. In addition, as will be seen in Part IV, there was consultation with the public at large after the initial international negotiations at Dumbarton Oaks and before final decisions were made, and public organizations were invited into consultation during the international negotiations at the San Francisco Conference, where the broad policy decisions were elaborated and presented in definitive form. Moreover, the American proposals entering into the negotiations among the major powers at Dumbarton Oaks were supplemented thereafter not only through these further consultations at home but also through further negotiations in Washington and abroad. All these activities and the preparations for them were one inclusive process and extended in scope far beyond the extraordinary arrangements for the development of postwar policy in other fields.

The preliminary international exchanges looking toward joint conversations among major powers on general organization for international security and peace began early in 1944 and interlocked with the preparation proceeding in the Informal Political Agenda Group. Together they constituted the direct chain of development leading from the Moscow Conference to the Dumbarton Oaks Conversations. In order to describe this chain clearly, it is, however, desirable first to take into account the other international negotiations that were proceeding.

CHAPTER XI

International Discussions and Conferences, Spring–Autumn 1944

THE INTERNATIONAL conferences and discussions held in 1944 were for the most part crowded into the spring and the autumn months. They varied in scope from matters of wide and basic policy concern to problems confined to a single interest, and they varied in character, certain ones including many governments while others were limited to but two major powers.

THE EUROPEAN ADVISORY COMMISSION

THE DECISION of the Moscow Conference to establish a European Advisory Commission provided a continuing body through which negotiations on the treatment of European enemy states were to be conducted during a year and a half among the United States, the United Kingdom, the Soviet Union, and, from November 1944, France. This Commission, on which Ambassador Winant was the United States representative, met in London from January 14, 1944, until superseded by the Council of Foreign Ministers under the Potsdam Agreement of August 1945. It devoted itself primarily to the questions that would be presented by the surrender and occupation of Germany, although its original terms of reference had been somewhat broader.

The Conference itself had referred to the Commission several matters that were before it at Moscow, notably, the United States proposal on the treatment of Germany, the Anglo-American proposal on France, and the question of Allied policy in liberated areas. Furthermore, it had been agreed there that the Commission would study and make joint recommendations to the three participating Governments on such European questions connected with the termination of hostilities as they might refer to it. More specifically, however, the Commission had been directed by the Conference to make detailed recommendations as soon as possible on the terms of surrender to be imposed upon each of the European enemy states and upon the necessary machinery to insure the fulfillment of these terms. In keeping with this latter directive, the Commission, when it met, decided to take up first the terms of surrender for Germany, and its subsequent discussions included only the additional questions of the Bulgarian armistice and of occupation policy in Germany and Austria. For reasons of policy and practical considerations of time, the armistice agreements with Rumania, Finland, with which the United States was not at war, and Hungary, and the civil-affairs agreements with the occupied Allied states were reached outside the Commission.

During the life of the Commission, the Office of European Affairs, with the assistance of the Division of Territorial Studies, was primarily responsible for supplying Ambassador Winant with the necessary background studies for his guidance on the Commission and with policy recommendations and directives. These studies and policy papers were developed in the several interdivisional country committees concerned with European enemy states, the Working Security Committee, and eventually the State, War, and Navy Coordinating Committee,[1] and certain of the economic committees. These papers were then reviewed in the Post-War Programs Committee, and the final directives were of course subject to clearance with the Secretary and, upon occasion, with the Joint Chiefs of Staff and the President before being sent. The same committee structure at the working level also reviewed documents prepared by Ambassador Winant's staff in London prior to their submission for approval at the top policy level in Washington. In September 1944, Hamilton Fish Armstrong was appointed Special Assistant, with the personal rank of Minister, to Ambassador Winant in connection with the latter's work on the Commission,[2] and from the summer of 1944 onward, the Ambassador's staff included Philip Mosely, Chief of the Division of Territorial Studies, who served there on detail as Political Adviser. By this time, it will be recalled, the Post-War Programs Committee was nearing completion of its review of the recommendations formulated in the country and area committees on European problems.

While the number of tripartite, and later quadripartite, agreements concluded in the European Advisory Commission prior to the end of the European war was small, the extensive documentation prepared for the use of the American representative on the Commission was to prove of great subsequent value when the period of actual occupation arrived.

---

[1] See pp. 347–48.

[2] Mr. Armstrong served only briefly in London, being appointed Special Adviser to the Secretary of State in December 1944; cf. p. 350.

THE WEST INDIAN CONFERENCE

IN MARCH 1944, the first session of the West Indian Conference was held under the auspices of the Anglo-American Caribbean Commission. Before the war, both the British and the American Governments had separately, in their respective spheres of responsibility, been attempting to alleviate the political, economic, and social difficulties of this region. With the United States acquisition in 1940 under 99-year lease of bases in the British West Indies, the desirability of joint efforts toward improving those conditions became apparent, particularly in view of the relationship between conditions of stability in the Caribbean and security requirements. The establishment of an Anglo-American Caribbean Commission for the purpose of "encouraging and strengthening social and economic cooperation" in this area between the United States and Great Britain and their dependencies had been announced on March 9, 1942.

This Commission, which had purely advisory functions, was composed of a British Section and a United States Section, under the chairmanship of Sir Frank A. Stockdale and Charles W. Taussig, respectively. It held a series of meetings in 1942–43 devoted primarily to wartime emergency problems. In August 1943, however, it established a Caribbean Research Council, for the consideration of long-range problems, and on January 5, 1944, it was announced that the British and American Governments had decided to inaugurate, under the auspices of the Commission, a "regular system of West Indian Conferences." This decision had grown out of consultations held in London in December 1942 by the two Co-chairmen of the Commission. The Conference would discuss "matters of common interest and especially of social and economic significance to Caribbean countries," and was designed to "broaden the base for the approach to Caribbean problems to include consultation with local representatives—not necessarily officials—of the territories and colonies concerned." Like the Commission, it would be purely advisory.

Both the Commission, and the Conference which met in Barbados March 21–30, 1944, were practical experiments in international cooperation on a regional basis to promote the advance of dependent areas and were conducted during a period when the whole problem of postwar policy toward dependent areas was being considered by the American and British Governments. They were in particular experiments along the lines of the regional commissions suggested for more general establishment in the informal British proposal of February 1943 with respect to dependent areas and later incorporated in the United States draft proposal on this subject presented at the Quebec and Moscow Conferences.[3]

---

[3] See pp. 189 and 198.

While this collaborative effort in the Caribbean was restricted in the first instance to two nations only and was therefore not as inclusive an arrangement as that contemplated under these proposals, the question of its extension to other countries with dependencies in this area was left open. The joint communiqué of March 9, 1942, establishing the Commission had stated that it would, "in its studies and in the formulation of its recommendations . . . necessarily bear in mind the desirability of close cooperation in social and economic matters between all regions adjacent to the Caribbean." [4] The Netherlands was already represented on the Caribbean Research Council, and the joint announcement of January 4, 1944, stated "Although these arrangements limit the Conference to United States and British participation the Conference will be free to invite participation of other countries on occasions."

While the development of these regional arrangements in the Caribbean can in no sense be attributed to the Department's work during the same period in preparation for the peace, the experience with these arrangements was reflected in the plans being formulated for international cooperation after the war in meeting the problems of dependent areas. The United States Co-chairman of the Commission and other staff members of the United States Section, which reported directly to the President but for administrative purposes was regarded as an integral part of the Department of State, were members of the interdivisional Committee on Colonial Problems established on September 23, 1943. This committee was kept currently informed of developments in the work of the Commission, and its views on certain problems before the Commission were solicited. The committee's first Chairman, C. Easton Rothwell, participated as an adviser to the Commission in the Barbados Conference.

THE STETTINIUS MISSION

IN THE spring of 1944, the urgency of certain immediate problems connected with the prosecution of the war and the stage of development that had been reached in the Department's preparation for the peace made desirable another informal exchange of views with the British. The approaching Normandy invasion necessitated Anglo-American agreement on the status of the French Committee of National Liberation. Joint action was needed in anticipation of the invasion to reduce to the minimum neutral trade with the enemy. The situation in the Near East required exploration by the two major

---

[4] On Oct. 30, 1946, an agreement was signed by the United States, the United Kingdom, France, and the Netherlands establishing a quadripartite Caribbean Commission, which became the prototype for the South Pacific Commission established in 1947.

Western Allies in order that they might currently coordinate their policies in this important strategic area. The progress of the war made it expedient to hasten the work of the European Advisory Commission and to advance the international consultations on postwar problems and policy as initiated the previous year. It was therefore agreed between the President and the Secretary in March that the Under Secretary, Mr. Stettinius, should undertake a special Mission to London. These London conversations began on April 7 and lasted until April 29, 1944.

The Under Secretary was accompanied on his mission by Isaiah Bowman, who was a member of the Informal Political Agenda Group and of the Secretary's "consulting group"; Wallace Murray and H. Freeman Matthews, Director of the Office of Near Eastern and African Affairs and Deputy Director of the Office of European Affairs, respectively; John L. Pratt, Consultant on Commercial Affairs; Robert J. Lynch, Special Assistant to the Under Secretary, who served as executive secretary for the Mission; and Louis J. Hector, Assistant to Mr. Stettinius. Both Mr. Bowman and Mr. Murray were members of the Post-War Programs Committee, and Mr. Matthews attended the meetings of this Committee as alternate for Mr. Dunn.

Discussions in the first instance were between Mr. Stettinius and, where postwar problems were concerned, Mr. Bowman and Prime Minister Churchill, Foreign Secretary Eden, and other high officials of the British Government. The Under Secretary undertook to keep the Soviet and Chinese Ambassadors in London informed of the course of these discussions, and also to talk with members of the governments-in-exile. Messrs. Murray and Matthews met principally with officials of the British Foreign Office, while Mr. Pratt was in touch primarily with British officials in the economic field.

Insofar as these conversations were concerned with the postwar period, they related in the main to the work of the European Advisory Commission, the occupation of Germany, continued cooperation with the Soviet Union, the projected world security organization, the "World Court," colonial policy, resumption of the Anglo-American economic conversations, the proposal for the establishment of a United Nations economic steering committee, postwar shipping policy, and the establishment of a "European Inland Transport Organization."

The Under Secretary was not authorized to go beyond an informal exchange of views with the British, and the discussions did not, therefore, result in positive commitments on postwar policy by either of the participating Governments. They did, however, serve to clarify the position of each on the problems presented. Those concerned with general international organization, the World Court, and colonial policy were of particular importance in the subsequent study and discussion of these questions within the Department.

Upon his return, the Under Secretary submitted a detailed report of his conversations in London to the Secretary and on May 8, summarized the discussions of current problems for the Policy Committee. Two days later, Mr. Bowman reported to a meeting of the Post-War Programs Committee on the discussions in which he had participated relating to the organization of the peace.

POLICY ADDRESS OF APRIL 9, 1944

WHILE Mr. Stettinius was in London and while the Post-War Programs Committee was working intensively on the entire range of problems on which recommendations were being submitted for decision, the Secretary, on April 9, 1944, delivered the third of his major addresses designed to explain current policy and to inform the public on impending steps in our preparations for the peace. Defining United States foreign policy as "the task of focusing and giving effect in the world outside our borders to the will of 135 million people through the constitutional processes which govern our democracy," the Secretary first drew attention to "three outstanding lessons" of recent years, which he described as follows:

" . . . In the first place, since the outbreak of the present war in Europe, we and those nations who are now our allies have moved from relative weakness to strength. In the second place, during that same period we in this country have moved from a deep-seated tendency toward separate action to the knowledge and conviction that only through unity of action can there be achieved in this world the results which are essential for the continuance of free peoples. And, thirdly, we have moved from a careless tolerance of evil institutions to the conviction that free governments and Nazi and Fascist governments cannot exist together in this world because the very nature of the latter requires them to be aggressors and the very nature of free governments too often lays them open to treacherous and well-laid plans of attack." [5]

In this connection, the Secretary referred to our decision after the fall of France in 1940 to defend ourselves and to assist those resisting aggression. He termed this "a major decision of foreign policy." The American people have since shown not only a determination to win the war but also a determination "to go on, after the victory, with our Allies and all other nations which desire peace and freedom to establish and maintain in full strength the institutions without which peace and freedom cannot be an enduring reality." This country could not, he declared, "move in and out of international cooperation and in and out of participation in the responsibilities of a member of the family of nations," since the "political, material, and

---

[5] *Department of State Bulletin*, X, 335–42.

spiritual strength of the free and democratic nations not only is greatly dependent upon the strength which our full participation brings to the common effort but . . . is a vital factor in our own strength."

On the basis of this fundamental development in United States foreign policy, the Secretary first discussed certain aspects of current policy with specific reference to the neutrals and to France and Italy, stressing in connection with the two latter states our national interest in a stable Europe after the war and in the development of democratic institutions there. He then turned to the "more far-reaching relations between us and our Allies in dealing with our enemies and in providing for future peace, freedom from aggression, and opportunity for expanding material well-being." He warned that solution of these problems required "the slow, hard process . . . of full discussion with our Allies and among our own people." Stating that such discussion was then in progress, he declared that the basis of our policy was soundly established, the direction clear, and the general methods of accomplishment emerging.

This basis, the Secretary said, lay in the lesson of recent history that "agreed and united action" among the free nations is "fundamental" and "must underlie the entire range of our policy." He asserted:

"However difficult the road may be, there is no hope of turning victory into enduring peace unless the real interests of this country, the British Commonwealth, the Soviet Union, and China are harmonized and unless they agree and act together. This is the solid framework upon which all future policy and international organization must be built. It offers the fullest opportunity for the development of institutions in which all free nations may participate democratically, through which a reign of law and morality may arise, and through which the material interests of all may be advanced. But without an enduring understanding between these four nations upon their fundamental purposes, interests, and obligations to one another, all organizations to preserve peace are creations on paper and the path is wide open again for the rise of a new aggressor.

"This essential understanding and unity of action among the four nations is not in substitution or derogation of unity among the United Nations. But it is basic to all organized international action because upon its reality depends the possibility of enduring peace and free institutions rather than new coalitions and a new pre-war period. Nor do I suggest that any conclusions of these four nations can or should be without the participation of the other United Nations. I am stating what I believe the common sense of my fellow countrymen and all men will recognize—that for these powers to become divided in their aims and fail to recognize and harmonize their basic interests can produce only disaster and that no machinery, as such, can produce this essential harmony and unity."

Having thus described the basis of our policy, the Secretary reviewed the stages of agreement already reached in the Atlantic Charter and the United Nations Declaration and at the Moscow, Tehran, and Cairo Conferences, but remarked upon their limitations in providing "a detailed blueprint for the future," and cautioned that the objectives set forth in the Atlantic Charter provided direction of policy but not specific solutions. He discussed in some detail, as will be seen later, the progress that had been made in our "work upon the form and substance of an international organization to maintain peace and prevent aggression and upon the economic and other cooperative arrangements which are necessary in order that we maintain our position as a working partner with other free nations." He concluded this address, as he had that in the previous September, by emphasizing the need for a nonpartisan approach to foreign policy. He stated:

"All of these questions of foreign policy . . . are difficult and often involve matters of controversy. Under our constitutional system the will of the American people in this field is not effective unless it is united will. If we are divided we are ineffective. We are in a year of a national election in which it is easy to arouse controversy on almost any subject, whether or not the subject is an issue in the campaign. You, therefore, as well as we who are in public office, bear a great responsibility. It is the responsibility of avoiding needless controversy in the formulation of your judgments. It is the responsibility for sober and considered thought and expression. It is the responsibility for patience both with our Allies and with those who must speak for you with them. Once before in our lifetime we fell into disunity and became ineffective in world affairs by reason of it. Should this happen again it will be a tragedy to you and to your children and to the world for generations."

CONFERENCES ON ECONOMIC AND SOCIAL PROBLEMS

ALTHOUGH the Department was not successful in its efforts to bring about an early resumption of the Anglo-American economic conversations and the establishment of a United Nations economic steering committee, a series of conferences of a specialized character in the economic, social, and cultural fields were held during the spring and summer of 1944 that led to important developments in postwar arrangements.

Social and Cultural Problems

Exploratory work in the field of postwar cultural relations, as noted earlier, had been initiated in the Department as early as the autumn of 1941. The possible need for an international agency in this field had early been recognized both by the Special Subcommittee on International Organization and the research staff and by the Division of Cultural Relations, where primary responsibility for the Department's cultural work rested. In connection with the meeting of the General Advisory Committee on Cultural Relations in February 1943,[6] Under Secretary Welles had raised specifically the question of the desirability of the "possible establishment and operation of an international cultural organization." That Committee the following June had stated its belief that "an international agency for educational relations and cooperation is an essential part of any provisional or permanent world organization," recommending that the Department of State "actively explore the possibility of the early organization of such an agency." By this time, the establishment of such an agency as part of the organization of the peace was being widely advocated in this country and abroad by educational leaders and by private organizations, some of the work of which stemmed from the earlier League of Nations activities in the furtherance of intellectual cooperation.

Although the outlines of a permanent organization in this field were being projected at an expert level, no specific proposal had as yet been developed in the preparation. Moreover, from the summer of 1942, emphasis began to shift in the Department's thinking from the general long-range problem of international cultural relations to the more immediate and specific one of postwar educational and cultural reconstruction, where it remained until after the Dumbarton Oaks Conversations. This development came in part from the realization of a practical and pressing need in this field to be met at the conclusion of hostilities; in part from the impetus given the planning to meet this need by the British-sponsored Conference of Allied Ministers of Education, which began on November 16, 1942, to convene periodically in London; and in part from the thought that out of the international machinery required to handle this particular problem and the experience thus acquired would develop more comprehensive and permanent arrangements for international collaboration in this field. Work was continued on this basis throughout 1943 and the first half of 1944 by the Division of Cultural Relations in collaboration with the Division of Political Studies, much consideration being given to related developments in connection with the Conference of Allied Ministers of Education, at whose meetings this Government was represented by an observer from May 1943.

The Conference of Allied Ministers of Education took steps in October 1943 to broaden the base of its membership, to strengthen its structure, and to explore the possible creation of an inter-Allied bureau of education that might become the permanent international agency in this field. Following this decision, favorable consideration was given in the Division of Cultural Relations to the possibility of transforming the conference into a United Nations cultural agency. That Division,

---

[6] Cf. p. 53.

upon receipt of an invitation from the conference to send regular representatives rather than observers to its next meeting, formulated specific proposals to this end. These were considered at a meeting of officers from the interested divisions with Assistant Secretary G. Howland Shaw on January 11, 1944. Four days earlier, on January 7, a group of American educators had met in Washington to be apprised of and to consider the Department's plans in this field.

Although contemplating establishment of a permanent cultural organization in due course, those responsible for the preparation in the field of international organization generally did not regard it as desirable that the plans for a specialized agency in the educational and cultural field should crystallize to the point of permitting the completion of negotiations for such an agency until after the general international organization had become more clearly defined. The proposals considered on January 11 were therefore revised, following that meeting, in the Division of Political Studies to assure the provisional and advisory character of the transformed conference as projected. The General Advisory Committee on Cultural Relations, at a meeting on February 18–19, approved the Department's proposal that this Government "cooperate in the creation of a United Nations provisional commission on educational and cultural reconstruction" and, as soon as established, "assume membership therein." At the same time it emphasized that this Government should "establish as an ultimate goal the creation of and full participation in a permanent international agency for educational and cultural relations within the framework of such world wide organization of nations as may be effected." The provisional organization, it stated, "should be so directed as to pave the way for the permanent international organization for educational and cultural relations." These recommendations were in general accord with those of the January 7 Conference of Educators.

On March 25, 1944, it was announced that this Government would send a delegation to the April 5 meeting of the Conference of Allied Ministers of Education in London comprised of Representative J. William Fulbright, of Arkansas; the Librarian of Congress, Archibald MacLeish, who had been a member of the Advisory Committee on Post-War Foreign Policy; John W. Studebaker, United States Commissioner of Education; Dean C. Mildred Thompson of Vassar College; Grayson N. Kefauver, Consultant to the Department of State in the cultural field; and Ralph E. Turner, Assistant Chief of the Division of Science, Education, and Art (previously Cultural Relations). Six days later, the Department issued its first statement of policy with respect to United States participation in "emergency educational and cultural rebuilding of the war-torn United Nations," which included the following declaration of purpose:

"In order to help the war-torn countries to help themselves in the rebuilding of essential educational and cultural facilities, the Department proposes to collaborate for the time being with the Conference of Allied Ministers of Education in London and to cooperate with the nations represented in this Conference, with the other United Nations, and with the nations associated with the United Nations in the war in forming, as soon as practicable, a United Nations organization for educational and cultural reconstruction. . . ."

The instructions to the United States Delegation to the conference, dated March 29, 1944, were drafted at a meeting of interested offices and divisions, including the Division of International Security and Organization, at which Assistant Secretary Shaw presided, but for lack of time did not come before the Post-War Programs Committee for review. The Conference of the Ministers of Education of the Allied Governments, meeting April 5-29, 1944, drew up a tentative draft agreement for a United Nations organization for educational and cultural reconstruction, from the consideration of which was subsequently to develop the proposal for a United Nations educational, scientific, and cultural organization. The tentative draft agreement which suggested more rapid development of a permanent organization in this field than had been contemplated by the Department, was considered by the Post-War Programs Committee on May 6, with a view to adjusting the draft to the maturing thinking in the Department on the question of international organization as a whole.[7]

Petroleum

Exploratory discussions with the British on petroleum questions were begun in Washington on April 18, 1944, and lasted until May 3. These discussions at the expert level resulted in a draft memorandum of understanding between the United States and the United Kingdom which was followed by formal Anglo-American conversations at Cabinet level in Washington, July 25-August 8.

The special committee on petroleum under the Taylor Committee had never functioned substantively, as already noted, and the preparations for these discussions were made in the first instance by a special interdivisional Petroleum Committee, established in December 1943 outside the framework of the postwar preparatory structure. This working committee was made up of representatives from the Department's interested geographic and other operating divisions. The documentation it produced was subject to the review of both the Post-War

---

[7] See p. 365.

Programs Committee and a new interdepartmental Petroleum Committee. The latter committee had been established on April 1, 1944, by the Cabinet Committee for the Anglo-American Petroleum Conversations, which had been set up on February 15, 1944, under the chairmanship of the Secretary of State. The draft memorandum of understanding mentioned above followed closely a proposed draft agreement prepared by the interdivisional working committee and reviewed in February, March, and April by the Post-War Programs Committee, which had endorsed the recommendation that with some amendment the proposed draft agreement should be used as the basis for discussion with the British. This position was approved by Secretary Hull.

The formal conversations with the British beginning July 25 developed the draft memorandum into the Anglo-American Petroleum Agreement signed on August 8, 1944. This agreement, which was submitted to the Senate for approval on August 24, was, however, not acted upon.[8]

The International Labor Organization

On April 20, 1944, the 26th session of the International Labor Conference convened in Philadelphia and concluded one month later. As previously noted, preparations for this meeting had been under way since the previous autumn in the Special Committee on Labor Standards and Social Security and the *ad hoc* group of its members, and also in the Interdivisional Committee on the Agenda of the ILO established in December 1943 under the chairmanship of Otis Mulliken. Primary responsibility for staff work on this matter in the Department of State rested thereafter in the newly created Division of Labor Relations, of which Mr. Mulliken became Chief, and in the Divisions of the Office of Special Political Affairs.

The Policy Committee on March 29, 1944, approved a revised draft of a resolution concerning the general scope and activity of the International Labor Office recommended by the Special Committee for introduction by the United States Delegation to the conference. On April 7 the Post-War Programs Committee considered a series of documents prepared by the interdivisional committee on the ILO agenda. These comprised the draft of a proposed instruction to the delegation and detailed commentaries on those agenda items bearing on foreign policy, particularly the items dealing with labor conditions in dependent areas; the relationship of the International Labor Organization to other international organizations, which raised serious questions in connection with the plans being formulated in the Depart-

---

[8] It was recalled at the request of the President the following January, and renewed negotiations resulted in a revised agreement, which, however, has yet to receive the Senate's consent to ratification. For the texts of these two agreements see *Department of State Bulletin*, XI, 154–56; XIII, 481–83.

ment for a general international organization to include an over-all economic organization; and the calling by the ILO of an international conference on postwar employment policies, which also raised serious questions since such a conference would tend prematurely to develop into a general economic conference. The documentation relating to dependent areas had been cleared with the Interdivisional Committee on Colonial and Trusteeship Problems. With some amendment, the Post-War Programs Committee approved the proposed instruction to the United States Delegation as the basis for this Government's position at the conference, deciding, however, to continue the practice heretofore followed of issuing no formal instructions to delegations to ILO meetings.

The government representatives on the United States Delegation to the conference were Secretary of Labor Perkins, Chairman, and Senator Elbert D. Thomas, with Assistant Secretary Berle and Carter Goodrich, United States Labor Commissioner, serving as alternates. The advisers to the delegation included officers from the Division of Labor Relations and the Division of Territorial Studies. At a meeting on June 21, the Post-War Programs Committee accepted a report on the conference "as evidence of the successful implementation of the general policy which it had previously approved." The convocation of a conference on postwar employment policies had not been made mandatory. No steps had been taken to expand the general scope and functions of the ILO, but the desirability of close cooperation between the Organization and any other specialized international agencies in the economic and social fields had been emphasized. The question of the future constitutional development of the Organization, including its relationship with other international bodies, had been referred to the Governing Body for consideration by a special committee, and the Governing Body had also been requested to appoint representatives to negotiate with international authorities concerning "any constitutional questions which at any time require immediate action." [9]

The Bretton Woods Conference

The Monetary and Financial Conference that met at Bretton Woods, New Hampshire, July 1–22, 1944, was the culmination of the international discussions on an expert level that had been in progress at the Treasury Department for more than a year.

On April 7, 1943, the Treasury had made public a letter from Secretary Morgenthau to the Finance Ministers of thirty-seven United and Associated Nations, enclosing the proposal for an international

---

[9] The Governing Body of the ILO at its meeting in January 1945 expressed its desire for association with the contemplated general international organization, which was later accomplished through agreement with the United Nations.

stabilization fund developed by the Treasury under the guidance of Harry D. White in collaboration with the interdepartmental American Technical Committee and inviting them to send their technical experts to Washington to discuss the proposal. The following day, the British Government released the plan drawn up by its experts headed by Lord Keynes. It was made clear, however, by both Governments that their respective proposals represented the views of their experts and involved no official commitments.

Aside from the earlier informal exchanges of views with the British in the course of the development of these two plans, discussions at the technical level with other countries were initiated in June. The discussions were conducted for the United States by the American Technical Committee and continued throughout the rest of 1943 and into 1944. They included an exchange of views with Soviet experts, who came to Washington early in 1944, and continuing exchanges with the British both during the Anglo-American Article VII discussions in the autumn of 1943, referred to above,[10] and in succeeding months. On April 21, 1944, the "Joint Statement by Experts on the Establishment of an International Monetary Fund" was released, setting forth the principal features of the proposal for an international stabilization fund upon which agreement had been reached among the United States, the United Kingdom, China, the Soviet Union, and other countries.

While these discussions had been concerned primarily with the creation of a monetary fund, the possible need for the establishment of some type of international lending institution had early been recognized by both the Treasury and State Departments. The Treasury proposal of March 1942 had included an international bank for reconstruction and development. By September 1943, a proposal for an International Investment Agency had been developed by the Division of Economic Studies in the State Department in consultation with other interested divisions and offices of the Department, which was fundamentally not very different from the Treasury proposal. The establishment of a bank was discussed briefly with the British during the Anglo-American monetary and financial discussions in September–October 1943, and late in November, the Treasury made public a "Preliminary Draft Outline of a Proposal for a Bank of Reconstruction and Development of the United and Associated Nations."

Considerable attention was given the bank proposal toward the end of the bilateral discussions that concluded early in 1944, but no joint statement on the proposed bank comparable to that issued on the fund had been formulated when, on May 26, it was announced

[10] See p. 190 ff.

that the President had called a Conference of the forty-four United and Associated Nations to meet at Bretton Woods in July to discuss the proposal for an International Monetary Fund and "possibly" the proposal for a Bank for Reconstruction and Development. At a preliminary meeting in Atlantic City the last two weeks in June, however, in which experts from the four major powers and thirteen other states participated, further refinement of the bank proposal was accomplished.

At Bretton Woods, agreement was reached on the creation of an International Monetary Fund and on the establishment of an International Bank for Reconstruction and Development, both of which, it was stipulated, should cooperate with "any general international organization" and with the specialized international agencies in related fields. The United States Delegation to the conference reflected in substantial degree the interdepartmental, official-public, and Executive-Congressional character of the American postwar preparation as a whole.[11] The advisers and technical secretaries to the Delegation and the technical officers of the conference were drawn largely from those who had participated in the work of the American Technical Committee or had otherwise been closely associated with the preparatory work for the conference.[12]

Other Consultations

There were in progress during the same period certain other international economic consultations for which the Department had a

[11] The Delegation was comprised of Secretary Morgenthau, Chairman; Fred M. Vinson, Director, Office of Economic Stabilization, Vice Chairman; Dean Acheson, Assistant Secretary of State; Edward E. Brown, President of the First National Bank, Chicago; Leo T. Crowley, Administrator, Foreign Economic Administration; Marriner S. Eccles, Chairman, Board of Governors of the Federal Reserve System; Miss Mabel Newcomer, Professor of Economics, Vassar College; Senators Robert F. Wagner of New York, Democrat, and Charles W. Tobey of New Hampshire, Republican, Chairman and ranking minority member, respectively, of the Senate Committee on Banking and Currency; Representatives Brent Spence of Kentucky, Democrat, and Jesse P. Wolcott of Michigan, Republican, Chairman and ranking minority member, respectively, of the House Committee on Banking and Currency; and Harry D. White, Assistant to the Secretary of the Treasury.

[12] Those drawn from the Department of State who had previously been associated with the preparation were: Technical Advisers, Messrs. Collado, Livesey, and Pasvolsky; Technical Secretary, John H. Fuqua; Secretaries and Assistant Secretaries of Technical Commissions and Committees, Messrs. Brown, Stinebower, and Young, Mrs. Eleanor Lansing Dulles, and Miss Ruth Russell. For a complete list of the Delegation and of the officers of the conference, see *Proceedings and Documents of United Nations Monetary and Financial Conference*, Department of State publication 2866, International Organization and Conference Series I, 3, vol. II, pp. 1130–33.

more direct responsibility than in the case of the Bretton Woods Conference and which reflected for the most part the work of the Special Committees.[13]   On March 24, 1944, the Post-War Programs Committee considered recommendations presented by Assistant Secretary Berle, Chairman of the Special Committee on International Aviation, in anticipation of his initiation the following month of a series of bilateral discussions on this question.   On April 13, recommendations on postwar shipping policy developed by the Special Committee on Shipping were considered by the Post-War Programs Committee with a view to arriving at a Departmental policy within which the special committee could carry on its further preparations for international discussions of this problem, which began in London on July 19, 1944.   On May 4 and again on May 17, the Post-War Programs Committee discussed policy recommendations presented by the Special Committee on Inland Transport in connection with a British proposal for a European inland transport organization to function in the transitional period after the war; these recommendations were to serve as a guide for the American representatives in discussions of this problem that took place in London, May 30–June 27, 1944.   On June 16, the Committee approved recommendations presented by Assistant Secretary Acheson, after consultation with members of the Senate Foreign Relations Committee, for changes in the draft constitution of a United Nations Food and Agriculture Organization prepared by the Interim Commission that had been established for this purpose by the FAO Conference the previous year.   In the formulation of all of these recommendations, the processes of the preparation already described were followed.

These economic consultations came to immediate fruition in two instances. On August 1, 1944, the FAO Interim Commission submitted its final report to the participating governments for approval. This final report included the draft constitution for a permanent organization, which should "constitute a part of any general international organization to which may be entrusted the coordination of the activities of international organizations with specialized responsibili-

---

[13] The exploratory talks on postwar rubber problems among the United States, the United Kingdom, and the Netherlands, which were held in London in August 1944 and which resulted in the establishment of an informal Rubber Study Group, had no direct connection with the extraordinary preparation under discussion here. As noted earlier, a special committee on rubber had been projected to function under the Taylor Committee, but had never been established. (See pp. 140–41.) However the United States Representative at these discussions was Bernard F. Haley, who had been the ranking Assistant Chief of the Division of Economic Studies before its absorption into the operating structure of the Department. The Rubber Study Group was to become the precursor of the study groups later proposed for the commodity field in the Habana Charter for an International Trade Organization.

ties." That same month, an agreement was reached in London among the Governments of the United States, the United Kingdom, Belgium, Canada, Greece, the Netherlands, Norway, and Poland and the French Committee of National Liberation, to which other of the United Nations subsequently adhered, on the establishment of a United Maritime Authority to function from the cessation of the European war until six months after the end of the war with Japan.

THE SECOND QUEBEC CONFERENCE

PRESIDENT Roosevelt and Prime Minister Churchill met for a second time at Quebec, September 11–16, 1944. Marshal Stalin, as before, had been invited to attend this meeting but had again indicated that military exigencies precluded his participation. The meeting was primarily military in character. No policy official of the Department accompanied the President to Quebec. The Joint Communiqué issued at its conclusion stated that the "President and the Prime Minister, and the Combined Chiefs of Staff, held a series of meetings during which they discussed all aspects of the war against Germany and Japan" and "reached decisions on all points both with regard to the completion of the war in Europe, now approaching its final stages, and the destruction of the barbarians of the Pacific".

Certain political matters were discussed at Quebec, however, and one important decision with far-reaching postwar implications was taken, namely acceptance by the President and the Prime Minister of the plan for the treatment of Germany after surrender presented by Secretary Morgenthau, who had accompanied the President to Quebec. This plan was in fundamental conflict with the recommendations on this matter made earlier that month by the Secretary of State and with the views of the War Department.[14] While this decision was later modified, it was to have an important bearing on the Government's subsequent position on this problem.

Agreement on the respective British and American zones of occupation in Germany, long at issue between the two Governments in the European Advisory Commission, was also reached at Quebec. A proposal to guide lend-lease to Britain in the period between the end of the European War and the defeat of Japan, designed to facilitate the reconversion of Britain's industry and the re-establishment of the British export trade, was also agreed upon by the President and

---

[14] Accounts of this decision and of the views held by the Secretaries of State and War have been made available in *Memoirs of Cordell Hull*, II, 1602–22, and in *On Active Service* by Henry L. Stimson and McGeorge Bundy (New York, 1947, 1949), pp. 568–83. Cf. also Henry Morgenthau, *Germany Is Our Problem* (New York, 1945), documentary foreword reproducing "Memorandum summarizing 'The Morgenthau Plan'."

Secretary Morgenthau. This matter had not come within the purview of either the departmental or the interdepartmental postwar preparatory work concerned here.

There was, in addition, some discussion by the President and the Prime Minister of the problems arising out of the Dumbarton Oaks Conversations then in progress in Washington, particularly the question of voting in the Security Council. This is described in chapter XIV.

CHAPTER XII

Proposals for General International Organization and an "Informal Conference"

HE PERIOD of concentrated preparation of the United States proposals on general organization for the maintenance of international peace and security covered seven months, from December 9, 1943, to July 8, 1944. The resulting views, refined and supplemented, were those that the United States set forth in the major power negotiations at Dumbarton Oaks.

The proposals were built during the same months that the United Nations were developing the momentum for sustained offensives in the war. In the south of Europe, the Allies opened battle in central Italy in May and captured Rome early in June. In eastern Europe, Soviet troops retook Odessa in April and Sevastopol in May and then pressed deeper into Rumania. The successful Allied landing in Normandy occurred June 6. By that time, in the Pacific the Allies had invaded Kwajalein and the Admiralty Islands, were fighting in Burma, and had landed at Hollandia in Dutch New Guinea and in Biak Island 900 miles from the Philippines. The United Nations were drawing near the battlegrounds where the final struggles would be fought to decision.

These welcome portents of future victory naturally increased the urgency for arriving at international agreement on organized means of maintaining world security and peace afterward. Having the same effect were the obvious desirability of rapidly following up the basic pledges on postwar organization embodied in the Declaration of Moscow and the fact that the Foreign Ministers at the Moscow Conference had agreed that a preliminary exchange of views should be undertaken in coming months on the problems of international organization for the maintenance of international peace and security. They contemplated that such exchange should be carried out in Washington first, as proposed by Mr. Molotov, and then in London and in Moscow.

The first step toward exchange on this basis occurred in November 1943. In cables to the American Embassies in London, Moscow, and

Chungking on November 18 this Government proposed, if the other three Governments concurred, to announce that the four parties to the Moscow Declaration would welcome adherence by all peace-loving states to the statement in paragraph 4 of the Declaration that "they recognize the necessity of establishing at the earliest practicable date a general international organization, based on the principle of the sovereign equality of all peace-loving states, and open to membership by all such states, large and small, for the maintenance of international peace and security." While this proposal received the approval of the Soviet Government only, it was in connection with its implications that the British Embassy on November 26, 1943, raised orally with the Department the question of the procedure involved in inaugurating the further exchanges among the four governments contemplated at the Moscow Conference. This conversation resulted in the expectation in both quarters that some exchange could begin within a reasonably short time. The matter was under consideration in the Department at that time, and the Embassy was informed that the question would be pursued as soon as the United States had "something definite to propose."

A prior decision on the substantive views on international organization that the United States should advance in such exchanges was imperative before procedural arrangements could be undertaken. Proposals were not yet in written form; their drafting and the progress in negotiations were to become concurrent developments.

The instrumentality for this drafting and also for recommending to the Secretary and the President the successive steps to be taken toward negotiations was the Informal Political Agenda Group.[1] The work was done with the cooperation of the War and Navy Departments and the Joint Chiefs of Staff. In the later stages, consultations with congressional and other political leaders were undertaken to reach decisions on the proposals. Several eminent private citizens were asked to review the ideas developed. The process of preparation in this field was accordingly complex despite the existence of a central group to concentrate on the work. It was faced with initial profusion of ideas on what was desirable and with uncertainty concerning what would prove practical. It was therefore replete with difficult choices.

"POSSIBLE PLAN"

THE SMALL Informal Political Agenda Group began on December 9, 1943, its concentration on "international organization discussions," as its minutes describe its work from this date forward. To and

---

[1] Cf. p. 169.

including December 23, it held ten meetings. On December 30, it resumed, fifty-two meetings being held between then and June 14, 1944, when the name "International Organization Group" was adopted at the suggestion of the Under Secretary. Under this name eight more meetings were held, ending July 8. On July 10, the Group was absorbed into the more inclusive American Group for conducting the Dumbarton Oaks Conversations.

In these seventy meetings the original membership of the Agenda Group continued almost unchanged. To the original members, who apart from Under Secretary Stettinius *ex officio*, were Messrs. Pasvolsky, Davis, Bowman, Taylor, Cohen, Dunn, Hackworth, and Hornbeck, with Mr. Notter participating for the staff, only Joseph C. Green, Special Assistant to the Secretary of State and a member of the Post-War Programs Committee, was added, on March 16, 1944. Participation of representatives of the armed services was contemplated from an early date, but the Group desired first to approach the problem of international organization for the maintenance of security from a political standpoint. The presentation of military views after political factors had been weighed was deemed the most effective method of work, since it would permit the military and political experts to join in drafting the final proposals on security aspects within a solid political framework. As the outlines of this framework became clarified, the Department, at the request of the Group on January 21, shortly afterward invited representatives of the armed services to meetings at which international security arrangements were to be discussed.

Meetings with these representatives were held on March 16 and 23, April 6, 13, 20, and 27, and May 11, 18, and 25, 1944. The attending officers were Maj. Gen. George V. Strong for the War Department, Admiral Arthur J. Hepburn and also Rear Admiral Roscoe E. Schuirmann (at the first three meetings) for the Navy Department, and Lt. Gen. Stanley D. Embick and Vice Admiral Russell Willson of the Joint Strategic Survey Committee of the Joint Chiefs of Staff. General Embick and Admiral Willson attended initially as observers in order to become informed of the plans being developed in the drafting stage, but such attendance was understood to be preliminary to the development and presentation of military views. The change to full participation by the armed service members occurred on April 4, when the Joint Strategic Survey Committee was authorized by Admiral Leahy to represent the Joint Chiefs "in furnishing to the State Department the necessary military guidance on the matter of the formulation of post-war policies." The Joint Strategic Survey Committee was further authorized, according to the letter of that date sent to the Secretary of State by Admiral Leahy, "to handle all such matters directly with the State Department, within the limits of the broad policies or principles established by the Joint Chiefs of Staff."

Fluctuating attendance of officers from the research staff in accordance with problems under discussion by the Group was customary in order to make specialized knowledge available to the meetings and, in the case of some problems involving technical drafting, to have the minutes of the discussion taken by the specialists working directly on the problems concerned. Except for some of the meetings in December, Messrs. Sandifer and Gerig and Miss Fosdick of the staff attended regularly, Miss Fosdick serving as assistant and continuing secretary. Additional experts from the staff, although never more than a very few at any one time, participated in single meetings or series of meetings on problems in their field. These included Donald C. Blaisdell, Philip M. Burnett, Clyde Eagleton, Bernard F. Haley, John D. Tomlinson, Lawrence Preuss, and Quincy Wright, Mrs. Esther C. Brunauer, Mrs. Alice McDiarmid, and Misses M. Margaret Ball and Pauline Reinsch. The officers attending in like manner from operating economic offices and divisions were Leroy Stinebower, who had previously been a participant from the research staff, Harry C. Hawkins, William A. Fowler, and John M. Leddy. C. Easton Rothwell and John H. Fuqua of the Secretariat of the Post-War Programs Committee and Miss Ruth B. Russell, assistant to Mr. Pasvolsky, were also present at a number of meetings, while Alger Hiss attended the two last meetings in July, when the Department arrangements for the coming negotiations at Dumbarton Oaks were being instituted.

Meetings throughout these seven months were approximately two hours in length and were usually held on Thursdays at 11 a. m. and Fridays at 4:30 p. m. In the last half of March and in April and May, the Thursday meetings were reserved for international security discussions with the representatives of the armed services, but additional or "2-a-day" meetings then had to be held on these or other days of the week. Although agenda were normally adhered to in the form sent to members in advance or agreed upon at a previous meeting, problems scheduled for discussion were occasionally deferred because of intervening developments, among which were the shifts in priority occurring after various White House discussions with the "consulting group."

The Group continued to work as informally as it had in its earlier phase, with *de facto* chairmanship by Mr. Pasvolsky and, at a number of meetings when security aspects were scheduled, by Mr. Davis or by Mr. Dunn. Drafts on given points prepared by individual members were discussed, but otherwise the basic drafting was done in the Division of International Security and Organization. The reservoir of essential materials and drafts previously prepared continued to be used,[2] and indications of the thinking abroad in official quarters were always at hand and studied as were the ideas developing among the public both here and abroad. In its drafting, the Group was bound only by its best judgment, not by earlier views. Since these meetings were for analytical and policy discussion and were relied upon to produce specific draft proposals, the work moved meeting by meeting to the building of agreement on the exact terms of a text. Detailed, though not stenographic, minutes were kept on the substantive reasoning and on preferred or alternative positions emerging from the discussions. A simple but complete system of documentation was maintained.

No votes were taken. As work advanced to the point of decision on the specific provisions to be recommended as proposals, any views or preferences contrary to the general sense of the Group were made the subject of an "alternative" placed in the text pending subsequent review or were written out as supplementary observations. In the course of consideration, each proposed provision was tested in terms of how it might work in practice, the test cases being drawn from actual instances in the history of the League of Nations and other international relations or, for this purpose, hypothetical problems posed as future possibilities. Texts were then refined in accordance with the findings and were often retested before the Group was satisfied with either their substance or the clarity of their phrasing. Since the draft texts of proposals had grown considerably in number by February 23, members were thereafter furnished with drafting books containing the provisions upon which preliminary agreement had been reached and the alternatives still under consideration. The staff brought these books up to date within hours after each meeting— and within minutes if a morning meeting was to be followed by an afternoon meeting, though this was not necessary more than a few times.

The Group's drafting during these seven months fell into five stages. The first was from December 9 to 17, 1943, inclusive. During this stage it considered, for illustration, such questions as when the general organization should be established, whether a provisional international organization should be attempted at the start, and whether the framework of the League of Nations should be used or a new organization established; it then clarified its general ideas on the desirable structure, functions, and powers for the organization. A "Possible Plan for the Establishment of an International Organization for the Mainte-

---

[2] Namely, the draft constitution written by the Special Subcommittee on International Organization, the "Charter of the United Nations" written by the staff, the "seven books" and commentary also written by the staff, and the drafts or parts of drafts written by members or staff officers. See pp. 110 and 176 and appendixes 13 and 23.

nance of International Peace and Security" was drawn up on broad fundamental lines in the second stage, December 21–23. This "Possible Plan" was drafted in response to a request from the President on the 21st during lunch with Secretary Hull after the former's return from Tehran and Cairo. Before its submission to the President on December 29, it was made the subject of several days of intensive discussion between the Secretary and a few members of the "consulting group," and at the suggestion of the Secretary, a memorandum commenting on the obligations of states under the "Possible Plan" had been written to accompany it.[3] This work was *ad hoc* by the members asked to assist; no meeting was called for this purpose.

The third stage began December 30, 1943, and lasted through March 15, 1944. At the outset of this stage, the Group considered particularly the problems that arose in connection with the supply and use of armed forces in enforcement of peace, including the constitutional problems that would be raised for the United States by participation in a world security organization empowered to use such forces. It also considered the relation and role of local and regional procedures and agencies with respect to the functions to be reposed in a world organization for peace and security. These problems, with their many ramifications in regard, for example, to regulation of armaments and armed forces, to the determination of threats to or breaches of the peace, and to the nature and powers of the executive council as the organ to be given enforcement powers, continued to be under consideration throughout January.

In February 1944, the Group turned back to the broader aspects of world organization as a whole. It gave renewed consideration to the general character and functions of the international organization as a whole and of its principal organs, beginning with the general assembly, executive council, international court, and secretariat. The obligations that members of the future organization should assume and a number of other questions, including those concerning membership in the organization, were involved in this consideration, as well as further questions that arose in relation to the subjects opened up for discussion in the January meetings. At the same time, commencing with the first of the meetings in February, attention was given to the specific topics to be suggested for study and discussion in the contemplated international negotiations. These matters were all carried over into the meetings in the first two weeks of March, increased attention being given to arrangements for security.

Thus by March 15—after which military representatives began to attend meetings—the Group had considered the political framework

---

[3] See appendix 33.

of the organization along five major lines: The general character and functions of an international organization, a general assembly, an executive council, an international court of justice, and arrangements for security. The latter included the following broad aspects: prevention and pacific settlement of disputes, regulation of armaments and armed forces, determination of threats to or breaches of the peace, nonmilitary measures of enforcement, supply and use of armed forces and facilities, and the nature and work of a security and armaments commission. The resulting papers constituted chapters of a charter and were intended for review by the Post-War Programs Committee and in due course—after further development, consultations with congressional leaders and others, and approval by the President—for use in the projected exchange of papers with the United Kingdom, the Soviet Union, and China.

Between March 16 and April 19, 1944, inclusive—the fourth stage— these papers were revised for the Secretary's use, primarily in the consultations he contemplated with Members of Congress. In the course of revision there were comprehensive discussions between the Secretary and various senior members of the Group on the main problems involved in the drafts. It will be recalled that in this period four meetings attended by representatives of the armed services were held. During these meetings all papers were opened for study and all security aspects of the problems at issue were re-examined in detail. In the meetings of the Group not attended by the military representatives particular consideration was given to the question of membership, including the right of withdrawal, to questions concerning the establishment of the organization, and to further examination of the general character and functions of the organization with reference especially to the general assembly, the executive council, and the international court. Attention in these meetings was also given to the nature of the general administrative arrangements that should be provided, including the question of what principal officers, such as the head of the secretariat and possibly a president, the organization might need. This stage of consideration resulted in the comparatively full draft "Possible Plan" that the Secretary used in his congressional consultations a few days later.

The fifth stage began April 20 and ended July 8. During these weeks, the drafts were more fully matured and became the proposals made by this Government for negotiation. The military representatives attended five of the meetings in this period and received the drafts and related papers on the whole "Plan." The full draft was supplemented and modified in the light of the congressional and other consultations then in progress and of the Group's own re-examination of the major problems it believed likely to arise in the then imminent Dumbarton Oaks negotiations. In the course of these meetings, further consideration was given to a large number of specific problems, including those concerning security arrangements, voting provisions, local and regional procedures and relationships, budgetary questions, and questions concerning entrance of this country into the organization, in view of the United States Constitution. In this period, the problems of dependent territories were discussed in terms of the possible establishment of international territorial trusteeships and of regional commissions for the development of dependent territories not placed under trusteeship. Several meetings were devoted to provisions concerning international economic and social problems within the structure of world security organization.

The Group's formulation of draft proposals in the economic and social fields had been postponed until over-all economic organization could be considered by the special interdivisional committee under Mr. Pasvolsky's chairmanship established in March.[4] Extensive study had been made early in the preparation of the problem of the coordination of international activities in these fields by the Subcommittee on International Organization and by the political research staff. A joint drafting group composed of research officers from the Divisions of Political Studies and of Economic Studies had begun work in December 1943 on a proposal for an over-all economic body within the framework of the general organization. The Group's "Possible Plan" as submitted to the President on December 29 stated that the organization should have "an agency for cooperation in economic and social activities."

Following the President's approval of the "Possible Plan" on February 3, 1944, a proposal was drafted in the Division of International Security and Organization early in March for the creation of a general economic commission and a general social commission. This proposal had been referred to the special interdivisional committee, composed of experts from both the political and economic offices, for consideration prior to its submission to the Informal Political Agenda Group. Thereafter, primary drafting responsibility for the concrete proposal to be made in this field rested for a time in the newly created Office of Economic Affairs, which, in collaboration with the Division of International Security and Organization, developed by the middle of June a draft proposal for an Economic Council. This draft, together with certain proposals formulated in the latter Division and designed to provide as well for the coordination of both economic and social activities, was considered at a series of meetings of the International Organization Group, beginning June 14. These meetings produced the definitive draft for an Economic and Social Council.

Similarly, the Agenda Group's consideration of specific proposals

---

[4] See p. 222.

with respect to dependent territories for inclusion in the "Possible Plan" was also long deferred, although provisions in this field had been contemplated as part of the plan for a general international organization from the beginning of the preparation in the Subcommittee on International Organization. The draft declaration of March 1943 on dependent peoples, however, which Secretary Hull had discussed with Mr. Eden at Quebec and with Mr. Eden and Mr. Molotov at Moscow, as described earlier, had left open the question of the relation of the arrangements projected therein to the proposed general organization. The amplification of this proposal desired by the Secretary had been begun in the interdivisional Committee on Colonial Problems late in the autumn of 1943, but no more definitive proposals had been formulated by the time the "Possible Plan" was sent to the President at the end of December. That "Plan" provided solely for "an agency for trusteeship responsibilities."

The interdivisional committee, which became the Committee on Colonial and Trusteeship Problems in January and then, in March, the Working Committee on Problems of Dependent Areas, continued its elaboration of the Secretary's original proposal throughout the early months of 1944, making only preliminary reference of certain basic recommendations to the Post-War Programs Committee in March.

It was not until May 10, following Mr. Bowman's return after accompanying the Under Secretary on his Mission to London, that the Informal Political Agenda Group began intensive consideration of specific proposals concerning dependent peoples for inclusion in the "Possible Plan." The British reaction to certain of the American ideas on problems concerning dependent areas had been consistently unfavorable. At the meeting of the Group on May 10 and at another two days later, Mr. Bowman reported in detail on the relevant aspects of his recent conversations in London, where with the express approval of the President he had discussed at length these problems with British officials, including the Prime Minister and the Colonial Secretary, Col. Oliver F. G. Stanley.

The Group's consideration of definitive proposals in this field continued into June. Documentation was provided by the above Working Committee and the Division of International Security and Organization. The resulting drafts, after clearance with the Office of Economic Affairs, were reviewed in the Post-War Programs Committee on June 15, 16, and 22 and, with some amendment, approved. A definitive proposal for territorial trusteeships was then incorporated by the Group in the "Possible Plan."

The subjects of discussion during the five stages in the Group's drafting had many interrelationships and thus often had to be taken up in a number of different connections. At most meetings several problems were scheduled for discussion; entire meetings were not usually devoted to any single problem. During the seventy meetings between December 9, 1943, and July 8, 1944, as many as thirty-six meetings, in whole or in part, considered the inherent character of any general international organization and the particular character of the specific organization under contemplation. The general assembly was discussed in thirty-four meetings, an executive council in fifty-three, an international court of justice in ten, pacific settlement of disputes in twenty-two, and determination of threats to or breaches of peace in fifteen. The Group took up the problems of initiation of enforcement action in seventeen meetings, nonmilitary measures in nine, and measures involving use of armed force in twenty-six. A security and armaments commission was discussed in fourteen, and regulation of armaments and armed forces in twenty-one. General administration, secretariat, and principal officers necessary for the organization were discussed in nine. Questions concerning the establishment and inauguration of the contemplated organization were before the Group at sixteen meetings. Regional procedures and agencies were particularly considered at seven meetings. Parts of thirteen meetings were devoted to the problems of territorial trusteeships and regional commissions in connection with dependent areas. Arrangements for economic and social cooperation and organization were the subject of twenty meetings in whole or in part.

The constitutional problems of American participation were taken up in connection with all subjects excepting some of a detailed, technical character. Similarly, the obligations and rights of members came into consideration at most meetings. The provisions for voting entered under the consideration of all problems relating to the functions and powers of the organization and the relationships of members to it. This basic question appeared at the start of the drafting and was not resolved to the satisfaction of all participants even by the last meeting of the Group.

EXCHANGE OF OUTLINES

No IMPORTANT step directed specifically toward arranging for negotiations on general international organization was taken for two months following the conversation at the Department on November 26, 1943, described above. On January 29, 1944, however, a member of the British Foreign Office, John Ward, and a member of the Post-Hostilities Planning Committee in London, Col. C. W. Walker, joined Paul Gore-Booth of the British Embassy in a further conversation at the Department on this question. In this conversation, an exchange of papers on posthostilities security arrangements, appropriately cleared as representing the views of experts, but on which official policy had not yet been determined, was projected subject to approval by higher authorities in order to obtain better understanding at an expert level of trends in thought and lines of preparation on both sides. Such preliminary exchange, however, did not take place before a more advanced procedure came under consideration in the spring of 1944. All steps toward exchange of views on substantive problems in this field then became direct moves leading into negotiations.

On February 1, 1944, further inquiries from the British Embassy were received in regard to the level of the future discussions and their coverage. A principal factor affecting this matter was that the views of the President on the basic ideas or "Plan" that the Secretary had presented to him on December 29 continued to be unknown. The Informal Political Agenda Group had proceeded for working purposes on the assumption of his general approval. The awaited approval was given on February 3, 1944, when the President, in discussion with the Secretary and some of the "consulting group," eliminated several of the alternatives that had been submitted on given points and initialed the paper. The drafting of specific United States proposals could now be expedited with no further uncertainty regarding the fundamental direction in which to move, and preliminary exchanges of views looking toward substantive negotiations could be carried forward with the other signatories of the Moscow Declaration.

At the Group's next meeting, February 8, it was told of the need to have a preliminary agenda with supporting papers for exchange purposes ready by March 15, and a projected outline was circulated and considered. On the same day, the British and Soviet Embassies were orally informed, on directive of the Secretary, by Assistant Secretary Dunn and Mr. Pasvolsky of the readiness of the United States to proceed toward "discussions" in Washington. The Department officials suggested that each of the three Governments prepare for exchange before these discussions papers on the general framework and functions of an organization for international peace and security and stated that an outline of proposed topics on which an exchange of views was believed necessary would be circulated shortly. The Embassies were also told that this Government would inform the Chinese as the discussions progressed; that, although at this stage we did not ask for Chinese participation in the discussions, we might later raise this question. The President had taken the position that after matters had proceeded a little further Generalissimo Chiang Kai-shek should be apprised but that for a time it would be well to restrict the number of those involved in these very confidential developments. The United States Embassies in Moscow and London were informed of the above steps by telegrams on February 10, 1944, with the explanation that at this stage no commitments by this Government were intended.

The Agenda Group on the same day was informed of the Secretary's desire to give an outline of principal problems to the British and Soviets within a week if practicable. The object of so doing was to have views covering all main problems prepared in advance of discussion in the light of a general knowledge of the thought of the other participants on what these problems were. The paper on which the Group began work was headed "Outline of Topics for Study and Discussion"; it was completed February 11.

Exchange of outlines began February 16. On that day the British Embassy handed to the Department a "Summary of Topics" as a suggested agenda for discussion, on which detailed papers would be sent from London later, and stated that the same was being communicated that day to the Soviet Government. It was made clear in this conversation that, before discussion of papers, some time would be taken for their study. The United States "Topical Outline," revised by the Group merely to put the topics in the form of questions, was handed to the British and Soviet Embassies on February 19, 1944.[5]

Comparison of the Outline and the Summary had already shown much similarity in the basic conceptions involved. At this time neither the British nor the American Government, however, knew whether such a preliminary paper was being prepared by the Soviet Government, and no indication of Soviet views was available for several weeks.

The Group now intensified its work on the papers to be exchanged under the Outline and completed those concerned particularly with security problems on March 3. A British *aide-mémoire* commenting on the Topical Outline was handed to the Department during a conversation on March 15, but the Group continued to draft on the basis of the Outline without seeking to reach any adjustment between its wording and that of the British Summary, since the variations were not serious. In the conversation on March 15, the question of a time schedule for exchange of papers was again raised, but the Department was as yet in no position to reply more specifically than heretofore.

On the same date, the Group's tentative proposals were distributed to the Post-War Programs Committee for review. This review did not end until April 7, owing to its interruption several times by other pressing matters. In the meantime, since the Group was responsible in the Department for perfecting the United States proposals in the first instance and for discerning in advance the foreseeable issues and difficulties likely to arise during international negotiations to establish a general international organization, it continued after March 15 to build and revise the proposals, taking into account the Committee's review as it was given. Moreover, no fundamental change of thought

---

[5] See appendix 34.

developed in the course of that review. Subsequently, problems coming up in the congressional and other consultations were immediately put under consideration as they arose. Thus, although a draft was ready by March 15, the proposals continued to be in process of refinement and completion by the Group through an unbroken chain of meetings for nearly four months longer.

Secretary Hull believed it timely in March to bring together for the public the basic principles underlying the Department's preparations, even though its specific proposals were still in the formative stage. A statement was therefore released to the press on March 21, 1944, entitled "Bases of the Foreign Policy of the United States," which summarized seventeen major aspects of this policy as the Secretary had set them forth over the past two years.[6] This step was one intended to provide the setting for the major address to follow and was taken just as major-power exchanges were beginning and as consultations with Members of Congress were invited on the proposals for international organization to be advanced by the United States.

The Secretary's address of April 9 was written while these consultations were being arranged and was connected both with the consultations and with further international exchanges. The time had come when developments in the direction of a general international organization were beginning to thread together into a single pattern of action.

CONGRESSIONAL AND OTHER CONSULTATIONS

WHILE CONSULTATIONS with Congress and with members of the general public had occurred earlier under the Advisory Committee, as has been observed, talks of a more definite character were now needed. The earlier consultations in 1942 and 1943 had been in the form of exploratory discussions, had involved no commitments on definitive views, and, although generally known to be occurring, were secret as to object and participants. The whole range of postwar problems had then been considered with Members of Congress on the basis of interchange of views on the possible courses of policy to adopt, and the Department thereby had the benefit of preliminary congressional advice. At that time and in the months since then, in-

---

[6] These seventeen aspects of policy related to "Our Fundamental National Interests, International Cooperation, International Organization Backed by Force, Political Differences, International Court of Justice, Reduction of Arms, Moscow Four-Nation Declaration, Spheres of Influence and Alliances, Surveillance Over Aggressor Nations, International Trade Barriers, International Finance, Atlantic Charter: Reciprocal Obligations, Sovereign Equality of Nations, Forms of Government, Non-Intervention, Liberty, Dependent Peoples." *Department of State Bulletin*, X, 275–76.

formal conversations had also taken place between the Secretary and Members of Congress at the Secretary's apartment or office, and numerous conversations with private citizens had been held. These were along lines customary in the Government, but they were all on a nonpartisan basis and dealt with future as well as current policy.

The object of the Secretary's consultations beginning in the spring of 1944 was to inform Members of Congress of the specific proposals in contemplation for the general organization and of the progress toward negotiation, to discuss the major questions that they or the Department foresaw, and to obtain their views and suggestions on these matters. The basic motive was to avoid a repetition of the divided attitude between the Executive and the Congress that had prevented participation by the United States in the League of Nations immediately after World War I and weakened the furtherance of our national interests thereafter. Consultation with the public was postponed, apart from a highly selective reference of proposals to a few private citizens, until after the possibility of unified major-power proposals had been clarified through informal negotiations. The explanation of basic objectives, the main concepts underlying the plans, and the procedure being followed were, however, set forth publicly even before the congressional consultations on the plans themselves actually commenced, and the broad policies to be advanced were outlined publicly before negotiations actually started on the substantive proposals.

The fact that the international exchanges to March 15, 1944, had raised a clear, though not yet fully developed, prospect that the major powers would begin detailed negotiations in the relatively near future, and the further fact that the possible United States proposals on the broad lines approved by the President were being rapidly matured in the Department, suggested that the time had come to seek congressional advice of a more explicit character. The Secretary discussed the matter with the President and then, on March 22, 1944, visited the Foreign Relations Committee to survey with the Senators developments under way. At that time he invited the Chairman to name a nonpartisan group to consider with him informally at the Department the possible plan being drafted for a general international organization. The group of Senators named in response by the Committee was composed of four Democrats, three Republicans, and one Progressive. Four had been members of the Advisory Committee: Senators Connally of Texas and Walter F. George of Georgia, Democrats, and Senators Wallace H. White, Jr., of Maine, and Warren R. Austin of Vermont, Republicans. Those new to such discussions were Senators Alben W. Barkley of Kentucky and Guy M. Gillette of Iowa, Democrats, and Senator Arthur H. Vandenberg of Michigan, Republican, and Robert M. LaFollette, Jr., of Wisconsin, Progressive. All eight had been active in considering the "Connally Resolution" of the preceding autumn. Since the selection of this Senatorial group took place gradually over several weeks, no meeting was held until it was completed.

On March 24, 1944, much of what Secretary Hull had said to the Senate Committee two days before was repeated to twenty-four Members of the House of Representatives with whom, at their request, he talked in his office. The Representatives in the group were all Republicans and were all serving their first term in the House: James C. Auchincloss of New Jersey; Frank A. Barrett of Wyoming; Ranulf Compton of Connecticut; Daniel Ellison of Maryland; Harris Ellsworth of Oregon; Angier L. Goodwin of Massachusetts; Robert Hale of Maine; Christian A. Herter of Massachusetts; Hal Holmes and Walt Horan of Washington; Harry P. Jeffrey of Ohio; J. Leroy Johnson of California; Walter H. Judd of Minnesota; Bernard W. Kearney of New York; Charles M. La Follette of Indiana; Clare Boothe Luce and John D. McWilliams of Connecticut; Chester E. Merrow of New Hampshire; Arthur L. Miller of Nebraska; Alvin E. O'Konski of Wisconsin; Norris Poulson of California; Winifred C. Stanley and Dean P. Taylor of New York; and Henry L. Towe of New Jersey. The Secretary, in sketching the foreign situation to these Representatives, stressed the importance of a nonpartisan approach to postwar problems and advised them of the work done during the past two years in which Members from both Houses of Congress had taken part. He said that he was about to resume discussions with Senators and Representatives of both parties upon the plan for international organization in its present form. He considered this to be desirable before such a plan was submitted for public discussion, lest it be debated controversially while still under development, and furthermore he wished to discuss the plan with our principal associates in the war before public discussion of it, since otherwise they might feel that there was a lack of cooperation on our part.

Promptly after these meetings, Secretary Hull with the assistance of a number of officers of the Department turned to the writing of his major address of April 9, 1944.[7] In this address he pointed out that any course of action toward international organization would obviously have to be acceptable abroad and to the American people at large, the Congress, and the Executive. In reaching acceptable proposals, he believed, details should not be discussed first, since this would risk divergence of opinion on the lesser problems involved, some of which might prove immaterial. We were therefore, he said, following a procedure which, though slow and difficult, he believed preferable. In his view:

---

[7] Cf., p. 233 ff.

". . . The only practicable course is to begin by obtaining agreement, first, upon broad principles, setting forth direction and general policy. We must then go on to explore alternative methods and finally settle upon a proposal which embodies the principal elements of agreement and leaves to future experience and discussion those matters of comparative detail which at present remain in the realm of speculation."

He then set forth the broad objectives of "an international organization to maintain peace and prevent aggression" and reported on the current status of our related preparation, saying:

". . . Such an organization must be based upon firm and binding obligations that the member nations will not use force against each other and against any other nation except in accordance with the arrangements made. It must provide for the maintenance of adequate forces to preserve peace and it must provide the institutions and procedures for calling this force into action to preserve peace. But it must provide more than this. It must provide for an international court for the development and application of law to the settlement of international controversies which fall within the realm of law, for the development of machinery for adjusting controversies to which the field of law has not yet been extended, and for other institutions for the development of new rules to keep abreast of a changing world with new problems and new interests.

"We are at a stage where much of the work of formulating plans for the organization to maintain peace has been accomplished. It is right and necessary that we should have the advice and help of an increasing number of members of the Congress. Accordingly, I have requested the Chairman of the Senate Committee on Foreign Relations to designate a representative, bipartisan group for this purpose. Following these and similar discussions with members of the House of Representatives, we shall be in a position to go forward again with other nations and, upon learning their views, be able to submit to the democratic processes of discussion a more concrete proposal."

Following this statement of intention to proceed first to consultation, next to the preliminary negotiation of a concrete plan, and then to public debate of this plan, the Secretary referred briefly to other problems that had also to be dealt with. He mentioned among these the treatment of enemy states, expansion of production and removal of trade barriers, maintenance and improvement of "the standard of living in our own and in all countries," provision of investment capital, stabilization of currency, development of communications and transport, and "the improvement of labor standards and standards of health and nutrition." He said he was unable in this address to "explain the work which has been done" in this connection, but he remarked that it had been "extensive" in these fields and that in "many of them proposals are far advanced toward the stage of discussion with members of the Congress prior to formulation for public discussion."

The Department had been apprised by the British Embassy on

the day preceding this address, April 8, of the Soviet reaction to the British Summary and the American Outline. Foreign Minister Molotov had stated on April 5, in a written reply to a British inquiry, that in his opinion fundamental questions should be discussed first. Examples of these were the relationship to exist between the general organization and the directing body, the method by which each of these would reach decisions, and the relation of mutual defense arrangements and any regional systems to the general security system. On certain other questions, clarification was needed; these included specifically those concerning the provision of bases for common use and the relationship between the international labor organization and the general security system. The Soviet Union, it was stated, did not regard acceptance of a list of topics as meaning settlement of all the topics in a favorable sense, or the order of topics on a list as being the order for discussion. The British list and the American list would undoubtedly assist in the coming discussions and, subject to the foregoing provisos, Mr. Molotov had no objection to their use as the basis of discussion in framing the program for negotiations on general security organization. He also did not object in principle to exchange of documents after the order of questions had been settled and those of first priority had been determined in negotiations in Washington. No direct message to Washington was received from Moscow.

In a telegram on April 17 to Under Secretary Stettinius, then on his Mission to London, Secretary Hull replied to inquiries received orally from the British, reported by the Under Secretary five days earlier, that the United States contemplated that the coming discussions in Washington should be, at least in the beginning, at the "higher technical level" rather than at a Cabinet level. He doubted that we would be ready for such talks as early as May, which the British were suggesting, since our readiness depended on the consultations with congressional leaders. At this time we did not expect to make any announcement of the discussions, but this might be reconsidered. Relative to a British suggestion of holding some discussions in Moscow, the Secretary said we would be glad to give thought to the matter.

On April 20, Mr. Hull again cabled the Under Secretary to say that no date for the Washington discussions could yet be set; that further study had led us to make some modification of several important points in our tentative proposals; and that the talks with congressional groups might result in additional modifications. He would therefore adhere to his plan for exchange of documents before undertaking discussions, even informally. As we had indicated to the British Embassy in Washington, we would also raise the question of China's participation when the documents were ready for exchange.

The situation was thus developing—with substantive discussion and any definite schedule of arrangements both deferred—when the detailed consultations with congressional leaders got under way in response to the invitation of March 24. A draft of tentative proposals was ready, though, as the Secretary had said, it was still undergoing change. It bore the date April 24, 1944.

The first meeting was held on April 25 in the Secretary's office. Seven of the eight appointed Senators were present: Senators Connally, Barkley, George, Gillette, Vandenberg, White, and Austin. The character of this and the further meetings was defined as informal, in which no member would be requested to give opinions or assume a commitment on the merits of the questions involved unless he wished. The Secretary described the cooperation of Senators and Representatives in the early part of the preparation, emphasizing the nonpartisan efforts so far made. He also stressed the need of developing support among peoples and governments for a suitable postwar program before confusion set in at the end of hostilities, the need of unity among the United States, United Kingdom, and Soviet Union if the general international organization were to succeed, and the need of informed public support on a nonpartisan basis in our own country. He handed to each Senator in strict confidence a copy of the April 24 draft of proposals, "Possible Plan for a General International Organization" and certain supporting documents. The Plan had six sections: I. General Character of an International Organization; II. A General Assembly; III. An Executive Council; IV. Arrangements for Security; V. An International Court of Justice; and VI. General Administration and Secretariat. Three other sections were noted as in preparation: VII. Arrangements for Economic and Social Cooperation; VIII. Arrangements for Territorial Trusteeship; and IX. Establishment.

The Plan was reviewed in general terms in this meeting, and the group was informed that copies of the same draft had just been handed for study and comment to three eminent jurists.[8] These men were former Chief Justice Charles Evans Hughes, Republican candidate for President in 1916; ex-Governor Nathan L. Miller of New York, Republican, who had been an associate judge of the Court of Appeals; and the Honorable John W. Davis, who had been Solicitor General of the United States, Ambassador to Great Britain, and Democratic candidate for President in 1924. The copies had been conveyed to them by Myron C. Taylor on behalf of Secretary Hull and with the approval of President Roosevelt. The Secretary in his letter of April 19, 1944, to Mr. Taylor asking that discussions with the three jurists be undertaken, as Mr. Taylor had suggested, wrote: "I am very anxious to have the benefit of their judgment on the gen-

---

[8] Not identified by name at this meeting.

eral plan and on the main provisions." After Mr. Taylor's preliminary discussions with the jurists and receipt of their observations, further talks with them were held, those in Washington being joined by Secretary Hull. These consultations afforded opportunity for additional and independent consideration of the proposed plan with highly capable citizens of legal training and exceptional experience in public and world affairs.

The second consultative meeting with the group of Senators took place on May 2, 1944. All eight were present. A later draft of the "Possible Plan," dated April 29, was given the participants after this meeting and was used henceforth; this differed from the previous draft chiefly in improved organization of material and more detailed provisions on peaceful settlement.[9] Discussion of substance characterized this meeting, since there had been opportunity for a week's study of the papers. The main questions raised dealt with (a) regional representation as a basis for council membership; (b) the need to consult with South American countries and to weigh the effect of the proposed international organization on the inter-American system; (c) major-power unanimity; (d) abstention from voting by parties to international controversies; and (e) the application of executive and legislative authority regarding the use of force. One question that arose was that if the international organization were established before the peace treaties were made, and if secret commitments had been made on peace settlements, might the United States be obligated to support a bad peace? This led to query and discussion whether there should be a provisional international organization until the peace settlements were made, the Secretary stating, however, that this had already been considered and rejected as impractical.

Secretary Hull expressed the view at this and subsequent meetings that for the United States to give up the idea of an organization to keep the peace, because of apprehension over the kind of peace that might be made, would be to give up the means whereby the making of a good peace could be facilitated and the peace itself progressively perfected thereafter. He pointed out further that such a decision would constitute a surrender of American leadership. It would leave the world at the end of the war without a program through which the basic principles enunciated in the Atlantic Charter, the Moscow Declaration, and the Connally Resolution could be realized and the international collaboration developed during the war carried over into the peace.

The third meeting was held May 12. Senator Austin was absent, and Senator White had to leave early. At this discussion the Senators were informed that the three jurists to whom the April 24 draft had

[9] See appendix 35.

been given had approved the essentials of the Plan. The Secretary had meanwhile conferred twice with former Chief Justice Hughes and had discussed the proposals with Mr. Davis and ex-Governor Miller at lunch.

The question of commitment to support a possibly bad peace was again of major concern at this meeting, as was the question of unanimity (or veto) and its relation to the power of the international organization to order military forces into enforcement action. The position of small states arose for discussion, and the remaining important questions raised in the preceding meeting, together with questions concerning the attitude of the Soviet Union toward future international cooperation, were considered at further length. While not all the Senators commented explicitly on whether the United States should proceed to international conversations with the other large nations, the consensus of the group was to that effect. The Senators themselves undertook to draft a statement accordingly.

The fourth meeting on May 29 was held on Senator Connally's initiative. Agreement on the wording of the projected statement had not been reached by the Senators. In this connection there was further discussion of the earlier question whether, before supporting an international organization to maintain peace, it would be necessary to know whether a good or bad peace would be made, with the organization obliged to support a possibly bad one. At the end of the meeting, Secretary Hull read to the group a draft statement on the four meetings, which he, with his advisers, had prepared and the tenor of which he had already discussed with the President. With the consent of all he gave the statement to the press later that day: [10]

"The first phase of the informal conversations with the eight Senators has been concluded. We had frank and fruitful discussions on the general principles, questions, and plans relating to the establishment of an international peace and security organization in accordance with the principles contained in the Moscow four-nation declaration, the Connally resolution, and other similar declarations made in this country. I am definitely encouraged and am ready to proceed, with the approval of the President, with informal discussions on this subject with Great Britain, Russia, and China, and then with governments of other United Nations.

"Meanwhile, I shall have further discussions with these and other leaders of both parties in the two Houses of Congress, and with others. The door of non-partisanship will continue to be wide open here at the Department of State, especially when any phase of the planning for a post-war security organization is under consideration."

---

[10] *Department of State Bulletin*, X, 510.

In the next three days, two lines of action were pursued. The first was in connection with the major-power exchanges. The Secretary met with Ambassadors Gromyko and Halifax on May 30 to inform them that the United States was ready to proceed with informal conversations as soon as their Governments were ready, and to request their Governments to fix an early convenient date to begin the "conference." In addition, he requested consideration of China's participation. The draft proposals were not conveyed at this time, the Secretary's suggestion being to have all the drafts "considered together" at the opening of the "informal conference." This seemed acceptable to the Ambassadors. That same day he reviewed developments with the Chinese Ambassador, Dr. Wei Tao-ming.

On the next day, May 31, speaking by telephone in the absence of Lord Halifax to the British Minister, Sir Ronald Campbell, the Secretary felt obliged to discuss the possibility that the Soviet Government, as at the Moscow Conference, might not agree to the participation of China in this informal conference, the Soviet Union not being at war with Japan.[11] Should this eventuate, the Secretary suggested having the conference in two series of talks, one with the Soviet Union at one time and the other with China at another time. This, in effect, had been done at the Cairo Conference, which was an Anglo-American-Chinese meeting preceding the Anglo-American-Soviet meeting at Tehran. The Secretary later on the same day informed the Chinese Ambassador of his suggestion, and on June 1, when the Soviet Ambassador called before leaving for Moscow, the Secretary advanced the same conditional possibility. On June 2, Generalissimo Chiang Kai-shek expressed his pleasure at the Secretary's suggestion. The Chinese Government was then promptly informed by telegram of the status of our views and plans in the sense already conveyed to the British and Soviet Ambassadors.

The second line of action after the public report on the Senatorial consultations was a statement by the Secretary, June 1, 1944, on one point that had come up in these consultations and had been made the subject of an inquiry from the press. This question concerned the role of small nations in the contemplated international security organization. The Secretary's statement asserted that the proposed organization was a "mutual affair," reflecting the "common interest" and "self-interest in every mutual sense" of both the large and the small nations. The Secretary further pointed out:

". . . As far as this Government is concerned, whenever I have said anything on this subject, it has always emphasized the all-inclusive nature of the world situation and our disposition and

---

[11] The Neutrality Pact between Japan and the U. S. S. R. continued at this time in full force, though not certain effect. Furthermore, reports indicated that relations between the U. S. S. R. and China were somewhat strained.

purpose to see that all nations, especially the small nations, are kept on a position of equality with all others and that, in every practicable way, there will be cooperation." [12]

While neither this Government nor any other could "give anybody a blueprint as to all the details of how these relationships between all the different nations will be gradually developed and perfected," he said, sovereign equality of all peace-loving states "irrespective of size and strength, as partners in a future system of general security" was the policy of the United States.

It was at this point that the Secretary's consultation with members from the House of Representatives on the Plan took place. The Representatives participating in the meeting in the Secretary's office on June 2, included members of the Committee on Foreign Affairs, but, more basically, constituted the House leadership for both parties. From the Democratic side were Representatives Sam Rayburn of Texas, Speaker; John W. McCormack of Massachusetts, majority leader; Sol Bloom of New York, Chairman of the Foreign Affairs Committee; and Robert Ramspeck of Georgia, majority whip; from the Republican side, Representatives Joseph W. Martin, Jr., of Massachusetts, minority leader; Charles A. Eaton of New Jersey, ranking minority member of the Foreign Affairs Committee; and Leslie C. Arends of Illinois, minority whip. Each was given a copy of the latest draft of the tentative proposals, which was a revision of the draft of April 29, and a general discussion of some length followed. The continuity of these specially arranged consultations was unavoidably interrupted at this juncture by the approaching recess of the Congress for the party conventions in this election year. The series was resumed later in the summer.

Additional, more general consultations were meanwhile under way and continued until later in June. On June 22, the Secretary conferred, without the draft Plan, with Senators Joseph H. Ball of Minnesota and Harold H. Burton of Ohio, Republicans, and Lister Hill of Alabama, and Carl A. Hatch of New Mexico, Democrats (often called the "B_2H_2" group), at their request. Moreover, in the period of these talks and until the party conventions had been held, Assistant Secretary Breckinridge Long and others were active for the Secretary in discussing with political leaders of both parties the planks concerning international organization to be incorporated in the party platforms.

A form of expert drafting consultation was also undertaken on behalf of the Secretary when Mr. Hackworth and Mr. Cohen of the Informal Political Agenda Group met with Judge Manley O. Hudson in New York, June 9–11 and 26, 1944, to consider article by article the

---

[12] *Department of State Bulletin*, X, 509.

proposals being developed for an international court of justice. Their meetings were held on the basis of drafts of a projected statute and a related "Introductory Note" concerning the existing Permanent Court of International Justice. These had been prepared by the two members of the Group, with the assistance of the research staff. They took into account not only the Statute of the existing Permanent Court and the draft proposals of the earlier Legal Subcommittee, but also the recent Report of the Informal Inter-Allied Committee on the Future of the Permanent Court of International Justice, the views of the Post-War Programs Committee as expressed concerning the court on March 20, 1944, and a proposal drawn up by the staff in light of all the foregoing.

Also, occasional conversations between individual representatives of interested public organizations and various officials occurred, either on or bearing upon the general problems of future international organization.

Beginning approximately with the first of the basic congressional consultations and with the steps described above toward an informal conference among the four governments, work continued to be pressed on the Plan. By June the draft used at the start of the consultations had been revised, added to, and rearranged into eleven sections. The former fourth section was replaced with one on Pacific Settlement of Disputes. Determination of Threats to the Peace or Breaches of the Peace and Action with Respect Thereto was inserted as section VI, and Regulation of Armaments and Armed Forces as section VII.[13]

With the "Possible Plan" about to become a final recommendation, and with the conclusion on June 2 of the congressional consultations on the Plan, another discussion with the President was considered desirable. It was also believed advisable, in view of increasing public discussion, which was partly reflected in the Secretary's statement of June 1, for the President to make a statement concerning the views and plans so far developed. A draft for this purpose was written in collaboration between the Secretary and some members of the Agenda Group on June 14 and was amended the following morning.

The Secretary and Mr. Stettinius, Mr. Bowman, Mr. Davis, and Mr. Pasvolsky of the Agenda Group discussed the proposed statement and plans later with President Roosevelt on June 15, and with limited amendments the statement was issued by the President that afternoon.[14] It mentioned the consideration given to suggestions received from groups, organizations, and individuals and emphasized "the entirely non-partisan nature of these consultations," devoting special attention to the "cooperative spirit" shown in the discussion of all

---

[13] The former sections VI–IX were renumbered to become VIII–XI.
[14] *Department of State Bulletin*, X, 552–53.

aspects of the postwar program. "This," it continued, "is a tribute to the political leaders who realize that the national interest demands a national program now."

The remainder of the short statement, as given below, constituted an announcement for public information and consideration of the broad framework of the "Possible Plan." It likewise, viewed in the light of the stress on nonpartisan participation in determining this framework, constituted an announcement to our Allies of the American unity that underlay this official position.

"The maintenance of peace and security must be the joint task of all peace-loving nations. We have, therefore, sought to develop plans for an international organization comprising all such nations. The purpose of the organization would be to maintain peace and security and to assist the creation, through international cooperation, of conditions of stability and well-being necessary for peaceful and friendly relations among nations.

"Accordingly, it is our thought that the organization would be a fully representative body with broad responsibilities for promoting and facilitating international cooperation, through such agencies as may be found necessary, to consider and deal with the problems of world relations. It is our further thought that the organization would provide for a council, elected annually by the fully representative body of all nations, which would include the four major nations and a suitable number of other nations. The council would concern itself with peaceful settlement of international disputes and with the prevention of threats to the peace or breaches of the peace.

"There would also be an international court of justice to deal primarily with justiciable disputes.

"We are not thinking of a superstate with its own police forces and other paraphernalia of coercive power. We are seeking effective agreement and arrangements through which the nations would maintain, according to their capacities, adequate forces to meet the needs of preventing war and of making impossible deliberate preparation for war and to have such forces available for joint action when necessary.

"All this, of course, will become possible once our present enemies are defeated and effective arrangements are made to prevent them from making war again.

"Beyond that, the hope of a peaceful and advancing world will rest upon the willingness and ability of the peace-loving nations, large and small, bearing responsibility commensurate with their individual capacities, to work together for the maintenance of peace and security."

CHAPTER XIII

"Tentative Proposals" and Negotiating Arrangements

THE FURTHER steps to refine the American proposals for a general international organization and to arrange major-power negotiations on this question were taken as situations demanding action were developing in all fields. The period of the spring and early summer of 1944 was a time of convergence both in war movements and in postwar developments.

Rome was liberated June 4. The successful breaching of the German sea wall of Europe by the cross-channel invasion of Normandy, June 6, D–day, decisively heralded eventual victory in Europe. The drive of the Allied forces inland then began swiftly to bring the policies to be applied in liberated areas to the operations stage in widening parts of Western Europe. Coordinate in timing with the drive in the West, the Soviet offensive across Poland, opening June 23, presaged "postwar" operations regarding Eastern Europe, where seriously conflicting forces were already in evidence, while the battles in the Balkans brought nearer the problems involved in the surrender of the Nazi satellites. Already, in March and April, negotiations looking toward withdrawal of an enemy state from the war had taken place with the Rumanians, albeit without immediate result. In the Pacific, the storming of Saipan by United States forces on June 15 was a long northward step toward Japan's home islands.

POSTWAR PREPARATION BY D-DAY

THE PROGRESS of the war toward military victory made it imperative to have available approved policy recommendations to guide this Government as the occasion arose in its discussions, negotiations, and actions with the other major Allies respecting both the enemy states and the liberated friendly nations. The Post-War Programs Committee, which had cleared a series of basic policy recommendations on the treatment of Germany, Rumania, Bulgaria, and Hungary by the end of May, concentrated in June primarily on recommended policy toward liberated European states. The interdivisional committees, particularly the committee on Germany, and the interdepartmental Working Security Committee, which was concerned with the problems relating to the European enemy states, accelerated their drafting of more detailed recommendations. Even recommendations already approved had constantly to be reviewed as the course of events unfolded and the nature of actual postwar conditions could be measured more exactly.

The military progress simultaneously increased the pressure toward completion of other aspects of postwar preparation. It did so particularly in regard to obtaining United Nations agreement, before the end of hostilities, on a general international organization for cooperation in maintaining peace and security. It was this problem that was fundamental to the postwar policy preparation in all other fields. The predication that a world security organization would exist was, for illustration, a weighty factor in policy recommendations on the territorial problems in areas affected by the war—from the standpoint of the organized cooperation it would signify, the obligations its members would assume, and related considerations including an anticipated lessening of pressures for local boundary changes designed to gain some wholly national strategic advantage. However, since it was the adopted policy to defer international commitments in the territorial field until after the war, except where the states directly concerned could reach a peaceable settlement, there was still time before the final decisions had to be made on most territorial problems. In many other parts of the American preparation, on the other hand, the stage was being reached where conclusion of international agreement was imperative if needed mechanisms were to be available when hostilities ceased.

As previously described, plans in several specialized economic and social fields had already become the subject of international negotiation. To a varying extent, each of them was influenced by the conceptions molding the "Possible Plan" for the world security organization, and the cumulative developments concerning all the projected functional organizations, as they were called, added to the urgency of clarifying the nature of the general organization and of determining its date of establishment. It was intended in the "Possible Plan," that the international organizations for specialized economic or other functions should be related to the general international organization in the sense that the latter would be an over-all organization with power to coordinate international activities in these functional fields. Obviously, therefore, the nature and timing of the establishment of the functional organizations were necessarily conditional upon the nature of the general organization and the prospects for its establishment. Consequently preparation in the specialized fields and in the field of general organization had to be closely integrated. This integration was achieved, within the Department, partly through participation, occasionally or continuously, by some of the same staff officers in the work in all these fields and partly through the process of review of all plans at the high technical level and by the Post-War Programs Committee. Where other Departments were also interested, it was accomplished through the various interdepartmental committees at the working and policy levels as already described.

The developments in the specialized fields of most immediate concern, as entailing negotiations for permanent functional international organizations during the spring and summer of 1944, have been discussed above. They were, in summary, the Conference of Allied Ministers of Education, which produced a tentative draft constitution for an educational and cultural organization; the Conference of the International Labor Organization, which provided for the further development of the ILO in the labor and social fields and for its eventual integration with other international organizations; the Bretton Woods Conference, where agreement was reached on the establishment of an international monetary fund and an international bank; and issuance by the Interim Commission on Food and Agriculture of a draft constitution for a permanent organization in this field. In each instance, the possible establishment in the future of an over-all organization was taken into account.

This network of international negotiations involved, though in differing measure, all of the United and Associated Nations in the construction of organized cooperation looking toward advancement of the general well-being and, thus, toward world peace and security. These negotiations as a whole were evidence of the general desire to create the economic and social organizations concerned by the close of hostilities in order, if possible, to have them available in handling the anticipated problems to be faced after victory.

In the political fields the problems had come by the date of the Allied landing in France on June 6 to be distinguishable into two broad types, one relating to immediate posthostilities arrangements and the other concerning international organization and security. Work was pressed on both, concurrently.

The preparations for immediate posthostilities arrangements were under the direction of Mr. Dunn. They were at various stages of advancement. Formulation of policy for the Far East was still in the stage of tentative recommendations from which more detailed preparations could proceed. Agreement on policy directives on certain problems regarding Germany was being reached in order to guide Ambassador Winant in the negotiations then under way in the European Advisory Commission. Final decision was being made on the policies to be applied in operations, either immediate or imminent, in the liberated areas.

The Far East Area Committee, composed of experts from the Office of Far Eastern Affairs, the Division of Territorial Studies, and other interested offices and divisions, was at work on a comprehensive series of papers being prepared at the request of the War and Navy Departments. The Civil Affairs Division of the War Department and the Occupied Areas Section of the Navy Department had asked the Office of Special Political Affairs on February 18, 1944, for the "recommendations and advice" of the State Department on "some of the fundamental questions which confront us in the planning, training and organization for civil affairs administration in Japan Proper, the Mandated Islands, and the countries occupied by Japan." An enclosure enumerating some of these basic questions accompanied this letter, which was to be followed by other similar requests. By May 15, twenty papers prepared in response by the interdivisional area committee and cleared by the Post-War Programs Committee had been transmitted to the War and Navy Departments. The basic document in this series set forth "the Post-War Objectives of the United States in Regard to Japan," [1] and the other papers dealt "principally with measures and policies for achieving" these objectives. These papers were described as being "in the nature of suggestions to the Army and Navy, prepared to accord with the situation as it can now be visualized, for the purpose of enabling CAD and OAS to prepare for the tasks ahead". Throughout the following summer and autumn, the interdivisional area committee on the Far East was engaged in the preparation of additional papers of this character for transmission to the War and Navy Departments.

The interdivisional committees on Germany and on the Balkan-Danubian area, composed of experts from the Office of European Affairs and its divisions, the Division of Territorial Studies, and other units having related economic or political interests, were working on the problems concerned with the European enemy states. The problems concerning Austria, not considered an enemy state, were handled by the committee on Germany. The policy papers prepared in these committees were being cleared first through the interdepartmental Working Security Committee, then by the Post-War Programs Committee and, where major economic questions were presented, interdepartmentally by the Executive Committee on Economic Foreign Policy. When approved, these papers were sent, as already noted, to Ambassador Winant in London, United States Representative on the European Advisory Commission. The committee on Germany was also preparing for the use of the War Department a series of recommendations concerning German education, in response to a request of April 5, 1944, from the Civil Affairs Division.

The interdivisional country and area committees working on prob-

---

[1] For text of basic document, see appendix 36.

lems of liberated areas and territorial adjustments, composed of experts from the geographic and economic offices and divisions and from the Division of Territorial Studies, were similarly clarifying American objectives in these areas and formulating policy recommendations to guide operations in the period of transition from war to peace. Their papers were being cleared through the Post-War Programs Committee, and such of the economic sections of these papers as needed interdepartmental clearance received it through the Executive Committee on Economic Foreign Policy.

In the case of Italy, the stage of operations had been reached with the conclusion of the Italian armistice in September 1943, and United States policy had begun to be implemented. The interdivisional committee on Italy concerned itself primarily with such long-range problems as those involved in basic political reform in that country and possible territorial adjustments that might arise at the time of the peace settlement.

A special *ad hoc* drafting committee, comprised of experts from the Division of Territorial Studies and from the Divisions of Eastern European, Central European, and Southeastern European Affairs was established in June 1944 at the suggestion of Secretary Hull to prepare an analysis of territorial disputes in Europe and elsewhere with a view to reducing the number of those that might require Allied negotiation. This committee continued its work into July and produced a basic policy paper on the settlement of territorial disputes in Europe, which was cleared by the Post-War Programs Committee on July 28, 1944.[2]

The second field of political preparation—international organization and security—was under the direction of Mr. Pasvolsky. Two *ad hoc* groups, both informal, were working in relationship with the Informal Political Agenda Group by June 6.[3] One of these groups had been set up five days earlier, at the suggestion on May 25 of the representatives of the Joint Chiefs on the Agenda Group, to hasten the consideration of whether interim consultative machinery should be established among the four major powers to implement particularly their commitment in paragraph five of the Moscow Declaration:

> "That for the purpose of maintaining international peace and security pending the re-establishment of law and order and the inauguration of a system of general security, they will consult with one another and as occasion requires with other members of the United Nations with a view to joint action on behalf of the community of nations."

---

[2] See appendix 37.

[3] This was in addition to the small group on the international court comprised of Messrs. Hackworth and Cohen, in consultation with Judge Manley O. Hudson. Cf. p. 267.

While this question naturally involved examination of the European Advisory Commission and the scope of its functions, the main point of concern was whether some form of recommendatory interim security commission was needed among the major powers to handle problems of global security—other than those concerning enemy states—during the transitional period before a general international organization could become operative. This group was also asked shortly to consider whether the peace settlements should be negotiated before a permanent international organization was established. This was a matter on which, as has been seen, a negative position had already been taken, but which had been discussed in the congressional consultations and which the Secretary wished to have reviewed.

The members of this *ad hoc* group were, in fact, most of those from the State, War, and Navy Departments on the Agenda Group, and its meetings constituted in effect extra meetings of that Group with the military representatives. The group was composed of Admiral Willson and General Embick representing the Joint Chiefs of Staff; General Strong representing the War Department; Admiral Hepburn, with Admiral Harold C. Train as his alternate, representing the Navy Department; and Mr. Dunn, with Mr. Matthews as his alternate, Mr. Hackworth, Mr. Pasvolsky, and Alger Hiss. The assisting technical experts were an officer of the Division of International Organization and Security, Mr. Sandifer, and the Secretary of the Policy Committee, Mr. Yost. Its eighth and last meeting was July 6.

The second *ad hoc* group, which came to be known as the "Armaments Committee," consisted of Joseph C. Green of the Agenda Group; Frederick Exton of the Department's Supply and Resources Division; General Strong; Admiral Hepburn, with Admiral Train as his alternate; Mr. Wilson, with Mr. Hiss as alternate from the Office of Special Political Affairs; and assisting experts on armament problems from the Division of International Organization and Security, Messrs. Sandifer, Donald Blaisdell, and Clyde Eagleton and Misses Marcia Maylott and Pauline Reinsch and from the Policy Committee Secretariat, Mr. Yost. By invitation Professors Edward M. Earle of the Institute of Advanced Study at Princeton, N. J., and Harold H. Sprout of Princeton University took part in two meetings. The primary objective of this high-level technical group was to make preliminary studies of the future agreements contemplated under the "Possible Plan" for regulation of armaments and armed forces, including manufacture and international traffic in arms. This group also studied problems of the possible "Security and Armaments Commission" and the agreements for provision of armed forces envisaged under that plan. These studies were desired in connection with the future implementation of the proposals being incorporated in the Plan, and while the studies of this *ad hoc* group were reflected in the discussions molding the Plan, its work was otherwise of an essentially long-range preparatory character. For these studies, the group held twenty-three meetings, commencing April 11 and ending July 27, 1944.[4]

As of June 6, 1944, the Agenda Group was working primarily on three aspects of the "Possible Plan," as it was still called. These were (a) the relation of regional to world-wide arrangements for pacific settlement of international disputes; (b) arrangements for dependent areas; and (c) refinement of the Plan especially from the standpoint of the position of the major powers in the proposed organization. While the Agenda Group as such did not directly undertake the steps currently in process among the signatories of the Moscow Declaration to arrange negotiations, its Departmental members did so with the assistance of the main staff officers of the Group.

The Informal Political Agenda Group was now about to be converted into "The International Organization Group," the first formal recognition of its existence and of the highly special function it had been performing since the previous December. Its last meeting as the Agenda Group was June 7, 1944. By this time it had largely completed, on the basis of the December 1943 memorandum of basic ideas, the draft "Possible Plan" in eleven sections.

For the last month of drafting, out of which the final Plan emerged, the renamed Group after June 7 concentrated most heavily on the precise economic and social arrangements to be included, to which several meetings were given over in whole or in part, and next most heavily on the provisions concerning dependent territories and on local and regional procedures in connection with security action. Budgetary and administrative provisions were considered at the meeting of July 5. By July 6, the full draft was available, now entitled: "Tentative Proposals for a General International Organization." At the last meeting of the International Organization Group, July 8, problems about which the members still had some questions were discussed, particularly regional arrangements and, very briefly, voting provisions.

The draft of the Tentative Proposals transmitted, as will be noted shortly, to the other three major powers was dated July 18, 1944. This draft was identical with the preceding draft of July 6 except for the omission, at the urging of the Joint Chiefs of Staff to avoid international discussion at this period in the war, of the section concerned with international trusteeship for dependent territories.[5] The basic framework of American policy on a postwar general organi-

---

[4] After Dumbarton Oaks, this group was reconstituted, following a discussion in the Policy Committee on Oct. 18, 1944, to consider certain long-range problems in the field of current armaments and arms traffic-control policy and continued to function intermittently into September 1945.

[5] See appendixes 38 and 39.

zation for the maintenance of international peace and security had been completed.

ARRANGEMENTS FOR DUMBARTON OAKS CONVERSATIONS

As the construction of the Tentative Proposals was being completed, efforts continued to arrange the necessary major-power negotiations concerning general international organization. The beginning of those efforts and their nature to June 2, 1944, has already been described. Diplomatic discussion among the four major powers was concentrated on procedural arrangements for exchange of papers before the informal conference that had been projected and toward obtaining agreement of views on several questions involved, including the time to begin such a conference. The views of the British Foreign Office as received by the Under Secretary through the British Ambassador, Lord Halifax, on June 5, favored having a conference on an "official" or high technical level in the near future, at any date after July 1, and, it was hoped, at a place outside the reach of the Washington heat at that time of year. Preference was expressed for exchange of papers before the actual convening of the conference, and also, if a single meeting of all Four Powers was not acceptable to the Soviet Government, for a conference in two series of Three Power discussions as the United States had proposed to the British Embassy for this contingency. Copies of the telegram setting forth these views were conveyed at once to the President and the Secretary.

The sense of urgency so reflected was also being felt by smaller nations. Dr. Eelco van Kleffens, acting on behalf of the Belgian, Luxembourg, Netherlands, and Norwegian Governments-in-exile, conveyed through the United States Embassy in London on June 9 a memorandum expressing the desire of these Governments to contribute to the settlement of the questions of the conditions to be imposed on Germany and of the political safeguards to be set up for their future security, possibly within a world-wide international system. He urged "all headway" on these matters. Official exchanges of views, or at least unofficial exchanges, with the Governments named were desired before final decisions were taken. This memorandum, it was stated, represented also the views "of a large number of occupied countries," and it was being conveyed to the British and the Soviet as well as the American Government.

This message arrived just after the Department requested the United States Ambassador in Moscow by telegram, on June 10, to ask Mr. Molotov "how long" before an answer to our invitation of May 30 might be received as "we are anxious to proceed." To this question, Mr. Molotov replied on June 13 that the Soviet Government was "actively working" and a reply would be made "in the very near future."

A second request was sent on June 27 to Ambassador Harriman to inquire when the Soviet acceptance might be forthcoming and stating we were most anxious to have the discussions initiated between July 15 and August 1, "the sooner the better." No reply being received in answer to this telegram, the request was reiterated in another telegram to the Ambassador on the evening of July 7, expressing the desire that the question of arrangements be taken up immediately with Mr. Molotov. The Ambassador might well recall to the Commissar, it was suggested, that the latter had initiated the suggestion to hold consultations in Washington, and say that the conversations would be informal and that, while we wished in these conversations to arrive at an understanding on major points in regard to the international organization, any understandings would be subject to final acceptance by each of the Governments. We would be glad to make available our drafts on the proposed organization for preparatory study and to receive any drafts from the Soviet Government, as soon as we were informed when the Soviet Government would find it convenient to start the conversations. A reply was also asked to the suggestion for a two-series conference. It was learned the next day that the British Ambassador in Moscow had also recently pressed Mr. Molotov for an answer.

The Soviet reply, dated July 9, 1944, was in the form of an *aide-mémoire* from the Soviet Embassy in Washington received the same day. It expressed readiness to confer on the suggested two-series basis, and agreed to start negotiations with the American and British Governments the beginning of August without preliminary exchange of papers. The Soviet Ambassador to the United States, Andrei A. Gromyko, was authorized to participate. The message proposed to limit discussion to questions of primary importance. In the Soviet view, these, briefly, covered the scope and character of the organization; safety (or security) measures for prevention of threat to and violation of peace and plans of combined actions; and methods and procedures of establishing the organization. These in general conformed with several of the broad questions suggested in the British Summary earlier in the year.

Secretary Hull on the following day informed the Chinese Chargé d'Affaires, Mr. Liu Chieh, of this reply and discussed with him particularly the prospect of two separate informal conferences. He stated that he had cabled London and Moscow that morning of his readiness to start the meeting on August 2. He informed the Chargé that we wished to talk with the British concerning a suitable time to hold meetings with the Chinese and perhaps have some discussion of the matter with the Soviets in order to have all parties satisfied, and he asked to have the suggestions of the Chinese Government after study of the matter. Thus, on July 10, a probable date of August 2 was being set for the coming informal conference, and it had not been decided whether the "Chinese" series of meetings would be after the "Soviet" series or concurrent with it.

At this juncture, information concerning our plans was conveyed to the governments of all the other American republics, Argentina excepted.[6] A conversation giving background information had already been held by the Secretary with the Ambassadors of the five Central American republics and of Panama on June 26, 1944. Initiation of general consultation with the other American republics, of a background character until it could become substantive after the projected conversations had been held, was undertaken on July 11. That day a telegraphic instruction was sent, after clearance in the Post-War Programs Committee four days earlier, to the United States Embassies in the capitals of all of the nineteen American republics which were members of the United Nations or associated with them.[7]

The nineteen Governments thereby apprised of developments were informed that studies were proceeding as rapidly as circumstances permitted and that conversations would shortly be initiated with the United Kingdom, the Soviet Union, and China, to be followed as soon as possible by exchanges of views with the other United Nations and the nations associated with them in the war. The United States, it was said, had devoted particular attention to the special relationship that exists between the United States and the other American republics, which it would take fully into account throughout the forthcoming conversations. It was urged that, for complete success, the subsequent exchanges of views contemplated should be based upon the most careful preparation by all the governments concerned.

Attention was called in this circular instruction to the President's statement of June 15 summarizing the broad views of this Government on the nature and functions of the contemplated organization. It was emphasized that as conversations progressed with other nations, the plans would "probably be modified," as the President had made clear at his press conference on May 30.

The Secretary's own characterization on June 1 of the establishment and maintenance of the proposed international organization as "a mutual affair" in which both the small and the large nations should at all times be especially interested was cited in connection with

---

[6] Argentina alone of the American republics was not included among the United and Associated Nations. It had failed to carry out its commitment to cooperate in the defense of this Hemisphere, and the American Ambassador, Norman Armour, had been called home for consultation in June 1944.

[7] Since the Foreign Minister of Mexico was then in Washington, he was informed directly through the Department, the telegram sent to the Ambassador in Mexico City being simply for his own information. A telegram was also sent to Buenos Aires solely for the information of the Embassy.

the fact that the first conversations were to be held with the United Kingdom, the Soviet Union, and China. On this point the instruction further stated that since the "major responsibility" for maintaining peace after the war "must inevitably" be borne by these three powers and the United States, no possibility existed of successfully establishing a general organization unless these four powers were prepared to support it. This Government, however, constantly bore in mind, as the President had emphatically stated on June 15, that the hope for an advancing and peaceful world depended on the ability and willingness of both the large and the small peace-loving nations "to work together" in maintaining international peace and security, each bearing responsibility commensurate with its respective capacity.

The instruction commented that it was the consistent policy of the United States to work closely with the other American republics in dealing with postwar problems of common interest and to insist that they have a full participation in international discussions and conferences dealing with policies and institutions of international cooperation. The United States believed that the inter-American system had an even more important role to fill in the future than in the past. Precisely what it would be must await clearer definition of the forms and functions of the general organization. In the meantime, exchanges of views should lay the groundwork for that role. The responses of the governments so approached as received over the next five weeks contained certain views on the character of the desired international organization, on equality of states in the future organization, on the continuation within any general organization of the inter-American system of collaboration, and on related matters.

As this consultation was being initiated, the efforts to arrive at definite negotiating arrangements among the four major powers became so active that telegrams and telephone calls began to cross each other. On July 12, the American Embassies in Moscow, London, and Chungking were instructed to inform the Foreign Offices there of the suggested date of August 2 to open "the conversations" in Washington and of our intention so to announce on July 15 unless there were objections.

A reply was also made on July 12 to the Soviet *aide-mémoire* of three days before. The replying *aide-mémoire* referred to the "Topical Outline" of February 17, handed to the Soviets February 19, and stated:

"As indicated in that outline, it is the view of this Government that the primary purpose of the proposed international organization is the peaceable adjustment of disputes, to which end it is recognized that the organization must possess the ultimate authority to use force as a measure of last resort. Consequently, in the view of this Government procedures for a peaceful adjustment of disputes must necessarily constitute an integral part of any effective scheme for an international organization. It is confidently believed that discussions of the structure of a world organization for the maintenance of peace and security will necessarily extend to consideration of procedures of pacific settlement and this Government will expect in the forthcoming discussions to state fully its views on this subject. This Government also expects during the course of the forthcoming discussions to express its views on the subject of possible arrangements for territorial trusteeship and of those aspects of international economic relations which concern the relationship of specialized economic and social agencies to the general organization, as distinguished from questions involving substantive policies in these fields. It is hoped that upon further consideration the Soviet Government will feel disposed to enter into preliminary discussion of these topics."

In conclusion, emphasis was placed on the following aspects of official United States thought concerning the "Conversations":

". . . this Government regards the forthcoming discussions as constituting an informal exchange of views, subject, of course, to eventual acceptance by the governments concerned of any understandings that may be reached. Moreover, it is to be anticipated that subsequent discussions with the other United Nations and continuing interchange of views between the three powers may well lead to modifications of the statements which it is to be anticipated will be jointly formulated as a result of the forthcoming discussions."

Ambassador Harriman reported on July 13 that Deputy Foreign Minister Vyshinsky wished formal confirmation that two separate series of conversations were planned, and also that this arrangement should be publicly explained. The British approval of an opening date early in August and of the proposed announcement arrived almost simultaneously with this message from Moscow.

By telephone call and by telegram on the 14th, Ambassador Harriman was told that two sets of concurrent but separate tripartite conversations were presently planned, and the holding of these conversations at Dumbarton Oaks in Washington was specifically mentioned by the Department for the first time. The full text of the proposed United States press statement as sent to Moscow and discussed by long-distance telephone on the 15th, however, spoke of the two series of meetings as being carried on either concurrently or with a short interval between and stated that after these conversations, discussions with the other United Nations would be held.

A new uncertainty now arose over the timing of the proposed announcement, which was to be made as soon as Soviet clearance was received, because of a report on the 15th from the American Embassy on the initial Soviet reaction to the reference to the discussions subsequently to be held with other United Nations. This was regarded by Mr. Vyshinsky as introducing a new element that raised questions of timing, scope of subjects, and representation in such discussions. Further discussion between Ambassador Harriman and Deputy Foreign Minister Vyshinsky ensued on the 16th. On the 17th unqualified Soviet approval of the proposed announcement was given. Since meanwhile both the British and Chinese Embassies had agreed to it, the following announcement by the Secretary was released to the press immediately:

> "The four governments signatory to the Declaration of Moscow are agreed that informal conversations and exchanges of views on the general subject of an international security organization will soon begin in Washington, probably early in August. It has been decided, following discussions with the other governments, that the first phase of the conversations will be between representatives of the United Kingdom, the United States, and the Soviet Union and that conversations on the same subject between representatives of the United States, the United Kingdom, and China will be carried on either at the same time or shortly thereafter. These conversations will be followed by discussions with the other United Nations."

The essential arrangements had been so far advanced by these developments through July 17 as to make possible the exchange of papers. Accordingly, copies of the "Tentative Proposals for a General International Organization," dated July 18, were handed in strictest confidence to the British, Soviet, and Chinese Embassies and also sent to London, Moscow, and Chungking on the same date.[8] Hope was expressed that copies of any similar proposals the others might have would be given to this Government for study prior to the meetings.

While the desired exchange was thus again urged, the questions of exact opening date and of whether the meetings should be in concurrent or successive series remained the immediate matters to resolve. These were considered further in an instruction from the Secretary to Ambassador Harriman late on the 18th, in which the opening date of August 2 and the plan to hold the two series concurrently continued to be favored.

The Soviet Government by *aide-mémoire* on July 20 proposed to start "approximately on August 10" and stated that it desired to have the two series in succession, expressing willingness to see either series come first. It did not think prior exchanges of papers necessary, considering that the purpose of "the informal discussions" themselves was to reach "a common point of view" on the main questions of the organization of security. It favored acceptance of a less binding basis of discussion in the beginning. It felt that such a preliminary discussion of views would possibly contribute to a more rapid arrival by the Allied Governments at drafts on the world security organization—such drafts would serve afterward as the basis on which an agreed draft by

---

[8] See appendix 38.

the three Governments could be worked out. After interchange of views in Washington, it concluded, the participating parties could present their proposals in written form.

In the American reply sent on July 22, similarly made by *aide-mémoire*, the suggested date of August 10 was accepted. Preference was expressed for holding the first cycle of meetings with the Soviet Delegation, which would be followed as soon as possible by the second cycle with the Chinese, provided this were satisfactory to the British. It was stated that we were prepared to consider in the forthcoming discussions any or all parts of the United States Tentative Proposals.

While efforts to reach agreement with the Soviet Government on arrangements rested briefly at this point, the British views, in the form of five memoranda on major aspects of general international organization, were received on July 22. Actual exchange of documents was thereby effected as among two of the parties to the scheduled "conversations."

The Chinese Embassy was informed by the Department two days later of the status of arrangements and that we proposed to keep the Chinese apprised of developments during the cycle of discussions with the British and Soviet representatives. In light of this intention, the hope was expressed to the Chinese that in the second cycle an accord could be reached without great delay. The Chinese Embassy had no objection to the proposed procedure, which had recently been suggested orally to the Department by the British Embassy in the interest of shortening the length of time the British officials participating in the "conversations" would have to remain in Washington, and this desideratum was again stressed by the Embassy on July 26. On that date, the British, in view of the Soviet desires, acceded to the delay of talks with the Chinese until after the first cycle. By this time, the British had also agreed to accept the latest proposed opening date of August 10.

Doubt of the Soviet ability to arrive so soon, however, had set in by July 26. The British Embassy pointed out to the Department on that day that their group would also find it difficult to arrive from London quite so early, unless their officials were to come by airplane. August 14 was then suggested in telegrams from Mr. Stettinius, Acting Secretary, to the United States Ambassadors in London and Moscow, July 28, and the new proposed date was immediately agreed upon by all and shortly announced.

However, late in the evening on August 4, Mr. Vyshinsky requested Ambassador Harriman to come to the Foreign Office. He there explained that the Soviet Government wished more time to study our Tentative Proposals, with a view to instructing the Soviet representatives on the American points, and consequently asked for postponement of meetings until August 21, 1944. The Ambassador commented in his cabled report that the Soviet representatives had been able to receive the draft proposals, which had been sent by courier, only on August 2 and were still translating them the next day. President Roosevelt was consulted concerning the request, and the British were immediately apprised of it. On the 7th, we telegraphed our acceptance of August 21 as the opening date and so informed the Chinese Embassy by telephone and announced it publicly that same day.

No further change proved necessary on this matter, the most procedural of those involved, which had taken five weeks to arrange. Ambassador Harriman received from Mr. Molotov on the 12th a note of appreciation for the postponement.

A full exchange of papers prior to the meetings, beyond that with the British, was delayed for some time further but, despite earlier indications to the contrary, was eventually accomplished. The Soviet Memorandum on the International Security Organization was presented to the Department on August 12. The Chinese paper on Essential Points in the Charter of an International Organization was received August 22. An earlier suggestion of Soviet views, moreover, had been received and considered in the Department. This was in the form of an article by "N. Malinin" in an issue of *Zvezda*, a Soviet literary publication. The article had been reported by Ambassador Harriman on July 24 to be of direct interest in reflecting official Soviet views, since the attention of the American Embassy in Moscow had been drawn to it, as worth special notice, before its publication. There was, of course, no certainty that the views in it would turn out to be those of the Soviet Government.

The negotiations concerning the main aspects of arrangements described above were supplemented by messages of an informational nature concerning the representatives being designated by each of the four Governments. The high level of the "informal conference" as envisaged from the outset was reflected in these designations. The exchanges of information on them were initiated formally by a cable from Secretary Hull to the American Ambassadors in London, Moscow, and Chungking on July 18, 1944. This cable requested that the Foreign Minister be informed that Secretary Hull would be the senior United States representative and would take part in consideration of basic policy, and that Under Secretary Edward R. Stettinius, would head the American Group in the more technical and detailed discussions. The list of representatives it contained, totaling seventeen, was tentative and was to be somewhat enlarged before its completion.

Information had already been received informally through conversation with British Embassy officials as early as June 26 indicating who several principal members of the British Group might be and naming Sir Alexander Cadogan, Permanent Under Secretary for Foreign Affairs, as the leader of the delegation. The Soviet *aide-mémoire* of July 9 had informed the Department that the participation of Ambassador Andrei A. Gromyko in the negotiations had been authorized. On July 12, conversations with officials of the Chinese Embassy showed that the Chinese Government was giving thought to the composition of the Chinese Group. After further information from all three arrived, though still not complete, the announcement of the American Group was made, August 1, 1944.[9] The statement emphasized that the meetings opening at Dumbarton Oaks would be "informal conversations" and repeated that they would be exploratory in nature.

Although a few more conversations were held between the Department and the Embassies of the three Governments in connection with the details of arrangements and additional informational telegrams on the several delegations were received, no further major matters arose before the "conversations," with one exception. This was the information conveyed orally by the British Embassy to Acting Secretary Stettinius, August 8, 1944, that, on instructions, the head of the British Delegation would be prepared on his arrival to discuss with the Secretary the possibility of a meeting of Foreign Ministers of the four major powers in September. After the arrival of the British Delegation, the Secretary, in a talk with the British Ambassador, Lord Halifax, and Sir Alexander Cadogan on August 14, suggested that "before" a meeting of the Foreign Secretaries "on international matters and especially to decide on any formal agreement possibly in September, it would be very important first to discuss steps toward conferring with the small nations." Secretary Hull added that if the four nations "should go on until they turned out to the world a completed document" and then sent "copies to the small nations in a 'take it or leave it' manner, as the whole movement would be construed, it would be difficult to avoid serious attacks" from various quarters. He asked that this suggestion be raised in the British Government for consideration.

No separate meeting of Foreign Ministers of the major powers occurred that was of the nature under discussion between August 8 and 14, 1944. The same question of the role of the smaller states raised by the Secretary in this regard, however, was the proximate cause for the new series of consultations within the United States on the Tentative Proposals, which developed in connection with a statement by Governor Thomas E. Dewey of New York five days before the Dumbarton Oaks Conversations opened.

---

[9] The full listing of the American and other groups is deferred to the next chapter on the Dumbarton Oaks Conversations.

NONPARTISAN SUPPORT OF "TENTATIVE PROPOSALS"

At the time of the consultations with the senatorial group and the three eminent jurists late in April and in May 1944,[10] and hence several weeks before the Republican Party Convention, steps were initiated to ascertain the prospects of a favorable statement by Governor Dewey, widely regarded as the leading candidate for the Republican presidential nomination, on international security organization. These steps were undertaken on the initiative of Myron C. Taylor and approved by Secretary Hull and by the President, with a view to assuring nonpartisanship on this matter in the approaching political campaign. After consulting with several eminent Republicans long active in Party positions, who, in turn, conferred with Mr. Dewey, and one of whom conveyed, in confidence, a copy of the April 29 draft of the "Possible Plan" to Governor Dewey, Mr. Taylor reported to the Secretary by memorandum. The memorandum, dated June 8, 1944, and thus sent prior to the nomination of a candidate by the Republican Convention, stated that "a direct approach" had not yet been made "in the matter we discussed." Caution in doing so, this memorandum continued, had been "dictated, on second thought, by the doubt whether a definitive statement might not be under some circumstances misused, and that he is only one of several in the field up to the moment." The memorandum concluded: "I am following the matter closely but do not want to make a wrong move at this time which might injure the project." No further developments in this direction were reported by the time Mr. Taylor wrote, on June 15, 1944, that at the President's request he was leaving for Rome, now that the German forces had evacuated that city, to resume his mission for the President to Pope Pius XII. Mr. Taylor was therefore unable to take any further direct part in the preparation, but on this trip he informed the Pope of the lines of American thought concerning the proposed general international organization.

The Republican Party Convention at Chicago, which nominated Governor Dewey for the Presidency and Governor John W. Bricker of Ohio for the Vice Presidency, adopted on June 27 a plank in its platform favoring

". . . responsible participation by the United States in post-war cooperative organization among sovereign nations to prevent military aggression and to attain permanent peace with organized justice in a free world.

"Such organization should develop effective cooperative means to direct peace forces to prevent or repel military aggression."

The Democratic Party Convention at Chicago, which nominated Franklin D. Roosevelt for a fourth term as President and Senator

[10] See p. 263 ff.

Harry S. Truman of Missouri for the Vice Presidency, adopted in its platform of July 29, a pledge

"To join with the other United Nations in the establishment of an international organization based on the principle of the sovereign equality of all peace-loving States, open to membership by all such States, large and small, for the prevention of aggression and the maintenance of international peace and security;

"To make all necessary and effective agreements and arrangements through which the nations would maintain adequate forces to meet the needs of preventing war and of making impossible the preparation for war and which would have such forces available for joint action when necessary."

Several weeks later, Governor Dewey issued a statement which strongly endorsed participation in an international security organization. The statement, dated August 16, 1944, referred, however, to recent reports concerning the Dumbarton Oaks Conversations and said: "These indicate that it is planned to subject the nations of the world, great and small, permanently to the coercive power of the four nations holding this conference."

Governor Dewey's statement then set forth a number of "fundamentals of future peace." These can only be indicated here, in summary, as follows: The view was expressed that the defeat of the principal enemy states "will be achieved primarily by the united power of Britain, Russia, China and the United States" and that to "insure that Germany and Japan shall never again be able to disrupt the peace of the world, these four Allies must maintain their present unity." The "responsibility to keep Germany and Japan disarmed should be shared with liberated peoples," it was stated, "but it cannot immediately be delegated to a world-wide organization while such organization is yet new and untried." Regarding the organizing of "permanent peace among the rest of the world, a very different attitude must be taken." In this respect, is was considered that peace was "a task of cooperation among equal and sovereign nations" and that it should be based on "freedom, equality and justice." Following further views on the work with which the world organization should be concerned and the bases on which peace should be founded, the statement concluded with objection to "proposals which amount merely to a permanent Four Power alliance to control the world."

The Secretary stated to the press on August 17 that the fears expressed were "utterly and completely unfounded." No "military alliance of the four major nations permanently to coerce the rest of the world," he said, "is contemplated or has ever been contemplated by this Government or, as far as we know, by any of the other governments." He explained that the purpose of the meeting at Dumbarton Oaks was to have "a discussion among the signatories of the Moscow Declaration" on establishing the kind of organization for peace and security envisaged therein, as "preliminary to similar discussions and early conference among all the United Nations and other peace-loving countries, large and small." The Secretary replied to press inquiry that he wished to keep international security organization out of Party politics and would "welcome conferences with others who come solely in a non-partisan spirit. . . ." He said he "would welcome such a conference with Governor Dewey."

The proposed conference was the subject of a telegram from Governor Dewey to the Secretary on the following day, stating "I am happy to accept your proposal . . . and to designate Mr. John Foster Dulles as my representative". Also, the belief was indicated in this telegram that in view of the progress of the war, effort to organize both temporarily and permanently for the establishment of lasting peace should be accelerated. To render the result "wholly bipartisan" and unitedly supported by the American people, Governor Dewey extended his fullest cooperation.

Three daily conferences in the Department between the Secretary and Mr. Dulles followed, beginning August 23 and ending August 25. The current draft of the Tentative Proposals was given to Mr. Dulles at the first conference. The Secretary also gave him a summary of their provisions dealing with subjects of special interest in the light of Governor Dewey's statement: position of small countries, pacific settlement and peaceful change, agreements for provision of armed forces and regulation of armaments, and control of Axis countries.

Much attention in these conferences was devoted to keeping the problem of the establishment of an international peace and security organization out of politics. The question of the distinction between "nonpartisan" and bipartisan arose in this connection. The Secretary believed that under our constitutional structure the party in power could alone have responsibility for execution of foreign policy, and that "bipartisan" was also inappropriate as limited to only two parties.

Since the Tentative Proposals were regarded favorably by Mr. Dulles, a draft joint statement to be issued to the press was discussed, together with the Proposals, on August 24 and again on the 25th. Following Governor Dewey's amendment by telephone to insert "full" in the sentence stating that "full public nonpartisan discussion of the means of attaining a lasting peace" was not precluded by the view that future peace should be kept "entirely out of politics," the statement was issued on August 25. This statement announced that there was "agreement of views on numerous aspects" of the subject, that the Secretary and Mr. Dulles expected "to continue to confer about developments" as they arose, and that whether there would be complete agreement of views would "depend on future developments."

The substantive aspects of these discussions clarified need of having an explicit stipulation inserted in the Tentative Proposals providing for "ratification by each country in accordance with its constitutional procedures" of the contemplated agreement under which armed forces would be placed at the disposal of the organization for enforcement of peace and security. A sentence to this effect was immediately written into the Tentative Proposals at the Secretary's direction.

Governor Dewey stated in a letter to the Secretary August 25 that he was "deeply gratified at the result of the discussions" and commented: "They constitute a new attitude toward the problem of peace." He then stated that he felt that war had been the only matter "above partisanship during a presidential campaign" heretofore, but that "if we are to have lasting peace, we must wage peace as we wage war. I feel that we are now making a beginning toward doing that and it is my hope that we shall have great success to that end." The Secretary considered the Governor's letter and the preceding conversations especially encouraging in their "heartening manifestation of national unity" on the foreign policy involved, as he wrote in reply to Governor Dewey on September 4, 1944. The Secretary's letter, as approved by the President, concluded with the suggestion that this correspondence be made public so that there might "be fuller public understanding of our common ground on this important subject," and this was done on September 6.[11]

The arrangements with Governor Dewey made in mid-August 1944 brought the political consultations on general international organization for peace and security to full circle. Continuation of congressional consultation, with the same groups of Senators and Representatives who were concerned in the discussions held in April, May, and June 1944, had been arranged just prior to the extension of consultations to include those of a primarily party character just described. On August 15, the Secretary had informed the senatorial group and the group of House leaders that the Dumbarton Oaks Conversations were to be on a technical or expert level, that the British in general favored the same principles embodied in the American document, and that he would inform them of any new fundamental principles that might be developed during the Conversations.

Accordingly, both congressional and party consultations—"nonpartisan" from the Department's standpoint, but increasingly called "bipartisan"—actively continued during the Dumbarton Oaks Conversations. The development of the nonpartisan policy as a whole since its institution by Secretary Hull in the spring of 1942 in connection with the preparation of our postwar foreign policy has been observed in earlier pages. It ultimately led to representation of both major Parties in the American negotiations on postwar problems. The first explicit step toward such representation in negotiating agree-

---

[11] *Department of State Bulletin,* XI, 255.

ment for the general international organization was taken shortly before the developments described immediately above. Participation by Henry P. Fletcher, general counsel of the Republican National Committee and diplomat of wide experience, as a member of the American Group to conduct the Dumbarton Oaks Conversations had been invited by Secretary Hull, July 1, and had been arranged by July 27, 1944. The latter was the effective date of his appointment as Special Adviser to the Secretary of State for postwar problems and plans, an unusual position which was created for Mr. Fletcher and which he occupied through the Dumbarton Oaks Conversations and until his resignation in December 1944. His membership on the American Group to conduct the Dumbarton Oaks Conversations was announced through the list released to the press on August 1, 1944.

While these international and domestic arrangements were being made for the "informal conference" to be convened at Dumbarton Oaks, the Tentative Proposals to be advanced there were being reviewed and final decisions on them made.

CHAPTER XIV

The American Group for Major Power Conversations

THE STUDY given the Tentative Proposals in the five weeks between their completion and the opening of the Dumbarton Oaks Conversations was intended to provide final briefing of the American negotiators for their conduct of the coming Conversations. It also provided a thorough review and some reconsideration of the Proposals. The arrangements for this study were purposely constructed to dovetail with the projected organization of the American Group for the Conversations and with that of the Conversations as a whole. Because of the flexibility that had distinguished the processes by which the Tentative Proposals had been prepared in the Informal Political Agenda Group, and that was contemplated for the major-power negotiations toward a common understanding on the problems involved in establishing a general international organization, the concept of "groups" was followed in all these arrangements. In keeping with this concept, the formal term "Delegation" was avoided by the Department.

Plans for this last readying stage prior to the start of substantive negotiations with the other major powers began to be considered in draft over-all memoranda as early as May 22, 1944. Definite arrangements developed first in connection with the staff. A meeting was held by Mr. Pasvolsky on May 29, attended by Messrs. Sandifer and Gerig of the Division of International Security and Organization and Alger Hiss, Special Assistant to Ambassador Wilson, Director of the Office of Special Political Affairs who was temporarily absent, to arrange the allocation of technical officers to work on what was then called the "Basic Instrument of the General International Organization." This Division and Office, as the staff responsible at a working level in this field, began at once to arrange the documentary materials required.

The necessary broader arrangements consumed much more time, since they involved plans for the American Group to conduct negotiations and also for the "informal conference," responsibility for which fell on the United States as host country. These arrangements, under the Secretary's general supervision, were directly in charge of Under Secretary Stettinius, acting with the assistance of Mr. Dunn to whom the work was reported administratively; of Mr. Pasvolsky who was charged with all substantive preparation; and of Mr. Hiss who was responsible for developing the administrative arrangements and was working directly with the Under Secretary on them. The Division of International Conferences was also called upon for assistance in selecting the site for the negotiations and in arranging the necessary facilities.

By June 22, the lines of the arrangements were becoming firm. An agenda, an organization of the American Group in three sections, and a steering committee were projected. This plan, by July 3, was being refined and supplemented. One of the memoranda being drafted dealt with the subject of relations with the press during the discussions, which was an ever present concern since, on the one hand, the substantive work was envisaged as necessarily secret while in the process of negotiation and, on the other, it was desired that the press should be supplied with the fullest information compatible with the nature and objective of the negotiations. The designation of representatives of each of the armed services was also undertaken at this time, and involved consultations with Admiral Leahy, the Chief of Staff to the Commander in Chief, Gen. George C. Marshall, the Chief of Staff of the Army, Assistant Secretary of War John J. McCloy, and Assistant Secretary of the Navy Ralph A. Bard. By July 11, a memorandum on the arrangements was completed.[1]

This memorandum envisaged the forthcoming discussions on international organization and security "as an informal interchange of views at a high diplomatic level, relating both to basic policies and to technical questions." The topics for discussion fell into "three broad categories," briefly, (I) structure and establishment, (II) arrangements for pacific settlement of disputes, and (III) security arrangements. Detailed discussions would correspond to these three categories, and hence would be conducted in three sections respectively. The members of the American Group would be allocated to these sections.

Secretary Hull was specified as the senior American representative to preside over the consideration of basic policies at the outset and over their further consideration at the end of the Conversations in the light of the technical discussions that would meanwhile have been held in the three sections. The Under Secretary would head the American Group in the detailed discussions, and would be chairman of the third section. It was contemplated that "in the American-British-Soviet

---

[1] See appendix 40.

phase of the discussion" a British official would act as chairman of the first section and a Soviet official of the second section, and that "in the American-British-Chinese phase" a Chinese official would be chairman of the second section. Although selection of the American Group was not yet completed, the memorandum allocated to the first section Messrs. Bowman, Grew, and Pasvolsky; to the second Messrs. Hackworth, Hornbeck, and Cohen; and to the third Messrs. Stettinius, Dunn, and Wilson, Admirals Hepburn, Willson, and Train, and Generals Embick, Strong, and Fairchild. All members and Assistant Secretary Long were expected to be present at all discussions except the technical discussions occurring in these three sections.

In regard to the advisers and the secretariat, the memorandum specified that the general adviser would be Mr. Notter, and there would be advisers from the four geographic offices of the Department. The secretariat would include assigned Army and Navy officers, and would function not only as assistants to the American Group but for the discussions as a whole. Mr. Hiss would act as executive secretary.

Headquarters for the discussions would be Dumbarton Oaks in Georgetown, the estate of Robert Woods Bliss, which had been deeded a few years earlier to Harvard University. The university rearranged its standing plans to make the estate available for this extraordinary purpose. While the facilities at Dumbarton Oaks would permit only a few offices to be available there for the individual groups participating, the British and Soviet delegations would have the use of their nearby embassies before and after the daily morning and afternoon meetings.

In conclusion, the memorandum stated that the American Group would immediately organize itself into three committees to accord with the three sections indicated. Mr. Stettinius would look to Mr. Pasvolsky as responsible for the first, to Mr. Hackworth for the second, and to Mr. Dunn for the third of these sections, and the whole group would meet each week. A small informal steering committee would also work from this time on. This would be composed of the Secretary, Chairman, Mr. Stettinius, Vice Chairman, Messrs. Dunn, Hackworth, and Pasvolsky, and Admiral Willson and General Strong.

A Tentative Agenda annexed to the memorandum set forth the larger points involved in the three categories of topics to be considered. The first, on the structure and establishment of the proposed international organization, covered six points: general structure and scope of the organization; the membership, functions, powers, and voting procedures of a general assembly; the membership, functions, powers, and voting procedures of a smaller executive body (executive council); administration and secretariat of the organization; arrangements for coordination of economic and other functional activities and agencies and the relation of such agencies and of any regional arrangements to the general organization; and procedure of establishment and inauguration of the organization.

Under arrangements for pacific settlement of disputes—the second category—four points were listed. These were methods of pacific settlement, regional and other procedures outside the general organization, procedures in the council and in the assembly, and the structure and functions of the "Court of Justice".

The third category, security arrangements, had seven points, the last of which was devoted to transitional aspects. The first six were the scope and character of joint action with respect to determination of threats to or breaches of the peace, to prevention or suppression of such threats or breaches, and to enforcement of decisions; methods of joint action not involving use of armed forces and methods involving use of armed forces; arrangements for provision of armed forces and facilities; relationship to mutual defense and regional systems; arrangements for regulation of armaments and the manufacture and traffic in arms; and structure and functions of an armaments and security commission. The seventh point was interim arrangements pending the effective functioning of the general organization in the field of security.

Secretary Hull handed this memorandum to President Roosevelt on July 12, 1944, together with the Tentative Proposals (in their July 6 form). The President had already received the draft of April 29, which had been used for most of the political consultations held since that date. All of the Proposals were constructed on the lines he had approved on February 3 with the exception of those on economic and social cooperation and on international trusteeship. To both of these only a reference had been made in the "Possible Plan" of December 29, 1943, and they were still regarded as "very tentative" when submitted to the President.

PRE-CONVERSATIONS BRIEFING AND REVIEW

THE PROJECTED working arrangements for the American Group had been put partly into effect even before this, inasmuch as the scheduled opening of the negotiations at this date was only a month distant. The Secretary on July 10, 1944, convened the Group for its first meeting, in order to inform members of the status of developments and to set in motion the proposed arrangements being put before the President. The Secretary remarked on the importance of bearing in mind the American concept of the full and free collaboration of states equal in status, which characterized the inter-American system, and stated that the United States was opposed to any groupings or federations that excluded recognition of the basic rights of individual member states. He felt it necessary to seek reasonable solutions in the forthcoming Conversations to the many problems involved in regional arrangements. Those in attendance were the Under Secretary, Messrs. Bowman, Cohen, Dunn, Grew, Hackworth, Hiss (for Mr. Wilson), Hornbeck, Pasvolsky, Notter and Carlton Savage (who was to assist the Secretary in maintaining a running account of the coming discussions), Admirals Willson and Train, and Generals Embick and Strong.

A total of eleven meetings of the full American Group were held before the negotiations, the four in July antedating the public announcement of the composition of the Group. The second meeting, on July 11, was held by Mr. Stettinius. This was concerned with getting the "three informal committees" started and assigning the staff to perform technical secretariat functions. General Muir S. Fairchild was present as a member for the first time. A number of the secretaries designated by this date also attended, and thereafter all the designated technical experts as a rule were present. The secretary of the first of the three sections or "informal committees"—later termed "groups"— was Mr. Gerig, with Messrs. Rothwell and Tomlinson and Miss Fosdick as assistant secretaries. For the second, Mr. Sandifer was secretary, with Mr. Preuss and Mrs. McDiarmid as assistant secretaries. Mr. Yost was secretary of the third, with Messrs. Blaisdell, Kirk, and Eagleton as the assistant civilian secretaries, and with several officers still to be assigned from the armed services. The officers shortly assigned were: from the Army, Col. William F. Rehm and Lt. Cols. Paul W. Caraway and W. A. McRae, and from the Navy, Capt. John M. Creighton.

The meeting of July 17, which was devoted to organizational details, was the first of the meetings of the Group to be held at Dumbarton Oaks itself. While the President's approval of the memorandum on arrangements was made known at this meeting, it was the following day that the Secretary read to the members in attendance at the fourth meeting in his office the message sent to him by President Roosevelt from aboard ship at sea. This message, dated July 15, concerned both the Tentative Proposals and the recommended arrangements.

> "I have read the memorandum with great interest and it has my approval. I like the plans for discussion and the preliminary outline of the proposals of a general international organization. Good Luck!"

Transmission of the Tentative Proposals to the other three Governments to be represented at Dumbarton Oaks was the principal subject of discussion at this meeting. It was on this occasion, July 18, at the instance of the members representing the Joint Chiefs of Staff and for the overriding military reasons of assuredly avoiding questions directly or indirectly related to the subject of postwar territorial settlements, that the decision was made to omit the section on international trusteeship from the Proposals and to remove this subject from the scope of matters to be raised by the United States in the Dumbarton Oaks Conversations.[2]   The possibility of a European High Commission for the interim period was also further considered at this meeting.

The American Steering Committee met for the first time on July 31.   Up to this time, its Departmental members had directed developments by conversations among section chairmen or in gatherings in the Under Secretary's office.   With the addition of Mr. Wilson, the Committee had reached its final membership of seven apart from Secretary Hull, who did not attend the meetings.   This committee met approximately every other day in this period.   It considered not only matters of working schedules, assignments, and usual steering matters, including informal social events for the foreign guests, but also certain special problems concerning the conduct of the major-power negotiations on which the United States should have suggestions.   It decided, for example, that, in order to permit greater latitude in the reconciliation of views during the negotiations, no stenographic record of the Conversations should be made.   Instead, informal and brief "running" minutes of opinions expressed, of proposals advanced, and of action taken should be kept, these to be made available to all delegations.   As this procedure was developed in the course of the actual negotiations, it required the taking of such minutes by assigned technical experts, the approval of the draft by the principal secretary of the section concerned, review by the general adviser, initialing by the executive secretariat, clearance with each of the other "delegations," and then the processing of the agreed record and its distribution before the next day's meeting.   A further subject of frequent discussion in this committee was information for the press.   The committee recommended that press correspondents should be invited to the opening session of the Conversations, and with the Secretary's approval it was so decided. Background talks with the press before and during the negotiations were similarly approved.

By August 1, 1944, when the members of the American Group were announced, the advisers and other officials had also been appointed. Aside from the general adviser already named in the memorandum approved by the President, the geographic advisers were: for Europe, Charles E. Bohlen, who was to keep in close touch with the Soviet Group,[3] and John D. Hickerson; for the Far East, Joseph W. Ballantine; for the Near and Middle East, Paul H. Alling, with Raymond A. Hare, alternate; and for Latin America, John M. Cabot.   Michael J.

---

[2] See appendix 39 for text of this section. The views of the Joint Chiefs of Staff were conveyed in writing by Gen. George C. Marshall to the Secretary of State under date of Aug. 3, 1944.

[3] Edward W. Nash of the Protocol Division also assisted in this duty.

McDermott was designated Press Relations Officer. G. Hayden Raynor was named special assistant to work with the Under Secretary in the negotiations. The executive secretariat was composed of Mr. Hiss, executive secretary; Mr. Rothwell, assistant executive secretary; three assistants, Donald B. Eddy, Col. David Marcus (United States Army), and Lt. Frederick Holdsworth (United States Navy),[4] and James F. Green as documents officer.

By the fifth meeting of the American Group, on August 7, Mr. Fletcher was able to attend, thus completing the Group. Meetings beginning at this time were all held at Dumbarton Oaks. Mr. Stettinius as Acting Secretary presided over the five meetings between the seventh and fifteenth, and by reason of the Secretary's developing consultations with Governor Dewey on August 16 and 17, Mr. Stettinius also was Chairman of the two meetings on those dates. This series constituted the review meetings of the American Group before the Conversations commenced.

In the meetings, beginning August 7, discussion largely centered on the Proposals. The minutes were separated into two parts: all so-called business matters of negotiation and arrangement reported to the meetings or raised there constituting Part I, and those on the substantive discussions, Part II. The purpose of this substantive discussion, aside from briefing all members thoroughly on the questions involved in each provision of the Tentative Proposals and on the reasons the given provision was favored, was to review the questions yet unsettled and likely to come up in the course of negotiation, and to arrive at proposals on them. As will be apparent from the preceding pages, it was impossible to pursue this study and consideration of the American position with exact knowledge of the Soviet proposals until after August 14, or of the Chinese proposals during any of this series, but the British views were available.

The substantive discussions in the full Group commenced after its three sections, now "groups," had begun to review the Proposals and to report their comment. A few shifts in their membership had been made. "Group I," composed of Mr. Pasvolsky, Chairman, Mr. Bowman, General Embick, Mr. Fletcher, Mr. Grew, and Admiral Hepburn, began work on July 19, 1944. The last two of its seven meetings were joint sessions with "Group II" to consider several difficult issues concerning pacific settlement and related voting procedures. "Group II," the members of which were Mr. Hackworth, Chairman, Mr. Cohen, and Mr. Hornbeck, started its meetings July 12, holding six meetings separately before the two joint meetings referred to above. "Group III," constituted of Mr. Dunn, Chairman, Generals Strong

---

[4] Additional assistance was made available later by the Army and Navy in regard to security, transportation, and other needed services.

and Fairchild, Admirals Willson and Train, and Edwin Wilson, convened July 13. It held eight meetings to and including August 18, several of which were held with Mr. Pasvolsky as acting Chairman. Minutes were not kept for the latter group but were kept for the first and second.

These three small study groups ended their meetings on the Thursday and Friday before the negotiations commenced. The groups were established for critical study of the Tentative Proposals, and to assist such study, papers entitled "Basic Questions" were placed before them. In these papers each section or chapter of the Tentative Proposals was made the subject of analysis by the staff of the Division of International Security and Organization. They were thus presentations designed to select and sharpen the important questions at issue through the entire range of the Tentative Proposals. They were written according to the following outline: the tentative United States proposal, including an interpretation where complexities were involved; the British proposal if available; League of Nations experience as provided in the Covenant and developed between the wars; and any alternatives for consideration in the case of any provision on which some query existed in the minds of the staff or had been raised in prior discussions in the Informal Political Agenda Group.

This documentation also presented as basic questions whether an interim consultative security commission for the period between the end of hostilities and the establishment of the permanent security organization should be proposed to deal with world security problems and, similarly, whether the European Advisory Commission should be reconstituted at the close of hostilities as a European High Commission having wider membership and competence. In addition, questions concerning the role of local and regional agencies in the maintenance of security and peace were analyzed in this series. The papers were completed, August 5, but by August 15 had been revised as "Basic Questions and Comparisons" in order to include in the analysis the Soviet proposals just received and translated and to take into account the discussions already held on the draft.

These papers formed the agenda for the final discussions of the American Group before entering the Dumbarton Oaks Conversations. Each member was supplied by the staff not only with the official texts of all proposals and the "Basic Questions" papers. He was also supplied with a summary of pertinent official statements and views by all governments; a working book containing a detailed commentary on every clause of the Tentative Proposals, including statements of alternatives rejected and the reasons for their rejection; and another working book of detailed papers, analyses of past experience relevant to the field of each member's assignment, and other reference documents.

Some of the amendments of the Tentative Proposals resulting from the thirty-nine days of discussion and review by the three "groups" were designed to improve clarity; others were made to take into account desirable modifications or additions that had been developed during this fundamental reappraisal of the Proposals. In these the views emerging from the congressional and other consultations were borne in mind. All were reported for discussion in the meetings of the American Group as a whole and it then made the decisions required, subject when consequential to the approval of the Secretary. Some of the changes were communicated as such to the other participating Groups during the negotiations; otherwise they were used to guide the American participants. Although the last meetings of the three small groups were on August 17 and 18, the meetings of the full American Group concluded on the morning of August 17, 1944. This meeting consisted of a last reading of the United States Tentative Proposals containing the amendments that had been approved.

The substantive amendments were of two kinds, those that filled out the Tentative Proposals and those that modified provisions. The most important of them were considered by Secretary Hull with Messrs. Dunn, Hackworth, and Pasvolsky on August 19. They related to eight questions, which reflected the nature of the review that had been given the Proposals in this period: Should the executive council have a right to impose terms of settlement of a dispute? Should great powers that are parties to a dispute be able to vote in decisions concerning such dispute? Should elected members of the council serve two-year terms or one? Should France have a permanent seat on the council and should the question of a permanent seat for a Latin American state— Brazil—be raised? Should the basic voting requirements in the council be two-thirds or a simple majority? Should there be provisions for withdrawal and for suspension of members? Should provision be made for *ad hoc* judges on the Court? And should the question of an Interim Security Commission and a European High Commission be raised in these conversations? It was decided that the last of these so-called "open questions" should not be raised in the coming conversations.

The amended Proposals, with certain adjustments made in consultation with the Secretary and a memorandum of recommendation on the first seven of the above questions, were taken up with the President on August 24. This discussion was attended by Messrs. Stettinius, Bowman, Dunn, Hackworth, and Pasvolsky. The President approved the Proposals. He also approved a recommended position that the United States should insist on the inclusion of economic and social matters in the scope of the organization. It was in the course of this talk that the President expressed preference for giving the name "The United Nations" to the new organization. At the same time he requested recommendations on its location. For the seat of the Court, he preferred The Hague. The definitive American position on all the open questions was not decided in this discussion. Those that remained unsettled were further discussed during the negotiations, which by this date were just starting.

These meetings of the American Group in July and August 1944 were a part of the far-from-finished preparation in this field. They marked, however, the end of the preparation to develop, through American study and effort alone, the views that we were to advance at Dumbarton Oaks.

The preparation so made was now to be completed through the processes of negotiation and through further thought during the interludes between negotiations—first among the major powers, later among the American republics and through diplomatic conversations with other powers, and finally among the United Nations as a whole. These final processes covered the span of the next nine months. They were wholly characteristic neither of usual international negotiations nor of usual formulation of policy. The Dumbarton Oaks Conversations inaugurated these final processes. At the same time, seen from the standpoint of August 1944, the negotiation of the major-power proposals which was the objective at Dumbarton Oaks marked by and large the end of advanced preparation in this field.

CHAPTER XV

Dumbarton Oaks Conversations and Political Consultations

THE DUMBARTON Oaks Conversations commenced on Monday morning, August 21, 1944, and were opened by Secretary Hull with a gavel made from the U. S. S. *Constitution*. They lasted a total of seven weeks, and were held in two phases: the first, ending September 28, between the representatives of the United States, the United Kingdom, and the Union of Soviet Socialist Republics; the second, beginning September 29 and ending October 7, between representatives of the United States, the United Kingdom, and China.

Since the Conversations were in the nature of meetings of high technical and diplomatic representatives to prepare joint views to refer back to their respective Governments for consideration, the discussions were held in secrecy. However, the opening sessions initiating each of the two phases were open to the press and photographers; the heads of the three participating Groups, especially after urging by the press for fuller news on August 24, issued joint communiqués approximately semiweekly; the President talked on the problems of international organization at some length during his press conference on August 29; the Under Secretary held some "off-the-record" talks with correspondents; and press conferences were held at the close of each phase.

The Conversations began energetically and with common desire for success. A high degree of cordiality and courtesy as well as of informality characterized all the discussions, even at the times of deadlock and during the occasionally prolonged periods of waiting in the first phase for instructions on specific issues. Realization was general that the movement of the war required rapid progress if the responsibilities of victory were to be met and full advantage taken of its opportunities. In Western Europe, Allied forces had landed in southern France on August 15, and on the 25th and 26th, Paris and Marseilles were freed and the Vichy regime terminated. By September 14, Brussels had been retaken; the Belgian Government had returned home; and Luxembourg had been freed. The Battle of Germany then opened as Allied forces crossed the German frontier.

301

In Eastern Europe, the Polish underground army was fighting against the Nazi forces in the Warsaw area; Bucharest was captured by Soviet forces at the end of August; Finland accepted the Soviet armistice terms on September 2; and Bulgaria asked the Soviet Union for an armistice on the 6th. The armistice with Rumania was signed in Moscow on September 12 and that with Finland a week later, the United States being a party to the first but not to the second of these agreements, since it was not at war with Finland. In the Far East and the Pacific, India was cleared of Japanese forces by August 17, and on September 14 and 15 successful landings in the Palau and Molucca islands were made by United States forces preparatory to the approaching battles for the liberation of the Philippines.

"SOVIET PHASE"

THE OPENING session of the Conversations at Dumbarton Oaks was attended by all the members of the three Groups, or "Delegations," representing the United States, the United Kingdom, and the Soviet Union.

The eighteen "representatives" heading the American Group have been named in preceding pages. The twelve civilian members included Secretary Hull, four former Ambassadors and one Ambassador-designate, the Under Secretary of State and two former Under Secretaries, and three members who had attended the Paris Peace Conference in 1919.[1] The membership included almost all of the Informal Political Agenda Group.[2] The six members from the armed services,

---

[1] It will be recalled that the civilian members were the Secretary; Edward R. Stettinius, Jr., Under Secretary of State and Chairman of the Group; Isaiah Bowman, President of Johns Hopkins University and Special Adviser to the Secretary of State on postwar problems and plans; Benjamin V. Cohen, General Counsel to the Office of War Mobilization; James Clement Dunn, Director of the Office of European Affairs, Department of State; Henry P. Fletcher, former Ambassador and Under Secretary of State, Special Adviser to the Secretary of State; Joseph Clark Grew, former Under Secretary of State and Ambassador to Japan, Director of the Office of Far Eastern Affairs, Department of State; Green H. Hackworth, Legal Adviser, Department of State; Stanley K. Hornbeck, Special Assistant to the Secretary of State and Ambassador-designate to the Netherlands; Breckinridge Long, former Ambassador to Italy, Assistant Secretary of State; Leo Pasvolsky, Special Assistant to the Secretary of State and Executive Director of the Committee on Post-War Programs; and Edwin C. Wilson, former Ambassador to Panama, Director of the Office of Special Political Affairs, Department of State. Those members who had attended the 1919 Paris Peace Conference as officials at the time were Messrs. Bowman, Grew, and Hornbeck. Other members had been present unofficially at that conference.

[2] Those not present were Myron C. Taylor, who, as already noted, had resumed his mission in Rome; Joseph C. Green, who was on leave; and Norman H. Davis, who had died July 1, 1944.

among whom were a former Commander in Chief of the United States Fleet and a former Deputy Chief of Staff, comprised the Chairman of the General Board of the Navy, the three members of the Joint Strategic Survey Committee of the Joint Chiefs of Staff, and two members of the Joint Post-War Committee of the Joint Chiefs.[3] There were no changes among the representatives during the Conversations.

The only change among the advisers to the American Group was that Joseph E. Johnson, Division of American Republics Analysis and Liaison, succeeded Mr. Cabot for the Latin American area in the closing week of the Soviet Phase of the Conversations.[4] Six technical experts from the staff, however, were added as assistant secretaries: Mrs. Esther C. Brunauer, Ralph J. Bunche, Walter M. Kotschnig, Miss Marcia Maylott, Norman J. Padelford, and Mrs. Pauline Reinsch Preuss. The remaining professional officers of the Division of International Security and Organization were called upon in the Department for expert aid on background factors as needed, and the personnel on documentary and administrative services were likewise drawn upon for assistance at Dumbarton Oaks. Michael J. McDermott, Special Assistant to the Secretary, was an active participant as Press Officer.

The United Kingdom "Delegation," as it was called in the notification of members sent to this Government, consisted in the first phase of the Conversations of the Permanent Under Secretary of State for Foreign Affairs, Sir Alexander Cadogan; the Legal Adviser of the Foreign Office, Sir William Malkin; Admiral Sir Percy Noble; Lt. Gen. G. N. Macready and his assistant, Maj. Gen. M. F. Grove-White; Air Marshal Sir William Lawrie Welsh;[5] the Secretary General of the Delegation, Gladwyn Jebb; A. H. Poynton of the Colonial Office; Col. Denis Capel Dunn, Military Assistant Secretary of the War Cabinet; Peter Loxley, Private Secretary to Sir Alexander Cadogan; Professor Charles K. Webster of the Research Department of the Foreign Office; Paul Falla of the Economic and Reconstruction Department of the Foreign Office; Paul Gore-Booth, First Secretary

---

[3] Admiral Arthur J. Hepburn, U. S. Navy, former Commander in Chief of the United States Fleet, Chairman of the General Board of the Navy Department; Lt. Gen. Stanley D. Embick, U. S. Army, former Deputy Chief of Staff, Chairman of the Inter-American Defense Board and Member of the Joint Strategic Survey Committee in the United States Joint Chiefs of Staff; Vice Admiral Russell Willson, U. S. Navy, Member of the Joint Strategic Survey Committee in the United States Joint Chiefs of Staff; Maj. Gen. Muir S. Fairchild, U. S. Air Force, Member of the Joint Strategic Survey Committee in the United States Joint Chiefs of Staff; Maj. Gen. George V. Strong, U. S. Army, Member of the Joint Post-War Committee in the United States Joint Chiefs of Staff; and Rear Admiral Harold C. Train, U. S. Navy, Navy Member of the Joint Post-War Committee in the Joint Chiefs of Staff.

[4] Sept. 25. For the advisers named earlier, see p. 293.

[5] These armed service officers were members of the Combined Chiefs of Staff.

of the Embassy in Washington; and A. R. K. Mackenzie as Press Officer. The British Ambassador, Lord Halifax, frequently attended the plenary meetings, and kept in close touch throughout this phase.

The Soviet Ambassador to the United States and Minister to Cuba, Andrei Andreyevich Gromyko, was Chairman of the Soviet Delegation. Arkadi Alexandrovich Sobolev, Counselor of the Soviet Embassy in London, was Deputy Chairman. The other members were Semen K. Zarapkin, Chief of the American Section of the Soviet Foreign Office; Maj. Gen. Nikolai V. Slavin of the Soviet General Staff; Rear Admiral Konstantin K. Rodionov, Chief of the Administrative Division of the Navy Commissariat; Professor Sergei A. Golunsky; Professor Sergei B. Krylov; Grigori G. Dolbin of the Foreign Office; Mikhail M. Yunin as Secretary; Valentin M. Berezhkov as Secretary-Interpreter; and Feodor T. Orekhov, Press Officer.

Secretary Hull gave the opening address on behalf of the President and himself, and was followed by the chairmen of the other two Groups. The Secretary said:

" . . . We meet at a time when the war is moving toward an overwhelming triumph for the forces of freedom. It is our task here to help lay the foundations upon which, after victory, peace, freedom, and a growing prosperity may be built. . . . this war moves us to search for an enduring peace—a peace founded upon justice and fair dealing for individuals and for nations."

After referring to the "lessons of earlier disunity and weakness" and the need of unity in view "of what modern war means," he spoke of the requirements for peace, including institutions through which to act in preserving peace. He then said:

"Success or failure of such an organization will depend upon the degree to which the participating nations are willing to exercise self-restraint and assume the responsibilities of joint action in support of the basic purposes of the organization. There must be agreement among all whereby each can play its part to the best mutual advantage and bear responsibility commensurate with its capacity."

These were conversations to reach a consensus on views to be recommended to the governments represented, the Secretary continued, and after similar consultations with China, the conclusions would be "communicated to the governments of all the United Nations and of other peace-loving nations." Our "further thought" was that "as soon as practicable these conclusions will be made available to the peoples . . . of all countries for public study and debate." It was a duty of the governments of peace-loving nations, he concluded, "to make sure that international machinery is fashioned through which peoples can build the peace they so deeply desire."

Mr. Gromyko spoke of decisive victory as "not far off" and said that in this war the "freedom-loving peoples . . . are striving to establish an international organization which would be capable of preventing the repetition of a similar tragedy and of guaranteeing for the peoples peace, security, and prosperity in the future." The organization, he envisaged, would be "based on the principle of the sovereign equality of all freedom-loving countries." In concluding, he expressed confidence that the discussions would be conducted "in a spirit of mutual understanding and in a friendly atmosphere. . . ."

Sir Alexander Cadogan mentioned the "large measure of agreement" noticeable in the provisional papers of the three Governments and the "general will" of the three "to achieve some kind of world organization, and . . . soon." He emphasized among other views that "individual nations, small and great, must be the basis" of the organization, that "peace, in the negative sense of absence of war, is not enough," and that "a measure of coordination between the various functional organizations" in economic and social fields must be arranged. Much depended on the efforts here, he said, "and some give-and-take will probably be required. . . ."

These three addresses set the broad direction for the work to be done. President Roosevelt, welcoming at the White House at noon on August 23 representatives to the four-Government Conversations, emphasized that "the four of us have to be friends, conferring all the time—the basis of getting to know each other. . . ." The work to be done would give "something to build on." [6]

In Moscow, Mr. Molotov said to the American Ambassador on August 22 that he had favorable reports of the opening of the Conversations, and felt that success was assured. He spoke also of his own respect for Secretary Hull and mentioned that Marshal Stalin was confident that he and President Roosevelt were in agreement on all fundamental questions.

Structure for the Conversations

After the opening plenary session, the organization of the Conversations was outlined at a meeting of the heads of the three groups of representatives. Each was accompanied by one or two associates: Messrs. Dunn and Pasvolsky were with Mr. Stettinius; Mr. Jebb with Sir Alexander Cadogan; and Mr. Sobolev and Mr. Berezhkov (interpreter) with Ambassador Gromyko. The Secretary was Mr. Hiss, serving in an international capacity. This Joint Steering Committee constituted on August 21 held eighteen meetings during the first phase—the phase formally described in the records as "Conversation A" but throughout the discussions called simply the "Soviet Phase" of the Conversations—plus a short additional special meeting at the end on a communiqué to be issued jointly to the press.

---

[6] *Department of State Bulletin*, XI, 197.

The Joint Steering Committee at this first meeting decided, in order to enable the Soviet representatives to resort to their native language from time to time, to recognize the use of both English and Russian during the Conversations. Mr. Stettinius was chosen permanent Chairman both of the Committee and of the Conversations, and on his insistence it was agreed that either of the other heads would so serve in his absence on any occasion. Holding of both morning and afternoon meetings was intended. The Committee agreed to have a record kept in the form of brief informal minutes cleared by all three Groups or Delegations. Concerning press releases, it decided to have the Chairman—and him alone—issue, after clearance with the other two heads, as much "procedural" information as possible. The papers submitted by all three Governments were to be taken as the basis of discussion. To start the Conversations in the plenary sessions of the next day, it agreed that the Soviet Group would first express its views, and then the American and British Groups would make their comments. The agreed-upon topics emerging from such initial exchanges and the question of what additional topics should be considered would then be clearer, so detailed discussion could be logically organized by the Committee.

The structure for the Conversations was largely clarified the next day in the second meeting of the Joint Steering Committee, which was held between the morning and afternoon plenary sessions—the only plenary sessions until the closing day of the first phase. Four subcommittees seemed to be necessary, the first as a drafting body, primarily to editorialize the drafts proposed in the Conversations by the substantive subcommittees, and the other three to correspond with those used by the American Group over the past several weeks as "working" sections. While each subcommittee had designated members, any of the delegation personnel were permitted to attend the meetings of these bodies.

The Drafting Subcommittee members were Sir William Malkin; Mr. Sobolev, accompanied by Mr. Dolbin; and Mr. Hackworth, assisted by others of the American Group including Rear Admiral Train. It was not considered to require a chairman. This subcommittee was staffed primarily with legal experts and was expected to be active only after discussion in the other subcommittees had advanced.

For the Legal Subcommittee, the following were named: Professors Golunsky and Krylov; Sir William Malkin, with another British member assisting; and Messrs. Hackworth, Cohen, and Hornbeck. This subcommittee, of which Mr. Hackworth was Chairman, held four meetings, August 24 and 31, and September 2 and 6.[7] It prepared the initial draft of joint proposals on the international court of justice.

---

[7] For the last two of these, formally cleared minutes were not kept.

The Subcommittee on General Questions of International Organization was a larger body composed of Messrs. Stettinius, Pasvolsky, Fletcher, Bowman, and Grew, Admiral Hepburn and General Embick; Ambassador Gromyko and Messrs. Sobolev and Zarapkin; and Sir Alexander Cadogan, Sir William Malkin, Mr. Jebb, and Professor Webster. It held four long meetings, August 23, 24, and 30, and September 4. The largest body was the Subcommittee on Security Questions, to which were named Ambassador Gromyko, Mr. Sobolev, General Slavin, and Admiral Rodionov; Sir Alexander Cadogan, Admiral Sir Percy Noble, General Macready, Marshal Sir William Welsh, Mr. Jebb, and Col. Capel Dunn; Messrs. Stettinius, Dunn, and Wilson, Admiral Willson, Generals Strong and Fairchild, and Admiral Train. Its two meetings were held on August 23 and 31. In constituting the two larger subcommittees, the Joint Steering Committee decided that since the heads or "chairmen of Groups" would be present, Mr. Stettinius should be the Chairman of each, with Mr. Gromyko taking the chair in his absence and Sir Alexander Cadogan in their absence.

These subcommittees began work by considering the principles and the basic questions involved in their respective fields to determine the topics to be covered. The topics were then transmitted to the Joint Steering Committee.

A significant decision of a structural nature was made by the Joint Steering Committee on Friday, August 25, on the basis of a suggestion made the preceding day in the Subcommittee on General Questions of International Organization to institute small "Formulation Groups." The decision was to institute such a group for each of the two larger subcommittees, with responsibility for drafting specific proposals as the subcommittees reached general agreement of views—a process already started and to which the first two weeks of the Conversations were to be devoted in considerable degree. This decision was put into effect on the next Monday afternoon, August 28.

The Formulation Group for the Subcommittee on General Questions of International Organization was composed of Mr. Pasvolsky; Mr. Jebb, with Mr. Webster as associate; and Mr. Sobolev, with Mr. Berezhkov, interpreter, as aide. The members of the Formulation Group for the Subcommittee on Security Questions were Mr. Dunn; Mr. Jebb, with Col. Capel Dunn as associate; and Mr. Sobolev, with Mr. Dolbin as aide. Mr. Notter attended with the American members of these groups throughout in his advisory capacity. Mr. Gerig was secretary of the first group and Mr. Yost secretary of the second, both acting in an international capacity.

The institution of the two Formulation Groups led immediately to questioning the need for the Drafting Subcommittee, which had been designated essentially as an editorial body, whereas the Formulation Groups, dealing with substance, were necessarily also performing the editorial tasks of avoiding duplication, inconsistencies, and unclear phrasing. Doubt of this need was strengthened when the Joint Steering Committee agreed on August 29 that Mr. Hackworth and Sir William Malkin should sit with the Formulation Groups, Mr. Sobolev already being a member.[8] The Drafting Subcommittee was not abolished, but it held only one meeting, near the close of this first phase, to consider the editorial form of the agreed Proposals.

The membership of the two Formulation Groups was so nearly identical that, although scheduled to meet in succession, they met together for their first meeting on August 28. The two groups continued to meet as one together for several days, and thus began immediately to lose separate identity, although for some time the distinction between the two was maintained on the basis of subject matter. By September 4, the records of the Joint Steering Committee refer to "the Joint Formulation Group" and after that more often merely to "the Formulation Group." The Group had no designated chairman, Mr. Pasvolsky simply serving as such from the start on request of the other members. Attendance by Admirals Willson and Train and General Fairchild and General Grove-White occurred upon occasion at the meetings during September, primarily when security questions were under consideration.[9] The three heads of the Delegations themselves joined in one meeting of the Group in its room at Fellows House adjoining Dumbarton Oaks.[10]

It was the Formulation Group in which not only the precise drafting and most of the exacting process of weighing the meaning and effect of each word and phrase in all proposals were carried out, but in which, with the sole exception of the Joint Steering Committee, the most detailed and analytical consideration was systematically given to all the provisions advanced for the international organization during the Dumbarton Oaks Conversations.

Since the Soviet representatives preferred informal discussions among a small number of persons rather than the less conversational consideration of questions in the main subcommittees or in plenary sessions, the Joint Steering Committee was more engaged after its first three meetings with basic substantive questions than is typical for such a body in international conferences. It spent little time on the schedule of discussion and other arrangements for the conduct of work, and from August 25 on it noticeably became the body in which the policy views of the three Delegations would be initially explored

---

[8] Mr. Hackworth thereafter was usually present. Sir William came to three meetings, in which drafting refinements were made.

[9] The Soviet military representatives did not attend.

[10] Sept. 8.

and issues outlined and in which final debates on controversial points would occur.

Particularly on the important issues, the final debates involved extensive consultation by each Delegation with its Government, with consequent increasing emphasis on the negotiating character of this Committee. There was frequent recurrence of debate on the same issues as the official positions taken were adjusted, instructions from the three Governments asked and received, compromises built and agreed views reached. Where it was "agreed to disagree," common views were at least reached on the disposition to be made of the unresolved issues. The work of the Joint Steering Committee was, accordingly, at the highest policy level.

The relationship between the Steering Committee and the Formulation Group was extremely close. The Committee alone could refer a matter to the Formulation Group, although at the outset some exceptions to this rule occurred, and the Group reported only to the Steering Committee. Controversial points when brought initially before the Joint Steering Committee were explored there and then, for the most part, referred to the Group for the drafting of a provision, or alternatives. The knottiest of the difficulties arising in the Formulation Group and not resolved there were, in turn, referred for appellate consideration to the Steering Committee. There they were debated by the heads of the three Delegations together with the four principal members of the Formulation Group—Messrs. Pasvolsky, Dunn, Sobolev, and Jebb—who always attended. Agreed views were then referred back to the Formulation Group for refinement, elaboration, and exact drafting, and views not agreed upon were the subject of further discussion by the Group in an effort to find acceptable formulas. Thus, the Formulation Group represented the highest expert level in the Conversations. However, through participation of the principal members of that Group as associates on the Steering Committee, the discussions in the Formulation Group at its expert level were inherently indistinguishable from those in the Steering Committee at its policy level except in one respect: the Steering Committee alone could conclude its discussions with decisions.

By its own wishes, the Formulation Group kept no minutes, and the only writing in its meetings was the drafting of texts. For the first seven days, it met both morning and afternoon, on several occasions for a total of seven or more hours a day—apart from other meetings its members attended earlier or later on some days.

Its first period of intense activity as an organized group covered two and a half weeks, August 28 through September 14, 1944, during which it held twenty meetings. The fact that the subcommittees almost without exception did not meet after the first few days of this period was the result of a decision of the Steering Committee on

August 31 to leave the Formulation Group free to work without interruption. Its principal members met alone several times after September 14 for prolonged discussions of the question of voting in the council, the Conversations by this time having arrived at an impasse on this matter. Eleven other questions before the Joint Steering Committee were still unresolved at this date, however, and also came under some consideration in these meetings.

The final period of the Group's activity comprised only one day, September 20, in which two long meetings of the Group were held to complete the drafting on pending questions in the light of the views agreed—or not agreed—upon in the Joint Steering Committee on the preceding day. The Group reported to that committee late in the afternoon. By the end of the day, the full draft was ready, and this text of September 20 was at once transmitted to the three Governments for approval. There were still, however, at that date a number of specific points on which governmental instructions were awaited by the Delegations.

Only two additional committee structures were evolved for the Conversations. The first was the "Group of Military Representatives of the Three Delegations." This started as a "special military subcommittee," but the name was changed to the less formal one of a "Special Informal Military Group." Its establishment was hardly the result of a decision. Rather it grew out of desires expressed in the meeting of the Subcommittee on Security Questions on August 23 for study of the technical aspects of a general proposal for an international air force corps advanced in the Soviet Memorandum. The nature of this proposal was not worked out in the Soviet paper, and when the possible interpretations of it were being developed at the subcommittee's meeting, the suggestion of its technical study by the professional service members naturally arose. The uniformed officers of the three Delegations being present, they were asked to study the matter as a special subcommittee. These members talked together informally throughout the first phase, but the only formal meetings of the Military Group, over which Admiral Willson presided and for which minutes were kept, were held on August 24 and 30. The first meeting covered the problems of provision of armed forces to the international organization as well as the specific question under reference. The second meeting, which was attended by most of the Formulation Group also, was given over to a continuation of the consideration of these problems and to discussion of the nature, functions, relationships, and other problems of a military advisory commission projected in connection with the work of the council of the organization.

A "Subcommittee on Nomenclature," the second additional body, was established on August 23 by the subcommittee on General Questions of International Organization. The duties of the new subcommittee were to recommend the names or titles for the international organization—for the basic instrument itself, the organs, and their officers. The members were Mr. Fletcher, Chairman, Messrs. Bowman and Pasvolsky; Professors Golunsky and Krylov; Sir William Malkin and Mr. Loxley. Its few meetings were entirely conversational, not organized in character, and without minutes. Its report was accepted by its parent subcommittee on September 4, 1944, and, with tentative reservations, by the Joint Steering Committee on September 12.

The names and titles recommended in this report were used thereafter in the drafting: "The United Nations," "Charter," "The General Assembly," "The Security Council," "President" for the presiding officers of these two principal organs, "Military Staff Committee," "International Court of Justice" to be used pending the drafting of a Statute for the Court, and "Secretary-General" for the principal officer of the "Secretariat." The Soviet representatives had initially reserved their position on several of these, not only for instructions but for reasons of language difficulties. For example, no word for "Charter" having exactly the same meaning as in the English language exists in Russian. Similarly, the word "President" was used to avoid the confusion in Russian and French that the word "Chairman" would cause. At the time of the report, provisions for "the Economic and Social Council" had not been formulated, and this name as used in drafting was accepted when the provisions for this Council were adopted.

Procedure Within the American Group

The Soviet and British Groups used their respective Embassies for most of their own meetings, though each also used its quarters at Dumbarton Oaks for some work. They came to the estate at the hour set for the first meeting of the day, normally 10:30 a. m. The American Group, on the other hand, carried on almost all its activities as a group at Dumbarton Oaks. The exceptions were Mr. Stettinius' almost daily talks with Secretary Hull, with whom he conferred either alone or accompanied by the members of the "consulting group" who were participating in the Conversations; talks with the President by the Secretary, the Under Secretary and, on occasion, the "consulting group" members; and one full Group discussion with Secretary Hull in his office. Secretary Hull himself discussed developments in the Conversations with the Secretaries of War and Navy at least once a week commencing August 29, 1944. Daily reports were prepared for the Secretary and the President, while a number of special memoranda were also sent to one or both of them on the larger problems that arose in the Conversations and required their consideration. As will shortly be seen below, these were used by the Secretary in his continuing congressional consultations.

The advisory and other technical staff of the Group frequently resorted to their home divisions in the Department for assistance, and there were some consultations with other officers of the Department by the Group members themselves, especially in regard to providing public information. The advisers for the European Area, Mr. Bohlen and Mr. Hickerson, had the special responsibility of keeping the American Embassies in Moscow and London apprised of developments, and all the geographic advisers to the Group had the duty of keeping it informed of the views being expressed abroad, which required work in and through the Department at all times. The representatives of the armed services likewise maintained close touch with the War and Navy Departments and the Joint Chiefs of Staff and on a number of occasions reported to the Group the views of the two Secretaries, the Chief of Staff, and the Joint Chiefs of Staff.

The arrangements within the American Group for its negotiating work, as has already been suggested, were similar to those adopted for the period of briefing and review, and the assignments of the American representatives to the various subcommittees of the Conversations corresponded in substantial measure to the subject matter on which each had concentrated in that preceding period. The full American Group met at 9 : 30 a. m., usually Monday through Saturday, in the former dining room which Mr. Stettinius once described as "the most used room" at Dumbarton Oaks. Its Steering Committee, composed of Messrs. Stettinius, Dunn, Hackworth, Pasvolsky, and Wilson, Admiral Willson and General Strong, with Messrs. Hiss and Raynor as secretary and assistant respectively, met only on call, and most informally. Special meetings confined to the Group members, the general adviser, the Chairman's special assistant, and the secretary of the Group were also held, although not frequently, to consider major critical issues being taken up with the Secretary and the President. These were, in effect, steering meetings with a temporarily enlarged participation.

The daily meeting of all American representatives, advisers, principal technical secretaries, and officers of the secretariat was the main organized basis of the American Group's functioning, since the members worked together on all problems and reached decisions in these meetings. Reports of all developments throughout the Conversations were given, during these meetings, including any views resulting from talks with the Secretary and President, and positions on the pending questions of the day were then determined. Necessary drafting was assigned, and plans on emerging matters were discussed. In September, particularly between the 4th and 8th, when drafts from the Formulation Group were under consideration, the entire Group, except those leaving for other meetings and a recess at lunch, stayed in session until late afternoon, work by some being continued thereafter until late at night. This same situation prevailed between the 11th and 20th, when the Conversations faced critical lack of agreement on the question of voting provisions and consideration had therefore to be given to the consequences of incomplete agreement on joint proposals. Either Mr. Long or Mr. Bowman served as Chairman when Mr. Stettinius was otherwise engaged.

A number of committees or "subcommittees" of the members were used by the American Group in conducting its work. These were created as need arose, although, since some problems were not solved or did not remain solved, certain of these *ad hoc* bodies assumed the nature of standing committees. The first of these was established on August 23, 1944, to assist Mr. McDermott, the Press Officer, in preparing recommendations for providing the press with fuller information. Those appointed were Messrs. Long, Bowman, and Fletcher. This committee reported the next day, but it was reappointed at once and several times more on this continuing need, each time with the addition of members until it at last included also Messrs. Cohen, Hornbeck, Wilson, Admirals Hepburn and Willson, and Generals Embick and Strong, with the general adviser, the special assistant, and the assistant secretary-general assigned to facilitate its work.

Another organized effort in a related connection was the assignment of Mr. Wilson, on August 31, as a committee of one to report on what was being done and should be done by the Department toward informing educational, religious, and other interested American public groups or organizations concerning developments, and toward enlisting their informed support of effective international organization. Mr. Wilson was asked to collaborate on this matter with John Dickey, Director of the Office of Public Affairs in the Department, and G. Howland Shaw, Assistant Secretary of State. The Group discussed the matter several times in September. In the course of such discussion, consideration was given to the possibility of reviving the project of a "Post-War Advisory Council" [11] or, alternatively, of holding after the Conversations occasional meetings of the leaders of these citizen organizations with the higher officers of the Department, current meetings being considered inadvisable in view of the nature of the Conversations. By September 11, these problems had been placed in the hands of the first-named committee, with Mr. Fletcher as Chairman, and the drafting of communiqués was added to its work.

A Subcommittee on Nomenclature and Location was appointed on August 30 by the American Group to recommend to it not only names and titles in connection with the organization, as in the case of the partly parallel body for the Conversations, but also the languages to

---

[11] See p. 213 ff.

be used by the organization and views on its location and that of its organs. The question of location stemmed immediately from the interest shown in this matter by the President in several recent talks with Mr. Stettinius and other officials. Prime Minister Churchill and Mr. Stettinius had begun to explore this matter when the Under Secretary had visited London on his mission earlier in 1944, and since then Mr. Bowman had been studying the many alternatives. The members of this "Fletcher Committee," as it was usually referred to, were, aside from Mr. Fletcher as Chairman, Messrs. Bowman, Cohen, and Hackworth, Admiral Hepburn, and General Strong. Mr. Hornbeck also joined in this work at times.

Additional problems were referred to this body from time to time, including such diverse matters as the drafting of a formula to provide for the continuous functioning of the Council of the organization, the consideration of Latin American views regarding world security organization being received in response to the circular telegram sent in July, and the drafting of recommendations, begun by September 6, 1944, relative to conferring with Latin American representatives on the proposals to result from the Conversations. For these latter matters, Mr. Wilson was added to the subcommittee, and Messrs. Notter, Cabot, and Gerig were assigned to assist. In connection with this work, it was understood that in accord with customary practice the British representatives were planning consultations with the members of the British Commonwealth of Nations, and were already providing information on the Conversations to the Dominions.

Study of the problem of United States representation in the organization being projected in the developing Conversations, which the Group had to consider even though only preliminarily, was placed in charge of the third committee of which Mr. Fletcher was Chairman. Its further members were Messrs. Bowman, Cohen, Grew, Long, Admiral Hepburn, and General Embick. This was a preparatory body, established to meet a need in advance of possible questions being raised, and no report was made.

A large amount of drafting was undertaken by the individual American representatives. The members from the armed services together drafted views on several occasions, and various members in groups of two or more not infrequently presented a draft on a point that they wished to have considered. The largest organized drafting effort by a committee of the American Group in connection with substantive proposals, however, took place in an *ad hoc* committee constituted on September 7.[12] This committee was created to

---

[12] There were *ad hoc* groups beside those mentioned above, for example, one to consider a request of certain Korean leaders to observe the Conversations. Such groups were of routine character.

condense and adjust the American proposals for an economic and social council, the subject to come before the Formulation Group late that afternoon. The members of this committee were Messrs. Bowman, Chairman, Cohen, Grew,[13] Hornbeck, Wilson, and General Strong. This work was not completed for several days, and meanwhile prolonged discussion by the full American Group took place on the drafts being prepared.

The last subcommittee used by the American Group was also established for substantive drafting. It was appointed on September 20 and 21, 1944, at the start of the last week of the Soviet Phase. The Group was confronted at that time with the selection of the important "open questions" that might still require consideration to complete the Proposals. It was then intended to annex a list of such questions to the Proposals when issued. The Group also wished prepared a memorandum for the Secretary, if he approved, to send to the President concerning the closing of the Soviet Phase. This subcommittee was composed of Messrs. Wilson and Cohen, with Messrs. Notter, Gerig, and Yost assisting. The Group considered the initial drafts at its night meeting on the 20th and the revised drafts in a meeting at 10:30 the following morning.

Stage One

As suggested by the foregoing, the Soviet Phase of the Conversations passed through a number of stages, although these tended to be obscured by the overlapping of the various threads of development and hence to have only approximate time limits. Secretary Hull's continuing nonpartisan consultations were interwoven with these stages.

The first stage was August 21–25, during which the committees and other group structures for conducting the discussions were organized, initial views presented, questions organized into agendas for discussion, and exploratory discussions begun. As noted above, the papers of all three Governments were used initially as the basis of these discussions, but thereafter, though without specific decision, the basic frame of reference in building joint proposals was the American Tentative Proposals. During these five days of presentation of views in the main subcommittees, the very substantial extent of common views on international organization among the three Governments had become evident, and most of the principal divergent conceptions had appeared.

It was during this opening week, as will be recalled, that Secretary Hull and Mr. Dulles, representing Governor Dewey, completed their

---

[13] Mr. Grew could not take part.

initial direct consultations in Washington.[14] The correspondence already described between the Secretary and Governor Dewey ensued over the next week [15] and continuing liaison between the Secretary and Mr. Dulles was also maintained through former Ambassador Hugh R. Wilson,[16] Republican and resident of the Capital, acting on request of Mr. Dulles and Governor Dewey. James Clement Dunn frequently served on behalf of the Secretary as the channel of detailed information to Mr. Wilson. Directly himself and through Mr. Wilson, the Secretary informed Mr. Dulles and Governor Dewey of developments including particularly his consultations with Members of Congress.

The Secretary's consultations with leaders in Congress resumed after the Party Conventions when, on August 23, the Secretary transmitted, to the members of the same senatorial group that had met with him in the spring, copies of the Tentative Proposals as sent to the other governments taking part in the Dumbarton Oaks Conversations. In these copies the additional provision resulting from the Secretary's conferences with Mr. Dulles had been inserted.[17] A copy of the proposals was also sent to Senator Elbert D. Thomas, Democrat of Utah, who had been active in the Advisory Committee during the previous two years and who joined the group at its first meeting with the Secretary during the Conversations. At this meeting,[18] on August 25, all additions and changes made since the draft of April 29, 1944, had been studied by the group were examined on the basis of memoranda written at Dumbarton Oaks for this purpose by Messrs. Bowman, Pasvolsky, Notter, and Gerig and Miss Fosdick. Chief attention in this meeting, however, was given to the problem of what authority in this Government could decide upon the use of force. This arose in connection with the power of the projected council of the proposed organization to order enforcement action and therefore involved the question of whether the American representative on the council could vote for such action on instructions from the Executive without trenching upon the exclusive power of the Congress to declare war. A possible requirement of congressional approval for specific uses of force was posed by this problem, which was clarified but left unresolved at this meeting.

---

[14] See p. 288.

[15] See p. 289.

[16] Mr. Wilson had taken part in the initial preparatory effort shortly after the start of the war and had returned to private life at the end of 1940. See pp. 22, 462.

[17] This concerned ratification of armed forces agreements. See pp. 288–89.

[18] All the former group were present except Senators Barkley and Gillette, who could not attend.

Stage Two

The second stage began during August 25 and carried through September 4. Although the exploratory character of the discussion continued to distinguish the Conversations for a week longer, it did so in diminishing degree. The new stage was especially marked by discussion of substantive issues in the Joint Steering Committee and drafting of first texts of joint proposals in the meetings of the Formulation "Groups." This development clearly denoted entrance upon more advanced work, although the views tending toward agreement were for the most part still tentative and in a few instances were subsequently altered.

The questions in the forefront at this stage were numerous. Among them were: Should economic and social as well as security matters be included within the scope of the projected organization? Should provision be made for withdrawal from membership, for suspension of the rights of a member, and for expulsion of a member? What should be the composition of the body to give military advice to the council? What should be the composition of the council? By what vote should the council reach decisions? Should members of the council that were parties to a dispute—including parties that were major nations with permanent membership on the council—have the right to vote or be required to abstain from voting in decisions by the council on the dispute? The latter was fundamental to the rights and obligations of members in the organization to the relation of large and small nations and to the basic principles on which the organization would function. The British came with the view that the votes of any parties to a dispute should not be taken into account. The American position, presented in this stage, was that a permanent member, like a non-permanent member, should not vote in connection with a dispute to which it was a party. The Soviet representatives held the contrary view. There was, however, no question concerning the general requirement of unanimity of the permanent members in reaching decisions on nonprocedural matters of peace and security, since from the outset there was no disagreement among the three Governments on this provision.

A further question, concerning membership, was raised in the Joint Steering Committee on August 28, 1944, and proved to have major significance. It was not agreed whether only the United Nations, of which there were thirty-five in this period, or also the eight "associated nations" which had not actually declared war but were contributing otherwise to the war effort should be initial members as proposed by the American and British Groups. In the course of the discussion of this question, Ambassador Gromyko stated that the "sixteen Soviet Republics" should be included among the initial members of the international organization. An attitude of reserve toward this proposal and anticipation of great difficulty from it was expressed by the other Chairmen present in their brief responses.[19]

The Soviet proposal was immediately the subject of consultation by Under Secretary Stettinius with Secretary Hull and the President, and by the Secretary and the Under Secretary with Ambassador Gromyko. Although the Soviet Ambassador volunteered that there should be no further reference to his proposal during the Conversations, on August 29 he indicated that on some other occasion his Government would probably raise the subject again. This matter was then considered in a telegram on August 31 from the President to Marshal Stalin. To this the Marshal replied on September 7, expressing the desire for an opportunity to explain to the President "the political importance" of this question.[20] In these exchanges, this Government's emphatic opposition to the Soviet proposal was expressed on the grounds that it might imperil the whole project for an international organization, and the suggestion made that it might more properly be presented for decision to the organization after it was established.

By decision at the White House, knowledge of this matter was closely restricted for two reasons: in order to give opportunity for diplomatic activity at high levels to persuade the Soviet Union to withdraw this suggestion or to allow it to lapse, and because of apprehension that wider information regarding it would risk creating by pressure of outraged opinion an immediate deadlock in negotiations perhaps fatally injurious to the establishment of the organization.[21] It was made known to the full American Group only on October 16, 1944, at a brief meeting in the office of Mr. Stettinius.

On the day after this question arose, August 29, the earliest drafts from the Formulation "Groups" began to arrive in the Joint Steering Committee. These drafts covered purposes, principles, membership, and principal organs. On that date, the practice of putting brackets

---

[19] This Government had previously been informed in a British *aide-mémoire* of Dec. 10, 1943, that the Soviet Government had requested representation on the War Crimes Commission for the "Ukraine, Bielo-Livonian, Moldavian, Lithuanian, Latvian, Estonian and Karelo-Finnish Republics," contending that these entities were no less sovereign than the British Dominions and that their war sufferings gave them a moral right to representation. The request had been rejected, but the implications of it, taken with the Soviet announcement on Feb. 11, 1944, of the autonomy of the constituent Soviet Republics in foreign affairs, were carefully studied in the Department. The possibility that some comparable request might be made in connection with the international economic organization under consideration during this period had been taken into account in a memorandum by the Under Secretary on Feb. 11, 1944, in which he expressed his opposition to the acceptance of any such proposal.

[20] For the single repetition of the Soviet view during the Conversations after Marshal Stalin's telegram, see below, pp. 327, 333–34.

[21] See, however, Part IV, pp. 396–97.

around any clause in a proposal, or around an entire proposal, was inaugurated by the Formulation "Groups" to signify a tentative phrasing of points on which any two delegations were at least generally agreed but on which disagreement from the policy standpoint or other reservation continued to be expressed by the third.[22] This practice enabled progress to be made in building the proposals, on the basis of common consent but without commitment, while unresolved issues continued to be discussed further in the Conversations, or were referred back to the Governments, or both.

By September 4 first drafts on the assembly, the council, arrangements for the maintenance of peace and security (covering pacific settlement of disputes, and threats to and breaches of international peace and security and action with respect thereto), and a draft on the court, had been prepared by the Joint Formulation Group. These comprised the first text, in eight chapters, of the eventual proposals resulting from the Conversations. There were many brackets in this text. Among the provisions so treated were those concerning the use of armed forces, regulation of armaments and armed forces, the role of the assembly in amending the charter, and voting in the council. So rapid was the progress in the first ten days of the Conversations, despite the "brackets", that on September 1, the Steering Committee of the American Group considered it possible to conclude the "Soviet Phase" in nine days, and to convene a general United Nations conference in eight weeks to complete the charter.[23] Progress began to be slower from September 4 on, however, as detailed questions of phrasing arose and as instructions on issues were awaited by the Soviet and, to some extent, the British Delegations.

During the second stage, the Secretary's consultations with Senators Ball, Burton, Hatch, and Hill had been resumed, on August 28, at which time these Senators had been given copies of the Tentative Proposals. The Secretary conferred with the leadership group from the House of Representatives the next day.[24] At both these meetings, the additions and changes to date in the Tentative Proposals being advanced at Dumbarton Oaks were discussed, and general approval was accorded them. Concurrently with these meetings, further thought was given to the problems raised in the previous meeting with the large senatorial group, first on the basis of a letter from Senator Vandenberg to the Secretary on August 29 and

---

[22] For example, see appendix 41.

[23] The date considered for the general conference was Oct. 25, 1944.

[24] Cf. above, p. 267. Representative Eaton was absent from the meeting of the 29th. In addition to such meetings, some correspondence with Members of Congress was as usual carried on with reference to specific matters in this field, as for example with Representative Emanuel Celler, Democrat of New York, on dependent areas and Palestine beginning Aug. 23.

then on the basis of a memorandum by Mr. Hackworth analyzing the uses of force under Executive authority in our national history. Copies of this paper, dated August 31, 1944, were made available to Sneators Connally and Vandenberg. Besides the further talks between the Secretary and individual Senators and Representatives over the next two weeks, there were also many other brief conversations by members of the American Group with Members of Congress, made possible by the attendance of many of the latter at the several official receptions held in turn by this Government and the British and the Soviet Embassies (and subsequently by the Chinese Embassy). These occasions afforded opportunity for all who took part in the Conversations to have direct congressional contact.

Stage Three

The third stage of the Conversations lasted approximately from September 4 through September 9. During it, the Joint Formulation Group arrived at its fourth draft of the projected proposals.

It was in these days that conciliation of opposing positions became increasingly doubtful on the issue of whether a major power when party to a dispute should have or not have a right to vote in decisions by the council on such dispute. To recognize such a right would, in effect, signify a veto by the major power that was a party in such a matter, in view of the agreed rule requiring in nonprocedural decisions unanimous concurrence by the major powers as permanent members of the Council. Soviet insistence that the right of vote should be kept by major powers in such cases had been voiced from the start of the matter's consideration on August 25 and 28, and when it continued unmodified in the discussions of the Joint Steering Committee, Secretary Hull had personally discussed the matter with Ambassador Gromyko, on August 31, without avail. On September 6 the Secretary, Under Secretary, and the President conferred on this and other problems at issue in the Conversations. President Roosevelt talked with Ambassador Gromyko and Mr. Stettinius early on the morning of September 8, and later that day the President cabled a personal message to Marshal Stalin, urging the necessity of reaching agreement and explaining why the United States favored denial of right of vote in such cases.

The Joint Formulation Group worked at this time particularly on the chapters providing for a secretariat, an economic and social council, the process of amendment, and regional arrangements, all but the first remaining within brackets. In accord with an earlier general disposition to postpone the drafting of a statute of the court until after the Conversations, the Legal Subcommittee concluded its meetings on September 6, with the concrete suggestion that representatives of the states to participate in the future general conference on the international organization should meet two weeks in advance of that conference for the purpose of preparing such a draft statute. By the last two days of this stage, the draft joint proposals had reached a length of eleven chapters, and the Joint Steering Committee, beginning on the 7th but notably on the 8th and 9th, removed brackets on several provisions, including particularly those for an economic and social council and for continuous session of the security council.

New or modified proposals concerning human rights and fundamental freedoms, and provisions concerning responsibility for control over former enemy states, interim arrangements for enforcement of peace until the new organization became effective, and membership of the organization, in addition to the continuing problems of voting, were coming under advanced consideration as this stage closed. There also remained unsettled the Soviet proposals concerning possible strategic bases for enforcement action and a possible international air force, and several proposals by other delegations, including one for assistance to states suffering loss through carrying out decisions of the security council. These questions had been discussed extensively by this time, but without agreement. The fifth draft of the joint proposals, compiled on the following Sunday to reflect the latest decisions by the Steering Committee, was thus still marked by many uncertainties. Nevertheless, the text was sufficiently developed to be sent to the participating Governments for comment.

It was during this short third stage that Governor Dewey made certain suggestions concerning the Tentative Proposals in a telephone conversation with the Secretary, September 6, and in a memorandum to the Secretary on the 8th. At the Secretary's request that if possible these suggestions be incorporated in the American Proposals, the three suggestions were immediately given attention by the American Group. Assurance that these ideas were shared and would be put forward in the Conversations was at once given to Mr. Dulles and Governor Dewey. The two specific suggestions made by Mr. Dewey were put in the American draft on the 9th, and were later incorporated in the final joint proposals. These concerned the right of nonmember states as well as member states to bring disputes or situations to the attention of the assembly or council, and explicit provision that such situations should include those that might lead to international "friction." The third suggestion made was that the text did not clearly show whether a condition, situation, or controversy arising from treaty provisions was included among matters that could be brought before the assembly or council. In this case, the point, on re-examination, still appeared to be implicit in the broad terms already adopted in the joint proposals relative to situations and disputes, and this same view appeared, from personal talks, to be held by the British. Furthermore, enumeration was generally opposed on the ground that it would call for inclusion of all possible factors, or else risk interpretation as excluding factors not mentioned. Therefore, no express reference to treaties was thought necessary.

Another consultation with the congressional groups had been intended early in this stage, but this was deferred to await more definite developments on questions not yet settled in the Conversations.

The stages through September 9, broadly speaking, comprised the part of the Soviet Phase of the Conversations devoted primarily to the construction of joint proposals. The rest of the Soviet Phase was principally characterized by negotiations to reconcile differing views and to dispose of the questions on which agreement was still lacking, rather than by the development of new proposals.

Stage Four

At the start of the fourth stage—September 11–20, 1944—the consideration of bracketed parts of the draft joint proposals was delayed pending receipt by the Soviet Delegation of further instructions. On the 12th, attention was given to the plans for some announcement at the end of the Conversations as a whole. Since the Soviet Delegation stated that it could not sign a Four Power communication, a plan for simultaneous release of one agreed announcement separately by each of the participating Governments was proposed and accepted. Although the recommendations on nomenclature already mentioned received favorable attention on September 12, they were tentatively approved only in part. This day was most notable for the progress made in eliminating some of the larger questions at issue. This progress was begun by withdrawal of the Soviet proposals concerning bases and an international air force, and, while certain other questions involving enforcement action were still left unresolved, views on the Military Staff Committee were brought into agreement.

Inclusion among the organization's purposes of cooperation in the solution of international economic, social, and other humanitarian problems as desired from the outset by the Americans and British was agreed upon September 13. An American proposal to have all positions in the organization filled without regard to race, nationality, creed, or sex was put under study in the Joint Steering Committee that day, and the sixth draft of the joint proposals was compiled. By the next day, the placement of interim or transitional arrangements in a separate and new chapter was agreed upon—though in brackets. An introductory statement was added to the joint proposals, giving "The United Nations" as the title of the organization and suggesting that the proposals be embodied in a charter. This progress was reflected in the seventh draft of the developing text, dated September 15. Sir Alexander Cadogan was called at this time to the Quebec Conference by Prime Minister Churchill, and no meetings of the Steering Committee were held on that day or the next.[25]

Before this brief interruption occurred, the Secretary's four main consultations in this stage had already taken place. The information conveyed in these consultations was drawn substantially from a memorandum of September 11, 1944, prepared for this purpose within the American Group at Dumbarton Oaks in the same manner as those for his preceding consultative meetings. This memorandum reported the status of each chapter of the joint proposals as so far developed, pointing out that all of the essential provisions of the Tentative Proposals had been agreed upon with some slight changes, fewer details, and the addition of a small number of new points.

The first of the four consultations started that same day, when the Secretary handed a copy of the memorandum to Hugh Wilson for Mr. Dulles. On the 12th Mr. Dulles telephoned to convey his pleasure over the progress shown in it; the Secretary mentioned the acceptance of Mr. Dewey's points and discussed particularly the question concerning the use of armed force that had come up in the last meeting of the senatorial group. He expressed to Mr. Dulles his apprehension lest the Soviet and British Governments come to feel that American participation in the enforcement of peace under the new organization could not be satisfactorily implemented. There were enough problems with the Soviets already in his opinion.

The second consultation was with the large senatorial group. Senators Barkley, Connally, George, Gillette, Vandenberg, and White were present at a meeting held on the 12th and were informed of the status of agreement attained in the Conversations. Satisfaction with this progress was expressed by the participating Senators, although out of anxiety over extreme attitudes that might possibly evolve in this country, question was voiced concerning the projected economic and social provisions. This and several other subjects, including the earlier problem of the power in this Government to decide on the use of armed force as this power was involved in the functioning of the projected organization, were then discussed. The latter problem, though characterized as "one-half of one percent of an otherwise 100 percent sound peace plan," was regarded by all as critical in relation to demonstrating, particularly to the Soviets at this difficult time, the firm American intention to seek an effective organization. The search for a solution of this peculiarly domestic problem took the

[25] Admiral Willson and General Fairchild were with the President at the Quebec Conference. Admiral Willson had with him the draft joint proposals as so far developed, as a precaution in case the President should need to consult them. Such need did not arise.

form in this meeting of exploring the domestic adjustments that would be required for our participation.

The last two consultations, with Representatives Arends, Bloom, Eaton, McCormack, Ramspeck, and Rayburn the next day, and with Senators Ball, Hatch, and Hill on the 14th, similarly covered the progress toward joint proposals in the Conversations and touched upon much the same questions. General belief that the economic and social provisions being advanced by the American Group were approximately in proper balance was expressed in these talks. The viewpoint was strongly presented by the Secretary in all meetings on these three days that the organization, if in existence when the time for conclusion of peace arrived, would exert a powerful influence toward a good settlement. He commented that he hoped for a United Nations Conference early in November, a hope that was not to prove realizable.

In the Conversations, the foremost among all unresolved issues continued to be that of voting in the security council. While in the preceding stage this issue had proved serious in substantive respects, it now posed the question whether to continue the Conversations in an effort to resolve the issue. Various formulas to find a way through this difficulty were considered. For example, the possibility of empowering the council to request, rather than to require, a major nation when party to a dispute to abstain from voting on its own case was explored, but discarded as inadequate. On the forenoon of September 13, it was learned that the Soviet Delegation's position, on instructions from Moscow, remained unchanged and that this was a "final" position. Nevertheless, on American initiative later that day, a compromise formula on the issue was drafted, informally and without prejudice to the positions that the Governments might adopt, by members of the Formulation Group.[26] This formula differentiated between decisions on pacific settlement and other decisions involving application of the rule of unanimity. This possible solution, while supported by both the Secretary and the Under Secretary of State as the maximum compromise we could accept, was advanced only at the technical level, as a possible basis for agreement, and was not presented officially. This effort reflected the heightened tension on this issue. Deadlock had been reached. Only a new proposal might offer hope of a solution.

Marshal Stalin's reply to the President's cable of September 8 on the subject was received on the 15th. Although conveying the Marshal's hope that the Conversations would have a successful outcome and that a solution of the voting question would be found, and expressing his view that the door to a solution still appeared open in the form of some special procedure for voting, as had originally been suggested

---

[26] See appendix 42.

but not specified in the American Tentative Proposals, this reply did not indicate any change in the Soviet position. Hence it gave no encouragement regarding acceptance of any compromise at this time. Prime Minister Churchill's views as reported by Sir Alexander Cadogan on his return from Quebec, September 16, were also adverse to considering compromise. Moreover, President Roosevelt himself was not then inclined to favor the new suggestion in the compromise formula.

Accordingly, by the 17th, the possibility of suspending the Soviet Phase of the Conversations and commencing the Chinese Phase came under discussion in the Joint Steering Committee. After consulting Secretary Hull, Mr. Stettinius conferred on that day with Mr. Gromyko to urge for the last time a change of position, and he discussed the whole situation with Sir Alexander Cadogan. It was ascertained definitely in those separate conversations, and in a further talk among the three together, that, while the situation was regarded as one of lack of agreement rather than of disagreement, no quick solution to the question of voting was in sight.

Whether, as a result, the proposals should be published in incomplete form raised serious doubts and much debate. At this point, Mr. Stettinius consulted with some of the American Group at Dumbarton Oaks and with Secretary Hull and the President by telephone. He then suggested a recess of the Conversations after the Soviet Phase, with resumption of the talks between the British, Soviets, and Americans on a date not later than November 15, to prepare complete proposals, which could serve as a basis for discussion at a full United Nations conference. This was considered in principle by the Joint Steering Committee on September 17. After Sir Alexander Cadogan and Ambassador Gromyko agreed to request instructions on this possibility, draft communiqués were prepared by the American Group and circulated immediately that day. There were two documents, a "short" communiqué to be issued at the end of the Soviet Phase and a "long" communiqué to be issued at the close of the entire Conversations. Consideration of these drafts was deferred, pending receipt of instructions.

On September 19, Mr. Stettinius reported in a memorandum to the Secretary: "Apart from relatively minor matters all essential recommendations have been agreed upon except the arrangements as to voting in the Council on which point we are at an impasse." In another memorandum on that date, he definitely raised for the American Group with the Secretary and the President the question whether this first phase of the Conversation should be continued longer. The memorandum set forth the opposing position of the three Delegations on the voting issue and the favorable view of the American Group toward the projected voting compromise. It also presented the divergent views in the Group regarding adjournment of this phase without agreement on the voting issue. In this situation, the Secretary asked the American representatives, advisers, and principal technical officers to his office for a discussion that afternoon. He emphasized in his remarks the need for patience and a friendly attitude in dealing with the Soviet Union, whose vital interests, he believed, required international cooperation. Much progress toward establishing an international organization had been made, he said, and "in any great endeavor such as this . . . there will be hitches now and then." We could "not expect . . . success fast."

Later that day, agreement was reached on several bracketed proposals and additional questions at a meeting of the Joint Steering Committee, held at Ambassador Gromyko's request. On September 20, further bracketed provisions and pending questions were decided in a meeting of that committee. The eighth draft of the joint proposals, dated the 20th, incorporated these developments and was transmitted that evening to the three Governments for their consideration.

The decision was made by the President on the morning of September 21, in a talk with Secretary Hull, Mr. Stettinius, Mr. Dunn, Mr. Pasvolsky, Admiral Willson, and General Embick, to adjourn the first phase of the Conversations on the understanding that the text of the joint proposals would soon be published, accompanied by a statement that the question of voting and certain other matters remained under consideration and would be the subject of further negotiations among the three Governments. A suggestion in this sense was communicated at once to Ambassador Gromyko and Sir Alexander Cadogan.

Stage Five

The last stage of the Soviet Phase commenced with this definite suggestion on September 21. It ended September 28.

The Secretary, in letters sent September 22 to the Senators with whom he had been conferring, projected further nonpartisan consultations with the congressional groups, but no meetings were held at this time. The election campaign was of course taking various members away from Washington, and ten days later the Secretary's illness precluded his continuance of activities of this nature. On September 23, Secretary Hull telephoned to Mr. Dulles to say that the Conversations had resulted in practical agreement aside from points to be cleared up before "the formal meeting" should take place. The principal point at issue was the voting question. The Secretary expressed anxiety over the critical stage reached especially with respect to the reaction of small nations and the possibility of "any large nation walking out. . . ." When Mr. Dulles expressed hope that the "bi-partisan aspect . . . be maintained," it was agreed, as he suggested, that "any concessions that would have to be made" would be "cleared with him. . . ."

The Joint Steering Committee held no meetings for the first six days of this stage, while waiting for the views of the Governments on the draft joint proposals. No major difficulty was anticipated in view of the generally acceptable wording of the still bracketed provisions. The main questions then awaiting decision, aside from the unresolvable one of voting in the security council, were the determination of initial membership of the organization, treatment of matters within the domestic jurisdiction of member states, provision for amendment of the charter, and provision, as proposed by the United States, for promotion of respect for human rights and fundamental freedoms.

The problem also remained of reaching agreement on the texts of the "short" communiqué to end the Soviet Phase and of the "long" communiqué to close the Conversations. The proposed texts communicated in preliminary form on September 17 [27] were considered in the meeting of the Joint Steering Committee on September 27, by which time instructions on both had been received by the British Delegation, but, it appeared, on only the "short" communiqué by the Soviet Delegation. The shorter communiqué was agreed upon immediately.

In considering the longer, there was discussion particularly of the provision for further steps to be taken by the four Governments "not later than November 15" to complete the proposals to be placed before the general conference of the United Nations. The British Government was of the opinion that no date should yet be specified. The Chairman of the Soviet Delegation believed that the further steps should be taken "if possible" by November 15. This specific date was therefore replaced by the phrase "as soon as possible," an amendment accepted reluctantly by the American Chairman. Approval of the longer communiqué was reserved, however, pending the receipt of instructions by the Soviet Delegation.

After this decision, and in the same meeting, Ambassador Gromyko stated that agreement by his Government on any date for the general conference of the United Nations would depend upon whether the British and the American Governments would accept the Soviet position on voting in the Security Council and the Soviet proposal that the Soviet Republics be initial members of the organization. Concerning the first of these provisos, the explanation was made that the Soviet Government continued to consider that the principle of the unanimity of the four great powers must be carried out unconditionally; on the second, no explanation was offered. Without comment

[27] After relatively minor changes had been suggested by the British, amended texts were circulated on the 26th, but the new texts arrived in Moscow too late for Soviet consideration and were therefore not used.

on either of these matters, the meeting turned to discussion of the timing of the publication of the communiqué, concluding that the next day would be too soon to arrange for its simultaneous release in the three capitals.

In the same meeting the remaining brackets were removed from the draft text of the proposals and agreement reached on its publication with a brief note that several other questions remained under consideration. The draft of the proposals to embody the agreements reached in this meeting was the ninth and last. It was approved on behalf of the three Governments in the closing plenary session on September 28. The longer communiqué was tentatively approved in that session, for issuance on October 9, and a final meeting of the Joint Steering Committee after the plenary session was devoted to efforts to assure complete agreement on it.[28]

Conversation A, or the Soviet Phase of the Dumbarton Oaks Conversations, officially ended on September 28, and the prearranged release of the "short" communiqué took place on the morning of September 29. This stated that the "Conversations between the United States, United Kingdom and Soviet Union Delegations . . . have been useful and have led to a large measure of agreement on recommendations for the general framework of the Organization, and in particular for the machinery required to maintain peace and security."

"CHINESE PHASE"

THE OPENING session of Conversation B—the "Chinese Phase" of the Dumbarton Oaks Conversations—was held immediately: Friday afternoon, September 29, 1944. Detailed discussion began the next Monday morning.

This last phase of the Conversations lasted but nine days. Rapid progress was possible since the Chinese views had already been taken carefully into account during the Soviet Phase and, after the earlier phase had exceeded expected limits, several informal American talks had been held with the Chinese representatives who had arrived on August 25. These preliminary and informational talks were in the interest both of normal courtesy and of facilitating the progress of the second phase when it could begin, and were in the special charge

---

[28] It was approved tentatively at this point in view of the indeterminate closing date of the Chinese Phase but also pending exchange of views between London and Moscow on a British proposal, with which the United States had agreed, to include in this communiqué a reference to the smaller United Nations Governments as participating in the enforcement of surrender terms. The paragraph containing such provision was in the end omitted, since the Soviet Government considered it beyond the scope of direct concern in the Dumbarton Oaks Conversations.

of Mr. Grew. The talks were held on the basis of the American Tentative Proposals and the Chinese "Essential Points." While the joint proposals being developed during the Soviet Phase were not reported in such talks in detail, their general outlines were indicated to the Chinese. Only a week-end of study of the final text of proposals resulting from the earlier phase was therefore necessary after September 29 before discussion of the Chinese points could begin.

The American Group as a whole had studied the Chinese views over the past four weeks and from time to time had considered plans for the coming Conversation with the Chinese. This study began shortly after the arrival of the Chinese paper when, on August 29, its initial analysis was assigned by the Group to Mr. Grew, Mr. Notter, the general adviser, and Mr. Ballantine, the geographic adviser on the Far East area. The President was given a copy of the Chinese paper on August 31 by Mr. Stettinius, with initial oral comments based on the analysis so far made.

Various dates for earlier beginning of the Chinese Phase had been projected by the American Group. On September 1, an opening date of the 11th of that month had been thought possible, and accordingly, on the 8th, Mr. Grew accompanied by the general adviser talked informally with Ambassador Wellington Koo, head of the Chinese Delegation, on the points of agreement and difference in the American and Chinese papers, and in broad terms indicated the nature of the joint proposals being formulated in the Conversations. When Monday the 11th arrived, with substantial advance despite pending questions, a date not more than a week later was the target. When on the 12th, it became clear that the first phase would continue for some time and that the Soviet Delegation continued to feel that until it was completed the Chinese Phase should not start, it was no longer feasible to aim at a definite date. The opening date of September 29 was not arranged definitively until two days before.

Meanwhile, as delay became prolonged, the inability of all the original British Delegation to remain for the conversations with the Chinese had been mentioned as a probability, and it eventuated that changes were required in the British Delegation. There were, however, no changes in the American Group.

The Chinese Delegation was composed of Dr. V. K. Wellington Koo, Ambassador to Great Britain, Chairman; Dr. Wei Tao-ming, Ambassador to the United States of America; Dr. Victor Chi-tsai Hoo, Vice Minister for Foreign Affairs; and General Shang Chen, Chief of the Military Mission to the United States as principal delegates, and as technical members: Dr. Chang Chung-fu, Director of the Department of American Affairs of the Ministry for Foreign Affairs; Dr. Kan Lee, Commercial Counselor, Chinese Embassy in Washington; Mr. Liu Chieh, Minister-Counselor, Chinese Embassy, and Secretary-General of the Delegation; Rear Admiral Liu Ten-fu, Naval Attaché to the Embassy; Maj. Gen. P. T. Mow, Deputy Director of the Commission on Aeronautical Affairs and concurrently Director of the Washington Office of the Commission on Aeronautical Affairs; Messrs. Pu Hsueh-feng, Counselor of the Supreme Defense Council; and T. L. Soong, Delegate to the United Nations Monetary and Financial Conference. Drs. S. H. Tan, C. L. Hsia, C. Y. Cheng, James Yu, Liang Yuen-li, and Chen Hung-chen were advisers. The secretaries were Tswen-ling Tsui, F. Y. Chai, C. K. Hsieh, and Dr. Mon-sheng Lin, with Wellington Koo, Jr., assisting the Chairman.

The Chairman of the British Delegation for the Chinese Phase was Lord Halifax, Ambassador in Washington. The other members were Admiral Sir Percy Noble, who was succeeded shortly by Commodore A. W. Clarke; Lt. Gen. Macready; Air Marshal Sir William Welsh, succeeded shortly by Air Vice-Marshal H. P. Willock; Sir George Sansom; Mr. Jebb, who served as acting Chairman when necessary; Maj. Gen. Grove-White; Professor Webster; Mr. Gore-Booth; Mr. Berkeley Gage; and Mr. Mackenzie as Press Officer. Sir Alexander Cadogan was able to remain as the British Chairman only for the opening session of this phase.

Presiding over the first plenary session on September 29, Secretary Hull spoke of China's "heroic efforts" in the war. Expressing appreciation for the work done by the representatives of the Soviet Union and United Kingdom in the earlier part of the Conversations, he said:

> ". . . I am fully convinced that the excellent work already done, and that which we are about to undertake, will carry us a long way toward complete understanding among our Governments and toward the wider understanding which the peace-loving peoples of the world so ardently desire."

Explaining that "the successful conclusion of these exploratory conversations will constitute only the first step in the formation of the international organization which we seek to establish," he looked ahead to full public discussion of "the joint recommendations" to be made at the end "of this phase of the conversations" and hoped that "a full United Nations conference may be convened at an early date to bring to fruition the work which has been initiated . . ." He urged that in "these deliberations we must never forget that millions of people throughout the world are struggling for an opportunity to live in freedom and security."

Ambassador Koo spoke of China's long-held belief in collective efforts to insure peace and security among nations. He declared that "all nations which love peace and freedom" have "a part to play in any security organization" and emphasized that all disputes should be settled solely by pacific means and that the organization must show decisiveness in acting by force when necessary. He also stressed the need for development of international law and for study and solution "of economic and social problems of international importance."

For the British Delegation, Sir Alexander Cadogan remarked the "very large measure of agreement" already existing among the three parties to this phase of the Conversations, not only on main objectives but "even in detail" on methods. The organization should be based on "the moral ideas on which our civilizations are founded." Responsibility should be commensurate with power, and the task was "to find the methods by which power may be rightly applied in the best interests of all nations." He hoped that "the memory of the danger" that the peoples of China and the British Commonwealth had narrowly escaped would bring "a unity to the world such as it has never before had." In this respect he emphasized that without "such common purpose and practice no institutions however well devised will have the necessary strength when the moment for action comes."

The principal organizational means for conducting the work in this second phase resembled those in the preceding one except that main subcommittees were not used. The Joint Steering Committee, occupying much the same position as previously, was composed of Mr. Stettinius, accompanied by Mr. Dunn, Mr. Grew, and Mr. Pasvolsky; Dr. Koo, accompanied by Dr. Hoo and and Dr. Liu; and Lord Halifax, accompanied by Mr. Jebb and Professor Webster.[29] Mr. Stettinius was named Chairman, and, as before, rotation was agreed upon, with Dr. Koo to serve in the absence of Mr. Stettinius, and Lord Halifax if they were absent. Also as before, the secretary was Mr. Hiss, acting in an international capacity. This Committee held two meetings on October 2, another on October 4, and its fourth and last on October 5.

The discussions in the plenary sessions of the full delegations in this phase were fuller in character than their earlier counterparts. This fact, together with changes in the work of the Formulation Group, rendered main subcommittees unnecessary. In addition to the formal opening plenary, three plenary sessions were held, on the 2d, 3d, and 7th of October, respectively.

The Joint Formulation Group in this phase was larger and more formal in its conduct of discussion than in the preceding period, and likewise differed in that, on request of the Chinese, it kept minutes. It met four times, on October 3, twice on the 6th, and on the 7th. Dr. Koo served as presiding officer and also as Chairman of the Chinese members, namely Drs. Hoo, Chang, and Liu, with Drs. Hsia, Liang, and Cheng as advisers and Messrs. Koo, Jr., and Tsui as secretaries. Mr. Jebb was acting Chairman of the British members throughout the meetings of this Group. His associates were Sir George Sansom,

---

[29] Dr. Hsia attended the first meeting in place of Dr. Hoo. In the absence of Lord Halifax, Mr. Jebb was the senior British representative.

General Grove-White, and Professor Webster, with Messrs. Gage and Mackenzie as combined advisers and secretaries. The acting Chairman of the American members throughout these meetings was Mr. Pasvolsky, the other members being Messrs. Dunn, Grew, and Hackworth and Admiral Train. The advisers and secretaries, aside from Messrs. Notter, Gerig, and Yost who continued as in the earlier phase, included Mr. Sandifer, Miss Fossdick, and Mrs. Brunauer. In the meetings of the 6th, however, most of the representatives, advisers, and secretaries of the American Group were present to hear the explanation and discussion undertaken that day of the provisions of the Proposals in their entirety.

The Group of Military Representatives of the Delegations held its single meeting on October 6. General Strong was its presiding officer, the members being Generals Shang and Mow, Admiral Liu, and Mr. Pu Hsueh-feng with Dr. Tan and Dr. Chen as counselors and secretaries, for China; Air Vice-Marshal Willock, Commodore Clarke, and General Grove-White for the United Kingdom; and Generals Strong and Fairchild and Admiral Train, with Messrs. Blaisdell and Eagleton, Colonel Caraway, and Captain Creighton as advisers and secretaries for the United States. This was the last of the organized committees used in the Chinese Phase.

The delegations carried on their work much as in the earlier phase. However, the American Group met but twice, October 3 and 7. It used no committees except the so-called "Fletcher Committee," which continued working on the questions of the possible location of the new organization and its organs and on the languages that should be given official status in their conduct of work. While reports to the American Group on these subjects were not completed at Dumbarton Oaks, the papers developed were used in the subsequent preparation in the Department. These two matters were not considered with the Chinese except to inform them that in the Soviet Phase postponement of discussion had been agreed upon informally. As before, Secretary Hull and President Roosevelt were kept informed of the progress of the Conversations by memoranda from the Under Secretary. However, Secretary Hull had been compelled by illness to leave his desk three days after opening the Chinese Phase, and it was no longer possible to discuss matters with him as fully or as frequently as heretofore.

The Conversations proceeded steadily and without encountering serious obstacles. The Joint Steering Committee tentatively decided on October 2 not to attempt to change the proposals and adopted the alternative procedure of placing in a separate document the additional points that China, the United Kingdom, and the United States believed should be included in the charter when drawn up. Two principal considerations were taken into account in this decision. The first was that the proposals, as written in the Soviet Phase, had been deliberately limited to the machinery and procedure considered essential for the organization and to statements of principle for the implementation of which machinery was provided. The second was that any changes in the proposals as drafted would require referral to the Soviet Government and therefore involve delay.

Discussions of a substantive character commenced in the Steering Committee the same day. A large number of questions were presented by the Chinese and examined on October 2 and during the next four days. Among the earliest of these was whether the use of force in self-defense was to be regarded as consistent with the purposes of the organization. Much consideration was given to the question of voting in the Security Council, though all in terms of analysis and possibilities for solution and without any further attempt to resolve the issue at this time.

Specific points to consider for inclusion in the proposals arose in the Joint Formulation Group on October 3. Aside from those postponed for study in connection with the statute of the court, withdrawn after analyzing the existing provisions of the proposals, or left for later consideration at the general United Nations conference where a complete charter would be written, three points led to the formulation of joint suggestions that day. These were that the charter should provide for settlement of disputes "with due regard for principles of justice and international law"; that the assembly should be responsible for studies and recommendations concerning the development and revision of the rules and principles of international law; and that the articles on the economic and social council should specifically provide for the promotion of educational and other forms of cultural cooperation. In the view of the Joint Steering Committee, these three suggestions were essentially clarifications that gave desirable emphasis to important aspects of the proposals or represented development of broad provisions already set forth in that document.

It was agreed at the Steering Committee's meeting the next day that these three matters should be discussed later with the Soviet Government in the hope of incorporating them in the charter at the general United Nations conference. For the present, they would be considered as additional to the questions left open at the close of the Soviet Phase and would accordingly not be presented with the joint proposals when issued.

In the same meeting, October 4, Mr. Stettinius referred to certain remarks made by the President the day before concerning the suggestion of the Soviet Delegation to extend membership to the Soviet Republics, which the President had characterized as "absurd." Ambassador Koo was then informed of the developments on this "very delicate question" and the opposition that had been expressed to the suggestion during the Soviet Phase. He was told that "in all probability it will never be possible to agree to the Soviet proposal," which the President, the Prime Minister, and the Generalissimo at "some later time" would probably have to take up with Marshal Stalin. The members of the Committee were urged to keep the matter in strict confidence. The view was expressed that "the whole civilized world would be shocked by such a proposal," which "if not handled properly" and if it became "a matter of gossip," would lead to violent criticism of the Soviet Union and "might jeopardize the success of the movement for an international organization."

After the meetings between October 4 and 6, during which the thorough examination made of the joint proposal as a whole was completed, an additional problem in establishing the new organization was considered. This problem was the transition from the League of Nations to the new organization, involving the liquidation of the League, the transfer of some of its continuing functions, and also the problem of membership for the United and Associated Nations that were members of the League. Of the League's forty-five members at this time, twenty-eight were United or Associated Nations. Of the forty-four United and Associated Nations, 15 were not members of the League, including of course the United States and the Soviet Union. While the initiation of action with respect to the League would rest with those nations that were members of the old organization and would enter the new, all the members of the new would be called upon sooner or later to have an opinion on this matter. In an informal gathering of the Joint Formulation Group early on October 7, this problem was explored and arrangements were made for an early exchange of "research papers" preparatory to an eventual Four Power proposal to the general United Nations conference.

PUBLICATION OF THE DUMBARTON OAKS PROPOSALS

APPROVAL OF the "Proposals For the Establishment of a General International Organization" and of the plans for their publication was given by the Secretary of State and the President on October 7, 1944. At that time—the last day of the Dumbarton Oaks Conversations—the next steps had not been fully considered. The American Group in its final meeting at 11 a. m. that day was informed of the President's thought, which had been developing for some weeks past, that a meeting should be held between himself, Prime Minister Churchill, and Marshal Stalin and that in the long run it would be best to have the question of voting in the Security Council dealt with "at the top level." [30] If such a meeting among these Heads of Government were not held soon, the Group was told, a meeting of the three Foreign Secretaries might be arranged.[31]

The British, Chinese, and American approval of the Proposals was announced in the closing plenary session just before noon, October 7, and the communiqué to close this phase was then agreed upon. In the concluding remarks, gratification that so much progress had been made in this phase and in the entire Conversations was expressed. On that day also a message of appreciation of the hospitality extended to the Soviet Delegation was sent by Ambassador Gromyko to Mr. Stettinius.

The Proposals were published on October 9, 1944, annexed to a communiqué issued simultaneously by each of the four Governments, which stated:

"The Governments which were represented in the discussions in Washington have agreed that after further study of these proposals they will as soon as possible take the necessary steps with a view to the preparation of complete proposals which could then serve as a basis of discussion at a full United Nations conference."

Copies of the Proposals were transmitted by this Government, shortly in advance of their general release, to the congressional consulting groups, the Senate Foreign Relations Committee, the House Foreign Affairs Committee, the Justices of the Supreme Court, Mr. Dulles, and to all American diplomatic missions.[32]

The Chairman of the American Group described the Proposals as "the unanimously agreed recommendations of the four delegations" that had taken part in the Conversations and as comprising "substantial contributions from each" delegation. "The few questions which remain for further consideration, though important," he said, "are not in any sense insuperable . . ." [33]

---

[30] Since a meeting of Prime Minister Churchill and Marshal Stalin in Moscow was imminent, President Roosevelt on Oct. 3 suggested to them that Ambassador Harriman be present as an observer, without power to commit this Government relative to any important matters that might be discussed and said that the President viewed this meeting as preliminary to a conference of the three Heads of Government to be held any time after the national election in this country. Telegram published in Robert E. Sherwood, *Roosevelt and Hopkins, an Intimate History* (New York, 1948), p. 834.

[31] In this regard, see above, p. 285. A further British suggestion, Oct. 4, that the Foreign Ministers of the participating governments hold a follow-up meeting is referred to in *Memoirs of Cordell Hull*, H, 1708. A meeting of Foreign Ministers eventuated only in connection with the Heads of Government conference at Yalta, four months later.

[32] See appendix 43.

[33] *Department of State Bulletin*, XI, 367.

In a statement issued on October 9, Secretary Hull commented that the Proposals were "neither complete nor final" and that "much work remains to be done," but he stated that they were "sufficiently detailed to indicate the kind of an international organization" that in the judgment of the four Governments "will meet the imperative need of providing for the maintenance of international peace and security." Reviewing then the American preparation in this respect, he said:

"We in this country have spent many months in careful planning and wide consultation in preparation for the conversations which have just been concluded. Those who represented the Government of the United States in these discussions were armed with the ideas and with the results of thinking contributed by numerous leaders of our national thought and opinion, without regard to political or other affiliations."

His "earnest hope" for the period ahead was that "discussion in the United States on this all-important subject will continue to be carried on in the same non-partisan spirit of devotion to our paramount national interest in peace and security which has characterized our previous consultations." In his concluding comments the Secretary said:

"It is, of course, inevitable that when many governments and peoples attempt to agree on a single plan the result will be in terms of the highest common denominator rather than of the plan of any one nation. The organization to be created must reflect the ideas and hopes of all the peace-loving nations which participate in its creation. The spirit of cooperation must manifest itself in mutual striving to attain the high goal by common agreement.

"The road to the establishment of an international organization capable of effectively maintaining international peace and security will be long. At times it will be difficult. But we cannot hope to attain so great an objective without constant effort and unfailing determination that the sacrifices of this war shall not be in vain." [34]

The President, in a statement also on October 9, commented that his impression of the Proposals was one of satisfaction "that so much could have been accomplished on so difficult a subject in so short a time." He stated that "from the very beginning of the war, and paralleling our military plans, we have begun to lay the foundations for the general organization for the maintenance of peace and security," and that this represented "a major objective for which this war is being fought . . ." [35] Three days later the President expressed the feeling of urgency that continued to mount after the close of the Conversations:

"We must press forward to bring into existence this world organization . . . There is no time to lose.

"It is our objective to establish the solid foundations of the peace

[34] *Ibid.*, p. 366.
[35] *Ibid.*, p. 365.

organization without further delay, and without waiting for the end of hostilities. There must, of course, be time for discussion by all the peace-loving nations—large and small. Substantial progress has already been made, and it must be continued as rapidly as possible."

He also announced that "further exchanges of views" with the other American republics would be undertaken by the United States "before the meeting of the general conference." [36]

It was noted in the Department that Marshal Stalin, in an address on November 6, 1944, concerning war and postwar matters generally, said in connection with his views on the means to prevent "fresh aggression" by Germany:

"There is only one means to this end, in addition to the complete disarmament of the aggressive nations: that is, to establish a special organization made up of representatives of the peace-loving nations to uphold peace and safeguard security; to put the necessary minimum of armed forces required for the averting of aggression at the disposal of the directing body of this organization, and to obligate this organization to employ these armed forces without delay if it becomes necessary to avert or stop aggression and punish the culprits.

"This must not be a repetition of the ill-starred League of Nations which had neither the right nor the means to avert aggression. It will be a new, special, fully authorized world organization having at its command everything necessary to uphold peace and avert new aggression.

"Can we expect the actions of this world organization to be sufficiently effective? They will be effective if the great powers which have borne the brunt of the war against Hitler Germany continue to act in a spirit of unanimity and accord. They will not be effective if this essential condition is violated."

In the same address, Marshal Stalin, when speaking specifically of the Dumbarton Oaks "Conference," referred to "talk of differences between the three powers on certain security problems." After stating that differences did exist and would "arise on a number of other issues as well," he commented

"The surprising thing is not that differences exist, but that there are so few of them and that as a rule in practically every case they are resolved. . . .

"What matters is not that there are differences, but that these differences do not transgress the bounds of what the interests of unity of the three great powers allow, and that in the long run they are resolved in accordance with the interests of that unity." [37]

The close of this intensive effort to obtain the joint proposals that resulted from the Dumbarton Oaks Conversations was a turning point for the preparation in the over-all field of international peace and

---

[36] *Ibid.*, pp. 397–98.

[37] Quoted as issued by the Soviet Embassy in Washington in its *Information Bulletin*, vol. IV, no. 117, Nov. 14, 1944, p. 4.

security.   The measure not only of the common interests of the major powers in this field but also of the difficulties to be overcome was now more exact than before, and the basis of the organization had been defined in most of its essential respects.

The necessary further preparatory activities in this field were pursued as rapidly as possible after the Conversations at Dumbarton Oaks and continued without interruption through the remainder of the wartime preparation of American postwar foreign policy.   Much as attention fastened upon them, however, they were but parts of the unfinished business of the preparation as a whole.

Part IV

THE UNFINISHED BUSINESS
WINTER 1944–SPRING 1945

"Many of the problems of the peace are upon us even now while the conclusion of the war is still before us. The atmosphere of friendship and mutual understanding and determination to find a common ground of common understanding, which surrounded the conversations at Dumbarton Oaks, gives us reason to hope that future discussions will succeed in developing the democratic and fully integrated world-security system toward which these preparatory conversations were directed."

——"The State of the Union," Annual Message of the President to the Congress, Franklin D. Roosevelt, January 6, 1945, *Department of State Bulletin*, XII, 27.

CHAPTER XVI

Transition from Extraordinary
Preparation to Operations

WITH THE joint Proposals achieved at Dumbarton Oaks by the four major governments in the United Nations coalition, all remaining American preparation of postwar policy entered the concluding stage. Work already well advanced was completed, or became merged with operations, in which preparatory work is at all times done on specific questions arising in the daily conduct of diplomatic relations.

The Dumbarton Oaks Proposals represented a decision among the four major powers on the future direction of their joint efforts toward world-wide peace and security. The decision was preliminary and incomplete, but it held out, in the circumstances, a promise of successful achievement. Though the Proposals had yet to be finished and the Charter had yet to be negotiated and ratified, the contemplated arrangements were such as to provide all the United and Associated Nations with an over-all framework for international relations and with a prospect of world order and advancement, in the light of which each nation could begin to orient its individual foreign policy. The intended permanent organization of international cooperation for peace—including, for the first time in history, all the major powers— was basic to the shaping of the entire future world order. Failure to complete the Proposals and to create the international organization was therefore nearly unthinkable, great though the obstacles to final agreement might be.

It was in this field that the preparation had so far been least assimilated into operations and in which operations were longest deferred. Only limited work of a primarily preparatory character remained in most other fields.

Since several questions had been left "open" by the Dumbarton Oaks Conversations, certain of which had to be resolved before a general United Nations conference to draft the Charter would become feasible, study of the open questions began immediately after October 9. It was predicated that such questions must be among the matters considered at an early meeting of heads of the United States, British, and Soviet Governments. At the same time, discussions with the other American republics concerning the Dumbarton Oaks Proposals had to be undertaken. Provision had to be made for the anticipated conversations in Washington with the diplomatic representatives of still other governments. And, the resumption of consultation with the Congress and participation in discussions of the Proposals with the public were no less requisite to the determination of the course of United States policy in so momentous a matter as a world security organization in which this country would be a member and a leader. In addition, manifold problems in connection with the war and in the economic and social fields, where action and such preparatory work as continued were intermingling, exacted constant attention.

Readjustments of structure for the conduct of the remaining preparation and for operations in fields in which the extraordinary preparatory work had ended had gradually come under consideration during the period of the Dumbarton Oaks Conversations. Thought on this problem developed rapidly in the two months thereafter. Such readjustments were believed particularly necessary in anticipation of the need for decisions in connection with the difficulties already appearing as an aftermath of military gains in Europe, with the negotiations and multitudinous operations that would be confronted as victory over the principal enemy states was attained, and with war settlements as they became possible. The nature of political, economic, and social forces in the post-hostilities period had become more plainly manifest, and the time was arriving when, in many parts of the world, new problems—anticipated and unanticipated—would be added to resurgent old problems that had remained unsolved in the years before the war submerged, redirected, or deepened them. It was equally apparent, from the progress of the Post-War Programs Committee and, in related matters, of the Policy Committee, from the outcome of the Dumbarton Oaks Conversations, and from the advances made toward establishment of specialized international economic and social organizations, that the bulk of essential preparatory work was done and that the remainder, with only certain exceptions, was becoming an adjunct to operations.

Thus the time was believed to have come when the preparation, in general, could be absorbed into the operational machinery and processes through which the Department would deal with the problems within its responsibilities during the war's final stage and the succeeding transitional period—machinery and processes influenced by the experience, structure, and methods of the preparation, but determined predominantly by "normal" operational requirements. The lines of reorganization were decided upon by December 20, 1944.

COURSE OF THE WAR, AUTUMN 1944

THE CONTRACTION of the theaters of war was making it clear that the postwar period was arriving—much as the war itself had arrived—step by step, in area after area, problem by problem. The postwar period was reached in some places and in some matters during the war; it did not arrive throughout the world at one time.

The sixth year of World War II had begun on September 3, 1944. By December 8, the United States had been in the war three years. In the great military theaters, the campaigns were growing in intensity and decisiveness as the fighting neared the homelands of the major enemy states. Yet, while the accumulating Allied advances assured victory, the enemy was exerting power so formidable that the final outcome was still distant, costly, and fraught with risks, both in Europe and in the Pacific and Asia.

United States forces engaged the Japanese Navy and landed on Leyte on October 19–20, beginning the months-long task of liberating the Philippines. A joint resolution of Congress, approved on June 29, 1944, paved the way for carrying out the pledge given by the President in the preceding August that "the Republic of the Philippines will be established the moment the power of our Japanese enemies is destroyed." When United States forces landed on Leyte, the President reaffirmed his promise that the Philippines would "take their place as a free and independent" nation when the Japanese invaders were driven out.[1] Enormously difficult operations were also pressed, successfully but slowly, by the Allies in Burma and to assist China. No postwar problem in this vast area of the war was immediately posed by these developments.

In Western Europe, the Allies in the late months of the year moved in central Italy to the heights near the valley of the Po. In the north, they continued their progress in France and in the Lowlands until a desperate German counter offensive into Belgium and Luxembourg—the last major challenge of the enemy in the West—began on December 16 and mounted in force until two days after Christmas.

No unusually disturbing problems within the realm of postwar policy were presented by the full or partial liberation accomplished through these military advances. Policy toward Italy, co-belligerent but under armistice conditions, was considered at the second Quebec Conference, and a joint statement of President Roosevelt and Prime Minister Churchill released on September 26, 1944, announced among other intentions that an "increasing measure of control" would gradually be handed over to the Italian Administration, that the Allied Control Commission would be renamed to drop the word "Control"

---

[1] *Department of State Bulletin*, IX, 91; XI, 455.

and that economic reconstruction should be started.[2]   On October 26, Acting Secretary Stettinius announced that the President would shortly nominate Alexander C. Kirk to be Ambassador to Italy.   Civil-affairs agreements to cover the period of military operations had been concluded in May and in July by the American and British Governments with the Governments-in-exile of the Netherlands, Belgium, and Luxembourg, and the latter two Governments had returned to their capitals in September.[3]   The United States, the United Kingdom, and the Soviet Union on October 23 recognized as the Provisional Government of France, the *de facto* authority established in Paris under Gen. Charles de Gaulle.   On November 11, France was invited by the United States, the United Kingdom, and the Soviet Union to join the European Advisory Commission, and on January 1, 1945, the French Provisional Government formally adhered to the Declaration by United Nations.

In view of the progress toward victory over Germany, the final determination of policy toward that country in the occupation period was put under special consideration at the highest interdepartmental level early in this period, as will be described shortly.   The treatment of Axis war criminals was made the subject of a formal statement by the Secretary of State on September 28 indicating various steps being taken to insure that neutral countries would not give asylum to such persons.   The work of the United Nations Commission for the Investigation of War Crimes was well under way in London by this date.[4]

In Eastern Europe, Soviet troops penetrated in October into East Prussia and into Hungary, where Nazi military control had been established the previous March.   The Bulgarian armistice was concluded in Moscow on October 28, 1944, leaving only Hungary as an Axis satellite.   Hungarian peace overtures had been made in Moscow earlier that month, but these preliminary negotiations had been suspended with the establishment of a German puppet regime in Hungary on October 16 and were not resumed until late December.[5]

The changing fortunes of war were affecting profoundly three of the Eastern European countries that were members of the United Nations: Greece, Yugoslavia, and Poland.   Local resistance forces in these states were active against the Nazis but were becoming increasingly divided among themselves.   In the face of such internal dissension, which more and more sharply involved the issues of Communism and attitude toward the Soviet Union, the return of their Govern-

---

[2] *Ibid.*, XI, 338.

[3] The course of the war did not permit the return of the Netherlands Government to The Hague until May 1945.

[4] See pp. 116, 186.

[5] The Hungarian armistice was signed in Moscow on Jan. 20, 1945.

ments-in-exile to power in these three countries had become a matter of serious question.

In Greece, where British forces were engaged against the enemy, the hopeful signs in the summer and early autumn that the resistance groups and the Government-in-exile had started toward a solution of their differences, when they joined together in a coalition government in anticipation of the liberation of Athens (October 1944), gave way rapidly to evidence that civil war was imminent. Such strife broke out early in December when the principal local resistance group (EAM), which had come under Communist domination, resorted to force against the coalition Government.

In Yugoslavia, a struggle for power was in progress between two opposing resistance groups—the Chetniks, headed by General Mihailovic, who supported the Government-in-exile, and the Partisans, led by General Tito, who in December 1943 had established an opposition provisional government. Negotiations had been in progress since June 1944 between General Tito and the Government-in-exile but were without result when national and Soviet forces drove the Nazis out of Belgrade, the Yugoslav capital, late in October. By the end of the year much of Yugoslavia had been liberated, but an effective agreement between the opposing resistance groups and the Government-in-exile for the administration of the liberated territory had yet to be achieved. In neighboring Albania, which had no government-in-exile, American and British efforts in the summer of 1944 to bring about a unification of resistance groups had been unsuccessful. The most effective of these groups, the National Liberation Front led by General Hoxha, which was similar in character to the EAM in Greece and the Partisans in Yugoslavia, had liberated with Allied military assistance three-fourths of that small country by October. It then declared its executive committee the provisional government.

In Poland, the long-continuing rift between the Soviet Union and the Polish Government-in-exile, arising directly from the Soviet territorial claims in eastern Poland, was having serious consequences, both political and military. It had resulted in the development of a strong Soviet-sponsored resistance group that had repudiated the authority of the Government-in-exile. It had also resulted in the anomalous situation at Warsaw in September, where, despite the fact that Soviet forces had taken its eastern suburb on September 14, the Polish patriot army in Warsaw, loyal to the Government-in-exile, was forced to surrender to the Germans on October 2. At the urging of the President and Prime Minister Churchill, negotiations were initiated in August among the Soviet Government, the Soviet-supported Lublin Committee of National Liberation, established in July 1944 to function in liberated Polish territory, and the Polish Government in London. These produced no agreement before full entry of Soviet forces into Warsaw, January 17, 1945. By this time, the Soviet Government had recognized the Lublin Committee as the provisional government of Poland, while the United States and Great Britain continued to recognize the Polish Government in London.

These developments in the closing months of 1944 necessitated the intensive application and adjustment of prepared policy regarding enemy states and liberated areas. This Government was thus confronted simultaneously with the perturbing questions concerning Eastern Europe and with the questions left open in the negotiations for the creation of the world security organization. Marked strain among the major Allied powers had begun to appear, which could gravely affect not only the peace but the prospect of rapid Allied victory in Europe. Upon the territorial problems created by the war or surviving from prewar years were now imposed the peculiarly unsettling and portentous difficulties which, unless held in check by successful efforts to maintain major power unity, would flow from expansion of Soviet control in the wake of Red military advances. Although President Roosevelt in an address on October 21, 1944,[6] expressed "faith" in the achievement of the "kind of world order which we the peace-loving nations must achieve," this task was one that now appeared to be increasing in complexity. The President said in the same address: "I am certain, for myself, that I do not know how all the unforeseeable difficulties can be met."

Much attention to the maintenance unimpaired of major power unity, for the sake of victory and of the future peace, was being given here and abroad at this time. Acting Secretary Stettinius in an address to the National Council of American-Soviet Friendship on November 16, 1944, spoke of "Differences in points of view and method of work" but expressed strong belief "that we shall work out whatever problems confront us in full realization that the greatest goals of each of us must be the common goals of both of us." [7]

During the preceding spring and summer, Great Britain and the Soviet Union had arrived at an arrangement defining their respective spheres of primary responsibility in Eastern Europe for the war period. This arrangement had been reluctantly accepted by the President because of military considerations but on a strictly limited trial basis and with the proviso that it did not involve the establishment of postwar spheres of influence in the Balkans. Between October 9 and 18, 1944, Prime Minister Churchill and Foreign Minister Eden met in Moscow with Marshal Stalin and Foreign Minister Molo-

---

[6] Address before the Foreign Policy Association, New York, N. Y., *Cong. Rec.*, vol. 90, part 11, appendix, pp. A4386–87.

[7] *Department of State Bulletin*, XI, 589.

tov in an effort, as reported later by the Prime Minister, to prevent misunderstandings and contrary policies. With respect to the issues that were arising among the United Nations, Foreign Minister Eden declared in the House of Commons on December 1 that "the fundamental truth remains that if we four [8] can stand together until victory is won, and afterward, there is no problem which we cannot solve. If we . . . fall apart, I do not care how good the international organization we build, or how perfect the machinery, it is not going to work at all." [9]

The foregoing is but a brief sketch of the circumstances of the time bearing on postwar policy, but it suffices to indicate the environment of difficulties in which consideration was undertaken of the means to conduct the remaining preparation on postwar security, political, and territorial problems. That consideration began both at staff and higher levels during the period of the last two weeks of the Dumbarton Oaks Conversations. It was well under way during November 1944, as over-all Departmental reorganization came under study.

At this point, when the extraordinary organization for postwar preparation had accomplished the bulk of the work originally projected for it, changes occurred in regard to the superior policy committees and the leadership of the Department.

The Post-War Programs Committee held its final meeting November 17, 1944. The Policy Committee's last meeting was twelve days later. Illness compelled Secretary Hull to submit his resignation November 21. His letter to the President of that date expressed "utmost regret" that, at a time when "complex and difficult conditions and problems . . . must be dealt with in the months and years immediately ahead," he could no longer make his full contribution. He wrote specifically in this regard of "the creation of the post-war peace organization," and the President, in his reply of the same date, commented that Cordell Hull had earned the title, "Father of the United Nations." [10] Mr. Stettinius was nominated on November 27 and took oath of office as Secretary of State on December 1, 1944.

Coincident with these developments, a specific decision was made to establish the State-War-Navy Coordinating Committee. This decision grew directly from the need for some such arrangement felt in the postwar policy preparation since the termination of Mr. Davis' Subcommittee on Security Problems the preceding year. It also reflected emerging operational requirements.

---

[8] The United States, the United Kingdom, the Soviet Union, and France.
[9] Parl. Deb., Commons, vol. 406, cols. 299–306.
[10] *Department of State Bulletin*, XI, 649.

Following informal discussion among members of the three Departments during and after the Dumbarton Oaks Conversations, a proposal for a committee of wide scope was agreed upon at a meeting of representatives of these Departments.   Mr. Stettinius, still Acting Secretary of State, then formally proposed to Secretaries Henry L. Stimson and James V. Forrestal on November 29, 1944, the appointment of a committee to represent the three Secretaries and to be charged with the formulation of recommendations to the Secretary of State "on questions having both military and political aspects" and with "coordinating the views" of the three Departments in matters of common interest.   This proposal was accepted December 1. James C. Dunn, then Director of the Office of European Affairs, was named the member for the Department of State and the Chairman. John J. McCloy, Assistant Secretary of War, and Artemus L. Gates, Assistant Secretary of the Navy for Air, were the other members.

The Committee began its meetings on December 19, when its interdepartmental secretariat had been organized.[11]   The advisers and deputies who began on that date to attend its meetings were Vice Admiral Russell Willson, Maj. Gen. John H. Hilldring, Col. R. A. Cutter, and John D. Hickerson, then Deputy Director of the Office of European Affairs of the Department of State.   This high ranking committee immediately turned its attention to the postwar problems remaining in the stage of preparation in connection with the treatment of Germany, Austria, and Japan and with the forthcoming conference of the American republics at Mexico City.

DEPARTMENTAL REORGANIZATION, DECEMBER 1944

MR. STETTINIUS, upon becoming Secretary, immediately instructed that a reorganization plan, designed to increase the Department's effectiveness, be drafted.   The projected structure was developed over approximately the next two weeks.   During this time, Joseph C. Grew was confirmed as Under Secretary, and, to fill vacancies left by the resignations of Mr. Berle, Mr. Long, and Mr. Shaw, three new Assistant Secretaries were placed in office.   These were William L. Clayton for economic affairs; Nelson A. Rockefeller for relations with the other American republics; and Archibald MacLeish to take charge of public and cultural relations.   Mr. Acheson continued as Assistant Secretary but now assumed responsibility for relations between the Department and the Congress and for international conferences.   By

---

[11] The Committee continued, under the name of the State-Army-Navy-Air Force Coordinating Committee, through June 30, 1949.   The original secretariat consisted of Fletcher Warren, Harold W. Moseley, Col. Wallace E. Whitson, Col. Charles W. McCarthy, and Keith Kane.

virtue of legislative authorization of two additional Assistant Secretaries, Mr. Dunn was named to supervise European, Far Eastern, and Near Eastern and African Affairs, and Brig. Gen. Julius C. Holmes was placed in charge of administration.

All these officials, with the exception of the last named, had taken part in one or another aspect of the postwar preparation. The new Secretary and Under Secretary had been members of the Post-War Programs Committee and of the American Group at the Dumbarton Oaks Conversations. Mr. Acheson had shared responsibility in all economic work. Mr. MacLeish had served on the Political Subcommittee of the Advisory Committee, Mr. Rockefeller on the Taylor Committee, and Mr. Clayton on a special committee under the Taylor Committee. Mr. Dunn had been especially active in the political, territorial, and security preparatory work. The Senate confirmed these appointments December 19, 1944.

Only limited changes were made in other positions at the superior level. Mr. Hackworth remained as Legal Adviser and engaged actively in the further postwar preparation. Mr. Pasvolsky continued as Special Assistant to the Secretary of State for International Organization and Security Affairs, in charge of "the work of preparing for a United Nations Conference to establish an International Security Organization." Both of these officials were designated as having rank equivalent to that of assistant secretary. Mr. Bohlen became Assistant to the Secretary of State and liaison officer with the White House and also participated in this preparation. Several new positions were created. However, most of these additions or changes of personnel, while concerned in varying degree with matters still postwar in character, were not primarily related to the remaining postwar preparation.[12]

The Policy and Post-War Programs Committees were transformed rather than abolished. The Secretary's Staff Committee, now instituted, in effect replaced both when it was charged with assisting the Secretary "in determining current and long-range foreign policy." This Committee accordingly considered the major policy problems of a postwar character of concern here. Its membership included, under the Secretary as Chairman, the Under Secretary, Assistant Secretaries, Legal Adviser, and the Special Assistant to the Secretary for International Organization and Security Affairs.

The new Coordinating Committee established at this time was responsible to the Under Secretary, who was its Chairman. Its membership was constituted of the Directors of Offices and Mr. McDermott as the Special Assistant to the Secretary for Press Relations. This body

---

[12] The reorganization was effectuated by Departmental order 1301 and Departmental designation 106, both on Dec. 20, 1944. *Department of State Bulletin*, XI, 777–813.

dealt especially with matters of policy or action arising in daily operations and questions of interoffice relations.   A small Committee on International Conferences at the Assistant Secretary level was also appointed at this time for the scheduling, organization, and conduct of conferences.[13] Its membership was constituted of Mr. Acheson as Chairman, Mr. Pasvolsky, and the Assistant Secretary in whose field any given conference was projected.

A Joint Secretariat succeeded the former separate secretariats of the Policy and Post-War Programs Committees.   That of the latter provided the principal model for the new Secretariat and thereby constituted a direct link with the secretariat activities that had been initiated by the research staff for the Advisory Committee in 1942.   Mr. Yost and Mr. Rothwell were named the Executive Secretaries of the new body.   The Secretariat, with minor modifications in designation, has continued to the present day, and the concept of superior Staff and Coordination Committees has been kept alive in certain current arrangements within the Department.

As noted, the substantive preparation for a general international organization continued under the charge of Mr. Pasvolsky, Special Assistant to the Secretary.   Mr. Bowman continued as Special Adviser to the Secretary of State, concentrating chiefly on postwar problems and especially on the general international organization.   Henry P. Fletcher was also named to continue as Special Adviser on these and related problems, but was unable to serve.[14] By a related appointment effective December 29, 1944, Hamilton Fish Armstrong became Special Adviser to the Secretary of State to advise on international political questions,[15] his work likewise centering chiefly on general international organization.

The staff work in that regard remained in the Office of Special Political Affairs, of which Ambassador Edwin C. Wilson continued as Director.   Under the new arrangements, however, general supervision of this Office was not continued under Mr. Dunn but was now vested in Mr. Pasvolsky, working directly with Secretary Stettinius, who maintained close touch with the administration of the Office and with its activities bearing upon international organization.

Several changes were made affecting the research staff and its work on the postwar preparation.   The Departmental announcement of December 20, after commenting that "prior to . . . January 15, 1944, the work of preparing for the peace and establishment of an inter-

[13] Mr. Acheson was relieved of this responsibility by Feb. 27, 1945, when individual superior officials were made responsible for the conferences in their respective fields.

[14] See p. 290.

[15] Cf. p. 229.

national security organization was organized on a study basis," stated that "the work of preparing for a United Nations Conference to establish an International Security Organization" would be continued by the divisions of the Office of Special Political Affairs. These divisions, however, were considerably altered. For some time changes had been developing. The Chief of the Division of International Security and Organization, Mr. Notter, had become Adviser serving under the Director of the Office, Mr. Wilson, shortly after the Dumbarton Oaks Conversations. In addition, also in connection with the new forms and conditions of work represented by the negotiations at Dumbarton Oaks, adaptation of this Division with its wide-ranging fields of activity to the last stage of preparation had been pressed by the Division itself, partly to anticipate the needs of final preparation and partly to complete the necessary staff adjustments before the time for operations was reached. Accordingly, the Division was now abolished, and its principal sections were made divisions all within the Office of Special Political Affairs.

There were three successor divisions, each charged with formulation and coordination of policy and action on the matters within its field. The Division of International Organization Affairs, with Durward V. Sandifer as Chief, was made responsible for matters regarding the establishment of the proposed United Nations organization, relations with that organization, and relations between it and specialized or regional agencies and organizations. The Division of International Security Affairs, with Joseph E. Johnson as Acting Chief and Donald C. Blaisdell as Associate Chief, was given responsibility for matters regarding the security phases of the proposed United Nations organization, including relations between it and regional security systems or arrangements, relations with the organization on security matters, and the relevant security aspects of United States foreign policy generally. The Division of Dependent Area Affairs, with Benjamin Gerig as Chief, was charged with responsibility for the matters concerning the activities of the proposed United Nations organization affecting dependent areas and peoples and the conduct of relations on such matters with the organization when established.

The Division of Territorial Studies, with David Harris as Acting Chief and Philip W. Ireland as Assistant Chief, was retained unchanged, but this was a temporary expedient pending completion of arrangements already begun for integration of its sections with the geographic offices and divisions and, to a lesser extent, with the economic offices and divisions. Its work by this date was conducted almost wholly in conjunction with these offices and divisions. Until its integration with them was accomplished in the course of the next two months, the preparatory papers of this Division for the most

part channeled directly to these offices and divisions, and only the
usual administrative matters pertaining to this Division came under
the supervision of Mr. Wilson and Mr. Pasvolsky.

All matters of postwar concern, other than those in the field of
international organization and the few further exceptions to be
noted below, were merged in the appropriate standing offices of the
Department.   There were twelve such offices, nine having responsibilities primarily for foreign policy and relations.   The determination
of policy recommendations on the postwar matters so allocated became essentially inseparable from the formulation of policy and coordination of action on the current matters with which each office was
charged.   In some cases, the divisions of these offices were specifically
directed to make studies or conduct work of postwar significance in
collaboration with one or another of the divisions still engaged in
completing the preparation for the international security organization.   Among such instances, for example, were the directives for
cooperation between the Division of American Republics Analysis and
Liaison and the Division of International Organization Affairs with
respect to inter-American organizations, meetings, and agreements.
The collaboration provided for between the Division of International
Labor, Social and Health Affairs and the Division of International
Organization Affairs in formulating recommendations and in maintaining liaison on labor, social, and health matters relating to the
operations of specialized international agencies in these fields was a
further illustration.   Such directives, however, involved essentially
only additions to the normal type of anticipatory work that attends
operations.

In general terms, it may be said that in the reorganization of
December 20, 1944, only transitional and temporary provisions were
made for the further preparation on postwar problems needed on a
special basis.   The provisions made at this time for the working of
the policy offices and divisions of the Department reflected in various
ways, however, the permanent absorption in the Department of the
methods developed in the extraordinary preparation.   This development is suggested by the following random quotation of phrases
or words from the Departmental Order concerned: "emerging problems," "background and policy studies," "basic country and area
policies," "long-range economic development projects," "preparation
for international discussions," "informal working relationships," "the
work of interdivisional and interdepartmental committees," "trends,"
"analysis of basic data," "research staff," "study," "special studies."

It was within the foregoing structure, extended by the interdepartmental committees that continued to function in connection with it,
that the terminal work of preparation was undertaken, described
below by main fields.

CHAPTER XVII

Remaining Economic and Social
Preparation and Conferences

IT HAS ALREADY been observed that, by autumn of 1944, no separate staffs and no extraordinary committee arrangements for postwar preparation in the economic and social field continued to exist in the Department. The remaining preparation on the many problems in this wide field was being carried forward through the ordinary operating structure of the Department and, interdepartmentally, through the Executive Committee on Economic Foreign Policy and its special and other committees, which continue, with some changes, to function to the present day.

During the period of the autumn of 1944 through the spring of 1945, definitive international agreement was reached on only one problem in this field—civil aviation. Negotiations were initiated or continuing, however, on several other problems, and great emphasis was being laid on certain fundamental economic policies, many of which had been developed in the course of the earlier preparation and attendant informal international discussions. The development of detailed plans and proposals on the basis of these broad policies and the furthering of the negotiations in progress were a major concern of the operating functional offices and divisions of the Department during this period. These activities were, in large degree, to come to fruition only after the war and over an extended period of months—in some cases, years.

The Executive Committee on Economic Foreign Policy was the main organ before which current and postwar problems continued to come for the interdepartmental consideration necessary on practically all matters in this field.[1] For the most part, no change in the structure of this Committee was made during the period here considered, but one new subcommittee of direct interest—that on Specialized International Economic Organizations—was established November 17, 1944. This subcommittee had the following terms of reference:

---

[1] The Interdepartmental Committee on Social Policy which has since functioned in a part of the field covered in 1945 by the Executive Committee was not established until the end of that year, its first meeting being in January 1946.

1. To formulate, within the framework of the proposals of the Dumbarton Oaks Conference, recommendations regarding:

A. The organization of such agency or agencies as may be required to carry out the economic programs, as approved by the Executive Committee, of the Committees on Private Monopolies and Cartels, Commodity Agreements, and Trade Barriers.

B. The relationship which should be established between such agency or agencies and the Economic and Social Council proposed by the Dumbarton Oaks Conference.

C. Such relations, if any, as should be maintained between such agency or agencies and the International Monetary Fund, the International Bank for Reconstruction and Development, the Food and Agriculture Organization, the International Labor Organization, and possible international organizations in other economic and social fields, such as aviation, shipping, communications, health, and narcotic trade.

D. Such elaboration of the proposals of the Dumbarton Oaks Conference as may be deemed desirable to facilitate any recommendations made under the above terms of reference.

2. To work closely with the Committees on Private Monopolies and Cartels, International Commodity Problems, and Trade Barriers in carrying out the above assignment.

The members of this subcommittee were Department of State: Charles P. Taft (chairman), Walter Kotschnig (vice chairman), Leroy D. Stinebower and John M. Leddy (secretary); Department of the Treasury: Harold Glasser, Raymond F. Mikesell (alternate); Department of Agriculture: Robert B. Schwenger; Department of Commerce: Frank A. Waring; Department of Labor: Carter Goodrich, A. F. Hinrichs (alternate); United States Tariff Commission: Lynn R. Edminster; Foreign Economic Administration: Miss Ethel Dietrich; Bureau of the Budget: Arthur Smithies (observer); War Production Board: William L. Batt (observer).

Within the Department, it will be recalled, the work on postwar economic problems was centered chiefly in two offices: the Office of Transportation and Communications, which had no Director and reported directly to Assistant Secretary Clayton; and the Office of Economic Affairs, under Bernard F. Haley after the appointment of Harry C. Hawkins in September 1944 as Economic Counselor at the London Embassy. On January 26, 1945, however, the Office of Economic Affairs, and also that of Wartime Economic Affairs, was abolished. In their places were established the Office of Commercial Policy, with Mr. Haley as Director, and the Office of Financial and Development Policy, with Emilio G. Collado as Director.[2] These new offices, together with the Office of Transportation and Communications, and their divisions had primary responsibility in the Department for developments concerning the specialized international or-

---

[2] *Department of State Bulletin*, XII, 175–76.

ganizations for economic and social cooperation. Some of their work was conducted through the new Subcommittee on Specialized International Economic Organizations.

No new or modified arrangements were evolved for the consideration of cultural problems, the Division of Cultural Cooperation (previously Science, Education, and Art) continuing to have the principal responsibility for preparing for a specialized international organization in the educational, scientific, and cultural field.

The work in all these fields was conducted in collaboration with the Division of International Organization Affairs insofar as organizational questions were involved. Recommendations were transmitted to the appropriate ranking officials of the Department or to the Staff or Coordination Committees, their reference depending on the character and importance of a problem, on whether it called for policy decision or implementation of determined policy, and on the timing of action involved.

Viewed from the standpoint of economic and social foreign policy, the winter of 1944–45 and the following spring were periods of pronounced activity. The conduct of the preparation leading to decisions now reflected in this activity has been described in earlier pages. The passage of many of the economic policy problems beyond the scope of this volume was denoted during this period by the requests of the Executive branch for legislative authorization, as in the case of the United Nations Food and Agriculture Organization and the Bretton Woods Agreement for an International Bank and Monetary Fund,[3] and for Senate consent to ratification, as in the case of the Convention on International Civil Aviation.[4] The period was marked by official declarations of policy or by reaffirmations of policy already enunciated.

As has been said, basic policy and even specific proposals in the economic and social field were more advanced at the outset of the preparation than in the political, territorial, and security fields. The views subsequently developed were therefore marked by a high degree of continuity with the prewar policy of the United States. Expansion of world trade, for example, had been a basic tenet of United States foreign policy in the thirties. The renewal for the fourth time of the Trade Agreements Act (first passed in 1934) on July 5, 1945, and the emphasis placed during the last winter and spring of the war by the President and by high officials of the State Department on international agreement for the reduction of trade barriers, the regulation of

---

[3] United States membership in the FAO and in the International Bank and Monetary Fund was authorized July 31, 1945. The FAO came into being Oct. 16, 1945, and the International Bank and Monetary Fund, Dec. 27, 1945. *Department of State Bulletin*, XIII, 252, 619–20, 1058–59.

[4] *Ibid.*, p. 437.

international cartel practices, and the adoption of a code of principles to govern commodity arrangements all stemmed from this same basic tenet. The preparation in the economic and social fields had resulted not so much in development of wholly new policy as it had in elaboration and modification of existing policies and in extension of their scope to meet anticipated postwar conditions. Special effort had been made toward the development of world-wide specialized international organizations, in order to obtain multilateral cooperation in the major fields of economic and social advancement. Policy regarding regional economic, social, and cultural arrangements in this Hemisphere had also been refined and expanded.

While, in general, implementation of agreed policy rather than completion of preparation characterized the closing months of the war in the economic and social field, the latter process was to some extent still in progress in this period. A summary of the main lines of activity relevant to the preparation, and which therefore does not attempt to sketch the full picture of the Department's economic activity from the autumn of 1944 through the spring of 1945, is presented below.

THE CIVIL AVIATION CONFERENCE

THE BILATERAL discussions of civil-aviation policy with the United Kingdom, the Soviet Union, China, Canada, India, New Zealand, Belgium, the Netherlands, and other countries, which had been initiated by the United States in April 1944,[5] made possible the convening of an international aviation conference in Chicago on November 1, 1944.

This conference, in which fifty-two nations participated and which the Danish and the Thai Ministers in Washington attended in a personal capacity, differed from the preceding wartime conferences in that such neutral states as Sweden, Switzerland, Turkey, Spain, and Portugal were represented. It also differed from previous conferences in that the Soviet Union at the last moment withdrew its delegation on the reported grounds that countries that had "conducted a pro-fascist policy hostile to the Soviet Union" were to be represented.[6]

The Chairman of the United States Delegation, and the President of the Conference, was Assistant Secretary Berle. The remaining members of the United States Delegation were Senators Josiah W. Bailey, Democrat of North Carolina, and Owen Brewster, Republican of Maine; Representatives Alfred L. Bulwinkle, Democrat of North Carolina, and Charles A. Wolverton, Republican of New Jersey; As-

---

[5] See p. 243.
[6] *New York Times*, Oct. 30, 1944.

sistant Secretary of Commerce for Air William A. M. Burden; Rear
Admiral Richard E. Byrd, U. S. N. retired; Mayor Fiorello H. La
Guardia, Chairman, United States Section, Permanent Joint Board
on Defense (Canada-United States) ; and L. Welch Pogue and Edward
P. Warner, Chairman and Vice Chairman, respectively, of the Civil
Aeronautics Board . As previously noted, Representatives Bulwinkle
and Wolverton were members of the Special Committee on Communi-
cations, of which Mr. Berle was Chairman, and Mr. Pogue was a mem-
ber of the Special Committee on International Aviation, of which Mr.
Berle was also Chairman. The American preparation for this Conference had been a primary concern of the Special Committee on
International Aviation and, within the Department, of the Office of
Transportation and Communications, then under Mr. Berle.

The Final Act of the Conference was signed on December 7, 1944.
It included a general air convention, providing among other things for
the establishment of an International Civil Aviation Organization;
an interim agreement providing for the creation of a Provisional International Civil Aviation Organization to function in this field until the
permanent organization could be established; two agreements on
transit and commercial entry rights—one known as the "Two Freedoms" and one as "Five Freedoms" document; and several resolutions
on other aspects of civil aviation. The provisions in both the convention and the interim agreement relating to the establishment of the
permanent and the provisional organizations, respectively, included
authorization for these organizations to enter into agreements with
other international bodies.[7] The agreements were accepted by this
Government on February 8, 1945, as executive agreements.[8] Senate
consent to ratification of the general convention was requested by the
President on March 12, 1945.[9]

PROPOSED INTERNATIONAL TRADE CONFERENCE

PARTICULAR EMPHASIS was placed during this final period of the preparation on the desirability of obtaining the agreement of our Allies
and also that of the Congress to certain basic postwar policies in the
international trade field. As will be recalled, the informal conversations with the British in the autumn of 1943 had, outside the financial and investment fields, been primarily concerned with the problems
of commercial policy, commodity policy, and international cartel

---

[7] The provisional organization came into effect June 6, 1945, and the permanent
organization, Apr. 4, 1947. *Department of State Bulletin*, XII, 1056 ; XVI, 809.

[8] *Ibid.*, XII, 198.

[9] Consent was received July 26, 1946, and the Convention was ratified Aug. 6,
1946. *Ibid.*, XII, 437; XV, 337.

practices, and conversations with the Canadians on these same subjects had followed early in 1944. Out of these conversations and the intensive work being carried on by the Special Committees on the Relaxation of Trade Barriers, on Commodity Agreements and Methods of Trade, and on Private Monopolies and Cartels, certain definite proposals had been evolved. These were considered by the Post-War Programs Committee in the spring and early summer of 1944.

The essence of these proposals was, in the field of commercial policy, the conclusion of a multilateral convention for the relaxation of trade barriers and the establishment of an international trade organization. In the field of commodity policy, it was the formulation of an international code of principles and the establishment of an international commodity organization. And in the field of cartels, it was the conclusion of a multilateral convention to forbid and prevent restrictive cartel practices and the establishment of an "International Office of Business Practices."[10] Complete agreement, however, on certain aspects of these proposals was lacking: for example, on the relative advisability from the standpoint of this Government of a bilateral or a multilateral approach to the problem of the reduction of trade barriers and on the degree of autonomy that should be enjoyed by the proposed specialized organizations. The Post-War Programs Committee reserved final judgment pending the further consideration of these aspects by the Executive Committee on Economic Foreign Policy on the basis of recommendations from its subcommittees,[11] but approved the general direction of the thought on these problems.

While work in these fields was continuing in the Department's Office of Economic Affairs and in the interdepartmental committees, the President and Secretary Hull, in an exchange of letters released to the press,[12] agreed that the elimination of cartel practices that "restrict the free flow of goods in foreign commerce" was a part of the same liberal commercial policy as the trade agreements program. The President in his letter of September 6 stated that this elimination could "be achieved only through collaborative action by the United Nations" and expressed the hope that the Secretary would keep his "eye on this whole subject of international cartels because we are approaching the time when discussions will almost certainly arise between us and other nations." In reply, the Secretary said on September 11:

"For more than a year the Department, together with other interested agencies, has been giving careful attention to the issues which

---

[10] See appendixes 44, 45, and 46.

[11] The former special committees on these problems had become subcommittees of the ECEFP.

[12] Sept. 8 and 13, 1944; *Department of State Bulletin*, XI, 254, 292–93.

you mention, as well as other related subjects. An interdepartmental committee was established at my suggestion, and has been giving constant and current consideration to cartel matters and the methods by which the objectives set forth in your letter may best be achieved and most appropriately be coordinated with other facets of our foreign economic policy.

". . . In the near future, and consistent with the pressing demands of the war upon your time, I want to present to you in more detail plans for discussions with other United Nations in respect to the whole subject of commercial policy."

Two and a half months later, work on these plans had progressed sufficiently to permit Assistant Secretary Acheson, in a statement on November 30, 1944, before the Subcommittee on Foreign Trade and Shipping of the House of Representatives' Special Committee on Post-War Economic Policy and Planning, to outline the thinking as it had developed to date in the Executive branch on commercial and commodity policy and on the cartel problem. Mr. Acheson announced the Department's intention "to seek an early understanding with the leading trading nations, indeed with as many nations as possible, for the effective and substantial reduction of all kinds of barriers to trade," and said:

". . . If exploratory discussions with representatives of other governments give encouragement to our efforts, a trade conference of the United and Associated Nations should be held at the earliest practicable date for the negotiation of an agreement for the reduction of all kinds of barriers to trade. This agreement would of course be submitted to the Congress for its consideration." [13]

A draft convention on commercial policy, prepared by its Subcommittee on Trade Barriers, had been submitted by this time to the Executive Committee on Economic Foreign Policy.

Also by this time, a basic document on commodity policy, drawn up by the Subcommittee on Commodity Agreements under the Executive Committee on Economic Foreign Policy, had been approved by this Committee and by the President. The thought in this document was reflected in Mr. Acheson's statement on November 30 when he said that it would be "desirable," in the case of commodity agreements, "to seek agreement between governments that all international commodity arrangements of this type should be based upon an acceptance of certain fundamental principles, in order to insure that such arrangements shall subserve the broader purposes of an expanding world economy."

Work on the cartel problem was less far advanced, and Mr. Acheson could state only that the Executive agencies of the Government were

---

[13] *Ibid.*, XI, 656–62. At this date the related problems of trade barriers, commodity agreements, and cartels were being discussed by Mr. Hawkins with British officials in London.

"attempting to determine the most fruitful means of reaching international agreement for the curbing of private restrictions on international commerce." The Subcommittee on Private Monopolies and Cartels was still in the process of formulating its definitive proposals in this field, which were not considered and approved by the Executive Committee on Economic Foreign Policy until the following March.

Mr. Acheson further asserted on November 30, however, that in addition to the International Labor Organization and the projected International Bank and Fund and Food and Agriculture Organization, there would also be needed "international organization as a continuing forum on the problems of international trade, commodity arrangements, and private business agreements." He specifically projected an international trade organization and an international agency to "facilitate cooperation between governments in the solution of international commodity problems." All these specialized organizations, Mr. Acheson said, would be brought into close relationship with the Economic and Social Council of the general United Nations organization envisaged at Dumbarton Oaks, in order to insure that their objectives and activities were "in fact harmonious and consistent with each other."

The fact that plans were maturing in all these fields was indicated by President Roosevelt's message to the Congress on February 12, 1945, in which he requested action on the Bretton Woods agreements.[14] He then stated:

"Nor do I want to leave with you the impression that the Fund and the Bank are all that we will need to solve the economic problems which will face the United Nations when the war is over. There are other problems which we will be called upon to solve. It is my expectation that other proposals will shortly be ready to submit to you for your consideration. These will include . . . broadening and strengthening of the Trade Agreements Act of 1934, international agreement for the reduction of trade barriers, the control of cartels, and the orderly marketing of world surpluses of certain commodities . . ."

The many considerations involved and the preliminary negotiations required were such, however, that it was not until almost the end of the year that the United States proposals for international agreement in the three additional fields mentioned by the President on February 12 were made public.

Several related steps occurred in the interval. The President urged, in a message to the Congress on March 26,[15] the extension of the reciprocal trade agreements program; this was authorized early in the sum-

mer. The Staff Committee, on May 18, 1945, approved recommendations looking toward the convening of an international conference on
trade and employment after certain preliminary steps had been taken.
These steps fall beyond the scope of this volume. They culminated
in the Anglo-American Financial and Trade Discussions held that
autumn and in the formal issuance following these discussions of the
United States "Proposals for Consideration by an International Conference on Trade and Employment." [16] The British, it was announced
in a joint statement issued simultaneously, were "in full agreement
on all important points in these proposals," and accepted them "as a
basis for international discussion." It was also announced that the
proposals had been circulated to other governments as a basis for discussion preparatory to the conference.[17]

The United States Proposals combined in one organization the three
specialized fields of commercial and commodity policy and cartels and
were based on the documentation prepared by the three subcommittees
of the Executive Committee on Economic Foreign Policy that were
working in these specific fields and by its Subcommittee on Specialized
International Economic Organizations.

OTHER SPECIALIZED AGENCIES PROJECTED

Six other lines of economic and social work were also at varying
stages of development in the terminal period of the postwar preparation. President Roosevelt mentioned two of these in his message to
the Congress on February 12, 1945, when he referred to proposals
being prepared in the fields of "shipping and radio and wire
communication."

---

[16] On Dec. 6, 1945. For text of proposals see appendix 47. The Anglo-American
discussions of postwar financial and trade problems, instituted in Washington in
the autumn of 1943, were resumed in London, under the chairmanship of Assistant
Secretary Clayton, in August 1945 following the Potsdam Conference. The recent
change in the British Government, however, made only preliminary discussion
possible at this time, and it was decided to postpone the formal discussions for a
month. These discussions opened in Washington on Sept. 11 and continued
until Dec. 6. As described in the joint statement issued by President Truman
and Prime Minister Attlee on Dec. 6, they were "concerned with the major problems affecting the basic economic and financial relations between the two countries, in the light of the provisions of article VII of the mutual aid agreement".
The subsequent international discussions under United Nations auspices, 1946–48,
based on these proposals, resulted in the General Agreement on Tariffs and Trade,
negotiated at Geneva in 1947, and in the Charter for an International Trade
Organization, negotiated at the Habana Conference in the winter of 1947–48. The
charter is currently awaiting ratification.

[17] *Department of State Bulletin*, XIII, 395, 905–29.

As noted earlier, the Post-War Programs Committee in April 1944 had reviewed the recommendations of the Special Committee on Shipping, which envisaged the possible formation of an international shipping organization, and a United Maritime Authority had been established as a wartime control agency in August 1944.[18]   Discussion of a permanent organization in this field, however, was not inaugurated until after the war.[19]

Recommendations on United States policy regarding international telecommunications, as formulated by the Special Committee on Communications, had also been reviewed by the Post-War Programs Committee.   This Committee on October 20, 1944, approved a series of recommended principles to be supported by the United States at any international conference in this field.   On the collateral question of a new international telecommunications organization, no position was taken at this time, the Special Committee having stated that it had "reached the conclusion that the preparatory work at present being undertaken had not progressed sufficiently to enable the committee to formulate a principle on this point." [20]

The advisability of a specialized agency for telecommunications had been considered, beginning in 1942, by the Economic Subcommittees and by the political staff in connection with the comprehensive study of international organization.   Subsequently the Special Committee on Communications and a small *ad hoc* group of that committee meeting in the Department of State considered at length the possible reorganization of the International Telecommunication Union with a view to strengthening it.   While no definitive proposals in this field were developed before the end of the war, the Staff Committee, on April 25, 1945, approved a recommendation for the holding of a World Telecommunications Conference. This Conference convened two years later and resulted in the reorganization and strengthening of the International Telecommunication Union, reflecting substantially the plans developed under the aegis of the Special Committee on Communications.[21]

---

[18] See p. 244.

[19] In February 1946, a month before the wartime agency was due to go out of existence.   No permanent organization has been established at the date of this writing, although a convention for an Intergovernmental Maritime Consultative Organization is now awaiting ratification and a provisional commission is functioning.

[20] An International Telecommunication Union, with a central bureau at Bern, had been established in 1932 to succeed the International Telegraph Union, in existence since 1865, but it had functioned somewhat ineffectually on an ill-defined basis.

[21] The Conference met at Atlantic City, N. J., July 1–Oct. 2, 1947. *Department of State Bulletin*, XVII, 1033–34, 1940–41.

The foreseeable difficulties concerning transport in Europe after the war were the subject of another development. The consultations on a possible European inland transport organization held in June 1944 [22] between the United States and the United Kingdom, with the Soviet Union represented by an observer, led to joint Anglo-American proposals projecting such an organization, an interim commission, and a conference of interested Allied powers. The Post-War Programs Committee approved on July 14, 1944, United States participation in the organization and interim commission. The conference, in which twelve Allied countries took part, convened in London on October 10. It considered a draft agreement establishing a European Inland Transport Organization (EITO) to function for at least two years after the defeat of Germany. After several sessions, however, the conference recessed on October 27, 1944, without taking any action.

As the German surrender became imminent, the Staff Committee on April 30, 1945, authorized United States participation in a Provisional Organization for European Inland Transport to meet immediate needs, and this organization was set up on May 8, 1945, by the Governments of Belgium, France, Luxembourg, the Netherlands, Norway, the United Kingdom, and the United States. The Staff Committee in its April 30 meeting also approved a draft agreement for a European Central Inland Transport Organization, which was subsequently established by the reconvened conference on September 27, 1945.[23]

The other specialized organizations in the economic and social fields, as developed since the close of the hostilities, had less direct roots in the wartime preparation on postwar problems. The most intensive work on a world health organization and on an international refugee organization was done after the close of hostilities.

The Special Subcommittee on International Organization in 1942–43 had envisaged some type of health agency within the general structure of future international organization and had explored such problems as the nature of such an agency, its relation to the projected general organization, and the method and timing of its establishment. The research staff elaborated the favorable views of the Subcommittee, and provided in its own draft "Charter of the United Nations" a technical organization for health. Following the publication of the Dumbarton Oaks Proposals, envisaging "international . . ., social and other humanitarian problems" within the competence of the new gen-

---

[22] See pp. 232, 243.

[23] This organization stemmed from the EITO considered in 1944. The other two "E" organizations, the Emergency Economic Committee for Europe and the European Coal Organization established in May 1945 and January 1946, respectively, were not specifically projected in the preparation and are therefore outside the scope of this volume.

eral organization, consultations on the question of an international health organization were initiated between the Department and the U. S. Public Health Service, and work was begun in the Department's Division of International Labor, Social and Health Affairs early in 1945 on a draft constitution for such an organization. Informal discussions were held with representatives of other interested governments. The product of these discussions found expression in the specific inclusion of international health among matters of concern to the United Nations and in the strong support given in the United Nations Conference at San Francisco to a joint Sino-Brazilian declaration that called for an international conference to form a health organization. The initiation of the future world health organization may be said to have stemmed from a long background of international interest covering almost the whole twentieth century, finding specific focus in the postwar preparations of this and other governments and in the joint declaration presented in the San Francisco Conference.[24]

The establishment of the International Refugee Organization was proposed only in the year after hostilities had ended.[25] Extensive work, however, had been done in this field during the war. It was conducted through the Department's regular channels, in consultation with Myron C. Taylor, who continued until near the end of hostilities to serve as the United States Representative on the Intergovernmental Committee on Refugees.[26] The work in this instance was in appreciable measure international, being done in connection with the Anglo-American conference on the refugee problem held at Hamilton, Bermuda, April 19–29, 1943, and with the Intergovernmental Committee, as well as with the War Refugee Board which was established by the President on January 22, 1944, as a temporary United States agency in this field. This work was concerned primarily with the immediate aspects of an urgent wartime situation.

The long-range aspects of the refugee problem, however, had also received extensive consideration. They were studied early in the preparation in connection with the plans being developed for UNRRA, the immediate problems to be faced from the security standpoint at the

[24] The World Health Organization came into being Apr. 7, 1948. The United States became a member on June 21, 1948.

[25] The proposal was advanced by the Special Committee on Refugees, of the Economic and Social Council of the United Nations, after the question of refugees and displaced persons had been considered by the General Assembly of the United Nations at its first session in January 1946. The International Refugee Organization came into existence Aug. 20, 1948. The United States had accepted membership in the organization on July 1, 1947.

[26] See p. 137. On Mar. 15, 1945, it was announced that Earl G. Harrison had been appointed to succeed Mr. Taylor as the United States Representative on the Intergovernmental Committee. *Department of State Bulletin*, XII, 452.

close of hostilities, postwar boundary and minority problems, and the projected International Bill of Rights.[27] The situation that would be faced as European areas were liberated and in the immediate postwar period became the primary concern of the Special Committee on Migration and Settlement created in 1943. This Special Committee prepared, at the request of the Joint Chiefs of Staff, a series of forty-five documents in the form of directives and suggestions to the United States Army on the problem of displaced persons in Europe during the period of direct military government. A summary of the policy recommendations involved in these documents was approved by the Post-War Programs Committee on June 21, 1944.[28] And on July 12, the Committee approved another series of documents prepared by the Special Committee, for the guidance of Supreme Headquarters of the Allied Expeditionary Force, relative to displaced foreign nationals in Germany and displaced German nationals. These policy recommendations all related to the immediate post-hostilities period, and their implementation was therefore considered to be the responsibility of the military authorities, who might request assistance from appropriate agencies, such as UNRRA.

No new specialized organization was projected in the course of this preparation, although it was realized that some form of specialized international agency might eventually be required to take care of all residual aspects of the refugee problem, including nonrepatriable refugees. This latter aspect became one of grave difficulty under the circumstances that in fact prevailed at the close of hostilities, particularly in Eastern Europe, including the Baltic. The United States in general believed that the freedom of choice of refugees whether or not to return to their homelands should be respected, and the circumstances when the fighting ended led to a continuing problem concerning displaced persons who felt themselves unable to return to their countries of origin. The International Refugee Organization provided a single international body whose responsibility it was to secure the repatriation or resettlement of the million displaced persons remaining in Central Europe.

In the cultural field, the further preparatory work in the Department on the tentative draft agreement for a temporary United Nations Organization for Educational and Cultural Reconstruction considered by the Post-War Programs Committee in May 1944,[29] moved slowly for some months during which the over-all purposes and relationships of such an organization were reconsidered in the light of developments concerning the general international organization. A revised text of

---

[27] See pp. 115–16.
[28] See appendix 48.
[29] See p. 238.

the draft agreement, dated May 30 and prepared in the Department,[30] was communicated to the British, Soviet, and Chinese Governments in August 1944 to serve as the basis for an informal exchange of views. The Department's consideration of this revised draft was not resumed until November, and it soon resulted in a much more far-reaching proposal. The essential characteristics of this new proposal were that it looked to the establishment of a permanent organization for educational and cultural cooperation almost simultaneously with the general international organization, and shifted the emphasis from reconstruction to longer-range objectives. This proposal, which was formulated through the collaborative efforts of the Division of Cultural Cooperation, the Division of International Organization Affairs, and the Office of Special Political Affairs, reflected the influence of the Dumbarton Oaks Proposals, with their philosophy and provisions regarding development of conditions essential for international peace.

The new proposal for a permanent organization in the educational and cultural field was approved in principle by the Staff Committee on February 2, 1945. The final draft of this proposal, dated March 8,[31] was made available by authorization of the Department on April 17 to the Conference of Allied Ministers of Education in London for its own information and use. This draft formed the basis for the revised proposals drawn up by the latter for consideration at a general United Nations conference. The conference, which met in London after the close of hostilities, reached an agreement for the establishment of a United Nations Educational, Scientific and Cultural Organization to have its seat in Paris.[32]

---

[30] See appendix 49.

[31] See appendix 50.

[32] The United Nations Conference for the Establishment of an Educational, Scientific and Cultural Organization met Nov. 1–16, 1945. The organization came into being on Nov. 4, 1946. United States membership was authorized July 30, 1946.

CHAPTER XVIII

Remaining Preparation on Territorial Problems

With its final series of recommendations concerning the Far East approved on November 17, 1944, the Post-War Programs Committee concluded its work on territorial problems. The term "territorial problems" throughout the preparation was interpreted to mean all the postwar political, economic, social, boundary, and security problems of individual countries so far as these problems might have concern for the United States. Beginning with the surrender of Italy in September 1943 and, to a rapidly increasing degree, from the summer of 1944 on, such problems in Europe were becoming matters for day-by-day decision and action. They thus came more and more within the usual operating responsibilities of the appropriate geographic offices and divisions of the Department.

In the spring and summer of 1944, the Post-War Programs Committee had approved a comprehensive series of recommendations on both transitional and long-range United States policy toward Germany, its satellites, and the Allied countries under its occupation. By the end of 1944, as will be recalled, the enemy had been expelled in whole or in part from most of these occupied states, and three of the four satellites were out of the war. The withdrawal of the fourth, Hungary, was a matter of weeks only, and the complete liberation of the occupied countries from enemy control was obviously imminent. The Post-War Programs Committee's recommendations on United States policy toward these states for the period immediately following their surrender or liberation were no longer recommendations for future action. They had become policy recommendations to be reviewed and adjusted in the light of existing circumstances for immediate implementation.

New as well as anticipated problems now came to the fore. Whether or not a particular problem had been the subject of preparatory work, the action taken represented current views and decisions by the operating offices and divisions. Those making these decisions had the benefit of the guidance available in the recommendations from

367

the preparation wherever applicable, but such applicability was determined by the forces and factors that had emerged or were emerging in the wake of the war in the areas directly affected. The only constant, continuing factor was the effort made throughout the preparation and the succeeding current operations to assure to the utmost degree possible the integrity of the national interests of the United States.

Within the Department, as already noted, the Staff and Coordination Committees now replaced, in the territorial as in other fields, the Post-War Programs Committee. The interdivisional country and area committees were retained, however, without basic reorganization and with only normal and occasional alteration in structure thereafter as the regular assignment of an officer was changed or as committees were modified by amalgamation, expansion of a field, completion of work, or rise of some new need. By the winter of 1944–45, these committees had become the organs through which, at a working level, policy recommendations for current and emerging decisions were developed for the consideration and review of the operational offices and at higher policy levels.

For administrative reasons, the geographic sections of the Division of Territorial Studies were not merged with these offices until March 1, 1945. Primary responsibility for the direction and utilization of their work during the interim period, however, rested in the operational offices. The officers of these sections, when their transfer to these offices had been completed, largely continued their participation on the interdivisional committees. The continuity of these committees was thus left substantially intact when the preparatory work and staff moved into operations.

The interdepartmental committees that were functioning before December 20, 1944, were also retained in the reorganization, including the major new committee of this character, the State-War-Navy Coordinating Committee (SWNCC), which had begun to function just prior to the reorganization. The earlier interdepartmental Working Security Committee, however, was now absorbed into an *ad hoc* SWNCC Committee on the Control of Germany, which in February 1945 became the State-War-Navy Coordinating Subcommittee for Europe, still under State Department chairmanship.

In the case of the principal enemy states, the action stage had not yet been reached, but the remaining preparation did not so much involve the formulation of basic policy recommendations as the elaboration and practical application of high policy decisions concerning Germany and of already agreed policy recommendations concerning Japan. The beginning of the transition from preparation to such decisions came first on the question of the treatment of Germany—

a transition that was more prolonged and complex than in the case of policy toward Japan. It was marked by the President's decision late in August 1944 [1] to establish an informal "Cabinet Committee on Germany" for the purpose of reaching an agreed policy on this question interdepartmentally and at the highest policy level. It was also marked, the following month, by certain broad and far-reaching decisions regarding Germany arrived at by the President and Prime Minister Churchill at the second Quebec Conference.

The "Cabinet Committee" was composed of the Secretaries of State, War, and the Treasury. The Committee met only a few times—on one occasion with the President—over a brief period before and im‑ mediately after the Quebec Conference. In this period, however, there were also individual discussions among the high officials con- cerned and a number of meetings of their associates.[2] At these meet- ings, the State Department was represented by ranking officers from the Office of European Affairs and its Division of Central European Affairs. A draft interim directive to the Supreme Commander of the Allied Expeditionary Force "regarding the military government of Germany in the period immediately following the cessation of orga- nized resistance" was drawn up by representatives of the State, War, and Treasury Departments on September 22, 1944. This document reflected not only the recommendations of the earlier extraordinary preparation but also the discussions in the "Cabinet Committee" and the decisions reached at the Quebec Conference. These discussions and decisions had likewise to be taken into account in the continuing work on a more definitive document by the Department's Interdivisional Committee on Germany, the interdepartmental Working Security Committee and its successor SWNCC subcommittee and the United States Delegation to the European Advisory Commission in London.

Following the Three Power conference at Yalta,[3] the President, in a memorandum to Secretary Stettinius on February 28, 1945, directed the Secretary of State to assume responsibility "for seeing that the conclusions, exclusive of course of military matters, reached at the Crimea Conference, be carried forward." The President asked the Secretary to confer with other Government officials on matters in their respective fields, and "to report to me direct on the progress you are making in carrying the Crimea decisions into effect in conjunc- tion with our Allies."

---

[1] Further information on the background of this decision is contained in Henry L. Stimson and McGeorge Bundy, *On Active Service in Peace and War*, p. 569.

[2] A more detailed account of these consultations is contained in *Memoirs of Cordell Hull*, II, 1604, 1608–09, 1614.

[3] See chapter XX, p. 391 ff.

This order resulted in the establishment of a new interdepartmental committee on March 15, 1945, at a meeting of the Secretaries of State, War, and the Treasury, the Foreign Economic Administrator, and a representative of the Secretary of the Navy. The new committee, known as the Informal Policy Committee on Germany, functioned under the chairmanship of Assistant Secretary of State Clayton.

Secretary of War Stimson named Assistant Secretary John J. McCloy to serve as his representative with General Hilldring as alternate. Secretary Morgenthau designated Assistant Secretary Harry D. White, with V. Frank Coe as alternate. The Foreign Economic Administrator, Leo T. Crowley, named H. H. Fowler as his representative, and Under Secretary Ralph A. Bard with Assistant Secretary Artemus L. Gates were subsequently named to represent the Secretary of the Navy. The secretariat of SWNCC served as the secretariat for this committee.[4]

The next step occurred while the new committee was getting under way. Following a meeting of high officials with the President on March 22, a memorandum was drawn up jointly by representatives of the State, War, and Treasury Departments, in order to reach an agreed view among these three Departments, summarizing "U. S. policy relating to Germany in the initial post-defeat period." This memorandum was approved by President Roosevelt on March 23 and was then introduced into the European Advisory Commission for consideration.[5] It served as the basis for directives later issued by this Government to the Commander in Chief of United States Forces of Occupation in Germany. On April 26, the Acting Secretary, Mr. Grew, transmitted to President Truman for his approval the first definitive directive for the military government of Germany. This directive had been in the process of development for some months, on the basis of the draft interim directive of September 22, 1944, by the Working Security Committee and later by SWNCC. The proposed directive had been placed before the Informal Policy Committee on Germany for revision in the light of the policy summary approved by President Roosevelt on March 23. The resulting directive was approved by President Truman on May 10, 1945, following consultation with the Joint Chiefs of Staff, for transmittal to General Dwight D. Eisenhower.[6]

---

[4] The Informal Policy Committee on Germany functioned until the end of August 1945, when the remaining matters on its agenda were transferred to SWNCC.

[5] Ambassador Winant circulated this document to the European Advisory Commission on Apr. 4, 1945, but it was never more than briefly discussed in the Commission.

[6] For text of directive to General Eisenhower, see *Department of State Bulletin*, XIII, 596–607.

On the same day the President approved a further directive, for the guidance of Edwin W. Pauley, the United States Representative on the Moscow Reparations Commission established by the Yalta Conference. This directive had been drawn up by the Informal Policy Committee on Germany on the basis of the Yalta decisions concerning German reparations and of the March 23 directive on general United States policy for the treatment of Germany in the initial post-defeat period.

These basic directives represented current policy decisions arrived at interdepartmentally at the highest policy level below the President, rather than policy recommendations for future decision. While the earlier preparation was reflected in these directives in various ways, the decisions at Quebec and Yalta, particularly in the economic field, had profound influence on them. The Department's Staff Committee was kept informed of these developments but itself took no active part in them.

Since the eventual victory over Japan was plainly less imminent in the first half of 1945 than victory in Europe, the transition from preparation to decision on the problem of the treatment of Japan began later than in the case of Germany. It was also confined to a much shorter period—essentially the months of July and August 1945. This was the period when President Truman, Generalissimo Chiang Kai-shek, and Prime Minister Churchill, in a proclamation issued from Potsdam on July 26, announced the terms for Japanese surrender and when the President, after the first Japanese offer of surrender on August 10, approved over the following month a series of basic instruments and directives concerning policy toward Japan at the time of surrender and in the initial period thereafter.[7]

The basic instruments and directives on Japan emanated from the State-War-Navy Coordinating Subcommittee for the Far East, which was under the chairmanship of the State Department. This subcommittee had been established in January 1945 by SWNCC first as its *ad hoc* Committee to Consider Problems Which Arise in Connection with Control of Pacific and Far Eastern Areas, but was shortly renamed. Beginning in February those participating in its meetings included the two senior officers of the Far East section in the Division

---

[7] These basic instruments and directives were: the Instrument of Surrender, a proclamation for issuance by the Japanese Emperor, and a directive to the Supreme Commander for the Allied Powers, which were approved by SWNCC and by the President on Aug. 12, 1945; General Order No. 1 concerned with military stipulations and directives approved by the President later that month; and a general directive entitled "United States Initial Post-Surrender Policy for Japan", approved by the President on Sept. 6. For the texts of these documents, see *Occupation of Japan: Policy and Progress*, Department of State publication 2671, Far Eastern Series 17.

of Territorial Studies, who were also ranking members of the Department's interdivisional Area Committee on the Far East, George H. Blakeslee and Hugh Borton. Among the representatives of the War and Navy Departments on the Subcommittee during the period of concern here were General Strong and Admiral Train, each of whom had long been associated with the preparation in the Department of State.

The basic instruments and directives drawn up in the Far East Subcommittee had undergone a lengthy process of review by the Joint Chiefs of Staff and the full State-War-Navy Coordinating Committee, and consequent revision, before approval by the President. Allowing for the adjustments required by developments since the autumn of 1944, the basic policy decisions directly concerning the problems of surrender and occupation of Japan reflected in these papers and in the Potsdam Proclamation involved no radical departure from the policy recommendations made on these problems by the Post-War Programs Committee. This Committee had explicitly recognized in making its recommendations that future developments might make some of the procedures and policies advocated not "entirely applicable." The Yalta Agreements on the Far East made in the same intervening period related only indirectly to surrender and occupation policies and procedures and did not derive from the preparation.

As noted above, the problems of liberated areas so far as they concerned individual countries had become matters for day-by-day decision and action by this final period of the war. The more general question of major-power policy raised by these problems, however, was still to some degree within the scope of the preparation because of its far-reaching implications regarding continued cooperation among the major Allies and of its relationship to the plans, now in their final stage of development, for a general international organization. The question arose specifically from the circumstances developing in Eastern Europe, particularly in connection with the re-establishment of governments in Greece, Poland, and Yugoslavia and in the ex-satellite states, as already noted, where a marked divergence had appeared in the policies of the United States and Great Britain on the one hand and of the Soviet Union on the other.

Preparatory to the Crimea Conference and on the basis of suggestions made by the Office of European Affairs on January 8, 1945, proposals were drafted for the immediate establishment, as a joint temporary agency, of an emergency high commission for liberated Europe, together with the issuance of a Four Power declaration of policy toward liberated areas by the Governments of the United States, the United Kingdom, and the Soviet Union and the Provisional Government of France.[8] The purposes of these proposals, in the words of the recommendation formulated, were to meet the

". . . urgent need for these four nations to achieve unity of policy, and joint action, with respect to:

"1. Political problems emerging in the former occupied and satellite states of Europe, such as the return of certain exiled governments, the setting up of provisional regimes, the maintenance of order within countries, and the arranging of early elections where necessary to establish popular and stable governments;

"2. Immediate economic problems such as the care for destitute populations and the restoration of functioning economic life of particular countries."

An initial discussion of these problems and their relationships to the plans for international security organization and to the winning of the war itself was held on January 10, 1945, between Assistant Secretary Dunn, Mr. Pasvolsky, Mr. Bohlen, and the Director and Deputy Director of the Office of European Affairs, H. Freeman Matthews and John D. Hickerson, respectively. Subject to the review of the above-named superior officers, drafting was placed in the hands of an *ad hoc* group from the Office of Special Political Affairs and its Divisions, composed of Messrs. Wilson, Notter, Sandifer, Gerig, and Joseph E. Johnson and Miss Fosdick, working with the collaboration of Robert W. Hartley of Mr. Pasvolsky's office. The recommendations and papers on a joint declaration and an emergency high commission were completed January 16, 1945. After approval by Secretary Stettinius, in discussion with his ranking associates in the Department, they were transmitted by him to the President, together with the papers on other questions within the concern of the Department of State in connection with the Crimea Conference.[9]

The continuing work on the treatment of Germany and Japan, described above, and the formulation of proposals for major-power agreement on Allied policy in liberated areas were the last activities in the territorial field that were in any measure identifiable with the special preparation on postwar policy problems.

---

[8] See appendix 51.
[9] See p. 394.

CHAPTER XIX

Continuing Preparation for General International Organization

ALTHOUGH THE proposals resulting from the Dumbarton Oaks Conversations encompassed most of the fundamental aspects of the international security organization, the remaining preparatory work was prolonged and some of it was difficult. An appreciable amount of this work was done in anticipation of the Crimea Conference to which the preparation looked for the decisions essential to further progress in creating an international security organization.

While policy recommendations on the questions pending were being determined, further congressional consultations were held and participation in public discussion undertaken. These activities are discussed immediately below, but description of the exploratory talks with representatives of the other American republics, which took place concurrently, is deferred for presentation in connection with the Mexico City Conference, to which they were related.

THE "OPEN QUESTIONS"

IT WILL BE recalled that when the Dumbarton Oaks Proposals were published, October 9, 1944, not only the voting question but several other questions had been left "open" and that a full United Nations Conference was contemplated as soon as agreement had been reached on certain of these questions among the governments that had taken part in the Dumbarton Oaks Conversations. It was to the six open questions that Under Secretary Stettinius referred in a memorandum to Secretary Hull, October 14, 1944, commenting that the Dumbarton Oaks Conversations had reached "only ninety percent" agreement. The "open" status of these questions had resulted from failure to agree in the case of two questions considered intensively in the Conversations, from agreement to postpone several questions not regarded as immediate, and in the case of trusteeship from unreadiness to hold discussion.

The two questions that had been the most difficult in the Conversations were also the most urgent: voting in the Security Council and initial membership of the organization. Location of the organization's headquarters was a question that had been foreseen in the Conversations but, aside from sporadic private talks, had not been discussed; with this question was associated the matter of official languages to be used in the organization, which did not appear to present critical difficulty. Territorial trusteeship had not been taken up in the Conversations, apart from informal expression of interest by each of the foreign governments at Dumbarton Oaks in its future consideration with a prior exchange of papers. A consensus had rapidly been reached in the discussion at Dumbarton Oaks bearing on the statute of the court to defer its drafting to a meeting of jurists. The last question was the transition from the League of Nations to the new organization, which had only been raised informally and outside the agenda in the Chinese Phase of the Conversations. Aside from these questions there were also, of course, the three additions to the Proposals on which the Governments represented in the Chinese Phase had agreed to consult the Soviet Government in due course, but on these no special preparation was required.

Although work on the six open questions began promptly after October 9, no organized procedure of preparation was instituted then. Superior structure was soon created, on a temporary basis, but no fixed group or committee at a working level was developed. Frequent drafting meetings, however, were held by the Special Assistant to the Secretary in charge of the substantive work in this field.

The superior committee was composed of Acting Secretary Stettinius, presiding, and Messrs. Hackworth, Dunn, Pasvolsky, and Wilson, with the executive assistance of G. Hayden Raynor as Special Assistant to the Under Secretary.[1] Its purpose was to guide the "follow-through" work on the open questions, with a view to conferring with the President as soon as possible in regard to the policies to be adopted on these questions and to determining the further steps to be taken toward the eventual United Nations conference to write the Charter. Mr. Stettinius was able to report in the first meeting of this committee on November 1, 1944, that the President's general plan was to cover all the open items requiring decision in a conference with Prime Minister Churchill and Marshal Stalin but that arrangements for such a conference were not completed. On the same occasion, the committee agreed upon the importance of having, after such a meeting of the three heads of government, a meeting of the Foreign Ministers of the American Republics.

[1] Mr. Raynor became Special Assistant to the Secretary of State after Dec. 20, 1944. Mr. Stettinius was Acting Secretary of State Oct. 21–Nov. 30, 1944, becoming Secretary of State Dec. 1, 1944.

In the second meeting, November 2, the possibility of exchanging, among the Dumbarton Oaks conferees, papers on international trusteeship was suggested, and it was decided to ask for a naval representative and a military representative to join in the next meeting to consider this matter. There was also agreement that, in the absence of Secretary Hull, Acting Secretary Stettinius should undertake after the election to resume consultations with the congressional groups.

Admiral Willson representing the Navy Department and General Strong temporarily representing the War Department attended the third meeting on November 8, bringing the total group to seven. This meeting touched on several of the pending questions, but especially on two. On one of these, trusteeship, consideration was inconclusive. The other, voting, was discussed on the basis of a memorandum written by a small number of experts drawn from among the senior officers of the Office of Special Political Affairs and its Divisions, working with Mr. Pasvolsky and his Executive Assistant, Mr. Hartley. This group consisted largely of the same experts who had been concerned with this complex problem during the life of the earlier Informal Political Agenda Group. The memorandum under consideration embodied the conclusions reached in a discussion held on the previous Saturday by Messrs. Dunn, Hackworth, and Pasvolsky and attended by the drafters.

The issue continued to appear precisely as it had during the Dumbarton Oaks Conversations. It was not the requirement of unanimity among permanent members in reaching decisions on substantive matters in the Security Council. Full agreement existed in that respect. The issue was whether any permanent member when party to a dispute before the Council would be denied a right to vote in reaching the decisions on that dispute during the time its peaceful settlement was being sought by the Council—namely, while the Council was performing its conciliatory and quasi-judicial functions in behalf of pacific settlement of disputes. When, however, the Council's functions of determining the existence of a threat to or breach of peace and of suppression of such a threat or breach were called into play, this issue was not involved, since these functions were of an enforcement character and need of unanimity among the major powers was regarded as controlling.

The paper of alternatives considered at the meeting on November 8 supported the above limitation on the unanimity requirement where peaceful settlement was concerned. Such a limitation was regarded as a "compromise," since under it no state would be able to be a judge in its own case when pacific settlement of that case was at issue, and yet the unanimity requirement would not otherwise be affected. This was the basis of the compromise formula that had been conceived at

Dumbarton Oaks among the senior American representatives on the Formulation Group, and put forward, but without official endorsement, in the Conversations at that time. Preference for the compromise formula was now expressed after the full analysis presented in the November 8 meeting, and papers on it were then drafted for the Acting Secretary.

A related question was the size of the majority vote required for Council decision. Since the uneven number of eleven members, of whom six were nonpermanent was projected, the provision incorporated in the compromise formula was for decision by seven votes. In matters other than procedural, the seven would have to include the votes of the permanent members excepting any required to abstain by reason of being party to the dispute or situation being voted on.

On November 15, these and additional papers on other open questions were discussed by the Acting Secretary, accompanied by Mr. Hackworth and Mr. Pasvolsky, with the President. The President approved the compromise formula as the position that should be taken by this Government.[2] With this decision, the word "compromise" became inapplicable from the American standpoint, since henceforth this constituted our preferred formula for resolving the contending positions among the major powers on the question. Although anticipatory of intervening developments, it may be noted here that the formula thus approved on November 15, 1944, was the same formula— with a minor clarification of the intended reference at one point—presented and agreed upon without change at the Crimea Conference. This formula was eventually embodied in the Charter of the United Nations with only the necessary adjustment of citations to refer to the Charter instead of the Dumbarton Oaks Proposals and of "should" to "shall."

In the same conversation with the President, approval was received for the recommendation presented regarding invitations to the full United Nations conference and initial membership in the general international organization. Thereafter, our position was to favor inviting only signatories of the United Nations Declaration to the conference. It was decided to urge this view upon the six American republics that had so far not declared war and not signed that Declaration, and hence still had the status of Associated Nations. The question of location of the world organization was left to the future United Nations conference.[3] On the fourth open question, the President took the position that the principle of international trusteeship should be firmly established and that the international organization should provide adequate machinery for this purpose. He directed that

---

[2] For text of memorandum approved by the President, see appendix 52.
[3] The related matter of "official languages" was not raised.

the Department of State proceed in consultation with the military and naval authorities to a further examination of tentative proposals on this subject. The two remaining open questions, concerning the Statute of the Court and the transfer of the functions of the League, were not raised. On the former, no decision was as yet required. On the latter, the question was one on which proposals from the United Kingdom and China were still being awaited.

With the Presidential approval of these policy recommendations on November 15, the urgent preparation in this field before the Crimea Conference was chiefly that required on the voting question and on the question of trusteeship. During the three weeks before negotiations on the voting formula were initiated early in December 1944, however, participation in the public discussion of the Dumbarton Oaks Proposals received much emphasis in the Department, and congressional and party consultations were resumed.

PUBLIC DISCUSSION

WITH THE CONCLUSION of the Dumbarton Oaks Conversations, the Department undertook to respond as fully as work permitted to the many requests being received from organizations of interested citizens, active in developing an informed public opinion, for officers to give addresses on the Dumbarton Oaks Proposals. In encouraging the fullest possible study of the Proposals, the Department allowed these officers for the first time to engage extensively in "off-the-record" discussions for the dual purposes of clarifying the new and difficult problems involved in the Proposals and of obtaining at the same time information concerning the views of the public on these problems.

Such discussions were arranged by interested public organizations, which, with the Department's cooperation, systematically provided for special meetings on the Proposals in practically all parts of the country. Members of the American Group from private life who had served at Dumbarton Oaks and several members from the War and Navy Departments took part in these discussions, in addition to the higher officers of the Department of State and the staff experts in this field. In the two weeks' period, December 5 to December 19, 1944, for example, five State Department groups took part in forty-five meetings on the Proposals in sixteen widely scattered cities. Frequent off-the-record meetings of leaders of these public organizations were held in the Department for the same purposes, and for the first time panel discussions were arranged for some of these meetings, in which a large proportion of the high officers of the Department participated. Meetings began on October 14, and by December 20 the Department had participated in some 115 such discussions.

These undertakings after the Dumbarton Oaks Conversations represented an important new part of the work of the Office of Public Affairs and of its Director, Mr. Dickey, and, after December 20, 1944, of Mr. MacLeish, the new Assistant Secretary in whom responsibility for this work was now vested. While this participation in the public consideration of national policy toward a general international organization for the maintenance of peace and security was most extensive in the winter months following the Dumbarton Oaks Conversations, it marked a new development in relationships of the Department of State and the public, which has since been maintained without essential change. Approximately one hundred public organizations, including churches, took part in these efforts to facilitate and encourage wide public discussion of this basic postwar foreign policy. Referring to their activities, Secretary Stettinius said on December 15, 1944: [4]

"I am particularly gratified by the understanding and vigor with which the proposals have been discussed and continue to be debated by our own people. Much of that discussion has been fostered by organized groups of citizens conscious of their responsibility to promote public understanding of the great national and international issues which confront us. Not only organizations specialized in the study of international relations, but business, labor, and farm groups, service clubs and associations of ex-servicemen, women's organizations and religious societies, professional associations and groups of educators are spreading an understanding of the Dumbarton Oaks proposals throughout the country. By their work these organizations are making one of the most important contributions that can be made at this time toward the establishment of a strong and workable international organization in which our country will have an active share commensurate with its position as a world power.

"These organized efforts to promote a clear understanding of the proposed international organization for the maintenance of peace promise well for the future. It is only through public discussion, knowledge, and understanding that the peace to come can rest upon firm foundations of popular support and participation—and thus be truly a people's peace."

The views of the public received through these channels, and in letters from individual citizens and from organized groups, were the subject of regular study and report to all superior officers of the Department of State concerned with the improvement of the Proposals and the final steps in the negotiation of the Charter. Such study was conducted by the Office of Public Affairs, where it has since continued, and by the Division of International Organization. This division at the time contained most of the Department's experts in this field, a part of whose time was currently devoted to the public discussions just described.

---

[4] *Department of State Bulletin,* XI, 741.

At the same time, the views of the governments of the other United Nations on the Proposals were being received through their diplomatic missions in Washington, occasionally from visiting foreign officials, and through United States diplomatic missions abroad. The reactions of European religious leaders were reported by Myron C. Taylor in communications to the White House, while the views of private individuals abroad were received through the reports of United States missions and in letters and press accounts. All these expressions of opinion were likewise studied, and during the winter of 1944–45 they increasingly provided the remaining preparation with explicit information on world opinion in connection with the future Charter.

CONGRESSIONAL AND PARTY CONSULTATIONS

By the time congressional consultations were resumed soon after the election in 1944, the mimeographed copies of the Dumbarton Oaks Proposals sent with letters to the participating Senators and Representatives on October 9, 1944, had been given considerable study, as was indicated in the comments that were being received by Secretary Hull or Acting Secretary Stettinius. John Foster Dulles, in a letter to the Secretary October 13, mentioned Governor Dewey's appreciation of the Proposals and said that he wanted to add his "own word of appreciation." He commented that while some of their "imperfections and inadequacies" might be dealt with before the Proposals became definitive, others might have to be dealt with after the organization was started. The main thing was to get started, and he felt that the Proposals brought this "within the realm of early possibility."

At Mr. Hull's suggestion, Mr. Stettinius on October 19 set up a committee to give continuing attention to the congressional and the party consultations for the purpose of avoiding partisanship in regard to the establishment of the general international organization. The committee was composed of Mr. Stettinius, Assistant Secretary Long, and Messrs. Hackworth, Dunn, and Savage. Since Mr. Dunn had recently been in touch on developments in this field with Hugh Wilson, who, in turn, was in contact with Mr. Dulles, the committee requested Mr. Dunn to continue this relationship. Steps were also taken by the committee to raise with staff members at the White House the desirability of assuring that the general undertaking to keep the problem of establishing the security organization "out of politics" would be fulfilled.

Consultation with Senators Connally, Barkley, George, Gillette, Vandenberg, Austin, White, and La Follette recommenced on November 24, 1944, in a long meeting held by Acting Secretary Stettinius, and attended by Messrs. Hackworth, Pasvolsky, Wilson, Hiss, and Raynor. The open questions and "the prospective timetable" of next steps toward the drafting of the Charter were presented and discussed. The problem of handling disputes arising from treaties was considered at length. A searching examination was made especially of the voting question as it had been left unsettled at Dumbarton Oaks. The specific issue of a permanent member's voting in the Security Council on a dispute involving that member, and the voting formula being favored for resolving that issue were before the Senate Group for the first time. No collective judgment was sought, but general satisfaction with the proposed voting position was expressed by the meeting.

An equally long consultation took place with leaders of the House of Representatives on December 4, 1944. This meeting, covering much the same broad ground as that with the Senators, was attended by Speaker Rayburn, Minority Leader Martin, Representatives Bloom, Ramspeck, Arends, and Eaton, Secretary Stettinius, Under Secretary Grew, and Messrs. Hackworth, Dunn, Pasvolsky, Wilson, Hiss, and Raynor. Each of the open questions was considered, though at varying length. In particular, the voting issue, trusteeship, and the problem of authorization of use of force were analyzed.[5]

Two days later, on the 6th, Secretary Stettinius met with Senators Burton, Hatch, Ball, and Hill to bring them up to date on developments since Mr. Hull had last talked with them. On December 8 he similarly consulted with Mr. Dulles.

NEGOTIATIONS ON THE VOTING FORMULA

CONCURRENTLY, NEGOTIATIONS with the United Kingdom and the Soviet Union on the compromise voting formula were being inaugurated. The negotiating papers on the voting formula had been drafted during the three weeks' period after Mr. Stettinius' conversation with the President on November 15, 1944. They had been prepared in the Department in the same manner as the recommendations on all the open questions considered in that conversation.

The initiating telegrams to open negotiations were sent directly by President Roosevelt, December 5 and 6, 1944, to Marshal Stalin, in the form of a message conveyed through Ambassador Harriman, who was asked to discuss the question with the Marshal, and to Prime Minister Churchill. Citing the continued delay in completing arrangements for an early meeting of the heads of the three governments and the conse-

---

[5] This latter problem was finally resolved in the "United States Participation Act of 1945", approved Dec. 20, 1945, Public Law 264, 79th Cong., 1st sess., 59 Stat. 619.

quent delay in convening the general United Nations conference, these telegrams proposed the voting formula, gave a broad explanation of its significance, and strongly urged its favorable consideration. A suggestion was made in their concluding paragraphs that representatives be designated by each of the three heads of government to meet at an early date to complete the Dumbarton Oaks Proposals with a proposal on the voting question and to consider arrangements for promptly convening the projected general conference. The suggested meeting, as was explained in another telegram, was contemplated as informal with only two or three representatives from each government. Ambassador Winant in London and Lord Halifax in Washington were informed.

Ambassador Harriman's interview with Marshal Stalin did not take place until December 14. At its conclusion Marshal Stalin said he wished to have the matter studied before he expressed an opinion. On December 22, the status of developments was reported orally by Secretary Stettinius to the President who indicated some "displeasure" that things were moving so slowly in this field.

The Soviet judgment on the formula, stated by Foreign Minister Molotov in a conversation with the Ambassador on December 26, was that unity among the major powers must be maintained from the very inception of a dispute without any exceptions. It was agreed, nevertheless, that the matter would be kept open for personal discussion between the President and the Marshal. The Ambassador, reporting this talk, conveyed his impression that the Soviet leaders did not wish to have the Council consider any subject without their approval, fearing differences between the major powers if there were exceptions to the unanimity rule. Marshal Stalin replied directly to the President that same day, saying that he saw no possibility of agreeing to the formula. He argued, in explaining his view, that a split among the Great Powers, with fatal consequences, could ensue from any limitation upon unanimity.

No word having been received with respect to the British position on the formula, the Secretary of State on December 29, 1944, requested Ambassador Winant to stress to the Prime Minister or Foreign Minister Eden the President's desire to have a reply at the earliest possible date. The Ambassador reported on the 31st and again on January 2, 1945, that Mr. Eden had not yet completed his examination of the formula.

The year 1945 thus began with continuing Soviet opposition to any compromise on the voting question and with uncertainty concerning the British attitude on the matter. It appeared that a further conversation between Secretary Stettinius and the President must soon be held, and preparation of the papers for such a talk was begun. The Department's officers working on the critical problems still impeding the establishment of the general international organization considered, in drafts made during the first week of January 1945, the alternative courses that might have to be weighed if, in the words of an important memorandum of this time, the "dangerous drifting going on now" were to be arrested. Settlement of the main open questions in this field at a meeting of the three heads of government was held to be "almost indispensable." At the same time, on the basis of a directive issued December 22, 1944, by the Secretary of State and subsequent specific allocations of work by the Staff and Coordinating Committees among the Department's offices, drafting had started on all memoranda needed from the Department for the information and policy guidance of the President "in connection with his meeting with Marshal Stalin and Prime Minister Churchill".

On January 6, 1945, the President, stating in his annual message to the Congress that the United Nations were an "association" of peoples—and that "the peoples' hope is peace," commented:

"It will not be easy to create this peoples' peace. We delude ourselves if we believe that the surrender of the armies of our enemies will make the peace we long for. The unconditional surrender of the armies of our enemies is the first and necessary step—but the first step only.

"We have seen already, in areas liberated from the Nazi and the Fascist tyranny, what problems peace will bring. And we delude ourselves if we attempt to believe wishfully that all these problems can be solved overnight."

In this regard, he further said:

"The nearer we come to vanquishing our enemies the more we inevitably become conscious of differences among the victors.

"We must not let those differences divide us and blind us to our more important common and continuing interests in winning the war and building the peace."

After considering "the misuse of power" as implied in the term "power politics," and saying that "Perfectionism, no less than isolationism or imperialism or power politics, may obstruct the paths to international peace," President Roosevelt urged against repeating the attitudes taken in "our disillusionment" at the end of the last war. He admitted to feeling "concern about many situations—the Greek and the Polish for example," and said such situations "are not . . . easy or . . . simple to deal with. . . ." But, he impressed upon his domestic and foreign audiences, the many specific and immediate problems connected with the liberation of Europe must not be permitted "to delay the establishment of permanent machinery for the maintenance of peace." [6]

---

[6] H. Doc. 1, 79th Cong., 1st sess., serial vol. 10969.

Two days later, further discussion of the voting formula took place between the President and Secretary Stettinius, accompanied by Messrs. Dunn, Pasvolsky, and Bohlen. In this long and thorough discussion on January 8, the President said he was determined to press for a decision but that he was puzzled by how to approach this problem. He asked whether another formula had been found since the Soviet objection was received. In the ensuing analytical discussion of the compromise formula and its operation in terms of the problem of unanimity, it was remarked by the Departmental officials that "our discussions with Congressional leaders, with many individuals and groups throughout the country and with representatives of the American republics and of other United Nations have convinced us that the unanimity rule needs to be modified at least to this extent." Specific examples to test how the formula would work in practice were brought up by the President and the others. The President then expressed himself, in the words of the report of the discussion written on the same day, as "satisfied that something like our formula was necessary and that he would make every effort to convince the Russians that it was essential from the point of view of our position."

Three days later, January 11, 1945, President Roosevelt conferred with a subcommittee of the Senate Foreign Relations Committee: Senators Connally, Barkley, and Thomas (Democrats), Vandenberg, White, and Austin (Republicans), and La Follette (Progressive). At this meeting he discussed the situation in Eastern Europe, and the voting formula, and informed them of the Soviet proposal at Dumbarton Oaks on membership. Under Secretary Grew and Assistant Secretary Acheson, who were present at this meeting, reported to the Staff Committee that the President had indicated that he himself was unsure whether the Soviet position on unanimity was a bad position and that we might have to yield to them on this point, but that, in his view, the Soviet Government would yield on its proposal of "votes" for the sixteen Soviet Republics. Secretary Stettinius conferred with the Senate Foreign Relations Committee as a whole on January 17, and discussed again various open questions, and policy toward liberated areas. These were the last congressional consultations, prior to the Crimea Conference, that bore directly on the remaining preparation in the field of the general international organization. The Secretary, however, on January 19, suggested that during his absence Mr. Acheson and others continue to meet with the Senate Foreign Relations Committee.

Word of the favorable British reply on the voting formula was received orally from the British Embassy January 13 and was confirmed in writing the next day. By this time, a memorandum analyzing how the formula would operate in the case of each foreseeable kind of decision under the Dumbarton Oaks Proposals was ready. As this draft was developing, two discussions of the problem had been held in the Department with Ambassador Gromyko on his initiative, that of January 11 dealing almost wholly with the voting question and that of the 13th dealing also with the other open questions in some detail. In both conversations, the Ambassador referred briefly to the continuing importance to his Government of its view that Soviet Republics should become initial members of the organization and that the Associated Nations and neutrals ought not to be included, but he was informed that we had "no new thoughts" on these matters. The two discussions were of unusual length, and permitted a thorough examination of a "straight unanimity rule," of various alternative compromises, and of the formula proposed by the United States. On January 15, 1945, copies of the memorandum analyzing the American formula were handed informally to Ambassadors Halifax and Gromyko.[7]

Memoranda for the President on Open Questions

These exchanges were the last negotiations on the proposed organization before the Crimea Conference convened. Simultaneously, memoranda for the President on the main open questions to be considered at that conference were completed. On January 16, they were put in the "Book" for the President, together with the more numerous memoranda, written in the operational sections of the Department and devoted to problems not within the scope of the remaining preparation. The "Book" was transmitted shortly thereafter to the President by Secretary Stettinius.

Of the six memoranda in the field of general international organization, the first was concerned with the voting question. It comprised, in fact, separate papers of analysis, proposal, background, and developments. The second memorandum on the composition of the Security Council dealt principally with the changed status of France and its possible participation as a sponsoring power in calling the general United Nations conference.[8] The third was on maintaining the position taken at Dumbarton Oaks that the nations to be invited to the general conference should be the 44 United and Associated Nations.

---

[7] See appendix 53.

[8] The Dumbarton Oaks Proposals had projected the inclusion in due course of France as one of the permanent members of the Security Council. The condition attached at the time of the Conversations to French tenure of a permanent seat was now regarded as having been met by virtue of the recognition that had been accorded the Provisional French Government, French membership on the European Advisory Commission, and the French signature of the Declaration by United Nations.

The fourth, on dependent territories, reported upon the status of the international trusteeship question and of the tentative draft proposal in this field still under consideration by this Government. The fifth dealt with the projected meeting of jurists to prepare a draft statute for the International Court of Justice, and the last considered "the liquidation of the League of Nations." There was no memorandum on the deferable question of location of the organization and the related matter of official languages.

These papers completed one step of the remaining preparation for a general international organization. They had been developed by the same senior experts of the Office of Special Political Affairs and its Divisions who have already been referred to as the working-level group that was meeting with Mr. Pasvolsky for this purpose. They met together with sufficient regularity between January 1 and February 10, 1945, to have summary minutes kept of their eighteen meetings, and inasmuch as a superior committee for these terminal aspects of preparation had failed to materialize, though it was persistently projected, their papers were reviewed only by the individual superior officials directly or indirectly concerned. This working group, known informally as "Mr. Pasvolsky's Committee" in the six weeks it functioned, ceased to exist as a group when several of its members left for their assignments at the Mexico City Conference.[9]

Aside from the work described above and the major question of trusteeship considered below study was especially given throughout these months to improvements that might be made in the Dumbarton Oaks Proposals in the course of their transformation into a Charter and to additional provisions that it might be desirable to incorporate in the Charter. Among these, for example, were possible provisions concerning freedom of information and religious liberty, both of which involved the subject of an international bill of rights, and the provision already in the Proposals, but not yet given the position of a basic principle, for promotion of "respect for human rights and fundamental freedoms." Informal interdivisional meetings of interested officers were held for consultation on these problems and for review of papers, Mr. Pasvolsky's Committee serving as the focal point for the completion of the necessary work on these problems. In general the drafting was carried out in the Division of International Organization Affairs.

---

[9] The original members of this group were Messrs. Pasvolsky, Wilson, Hiss (until he left for Yalta), Notter, and Hartley. Toward the end of January, Messrs. Sandifer, Gerig, and Johnson joined the group.

INTERDEPARTMENTAL CONSIDERATION OF TRUSTEESHIP

ON THE QUESTION of international trusteeship, much difficult work was still to be done. This question required, and was accorded, exceptional emphasis in the remaining preparation because of its intrinsic importance to fundamental American foreign policy in almost all its aspects, and because of its profound bearing upon American national security not only in future years but in the attainment of victory in the final crucial stages of the war. As has been seen, a tentative proposal for international trusteeship had been prepared and approved by the Post-War Programs Committee before the Dumbarton Oaks Conversations, but for military considerations it had not been put forward in those Conversations.[10] It was clear as a matter of policy at that time, however, that the President approved the principle of trusteeship. He had written on July 10, 1944, to the Joint Chiefs of Staff: "I am working on the idea that the United Nations will ask the United States to act as Trustee for the Japanese mandated islands."

The attention given to this matter in the Department during the two weeks after the Dumbarton Oaks Conversations was on the basis of a draft letter addressed to the Chief of Staff, Gen. George C. Marshall, intended for prior informal discussion with the Joint Chiefs of Staff. This draft letter proposed that the chapter of the "Tentative Proposals" withheld from the Conversations should now be sent to the other three major powers to inaugurate the exchange of views considered necessary before the general United Nations conference. The consideration of the whole matter was undertaken by an *ad hoc* group of officers comprised of Messrs. Pasvolsky and Dunn at the policy level and at the working level of Henry S. Villard of the Near Eastern Office, Robert B. Stewart of the European Office, Harley Notter of the Office of Special Political Affairs, Benjamin Gerig, Donald C. Blaisdell, James F. Green, and Ralph Bunche from the Divisions of the latter Office and C. Easton Rothwell, then Executive Secretary of the Post-War Programs Committee. In lieu of the projected letter, a number of informal conversations with Admiral Willson of the Joint Chiefs of Staff were held during this period by superior officers in the Department of State.

On December 30, 1944, Secretary Stettinius proposed in letters to Secretaries Stimson and Forrestal that representatives of their Departments join with the Department of State in preparing a draft proposal for eventual incorporation in the final United Nations Charter and for possible early discussion with the other major Allied powers, which would set forth general principles and provide for international

---

[10] See pp. 276, 295.

trusteeship machinery.   The Department of State was working on this draft, it was stated, with the intention, as heretofore, that the application of trusteeship to specific territories would be left for future determination.[11]

The draft proposal referred to was a revision of the paper withheld from the Dumbarton Oaks Conversations.   It did not, however, encompass all the problems of policy concerning dependent areas on which papers were then being developed in the Department of State. Chief among these additional papers, as they were being drawn up in the interdivisional committee on dependent areas and within the Division of Dependent Area Affairs, were two: one on minimum standards applicable to all non-self-governing areas, including colonies and other types of dependencies as well as trust territories, and the other on regional advisory commissions to assist the authorities responsible for dependent territories in the discharge of their international obligations for the development and welfare of these territories and their peoples.

An Interdepartmental Committee on Dependent Area Aspects of International Organization was promptly created pursuant to informal agreement among the Departments concerned.   The State Department representatives on this ranking Committee were appointed by the Staff Committee on January 5, 1945: Mr. Pasvolsky, Chairman, Assistant Secretaries Dunn, Rockefeller, and Clayton, and Isaiah Bowman.   The War Department and Air Corps were represented by Generals Embick and Fairchild, respectively, the Navy Department by Admiral Russell Willson, and the Interior Department by Under Secretary Abe Fortas.[12]   The United States Commissioner on the Anglo-American Caribbean Commission, Charles W. Taussig, attended as an expert on relevant Caribbean problems.   The other members were Messrs. Wilson, Director of the Office of Special Political Affairs and the Committee's Acting Chairman when necessary; Charles P. Taft, Special Assistant to the Assistant Secretary for Economic Affairs and alternate for Mr. Clayton; Benjamin Thoron, who accompanied Mr. Fortas for the Interior Department; and Messrs. Haley, Director of the Office of Commercial Policy, and Gerig and Green from the staff of the Division of Dependent Area Affairs.[13] The Committee's meetings began on February 2, 1945.

---

[11] See appendix 54.

[12] The military and naval representatives were all members of the Joint Chiefs of Staff.   The interest of the Interior Department stemmed up from its responsibilities for administration of certain territorial possessions of the United States.

[13] Admiral Willson's alternate on one occasion was Admiral Harold C. Train; Mr. Wilson's on one occasion was Alger Hiss; and Avra Warren accompanied Mr. Rockefeller once.

In the interval, informal discussions took place in the State Department between Col. Oliver F. G. Stanley, British Minister of State for the Colonies, and Departmental officials on the possibilities of regional commissions for colonial territories, of a declaration of standards for administration of all dependent territories, and of trusteeship. There was recognition, most fully expressed in the discussion on January 18, of the heightening urgency for effecting an exchange of papers on trusteeship before the projected general United Nations conference convened.

The immediate problem in the remaining preparation on this question, however, was not international. Rather, it was to arrive at an agreed policy proposal within this Government that would satisfactorily take into account all the vital national interests of the United States involved in this complex question, including especially provision for the security of the United States in the Pacific. Congressional interest in the disposition to be made of the Pacific islands not under the control of an Allied power was strongly expressed in this period, and a subcommittee of the Committee on Naval Affairs of the House of Representatives was appointed on January 23 to study this matter. That same day, the Secretary of War set forth in a memorandum to Secretary Stettinius his views as expressed in a discussion of the previous day on the basic considerations relative to our national security involved in the projected trusteeship plan, and shortly thereafter, further interdepartmental discussion of this problem occurred at the Assistant Secretary level.

The necessity of responding to the approaches of other governments concerning our views on a trusteeship system was stressed by the Chairman at the initial meetings of the Interdepartmental Committee. At the third meeting, on February 13, he announced the Crimea decision to include a trusteeship system in the proposals for a general international organization. The Joint Chiefs of Staff conveyed to Secretary Stettinius, through a memorandum from the Chairman of the State-War-Navy Coordinating Committee on February 26, 1945, their concurrence in the Secretary's proposal nearly two months earlier regarding interdepartmental preparations for international discussion of trusteeship and their views concerning United States security requirements that should be recognized in such discussion. This memorandum also conveyed the hope of Secretaries Stimson and Forrestal that the State Department's formulation of the proposal on trusteeship would proceed expeditiously and their intention to accord it prompt consideration when it was ready.

In its second meeting on February 8, the Interdepartmental Committee had developed certain essential differentiations between strategic and nonstrategic areas for trusteeship purposes and arrived at the concept that the former should come within the purview of the Security Council, where the unanimity requirement would be operative This was the basic concept on which the long-sought agreed policy wa to be constructed. On March 2, in its sixth meeting, the drafting of a definitive proposal was begun by the Committee. Three of its members, however—the Chairman, Assistant Secretary Rockefeller, and General Embick—were absent on assignment to the United States Delegation attending the Conference at Mexico City, which had convened February 21.

Agreement on a trusteeship proposal, while advanced by the work so accomplished, was, however, not immediately reached. The further steps taken occurred mainly after the Mexico City Conference had been held and all officials concerned had returned to Washington and can best be described after consideration has been given to the Crimea and Mexico City Conferences.

CHAPTER XX

International Conferences
February–March 1945

BOTH IN THE meeting of the three heads of Government at Yalta early in February and in the inter-American conference at Mexico City beginning later that month, the postwar preparation was involved, and the resulting decisions strongly influenced the subsequent preparatory work. In both instances, however, these relationships were confined to only certain of the matters discussed at the conferences.

THE CRIMEA CONFERENCE

WHEN PRESIDENT Roosevelt, Prime Minister Churchill, and Marshal Stalin met at Yalta on the Crimean Peninsula, February 4–11, 1945, fourteen months had elapsed since their last meeting. The forces of the Western Allies were now attacking inside Germany close to the Rhine. Only Norway, Denmark, and a part of the Netherlands were still occupied. On the Eastern front, Soviet troops had crossed Poland and were fighting along the Oder in Germany, at some places less than a hundred miles from Berlin. At one point, north of Breslau, they had crossed the Oder. Northern Italy, however, had not yet been cleared of the enemy, and fighting was still in progress in Austria, Czechoslovakia, and Yugoslavia, and also in Hungary, where German forces were still resisting expulsion, although an armistice had been signed by the United States, the United Kingdom, and the Soviet Union with the Provisional National Government of Hungary shortly before. In the Far East, though the liberation of the Philippines had not yet been accomplished, United States troops recaptured Manila on February 4; the Burma Road, closed for nearly three years, was again serving as a supply route for China; and more frequent bombing of the Japanese home islands had begun.

Thus, as the Crimea Conference convened, the defeat of Germany was expected in a matter of months,[1] even though the Battle of the Bulge had left among the Allies a degree of uncertainty and some

---

[1] Dwight D. Eisenhower, *Crusade in Europe* (New York, 1948), pp. 366–86.

pessimism over how soon Germany could be forced to surrender. Thereafter invasion of Japanese home territory could be undertaken. The islands directly to the southeast and southwest of Japan proper were becoming increasingly vulnerable to assault and the final costly battles on the main islands of Japan were expected to open late in the autumn.

Because of the imminence of victory over Germany and, therefore, of the time when the entire United Nations war effort could be concentrated against Japan, and because the "postwar" period was already being entered in those areas wholly or partly free from enemy occupation and in the ex-satellite states, there was an emphasis at the Crimea Conference on immediate and longer-range postwar problems that had not characterized previous great power conferences with the exception of that held at Moscow. There was, moreover, emphasis for the first time on specific decisions in this field.

Military decisions of great importance were made at Yalta, as at the previous conferences, and these, as before, continued to be of major concern to the heads of the three powers leading the war effort of the United Nations coalition. High ranking military, naval, and air officers composed half of the American group accompanying the President. The Conference went further, however, and arrived at basic decisions on many political problems which were to have a far-reaching effect on postwar arrangements. In anticipation of the political character of the Conference, the three heads of government were accompanied to Yalta by their respective Foreign Ministers.[2]

The extraordinary preparation so far as it still continued had been directed, as has been seen earlier in this Part, toward decisions on only certain of these political problems. The papers on these particular problems carried by the Secretary of State to the Conference were directly addressed to the question of the voting formula; the question of inviting the Associated Nations, together with the United Nations, to the future general conference and of limiting the invitations to these only; the question of provision for trusteeship in the Charter to be written at the general conference;[3] and several questions of detail con-

---

[2] The following American civilian officials along with Secretary Stettinius accompanied the President to the Conference: Harry L. Hopkins, Special Assistant to the President; former Supreme Court Justice James F. Byrnes, Director, Office of War Mobilization and Reconversion; W. Averell Harriman, Ambassador to the Soviet Union; and three officers of the Department of State, H. Freeman Matthews, Director of the Office of European Affairs, Alger Hiss, Deputy Director of the Office of Special Political Affairs, and Charles E. Bohlen, Assistant to the Secretary of State. It will be recalled that both Ambassador Harriman and Mr. Bohlen had participated in the earlier meetings at Moscow and Tehran and that Mr. Bohlen and Mr. Hiss had attended the Dumbarton Oaks Conversations.

[3] For this paper and the covering memorandum, see appendix 55.

cerning the calling of the general conference. Papers in the latter group included a list of nations invited to the three prior United Nations Conferences at Hot Springs, Atlantic City, and Bretton Woods, and a draft of the invitation to the future conference, together with a draft announcement on that conference and suggestions on its location and a paper on the composition of the United States Delegation to it. With the exception of this last question, which was of concern only to the United States, the agreements sought on such matters were obviously those deemed essential to the convening of the future conference to draft the Charter. Accordingly, from the standpoint of the remaining extraordinary preparation, the Crimea Conference constituted in these respects a stage of decision at the highest policy level, as had the Dumbarton Oaks Conversations at the highest level of technical competence, that brought the preparatory work for the general international organization very near conclusion.

Although a number of the decisions reached by the Conference were on postwar arrangements of concern to this volume, the larger number of the decisions fall outside its scope. To take as an example the decisions of the Conference with regard to the occupation and control of Germany after its defeat, it has been observed that the extraordinary preparation on this problem had rapidly terminated after the Post-War Programs Committee had approved the recommendations of the preparation, and consideration of policy had begun at a Cabinet level in September 1944, as part of the process of reaching Presidential decision on the State Department's recommendations. The transition thereafter made to the usual advance preparation on specific issues, normally attending current operations, had been recognized in the reorganization of the Department of State on December 20, 1944, under which the officers working on Germany in the Division of Territorial Studies were being absorbed administratively into the operating offices and divisions by the time of this Conference, and in the activities of the State-War-Navy Coordinating Committee beginning December 19, 1944. With the military problem of the entrance of the Soviet Union into the war against Japan [4] and the Far Eastern territorial conditions that by agreement of the three heads of government were attached thereto, the extraordinary preparation had not been concerned. With respect to the establishment of "the Polish Provisional Government of National Unity," to the future frontiers of Poland, and to the formation of a new government in Yugoslavia, it has already been noted that the problems at issue had entered into the

---

[4] The Soviet Union declared war on Japan as of Aug. 9, 1945. This was three days after the first atomic bomb was dropped on Hiroshima and the day after the second was dropped on Nagasaki.

operations stage during 1944. The question of the treatment of war criminals had long since become a matter for operations, with the establishment, mentioned earlier, of the United Nations War Crimes Commission in London late in 1943.

The American proposals with respect to liberated Europe, to come before this crucial conference, were of active concern to the conduct of the remaining postwar preparation. These proposals, on which the President had not yet definitely ruled, were discussed informally by Secretary Stettinius and Foreign Minister Eden on the way to the Crimea, at Malta on February 1, 1945. The point of view on this matter taken in the extraordinary preparation was set forth in a memorandum for the use of Secretary Stettinius, in which the "cognate importance" of the projected high commission for liberated Europe [5] was emphasized as "the most powerful antidote that we can devise for the rapidly crystallizing opposition in this country to the whole Dumbarton Oaks idea on the score that the future organization would merely underwrite the system of unilateral grabbing." In his talk with Mr. Eden, the Secretary stated, however, that the President had misgivings that the proposed European high commission might prejudice the prospects of world organization. On February 4 the President expressed to Secretary Stettinius his unfavorable impression of the record of the European Advisory Commission, and said that, rather than to establish another commission, he preferred to have meetings of the Foreign Ministers to handle the necessary work regarding liberated areas. A further objection to the proposed high commission was that the United States would be loath to assume the responsibilities in regard to the internal problems of the liberated countries that such a standing high commission would unavoidably entail.[6] This, in the circumstances, was a view applicable predominantly to Eastern European countries.

As it eventuated, the proposal for a commission on liberated Europe was not placed before the Conference, but the proposed joint declaration was advanced with certain changes, several of which were necessary to delete references to the high commission.[7] With limited additional amendment in the Conference itself, this Declaration "to concert during the temporary period of instability in liberated Europe the policies of their three Governments to assist the peoples" of former enemy occupied and ex-satellite states in Europe "to solve by demo-

---

[5] See p. 372 and appendix 51.

[6] The records do not clearly show whether this view was one held by the President or represented the view of an adviser.

[7] See appendix 56 for text presented at Yalta.

cratic means their pressing political and economic problems" was adopted on February 10, 1945.[8]

Secretary Stettinius and Foreign Minister Eden, on February 1, 1945, aboard H. M. S. *Sirius* at Malta, also had a brief discussion, in which there was agreement of views, on the voting formula and on plans for consultation with China and France regarding the formula and the calling of the future conference as soon as practicable.

The voting formula was considered by the three heads of government in a plenary meeting at Livadia Palace, Yalta, late in the afternoon of February 6. At this meeting, attended by the Foreign Ministers and a number of other civilian members from each delegation, Secretary Stettinius gave the initial explanation of the formula.[9] There ensued the only full length discussion of the formula among the three heads of government during the Crimea Conference, and it ended, at the suggestion of Marshal Stalin, with the matter being put under study.

At the plenary meeting the next afternoon, February 7, 1945, Foreign Minister Molotov stated that certain questions involved in the voting formula had become much clearer by reason of the explanation and discussion the day before. It now appeared, he said, that the formula would secure the unanimity of the three powers in guaranteeing peace and security after the war. Adding that maximum unity among these three great powers had been the Soviet position at Dumbarton Oaks and that the Dumbarton Oaks Proposals and the modifications now suggested by President Roosevelt would secure collaboration by all nations great and small after the war, Mr. Molotov then stated that the voting proposals were "acceptable." Continuing his statement, Mr. Molotov spoke next of the participation of Soviet Republics in the security organization. He did not present this Soviet proposal in the all-inclusive form it had taken at Dum-

---

[8] For text of this declaration, see *Department of State Bulletin*, XII, 215. The declaration set forth the following specific purposes:

"To foster the conditions in which the liberated peoples may exercise these rights, the three governments will jointly assist the people in any European liberated state or former Axis satellite state in Europe where in their judgment conditions require (A) to establish conditions of internal peace; (B) to carry out emergency measures for the relief of distressed peoples; (C) to form interim governmental authorities broadly representative of all democratic elements in the population and pledged to the earliest possible establishment through free elections of governments responsive to the will of the people; and (D) to facilitate where necessary the holding of such elections."

[9] For the explanatory statement made by Secretary Stettinius in this plenary session, which set forth the United States position on freedom of discussion that later became an issue during the San Francisco Conference, see appendix 57.

barton Oaks, however, naming only the Ukraine, Byelorussia, and Lithuania and remarking that "at any rate two" of these had full right to be considered original members.

The President welcomed the Soviet accession to the voting formula without discussion. He, then, after raising the question of inviting the Associated Nations to the future conference on the Charter and mentioning that different views were held among the three heads on the question of giving "more than one vote" to "the larger nations," moved, and it was agreed, that the matter of membership be referred to the Foreign Ministers for study, along with the questions of the time and location of the general United Nations conference and the states to be invited to it. Following some discussion of this motion, during which the President indicated to the Prime Minister and to the Marshal that he felt strongly that the Soviet proposal on membership must be studied before he could express an opinion on it, the matter was referred to the Foreign Ministers. The Foreign Ministers met promptly on these matters and reported to the next day's meeting of the three heads of government.

Agreement was reached in that plenary meeting, on February 8, to invite the eight Associated Nations and Turkey, provided they declared war on either Germany or Japan or both by March 1, 1945, and thereby qualified themselves as United Nations.[10] Saudi Arabia was added to this list near the close of the Conference. The inclusion of Denmark was favorably considered, but its status as an occupied country without a government-in-exile was regarded as precluding an invitation at this time.

The admission of the Ukrainian and Byelorussian Soviet Socialist Republics as original members of the international organization when established was also considered on February 8. It was decided that at the general United Nations conference the delegates of the United Kingdom and the United States would support a Soviet proposal, if made, that two Soviet Republics be admitted to original membership in the general international organization.[11] The two

---

[10] The eight Associated Nations were Chile, Ecuador, Paraguay, Peru, Uruguay, Venezuela, Egypt, and Iceland.

[11] Secretary Stettinius in a note addressed to the Soviet Ambassador in Washington, Mar. 29, 1945, replying to a Soviet note of Mar. 25 on representation of the Ukrainian and White Russian Soviet Socialist Republics in the discussions at San Francisco, once these republics had been accepted by the Conference as original members of the new organization, stated that this specific question had not been raised by the Soviet Delegation at the Crimea Conference. The Secretary further stated that, pending the decision of the Conference on initial membership of these republics in the proposed organization, there appeared to be "no grounds at this stage for raising the question of the representation of the Ukrainian and White Russian Republics at the Conference itself."

then indicated by Marshal Stalin were the Ukraine and Byelorussia. It was further decided, on the basis that these two were already at war as components of the Union of Soviet Socialist Republics, that they should not sign the Declaration by United Nations.

A Soviet suggestion was made on February 11, to insert in the final text of the communiqué to be issued at the close of the Conference, that it had also been "resolved to recommend" to the future United Nations conference to invite the two Soviet republics as original members. This suggestion was withdrawn by Marshal Stalin after discussion brought out that, if this statement were to be included, the issuance of the communiqué would have to be delayed in order to permit prior consultation with the British Dominions and that it would be necessary to include an explanation of the American position. During the period in which this matter was being considered, February 8–11, the President obtained the concurrence of the other two heads in an equal number of votes for the United States in the assembly of the international organization, if this should be deemed necessary in the United States. On March 29, 1945, these agreements were made known by the White House, and on April 3 they were the subject of a statement by the Secretary of State in which the President's decision not to request the two additional votes for the United States was announced.[12]

The Crimea Conference decision on the question of international trusteeship, readily arrived at, was made closely pursuant to the recommendations submitted by the Department to the President but on which he had made no ruling before his departure. This decision provided that the five nations to have permanent seats on the Security Council should consult together on this question before the United Nations conference and that trusteeship would apply only to (a) existing mandates of the League of Nations, (b) territories detached from the enemy as a result of the present war, and (c) any other territory that might voluntarily be placed under trusteeship. It also provided that no discussion of actual territories was contemplated in the preliminary consultations or at the future conference and that it should be a matter for subsequent agreement which territories in the above categories would be placed under trusteeship.

Agreements on other matters of concern to the remaining preparation were two, as follows: The United States Government on behalf of the three powers would consult the Government of China and the

---

A public statement of the Secretary of State on this matter, Apr. 3, 1945, pointed out: "No agreement was, however, made at Yalta on the question of the participation" of the two Soviet Republics "in the San Francisco Conference." *Department of State Bulletin*, XII, 600–01.

[12] *Ibid.*, pp. 530 and 600–01. For consideration of this action by the Department, see below, p. 422.

French Provisional Government in regard to the decisions of the Crimea Conference bearing on the proposed world organization before announcement of these decisions. The general United Nations conference would be held April 25, 1945, at San Francisco, and the invitation, the draft of which was approved, would be issued by the United States Government on behalf of itself and of the Governments of the United Kingdom, the Union of Soviet Socialist Republics, and the Republic of China and of the Provisional Government of the French Republic.[13]

The suggested list of principal United States Delegates to the general conference was naturally not a subject of discussion by the Crimea Conference, but it was approved by the President during the Conference, February 11. Further mention will be made of this step, in connection with the description of the pre-San Francisco preparations.

Meantime the Mexico City Conference had been called. Secretary Stettinius went from Yalta to Mexico City to lead the American Delegation at this Conference, in which not only problems primarily inter-American in character but also certain major questions relating to general international organization were considered.

THE MEXICO CITY CONFERENCE

THE IMPETUS for the convening of a conference of American republics sprang from several sources, some regional in background and objective, others broadly international in origin and scope. Political, economic, and social problems of common American interest raised by the war or foreseeable after the war were pressing for joint consideration. This need had accumulated because of the postponement of the periodic conference of American states during the war and the lapse of time since the last consultative meeting of Foreign Ministers, which had been held at Rio de Janeiro in 1942. The Conference primarily originated in and was conducted through operational channels, and in large measure the matters to come before it lay within the scope of operations in the Department of State and the other Departments and agencies of the Government having related interests.

The problems of world security organization and the relationships of the inter-American system to the world organization in the aftermath of the war and the longer future were, however, likewise of much concern in all quarters and required inter-American consideration.

---

[13] For texts of the communiqué issued by the three heads of government at the conclusion of the Crimea Conference and of the Protocol of Proceedings of the Conference, subsequently released, see, respectively, the *Department of State Bulletin*, XII, 213–16, and Department of State press release 239 of Mar. 24, 1947.

These were the problems of direct interest to the remaining preparation. Consultation on these problems had begun, as will be recalled, with the exchanges of views inaugurated with the nineteen Latin American republics included among the United and Associated Nations in the circular telegram of July 11, 1944, relative to the problems of establishing a general international organization.[14]

The Committee on Post-War Programs contemplated on July 7, 1944, when it considered the proposal for this exchange of views, that in due course a fourth meeting of the Foreign Ministers of the American Republics might take place on the problems in this field. The exchanges of views were initiated, however, without that prospect definitely in mind.

Further informative steps and diplomatic discussions followed while the Dumbarton Oaks Conversations were under way. Secretary Hull informed the governments of these nineteen other American republics by a circular telegram of September 6, 1944, that their comments concerning international organization received in the past several weeks were being kept in mind and apprised them in general terms of the progress being made at Dumbarton Oaks. In discussions with the Ambassadors of these republics in two groups on September 15 and 16, he summarized the Conversations to date, commented on the views and efforts of the United States toward international security organization, and stated that after the Conversations he wished to discuss the Joint Proposals with the Ambassadors and to explain any points on which they might have questions. At that time he stressed, as did also Norman Armour, then Director of the Office of American Republic Affairs, who was present with the Secretary at these talks, that the United States was trying to preserve on a world-wide basis the principles developed in this Hemisphere and that the inter-American system would have an important role in the framework of the world organization. Both the intention to have further exchanges and the belief that the inter-American system "must play" a "strong and vital role" within the world-wide framework being envisaged were repeated by President Roosevelt in his address three days after the Dumbarton Oaks Proposals were published.[15] Some mention of the desirability of a consultative meeting had been made in related diplomatic talks that had occurred up to this time, but in indefinite terms and with uncertainty regarding its practical possibility at any early date.

The American Group at the Dumbarton Oaks Conversations had on more than one occasion discussed the most desirable ways and the

---

[14] See above, p. 279. Argentina was not included.
[15] Address on Columbus Day, Oct. 12, 1944, *Department of State Bulletin*, **XI**, 397–98.

best time to undertake discussions with the other American republics, and steps toward this end were promptly taken at the close of the Conversations. A reception given by Under Secretary Stettinius to the Chiefs of Diplomatic Missions from the other American republics at Blair House on October 12, 1944, began a series of meetings for systematic but informal interchange of views on the Dumbarton Oaks Proposals. As soon as time had been allowed for comments to be received from at least some of their governments, another "Blair House Meeting" with the chiefs of these missions was held, October 26.[16] This was attended by several visiting United States Ambassadors as well as by several ranking officials of the Department, two of the military and naval representatives, and most of the senior staff members who had taken part in the Dumbarton Oaks Conversations. Similar meetings were held thereafter, mainly in the Department of State.

In the third meeting, on November 9, a Committee of Coordination was appointed to summarize the comments made on the Proposals and the suggestions being received, its membership being constituted of the Ambassadors of Mexico, Uruguay, Venezuela, and Brazil, and Mr. Armour, whose place on the Committee was taken by Nelson A. Rockefeller when the latter was appointed Assistant Secretary of State. Ambassador Carlos Martins of Brazil was subsequently named chairman of this Committee, and John M. Cabot served as secretary. Some of the Committee's staff work was done in the Department, including a collation, prepared in the Division of International Organization Affairs, of the comments and suggestions received from other American republics and of the Dumbarton Oaks Proposals.

After the third meeting, Mr. Stettinius, then Acting Secretary, publicly spoke of being "encouraged by the support that the American republics are showing for the basic ideas" embodied in the Proposals,[17] and in his consultation with Senate leaders on November 24, already referred to in another connection,[18] he noted that his statement had received the prior approval of the Chiefs of Mission. He mentioned also to the Senate group on that date that individual suggestions for improvement of the Proposals were being presented by a number of the Ambassadors.

By this time, a consultative meeting with the Foreign Ministers of the other nineteen participating American republics was being projected [19] to meet January 10, 1945, if practicable. The nature of the desired meeting was clarified as being, in the words of a memorandum

[16] *Ibid.*, XI, 525.
[17] *Ibid.*, p. 565.
[18] See above, p. 380.
[19] *Department of State Bulletin*, XI, 630.

written in the Department of State soon afterward, "not a regular consultative meeting of Foreign Ministers but an inter-American meeting held in accordance with the practice of the American republics to consult together on matters of mutual interest."

By the fourth meeting with the Ambassadors, December 29, 1944, Secretary Stettinius was able to report that the opinion being expressed through diplomatic channels evidenced progress toward the holding of an inter-American conference. He emphasized that at such a conference, the governments represented could continue their thinking on the major issues being considered in the present informal meetings. The understanding of each other's viewpoints gained in these exploratory meetings, he felt, would contribute not only to that conference but to the subsequent general United Nations conference. Mr. Rockefeller emphasized in the same meeting that the developing inter-American conference was not to be defined as a meeting solely of Foreign Ministers.

The plan to hold such a conference became definite as the new year began, and on January 13, 1945, announcement was made of its place, Mexico City. Within a few more days, the date of its opening, February 21, had been definitely decided. The informal exchanges, however, continued and were even intensified until the participants had to start for Mexico City. Five more meetings were held with the Ambassadors: January 5, 26, and 31, and February 5 and 9, 1945, during which the thorough paragraph-by-paragraph discussion of the Dumbarton Oaks Proposals for which the meetings had been instituted was completed. The object of these exchanges from the outset, as stated by Mr. Rockefeller in the fourth meeting, was not to achieve "unified views" or "closed views" but clarification of the Proposals and of the related suggestions received from the participating American republics, with the expectation thereby of arriving at "common informed understanding" in support of the Dumbarton Oaks Proposals and their improvement. These meetings, accordingly, did not constitute a negotiation on the problems concerned but instead a close examination of them in advance of the general United Nations meeting to draft the Charter.

The Inter-American Conference on Problems of War and Peace held by the American republics collaborating in the war effort had a notably broad agenda, for which various of the participating states proposed items. Those suggested by the United States had been developed in December 1944, and an exploratory proposal of an agenda was communicated by circular telegram, January 5, 1945, to the other participating governments. The main headings and subheadings of the United States proposed agenda were also transmitted to President Roosevelt and were approved on January 18, 1945. Its four principal headings were I. Further Cooperative Measures for the Prosecution of the War to Complete Victory; II. Consideration of Problems of International Organization for Peace and Security; III. Consideration of the Economic and Social Problems of the Americas; and IV. Other Matters of General and Immediate Concern to the Participating Governments.

The second heading covered the points of active interest for the remaining extraordinary preparation, including not only matters concerning world organization but several aspects of the further development and strengthening of the inter-American system and its relation to world organization. In its work on these matters, the preparation took into consideration the materials already developed by inter-American organizations, particularly those available from the Inter-American Juridical Committee, the Pan American Union, and former conferences, as well as the views presented in the above informal consultations.

The preparation began actively to consider in January 1945 two other specific problems of major importance. One related to possible regional arrangements, within the inter-American system, for enforcement of peace and security. This envisaged measures not involving the use of armed force, as well as measures that would involve the use of armed force. The other problem related to a Colombian suggestion concerning the possibility of "joint guarantee of boundaries" of the respective American republics, the broad conception of which had been approved in principle by President Roosevelt in conversation with President Eduardo Santos of Colombia and Assistant Secretary Rockefeller on January 9, 1945. These problems called for searching consideration of the question of self-defense against threats or acts of aggression, and of the nature of arrangements and procedures for dealing with matters appropriate for regional action in connection with the maintenance of international peace and security. The initiatory role in developing United States views on the inter-American aspects of these problems was operational, while the initiatory role as regards their general international aspects and with respect to the relationship of regional arrangements to those of a world organization lay with the remaining extraordinary preparation. The intermingling of these two aspects of the work was reflected in the structural arrangements employed to arrive at the United States policy recommendations on the manifold problems to be considered at the approaching conference.

The preparatory work for the coming conference evolved, like the conference itself, in relation to the informal consultations on general international organization. Beginning October 17, 1944, a joint group, composed of staff experts drawn from divisions of the operating office—the Office of American Republic Affairs—and from the Office of

Special Political Affairs and its divisions, acted in an advisory and recommendatory capacity for these consultations. This informal joint group was in effect the successor of the Subcommittee on International Organization that had functioned under the Latin America Area Committee. It was later absorbed into a new and formalized structure, created at the end of the year, through which all advance work for the conference, both of extraordinary and of usual preparatory character, was completed between January 1, 1945, and February 12, 1945.

A Steering Committee of superior officials headed the new structure and was authorized to approve recommendations submitted to it, to make recommendations to the Secretary of·State, and to give final approval to the arrangements for the conference to be proposed by this Government to the Governing Board of the Pan American Union. This Committee, composed of Assistant Secretaries Rockefeller, Chairman, Acheson, and Clayton, Mr. Pasvolsky, and the Director of the Office of American Republics Affairs, Avra M. Warren, convened formally under its mandate only once—after the substantive papers were ready for its approval.

Principal activity at a policy level during the period in which papers were being developed was vested in a Policy Committee. This Committee was charged to "determine policy with regard to all matters on the agenda in light of our relations with the other American republics and to give appropriate instructions to the committees mentioned hereafter." Mr. Rockefeller served as its Chairman, the further membership being constituted of his assistants and the appropriate officers from the Office of American Republic Affairs,[20] with the addition of Mr. Berle, at this date Ambassador to Brazil. This Committee held 18 meetings January 17–February 7, 1945.

Two "working groups," or committees, were established. One was for economic problems, reporting to Assistant Secretary Clayton who had responsibility for the development of United States policy and proposals in this field. Since all work on this subject was operational, its description must be omitted here, although it is to be noted that resolutions on economic subjects to be introduced in the conference were discussed with the ECEFP and with Members of Congress before the United States position was made definitive. The other working group dealt with political problems, among which were the problems of inter-American relationships and world organization still of concern to the preparation. The members of this latter group were Avra Warren, Chairman, John M. Cabot, Vice Chairman, John Dreier, Louis

---

[20] The constant core of its membership was composed of Avra M. Warren, Dana C. Munro, John E. Lockwood, John C. McClintock, Dudley B. Bonsal, John M. Cabot, William Sanders, and John C. Drier, with Robert G. McGregor, Jr., and Harry W. Frantz frequently participating.

J. Halle, Jr., Joseph E. Johnson, Miss Marcia V. N. Maylott, Harley Notter, and William Sanders. Dudley Bonsal, Executive Secretary of the Policy Committee, referred to above, and his assistant, James Espy, also usually took part. This group, like the informal joint group from which it developed,[21] usually met daily, and it normally joined the meetings of the Policy Committee to consider the drafts that the group had formulated. Necessary liaison on agenda matters with the War and Navy Departments, and particularly with the United States officers assigned to duty with the Inter-American Defense Board, was conducted through operational channels.

The above structure was superseded on February 13, 1945. That day the United States Delegation met for general organizing purposes before leaving for the Conference in Mexico City. Since the Delegation included a large proportion of the officers active in the advance work—the superiors as "advisers" and the experts as "technical officers"—the organization of the Delegation was such as largely to continue at the Conference the allocation of functions followed in preparing for it.

The United States Delegate and Alternate Delegate were Secretary Stettinius and Assistant Secretary Rockefeller, respectively. The special congressional advisers, constituted on a bipartisan basis, included two members of the Senate Foreign Relations Committee, Senators Tom Connally and Warren R. Austin, and two members of the House Foreign Affairs Committee, Representative Luther A. Johnson serving in the place of Representative Sol Bloom, who could not attend, and Representative Edith Nourse Rogers, Republican of Massachusetts. As will be recalled, the first three of these congressional members had participated in the extraordinary preparation under the Advisory Committee on Post-War Foreign Policy and in the later congressional consultations. These same members, although taking part in other fields of the Conference, in which Congresswoman Rogers was especially active, devoted their attention particularly to the major problems on which the postwar preparation was still continuing.

The Delegation was broadly representative of interested Departments and agencies of this Government. Over a third of the advisers had been active in the extraordinary preparation, serving on the committees in the political and security fields or on one or more of the general and special economic committees. These included Generals Embick and Strong, Admiral Train, Mr. Berle, Mr. Clayton, Oscar Cox, Green H. Hackworth, Eric A. Johnston, Miss Katharine F. Len-

---

[21] The members of the former joint group, which informally had the name of the Latin America Working Committee, had been Messrs. Cabot, Notter, Johnson, and Ivan Stone, and Miss Maylott, all but the first and third being from the research staff.

root, Leo Pasvolsky, Warren Lee Pierson, Wayne C. Taylor, and Leslie A. Wheeler.[22]   Only a small proportion of the technical experts, on the other hand, were drawn from among the officers active in the preparation on postwar problems.

At the Conference, the problems of concern to the extraordinary preparation, though now also of concern to the normal operations through which American foreign policy and relations are carried out, were within the purview particularly of committee II, World Organization, and committee III, Inter-American System.   The important substantive resolutions in regard to economic and social advancement were considered in committees IV and V, and several projects of widespread interest on military subjects, elimination of centers of subversive influence, and war crimes were placed within the jurisdiction of committee I.   Texts were coordinated by committee VI and adopted in Plenary Session.   Of the sixty-one resolutions adopted, only a small number were directly pertinent to the remaining preparation.

Secretary Stettinius was elected Chairman of committee II, of which the Honorable Guil'ermo Belt of Cuba was Vice Chairman and the Honorable Caracciolo Parra Pérez of Venezuela was Reporting Delegate.   The resolution "On Establishment of a General International Organization" (resolution XXX) resulting from this committee's intensive discussions was based on a Mexican proposal and declared the determination of the American republics to cooperate in the establishment of a general international organization "based upon law, justice and equity."   This resolution endorsed the Dumbarton Oaks Proposals as a basis for the setting up of a world organization to achieve peace and promote the welfare of all nations.   At the same time the resolution set forth the following points which, in the opinion of the participating Latin American governments, should be taken into consideration in formulating the Charter at the San Francisco Conference:

"a) The aspiration of universality as an ideal toward which the Organization should tend in the future;
"b) The desirability of amplifying and making more specific the enumeration of the principles and purposes of the Organization;
"c) The desirability of amplifying and making more specific the powers of the General Assembly in order that its action, as the fully representative organ of the international community may be rendered effective, harmonizing the powers of the Security Council with such amplification;

---

[22] The full list of the Delegation is contained in the Report Submitted to the Governing Board of the Pan American Union by the Director General, entitled *Inter-American Conference on Problems of War and Peace*, Mexico City, February 21–March 8, 1945 (Pan American Union, Washington, D. C., 1945), pp. 105–6.

"d) The desirability of extending the jurisdiction and competence of the International Tribunal or Court of Justice;

"e) The desirability of creating an international agency specially charged with promoting intellectual and moral cooperation among nations;

"f) The desirability of solving controversies and questions of an inter-American character, preferably in accordance with inter-American methods and procedures, in harmony with those of the General International Organization;

"g) The desirability of giving an adequate representation to Latin America on the Security Council."

From committee III, presided over by the Honorable Alberto Lleras Camargo of Colombia, emanated the declaration and recommendation of "Reciprocal Assistance and American Solidarity" (resolution VIII), formally called the Act of Chapultepec, which was an outgrowth of the Colombian suggestion referred to above. This resolution declared that "every attack of a State against the integrity or the inviolability of the territory, or against the sovereignty or political independence of an American State, shall . . . be considered as an act of aggression against the other States which sign this Act." It provided for consultation among the members "in order to agree upon the measures it may be advisable to take," subsequent action to be taken under the constitutional powers and processes of the individual members. The measures set forth encompassed not only procedures not involving use of armed force, but for the first time within the inter-American system, "the use of armed force to prevent or repel aggression." In its closing part it recommended the subsequent conclusion of a treaty to meet threats or acts of aggression.[23] It was specifically provided that the arrangements and procedures contemplated in the declaration and the recommendation should be consistent with the purposes and principles of the future Charter of the general international organization. The same committee also considered the resolution (IX) on "Reorganization, Consolidation and Strengthening of the Inter-American System," introduced by the United States Delegation. This resolution, among other far-reaching provisions, contemplated that the regional system should "maintain the closest relations with the proposed general international organization." [24]

These resolutions concluded the process of organized consultation with other American republics bearing wholly or in appreciable

---

[23] Negotiated at Rio de Janeiro in 1947 as the Inter-American Treaty of Reciprocal Assistance, which became effective in 1948.

[24] For a detailed account of this Conference, see *Report of the Delegation of the United States of America to the Inter-American Conference on Problems of War and Peace*, Department of State publication 2497, Conference Series 85.

measure upon the subjects of negotiation at the San Francisco Conference.

A number of steps toward calling that conference were taken by Secretary Stettinius while attending the Mexico City Conference and during the same period by the Department of State in Washington. These steps set in motion the activities with which the extraordinary preparation concluded.

CHAPTER XXI

End of Preparation
For General International Organization

INVITATIONS TO the United Nations Conference to be held on April 25, 1945, at San Francisco, California, "to prepare a charter for a general international organization for the maintenance of international peace and security" were issued as the foregoing inter-American resolutions were being adopted. It had required almost exactly five months after the last session of the Dumbarton Oaks Conversations to make possible this further step toward the Charter of the United Nations.

INVITATIONS TO THE SAN FRANCISCO CONFERENCE

DURING THE three weeks after the Crimea Conference, consultations were carried out with the Chinese Government and with the Provisional French Government in regard to the text of the invitations and the nations to receive them, the voting formula, the time and place of the conference, and the association of these powers with the three governments represented at Yalta as joint sponsors of the conference. These consultations were initiated on February 12, 1945, by the United States acting on behalf of the three originating powers, as had been agreed upon at Yalta and as had been recommended to the President by the Secretary of State. Since the time required for such consultation entailed delay in announcing the Yalta agreement on voting procedure, that agreement was discussed over the week-end of February 16 by Assistant Secretary Acheson with the larger Senate group regularly consulted on the problems of establishing a general international organization, and by Acting Secretary Grew with the smaller senatorial group, which had also been consistently included in the Department's discussions of these problems.

President Roosevelt, by telegram on February 23, informed Secretary Stettinius at Mexico City and Acting Secretary Grew in Washington that he was leaving the decisions concerning the date of issuance of the invitations and the publication of the voting formula to the

Secretary of State without further reference to the President, but he expressed a preference for having the invitations issued before March 1. By the time of this telegram, the Chinese Government had approved the voting formula and agreed to join with the United States, the United Kingdom, and the Union of Soviet Socialist Republics in sponsoring the forthcoming conference and the invitations to it. The Provisional French Government, in a note handed Ambassador Jefferson Caffery in Paris on February 24, agreed to participate in the conference. It stated, however, that it could not undertake sponsorship unless the text of the invitation set forth the French desire for the adoption of certain unspecified amendments to the Dumbarton Oaks Proposals, in the formulation of which it had not participated, and unless the invitation stated that these amendments would serve as a basis for discussion at the San Francisco Conference together with the Proposals themselves.

These French conditions were not consistent with the Crimea decision that the Dumbarton Oaks Proposals, supplemented by the voting formula, should serve as the basis for discussion at San Francisco. Efforts toward removing the conditions to the French acceptance of sponsorship proved unproductive, although the issuance of the invitations was delayed five days in an attempt to find acceptable phrasing that would to some extent accommodate the French wishes. Accordingly, there were but four sponsors. Shortness of time precluded more protracted negotiation with the French to obtain their agreement to the Proposals, and this Government took the view, furthermore, that all the nations participating in the conference, including the sponsoring powers, would be free to introduce proposals and comments for the consideration of the conference.

The invitations, together with a statement approved by the President commenting analytically on the proposed voting formula contained in the text of the invitations, were issued by this Government at 12 noon March 5, 1945, eastern war time, and released in Washington at the same time. The four sponsoring Governments suggested in their invitations that the Conference "consider as affording a basis for . . . a charter the proposals" resulting from the Dumbarton Oaks Conversations "which have now been supplemented by the following provisions. . . ." The voting formula, as approved by President Roosevelt November 15, 1944, and accepted at Yalta, was then quoted:

" '1. Each member of the Security Council should have one vote.
" '2. Decisions of the Security Council on procedural matters should be made by an affirmative vote of seven members.
" '3. Decisions of the Security Council on all other matters should be made by an affirmative vote of seven members including the concurring votes of the permanent members; provided that, in decisions under Chapter VIII, Section A, and under the second sentence of

Paragraph 1 of Chapter VIII, Section C, a party to a dispute should abstain from voting.' " [1]

The text of the invitation was read by Secretary Stettinius to committee II, in the Castle of Chapultepec, Mexico City, at the same time that it was released in Washington.

The sponsors' invitations were addressed to each of the nations at war by March 1, 1945, with Germany or Japan, or with both. [2] By that date, Turkey, Saudi Arabia, and all former Associated Nations except Iceland had qualified for membership in the United Nations. Poland, the remaining member of this wartime association, could not be invited because it was still without the representative government contemplated under the Yalta Agreement concerning that country. Subsequently, on March 30, invitations were extended to Syria and Lebanon after these two states had adhered to the United Nations Declaration. [3]

President Roosevelt meanwhile had returned to Washington, and addressed the Congress, March 1, on the Crimea Conference. Because consultation on French sponsorship was still in progress, he had to state that it was "not yet possible to announce the terms of the agreement" on the voting procedure. He spoke of the hope and expectation that the San Francisco Conference would "execute a definite charter of organization under which the peace of the world will be preserved and the forces of aggression permanently outlawed." He then added:

---

[1] These provisions, as stated in the invitations, were for section C of chap. VI of the Proposals. *Department of State Bulletin*, XII, 394, 396. Subsequently, on Mar. 24, 1945, a further explanatory analysis of this formula was issued by the Department, in which the United States position that there was nothing in the voting formula to preclude the Organization from "*discussing*" any dispute or situation which might threaten the peace and security by the act of any one of its members" was categorically stated. *Ibid.*, p. 479.

[2] These were Commonwealth of Australia, Kingdom of Belgium, Republic of Bolivia, United States of Brazil, Canada, Republic of Chile, Republic of Colombia, Republic of Costa Rica, Republic of Cuba, Czechoslovak Republic, Dominican Republic, Republic of Ecuador, Kingdom of Egypt, Republic of El Salvador, Empire of Ethiopia, Kingdom of Greece, Republic of Guatemala, Republic of Haiti, Republic of Honduras, India, Empire of Iran, Kingdom of Iraq, Republic of Liberia, the Grand Duchy of Luxembourg, United Mexican States, Kingdom of the Netherlands, Dominion of New Zealand, Republic of Nicaragua, Kingdom of Norway, Republic of Panama, Republic of Paraguay, Republic of Peru, Commonwealth of the Philippines, Kingdom of Saudi Arabia, Republic of Turkey, Union of South Africa, Oriental Republic of Uruguay, United States of Venezuela, Kingdom of Yugoslavia.

[3] Actual signature of the Declaration by Lebanon, Saudi Arabia, and Syria took place Apr. 12, 1945. The final total number of United Nations, 47, was attained with these signatures.

"This time we shall not make the mistake of waiting until the end of the war to set up the machinery of peace. This time, as we fight together to get the war over quickly, we work together to keep it from happening again."

Saying that he was "well aware" that the Senate must consent to the ratification of the Charter, he announced:

'The Senate of the United States, through its appropriate representatives, has been kept continuously advised of the program of this government in the creation of the international security organization.

"The Senate and the House of Representatives will both be represented at the San Francisco conference. The congressional delegates to the San Francisco conference will consist of an equal number of Republican and Democratic members. The American Delegation is—in every sense of the word—bipartisan."

In this address, the President more than once emphasized that the resulting plan would not be perfect. He said that whatever was "adopted at San Francisco will doubtless have to be amended time and again over the years, just as our own Constitution has been." Nevertheless, he stated in conclusion:

"There will soon be presented to the Senate of the United States and to the American people a great decision which will determine the fate of the United States—and of the world—for generations to come.

"There can be no middle ground here. We shall have to take the responsibility for world collaboration, or we shall have to bear the responsibility for another world conflict." [4]

The time between these developments in the first week of March 1945 and the opening session of the United Nations Conference at San Francisco in the last week of April constituted a preconference period of approximately seven weeks. In this period, the several aspects of the remaining preparation for a general international organization were either concluded or the way made ready for their conclusion early in the Conference itself.

The Conference, as such, did not constitute part of the preparation, but rather provided the occasion for the ultimate utilization in negotiation of the proposals developed through the extraordinary preparation in this field. Nevertheless, it was in the special consultations held during the opening days of the Conference that the preparation was concluded. Accordingly, the Conference is described here only in so far as seems necessary to complete the description of the terminal work of preparation and the context of developments in which it was accomplished.

---

[4] Text printed in *Department of State Bulletin*, XII, 321–26 and 361.

Three principal aspects of work having a substantive character were outstanding in the preparation during this period of seven weeks: joint proposals for the Statute of the International Court of Justice; proposals for international trusteeship; and recommendations for additions to, or modifications of, the Dumbarton Oaks Proposals in the light of the views and suggestions received from other governments and from the American public, or of further study by officials concerned with this broad field. Preparation on each of these aspects took place concurrently.

Integrally related to them were the further congressional consultations held in the Department during March, the assembling of the United States Delegation for the announced conference, and the pre-conference work with the Delegates beginning in March. These developments will be described first.

CONCLUDING CONGRESSIONAL CONSULTATIONS

THE CONSULTATIONS with the large Senate consulting group on the morning of March 15, 1945, with the "B_2H_2" group of Senators on the afternoon of that day, and with the group of leaders of the House of Representatives on the morning of the 16th, were held by Secretary Stettinius as soon after his return from the Crimea and Mexico City Conferences as arrangements could be made. The subjects common to the three consultations were "Plans for the World Security Conference at San Francisco," "The Yalta Conference," and, though more in a reporting sense than as a matter for discussion, "The Mexico City Conference." The Secretary mentioned in all three gatherings that arrangements were "now going forward for a preliminary meeting of United Nations lawyers to be held on April 9 in Washington" and that discussion of trusteeship was being undertaken among the State, War, and Navy Departments "looking toward an agreed United States position," which was essential before international consultations on this subject could take place among the sponsor powers.

The consultative meeting with the larger Senate group was attended by Senators Connally, Barkley, Gillette, and Thomas (Democrats) and Vandenberg, Austin, and White (Republicans), with Messrs. Stettinius, Acheson, Dunn, Pasvolsky, Rockefeller, Hackworth, Matthews, Bohlen, Raynor, and Charles P. Noyes [5] present for the Department of State. Consideration was given, in connection with our views on the Charter, to the intention of providing through separate legisla-

---

[5] Appointed Assistant to Secretary Stettinius ten days earlier. Senators George, Democrat, and La Follette, Progressive, of the group were absent from this meeting.

tive authorization after the international organization had been established military, naval, and air contingents for use by the projected Security Council of the organization; to the provision to be made in the Charter respecting regulation of armament; and to the Soviet Union's general attitude toward participation in the proposed international organization.[6] Problems relating to the designation and powers of the United States "Delegate" to the United Nations after ratification of the Charter were also briefly mentioned, and the progress of the negotiations to establish a Polish Government representing all the major political parties in Poland was reviewed.

In the next consultative meeting, which was attended by Senators Ball, Burton, Hatch, and Hill and by the same members of the Department with one exception,[7] the voting formula, trusteeship, and the position of France in regard to the coming conference were major topics. Those present at the third meeting were Representatives Rayburn, McCormack, Bloom, and Ramspeck (Democrats) and Martin, Eaton, and Arends (Republicans), again together with the same Department members. Discussion on this occasion largely concerned the court, the voting formula, and trusteeship.

While an allusion was made in the latter gathering to the possibility of a further meeting in the Department perhaps a month hence, these three meetings proved to be the last in the long series of organized congressional consultations, which had been inaugurated one year before and which, in effect, had succeeded the discussions with Members of Congress in the weekly meetings during 1942–43 of the Subcommittee on Political Problems under the Advisory Committee on Post-War Foreign Policy. However, the participation on the United States Delegation to the San Francisco Conference of the two Senators and the two Representatives having direct responsibility for the majority and the minority leadership of the Senate Foreign Relations Committee and the House Foreign Affairs Committee, respectively, had already been announced. The first of the preconference meetings of the Delegation had taken place, as will be seen below, just before these last congressional consultations were held. "Nonpartisan" congressional and party consultation in the preparation of United States policy proposals was thus transformed into participation on a "bipartisan" (as described by the President) basis in the decisive negotiation of those proposals.

---

[6] This meeting with Members of the Congress and the two others next described were before the release by the White House of information on the question of "three votes" already referred to above, p. 384, and no discussion of it appears in the records.

[7] Mr. Bohlen could not attend this meeting.

By the middle of March 1945, accordingly, the structure used by the Delegation to the San Francisco Conference had taken form sufficiently to supplant the prior arrangements for congressional consultation in this field and, not long after, those for party consultation as well. *Ad hoc* consultations continued to occur not infrequently in the preconference period between Senators and Representatives and ranking Departmental officials, but such talks were on an individual footing and were mainly, though not exclusively, held with the two Senators and the two Representatives named to the Delegation.

THE UNITED STATES DELEGATION

CONSIDERATION OF the composition of the United States Delegation to the projected United Nations conference, particularly of the members to have the rank of delegate, was initiated by the preparatory staff promptly after the Dumbarton Oaks Conversations. The most active consideration of this problem, however, occurred in late December 1944 and early January 1945, and the suggested list of United States Delegates—though not of the entire Delegation—was arrived at prior to the Crimea Conference. The final recommendations submitted to the President were formulated at the highest official level of the Department, and while the officers engaged in the preparation contributed to these recommendations, they reflected primarily an over-all Departmental judgment.

After mid-January 1945, the work of the remaining preparatory structure was almost exclusively substantive in character, centering upon the completion of United States proposals in regard to the Charter. This development was clarified by the differentiation made near the outset of the preconference period, on March 16, 1945, between such remaining preparation on the one hand and the administrative problems and arrangements concerning the Delegation and the Conference itself on the other.

The division of the total conference burden was made on that date in order to concentrate in different superior officials the two main types of work that had devolved upon the Department on behalf of this Government as a participant in and as host to the Conference. The substantive work was continued under the responsibility of the ranking official, Mr. Pasvolsky, who under the Secretary of State had been charged throughout the preparation with such work. The administrative responsibility for the composition and working structure of the Delegation and for the Secretariat of the Conference and related arrangements was vested by the Secretary of State in Mr. Dunn, his ranking assistant in these respects throughout the preconference period.

The two lines of work were coordinated by the Secretary of State and his own office assistants, particularly G. Hayden Raynor and Robert Lynch. Various superior officials were consulted or called upon to assist and Mr. Pasvolsky and Mr. Dunn conferred at intervals on problems of common concern. Immediately below the rank of Assistant Secretary or its equivalent, however, the differentiation between the two lines was such that those concerned with the administrative arrangements did not take part in the remaining substantive preparation. This distinction was maintained in the daily activity preparatory to the Conference and was reflected in the meetings of the Delegation. Only the four earliest meetings, before the Delegation concentrated on substantive problems, were attended by officers having administrative responsibilities in connection with conference arrangements.

At the office level, the arrangements were in charge of Alger Hiss, who was appointed by the Secretary to be Director of the Office of Special Political Affairs, effective March 19, and who was designated by the Secretary to organize the arrangements, with John C. Ross, Director of the Office of Departmental Administration, as deputy for that purpose. These two senior officers later became, respectively, the Secretary General and the Deputy Secretary General of the Conference.

Most of the other officers assisting in the making of the Conference arrangements under the direction of Messrs. Hiss and Ross were drawn from the Staff Committee Secretariat, from the Department's various operating offices and divisions, and from the Foreign Service. These officers were later assigned to carry out the responsibilities of the Secretariat for the Conference as a whole.[8] They, together with the two senior directing officers, were therefore called upon to perform their duties at the Conference on an international basis, and to begin to act

---

[8] In addition to the officers of the Conference named above, a large Secretariat was needed for the Conference itself. This was principally provided, as noted above, through assignment to these temporary Secretariat posts from the Department of State, including the Foreign Service, but also from other parts of the Government and from private life. Moreover, other participating Governments made available certain personnel, particularly in the language fields. Those serving on the Secretariat who had formerly had experience on the staff of the extraordinary preparation, or were assigned from the existing preparatory staff, were Messrs. Rothwell (the Executive Secretary), Berdahl, Brown, Chamberlin, Chase, Gideonse, Green, Halderman, Ireland, Kirk, Maktos, Masland, Myers, Padelford, Pfankuchen, Power, Stone, Vandenbosch, Wood, and Yale; Misses Armstrong, Ball, Fluegel, and Sullivan; and Mrs. Preuss. Several others, including Messrs. Dreier, Guthe, Kelchner, and Stewart, had been to some extent associated with the preparation in their operational capacities. For a complete list of officers of the Conference, see *The United Nations Conference on International Organization: Selected Documents*, 1946, Department of State publication 2490, Conference Series 83, pp. 25–35.

on this basis even in the preconference period. The work and development of the Conference Secretariat did not, however, constitute an integral part of the remaining extraordinary preparation under exposition here.

In contrast, the work on the procedures and administrative arrangements that were needed for the United States Delegation was undertaken by the same group of staff experts from the component divisions of the Office of Special Political Affairs who were taking part in the remaining substantive preparation, with Mr. Sandifer, Chief of the Division of International Organization Affairs, acting as liaison officer between this group and those at higher levels in charge of the administrative arrangements as a whole. This smaller number of officers were also to perform the secretariat duties for the United States Delegation, serving, of course, on a strictly national basis. Normally these officers also functioned as technical experts on the Delegation. This was in conformity with the practice established early in the preparation of having professional experts themselves undertake whatever secretariat duties were required. To a degree, therefore, the work of the United States Delegation Secretariat was a function of the remaining preparation, and at the technical level this Secretariat provided the necessary integration with the Conference Secretariat.

As noted earlier, the President, while at the Crimea Conference, had approved on February 11, 1945, the recommended list of eight delegates. These were Secretary of State Edward R. Stettinius, Jr., Chairman; the Honorable Cordell Hull, Senior Adviser; Senator Tom Connally (Democrat); Senator Arthur H. Vandenberg (Republican); Representative Sol Bloom (Democrat); Representative Charles A. Eaton (Republican); Commander Harold E. Stassen (Republican), former Governor of Minnesota and at this time in the United States Naval Reserve on active service, who in his general capacity represented the public and particularly the veterans' interest, in the maintenance of future peace and security; and Miss Virginia C. Gildersleeve, Dean of Barnard College, who represented no political party but rather the interests of American women in this field and, in general, the interest of the public at large.[9] Mr. Hull, though in improved health, was not able to join the Delegation either in its preconference work or at San Francisco. Though the number of active Delegates was thus reduced to seven, Mr. Hull was kept in close touch with the work of the Delegation by telephone and telegraph. The other Delegates and a number of officials of the Department of State convened in their first meeting on March 13, 1945. This meeting in the Department instituted the series of formal Delegation meetings that henceforth provided the authorized body to arrive at the concluding recommen-

_____

[9] The list was published Feb. 13, 1945, *Department of State Bulletin,* XII, 217.

dations on United States proposals in regard to the Charter of the United Nations.

The selection of the advisers to the Delegation occurred gradually over several weeks. Eleven were appointed as "Department of State" advisers. Of these, Messrs. Dunn, Hackworth, and Pasvolsky, together with the two Special Advisers to the Secretary, Messrs. Bowman and Armstrong, were of superior rank and constituted in fact "general" or "principal" advisers of the Delegation, as they were sometimes called. It was intended that these five should function in all fields and especially as senior negotiators. Charles W. Taussig, Chairman of the United States Section of the Anglo-American Caribbean Commission, was adviser with particular reference to trusteeship. John D. Hickerson, Deputy Director of the Office of European Affairs, and Avra M. Warren, Director of the Office of American Republic Affairs, who had recently been associated with the relevant problems of international organization that had been considered at the Mexico City Conference, were advisers charged with responsibility for negotiations with delegations on the entire range of problems concerned in the Conference, Mr. Warren to act exclusively in relation to the delegations of the other American republics. Messrs. Notter and Stinebower, the advisers who had been the respective heads of the political and economic staffs of experts gathered for the postwar work in the Department, had wide general responsibility in their fields and functioned as negotiators in any absence of the United States Delegate on the Conference commissions and committees to which each was assigned.[10]

The inclusion of John Foster Dulles, whose acceptance of Secretary Stettinius' invitation of April 2 completed the appointments to the "Department of State" advisers on the Delegation [11] and who served largely as a "principal" adviser, brought directly into the concluding preparation in this field the representative through whom, and with whom, the party consultations inaugurated by Secretary Hull with Governor Thomas E. Dewey in the previous summer had been carried on. Substantial negotiating responsibility on various major problems was carried by Mr. Dulles in the Conference commissions and committees and in related meetings.[12]

---

[10] Charles P. Taft was also named as an adviser from the Department of State, but did not attend the Conference.

[11] The letter of acceptance, Apr. 4, 1945, is published in the *Department of State Bulletin*, XII, 608.

[12] Assistant Secretaries Holmes, Rockefeller, and MacLeish and Adlai E. Stevenson, Special Assistant to the Secretary of State to work in the public relations field on matters relating to postwar international organization, were also present at the Conference in pursuance of their regular responsibilities in the Department of State.

Seventeen advisers were appointed to represent other Departments and agencies. These appointments were all made on the nomination of these other Departments and agencies at the request of the Department of State in March, and were automatically accepted. Those from the War and Navy Departments and the Joint Chiefs of Staff included Generals Embick and Fairchild of the Joint Strategic Survey Committee of the Joint Chiefs of Staff; Admiral Hepburn, Chairman of the General Board of the Navy, Admiral Willson of the Joint Strategic Survey Committee; and Admiral Train of the Joint Post-War Committee of the Joint Chiefs of Staff. Each of these had long experience in the extraordinary preparation. Assistant Secretary John J. McCloy, Maj. Gen. R. L. Walsh, and Brig. Gen. Kenner Hertford of the War Department and Assistant Secretary Artemus L. Gates of the Navy Department, completed the advisers representing the armed services.

On the civilian side, Abe Fortas, Under Secretary of the Interior; Assistant Secretary of the Treasury Harry D. White; Frank A. Waring, Special Assistant to the Secretary of Commerce; and Oscar Cox, Deputy Administrator of the Foreign Economic Administration, had participated in various interdepartmental phases of the preparation. The other civilian advisers were the Solicitor General of the United States, Charles Fahy; Assistant Secretary Charles F. Brannan of the Department of Agriculture; Assistant Secretary Daniel W. Tracy of the Labor Department; and Donald C. Stone, Assistant Director of the Bureau of Budget.

In the fiscal field, four Members of Congress were invited by Acting Secretary of State Grew on April 25 "to proceed to San Francisco at an appropriate time to confer with the United States Delegation on the budgetary problems which will arise later at the United Nations Conference on International Organization." This group was again bipartisan. It consisted of Senators Pat McCarran, Democrat of Nevada, and Wallace H. White, Jr., Republican of Maine, and of Representatives Louis C. Rabaut, Democrat of Michigan, and Karl Stefan, Republican of Nebraska, the Chairmen and the ranking minority members, respectively, of the subcommittees for the Department of State of the Senate and House Committees on Appropriations.[13] Senator White, it will be recalled, had been a member of the Subcommittee on Political Problems of the Advisory Committee on Post-War Foreign Policy.

---

[13] *Department of State Bulletin*, XII, 802. Senator White was unable to attend, but Senator McCarran and Representatives Rabaut and Stefan subsequently consulted with the Delegation in San Francisco. *Report to the President on the Results of the San Francisco Conference*, June 26, 1945, Department of State publication 2349, Conference Series 71, p. 256. Certain other Senators also visited San Francisco and consulted with the Delegation during the Conference.

The fourteen political and liaison officers on the Delegation included several officers of the Department of State who had been connected with the preparation in its later stages, particularly Joseph W. Ballantine, Charles E. Bohlen, and Henry S. Villard.[14] These fourteen officers were responsible for assisting in negotiations with the delegations from countries situated within the area of particular concern to their respective offices in the Department.

The composition of the Delegation at its technical level also showed the marked extent to which the structure for the extraordinary preparation in this field was carried over into the negotiating structure. The technical experts on the Delegation, who rendered direct assistance to Delegates, were drawn very largely from the special staff for that preparation. The officers from this staff included the three chief technical experts, Messrs. Sandifer and Gerig, who also served respectively as the Secretary General and Deputy Secretary General of the Delegation, and Joseph E. Johnson, who had not joined the special staff until December 1944 but who had previously participated briefly in the Dumbarton Oaks Conversations. Other technical experts who had taken a direct part in the preparation were Messrs. Hartley, Blaisdell, Bunche, Kotschnig, Preuss, Young, Cordier, Eagleton, Howard, Reiff, Tomlinson, Adams, Buehrig, and Roberts, Miss Fosdick who also served as Special Assistant to the Secretary General, Miss Maylott, Mrs. Brunauer, and Mrs. McDiarmid; William Sanders had joined the special staff just prior to the Conference.

Of the remaining technical experts on the civilian side, Carlton Savage had assisted the Secretary in his congressional consultations in this field. Otis E. Mulliken had been closely associated with the work on labor and social problems, as had Bryn J. Hovde on cultural problems, while Miss Marjorie M. Whiteman had assisted Mr. Hackworth on legal problems and had been his special assistant at the meeting of the Committee of Jurists discussed below. Philip C. Jessup, professor of international law at Columbia University, continued as a technical expert on the Delegation the work, shortly to be described, that he had begun in connection with the joint proposals for the Statute of the Court.

---

[14] Several others, including Paul H. Alling and John M. Cabot, had been to some extent associated with the work in their operational capacities.

Since the description of the Delegation in this volume does not include a substantial number of its personnel, as, for example, the special assistants and assistants to the Chairman, the assistants to Delegates, the public liaison officer and his special assistants, who were important in the Conference but whose work is not entirely germane here, reference is made for a full list of the Delegation to the Department publication *The United Nations Conference on International Organization: Selected Documents*, previously cited, pp. 59–63.

The Delegation's technical experts included also a number of Army, Navy, and Air Force officers, one of whom, Lt. Bernard Brodie, United States Naval Reserve, was on detail to the Department of State on the staff of the Division of International Security Affairs, a part of the preparatory staff. Col. P. M. Hamilton and Commodore T. P. Jeter, United States Navy, were from the Joint Post-War Committee of the Joint Chiefs of Staff, while Lt. Frederick Holdsworth was of the Joint Strategic Survey Committee of the Joint Chiefs. Col. Charles H. Bonesteel, 3d, was of the War Department General Staff and Lt. Col. W. A. McRae was of the Army Air Forces. Several of these experts had been associated for varying periods with their superior officers in the conduct of the preparation.

The important documentary and related forms of assistance required by the Delegations were supplied in large measure by professional officers drawn mainly from the preparatory staff.[15]

Attendance at Delegation meetings was restricted and was somewhat smaller in the preconference period than later. Active participation in meetings was as a rule confined to Delegates, the "Department of State" advisers, the ranking advisers from the War and Navy Departments and the Joint Chiefs of Staff, and the Secretary General of the Delegation. Other advisers took part upon occasion when matters of concern to their respective Departments and agencies were under discussion, as did, in their respective fields, Assistant Secretaries Rockefeller, MacLeish, and Holmes, and Mr. Stevenson. The chief technical experts Messrs. Gerig and Johnson, the Special Assistant to the Chairman Mr. Raynor, and two of the technical experts, Mr. Hartley and Miss Fosdick, regularly attended the Delegation meetings, and three assistants to the congressional members of the Delegation, Messrs. Boyd Crawford, Robert V. Shirley, and Francis O. Wilcox, were usually present. The Delegation press officer and public liaison officer frequently attended. Individual technical experts were invited when matters within their particular competence were under consideration. Assigned technical experts, and particularly Miss Fosdick, also served as recording secretary for the meetings.

The Delegation did not function in the Conference or before on the basis of official instructions: it formulated its own views, and, apart from those of such importance that they were submitted as recom-

---

[15] Those from this staff were Mrs. Virginia F. Hartley, George V. Blue, Philip M. Burnett, and Lawrence Finkelstein, and Misses Alice Bartlett, Suzanne Green, Elizabeth Driscoll, M. Kathleen Bell, Jean Turnbull, Betty Gough, Jeannette E. Muther, and Jane Wheeler. Miss Louise White, also a member of the staff, served as administrative officer for the Delegation. For the additional personnel, drawn from the State and War Departments, see *ibid.*, p. 63.

mendations through its Chairman to the President for his approval, the Delegation negotiated directly on the basis of the views it formulated, the President being kept constantly informed of all developments. In the preconference period, its views took the form almost wholly of recommendations. Its nearest approach to negotiation in this period was the presentation of its views to the Secretary of State on his request for guidance, in his own preconference negotiations with the other sponsoring powers, on questions relevant to the coming conference. Its conclusions were determined at all times on the basis of majority approval, any Delegate holding contrary views being free as an individual to discuss them publicly, but every effort was made to reach a fully considered view that would represent unanimous agreement or at least assent to the consensus of the majority. For the remaining extraordinary preparation, the Delegation, after it convened, was the final authority for the determination of recommendations, and on matters that did not need to be referred to the President, the final authority for decision.

The four earliest Delegation meetings, held on March 13, 23, and 30, and April 3, were on a weekly basis, were somewhat preliminary in character, and were sometimes not complete in membership. Thereafter, the Delegation met more frequently—April 9, 10, 11 (two meetings), 12, 16, 17, and 18, at which point it ended its meetings in the Department and convened next in San Francisco.

The first of these meetings, March 13, was divided into two parts, the Delegates being received by the President between the two. Discussion was chiefly of Delegation arrangements. Attending Departmental officers were present only on request of the Secretary, designations to service on the Delegation still being under consideration.[16] Between this meeting and the next, the decision was made by the Secretary of State, on March 21, to name the coming conference "The United Nations Conference on International Organization."

The second meeting, March 23, was devoted primarily to consideration of inviting "private national organizations" to be represented at the Conference. A proposal to do so had previously been considered favorably by the Secretary's Staff Committee, to which periodic reports on developments with respect to the Conference were made

---

[16] Attendance at the first meeting was made public in the *Department of State Bulletin*, XII, 435. It may be noted that all of the Delegates came to the first meeting, but that Commander Stassen and Dean Gildersleeve were unable to come to the second meeting, and the former could not attend the third and fourth. Under Secretary Grew and Assistant Secretaries Acheson and MacLeish attended several of the preconference meetings, besides officers who were already or later assigned to the Delegation. Mr. Grew presided at the times Secretary Stettinius was absent.

throughout this preconference period. After approval of this general plan by the President on March 29, forty-two such organizations—closely approximating the list compiled for the projected Advisory Council in 1944—were invited to send a representative each to serve in the capacity of consultant to the Delegation.[17]

This meeting was also a divided one, the Delegates being again received by President Roosevelt during it. The President on this occasion informed them of the status of the agreement on the "three votes" question as reached at the Crimea Conference. This same question was considered at Secretary Stettinius' suggestion in executive session with the Delegates at the start of their third meeting, March 30, and again at the beginning of their fourth meeting, April 3. The Staff Committee had recommended, April 2, on the initiative of officers concerned with the preparation, that the United States request no more than one vote. After being cleared by the Delegates, who were immediately consulted, this recommendation was submitted to the President and announced as the United States position on April 3.[18]

These were the last meetings in which matters of arrangements and organizing problems were prominent on the agenda, and the meeting of April 3 was the transitional meeting leading toward the substantive discussions commencing April 9. The advisers so far as appointed were admitted to the meeting on the 3d, and general plans for their work were presented at that time. Attendance of the advisers from other Departments and agencies was substantially complete by this time but the list of those from the Department of State was not filled until a few days later.

The same day, April 3, Secretary Stettinius issued a press statement expressing the judgment of this Government that "the rapid tempo of military and political developments, far from requiring postponement of the San Francisco Conference on International Organization, makes it increasingly necessary that the plans for this Organization worked out at Dumbarton Oaks be carried on promptly." The Secretary also asserted that we had "moreover received no indication that any government believes that the Conference should be postponed." In this statement were reflected, on the one hand, the rapid advance of the Allied armies toward Berlin from both the East and the West, bringing with it the strong possibility of an early Ger-

---

[17] *Ibid.*, pp. 724–25. Among the representatives were a number who had earlier been associated with the preparation, particularly Clark M. Eichelberger, Robert J. Watt, James T. Shotwell, Philip Murray, and James G. Patton. Groups including but not restricted to the consultants appeared upon occasion before the Delegation to represent such special interests as agriculture, business, labor, and education.

[18] See p. 396.

man collapse and hence the precipitation soon of vastly difficult problems concerning Germany; and on the other hand, the growing differences between the Soviet Union and the other sponsoring powers, particularly over policy in Eastern Europe. This deterioration in Allied unity was manifest in such specific preconference issues as the question of inviting the Polish Provisional Government functioning in Warsaw to attend the Conference, of seating delegations from the Ukrainian and Byelorussian constituent republics at the Conference, of the presidency of the Conference, and Marshal Stalin's evident intention not to send Mr. Molotov to San Francisco despite warnings by President Roosevelt that such a decision would be construed as lack of Soviet interest.[19]

It was at this difficult juncture that the Delegation started its review of the Dumbarton Oaks Proposals and its consideration of the changes and additions suggested by the preparatory staff and by Delegates themselves. Two related steps, of which the Delegation was kept informed, were in progress as this work was carried through, and these steps will be discussed before the review process is described.

THE UNITED NATIONS COMMITTEE OF JURISTS

THE DRAFTING of the United Nations proposal for a statute of the International Court of Justice was done between April 9 and 20, 1945.

United States preparation for the proposed statute had been completed before the Dumbarton Oaks Conversations, with the sole exceptions of one point settled the second day of the Conversations and such adjustments in nomenclature as were necessary to conform with the terms used in the Dumbarton Oaks Proposals. As will be recalled, the United States proposals on an international court had developed from the initial study and drafting undertaken in 1942–43 by the Subcommittee on Legal Problems, which suggested an appreciable number of modifications in the Statute of the Permanent Court of International Justice. Early in 1944, additional drafting by the research staff ensued, followed in the spring by consideration of drafts in the Informal Political Agenda Group and special review by two members of the Group, Mr. Hackworth and Mr. Cohen. These two members, as noted earlier, consulted with Judge Manley O. Hudson in June 1944 and with the assistance of the research staff then formulated a revised draft proposal.

The new draft involved minimum adjustments in the Statute of the Permanent Court to adapt it for use as the statute of a new court, and

---

[19] See quoted messages in James F. Byrnes, *Speaking Frankly* (New York, 1947), p. 55.

was finished June 30. It was considered in the light of previous drafts on July 12 by "Group II" of the American Group to conduct the Dumbarton Oaks Conversations, the participants including Messrs. Hackworth, Cohen, and Hornbeck and from the staff, Messrs. Sandifer, Preuss, and Padelford, and Mrs. McDiarmid. Eleven basic questions were isolated as requiring superior decisions, among which were a number of staff suggestions derived particularly from the earlier draft made by the Subcommittee on Legal Problems. These questions were put before "Group II" for its further consideration on July 28 and 31, 1944. Revised basic questions were then drawn up by the staff on August 5, and were considered three days later by the whole American Group.

The consideration of these questions in the meeting of the Group on August 8 was definitely favorable to the establishment of a new court under a statute constructed by adaptation of the Statute of the existing Permament Court of International Justice. There was likewise approval of the proposals drafted for such provisions of the new statute as those concerning relationship of the court to the general international organization, membership, chambers of the court, jurisdiction over justiciable disputes, and advisory jurisdiction.

To study unsettled questions regarding nomination and election of judges, parties eligible to bring cases before the court, the practice of permitting national *ad hoc* judges, and amendment of the statute, a temporary subcommittee composed of Messrs. Hackworth, Cohen, Hornbeck, Bowman, Pasvolsky, and General Strong was created by the American Group at the same meeting. After consideration of these questions by the American Group on August 10, the only question still left unsettled was that concerning *ad hoc* national judges. There were conflicting opinions on this matter, and it was not settled until, during the Dumbarton Oaks Conversations, a decision was made by the Secretary of State not strongly to oppose, but unfavorable to, the practice. This view was announced to the American Group at a meeting on August 22, 1944.

What proved to be the final United States draft proposal for a statute of the international court of justice—written in the form of proposed revisions in the Statute of the existing Permanent Court of International Justice—was dated August 15, 1944.[20] This paper, not discussed in the Dumbarton Oaks Conversations, embodied the structural pattern of the new court that the American Group had in mind when the brief provisions concerning an "International Court of

---

[20] Printed in appendix 58. The text appears, with some variation in nomenclature, as "Jurist 5" in *The International Court of Justice: Selected Documents Relating to the Drafting of the Statute*, Department of State publication 2491, Conference Series 84, p. 57 ff.

.Justice" were developed as chapter VII of the Dumbarton Oaks Proposals. The publication of these Proposals on October 9, 1944, conveyed the first authentic general notice that a new court was contemplated by the four powers represented at Dumbarton Oaks as a principal organ of the future United Nations organization, and that its statute would be a part of the Charter. No criticism of this plan was expressed in memoranda or comments upon the Proposals received from other governments over the next several months. In the spring of 1945, when the tie came to arrive at joint proposals for the statute, no further substantive preparation within this Government beyond the paper of August 15, 1944, was believed to be necessary.

On March 24, 1945, an invitation to a meeting of a United Nations Committee of Jurists was sent by the United tSates, on behalf of the four sponsoring governments, to each of the governments being invited to the United Nations Conference on International Organization. When Syria and Lebanon became eligible to sign the Declaration by United Nations, invitations were sent to them also. With the exception of India and the Union of South Africa, all those invited accepted, and a total of forty-four nations participated in the meeting.

The invitations described the purpose of the meeting as "to prepare, prior to the San Francisco Conference, a draft of a statute to be submitted to that Conference for consideration" and stated "that if the work of the Committee of Jurists is not completed by the time the United Nations Conference begins, sessions should be continued at San Francisco." They suggested that each nation should appoint one representative to the Committee, to be accompanied, if desired, by not more than two advisers. The representatives and advisers appointed included six of the fifteen men who, in the next year, were elected members of the International Court of Justice.[21] Judge Charles de Visscher (Belgium) of the Permanent Court of International Justice and former Judge Wang Chung-hui (China) were among the national representatives present. In its work, the Committee also had the advice of Judge Manley O. Hudson of the Permanent Court, whom the Committee itself invited to attend.

With the President's approval, Green H. Hackworth, Legal Adviser in the Department of State and for several years a member of the Permanent Court of Arbitration, was designated on April 3, 1945, as the Representative of the United States on the Committee, and was elected its Chairman at the opening session on the 9th. After discussion in the Secretary's Staff Committee of the problem of possible precedent for the San Francisco Conference posed by a Soviet pro-

---

[21] Jules Basdevant (France), Charles de Visscher (Belgium), Green H. Hackworth (United States), S. B. Krylov (Soviet Union), Hsu Mo (China), and John E. Read (Canada).

posal that the representatives of the four sponsoring powers be co-chairmen of the Committee, Mr. Hackworth suggested an arrangement whereby representatives of the other three sponsor governments would be requested to take the chair in rotation from time to time, and this was approved by the Committee.[22]   Charles Fahy and Philip C. Jessup were designated as the United States advisers.

Since the statute was to become a part of the Charter, the United States Representative was authorized by his letter of designation from the Secretary of State "to consider with the committee not only the statute but also such other matters as are deemed necessary to determine the position and jurisdiction of the court within the proposed Organization".   He was to report the results to the Secretary of State and to the members of the American Delegation at the San Francisco Conference.   Mr. Hackworth's account of the proceedings was the basis of Secretary Stettinius' report to the President on April 23, 1945.

The Secretariat of the Committee was supplied by the United States.   It included Mr. Preuss, acting Associate Chief of the Division of International Organization Affairs, who was named principal secretary of the Committee, Mr. Maktos, the assistant secretary, and their assistants, Mr. Padelford (consultant), Mr. Halderman, Miss Maylott, and Mrs. McDiarmid.   These members were from the branch of the staff, which also included Messrs. Eagleton, Myers, and Reiff, working on the legal problems still under study.

The United Nations Committee of Jurists convened in plenary session in the Interdepartmental Auditorium, Washington, April 9, 1945.   Secretary Stettinius in his address of welcome to the Committee at this session set forth the anticipated nature of its work in the following words: [23]

"It is scarcely possible to envisage the establishment of an international Organization for the maintenance of peace without having as a component part thereof a truly international judicial body.

". . . If the statute of such a court is to form part of the Charter of the new international Organization, steps must now be taken to formulate such an instrument for consideration at the forthcoming conference of the United Nations at San Francisco. . . .

"The war-weary world is committing to your hands, in the first instance, the responsibility of preparing recommendations.   To your measured judgment the people of the world with faith in order under law entrust this important initial work."

---

[22] These representatives were G. G. Fitzmaurice of the United Kingdom, N. V. Novikov of the Soviet Union, Judge Wang Chung-hui of China.   Jules Basdevant of France was designated rapporteur.

[23] *Department of State Bulletin*, XII, 672.

Nine days later, April 18, the Committee unanimously adopted its "Report." The "Record of the Meeting of the Committee of Jurists For the Preparation of a Draft of a Statute for the International Court of Justice To Be Submitted to the United Nations Conference on International Organization," which contained the "Draft Statute" and the accompanying "Report of Rapporteur on Draft of Statute of an International Court of Justice,"[24] was signed in the last meeting on April 20, just in time to enable representatives to board a special train for the opening of the San Francisco Conference.[25] The papers themselves remained in Washington for initial processing; working sets arrived in San Francisco shortly after the Conference had begun.

The Statute of the Permanent Court of International Justice was the basis used by the Committee of Jurists in drafting. Since the official languages under that Statute were French and English, the Committee's "Drafting Committee," which began on April 14 to collate and finalize the full text of the proposed new statute as its parts were agreed upon, gave its attention to both English and French versions of all points. The final "Record," however, was signed by all representatives not only in those two languages, but also in Russian, Chinese, and Spanish [26]—a precedent later followed at the San Francisco Conference in the case of the Charter of the United Nations, including the Statute. On reference from Mr. Hackworth, the United States Delegation to the San Francisco Conference considered on April 17 the question of such multiple language signatures and agreed that he should not object to them.

The Draft Statute reflected an agreement by the Committee not to attempt definite recommendations on some questions on which there was strong support for differing views and on which political rather than primarily technical factors were involved. In five articles, accordingly, alternatives were presented. Four occurred in connection with the several provisions relating to the process of nomination of judges, the alternatives suggesting either a system of direct nomination by governments or the continuance of the indirect system used for the old Court. The fifth concerned the reference of cases to the new court, which, the alternatives suggested, should either be optional as under the old Court, or compulsory in certain types of cases.[27]

---

[24] For texts of these documents, see *The International Court of Justice*, pp. 98–133. Department of State publication 2491, Conference Series 84.

[25] *Department of State Bulletin*, XII, 759.

[26] Some signatures were given only on Apr. 30, at San Francisco.

[27] For the terms of the later United States recognition of the compulsory jurisdiction of the Court on Aug. 14, 1946, see *Department of State Bulletin*, XV, 452–53.

Early in the Committee's consideration of controversial questions of this character, Mr. Hackworth consulted the United States Delegation to the San Francisco Conference. The Delegation favored the optional formula for reference of cases to the new court and a proposal that the General Assembly should be able to request advisory opinions of the court. It suggested that Chief Justice Stone and former Chief Justice Hughes should be consulted on such questions as nomination and number of judges, and this was done.

The new Draft Statute, which was in substantial accord with the draft proposal presented by the United States and with the views of the United States presented in the course of the Committee's work, was the basis of the deliberations of the San Francisco Conference leading to the final Statute of the International Court of Justice. The Committee of Jurists thus completed the work of arriving at joint proposals on one of the major questions left "open" at the end of the Dumbarton Oaks Conversations.

Meanwhile, consideration of international trusteeship, the last of the "open questions" envisaged in the preparation as necessary to complete the Dumbarton Oaks Proposals, reached the decision level within this Government.

UNITED STATES PROPOSALS FOR TRUSTEESHIP

THE POSITION to be adopted by the United States in regard to international trusteeship continued to be in question throughout the preconference period. Active drafting of proposals was undertaken at the start and again briefly at the conclusion of the period, with developments during the several weeks between primarily focused on the fundamental question of policy involved.

The first definite proposals were more detailed than the final ones and were the product of discussions carried on in the Interdepartmental Committee on Dependent Area Aspects of International Organization. This Committee completed its work on March 15, 1945, having concentrated principally in its nine meetings on a paper entitled "Arrangements for International Trusteeship." [28] Some consideration had also been given to two companion papers, the one headed "Declaration Regarding Administration of Dependent Territories" receiving rather more attention than the other on "Regional Advisory Commissions." These, together with the paper on "Arrangements," were designed to form three parts of a chapter to supplement the Dumbarton Oaks Proposals. The drafts of all three papers as originally put before the Committee had been prepared in the Department of

[28] Cf. p. 387 ff.

429

State by the Division of Dependent Areas, with the reviewing assistance of the Department's interdivisional Working Committee on Dependent Areas, and they constituted revisions without basic change of the papers on the same subjects that had been cleared in the preceding year by the Post-War Programs Committee.

After each of the Interdepartmental Committee's meetings, however, the papers discussed, and particularly the main paper, were revised, in some respects substantially. Between meetings the problems involved were considered and solutions appraised or devised by the State Department representatives on this Committee, Mr. Pasvolsky and Mr. Dunn, and Messrs. Gerig and Bunche, who were their assisting staff members, and by Messrs. Wilson, Hartley, Johnson, Notter, and Sandifer, who did not attend the meetings. The Committee decided to omit from proposals to be initiated by the United States those dealing with regional commissions, although the paper on this subject was made ready for use in considering any document on this matter presented by another government. The presentation of such a paper by the British was anticipated, particularly after Colonel Stanley's visit in January 1945. The Committee also decided to embody the principles that had been set forth in the paper on administration in a separate declaration which might or might not be incorporated in the Charter.[29]

The final meeting of the Interdepartmental Committee, attended by Mr. Pasvolsky (Chairman), General Embick, Admiral Train, Messrs. Fortas, Rockefeller, Taussig, Thoron, Gerig, and Bunche, had before it the eighth draft of the paper on "Arrangements." The text, as amended in this meeting, March 15, was recorded as the ninth draft. It incorporated the basic distinction made in this Committee on February 8 between strategic and nonstratègic areas and provided for corresponding differences in international supervision. The strategic category was regarded as coming in some respects within the purview of the General Assembly and the Trusteeship Council but also as coming, in several major respects, within the scope of the Security Council and of the unanimity requirement in the voting procedure contemplated for that Council. This draft, among its five and a half pages of proposals, also made provision whereby territories in the three categories defined at the Crimea Conference[30] might be placed under trusteeship by means of negotiated "trusteeship arrangements."

The Interdepartmental Committee approved this draft, as representing agreement in the Committee, for transmission by the Department of State to the Secretaries of the War and Navy Departments and

---

[29] The Committee intended to meet further on such a declaration of principles but did not do so.

[30] See p. 397.

the Joint Chiefs of Staff. It believed that if after examination of the paper at that level, and by the Secretary of State and the President, nothing further needed to be done on it, the paper would be ready for exchange with the other sponsor powers and France.

This document, accordingly was submitted to the Secretary's Staff Committee in the State Department on March 17, 1945, for approval prior to its clearance with the other interested Departments and with the President. The Staff Committee had been informed three days earlier that further discussions at Cabinet level would probably be necessary, and this was to prove correct. Although the draft proposals under consideration had been formulated through interdepartmental collaboration, the fundamental question had still persisted unresolved whether from the standpoint of vital national security the Japanese mandated islands should be brought under *de facto* United States control within a system of international trusteeship constituting part of the general security system contemplated in the United Nations Charter, or whether, in order to assure the control necessary for our own peace and for the peace of the Pacific Area, the islands must be annexed. A collateral problem was that of announcing this Government's position if the latter view were sustained. As was made clear in the discussions, these were not questions concerning the objective of assuring national security interests with respect to the Pacific, on which views were identical from the beginning, but of how best to assure the national interests involved.

On March 20 the Secretary's Staff Committee approved the document, and decided to ask for an early meeting of the Secretary of State with the Secretaries of War and the Navy for the purpose of obtaining the formal clearance of the latter Departments prior to presenting the paper to President Roosevelt. Secretary Stettinius was away for the next several days, and upon his return he was orally informed by President Roosevelt, on March 29, that the latter would review the trusteeship paper in a week or ten days.

Steps were taken internationally while these developments between March 15 and March 29, 1945, were occurring. The Secretary of State instructed the American Ambassadors in London, Moscow, and Chungking on March 16, 1945, to raise certain questions of procedure for undertaking the consultation on trusteeship envisaged in the relevant Yalta agreement. This agreement, it will be recalled, provided for such consultation to be held before the San Francisco Conference among the five governments that were to occupy permanent seats on the Security Council. One question was whether to include France in such consultations, that nation not being a co-sponsor of the coming Conference; it was the thought of the Department that France should be included. The telegrams suggested that the consultations should be conducted at a technical level and preferably in Washington as soon as possible after April 1, 1945, following the exchange of papers that we hoped would be possible.

Following receipt of word from the British, Soviet, and Chinese Representatives of their readiness to participate, a telegram was sent to Paris on March 27 making the same proposal for preliminary conversations but mentioning "around" April 8 as the date. This was at once accepted, and by the end of March the Department had been informed of the definite or at least probable appointments of the British, Chinese, and French Representatives and of their expected early arrival. No information concerning a Soviet Representative had been received, but this did not delay matters in view of the fact that our own decision to embark upon such consultations could not be made until this Government had arrived definitively at a position on trusteeship.

On April 2 it appeared from a meeting of the Secretaries of State, War, and the Navy held in the War Department that the further consideration that would have to be given to this question must be undertaken with the President. The Department of State consequently, on April 9, transmitted a memorandum to the President reporting the views on this subject held respectively by the Department of State, with which the Interior Department concurred, and by the War and Navy Departments.[31] This memorandum, which emanated in its final form from drafting done in the Department at the Assistant Secretary level, recommended a prompt determination of the Government's position, and suggested that the President ask representatives of the State, War, and Navy Departments to "come down for a half hour's discussion of this subject, within the next few days . . ."[32]

President Roosevelt was resting at his home in Warm Springs, Georgia. He intended to be present at the opening session of the San Francisco Conference, and the initial draft of an address was being prepared for his consideration by the superior officials of the Department of State, to be sent him April 12. On Tuesday, April 10, 1945, he sent word to the Secretary of State saying: "Your message on International Trusteeship is approved in principle." He said he would see "your representative" and those of the Army and Navy "on the 19th." His message concluded: "That will be time enough. And if you have already left I will, of course, see you on the 25th."

---

[31] Secretary Harold L. Ickes of the Interior Department submitted his views to the President before the above memorandum had been completed. The other two Departments, according to the memorandum from the Department of State, intended likewise to present their views separately to the President.

[32] Participation directly by the Joint Chiefs of Staff in this conversation was also contemplated according to the views of the three Secretaries expressed in conversations the following day.

This memorandum was interpreted by the Secretary to mean that the trusteeship problem should be discussed at the San Francisco Conference and that the preliminary consultations among the five major powers should start after the conversation with the President on the 19th. The Secretary also believed that there would be sufficient time adequately to handle the consultations even with this delay.

Two days later, on the afternoon of April 12, President Roosevelt died, and Vice President Harry S. Truman succeeded to the Presidency.

Trusteeship was one of the principal problems on the status of which the Secretary of State briefed the new President the following day. Discussion of the best course for finally achieving the United States position ensued the same day within the Department of State and between it and the Interior Department. On the next day conversations were held among Secretaries Stettinius and Forrestal, Admiral King, and General Marshall, and then among Secretaries Stettinius, Stimson, and Forrestal. Further interdepartmental discussion and drafting took place on that week-end and on the 16th.

These efforts resulted in a general statement of proposed United States policy for submission to the President. The proposed statement was first placed before the United States Delegation to the San Francisco Conference, in executive session. The initial meeting of the delegation to consider this statement, April 17, was attended not only by all the military and naval advisers on the Delegation but also by Secretaries Stimson and Forrestal, Special Assistant to the Secretary of War Harvey H. Bundy, Assistant Secretary of the Navy Artemus L. Gates, and Special Assistants to the Secretary of the Navy Maj. Mathias F. Correa and R. Keith Kane. The Delegation met again on this subject the next morning, Mr. Bundy attending for Secretary Stimson and Major Correa and Mr. Kane for Secretary Forrestal. Under Secretary Fortas represented the Interior Department in these meetings. Besides the seven Delegates present—Secretary Stettinius, Senators Connally and Vandenberg, Representatives Bloom and Eaton, Commander Stassen and Dean Gildersleeve—the others attending both meetings were Messrs. Dunn, Hackworth, Pasvolsky, Bowman, Armstrong, Taussig, Hickerson, Notter, Dulles, Sandifer, Raynor, Gerig, Hartley, Blaisdell, and Bunche and Miss Fosdick.

Marked clarification resulted from the thorough consideration given to the problem in the meeting of the 17th. The proposed statement was revised immediately afterward by Messrs. Pasvolsky, Bowman, Dulles and the military and naval representatives, and the revised document was approved by all concerned with only minor amendments in the opening hour of the meeting on the 18th. It was then recommended to President Truman as a directive to be given by him to the Delegation. The President discussed it at the White House later on April 18 with the Secretaries of State, War, and the Navy, and approved it.

Since the fact of this determination of a United States position on trusteeship was immediately the subject of press and other public comment, thought was given by the President and the Secretaries of State, War, and the Navy to the possible issuance of a press statement. The draft text that the three Secretaries agreed to recommend to the President for release, if he desired, was conveyed to him with a memorandum from the Secretary of State, April 20. The draft text read as follows:

"The United States Government considers that it would be entirely practicable to devise a trusteeship system which would provide, by agreements, for (1) the maintenance of United States military and strategic rights, (2) such control as will be necessary to assure general peace and security in the Pacific Ocean area as well as elsewhere in the world, and (3) the advancement of the social, economic, and political welfare of the inhabitants of the dependent territories.

"It is not proposed at San Francisco to determine the placing of any particular territory under a trusteeship system. All that will be discussed there will be the possible machinery of such a system. It would be a matter for subsequent agreement as to which territories would be brought under a trusteeship system and upon what terms."

This statement, however, was not issued, the Secretary having said in his transmitting memorandum that, inasmuch as "our preliminary negotiations" with the other four major powers contemplated under the agreement reached at Yalta had not taken place and might be affected by such a statement, he considered it advisable to make no statement until they had been concluded.

By this time, most of the members of the United States Delegation had left for San Francisco. On the day of departure, however, the main paper of proposal as it had emerged from the Interdepartmental Committee on March 15, 1945, was again brought under consideration. The purpose of revising this long paper was to shorten and adjust it to the ideas and policy views developed during the intervening weeks through the intensive efforts just described. It had been suggested in the Delegation that a short draft of proposals was preferable. Commander Stassen had presented his views in the form of a short draft at the close of the meeting of April 18, and at his suggestion an informal meeting of some of the Delegates, advisers, and technical officers was held that afternoon just before they took the train for San Francisco. On the basis of the general ideas resulting from this meeting, a new draft was drawn up on the train by a

"Technical Group" composed of Messrs. Pasvolsky, Taussig, Notter, Sandifer, Gerig, Johnson, Hartley, and Bunche.

The new paper, after clearance by telegraph with the War and Navy Departments at Washington, was considered by the Delegation at San Francisco on April 26. It was adopted with three clarifying amendments desired by those Departments. This, the sixteenth draft made since the beginning of interdepartmental consideration early in 1945, was the final paper wholly based on United States preparation. It constituted the proposals advanced by this Government in the major power consultations on international trusteeship which ensued, as will shortly be noted, in connection with the San Francisco Conference.

COMPLETION OF UNITED STATES PROPOSALS

APART FROM the work just described directed toward the formulation of joint proposals for a Statute of the International Court and the determination of United States proposals for an international trusteeship system, the substantive preparation undertaken immediately before the San Francisco Conference comprised primarily a review of the Dumbarton Oaks Proposals. This review was conducted directly by the United States Delegation and, as completed at San Francisco, constituted the last over-all consideration of United States policy proposals for a general organization.

The death of President Roosevelt, and the succession of Harry S. Truman to the Presidency on the evening of April 12, 1945, came as this review was in progress. Within the hour after taking his oath of office, the new President stated that the San Francisco Conference would proceed,[33] and on the next day Secretary Stettinius announced that "President Truman has authorized me to say that there will be no change of purpose or break of continuity in the foreign policy of the United States Government." [34]

The United States Delegation began its review with the first of its "regular" or "daily" meetings, Monday, April 9, 1945.[35] It had two general purposes in mind: to arrive at recommendations on any new proposals the United States should advance in consultations with the other sponsor powers and in the Conference itself, and to determine the position that should be taken toward proposals offered by other governments so far as these were available for consideration. The Delegation was informed by Secretary Stettinius that the already

---

[33] *Department of State Bulletin*, XII, 722.

[34] *Ibid.*, XII, 669.

[35] This was the fifth meeting of the Delegation. The preceding four were *ad hoc*. Cf. above, p. 421.

defined positions of this Government, our joint sponsorship of the Dumbarton Oaks Proposals, and the supplemental provision for voting in the Security Council as agreed to at Yalta did not leave "very much elbow room" for changes. Alterations in the basic relations of organs, in the obligations of member states, and in the balance between organs, between regional organizations and the general organization, and between large and small states, as they were set forth in the Proposals would therefore require most careful consideration. There was greater freedom, however, to propose additions believed to be necessary or desirable for the completion of the Charter as a legal instrument. A distinction between "changes" and "additions" thus arose and was maintained for some time, but the former came to stand for both.

Eight meetings in which review was the main object were held, April 9–12 and 16–18.[36] The discussion dealt mainly with basic ideas and normally left questions of precise phrasing for later consideration in connection with the drafting of the Charter in the Conference. When consensus was not self-evident, the opinion of the Delegation on any point was ascertained by majority vote, but, as has been noted, an agreed view was consistently sought. For the most part, the Delegation convened early each morning and proceeded methodically through a binder of papers entitled *Proposals and Suggestions for Consideration, Book Two*.[37] These papers, prepared by the staff, summarized the most significant suggestions for Charter provisions advanced to date by any source, official and unofficial, and included the specific suggestions developed since Dumbarton Oaks by officers engaged in the extraordinary preparation.

These suggestions had been derived from problem papers written between November 1944 and January 1945 by the staff, under Mr. Pasvolsky's direction, on each provision of the Dumbarton Oaks Proposals. The papers set forth every foreseeable problem that might arise in negotiations, a recommended position on each, and an analysis of both the problem and the recommended position. In these papers, new provisions were also suggested when considered desirable to produce a complete Charter. Furthermore, alternatives were presented wherever available for those suggestions marked as "preferred." These alternatives, of which analytical appraisals had also been made, incorporated the specific proposals of the Delegates already expressed publicly, and for the most part in communications to the Department as well, and set forth the specific views of Senators and

---

[36] Two meetings were held on the 11th.

[37] Book Three set forth in detail all proposals and suggestions that had been received. Book One contained basic reference papers.

Representatives not taking part as Delegates, of numerous private citizens, of religious groups, and of scholarly and other organizations in the United States. The individual reactions of the twenty-three governments commenting on the Proposals in advance of the Conference, the joint views of the Inter-American Juridical Committee, and the views of nineteen Latin American republics embodied in the Mexico City Conference resolution regarding the Proposals were similarly taken into account. The wide range of general comment and opinion drawn upon further included the views of individual foreign officials, the reports of Myron C. Taylor from Rome, and suggestions in the American and foreign press.

In addition, specific suggestions on the provisions relating to the Economic and Social Council were available in recommendations received from the Executive Committee on Economic Foreign Policy, based on interdepartmental study of the economic aspects of the Covenant of the League of Nations, the Atlantic Charter, and Article VII of the Mutual Aid Agreements. Interdepartmental views on security provisions were received on April 16 from an *ad hoc* Committee on Security Aspects of the Preparation for the United Nations Conference. This body, though not formally a subcommittee of the Delegation, consisted mainly of the civilian and military advisers and experts assigned or being assigned to the Delegation.[38] Under the chairmanship of Mr. Dunn, and with Joseph E. Johnson as secretary, this Committee considered the provisions on international security in the Dumbarton Oaks Proposals at four meetings, April 3–11, as a special study to facilitate the Delegation's review.

The Delegation was informed at its first "review meeting" that the Dumbarton Oaks Proposals and the views agreed upon in the Delegation from day to day would be redrafted by the staff in the form of exact articles for a Charter as a legal instrument. A preliminary draft of this nature had, in fact, already been made between March 21 and April 5 by a group of five of the staff. The redraft was now prepared in consultation with Senator Connally, by a group under Mr. Pasvolsky, composed of Messrs. Notter, Johnson, Tomlinson, Gerig, and Hartley and Miss Fosdick.[39] This drafting was conceived as a part of the concluding preparatory work in this field. It was undertaken not only in anticipation of Conference needs and in order to ascertain the nature of the technical drafting problems likely to be encountered in phrasing the Charter in legal terminology but also

---

[38] The Committee was joined occasionally by officers not assigned to the Delegation, particularly Assistant Secretary of State Julius C. Holmes.

[39] Of the preceding group Mr. Eagleton and Mrs. McDiarmid had been assigned to work with the Committee of Jurists, and Mrs. Brunauer was assigned to other conference work.

to discover any difficulties or inadequacies in the Proposals to which the attention of the Delegation should be called. This United States draft of a Charter could not be finished before the Conference, but its completed chapters were utilized by United States advisers and experts at San Francisco.

The Delegation began its review of the Proposals by considering the suggestions for the name of the future international organization. "The United Nations" continued to be favored.[40] Consideration of the preamble was deferred after a short discussion. The "purposes" were then re-examined, followed by the "principles," the General Assembly, membership, and "organs" as a whole. Next, on April 11, arrangements for economic and social cooperation were taken up. Arrangements for the maintenance of international peace and security and transitional arrangements were considered April 12 and 16. The attention given April 17 and 18 to the subject of international trusteeship has already been noted in the preceding section. In the long meeting on the 18th, however, a number of other problems were also examined. These included particularly the provisions concerning domestic jurisdiction and amendment of the Charter and, in that connection, the possibility of a new provision for a United Nations conference to revise the Charter after a term of years. They also included the question of whether provision for withdrawal should or should not be made. Some further consideration was also given to provisions for economic and social cooperation, on the basis of additional preparatory work by the advisers in the economic and social fields.

The Delegates were at all of these "review meetings" with the exceptions of Commander Stassen, who was arranging leave from his naval staff post during the first four meetings of this series, and of Senator Connally and Representative Bloom, on one occasion each, because of congressional duties. Of the advisers, Mr. Dunn, Mr. Bowman, and Mr. Armstrong were present at all but one meeting, Mr. Pasvolsky and Mr. Dulles at all, Mr. Hackworth at four, Mr. Hickerson at three, Mr. Notter at seven, and Mr. Stinebower at two.[41] Assistant Secretaries of State Acheson and Rockefeller joined the earliest two meetings.[42] Mr. Raynor attended all. Of the Delegation's chief technical officers, Mr. Sandifer took part in four meetings, Mr. Gerig in all, and J. E. Johnson in three. Except for Mr. Hartley who was

---

[40] In the conference "The" was dropped.

[41] Charles P. Taft attended until Mr. Stinebower had been designated adviser.

[42] In addition, John S. Dickey and Alger Hiss participated in connection with public relations and conference arrangements, respectively, during portions of one meeting.

usually present, experts came as required for their special competence.[43] Miss Fosdick took the summary minutes required.[44]

Participation of advisers from other Departments was noteworthy beginning April 11, when Messrs. Brannan, Cox, Waring, and White took part, and the next day when military advisers joined the meetings. General Embick, Admiral Willson, and General Fairchild participated in all or part of the meetings held April 12, 16, 17, and 18, Admirals Hepburn and Train and General Hertford in the last three, and Messrs. Fortas and Taussig in the last two. The military experts attended the same four meetings, Colonel Bonesteel all four, Colonel Hamilton and Lieutenant Colonel McRae three, and Colonel Ladd two.

The most important results of the review were embodied for his information in a "Memorandum For The President" dated April 19, 1945.[45] The changes in the Dumbarton Oaks Proposals and the additions referred to in this memorandum were unanimously supported by the Delegation. This four-page paper also indicated a number of questions on which formulation of definitive views was deferred. These included the wording of the preamble, possible changes of wording regarding economic and social cooperation, and the possibility of having provisions in the Charter for defining the right of self-defense, for withdrawal, and for a future conference to review the Charter. The President, who on April 17 had told the Delegates that he was "counting on *them*" and who left them wide power of discretion in determining the course to take, was informed by this memorandum that the Delegation would "reserve our final positions on all these, of course, until we learn the views of other governments."

Although in some respects final positions were settled only as the Conference itself arrived at decisions, the reference in this memorandum to "other governments" was applicable, at this point in developments, particularly to the other sponsoring governments. Consultations were shortly to occur among the four sponsors, and it was during these consultations that the definitive views of the Delegation, so far as directly germane to the extraordinary preparation, were completed.

While consultation had not been firmly agreed upon by the beginning of the Delegation's review meetings on April 9, it had become the subject of active consideration by the four powers and was arranged on April 10. Under the Yalta Agreement, the sponsoring governments had accepted the Dumbarton Oaks Proposals together with the

---

[43] These included on four occasions Donald C. Blaisdell; on three Mr. Savage; on two Messrs. Sanders, Cordier, and Kotschnig; and on one occasion each, Mr. Howard and Mr. Eagleton.

[44] To take minutes for part of a meeting, Mrs. Brunauer and Messrs. Buehrig, Bunche, and Leddy attended once each, and John D. Tomlinson twice.

[45] Appendix 59.

voting formula "as affording a basis" for the Charter.   In accordance with this agreement, the Department of State, in a memorandum transmitted to the British, Soviet, and Chinese Embassies on March 28, 1945, proposed that the sponsoring governments consult on any "substantial" changes in the Proposals that any of the four governments desired to suggest to the Conference, each government, however, to remain free to make suggestions in the Conference commissions and committees to improve the Charter within the framework of the Proposals.[46]   In discussion on April 10 between the Secretary of State and the British, Soviet, and Chinese Ambassadors in connection with organizational arrangements for the Conference, agreement was reached that the four Delegations would consult on proposals made by any country that would change directly or affect indirectly the character of the Dumbarton Oaks Proposals, or that were important in other respects.[47]   It was made clear early in this discussion that—contrary to a Soviet suggestion—the consultation would not signify an agreement to "concert" the views of the delegations of the sponsor powers on all matters proposed by any of them or by other delegations. Furthermore, it was clarified by Secretary Stettinius at the conclusion of the discussion that this "agreement to consult" was "not an agreement in advance to agree."

The agreement on April 10 led to the so-called "Big Four" consultations which were held April 23–May 4, 1945, inclusive.   At the time of the agreement it was known that Foreign Ministers Anthony Eden and T. V. Soong would head their respective delegations at the beginning of the Conference and were soon to arrive in Washington. That the consultations could take place on the highest ministerial level without exception was ascertained on the evening of April 13 from a telegram sent to the Secretary of State by Ambassador Harriman immediately following a conversation with Marshal Stalin and Foreign Minister Molotov concerning the death of President Roosevelt.   At the Ambassador's suggestion, Marshal Stalin had decided that although it was difficult for Mr. Molotov to leave Moscow at that time, the Foreign Minister would attend the San Francisco Conference if only for a short time, stopping en route in Washington to see President Truman.   On April 23, Mr. Molotov called upon the President, who had by then conferred with Mr. Eden and Mr. Soong.   That

---

[46] See appendix 60.

[47] This was a meeting of the so-called "Informal Organizing Group on Arrangements for the San Francisco Conference".   Attending Department officials and officers on Apr. 10 included Messrs. Dunn, Pasvolsky and Raynor, together with Messrs. Hiss (secretary), Ross, and Charles F. Darlington of the Conference Secretariat being formed at this date.   This organizing group had held its first meeting Apr. 3, 1945.

evening the first consultative meeting of the Foreign Ministers of the four sponsoring governments was held, 9 : 35–11 : 15 p. m., in the Department of State.

Major questions of organization for the Conference and admission of states to the Conference comprised the business of this Washington meeting and of the first four meetings in San Francisco, April 25, 27, 28, and 30.[48] Furthermore, these five meetings and also, in the main, the discussion at dinner on May 1, which was considered the sixth meeting, were diplomatic exchanges not specifically concerned with Charter proposals.[49] To this there were two exceptions. The first was a statement by Mr. Molotov, without discussion, in the Washington meeting that his Government approved the three Chinese proposals agreed upon at Dumbarton Oaks. These had been communicated by the Department of State to the Soviet Ambassador on March 16, 1945.[50] The second occurred in the discussion at the dinner on May 1, which constituted the transition to substantive consideration of Charter provisions. During the dinner, some discussion of regional arrangements arose, particularly in relation to the Soviet mutual assistance pacts, and Mr. Molotov suggested that a provision be added to the Proposals to permit the action against German aggression provided for under such pacts. Following an inquiry by Mr. Stettinius whether consultations on suggested changes in the Dumbarton Oaks Proposals could not be completed before Mr. Molotov had to return to Moscow, that objective was agreed to, and the five remaining consultative meetings, May 2–4, 1945, dealt exclusively with Charter proposals.

The Conference had convened April 25, 1945, and meanwhile occupied itself with the determination of its own organization as a working body and of various other administrative and procedural arrangements; admission to the Conference of Byelorussia, the Ukraine, and Argentina—none of which were signatories of the Declaration by

---

[48] Among the questions, which included the presidency of the Conference and the maintenance of equality of position among the major powers in that regard, official languages, plans for the opening sessions, committees and allocation of positions on them, etc., were the difficult matters of admission of the two Soviet republics, or Argentina, and of Poland. The first of those matters was taken up Apr. 23 while the last two were considered Apr. 28 with the Foreign Ministers of Brazil, Chile, Mexico, and Venezuela taking part.

[49] In these meetings Secretary Stettinius was accompanied regularly by Mr. Dunn and usually by Mr. Bohlen, once by Senators Connally and Vandenberg and Mr. Rockefeller, on two occasions by Ambassador Harriman, and once by Mr. Raynor. Mr. Hiss and Cabot Coville of the Secretariat attended the two earliest meetings, and the latter also attended to take the minutes of the meeting on the 30th.

[50] Public announcement that the Soviet Government joined in sponsoring the Chinese proposals was made by Mr. Stettinius at San Francisco on Apr. 24, 1945.

United Nations; [51] and the opening addresses of delegates. These were activities pertaining to the Conference rather than to the completion of preparation under exposition here.

Although the earliest meetings of the United States Delegation, April 23–25, were similarly devoted to the problems of organizing the Conference and the Delegation's own working structure, consideration of changes to be proposed or supported in connection with the Dumbarton Oaks Proposals was resumed in the Delegation meeting April 26, 9 : 30 a. m. to 1 p. m. Changes to be proposed by the United States were designated "A", those to be supported, "B".

The Delegation at this time re-examined certain of the positions reported to the President a week before, such as those referring to treaty obligations and "principles" and took up the points that had been deferred or not yet considered. These included such questions as the extent of the organization's powers to recommend terms of peaceful settlement in an international dispute; relationship of the organization to nonmember states in matters of maintenance of international peace and security; the empowering of the General Assembly to propose treaties; matters concerning the Secretariat of the organization; amendment of the Charter and a future conference to revise the Charter; the question of a provision for withdrawal; [52] and possible explicit provision for the exercise of the right, regarded as implicit, of self-defense. On certain of these questions memoranda were requested of the advisers—and in the case of the self-defense provision, a specific draft. At the meeting on the morning of April 27, consideration returned once more to arrangements for economic and social cooperation and specifically to provision for educational and cultural cooperation. The evening meeting of that date continued the discussion of several of the same points and took up briefly registration of treaties, provision against the undertaking of obligations inconsistent with the future Charter, and regional arrangements.

By the end of the evening on April 27, 1945, the Delegation had finished its systematic review.

Questions of two types, however, remained at that time. The first related to the proposals of the Committee of Jurists for an international court. The main issues in this connection, which were discussed

---

[51] Denmark, also not a signatory of the Declaration, was admitted at a later date, June 5.

[52] No provision for withdrawal was included in the Charter. This question was handled through a Declaration on Withdrawal developed in Committee I/2 of the San Francisco Conference and accepted by the Conference. For text of this Declaration, see *The United Nations Conference on International Organization: Selected Documents*, Department of State publication 2490, Conference Series 83, pp. 525–26.

the morning of May 2, concerned whether the court was to be viewed as a new body or as the "old" revised,[53] whether to favor compulsory or optional jurisdiction by the court, the method of nominating judges, and the functional relationships of the court to other organs of the organization, including, for example, the rendering of advisory opinions on request of the General Assembly, and the reference of cases to the court. The second type of questions related to the suggestions received by May 2 from the advisers on economic and social aspects of the Charter and from the consultants to the Delegation. The latters' suggestions concerned additional provisions for cultural cooperation, education, and human rights and fundamental freedoms, and a new provision for a commission on human rights. These were considered in a late afternoon meeting on the same day, 5 : 30 p. m. to 8 : 30 p. m.

The results of this long process of final review were incorporated in a paper, "Changes in Dumbarton Oaks Proposals as suggested by the United States Delegation", dated May 2, 1945.[54]   This was the paper exchanged on the same date with the delegations of the other sponsor powers, which also on this date circulated their papers under the title of "amendments."

In its meetings on May 2, especially in the late afternoon meeting, the Delegation's work began to be interrelated with the sponsors' consultations. This development came about as a consequence of informal discussions among principal advisers of the four delegations, which had commenced Sunday morning, April 29, in Mr. Pasvolsky's office and were being held daily. Attention could thus be given by the Delegation to the specific proposals that, it was informed, were about to be considered by the Foreign Ministers. While the text of the Chinese "amendments" had not yet been received by the Delegation, the discussion on May 2 of the texts of the British and Soviet "amendments" demonstrated that certain United States changes could be withdrawn as involving only verbal differences.

At 9 p. m. on May 2, in the penthouse of the Fairmont Hotel, the first meeting of the Foreign Ministers to consider the specific "changes" and "amendments" began. Secretary Stettinius was accompanied by Senators Connally and Vandenberg, Commander Stassen, Ambassador Harriman who assisted the Secretary in a negotiating capacity at intervals during the Conference, Assistant Secretary MacLeish, and Messrs. Pasvolsky, Dunn, Bowman, Armstrong, Dulles, Raynor, and Sandifer (secretary). Mr. Eden was accompanied by Sir Alexander Cadogan, Sir William Malkin, H. M. G. Jebb, C. K. Webster, and an interpreter. With Mr. Molotov were Ambassador A. A. Gromyko, and

---

[53] The Delegation left this to negotiation ; the Conference decision, with United States concurrence, was for a new court.

[54] Appendix 61.

K. V. Novikov, S. K. Zarapkin, A. A. Sobolev, S. A. Golunsky and S. B. Krylov, and an interpreter and two further aides.[55] Dr. Soong was accompanied by Ambassador V. K. Wellington Koo, Victor Chitsai Hoo, Ambassador Hsu Mo, and Liang Yuen-li. Mr. Stettinius served as Chairman. The Chinese paper, now available, was considered first; then the order of the Dumbarton Oaks Proposals was followed by paragraphs, the four governments' suggestions being taken up as the applicable paragraph of the Proposals was reached. While decisions were not pressed for in this meeting, progress on decisions was made through most of the first six chapters of the Proposals.

The seven United States Delegates attended the second consultative meeting on the morning of May 3, Secretary Stettinius being accompanied by the same advisers except for Mr. Dulles, by Mr. Bohlen, and again by Mr. Sandifer as secretary.[56] The other Foreign Ministers were accompanied as before, except for the addition of Clement R. Attlee to the British group; V. V. Kuznetsov and G. P. Arkadiev to the Soviet; and Wang Chung-hui to the Chinese. Discussion began with chapter VI, section D, of the Dumbarton Oaks Proposals and covered the remaining chapters by the device of leaving unresolved certain questions for further consideration, by agreeing to forego further consultation on a British proposal concerning the International Labor Organization, and by assigning questions in three instances to subcommittees.

The first of the three subcommittees was "on domestic jurisdiction" and was made up of Mr. Dulles and Mr. Hackworth, Sir William Malkin, Professor Golunsky, and Dr. Wang. Its report was considered in the third consultative meeting, on the same day, May 3, at 9:40 p. m., but was not agreed upon.

The second was "on treaties." In this instance, the persons appointed were joined by additional members of delegations, the subcommittee thus being comprised of Secretary Stettinius and Mr. Pasvolsky (chairman), with Mr. Dunn and Mr. Hartley (secretary) also attending; Mr. Eden (not attending its meeting on this date), Sir Alexander Cadogan, and Mr. Jebb, with Sir William Malkin and Professor Webster, and an assistant; Foreign Minister Molotov and Ambassador Gromyko with Mr. Sobolev, Professor Golunsky, and two assistants; and Ambassador Koo and Dr. Wang, with Dr. Hoo and Dr. Liang. The question at issue before this body, which was presented by a United States proposal and by a British redraft of it, was whether the General Assembly should be enabled to consider international "situations arising out of any treaties or international engagements." On

---

[55] Not identified in the records.

[56] Additional technical experts, including Messrs. Gerig, Johnson, and Hartley, attended subsequent consultative meetings of the Foreign Ministers.

this problem Soviet views continued to differ from those of the other participants.

The third subcommittee was "on Commissions under the Economic and Social Council" and consisted of Mr. Bowman, Mr. Attlee, Mr. Kuznetov, and Dr. Hu Shih. Its report was made to the evening consultative meeting on May 3 and agreed upon.

Midnight of the next day, Friday, May 4, had been set by a decision of the Conference a week earlier, as the deadline for the receipt by the Conference of any new substantive proposals. At the start of this day, the items pending before the consultative meetings included such questions as domestic jurisdiction, situations arising out of treaties or international engagements, regional arrangements, Security Council recommendations of terms of settlement for international disputes, and the related problem of whether enforcement measures could or could not be applied in connection with such terms.

Aside from the first item, on which no new points were at issue, these questions were intensively reconsidered by the United States Delegation at its 9 o'clock morning meeting on this day of many meetings. A further and fuller examination was also made by the Delegation at this time of the right, still viewed as implicit in the Proposals, of self-defense by a nation if attacked. The specific problem was whether this right included action on a regional or other special basis. Certain aspects of the latter question with specific reference to the enemy states had been raised not only by the Soviet suggestion but particularly by a French proposal now before the Conference. Further, the Act of Chapultepec, and the inter-American treaty contemplated thereunder, no less directly raised query whether the right of self-defense should not in some way be explicitly recognized in the Charter.

The "subcommittee on treaties" met briefly in mid-morning, May 4. Mr. Eden joined the British members in this meeting, and Assistant Secretary of War McCloy and Messrs. Bowman and Dulles joined the American members. The meeting put under study a United States draft specifying the General Assembly's power to make recommendations for peaceful adjustment of situations "regardless of origin," the quoted phrase replacing the much contested words "arising out of any treaties or international engagements." In a later meeting of this subcommittee at 5 : 15 p. m., which a French Delegate, Henri Bonnet, and his advisers had been invited to attend, agreement in principle—but not final agreement—was reached on this new draft provision. Consideration had also been given at the subcommittee's morning meeting to what changes, if any, should be made in the Proposals in connection with enforcement action under regional or other special arrangements.

Discussion of this question continued in the afternoon meeting, but was inconclusive.

The fourth meeting of the Foreign Ministers, at noon that day, accepted the report of the "subcommittee on domestic jurisdiction," which combined United States and Soviet suggestions, and agreed on provisions defining the Security Council's powers with respect to terms of settlement. The fifth meeting of the Foreign Ministers, 6 : 30–8 : 35 p. m., considered a new United States formula on the question of enforcement action under regional or other special arrangements, which had been approved by the United States Delegation in a half-hour discussion at 7 : 10 p. m., during which the Foreign Ministers' meeting recessed. While some advance was made at this meeting, it fell short of final agreement on either the "regardless of origin" paragraph or the new regional formula.

The last consultative meeting of the four Foreign Ministers was held at 10 : 15 that evening to consider these two unresolved questions. It, however, closed at 11 : 15 p. m. with agreement only that each delegation would have to submit separately to the Conference such of its suggested changes in the Dumbarton Oaks Proposals as had failed to obtain joint sponsorship during the consultations. This agreement was reached with the hope, as expressed by the Chairman, that consultations on the unresolved questions could continue at a later stage of the Conference.

One further major question, international trusteeship, was brought up in the Foreign Ministers' consultations. This was raised merely to obtain approval, which was given, for the submission of individual national, instead of joint, proposals on this problem, in view of the May 4 deadline for receipt of new proposals. As the United States Delegation noted, waiver of that deadline in this special case pending agreement on joint proposals involving lengthy negotiations, would be undesirable since it would leave the Conference committee in this field without proposals from the major powers to consider along with the proposals already received from other delegations.

The consultations on trusteeship were held at the Fairmont Hotel, but they were separate from those of the Foreign Ministers and differed in two general respects: those on trusteeship were held at the Delegate, not Foreign Minister, level, and were among the four sponsor powers and France. The "Preliminary Consultations on Trusteeship by Representatives of the Five Powers" commenced on the evening of April 30 and this group met for the second time on the evening of May 3. The representatives in these two meetings were Commander Stassen for the United States, whom the others designated Chairman; the Viscount Cranborne for the United Kingdom; Mr. Sobolev for the Soviet Union; Dr. Koo for China; and Paul

Emile Naggiar for France in the first and René Pleven in the second. For the United States, the advisers at these meetings were Assistant Secretaries McCloy and Gates of the War and Navy Departments, respectively, and Under Secretary of the Interior Fortas, with the addition of Mr. Taussig at the second.[57] Messrs. Gerig and Bunche were the assisting experts, the latter serving as secretary of the consultations.

The United States proposals as completed April 26 were presented at the first meeting, but the other participants desired to study these proposals before submitting their own. The British paper, which did not distinguish between strategic and nonstrategic areas, was distributed at the second meeting, May 3, but only exploratory discussion of it was undertaken. No other proposals were forthcoming at this point. With another meeting not feasible before May 5 and with the position of three of the participants yet to be fully stated, it became clear that the consultations so long contemplated on trusteeship could now only provide a partial exchange of views before substantive discussion of this subject began in the Conference committee. Agreement on a common draft would obviously require much time. Accordingly, individual papers were submitted to the Conference on May 4 by the United States, by the United Kingdom, and also by France.

At the end of the "Big Four" consultations shortly before midnight May 4, 1945, and as the sponsors' "joint proposals" for amendments to the Dumbarton Oaks Proposals together with the individual amendments of each sponsor were being printed for immediate circulation to all delegations, Secretary Stettinius sent to the President, Mr. Hull, and Acting Secretary Grew his "daily message." It was through these messages that, aside from frequent telephone conversations to obtain counsel or the President's approval, he regularly reported on developments in the Conference.

After explaining in this telegram of May 4 the status of agreement so far reached on the amendments, Secretary Stettinius gave as his estimate that it would be possible in due course to reach agreement on the two questions that had remained unresolved in the consultations. He reported that the four Foreign Ministers had agreed that France would take part beginning the following week in any conversations among the sponsors regarding the conduct and organization of the Conference. The Secretary then concluded with the following statement on the work of the Conference:

---

[57] Admirals Willson and Train, Generals Embick and Fairchild, and Mr. Kane were usually present after the third meeting. Representative Bloom and Mr. Bowman also attended upon occasion.

"Seven of the committees of the Conference met today and organized themselves. Others will meet tomorrow for this purpose. They will not begin actual substantive work until Monday."

With the developments reported in this telegram, and its indication that the substantive Conference work—postponed until the new proposals of the four sponsor powers were ready—was about to begin, the extraordinary preparation of United States postwar foreign policy for a general international organization ended: May 4, 1945.

As had been specifically desired from the Moscow Declaration of 1943 onward, the preparation of final United States policy recommendations in this field had been completed in the form not only of national views, but of views advanced jointly by the four major powers. The views of other governments, and indeed all available ideas from both public and private sources, had been taken into account in the preparation and would be considered by the Conference. But it was believed that the foundation for final decisions must necessarily be provided through the joint action of the major powers, which alone had the capacity to wage world-wide war and therefore had special responsibility in the maintenance of universal peace.

Secretary Stettinius commented as follows upon the preparatory effort in his address during the first plenary session of the Conference: [58]

"In the preparations for this Conference we have sought from the beginning to build with vision and with justice, but to build always upon the realities and upon hard-won experience.

"To build upon a millennial idealism, however fine in theory, would be to build upon quicksand. To build only on the collaboration and interests of the major nations would be to deny the community of interests of all nations.

"We have sought instead to assure that the strength of the major nations will be used both justly and effectively for the common welfare—under the law of a world charter in which all peaceful nations are joined together.

"We began by seeking common understanding among the sponsoring nations on basic objectives and on the essential machinery for action. These are the nations which have united their strength against the aggressors so successfully in this war. We proceed now by seeking agreement among all the nations, large and small, which have been united against the common enemy."

Upon their publication on the morning of May 5, 1945, the "Joint Proposals" and the three accompanying "Proposals by the United States" [59] resulting from the extraordinary preparation became the basis, together with the proposals of other nations at the Conference,

---

[58] Apr. 26, 1945. *Department of State Bulletin*, XII, 792–95.

[59] Appendixes 62 and 63. Also in *Department of State Bulletin*, XII, 851–55.

for diplomatic negotiation and international decision upon the terms of the treaty that is the Charter of the United Nations.

When the Conference entered its "working-committee stage" on Monday May 7, after study on Saturday and Sunday of the amendments offered by the sponsors and by the other participating nations, hostilities were ending in Europe. The unconditional surrender of Germany was proclaimed by President Truman May 8, 1945. The Conference remained wholly a wartime one, however, the United States Delegation declaring through its Chairman: "The fighting is not yet over. We have still to win the same full final victory over Japan. . . ."[60]

The requirements of the task before the Conference—fundamental in their analytical and philosophical aspects and exacting with respect to the phrasing of each sentence of the developing Charter—took fifty-one days to fulfill. As this "working-committee stage" began, Secretary Stettinius reported to the President that the two amendments left unsettled in the consultations of the four Foreign Ministers had, late on the evening of May 6, been agreed to by Mr. Molotov, thus completing "substantial agreement" among the sponsor powers "on the outstanding issues before the Conference."

The many significant questions that arose during the working stage of the Conference are beyond the province of this volume.[61] Few were wholly new; some arose from divergent interpretations of agreed provisions; still others stemmed from differing views on the responsibilities to be vested in the organization and the distribution of power among its organs. The provisions in the Charter respecting both self-defense in the event of armed attack and the role of regional arrangements in relation to the functioning of the world security organization were among the most basic issues faced in the Conference, and an agreed position on these two questions that would take into account the views of other participating nations was not reached among the four sponsors and France, "the Big Five," until May 21. That a veto under the voting formula agreed to at Yalta could not prevent discussion by the Security Council of any international dispute or situation

---

[60] Statement for the United States Delegation by the Secretary of State, May 8, 1945; *Department of State Bulletin*, XII, 887.

[61] For a discussion of these questions as they were resolved by the Conference, see *Charter of the United Nations, Report to the President on the Results of the San Francisco Conference by the Chairman of the United States Delegation, the Secretary of State*, June 26, 1945. Department of State publication 2349, Conference Series 71.

was another crucial issue.[62]   Among others were the objectives of international trusteeship, certain specific provisions raised for inclusion among "purposes and principles," the scope of international economic and social cooperation, and the extent of the power of discussion and recommendation to be vested in the General Assembly.

To examine or review the amendments advanced by the other participating nations, the heads of the delegations of the sponsor powers and France instituted a new series of "informal consultations" on May 7.[63]   Their deputies also met regularly to give high-level technical and advisory consideration to these amendments in advance.[64] Separately conducted five power consultations on trusteeship continued and resulted on May 14 in an agreed "Working Paper" which was developed thereafter by the continuing consultations and by the Conference committee in this field into chapters of the Charter.[65]

The Dumbarton Oaks Proposals and the sponsors' amendments of May 4, which provided the framework for the organization and the basis of discussion in the Conference, were refined, adjusted, and filled out to become the Charter of the United Nations through the collective

---

[62] Interpretation to this effect was specifically agreed upon only through direct reference to Premier Stalin and Foreign Minister Molotov on June 6, 1945, during talks initiated by the United States and conducted in Moscow by Mr. Hopkins and Ambassador Harriman, accompanied by Mr. Bohlen. This interpretation had, however, been put forward by the United States at the Yalta Conference and had received tacit acceptance there in the agreement on the voting formula; see appendix 57. For the statement made by the delegations of the four sponsor powers on the voting question on June 7, see *The United Nations Conference on International Organization: Selected Documents,* Department of State publication 2490, Conference Series 83, pp. 751–54.

[63] These were usually called meetings of heads of the Delegations of the Five Powers but were termed in the minutes "Informal Consultations of the Foreign Ministers and Ambassadors of the United States, United Kingdom, Soviet Union, China, and France." The Soviet, British, and French Foreign Ministers departed in the first week of this series.

Informal group meetings also occurred, especially among the Latin American, Arab, and the British Commonwealth Delegations.

[64] Beginning May 8. The deputy for the Chairman of the United States Delegation was Mr. Pasvolsky, with Mr. Hartley assisting. These Deputies also considered the Interim Arrangements under which a Preparatory Commission was established by the Conference, effective June 26, 1945, to arrange for the first sessions of the Organs of the United Nations under the Charter. There were, in addition, other forms of consultation among the major powers, though at an adviser level, the most continuous of these being in the economic and social field, in which Messrs. Stinebower and Waring participated for the United States.

[65] This "Working Paper" did not represent Five Power agreement on all the points contained, and its presentation to the Conference was without prejudice to the right of the five participating powers subsequently to advance their individual views and to propose amendments. For text of this paper, see appendix 64.

effort of the representatives of fifty nations. These informed men and women—many of whom had had direct experience with the critical difficulties characterizing international relations throughout their generation, and some of whom, besides the Americans, had made a special effort of preparation for the peace—brought their individual experience and thought to bear on the decisions to be made by the Conference through a searching and lengthy process of debate, negotiation, and drafting.

President Harry S. Truman arrived in San Francisco on June 25 to address the closing session of the Conference on the following day. He approved the draft Charter, and attended its signing on June 26 by the United States Delegates: the Secretary of State, the two Democratic and Republican leaders of the Foreign Relations Committee of the Senate, the two Democratic and Republican leaders of the Foreign Affairs Committee of the House of Representatives, and the two Delegates from the general public. The "Father of the United Nations", Cordell Hull, signed the Charter later in Washington.

The seal of approval was placed on the extraordinary United States preparation for a general organization for the maintenance of international peace and security when the consent of the Senate to ratification of the Charter of the United Nations was granted, July 28, 1945, by vote of 89 in favor, with but two against, and with no reservation, and when the United States ratification was deposited in the Department of State on August 8, 1945. This was almost exactly four years after "the establishment of a wider and permanent system of general security" had been projected by President Roosevelt and Prime Minister Churchill in the Atlantic Charter.

The preparation had been completed before the end of hostilities in Europe. The United States decision approving the Charter was made before the formal surrender of Japan on September 2. The Charter entered into effect October 24, 1945.

Appendixes

Division for the Study of Problems of Peace and Reconstruction

The functions of the Division should be as follows:

1. To assemble information, ideas, and views, bearing on the problems of peace and reconstruction through

a. Special reports from our missions abroad;

b. Contacts with other Departments and agencies of the Government;

c. Informal contacts with appropriate unofficial groups in this country; with similar groups abroad; and with such international agencies as the League of Nations, the International Labor Office, the Bank for International Settlements, the International Chamber of Commerce, etc.;

d. Contacts with informed individuals;

e. Study of published and other available materials.

2. To build up systematic files of data and ideas on the following groups of topics, in their relation to the problems of peace and reconstruction:

A.

a. Commercial policy and relations;

b. Monetary problems;

c. Problems of investment and credit;

d. Other problems of economic relations.

B.

a. Territorial claims and problems of territorial adjustment;

b. Population and migration problems;

c. Possibilities of political arrangements for the maintenance of peace;

d. Problems of machinery for revision of treaties and peaceful settlement of disputes.

C.

a. Problems of limitation and reduction of armaments;

b. Problems of belligerent and neutral rights and obligations;

c. Problems of the humanitarian aspects of warfare.

D.

a. Methods of limitation of national sovereignty;

b. Problems of general machinery of international cooperation;

c. Other relevant problems.

---

[1] Attachment to memorandum of proposal discussed Dec. 27, 1939.

3. To study and analyze the materials assembled, and, if necessary, to engage in appropriate research activities;

4. To prepare for the use of the Intradepartmental Committee factual and/or analytical memoranda on various topics and on proposals and suggestions coming from various sources; and to record the Committee's proceedings.

It is not anticipated that the Division would engage in extensive research activities, at least for some time to come. At the outset, its work should be directed toward assembling and studying materials which are available; preparing appropriate instructions to the Missions; and attempting to influence the research activities of unofficial organizations in the direction of studying such problems or aspects of problems as would be of value to the work of the Division. Later on, if important lacks should appear in the materials gathered and systematically analyzed by the staff of the Division and if there should appear to be no promising chance of supplying the needs through outside agencies, the Division might have to develop its own research activities. For the present, therefore, the Division would not require more than a small staff, which could easily be recruited in the main by detail from the Foreign Service and from some of the existing Divisions in the Department.

APPENDIX 2
January 3, 1940

Subcommittee on Economic Problems of the Intradepartmental Committee on Peace and Reconstruction: Program of Work

I. OBJECTIVES

The objectives of the Subcommittee's work should be to assemble information and ideas, on the basis of which our Government will be able to

1. Prepare for possible participation in a Conference;
2. Prepare for participation in reconstruction efforts during the post-Conference period;
3. Attempt to influence the policies and actions of other governments prior to the Conference.

II. CURRENT PROBLEMS

The Subcommittee should proceed on the obvious basic assumption that whatever economic order may result from a Conference and the reconstruction efforts of the post-Conference period must grow, in large measure, out of the conditions which will develop during the pre-Conference period. Hence the importance of objective No. 3 above. As part of the basis for pursuing this objective, the Subcommittee should give its attention to five principal fields, as follows:

1. Commercial policy and relations.
2. Monetary policy and relations.
3. Credit and investment relations.
4. Production trends.
5. Price trends.

In connection with each of these fields, the following data are needed for as many countries as might seem to be desirable, such data to be currently kept up to date:

1. Statistical position.
2. Government action.
3. Influencing factors other than government action.
4. Relation of current developments abroad to basic ideas advocated by the Government of the United States.
5. Relation of current developments abroad to the interests of the United States.
6. Action taken or in contemplation by the Government of the United States with respect to particular developments.

A part of the Subcommittee's task should be to advise whether or not any particular action on the part of our Government mentioned above should be utilized as an opportunity to call the attention of other governments to basic ideas advocated by us. Similarly, the Subcommittee should advise whether or not such representations should be made in connection with any development abroad with respect to which no action on the part of our government is taken or is in contemplation.

The Subcommittee should also build up a factual and analytical file, currently kept up to date, on policy and actions of the Government of the United States in the five fields indicated above.

III. Broad Problems

In addition to data and ideas with reference to the subjects indicated above, the Subcommittee should secure the necessary data and prepare analytical reports on the following broad topics:

1. Character of a desirable economic world order.
2. How much of such a world order appears to be practicable on the basis of certain assumptions.
3. How much can be achieved through the peace conference.
4. What should be the direction and machinery of post-conference effort.
5. What policies would be necessary for the United States as a contribution to the establishment of such a world order.
6. On the assumption that the United States would be willing to pursue such policies, what contribution would have to be made by the other countries.
7. Relation of an economic program to political relations, disarmament, and other factors.

IV. Basic Analyses

As background material for its work in connection with Parts II and III of this outline, the Subcommittee should prepare or secure basic analyses on the following topics, and possibly others:

1. Economic provisions of the treaties of peace.
2. Economic policies pursued by the principal countries, 1919–1939.
3. Various types of government action in the economic field, especially during the last decade.
4. International economic efforts, 1919–39.

V. Proposals and Plans

Finally, the Subcommittee should study and analyze proposals and plans put forward in various quarters.

APPENDIX 3
January 15, 1940

Subcommittee on Economic Problems of the Advisory Committee on Problems of Foreign Relations

OUTLINE OF A MEMORANDUM ON THE BASES OF AN ECONOMIC SETTLEMENT

The Memorandum to be prepared along the lines of the following outline would be intended to serve as a program of action, which might be submitted as a basis of discussion to a Conference of Neutrals and/or to a more general Economic Conference. The topics covered in Part A should be embodied in a General Declaration to be adopted by the Conference. The topics covered in Part B should find expression in Resolutions and Conventions.

Part A: General Questions

I. The Desired Objectives
II. The Interdependence of Economic and Political Factors
III. The Interlocking of Commercial, Financial, Monetary, and other Economic Policies
IV. Types of Action

Part B: Technical Questions

I. Commercial Policy

1. Desirable Machinery of Trade Relations
2. Tariff Matters
3. Governmental Quantitative Controls
4. Most-favored-nation treatment
5. Regional Arrangements
6. Subsidies, Dumping, and other Forms of Unfair Competition
7. Indirect Protectionism

II. Problem of Raw Materials

1. Is there a Specific Raw Materials Problem?
2. Governmental Commodity Controls
3. Producers' Agreements
4. Machinery of Possible Action in the Light of Past Experience

III. Credit and Investment Policy

1. Probable Credit and Investment Needs of the Post-War World
2. Problems of Commercial Credit
3. Problems of Long-term Credit
4. Problems of Existing Indebtedness
5. Problems of Machinery of Credit and Investment

IV. Monetary Policy

1. Type of Monetary Arrangements Necessary for the Promotion of Trade, Credit, and Investment Relations
2. Problems involved in the Establishment and Maintenance of Such Arrangements

V. Other Factors in International Economic Relations
VI. General Machinery of International Action
VII. Problems of the Transitional Process
VIII. Contributions of Policy to be made by the United States in the Various Fields on Condition that Appropriate Policies would be adopted by other Countries

NOTE: In the initial stages, Sections VII and VIII would have to be worked out on the basis of various assumptions.

APPENDIX 4
February 29, 1940

[Memorandum, Pasvolsky to the Secretary (Hull)]

The following plan appears to offer the most feasible method of securing interdepartmental cooperation in connection with our economic consultations with neutrals:

A special interdepartmental committee should be created, to be known as Interdepartmental Advisory Committee on Economic Consultations with Neutrals. It should consist of representatives of the Departments of State, Treasury, Commerce and Agriculture, the Tariff Commission and the Export-Import Bank. As need arises, other Departments or Agencies might be invited to send their representatives. The committee should be under Department of State chairmanship and should have the following functions:

1. To draw up a formulation of our position as regards the implementation of the policies broadly set forth in our initial statement to the neutral nations, especially with respect to the specific policies and actions which we might, under appropriate conditions, be willing to pursue; and to make recommendations with respect thereto;

2. To consider replies and comments of a substantive nature received from the other governments with the view to determining our position with respect to them, and to make appropriate recommendations; and

3. To engage in, or arrange for, necessary studies in connection with the above.

For the purpose of carrying out the third function, the committee should, from time to time, set up small subcommittees to deal with specific topics.

The committee should be created for the special purpose of aiding in the conduct of consultations with other nations as to future economic arrangements. It should work in close contact with existing permanent committees in the various fields, which would, naturally, continue to carry out their normal functions. For example, it should refer all questions involving our basic commercial policies to the Executive Committee on Commercial Policy; all questions of trade-agreement arrangements and technique to the Committee on Trade Agreements; etc.

If you approve this plan, I would suggest that you discuss the matter in a broad way with the Secretaries of the Treasury, Commerce and Agriculture. I attach a memorandum of suggestions for such conversations.[2]

---

[2] Not printed.

APPENDIX 5
May 1, 1940

Memorandum [by Hugh R. Wilson] Arising From Conversations in Mr. Welles' Office, April 19 and 26[3]

I shall endeavor to set down subsequently a summary of the type of agreement which, in the opinion of the conferees, seems the most practical, but before doing so, think it advisable to make certain explanatory remarks. The questions of naval limitation or regulation and blockade were discussed at some length, most of us feeling that unless some solution of the naval problem is found, any suggestion as to land and air forces is unlikely to succeed. I need not enlarge on this discussion, it will be remembered by the participants. Also the discussion brought out the fact that to achieve disarmament and a force to make it effective, some machinery for political decision must exist, and that responsibility for the operation of an international force must rest with this body and not with an individual.

The project follows:

1. *Political Body* (regional in character)

Some explanatory remarks are necessary. It seems clear that there must be in Europe such derogation to the sovereignty of states as will make for quick and decisive action by the body. This involves the abolition of the rule of unanimity. But the practical power will reside, as always, in the hands of the Great Powers unless, which is unlikely, we can conceive of a Federated Union along the pattern of the United States. Hence in some form, perhaps in that of an Executive Committee, the Great States must be able to consult at once and decisively.

There are obvious economic advantages to be gained by the establishment in Europe of various blocs or free trade groups of states. There are political advantages as well which might flow from such formations, and if we consider each bloc as a political unit for the purposes of European administration it is possible to see a type of Executive Committee or Political Body which might function provided sovereignty could be curtailed to a point of agreement by each bloc to abide by a majority or two-thirds decision of the members of the body.

The blocs might be distributed as follows:

(1) Great Britain
(2) France (These two nations may or may not serve as separate blocs, in accordance with their post-war political development)
(3) Italy
(4) Germany
(5) Iberian Peninsula
(6) The Oslo group
(7) The Eastern Baltic States and Poland
(8) The Danubian States (Bohemia-Moravia, Slovakia, Hungary, Yugoslavia)
(9) The Balkan States (Rumania, Bulgaria, Greece).

The Political Body might consist of one member from each of these groups. The presidency might rotate each year in accordance with the precedent of the Federal Council of Switzerland.

---

[3] Addenda papers not printed.

The Political Body should exercise several functions either directly or by delegation to appropriate agencies.

(a) Reference of justiciable cases to the Permanent Court (as below).

(b) The functions of mediation and arbitration of disputes not arising under law, or those brought about by changed conditions. This is the safety-valve function and is proved indispensable by the experience of the past twenty years.

(c) Providing for treaty revision.

(d) To consider action on decisions reached and forwarded by the Permanent Disarmament Commission (see below).

(e) The power to issue command for action to the International Force.

(f) To consider reports from the Permanent Group (as below) and take appropriate measures.

2. *Permanent Court of Justice*

There should be a court of justice, perhaps the Permanent Court, to handle justiciable cases. The rules and constitution of the Permanent Court, however, would have to be modified to fit altered circumstances arising from the war. For instance, the dependence of the Court upon the League Council might have to be severed.

3. *Permanent Group*

There should be established a permanent group whose duty it would be to watch over events in the various countries and to announce to the Political Body any situation, together with recommendations for its treatment, which in the judgment of the group is likely to become acute and to lead to disturbance. The group should consist of selected individuals rather than government appointees, recognized for their wisdom, character and experience. The group should have wide powers for travel and investigation and perhaps for the maintenance of representatives in the various countries to furnish periodic reports of conditions.

4. *The International Force* (regional in character)

An international force shall be constituted under the following conditions:

(a) It shall consist of bombing planes and fighting planes for their protection.

(b) It shall be established at suitable strategic points either upon neutral soil, or, if this prove impracticable or inadvisable, upon internationalized soil, islands perhaps.

(c) Its personnel should be recruited from small neutral states.

(d) There should be a commander and several successors, all of neutral states, who have supreme authority as to operation but are subordinate to the Political Body as to the decision to begin operations and against which state to begin.

(e) Plants for production of such planes should also be situated in the neutral or internationalized zone.

(f) Contributions for the creation and maintenance of the force should be made immediately and for a considerable period in advance, say ten years.

5. *Disarmament Provisions* (primarily regional but with possible participation, for limited purposes, of states of the world).

(a) Abolition of bombers and prohibition of manufacture thereof, prohibition against bombing.

(*b*) Abolition and destruction of all mobile weapons of greater calibre than can be carried by a man or a horse twenty miles in twenty-four hours.

(*c*) Limitation on fighting and observation planes.

(*d*) Limitation on recruits (number and length of service).

6. *Permanent Disarmament Commission* (primarily regional but with possible participation, for limited purposes, of states of the world).

A permanent disarmament commission should be set up for the purpose,

(*a*) of continuing the study of disarmament methods and their application over and above those provided for in the disarmament agreement

(*b*) of verifying the operation of the disarmament agreement, both through reports and by means of inspection on the spot

(*c*) of watching import and export of arms, chemicals, et cetera, including inspection of factories for arms production in countries parties to the agreement

(*d*) of reporting to the Political Body any infraction of agreement

(*e*) of summoning the Political Body into being immediately in the case of serious infraction.

7. *Technical Commission* (worldwide in scope)

A permanent technical commission should be set up for the purpose,

(*a*) of study of trade policy, credit and monetary policy, international public projects, transportation, public health, intellectual cooperation, social problems, et cetera

(*b*) of examining the operation of existing agreements, and

(*c*) of arranging for negotiations of new agreements and making recommendations to the governments for changes necessitated by altered conditions.

APPENDIX 6
December 18, 1940[4]

Interdepartmental Group To Consider Post-War Economic Problems and Policies

ORGANIZATION OF WORK

The Group is an interdepartmental committee whose function it is to organize, direct, and review studies bearing on the problems of post-war international economic relations, especially from the viewpoint of possible alternatives of foreign economic policies for the United States. It works or proposes to work through the sub-committees indicated below. *The sub-committees already set up and at work are marked with an asterisk.*

I. *Sub-committees on Regional Studies*

The function of these sub-committees is to study several regions from the viewpoint of the economic aims and current economic practices of the nations respectively predominant in each of the regions, as well as of the economic structure

---

[4] Memorandum of agreed views reached in meeting of group Dec. 17, 1940.

and possibilities of each region under various assumptions as to the outcome of the war. The regions selected are as follows:

1. Germany and the Continent of Europe*
2. Japan and the Far East*
3. Soviet Russia*
4. The British Commonwealth*
5. The United States and the Western Hemisphere

II. Sub-committees on Commodity Studies

The function of these sub-committees is to prepare studies of world production, trade, and consumption of the principal basic commodities as of the pre-war period, and to examine the possibilities of alterations in the pre-war statistical picture in the areas which are the subjects of regional studies as a result of three types of policy: intensification of existing production or development of new production; substitution; regulation of consumption. The commodities or groups of commodities selected for study are as follows:

1. Foodstuffs, fats and oils*
2. Fibres*
3. Rubber, hides and skins*
4. Coffee, tea, cocoa, spices, tobacco*
5. Metals*
6. Fuels*
7. Lumber, pulp and paper*
8. Chemicals and other non-metallic mineral raw materials*

III. Sub-committees on Subject Studies

The function of these sub-committees is to prepare memoranda in each of the selected fields giving a description and an appraisal of the various systems and policies practiced or proposed in recent years. The fields selected are as follows:

1. Commercial Policy*
2. Monetary and Financial Policy
3. Transportation
4. Population Movements.

IV. Sub-committee on Alternatives of Foreign Economic Policy for the United States

The function of this sub-committee, which is to be set up later, will be to utilize the materials prepared by the other sub-committees for the purpose of setting forth and appraising the various alternatives of desirable and feasible foreign economic policies which are likely to be open to the United States on the basis of various assumptions as regards both domestic and international considerations and with respect to both long-range objectives of policy and the immediate post-war situation.

---

* For explanation of asterisk, see text above.

April 11, 1941

[Memorandum, Pasvolsky to Under Secretary Welles]

I have the following suggestions:

1. The time seems to be opportune for reviving the Advisory Committee on Problems of Foreign Relations.

2. The Committee should be reconstituted as a single body, rather than as a large group subdivided into three sub-committees.

3. The Committee should continue to be under your chairmanship, and a new vice-chairman should be appointed to replace Hugh Wilson.[5]

4. The Committee should, at this stage, have the following principal functions:

  a. To resume and continue the discussions which were begun last year after your return from Europe on the subject of the organization of peace. I expect that the Division of Special Research will be in a position to place before the Committee, as a basis for its discussions, appropriate documentation and analyses of proposals put forward from various quarters.

  b. To review plans for economic action as they are worked out by the Inter-departmental Group to Consider Post-war International Economic Problems and to direct negotiations on this subject with Great Britain and other countries as and when such negotiations are undertaken. In this connection, it will be necessary to reorganize the Interdepartmental Group to make it more effective for the purpose in view.

5. The following, in my opinion, should, in one way or another, be associated with the work of the Committee:

Mr. Welles	Mr. Long
Mr. Berle	Mr. Feis
Mr. Acheson	Mr. Duggan
Mr. Norman Davis	Mr. Atherton
Mr. Hackworth	Mr. Savage
Mr. Hornbeck	Mr. Reber
Mr. Dunn	Mr. Edminster
Mr. Pasvolsky	Mr. Hawkins

All of these, I think, would have something to contribute. Alternatively, it might be possible to constitute the first eight persons on this list (or, perhaps, a somewhat differently constituted group) as regular members and to bring in from time to time, as subjects come up which are of special interest to them individually, such of the others—and, perhaps, still others whose names do not appear here—as would have a special contribution to make with respect to any particular subject.

---

[5] Retired Jan. 1, 1941.

APPENDIX 8
A.   July 28, 1941
B.   February 23, 1942

[A. Draft of Article VII of a "Lend-Lease" Agreement Approved by the President for Discussion with the British Government; Handed by Assistant Secretary Acheson to John Maynard Keynes July 28, 1941]

ARTICLE VII

"The terms and conditions upon which the United Kingdom receives defense aid from the United States of America and the benefits to be received by the United States of America in return therefor, as finally determined, shall be such as not to burden commerce between the two countries but to promote mutually advantageous economic relations between them and the betterment of world-wide economic relations: they shall provide against discrimination in either the United States of America or the United Kingdom against the importation of any product originating in the other country; and they shall provide for the formulation of measures for the achievement of these ends."

[B. Text of Article VII of the Mutual Aid Agreement between the Governments of the United States and the United Kingdom, signed and sealed at Washington February 23, 1942.[6] Identical text in subsequent agreements made under the Lend-Lease Act of March 11, 1941]

ARTICLE VII

"In the final determination of the benefits to be provided to the United States of America by the Government of the United Kingdom in return for aid furnished under the Act of Congress of March 11, 1941, the terms and conditions thereof shall be such as not to burden commerce between the two countries, but to promote mutually advantageous economic relations between them and the betterment of world-wide economic relations.   To that end, they shall include provisions for agreed action by the United States of America and the United Kingdom, open to participation by all other countries of like mind, directed to the expansion, by appropriate international and domestic measures, of production, employment, and the exchange and consumption of goods, which are the material foundations of the liberty and welfare of all peoples; to the elimination of all forms of discriminatory treatment in international commerce, and to the reduction of tariffs and other trade barriers; and, in general, to the attainment of all the economic

---

[6] *Department of State Bulletin*, VI, 192.

objectives set forth in the Joint Declaration made on August 12, 1941, by the President of the United States of America and the Prime Minister of the United Kingdom.

"At an early convenient date, conversations shall be begun between the two Governments with a view to determining, in the light of governing economic conditions, the best means of attaining the above-stated objectives by their own agreed action and of seeking the agreed action of other like-minded Governments."

APPENDIX 9
September 12, 1941[7]

Proposal for the Organization of Work for the Formulation of Post-War Foreign Policies

1. The task of formulating post-war foreign policies, which involve, of course, this country's attitude toward and participation in the organization and maintenance of peace and the promotion of sound international economic relations, relates to three groups of problems, as follows:

    a. Political and territorial arrangements;
    b. Armament arrangements;
    c. Trade and financial relations.

These problems are closely interrelated and can be considered fully and adequately only under some unified auspices and well-defined leadership.

2. Policies with regard to these problems are of concern to several departments and agencies of the Government. Among these, however, the Department of State has, by the very nature of the problems themselves, always had and has today by far the greatest share of responsibility.

Problems relating to political and territorial arrangements fall predominantly into the province of the Department of State. They cannot, however, be usefully considered apart from the other two groups of problems.

Problems relating to armament arrangements, while they concern the War and Navy Departments on the technical side, fall into the province of the Department of State on the all-important diplomatic side. Moreover, they cannot usefully be considered apart from the problems relating to political and territorial arrangements.

Trade and financial relations, while they concern several departments and agencies of the Government, similarly cannot usefully be considered apart from the problems relating to political and territorial arrangements and, in somewhat lesser degree, the problems relating to armament arrangements. Moreover, on the all-important negotiation side, economic problems fall predominantly into the province of the Department of State.

While it is thus clear that many departments and agencies of the Government should participate fully in the work of formulating an effective program of foreign policy designed to implement the principles expressed in the eight points of the Roosevelt-Churchill statement, it is equally clear that the task involved logically requires that leadership in the preparation of such a program should be

---

[7] Memorandum, Pasvolsky to the Secretary (Hull), transmitting memorandum of same date not printed.

exercised, under the President, by the Department of State, or, more specifically, by the Secretary of State.

3. The Department of State, recognizing its primary responsibility in this field, has, since the outbreak of war in Europe, taken some steps to meet this responsibility. In January, 1940, a departmental Advisory Committee on Problems of Foreign Relations was established. It was made up of officials of the Department and two prominent persons outside the Department. It was active for several months, but has been inactive since. In May, 1940, the Department took the leadership in organizing an informal Interdepartmental Group to Consider Post-War International Economic Problems and Policies. This Group, which is still in existence, brought together, under the chairmanship of Mr. Pasvolsky, experts of the Departments of State, the Treasury, Commerce and Agriculture, the Tariff Commission, the Federal Reserve Board, and the Army and Navy Munitions Board. In the summer of 1940, when the Group was working on an economic program for the Havana Conference, its meetings were attended also by experts of the Reconstruction Finance Corporation, the Export-Import Bank, and the Commodity Credit Corporation. The Group has been inactive for the past few months, partly because of the increasing preoccupation of the various departments and agencies with current problems and partly because of the inherent difficulty of carrying on work of this kind on a purely informal basis. In February, 1941, there was set up in the Department a Division of Special Research, charged, among its other duties, with the conduct of studies in the field of post-war problems. The Division has been increasingly active in this field. Finally, the Department has had very useful cooperation of the Council on Foreign Relations and of other groups outside the Government working in this field. There is clearly a need now for expanding the Department's own work and its leadership in the entire field.

As matters stand today, several departments and agencies of the Government are carrying on programs of study in the economic field, more or less sporadically and independently of each other. Moreover, in the Executive Order of July 30, establishing an Economic Defense Board under the chairmanship of Vice President Wallace, the Board was directed (Article 3, paragraph 3) to "make investigations and advise the President on the relationship of economic defense measures to post-war economic reconstruction and on the steps to be taken to protect the trade position of the United States and to expedite the establishment of sound peace-time international economic relationships."

Under these circumstances, there is grave danger that work with respect to post-war economic policies will either be done independently by several agencies of the Government or else that it will be coordinated under other leadership than that of the Department of State; will be hopelessly intermingled with the consideration of war problems, since the emphasis in the Economic Defense Board must of necessity be on war rather than on post-war questions; and will be carried on in more or less complete isolation from work on the other groups of problems and policies involved in post-war reconstruction. This latter work must necessarily be done by the Department of State, although even here there is some danger that independent activities along these lines might be undertaken by Colonel Donovan's organization, again resulting in an intermingling of war and post-war problems.

The fact that the Department is represented on Vice President Wallace's Board can scarcely create for it an adequate position of leadership or provide for sufficient integration of the entire work in its several phases (political, territorial, armament, economic). If ultimate confusion and loss of valuable time are to be avoided, the task of formulating post-war foreign policies should be safeguarded from being subordinated to the work involved in meeting current war problems and should logically be organized under the formal and active leadership of the Department of State.

4. This can best be done in one of two ways, as follows:

A. For the President to announce publicly that he has assigned to the Secretary of State primary responsibility for preparatory work on all phases of post-war foreign policies, with authority to appoint an Advisory Committee on Post-War Foreign Policy under his own chairmanship, or a chairman of his designation, and to set up such working facilities as he might find desirable.

B. For the President to appoint an Advisory Committee on Post-War Foreign Policy, designating the Secretary of State as Chairman and empowering him to create the necessary organization. Plan A is far preferable to plan B, and there exists a good precedent for it. This is what was done very effectively in the case of the Trade Agreements Program. There is even more cogent reason for it in this case because of the greater variety of the problems involved and the greater measure of responsibility developing on the Department of State with regard to these problems.

5. In either case, it would be highly desirable that Vice President Wallace should be a member of the Advisory Committee. Accordingly, the Committee might be made up as follows:

Secretary of State, Chairman
Under Secretary of State, Vice Chairman to act as an alternate for the Chairman when necessary
Vice President Wallace
Four or five prominent persons outside the Department of State
Four or five officials of the Department of State

One of the Department of State members of the Committee should be designated as its Executive Officer and be charged with responsibility for the administrative phases of the work and for the coordination of the research and other activities needed for the functioning of the Committee itself and of its subcommittees.

6. The Advisory Committee should operate through three subcommittees as follows:

Political and Territorial Problems. This subcommittee should consist of some members of the Advisory Committee, the Political Advisers of the Department of State, and possibly some additional members.

Armament Problems. This subcommittee should consist of some members of the Advisory Committee, some competent officers of the Department, and, at some stage, of representatives of the War and Navy Departments.

Subcommittee on Economic and Financial Problems. This subcommittee should be entirely interdepartmental in character and should consist, in addition to some members of the Advisory Committee, of competent officials of the Departments of State, Treasury, Commerce and Agriculture, as well as of the Tariff Commission, the Federal Reserve Board, and, perhaps, other agencies. It should be in close contact with agencies, within and outside the Government, working on domestic post-defense problems. The subcommittee should replace the existing informal interdepartmental group.

7. Under this arrangement, the Advisory Committee would be the central guiding and coordinating body, while the subcommittees would be responsible for work in their respective specialized fields. The research work and the drafting of memoranda and documents would be done by the Division of Special Research

and other appropriate divisions of the Department of State, by similar divisions of other departments and agencies of the Government, and by such non-governmental agencies as the Council on Foreign Relations and any others that might be willing to cooperate with the Government in this respect. All such activities would be under the direction of the subcommittees in their respective fields, operating under the authority of the Advisory Committee. Recommendations to the President would be submitted solely through and in the name of the Chairman of the Advisory Committee, i. e., the Secretary of State.

8. In this manner, it would be possible to mobilize for the end in view and to the greatest advantage the entire resources of the Government and the best brains outside the Government. The work would proceed expeditiously, with a minimum of overlapping as among the various agencies of the Government, with responsibility clearly and properly allocated, and with possible differences of opinion among the participants reduced to their essentials by the time the results reach the President.

APPENDIX 10
May 10, 1943

[Memorandum (Notter) to the Secretary (Hull)]

S: Mr. Secretary

The schedule of the subcommittees on post-war problems meeting this week is as follows:

Thursday, May 13, 2:30 p. m.
Joint meeting of the Special Subcommittee on International Organization and the Subcommittee on Security Problems.
Subjects: Revised draft of General United Nations Protocol for the War and Transition Period; draft of Protocol for a Four-Power Security Agreement.
Place: Conference Room (474).

Friday, May 14, 3:00 p. m.
Special Subcommittee on Legal Problems.
Subject: International Judicial Organization.
Place: Mr. Hackworth's Office.

Friday, May 14, 5:00 p. m.
Subcommittee on Territorial Problems.
Subjects: Palestine; Syria and the Lebanon.
Place: Conference Room (474).

Saturday, May 15, 10:30 a. m.
Subcommittee on Political Problems.
Subject: Underlying questions concerning future international juridical organization.
Place: Your Office.

The Committee on Post-War Economic Policy will not meet until June 4.

Agenda for the Meeting of May 8, 1943

1. Opening Statement.
2. Discussion of the questions raised with respect to Political Action.
3. Reading of the questions on Juridical Procedures to be discussed at the next meeting, for the purpose of helping the members of the Committee to give some thought to these problems in the meantime.

[Attachments]

May 8, 1943

OPENING STATEMENT

The discussion last Saturday dealt with the question

What is involved in safeguarding our security by preventing another war?

The discussion proceeded on the assumption that the answer to this question involves four principal types of action, as follows:

1. Political action to prevent differences between nations from arising or from reaching the state of conflict.
2. Juridical procedures to deal with such differences as cannot be adjusted by political action.
3. Enforcement procedures.
4. Concerted action, especially in the field of economic development and progress.

The consensus of opinion last Saturday pointed to the need of creating international machinery to provide an effective vehicle for these various types of action. Before serious consideration can be given by this Committee to the precise forms of such international machinery, it is necessary to explore the extent to which, in the judgment of the members of the Committee, the United States should be prepared to participate in each of the types of action indicated. Such exploration must, of course, itself be tentative. It should be intended to provide a foundation upon which to base realistically proposals for the forms of international machinery.

We propose to devote the next three or four meetings to such an exploration. At the meeting today, we shall take up certain questions relating to political action for the prevention of wars. At the meeting next week, we shall examine certain questions relating to juridical procedures; and at the following meeting, questions relating to enforcement procedures. After that, we shall take up for more detailed examination questions relating to concerted action in the field of economic development and progress.

---

[8] Memoranda (Pasvolsky and Staff) to the Chairman of the Subcommittee on Political Problems (Secretary Hull).

For discussion on May 8, 1943

I. POLITICAL ACTION

With regard to political action for the prevention of wars, it is necessary to examine the following propositions and questions:

1. Political action for the prevention of wars requires that an international body or bodies be established to which any participating nation can bring for consideration any difference threatening the peace that may arise between it and another nation when direct negotiations have failed. Such a body should possess the right to require that differences between nations, not referred to it by either of the parties, be brought before it for consideration, whenever in its judgment such differences threaten international peace. Would the United States be willing, as a member of such a body, to appear before it when the United States is a party to a controversy—on condition, of course, that all other member nations accept a similar obligation?

2. Should the procedure operate on a regional or universal basis, or on a combination of the two? If the latter be the case, should, for example, a difference between two European countries be brought before a European body, but a difference between a European and an American country be brought before a universal body? In the case of regional procedure, should the United States participate in any non-American regional body?

At this stage, the problem of political action should be considered apart from the problem of the use of concerted measures to compel non-recourse to war as a means of settling international disputes. This latter problem will be examined at a later stage of the discussion.

For Discussion on May 15, 1943

II. JURIDICAL PROCEDURES

With regard to juridical procedures for the prevention of wars, it is necessary to examine the following propositions and questions:

1. International action for the prevention of wars requires the establishment of an international court or courts to which disputes which threaten the peace between nations and which have not otherwise been settled must be referred for adjudication and final decision. To what extent should the United States be willing to accept for itself the obligations growing out of its participation in such juridical machinery?

2. Should the juridical procedure operate on a regional or universal basis, or on a combination of the two? If the latter be the case, what should be the respective jurisdictions of regional and world courts, and what should be the geographic basis of United States participation?

At this stage, the problem should be considered apart from the problem of enforcement of court decisions, which will be taken up at the next stage of discussion.

For Discussion on May 22, 1943

III. ENFORCEMENT PROCEDURES

The problem of enforcement procedures requires the examination of the following questions:

1. Should the United States participate—and to what extent—in joint international action, including the use of force if necessary, designed (1) to prevent

or repress violation of stated international obligations; (2) to prevent or repress other national acts that may threaten international peace; (3) to enforce decisions of international courts?

2. Should the procedures involved operate on a regional or universal basis, or on a combination of the two? If the latter be the case, what should be the relative scope of regional and universal enforcement procedures, and what should be the geographic basis of United States participation?

3. Should the United States participate in a general agreement for the limitation of armaments, and should it be willing to accept an obligation to set both maximum and minimum limits of its armed forces?

APPENDIX 12
March 17, 1943

Memorandum For The President

Herewith is attached amended draft relating to dependent peoples, dated March 9, 1943.

C[ORDELL] H[ULL]

[Attachment]

March 9, 1943

DECLARATION BY THE UNITED NATIONS ON NATIONAL INDEPENDENCE

In the Declaration signed on January 1, 1942, the United Nations pledged themselves to a complete victory in this war for the preservation of liberty, independence, human rights and justice. They also proclaimed their resolve to attain, for themselves and for the human race as a whole, the objectives stated in the Joint Declaration of President Roosevelt and Prime Minister Churchill dated August 14, 1941, known—from the region in which it was formulated—as the Atlantic Charter. That Charter sets forth certain fundamental principles and purposes, applicable to all nations and to all peoples, among which are the following:

Respect for the rights of all peoples to choose the form of government under which they will live;

Restoration of sovereign rights and self-government to those who have been forcibly deprived of them; and

Establishment of a peace which will afford to all nations the means of dwelling in safety within their own boundaries, and which will afford assurance that all the men in all the lands may live out their lives in freedom from fear and want.

By their adoption of the Atlantic Charter as an integral part of the Declaration of January 1, 1942, the 31 United Nations have thus affirmed their determination that the independence of those nations which now possess independence shall be maintained; that the independence of those nations which have been forcibly deprived of independence shall be restored; that opportunity to achieve independence for those peoples who aspire to independence shall be preserved, respected, and made more effective; and that, in general, resolute efforts will be made to create a system of world security which will provide for all nations and all peoples greater assurance of stable, peace and greater facilities for material advancement.

The carrying out of these pledges imposes important responsibilities upon those peoples who possess or who are seeking to regain independence and upon all peoples who aspire to independent status. The particular pledge that peoples who aspire to independence shall be given an opportunity to acquire independent status is, therefore, in varying degrees, of concern to all of the United Nations and to all nations and peoples which now, or which may hereafter, cooperate in carrying forward and applying the provisions of the Atlantic Charter. The effectuation of that pledge requires that all such nations and peoples collaborate to that end with each other to the fullest practicable extent. Accordingly, the United Nations hereby make the following Declaration:

I

1. It is the duty and the purpose of those of the United Nations which have, owing to past events become charged with responsibilities for the future of colonial areas to cooperate fully with the peoples of such areas toward their becoming qualified for independent national status. While some colonial peoples are far advanced along this road, the development and resources of others are not yet such as to enable them to assume and discharge the responsibilities of government without danger to themselves and to others. It is, accordingly, the duty and the purpose of each nation having political ties with colonial peoples:

a. To give its colonial peoples protection, encouragement, moral support and material aid and to make continuous efforts toward their political, economic, social, and educational advancement;

b. To make available to qualified persons among the colonial peoples to the fullest possible extent positions in the various branches of the local governmental organization;

c. To grant progressively to the colonial peoples such measure of self-government as they are capable of maintaining in the light of the various stages of their development toward independence;

d. To fix, at the earliest practicable moments, dates upon which the colonial peoples shall be accorded the status of full independence within a system of general security; and

e. To pursue policies under which the natural resources of colonial territories shall be developed, organized and marketed in the interest of the peoples concerned and of the world as a whole.

2. It is incumbent upon all peoples that aspire to independence to exert themselves in every feasible way to prepare and equip themselves for independence—socially, economically, and politically—to the end that they may, as soon as possible, be able to create, conduct and maintain, for, by and of themselves, efficient structures of stable self-government based on sound principles of social and political morality. In the present moment of world emergency, the capacity and desire of such peoples for the enjoyment of freedom can best be demonstrated by their contribution now toward the defeat of the Axis foes of all freedom and independence.

3. The carrying out of the policies above declared will necessarily call for much and continuous consultation and collaboration between and among the nations which are directly responsible for the future of various colonial areas and other nations which have substantial interests in the regions in which such

areas are located. In order to provide an effective medium for such consultation and collaboration, there shall be created in each region, by agreement of the nations thus concerned, a commission on which each of those nations shall be represented and in the work of which the various colonial peoples concerned shall have appropriate opportunity to participate and to have or to achieve representation.

II

1. As a result of the last war, peoples in several areas still unprepared for full independence were released from political ties with nations formerly responsible for them. Other peoples in like status may be similarly released from their former political ties as a result of this war. It is the purpose of the United Nations to assume with respect to all such peoples a special responsibility, analogous to that of a trustee or fiduciary. The United Nations hereby recognize it as their duty to give the fullest cooperation to such peoples in their efforts to prepare themselves for independence through political, economic, social, and moral advancement—and eventually to arrange for their assumption of independent status. To this end, they recognize it as their duty to observe in the case of such peoples each of the policies, obligations and methods hereinbefore set forth for observance by independent countries toward their own colonial peoples.

2. In order to carry out effectively the purposes and functions described in the preceding paragraph, the United Nations propose to establish, as soon as circumstances permit, an International Trusteeship Administration composed of representatives of the United Nations and of all other nations which now, or which may hereafter, cooperate in carrying forward and applying the provisions of the Atlantic Charter. The Administration will operate through regional councils composed of representatives of the nations having major interests in the respective regions. The machinery of each council will be so designed as to give the peoples of the territories held in trust in its region full opportunity to be associated with its work.

Appendix 13
July 14, 1943 [9]

Draft Constitution of International Organization

Preamble

The United Nations,

Having dedicated themselves to the principle of peaceful relations between states, and

Having subscribed to a common program of human rights,

Hereby establish and agree to maintain the instrumentalities by which peace and human rights may be assured.

---

[9] Document of the Special Subcommittee on International Organization. Brackets in this paper as in the original.

Article 1

MEMBERS OF THE INTERNATIONAL ORGANIZATION

1. The membership of the International Organization shall reflect the universal character of the international community.

2. All qualified states and dominions shall be Members of the International Organization. The Council shall decide as to the nature of the qualifications.

Article 2

ORGANS OF THE INTERNATIONAL ORGANIZATION

1. The action of the International Organization under this instrument shall be effected through an Executive Committee, a Council, a General Conference, a Secretariat, a Bureau of Technical Services, and such other bodies as may be recognized or established by the International Organization.

Article 3

THE EXECUTIVE COMMITTEE

1. The Executive Committee shall be composed of representatives of the United States of America, the United Kingdom of Great Britain and Northern Ireland, the Union of Soviet Socialist Republics, and China. The Council by unanimous vote may designate additional Members.

2. Other Members of the International Organization may, by the unanimous vote of the Executive Committee, be invited to participate in the discussion of designated problems.

3. The Executive Committee shall have responsibility in matters of international security as laid down in Article 10.

4. Powers reserved to the Council may, in emergency cases when the Council is not in session, be exercised by the Executive Committee.

5. The General Secretary shall act as permanent chairman of the Executive Committee. The Executive Committee, through the General Secretary, shall keep the Council currently informed of its work. The Executive Committee shall establish rules governing its own procedure.

6. Except as otherwise expressly provided in this instrument, decisions by the Executive Committee shall be by a unanimous vote of the Members present. Questions of procedure may be decided by a majority of the Members present.

Article 4

THE COUNCIL

1. The Council shall be representative, directly or indirectly, of all the Members of the International Organization.

2. It shall be composed of eleven representatives including one representative designated by the United States of America, one by the United Kingdom of Great Britain and Northern Ireland, one by the Union of Soviet Socialist Republics, one by China, two by the group of European states, two by the group of American states, one by the group of Far Eastern states, one by the states of the Near and Middle East, and one by the British Dominions. Each of these states and groups of states shall arrange the method of selection and the tenure of office of its representatives. The states composing each group are listed in an Annex to this instrument.

3. Changes in the number of Members of the Council may be made by a majority vote of the General Conference with the concurrence of the Executive Committee.

4. Any Member of the International Organization not directly represented on the Council shall be entitled, subject to approval by a majority of the Council, to attend and be heard during the consideration of matters which specially affect the interests of that Member.

5. The Council shall have authority to supervise and coordinate the work of the various organizations, bureaus, committees or commissions which may be recognized or established under this instrument, and report periodically thereon to the General Conference. It may also deal with any situation or condition which may threaten an impairment of the good relations among peoples.

6. The General Secretary shall act as permanent chairman of the Council. The Council shall establish rules governing its own procedure and otherwise perfect its organization.

7. At meetings of the Council each state or group of states shall have one representative and one vote. Except as otherwise expressly provided in this instrument, decisions by the Council shall be by a two-thirds majority of the Members present, provided all the Members of the Executive Committee concur. Questions of procedure may be decided by a majority of the Members present.

8. The Council shall remain in permanent session. It may recess from time to time, subject to call by the chairman at his own discretion or at the request of any two or more Members. It shall regularly meet at the seat of the International Organization. It may hold special meetings at such other place or places as may be agreed upon or as may be deemed by the chairman, in any emergency, to be most convenient.

ANNEX

Representatives on the Council, other than representatives of the United States of America, the United Kingdom of Great Britain and Northern Ireland, the Union of Soviet Socialist Republics, and China, shall be elected by the groups of states listed below.

Group of European States (2 representatives)		Group of Far Eastern States (1 representative)	
Albania	Luxemburg	China	Philippines
Austria	Netherlands	Japan	Thailand
Belgium	Norway	[Korea]	
Bulgaria	Poland		
Czechoslovakia	Portugal	*British Dominions*	
Denmark	Rumania	(1 representative)	
Estonia	Spain	Australia	United Kingdom of
Finland	Sweden	Canada	Great Britain
France	Switzerland	[India]	and Northern Ire-
Germany	United Kingdom of	New Zealand	land
Greece	Great Britain and	Union of South	
Hungary	Northern	Africa	
[Irish Free State]	Ireland		
Italy	Union of Soviet So-		
Latvia	cialist Republics		
[Liberia]	Yugoslavia		
Lithuania			

| *Group of American States* | | Salvador | Venezuela |
| (2 representatives) | | Uruguay | |

Argentina	Guatemala
Bolivia	Haiti
Brazil	Honduras
Chile	Mexico
Colombia	Nicaragua
Costa Rica	Panama
Cuba	Paraguay
Ecuador	Peru
United States of America	Dominican Republic

Group of Near and Middle Eastern States

(1 representative)

Afghanistan	[Liberia]
Egypt	Palestine
Ethiopia	[Sa'udi Arabia]
Iran	[Syria]
Iraq	Turkey
[Lebanon]	

Article 5

THE GENERAL CONFERENCE

1. The General Conference shall be composed of representatives of all Members of the International Organization accepting the obligations of membership, and having governments capable of discharging the duties incumbent upon Members of the International Organization.

2. The General Conference shall have authority to act upon any matter of concern to the international community, and such special matters as may be referred to it by the Executive Committee or the Council. As to matters falling specifically within the scope of functions of the Executive Committee or of the Council, and which have not been referred to it by these bodies, any action of the General Conference shall take the form of recommendations. In the case of specific questions pending before the Executive Committee or the Council, action by the General Conference shall be subsequent to that of these bodies.

3. The General Conference, at the request of the Executive Committee, shall give such assistance in the application of security measures as may be deemed necessary for the restraint of aggression and the maintenance of peace.

4. With respect to the various organizations, bureaus, committees, or commissions which may be recognized or established under this instrument, the General Conference shall have the authority to secure their technical advice, to initiate action through these bodies, and to set up other agencies for specific purposes.

5. The budgetary estimates of the International Organization and its constituent bodies shall be subject to examination and approval by the General Conference and by the Council, which shall determine the method by which the necessary funds shall be provided and properly allocated among the Members.

6. The General Conference may, with the approval of the Council, accept voluntary contributions for defraying current expenses or establishing an endowment for general or specific purposes.

7. Each member of the General Conference shall have one vote. Except as otherwise expressly provided in this instrument, decisions by the General Conference shall be by a two-thirds majority of the Members present. Questions of procedure may be decided by a majority of the Members present.

8. The General Conference shall meet annually in regular session. It shall convene in special session at the call of the President acting at his own discretion or on request of the Executive Committee, or of the Council.

9. The President of the General Conference shall be chosen by majority vote from among its members. He shall hold office for a period of one year, and shall not be eligible to succeed himself for reelection.

10. The General Conference shall establish rules governing its own procedure and otherwise perfect its organization.

Article 6

THE GENERAL SECURITY AND ARMAMENTS COMMISSION

1. The General Security and Armaments Commission shall be established by the Council as a permanent advisory and administrative agency to assist the Council and the Executive Committee in giving effect to the provisions of this instrument relating to the application of security measures and the control of armaments according to the procedure of Article 10.

2. The Commission shall be expert in character and be widely representative of the members of the United Nations. It shall be composed of military, naval, aviation, and civilian representatives of the states and groups of states represented on the Council. Additional representatives may be designated by the Council. Each member of the Commission may be accompanied by alternates and experts. The Commission may set up a panel of special experts, and may appoint committees whose number, composition, and functions shall be subject to approval by the Council.

3. The General Security and Armaments Commission shall be charged with the following specific duties: (a) to study the quantitative limitations of armaments as provided in Article 10; (b) to supervise and report to the Council on the execution and maintenance of armaments stipulations as laid down by the Council, and to advise on any modifications; (c) to study all technical matters pertaining to the application of security measures, and to take charge of the technical coordination of security measures instituted by the Council or the Executive Committee.

4. An Armaments Inspection Commission shall be established by the Council to carry out the duties of armaments inspection laid down in Article 10, paragraph 7. It shall act under the authority of the General Security and Armaments Commission, and be composed of military, naval, aviation, and other technical experts, a majority of whom shall be nationals of states other than those having individual representation on the Council. It shall report regularly to the Council through the General Security and Armaments Commission.

Article 7

THE SECRETARIAT

1. A permanent Secretariat shall be established at the seat of the International Organization. It shall comprise a General Secretary and such secretaries and staff as may be required.

2. The General Secretary shall be appointed by the Council with the approval of a majority of the General Conference. His tenure of office shall be indefinite, subject to removal for cause by a two-thirds majority of the General Conference. The secretaries and staff shall be appointed by the General Secretary with the approval of the Council. In making appointments the widest distribution among nationalities shall be made that is compatible with technical efficiency.

3. The officials of the permanent Secretariat shall be exclusively international officials, having international and not national duties. They shall on appointment make a declaration of loyalty to the International Organization agreeing to discharge their duties and regulate their conduct with the interests of the International Organization alone in view and not to seek or receive instructions from any Government or other external authority.

4. The General Secretary, or officials designated by him, shall act in that capacity at all meetings of the General Conference, of the Council, and of the various organizations or committees falling within the framework of the International Organization.

5. The secretarial staffs of other organizations, bureaus, or commissions, established within the framework of the International Organization but not located at the central seat of the Organization, shall be subject to the general staff regulations governing the central secretariat. The direction of these secretariats shall be in charge of the principal secretary or director of that office or bureau.

6. All positions under, or in connection with, the International Organization shall be open equally to men and women.

7. Officials of the International Organization when engaged on the business of the Organization shall enjoy diplomatic privileges and immunities.

Article 8

THE JUDICIARY

1. A permanent court of international justice and such additional international tribunals as may be found to be necessary shall be maintained. The General Conference shall establish a committee of jurists which shall make recommendations concerning necessary alterations or revisions in the Statute of the Permanent Court of International Justice, and concerning the establishment of additional tribunals.

Article 9

PEACEFUL ADJUSTMENT

1. The Members of the International Organization agree to facilitate a settlement of all their differences by peaceful means in accordance with the procedures set forth in this instrument.

2. Any condition whose continuance might disturb the peace or the good understanding between nations, or any dispute which if unsettled might lead to a rupture, shall be settled by direct negotiation, by negotiation through intermediaries, by recommendation of the Council or the General Conference, or by judicial decision.

3. Any state shall have the friendly right to bring to the attention of the Council or the General Conference any condition or dispute which in its view may disturb the peace or the good understanding between nations:

(*a*) If the action is initiated by any party directly involved in such condition or dispute, the Council or the General Conference may institute the procedure of paragraph 4 by a majority vote.

(*b*) If the action is initiated by a state not directly involved, the Council or the General Conference may institute the procedure of paragraph 4 by a two-thirds vote.

4. If the Council or the General Conference decides that action should be taken, the Council shall cause an investigation to be made and shall cause such action to be taken as it may deem necessary to facilitate a settlement. If the Council fails to effect a settlement in this manner, it shall make a report on the whole case to the General Conference, including recommendations for a settlement which it deems just and equitable.

5. The General Conference, taking into account the report of the Council, any opinions rendered at the request of the Council or otherwise by the Permanent Court of International Justice, and any additional considerations, shall make such recommendations for a settlement as it may deem just and equitable. If these recommendations are approved by a three-fourths [vote] of the Members present, exclusive of the parties, it shall be the duty of the parties to give effect to them.

Article 10

SECURITY AND ARMAMENTS

1. Any menace to the peace of nations, wherever it arises, is a matter of vital concern to all states. The International Organization through its Executive Committee or Council, shall take any action necessary to safeguard or restore peace.

2. In the event of a breach, or imminently threatened breach, of the peace between nations, the Chairman of the Council, on consultation with such members of the Executive Committee as may be available, shall request the parties to desist from any action which would further aggravate the situation and shall forthwith summon a meeting of the Council. The Council shall request the parties to restore or maintain the position existing before the breach or threatened breach of the peace and to accept procedures of peaceful settlement. The state or states failing to comply with this request within the time specified shall be presumed to intend a violation of the peace of nations and the Executive Committee or the Council shall apply all the measures necessary to restore or maintain the peace.

3. Members of the International Organization undertake in no case to give a state, declared by the Council to be threatening or committing a violation of the peace, assistance of a character which in the opinion of the Council would aggravate the dispute.

4. Members of the International Organization agree to make available for action taken under paragraph 2 to restore or maintain peace such armaments, facilities, installations, strategic areas and contingents of armed forces, and to afford such freedom of passage through their territories, as the Council or the Executive Committee, advised by the General Security and Armaments Commission, may determine to be necessary for this purpose, having regard for the geographical position, regional or special obligations, and relative resources of member states. All national forces and facilities shall operate under their national authorities subject to the general control of the Executive Committee and the technical coordination of operations provided by the General Security and Armaments Commission.

5. Member States agree to carry out such measures of an economic, commercial, or financial character as the Council or the Executive Committee shall determine to be necessary for the successful prosecution of action undertaken in accordance with this Article. They mutually agree to support one another in compensating excessive losses resulting from the execution of these measures, and in resisting any measures of reprisal resulting from such action.

6. Members of the International Organization undertake to keep the general level of their armaments at the lowest point consistent with the effective discharge of their respective obligations for maintaining international security, and consistent with their internal domestic security. They accordingly agree that the Council, acting on the advice of the General Security and Armaments Commission, and taking into account the special responsibilities for security assumed by some states, and the collective responsibility assumed by all, shall establish

the minimum and maximum limitations on armaments and the regulations of previously agreed categories of armaments potential to be observed by all members. These limitations and regulations shall be subject to modification and amendment by the Council.

7. The limitations and regulations established under paragraph 6 shall be enforced by a system of inspection carried out by the Armaments Inspection Commission under the direction of the General Security and Armaments Commission. Member States agree freely to accord to the Commission every facility for the effective discharge of its mission.

8. Any action by the Council under this Article shall require a two-thirds majority vote including three-fourths of the states members of the Executive Committee.

Article 11

ECONOMIC AND SOCIAL COOPERATION: BUREAU OF TECHNICAL SERVICES

1. There shall be established as a part of the International Organization a Bureau of Technical Services. Subject to the general supervision of the Council, the Bureau of Technical Services shall assist the Council, the General Conference, and the Members of the International Organization in developing, on the basis of mutual and common interest, international collaboration in fields other than military security with a view to making the most effective use of the world's human and material resources, to increasing the wealth and improving the standards of living of all nations, and to promoting social security, economic stability, general well-being and peace throughout the world.

2. The Bureau of Technical Services shall be under an Administrative Director selected by the Council on the basis of his internationally recognized technical and administrative competence. It shall be organized with the following sections, each in charge of a Director also selected by the Council in consultation with the Administrative Director on the basis of internationally recognized technical competence: (a) General Economics and Finance, (b) Labor, (c) Trade and Industry, (d) Agriculture, (e) Communications, (f) Health, (g) Relief and Social Welfare, (h) Trusteeship, (i) Migration and Resettlement, and (j) Education and Cultural Relations. The Council may from time to time alter the number of sections and define the scope of their work.

3. The sections of the Bureau shall be so organized as to have in their respective fields adequate technical competence in research, program-development and administration. Subject to the direction of the Council, these sections shall cooperate with other international agencies functioning within the fields of their interests, and act as liaison between such agencies and the International Organization.

4. The Council or the General Conference, with the assistance of the sections of the Bureau, may establish committees or convene conferences of qualified experts to consider matters within designated fields of interest, and they may make provision for cooperation with other international agencies functioning in such fields to the extent found to be desirable and practicable. [See Interpretative Note to Article 11].

5. The Council and the General Conference shall have authority to call upon the sections of the Bureau, and upon the committees or conferences referred to in paragraph 4, for technical advice and assistance and to request them to undertake specific technical assignments. The Directors of the various sections of the Bureau and representatives of other international agencies may be invited by the Council to participate in the discussions of any subject in which they may be specially interested.

6. To assist the Council in coordinating the work of the Bureau of Technical Services and of the various committees and conferences, there shall be established an Administrative Committee composed of the Administrative Director, as Chairman, and the Directors of the various technical sections. The Members of the staff of the Bureau and representatives of other international agencies may be invited to participate in the discussion of designated problems. To facilitate the task of coordination, the Council shall define the jurisdiction of the various sections, committees and conferences, and arrange for the joint consideration of problems of interest to more than one of them.

7. The Administrative Committee shall meet periodically and at the call of the Chairman. It shall examine the reports of the various technical sections, committees and conferences, and of other international agencies functioning within the same or related fields, and shall submit these reports together with its own report and recommendations to the Council and the General Conference for action by these bodies or by the Members of the International Organization.

8. The sections of the Bureau, the various committees and conferences, and any other international agencies which depend for their budgetary requirements on the International Organization shall submit their annual budgetary estimates for review by the Administrative Committee. The Administrative Committee shall transmit such estimates with its own recommendations to the Council and the General Conference.

Interpretative Note to accompany Article 11

1. The functions of the agencies envisaged in Article 11 (paragraph 2) shall include the following:

(*a*) General Economics and Finance

> an agency or agencies to assist in the task of economic reconstruction, to facilitate access to the trade and raw materials of the world, to encourage mutually advantageous programs of industry and agriculture, and to cooperate in bringing about such conditions of exchange and credit as will encourage private and public investment necessary for effective use of the world's resources and the improvement of standards of living;

(*b*) Labor

> an agency or agencies to assist in industrial and labor rehabilitation to promote among all peoples improved labor standards, economic advancement, and social security, and to prevent all forms of slavery and forced labor;

(*c*) Communications

> an agency or agencies to facilitate mutually advantageous regulation of air navigation, telecommunications, and of transit by land and sea;

(*d*) Health

> an agency or agencies to prevent the rise and spread of epidemics, to effect cooperation for the improvement of public health, to raise the standard of nutrition, and to combat the illicit traffic in drugs dangerous to public health;

(*e*) Social Welfare

> an agency or agencies to deal with problems of relief, migration and resettlement of peoples, the protection of young people, and the suppression of traffic in women and children;

(f) Education and Culture

an agency or agencies to further the mutual understanding of the ideals and outlook of peoples by increasing the facilities of cultural inter-change, to promote participation in common enterprises in education, the arts and sciences, and to prevent the dissemination of propaganda which might embitter the relations between peoples.

2. The General Conference and the Council, in carrying out the purposes of Article 11, may take into account and utilize the services, to the extent which may be practicable, of the various existing agencies for international cooperation, such as:

The International Labor Organization
The Economic and Financial Organization
The Health Organization
The Communications and Transit Organization
The Intellectual Cooperation Organization
The Social Questions Committee

as well as any committees and conferences which may have been established by the United Nations.

3. The General Conference and the Council, advised by the Administrative Committee, shall also consider, in consultation with the competent authorities of the international technical organizations of a primarily administrative charac-ter, what relationship with the International Organization would be mutually advantageous. Such administrative bodies might include:

The Universal Postal Union (1875)
The International Bureau of Weights and Measures (1876)
The International Bureau for the Protection of Industrial Property (1884)
The International Telecommunications Union (1926)
The International Hydrographic Bureau (1919)

Article 12

TRUSTEESHIP

1. To those non-self-governing territories which are inhabited by peoples not yet able to stand by themselves, the principle of trusteeship shall be applied in their governance in accordance with which the welfare of the inhabitants and the general interest of other peoples shall be assured under the authority and super-vision of the International Organization.

2. The trusteeship over any such people shall be effected through the agency of a state or a group of states, acting under the supervision of a Regional Council, and all performing their trust under the authority of the Council of the Inter-national Organization according to the distribution of powers set forth in the Trusteeship Protocol attached to this instrument.

3. The territories to be so administered, and the designation and composition of the administrative and supervisory authorities, shall be determined by the Council of the International Organization. Provisionally, or until the Council decides that the trusteeship shall be altered or terminated, the administrative and supervisory authorities and the territorial dispositions under them shall follow the plan laid down in Annex III of the Trusteeship Protocol.[10]

4. The Administration in each territory shall exercise its authority according to a charter which shall set forth the duties, responsiiblities and powers deemed

---

[10] Not printed.

by the Council of the International Organization to be most suitable to the stage of development of the peoples in that territory, having regard to social and economic conditions, to factors affecting general security, and other circumstances. All charters, however, shall contain provisions to assure:

(a) the preparation and education of the inhabitants for self-government;
(b) protection of the inhabitants from exploitation, and the promotion of economic and social justice;
(c) abolition of all forms of slavery and forced labor;
(d) control over the liquor and drug traffic, and the traffic in arms;
(e) freedom of conscience;
(f) establishment and maintenance of non-discriminatory commercial treatment;
(g) promotion of equality of economic opportunity consistent with the safeguarding of the interests of the local inhabitants.

5. The Council of the International Organization and the Regional Supervisory Councils shall have the right of inspection in the territories brought under the Trusteeship.

6. The inhabitants of the territories shall have the right of petition directly to the Regional Supervisory Council of that area in conformity with the regulations or conditions prescribed by the Supervisory Council or the Council of the International Organization.

7. The Council of the International Organization shall in each case determine the terms and conditions under which the trusteeship shall be altered or terminated.

Article 13

REGIONAL ARRANGEMENTS

1. Nothing in this instrument shall be deemed to affect such regional arrangements, associations or agreements, now existing or which may be entered into, provided these arrangements are not inconsistent with the aims and purposes of this instrument. The Council or the General Conference may encourage the establishment of such arrangements, associations or agreements, when deemed desirable to give effect to the general purposes of the International Organization.

2. In the event that any controversy arises as to the consistency of such arrangements, associations or agreements with the aims and purposes of this instrument, the Council may refer the legal aspects of the question to the Permanent Court of International Justice for an opinion.

Article 14

TREATIES

1. This instrument shall form a part of the supreme law of each Member State, any contrary provision in its treaties or other international acts notwithstanding.

2. The Members of the International Organization undertake not to conclude or continue any treaty or other international act which is inconsistent with the provisions of this instrument.

3. Every treaty or other international act entered into by Members of the International Organization with any Member or non-Member shall be submitted to the Secretariat for registration and prompt publication. The texts of treaties so registered and published shall be regarded for purposes of the International Organization as the authentic texts.

Article 15

EXPENSES

1. The expenses of the International Organization shall be borne by the Members in proportions determined by the General Conference and the Council.

2. Regulations for the financial administration of the Organization shall be approved by the General Conference and the Council.

3. A Treasurer shall be appointed by the Council with the approval of the General Conference.

4. The Treasurer shall receive and administer all funds of the International Organization.

Article 16

AMENDMENTS

1. Amendments to this instrument shall take effect upon their approval in the General Conference by a vote of three-fourths of the Members present, including the affirmative vote of each of the Members of the Executive Committee present, provided that no amendment proposed shall be voted upon by the General Conference without first having been submitted by the General Secretary to the States Members at least nine months prior to action by the Conference.

APPENDIX 14
December 3, 1942 [11]

Bill of Rights

Article I

Governments exist for the benefit of the people and for the promotion of their common welfare in an interdependent world.

Article II

All persons who are willing to work, as well as all persons who through no fault of their own are unable to work, have the right to enjoy such minimum standards of economic, social and cultural well-being as the resources of the country, effectively used, are capable of sustaining.

Article III

1. All persons shall enjoy equality before the law with respect to life, liberty, property, enterprise and employment, subject only to such restrictions as are designed to promote the general welfare.

2. No person shall be deprived of life, liberty or property except in accordance with humane and civilized processes provided by law.

Article IV

All persons shall enjoy freedom of conscience, of religious belief, and of public and private worship, provided that the exercise of these rights does not conflict with public order or good morals.

---

[11] Document of the Special Subcommittee on Legal Problems.

Article V

All persons shall enjoy freedom of speech and of the press, and the right to be informed, subject only to the restraints necessary to the maintenance of public order and good morals.

Article VI

All persons shall enjoy the right, acting individually or in concert, peacefully to petition the government for a redress of grievances or to address complaints to the public authorities.

Article VII

All persons shall enjoy the right to assemble peaceably and to form associations for political, cultural, social and economic purposes, subject to the right of the state to take reasonable measures for the maintenance of public order and the prevention of subversive activities.

Article VIII

All persons shall enjoy an equal right of participation in education publicly provided. Persons receiving public education shall not be obliged to participate in religious instruction in a faith to which they or their parents do not adhere.

Article IX

1. The right of the people to be secure in their persons, houses, papers and effects from surveillance, search, seizure, arrest and detention shall not be denied or abridged except by orderly process determined by law and upon the establishment or probable cause.

2. No measures of unnecessary severity shall be used in making arrests. A person arrested for any cause shall be brought promptly before a competent judicial authority who shall within a reasonable time hold a hearing and either release the arrested person or issue an order, giving reasons for his detention. If the person detained is not charged with the commission of a crime, he shall have the right to have the propriety of his detention reconsidered by such authority at reasonable intervals.

Article X

1. In all criminal proceedings the accused shall not be subjected to threats or intimidation. He shall be presumed to be innocent until he is proved guilty, and he shall enjoy the right to a speedy, fair and public trial by an impartial court.

2. The accused shall enjoy the right to be informed of the nature and cause of the accusation against him, to be confronted with the witnesses against him, to have compulsory process for obtaining witnesses in his favor, to have the assistance of counsel for his defense, and to petition the court for his release.

Article XI

Cruel and unusual treatment shall not be inflicted in the detection, prevention or punishment of crime, nor excessive bail required, nor excessive fines imposed.

Article XII

No person shall be punished except in virtue of a law in force prior to the commission of the offense, and no penalty shall be imposed in excess of that in force at the time the offense was committed.

Article XIII

Any person charged with the commission of a crime shall be tried only before a court having jurisdiction over him in accordance with the preexisting law.

Article XIV

After having been duly acquitted of a crime no person shall be tried again for the same offense.

Article XV

No state shall deny to a person born within its territory the citizenship of the state unless he acquires at birth citizenship in another state.

Article XVI

These human rights shall be guaranteed by and constitute a part of the supreme law of each state and shall be observed and enforced by its administrative and judicial authorities, without discrimination on the basis of nationality, language, race, political opinion, or religious belief, any law or constitutional provision to the contrary notwithstanding.

APPENDIX 15
June 25, 1943 [12]

Tentative Proposal for Revision of the Statute of the Permanent Court of International Justice

Article 1

The Permanent Court of International Justice is reconstituted in accordance with the provisions of this Statute.

CHAPTER I
ORGANIZATION OF THE COURT

Article 2

The Permanent Court of International Justice shall be composed of a body of fifteen judges elected regardless of their nationality from among persons of high moral character and juridical eminence. No person shall be eligible for initial election who has passed the age of sixty-five years.

Article 3

1. At the time of constituting the Court, and thereafter as vacancies occur, the Council of the International Organization shall by majority vote of the members present, subject to confirmation by the General Conference of the International Organization by majority vote of the members present, appoint a Nominating Committee of nine persons of high eminence who, while fulfilling the function of presenting nominations, shall represent only the international community. The Committee shall be convened in the first instance on the call of the Chairman

[12] Initial proposal of the Special Subcommittee on Legal Problems.

of the Council and thereafter on the call of the Registrar of the Court. Upon the completion of the election for which it was appointed to serve, the Committee shall cease to exist.

2. At the time of the initial election of judges, the Committee shall nominate thirty persons. At subsequent elections it shall nominate three persons for each place to be filled.

3. From the nominations so made, the Council, by a majority vote of the members present, shall elect the judges of the Court, subject to confirmation in each case by the General Conference by majority vote of the members present.

4. If the General Conference fails to confirm any person elected by the Council, the Council shall, subject to confirmation by the General Conference, elect an additional judge from the list of nominees.

5. If the list of nominees is exhausted and a place on the Court remains unfilled, the Nominating Committee shall submit additional names as provided in paragraph 1. This procedure shall continue until all places are filled.

Article 4

At every election the Nominating Committee, the Council and the General Conference shall bear in mind that not only should all judges of the Court possess the qualifications required, as well as competence in the use of one of the official languages, but that the whole body should be so constituted as to represent the main forms of civilization and the principal legal systems of the world.

Article 5

1. The judges of the Court shall be elected for nine-year terms and shall be eligible for reelection.

2. They shall retire upon attaining the age of seventy-five years. They shall continue to discharge their duties until their places have been filled, and they may, at the discretion of the President of the Court, finish a term of Court then in progress.

3. In the case of the resignation of a member of the Court, the resignation shall be addressed to the President of the Court for transmission to the Chairman of the Council. This last notification makes the place vacant.

Article 6

No member of the Court shall exercise any political or administrative function or pursue any other occupation of a professional nature. Any doubt on this point shall be settled by the decision of the Court.

Article 7

1. No member of the Court may participate in the decision of any case in which he has previously taken an active part as agent, counsel or advocate for one of the contesting parties, or as a member of a national or international Court, or of a commission of inquiry, or in any other capacity.

2. Any doubt on this point shall be settled by the decision of the Court.

Article 8

1. A judge shall be subject to removal when, in the unanimous opinion of the other judges, he has ceased adequately to fulfill the functions of his office.

2. Formal notification of a decision to this effect shall be made to the Chairman of the Council by the Registrar. This notification makes the place vacant.

Article 9

Whenever a judge has absented himself from more than one-fourth of the sessions of the Court over any two-year period, excepting authorized vacations, such fact shall be brought to the attention of the Court by the Registrar, and unless within a succeeding period of sixty days of such notice the other judges by unanimous vote decide that the absence has been for reasonable cause, the Registrar shall notify the Chairman of the Council that the place has become vacant. This notification makes the place vacant.

Article 10

The members of the Court and the Registrar of the Court including their immediate families and official personnel, when traveling to or from the seat of the Court or when in residence at the seat of the Court, shall enjoy diplomatic privileges and immunities.

Article 11

Every member of the Court shall, before taking up his duties, make a solemn declaration in open court that he will exercise his powers impartially and conscientiously.

Article 12

1. The Court shall elect its President and Vice-President for a term of three years; they may be re-elected.

2. It shall appoint its Registrar.

Article 13

The seat of the Court shall be at The Hague.

Article 14

The Court shall remain permanently in session except during the judicial vacations, the dates and duration of which shall be fixed by the Court.

Article 15

1. If, for some special reason, a member of the Court considers that he should not take part in the decision of a particular case, he shall so inform the President.

2. If the President considers that for some special reason one of the members of the Court should not sit on a particular case, he shall give him notice accordingly.

3. In event of disagreement between the members of the Court and the President, the matter shall be settled by the decision of the Court.

Article 16

1. The full Court shall sit except when it is expressly provided otherwise in this instrument. A quorum of nine judges shall suffice to constitute the Court.

2. The Rules of the Court may provide for allowing one or more judges, according to circumstances and in rotation, to be dispensed from sitting, *provided* that the number of judges available to constitute the Court is not reduced below eleven.

Article 17

1. In order to facilitate the work of the Court, the President may from time to time with the concurrence of the other members of the Court establish one or more chambers composed of not less than three members of the Court, to continue for such periods as he may direct. The President is empowered to

make such assignments of judges as may be necessary to enable a chamber to perform its function. Three judges shall be necessary to constitute the quorum of a chamber.

2. The President of the Court may assign to a chamber thus established particular cases, or particular classes of cases, *provided* that neither party objects.

3. The chambers shall exercise their jurisdiction within the same general limitations as are provided in this statute for the Court as a whole.

Article 18

The decision of a chamber established under Article 17 shall be final if any time prior to the rendering thereof the parties agree that it shall be final. Either party may, within two months following the date of the rendering of the decision, petition the full Court for an order requiring the Chamber to submit the decision for review. In the absence of such a petition the decision shall become final two months after the rendering thereof.

Article 19

The Court shall frame rules for regulating its procedure and that of any chamber created by it.

Article 20

If the Court includes upon the Bench a judge or judges of the nationality of one only of the parties (or joint parties), he or they shall retire from consideration of the case if requested to do so by the other party.

Article 21

1. The annual salaries and necessary emoluments of the judges shall be fixed by the General Conference of the International Organization on the recommendation of the Council. The salaries may not be decreased during the term of office.

2. The salaries of the Registrar and other personnel of the Court shall be fixed by the General Conference on the recommendation of the Court.

3. Matters relating to retirement annuities for the judges and other officials of the Court (as well as those relating to traveling expenses) shall be fixed by regulations of the General Conference.

Article 22

The expenses of the Court shall be borne by the International Organization in such a manner as shall be decided by the General Conference upon the proposal of the Council.

CHAPTER II

COMPETENCE OF THE COURT

Article 23

Any state, or any agency of the International Organization which is so authorized by terms of the instrument by which it was created, may be a party to cases before the Court.

Article 24

1. The jurisdiction of the Court shall comprise all cases involving disputes as to the respective rights of the parties which the parties refer to it or which, in the event that a threat to the peace exists, may be referred to it by the Council; and all such matters specially provided for in treaties and conventions in force.

2. Any state or any international organization eligible under Article 23 may at any time declare that it recognizes as obligatory *ipso facto*, and without special agreement, in relation to any other state or international organization eligible under Article 23, the jurisdiction of the Court in all or any cases involving disputes as to the respective rights of the parties. This declaration may be made unconditionally or on condition of reciprocity on the part of several or certain states, or for a certain time.

3. The Court shall have the power upon the petition of any interested party or parties eligible to institute proceedings under Article 23, to declare rights and other legal relations of such party or parties, provided that the case is submitted to the Court in accordance with the terms of this Article. Such declaration shall have the force and effect of a final judgment, whether or not further relief is or could be claimed.

4. The Court shall have the power to give an advisory opinion upon any dispute or question referred to it by the Council or the General Conference. In the exercise of its advisory functions, the Court shall be guided by the provisions of this Statute which apply in contentious cases to the extent to which it recognizes them as applicable.

5. In any case arising under this Article, notice shall be given to all interested parties, and such parties shall be given an opportunity to be heard.

6. In the event of a dispute as to whether the Court has jurisdiction, the matter shall be settled by the decision of the Court.

Article 25

The Court shall have jurisdiction in its discretion to review a decision of any international court or tribunal, provided that the application for review is made in accordance with an agreement entered into by the parties. Any dispute as to the right of petition under such agreement shall be submitted for decision to the Court.

Article 26

The Court shall apply:

1. International conventions, whether general or particular, establishing rules expressly recognized by the contesting States;

2. International custom, as evidence of a general practice accepted as law;

3. The general principles of law recognized by civilized nations;

4. Judicial decisions and the teachings of the most highly qualified publicists of the various nations, as subsidiary means for the determination of rules of law.

Nothing in this article shall prejudice the power of the Court to decide a case *ex aequo et bono*, if the parties agree thereto.

Article 27

The decision of the Court has no binding force except between the parties and in respect of that particular case.

Article 28

The judgment is final and without appeal. In the event of dispute as to the meaning or scope of the judgment, the Court shall construe it upon the request of any party.

Article 29

1. An application for revision of a judgment can be made only when it is based upon the discovery of some fact of such a nature as to be a decisive factor.

which fact was, when the judgment was given, unknown to the Court and also to the party claiming revision, always provided that such ignorance was not due to negligence.

2. The proceedings for revision will be opened by a judgment of the Court expressly recording the existence of the new fact, recognizing that it has such a character as to lay the case open to revision, and declaring the application admissible on this ground.

3. The Court may require previous compliance with the terms of the judgment before it admits proceedings in revision.

4. The application for revision must be made at latest within six months of the discovery of the new fact.

5. No application for revision may be made after the lapse of ten years from the date of the sentence.

Article 30

1. Should a State consider that it has an interest of a legal nature which may be affected by the decision in the case, it may submit a request to the Court to be permitted to intervene as a third party.

2. It will be for the Court to decide upon this request.

Article 31

1. Whenever the construction of a convention to which States other than those concerned in the case are parties is in question the Registrar shall notify all such States forthwith.

2. Every State so notified has the right to intervene in the proceedings; but if it uses this right, the construction given by the judgment will be equally binding upon it.

CHAPTER III

PROCEDURE OF THE COURT

Article 32

1. The official languages of the Court shall be French and English. If the parties agree that the case shall be conducted in French, the judgment will be delivered in French. If the parties agree that the case shall be conducted in English, the judgment will be delivered in English.

2. In the absence of an agreement as to which language shall be employed, each party may, in the pleadings, use the language which it prefers; the decision of the Court will be given in French and English. In this case the Court will at the same time determine which of the two texts shall be considered as authoritative.

3. The Court may, at the request of any party, authorize a language other than French or English to be used.

Article 33

1. The Court shall have the power to indicate, if it considers that circumstances so require, any provisional measures which ought to be taken to reserve the respective rights of either party.

2. Pending the final decision, notice of the measures suggested shall forthwith be given to the parties and the Council.

Article 34

1. The parties shall be represented by agents.

2. They may have the assistance of counsel or advocates before the Court.

Article 35

1. For the service of all notices upon persons other than the agents, counsel and advocates, the Court shall apply direct to the government of the State upon whose territory the notice has to be served. The same provision shall apply whenever steps are to be taken to procure evidence on the spot.

2. At the request of the Court, a state shall take all steps, within its territory and compatible with its public interest and security, to obtain the execution of letters rogatory, the taking of depositions, and the production of all documents or exhibits, whether or not the state applied to is a party to the proceeding for which such evidence is required.

Article 36

The Court may, at any time, entrust any individual, body, bureau, commission or other organization that it may select, with the task of carrying out an enquiry or giving an expert opinion.

Article 37

1. Whenever one of the parties shall not appear before the Court, or shall fail to defend his case, the other party may call upon the Court to decide in favour of his claim.

2. The Court must, before doing so, satisfy itself, not only that it has jurisdiction, but also that the claim is well founded in fact and law.

Article 38

1. All questions shall be decided by a majority of the judges present at the hearing.

2. In the event of an equality of votes, the President or his deputy shall have the decisive vote.

Article 39

1. The judgment shall state the reasons on which it is based.

2. If the decision is not unanimous, the votes of the judges shall be recorded. Judges disagreeing with the opinion of the Court or part thereof shall be entitled to state succinctly their separate views.

Article 40

Unless otherwise decided by the Court, each party shall bear its own costs.

CHAPTER IV

AMENDMENTS

Article 41

Amendments to this instrument which are adopted by a two-thirds vote of the states represented in the General Conference shall take effect when ratified by three-fourths of the states that have subscribed to this instrument, including three of the four states having direct representation on the Executive Committee.

Poland: Ethnic Composition of the Population East of the Soviet-German Demarcation Line of September 28, 1939

I. ETHNIC DATA FOR THE AREA AS A WHOLE

The territory which was occupied by the Soviet Union in 1939 had an approximate area of 78,700 square miles and a population, according to the Polish census of 1931, of 11,850,571. This population, according to the statistics on mother-tongue, was made up of the following nationalities:

	Number	Percent		Number	Percent
Poles	4, 733, 046	39. 9	Russians	119, 269	1. 0
Ukrainians	4, 055, 365	34. 2	Lithuanians	75, 949	0. 6
White Russians	986, 605	8. 3	Germans	83, 850	0. 7
"Local" (Ukrainians and White Russians)	707, 088	6. 0	Jews	1, 036, 576	8. 7
			Czechs	31, 000	0. 3

II. ZONES OF ETHNIC SETTLEMENT

1. Northern Zone

In general, the northern half of eastern Poland is populated by Poles and White Russians, with some 75,000 Lithuanians living in the districts adjoining the pre-1939 Polish-Lithuanian frontier. A strongly Polish-speaking zone extends northeastward from the solid Polish bloc of central Poland to the pre-1939 Soviet-Polish frontier.

The *województwo* (province) of Bialystok (all but a small fraction of which was included in the Soviet-occupied area) is strongly Polish in character. Thence, the zone of Polish settlement extends eastward to the former Polish-Soviet frontier, embracing the northern *powiaty* (administrative districts) of the *województwo* of Nowogródek (Szczuczyn, Lida, Wolozyn and Stolpce), and northeastward along the former frontier between Poland and Lithuania, through the western *powiaty* of the *województwo* of Wilno (Wilno-Troki, Oszmiana, Swieciany and Braslaw). In each of these eight *powiaty* the Poles have an absolute majority; lumped together, these eight districts show a Polish-speaking population of 920,137, or 70.1 percent of their total.

The remaining eight *powiaty* in the two *województwa* of Wilno and Nowogródek show a White Russian total of 551,322 (53.3 percent), as against a Polish total of 395,445 (38.3 percent). The White Russians are strongest in the extreme northeastern corner of former Poland and in the *powiaty* of Nowogródek and Nieświez.

A line separating districts with Polish majorities or pluralities from those in which the White Russians are the most numerous linguistic group would follow the administrative boundary between the *powiaty* of Braslaw and Dzisna, then cut across Postawy (in which Poles and White Russians have approximately equal representation) to the junction of the Postawy-Swieciany boundary with the northern boundary of Wilejka, thence following the western boundaries of

---

[13] A factual background paper.

Wilejka and Molodeczno to the former Polish-Soviet frontier; following that line southwards as far as the administrative boundary between the *powiaty* of Stolpce and Nieświez, it would then turn westward and follow the northern boundaries of Nieświez, Baranowicze, Nowogródek and Slonim, to meet the eastern boundary of the *województwo* of Bialystok at the junction of the Szczara and Niemen Rivers. The eastern sector of the *województwo* of Wilno and the southern sector of that of Nowogródek would thus fall within White Russian-speaking territory, but these two areas would be separated by a strip of territory in which the Poles form the majority. The *powiat* of Baranowicze also has a slight Polish majority but it is surrounded by predominantly White Russian district; accordingly, it falls on the White Russian side of a hypothetical ethnic line.

The totals reported for the two *województwa* of the northern zone (Wilno and Nowogródek) are as follows:

		Percent			*Percent*
Poles	1, 315, 582	56. 4	Lithuanians	69, 337	3
White Russians	703, 141	30. 1	Jews	185, 853	8

2. Central Zone

The *województwo* of Polesie, which extends from the Bug River, in the Brest-Litovsk area, through the Pripet marshes to the former Soviet-Polish frontier, is overwhelmingly non-Polish. The census statistics show only 75,338 White Russians and 54,047 Ukrainians, as against 164,106 Poles, (14.5 percent) but 707,088 inhabitants (62.5 percent) are listed as "local". These are probably White Russians and Ukrainians, in any case, non-Poles. Polish spokesmen admit freely that this "local" population is White Russian and Ukrainian in language, religion and customs, but deny that it has any degree of White Russian or Ukrainian national or political consciousness. In this area the traditional line of cleavage has been Catholic (Polish) and Orthodox (White Russian and Ukrainian), divisions which largely coincide with the social cleavage between upper class (landowners and officials) and peasantry.

The *województwo* of Wolyń, directly south of Polesie, has a total population of 2,085,574, of whom 1,426,872 (68.4 percent) were reported as Ukrainian-speaking, and only 346,640 (17.1 percent) as Polish-speaking. There were also, in 1931, 46,883 Germans in this province, more than half of the German-speaking population of Eastern Poland, as well as a greater number of Jews (205,545) than in any other *województwo*.

In the two central *województwa* together, the Polish-speaking element comprises only 15.9 percent of the total population, and is in the minority in every political subdivision (*powiat*).

3. Southern Zone

South of the *województwo* of Wolyń lies Eastern Galicia, which includes the *województwa* of Tarnopol, Stanislawów, and the eastern part of Lwów. In this thickly populated area, with its 4,959,910 inhabitants, the Ukrainians have an absolute majority (51.9 percent), and the Poles represent 40 percent of the population. In the southeastern province of Stanislawów the Ukrainians are a majority in every *powiat* and make up 68.8 percent of the total population of 1,480,285; the Polish share is only 22.4 percent.

In the *województwa* of Lwów (eastern part) and Tarnopol, Poles and Ukrainians are fairly evenly balanced. This territory forms a corridor of mixed population bounded on the north and on the south by solidly Ukrainian-speaking areas; it extends eastward from the Soviet-German partition line of 1939, in the vicinity of the city of Przemyśl, all the way to the pre-1939 Polish-Soviet frontier. Its total population in 1931 was 3,479,625, of whom 1,651,756 (47.5 percent) were Polish-speaking, and 1,549,965 (44.5 percent) were Ukrainian-speaking. The two nationalities are evenly balanced in nearly every *powiat;* in only a few instances is the majority of one over the other as much as two-to-one. The heaviest Ukrainian majorities are found in the districts on the edges of the corridor of mixed population, bordering on the *województwo* of Wolyń to the north and on Carpathian Ruthenia and the *województwo* of Stanislawów to the south.

Running through the center of the corridor is a narrower strip, never more than about fifty miles wide, in which Polish majorities are consistent. These majorities are strongest in the vicinity of the city of Przemyśl, in the city and *powiat* of Lwów (where the 1931 census reported are 278,924 Polish-speaking and 93,532 Ukrainian-speaking persons), and in the area between the city of Tarnopol and the former Polish-Soviet frontier. This predominantly Polish strip includes the following *powiaty:* Przemyśl (eastern half), Mosciska, Rudki, Lwów (in the *województwo* of Lwów), and Kamionka Strumilowa, Przemyślany, Zloczów, Zborów, Tarnopol, Trembowla, Skalat and Zbaraz (in the *województwo* of Tarnopol). The number of Poles in this area is 853,960 (56.7 percent of the total population of 1,506,132), and the number of Ukrainians 490,224 (32.6 percent).

No line of ethnic division can be drawn through Eastern Galicia from north to south. The only possible lines run east and west, from the San River to the pre-1939 Polish-Soviet frontier, separating the strip of districts with Polish majorities from the predominantly Ukrainian-populated territory to the north and to the south. These lines are based purely on the language statistics.

III. ETHNIC CHARACTER OF THE POPULATION NEAR THE SOVIET-GERMAN LINE OF PARTITION

In the north, the Soviet-German line of partition cut through solidly Polish-populated territory. The *województwo* of Bialystok, lying almost entirely east of the line, is strongly Polish in character, especially its western districts. The northernmost *powiat*, Suwalki, which was joined to East Prussia pursuant to the Soviet-German agreement of September 28, 1939, is also overwhelmingly Polish. The eastern districts are more mixed, but the Poles, according to the census of 1931, are the most numerous nationality even there.

Where the line followed the Bug River along the western boundaries of the *województwa* of Polesie and Wolyń, it marked a rough lines of separation between Polish and non-Polish nationalities. All the *powiaty* of Polesie and Wolyń have non-Polish majorities, even the westernmost ones along the Bug River.

Where the line ran from the Bug to the San River (roughly, a straight line between Sokal, on the Bug, and Jaroslaw, on the San), it bisected a number of *powiaty* where the Polish-speaking and Ukrainian-speaking elements are fairly evenly balanced, with the latter having numerical superiority in Sokal and Rawa Ruska, the former in Lubaczów.

Along the San River, which the partition line of 1939 followed from the city of Jaroslaw to the former Polish-Czechoslovak border, the districts on the left bank, which fell to the Soviet Union, have Ukrainian majorities, with the exception of the eastern part of the *powiat* of Przemyśl (including the city of that name). The city of Lwów, which is less than one hundred kilometers east of the partition line, has a large Polish majority. In general, the San River is the dividing line between the overwhelmingly Polish-speaking part of the *województwo* of Lwów, to the west, and the mixed Polish and Ukrainian part to the east. The 1931 statistics give the Poles a slight majority in the eastern part, 862,642 as against 821,810. No sharp line of ethnic division can be drawn through this area. The line of September 28, 1939, left many Poles to the Soviet Union; but a line drawn to the east of the city of Lwów leaves almost as many Ukrainians in Poland.

IV. Ethnic Composition of the Territory Ceded by the Soviet Union to Lithuania, October 10, 1939

The area ceded by the Soviet Union to Lithuania on October 10, 1939 included the city of Wilno and the eastern parts of the *powiaty* of Braslaw, Swięciany and Wilno-Troki (all in the *województwo* of Wilno), plus a small corner of the *powiat* of Lida (in the *województwo* of Nowogródek). In each of these units the Poles outnumber the Lithuanians. The total population of the area (1931 census) was approximately 467,700, of whom 69.6 percent were Polish-speaking, 14.3 Yiddish-speaking, 8.8 percent Lithuanian-speaking, 3.7 percent Russian-speaking and 3.1 percent White-Russian-speaking. In the city of Wilno, with a population of 195,071, there were 128,628 Polish-speaking persons, 54,596 Yiddish-speaking, 7,372 Russian-speaking, 1,737 White-Russian-speaking, and 1,579 Lithuanian-speaking.

The Polish Census of 1931

While the Polish statistics of 1931 represent the best available data, their present usefulness is limited. In the taking of the census, political pressures undoubtedly maximized the registered total of Polish-speaking inhabitants at the expense of the non-Polish nationalities; to what degree this occurred is uncertain. Ukrainian nationalists have claimed repeatedly that the Polish census understated the number of their people. Foreign Commissar Molotov, in a speech of October 31, 1939, asserted that Soviet-occupied Eastern Poland contained seven million Ukrainian inhabitants and over three million White Russians; these estimates are much higher than the official Polish figures for 1931.

Since the census of 1931 the makeup of the population has undergone notable changes. Before the outbreak of war in 1939 the government of Poland fostered the settlement of Polish farmers in the eastern provinces. Since September 1939, the Polish element has been much reduced, perhaps by over one million, through the flight of many Poles to neighboring countries and through the migration and deportation of Poles to the interior of the Soviet Union. The German invasion and occupation have brought about further drastic changes, including extermination of a great part of the Jewish population and the transfer of forced labor to other areas under German domination. The actual situation upon the cessation of hostilities, can be determined only by detailed investigation on the ground.

Polish-Soviet Frontier: Alternative Boundaries

1. DESCRIPTION OF ALTERNATIVE BOUNDARIES [15]

The following ten lines, which cover most of the possible compromises between the frontier of 1938 and the Soviet-German partition line of September 28, 1939, will be discussed in terms of 1) their strategic implications for the two states and for general security in Europe; 2) the way in which they divide the various ethnic groups inhabiting the disputed area; 3) their probable economic advantages and disadvantages to the two states; 4) their bearing upon communications and transportation.

A. *The Soviet-German Partition Line of 1939*

This line followed the former Polish-Lithuanian boundary southwestward from the frontier of Latvia to the southernmost tip of Lithuania, then cut across the base of the Suwalki salient (leaving the *powiat* of Suwalki and part of that of Augustów to Germany) then followed the boundary between Poland and East Prussia and the Pisa and the Narew Rivers to the city of Ostrolęka, then ran in a southwesterly direction to meet the Bug River near the town of Malkinia; it followed the Bug upstream as far as the town of Krystynopol, in Eastern Galicia, turned west and ran in a nearly straight line to a point on the San River near Sieniawa, then followed the San River upstream to the old border between Poland and Czechoslovakia.

In the consideration of this line as a possible Polish-Soviet boundary the point where the Pisa River crosses the boundary of East Prussia will be taken as the northern terminus; the Suwalki district thus falls on the Soviet side of the line.

B. *The Curzon Line of 1919 and its Continuation Through Eastern Galicia*

On December 8, 1919, the Supreme Council of the Allied and Associated Powers recognized the right of Poland "to proceed with the organization of a regular administration" in the territory west of a line which followed the Bug downstream from the northern border of Eastern Galicia to the administrative boundary between the districts of Bielsk and Brest-Litovsk, then ran in a general northeasterly direction to pass east of the town of Hainowka and reach the Lososna River, near its source; it followed the Lososna River, with some deviations, to its confluence with the Niemen River, then followed the latter past Grodno to the district of Suwalki, the eastern and northern Boundary of which it followed, with slight deviations, to the border of East Prussia.

The line which the Supreme Council accepted, in 1919, as the western boundary of Eastern Galicia, for which a special status was under consideration, was a continuation of the Curzon Line. It followed the southern boundary of the province of Lublin as far as Belzec, then turned south to follow the western boundaries of the districts of Rawa Ruska, Jaworów, Mosciska, Sambor, Stary Sambor and Turka.

---

[14] A problem paper. In B below, the reference to the "Curzon Line" is to the line of Dec. 8, 1919, to which the name of Lord Curzon became attached in 1920. All the following footnotes in appendix 17 are in the original document.

[15] See Map 13, Polish Series (Eastern Poland: Distribution of Population). [Printed as appendix 19.]

C. *Line "C"*

This line follows the eastern boundary of the province (*województwo*) of Bialystok from the former Polish-Lithuanian border to the Bug River, and the Soviet-German partition line of 1939 thereafter.

D. *Line "D"*

This line is identical with line "C" as far as the northern boundary of Eastern Galicia; from that point it continues along the Bug River upstream to the city of Kamionka Strumilowa, whence it runs due south and follows the eastern boundary of the province of Lwów to the point where it meets the Bóbrka-Przemyślany road; it then turns west to run south of the city of Bóbrka to the point common to the three districts (*powiaty*) of Lwów, Bóbrka and Zydaczów, and follows, with slight deviations, the eastern boundary of the province of Lwów to the former Polish-Czechoslovak frontier. This line follows an alternative western boundary of Eastern Galicia proposed by the British Delegation to the Peace Conference in 1919.

E. *Line "E"*

This line follows the eastern boundaries of the following districts leaving them all within Poland: Swięciany, Wilno-Troki, Oszmiana, Lida, Szczuczyn, Wolkowysk, Bielsk; it then follows the Soviet-German partition line of 1939 from Niemirów (the point where the administrative boundary between the districts of Bielsk and Brześć-nad-Bugiem meets the Bug River) to the former frontier between Poland and Czechoslovakia.

F. *Line "F"*

This line is identical with Line "E" as far as the point common to the three districts of Bielsk, Brześć-nad-Bugiem and Pruzana; it then follows the eastern boundaries of the following districts, leaving them all within Poland: Brześć-nad-Bugiem, Luboml, Wlodzimierz, Sokal, Zolkiew, Lwów, Bóbrka, Zydaczów and Kalusz.

G. *Line "G"*

This line follows the eastern boundaries of the provinces of Bialystok and Lublin, then the southern boundary of Wolyń and the eastern boundary of Tarnopol thus leaving to the Soviet Union the four eastern provinces of Wilno, Nowogródek, Polesie and Wolyń.

H. *Line "H"*

This line is identical with Line "G," except for the attribution to Poland of the three districts of Brześć-nad-Bugiem, Luboml and Wlodzimierz.

I. *Line "I"*

This line is identical with Line "F" from the border of Lithuania to the border of Eastern Galicia, whose northern and eastern boundary it follows to the point common to the pre-1939 frontiers of Poland, Rumania and the Soviet Union.

J. *Line "J"*

This line is identical with Line "B" (Curzon Line) as far as the northern border of Eastern Galicia, then continuing along the Bug River upstream to the city of Kamionka Strumilowa, and running south along the boundary between the provinces of Tarnopol and Lwów, then along the boundary between Tarnopol and Stanislawów, to terminate at the former Polish-Rumanian frontier near Zaleszczyki.

II. STRATEGIC CONSIDERATIONS

1. *Soviet Strategic Aims*

The territory between Line "A" and the former Polish-Soviet frontier provided a cushion for absorbing the German attack in 1941; the time which the Soviet armies won by fighting delaying actions in former Polish territory may have been a crucial factor in saving Moscow and Leningrad from capture in 1941. On the other hand, it is sometimes maintained that the severe losses suffered by the Red Army in battles of encirclement west of the main line of fortifications along the old Soviet-Polish frontier were too high a price to pay for the time gained. Whatever the military value of this territory to the Soviet Union in 1941, the Soviet Government will probably see strategic advantages in recovering it. Following rivers for most of its length and anchored on the Carpathian Mountains at its southern end, the line of 1939 (Line "A") could be fortified and made more defensible than the frontier of 1920–1939. From the Soviet viewpoint, all the alternative boundaries to the east of this line would be less satisfactory, since they reduce the width of the protective area which could be used for defensive fighting.

Should the Soviet Union desire to play an active role in Central Europe, it would prefer Line "A" to the other suggested boundaries. Central and Western European nations may look with some apprehension on the extension of Soviet [territory] so far to the west.

2. *Polish Strategic Aims*

Poland will be in a difficult military position, no matter where the boundary is drawn, and will have to depend for security upon allies among the Great Powers or upon a collective security system. Insofar as Poland's strategic interests are served by keeping the eastern boundary as far as possible from Warsaw and the heart of Poland, Line "A" is the least favorable, and the former Polish-Soviet boundary the most favorable.

3. *The Northern Sector*

The strategic problems in the northern sector are connected with the question of the future disposition of Lithuania. If Lithuania again becomes a Soviet Republic, the Wilno region would probably go to the Soviet Union; otherwise it would be a thin and highly exposed Polish salient projecting into Soviet territory. Lines "E," "F" and "I" would thus be eliminated from consideration.

Line "A", which at one point runs within one hundred kilometers of Warsaw, would put Poland in a difficult strategic position. The "Curzon" line (Lines "B" and "J") would be less objectionable to the Poles on this score, and those which follow the eastern border of the province of Bialystok (Lines "C", "D", "G" and "H") are even better.

If Lithuania becomes independent and enters into close association with Poland, lines "E", "F" and "I", which leave the city of Wilno and five additional districts to Poland, would give Poland a larger block of territory in the north but no special strategic advantages. Wilno, though an important point in any Polish-Lithuanian plan of defense, would be in a very vulnerable location.

4. *The Central Sector*

There are only two alternative boundaries in the central sector, where seven of the lines ("A", "B", "C", "D", "E", "G", "J") follow the course of the Bug River, and the other three ("F", "H", "I") follow a line parallel to the Bug about forty kilometers to the east. The Bug makes a fairly good geographic boundary, although it is not a formidable barrier to military operations. The

Poles consider the line of the Bug to be uncomfortably close to central Poland. They would probably feel a greater sense of security if they held Brest-Litoysk, on the eastern bank, and an additional forty-kilometer-wide strip of territory. The Pripet marshes would not serve Poland as a defensive barrier if the Soviet Union held Brest-Litovsk, which lies immediately to the west of the marsh area and is connected by double-tracked strategic railways with Minsk and Kiev.

5. *The Southern Sector*

The strategic significance of the alternative boundaries in Eastern Galicia lies in their location with respect to the Carpathian Mountains. Those lines which terminate at the former Polish-Czechoslovak border near the source of the San River (lines "A", "B", "C", "E") bring the Soviet Union to the crest of the Carpathians along the whole northern border of Ruthenia. The most easily traversible passes through the northern Carpathians lie along this border. Three minor railways running through these passes connect the former Polish and Czechoslovak railway systems.

Possession of this Carpathian frontier would probably assure the Soviet Union of a large voice in the affairs of Central Europe. Bordering on the disputed territory of Ruthenia, which is inhabited by a Ukrainian-speaking population, it could make its influence felt in Czechoslovakia and in Hungary. Poland and Rumania would be deprived of the common frontier they possessed between 1920 and 1939. The strategic position of the Soviet Union in the face of a potentially hostile Polish-Rumanian bloc or larger East European grouping would be very strong. The possibility that any of the nations of Eastern Europe, singly or in combination, could defend themselves against the Soviet Union, would be small.

Lines "D" and "F" partition Eastern Galicia from north to south; they are slightly more favorable to Poland than the San River line. The Soviet Union would still have a Carpathian frontier, but it would be shorter, and the wedge of Soviet territory between Poland and Rumania would be narrower. Under Line "D" the Soviet Union would have access to two Carpathian passes; under line "F" to but one, the Jablonica Pass.

Lines "G", "H" and "I" leave the whole of Eastern Galicia to Poland. The Soviet frontier would be about one hundred miles distant from the Carpathians, as before 1939. If Rumania should retain Bukovina, Poland and Rumania would have a common frontier, and the Soviet pressure upon Central Europe would be somewhat less than if Soviet territory extended to the Carpathians. Poland and Rumania would be directly connected by the strategic Lwów-Cernăuţi railway.

Line "J" is a compromise line running through Eastern Galicia roughly along the administrative boundary between the provinces of Lwów and Stanisławów, on the one hand, and Tarnopol on the other. This line leaves to Poland the crest of the Carpathians all the way to the border of Bukovina. Again, in the supposition of Rumania's retaining Bukovina it would give Poland and Rumania a common frontier and a belt of territory about one hundred kilometers in width east of the Carpathians. The Lwów-Cernăuţi railway, which would run within Polish territory at a distance of a few miles from the frontier, would probably be of little use to Poland in a defensive military campaign against the Soviet Union.

III. Ethnic Factors

1. *Ethnic Groups in Eastern Poland* [16]

The territory lying east of the Soviet-German line of September 28, 1939, (including the district of Suwalki, which was then annexed to East Prussia) had about twelve million inhabitants in 1931, according to the Polish census of that year. Forty percent were listed as Polish-speaking, 34 percent as Ukrainian-speaking, 8.2 as White Russian-speaking, and 1.1 percent as Russian-speaking. The Soviet Union could lay claim, on ethnic grounds, to 49 percent of the population of this area; this figure includes the White Russians, who are concentrated in the northern provinces, the Ukrainians, who inhabit the southern provinces, the Russians, who are scattered throughout the whole area, and the "local" inhabitants of the province of Polesie. The "local" languages of this last-named group are variations and dialects of White Russian and Ukrainian, which the census-takers chose not to classify with those two main language groups.

The Polish-speaking population in the area east of the line of 1939 (Line "A") numbered 4,833,918 in 1931 and over five millions in 1939, according to official Polish figures. The Poles are the majority nationality in the Bialystok, Wilno and Lwów areas, and they represent a substantial element in the population elsewhere. Although the upper and middle class Poles, who made up the greater part of the landlord and professional classes before 1939, will be greatly reduced in number at the close of the war, the Polish peasantry will probably remain as a numerically important minority in both the White Russian and Ukrainian-populated regions. [17]

2. *Political Aspirations of the Different Ethnic Groups*

The language statistics, even if assumed to be one-hundred percent accurate, cannot be accepted as an infallible index of the aspirations of the various ethnic groups inhabiting Eastern Poland, particularly when they are limited to a choice between Polish and Soviet rule. It is probably safe to assume that the overwhelming majority of those whose mother-tongue is Polish would favor the restoration of Polish sovereignty. The aspirations of the non-Polish-speaking inhabitants are not so clear.

a. The White Russians.—The White Russian-speaking people of the northern provinces are a culturally backward peasant population, with no coherent political groupings or programs. They had both national and social grievances against the pre-1939 Polish regime; there was some sympathy with the Soviet Union and with Communism. Generally speaking, the White Russians seem to have welcomed the Soviet occupation in 1939, for it meant liberation from their Polish landlords and the distribution of land to the peasantry. Under Polish rule their living standards were so low that there could hardly be any strong objection, on economic grounds, to incorporation in the Soviet Union, despite the adjustments involved in the process of "Sovietization". In the cultural sphere the White Russians of former Poland would probably have greater opportunities for development in association with Soviet White Russia than as citizens of a reconstituted Poland.

b. The Ukrainians.—The case of the Ukrainians is somewhat different. They are more advanced, culturally and politically, than the White Russians. Especially in Eastern Galicia, the Ukrainians had developed both economic and political organizations intended to further the welfare and aspirations of the

---

[16] See T Document 218, "Eastern Poland: Ethnic Composition of the Population." [Not printed.]

[17] See Tables I and II for statistics on the ethnic groups on each side of the ten alternative boundaries. [Not printed.]

national community. The prevalence of individual peasant farms in this area has contributed to the growth of a strong feeling of Ukrainian nationalism directed against both Poland and the Soviet Union. Although the Ukrainians of Eastern Poland are divided by religion (some are Orthodox, some Uniate), by differing historical experience (some under Austria, some under Russia), and by varying shades of political opinion, they have been more or less united in their opposition to the Polish state. Very few, in the 1918–1939 period, favored incorporation in the Soviet Ukraine. Given a choice, the majority would probably favor an independent Western Ukrainian Republic, which might include Carpathian Ruthenia and northern Bukovina as well as Eastern Galicia and Volhynia. This solution seems politically impossible now, as it was in 1919.

The year and a half of Soviet occupation of Eastern Poland was not a happy experience for many of the former leading elements among the Ukrainian and White Russian population. The nationalist political parties were liquidated. The intelligentsia and "kulak" elements, and even some Communists, were persecuted. The collectivization of agriculture, gradually introduced in 1940 and 1941, can hardly have been welcomed by the peasants. Generally speaking, however, the elimination of the Polish ruling class and the fact that a distribution of land to the peasants preceded collectivization (which could then be introduced slowly and without the use of force), compensated for the "invasion" of Communist Party men and G. P. U. agents, the absence of political freedom, and the campaign against religion.[18]

The Ukrainians of this area, for the most part, consider the choice between Polish and Soviet rule as a choice between two evils. Union with the Soviet Ukraine would seem to be a more natural association for them than a return to Polish rule, which has a long record of bitterness and failure.

3. *Northern Sector*

While in the central and southern sectors Line "A" roughly follows the line of ethnic division between the predominantly Polish area and the area of mixed population, in the north it runs far to the west of any plausible ethnic line. It leaves outside Poland all but a fraction of the province of Bialystok and also the Wilno region (the five districts of Swięciany, Wilno-Troki, Oszmiana, Lida and Szczuczyn) ; in both these areas the Poles had a 70 percent majority in the census of 1931. This ethnically Polish territory, which contains one and one-half million of the nearly five million Poles living east of Line "A", is contiguous to the purely Polish territory west of Line "A".

The "Curzon" Line (Lines "B" and "J") more nearly approaches the line of division between strongly Polish and mixed territory, although in the absence of statistics on individual communes, it is impossible to tell how nearly they coincide. That part of the province of Bialystok which lies to the west of Lines "B" and "J" (including the Suwalki district) is overwhelmingly Polish. The only districts which have a substantial White Russian population are Grodno, Bielsk and Wolkowysk, which lie, wholly or in part, on the eastern or Soviet side.

Lines "C", "D", "G" and "H", following the eastern boundary of the provinces of Bialystok, are slightly more favorable to Poland. They leave to Poland an area with a large Polish majority and with a White Russian minority of about 200,000 living in the area adjacent to Soviet territory. A large Polish population, living in the provinces of Wilno and Nowogródek, would be left within the Soviet Union. The Poles in these two provinces outnumber the White Russians by a margin of nearly two to one (1,315,500 to 703,000) according to the Polish census statistics.

---

[18] See T Document 228, "Soviet Rule in Eastern Poland, 1939–1941." [Not printed.]

Lines "E," "F" and "I" leave to Poland five additional districts, including the strongly Polish city of Wilno. Although this region is not likely to fall to Poland unless Lithuania again becomes an independent state, Poland's claim to it on ethnic grounds is good. The census of 1931 listed 698,000 Poles, 78,000 White Russians, and 65,000 Lithuanians in these five districts. In the remaining parts of the provinces of Wilno and Nowogródek, which would fall to the Soviet Union, the Poles make up nearly half the population, 618,000 out of a total of 1,392,000. There are Polish majorities in some of the easternmost districts bordering on the former Polish-Soviet frontier.

4. *Central Sector*

The line of the Bug River was the eastern boundary of "Congress Poland" and makes a fairly clear division between Polish-speaking and non-Polish-speaking populations, although there are some 63,000 Ukrainians in the districts bordering the western bank of the river, and some 102,000 Polish-speaking persons in the three districts of Brześć, Luboml and Wlodzimierz, which border on the eastern bank. These three districts form the additional belt of territory left to Poland by Lines "F", "H", and "I"; all the other lines follow the course of the river. Their total population in 1931 was 452,000 of whom only 23 percent were Poles. There are no valid ethnic grounds for the inclusion of this area within Poland, except as compensation for the cession to the Soviet Union of predominantly Polish-speaking territory elsewhere.

In the remaining area of the provinces of Polesie and Wolyń, which falls to the Soviet Union under all alternative lines, there are only 408,000 Poles (14.7 percent) in a total population of 2,766,000.

5. *Southern Sector*

It is impossible to draw a line through Eastern Galicia which does not leave large numbers of Poles or Ukrainians under alien rule. Lines "A", "C" and "E" follow the line of the San River. This line is the least favorable to Poland; while the population to the west of it is almost purely Polish, nearly two million Poles, about two-fifths of the total population, inhabit the area east of the San River and would come under Soviet rule.

Line "B", which represents the continuation of the "Curzon" line in Eastern Galicia, runs somewhat to the north of line "A" in the Rawa Ruska region, and to the east of it in the Przemyśl region. It leaves to Poland a slightly greater area of mixed population, in which Poles and Ukrainians are fairly evenly balanced; this area includes the city of Przemyśl, which is strongly Polish.

Line "D" was suggested by the British Delegation at the Peace Conference of 1919 as a possible boundary between Poland and an autonomous state of Eastern Galicia. It follows roughly the eastern boundary of the province of Lwów. The total population of the Eastern Galician territory lying between Line "D" and Line "A" was 1,795,000 in 1931, of whom 831,000 (46 percent) were Poles, and 777,000 (43 percent) were Ukrainians. Line "D" leaves the strongly Polish city of Lwów to Poland.

Line "F" leaves to Poland a somewhat larger share of the territory of Eastern Galicia, including the western half of the province of Stanislawów. This added area, which has a population of almost half a million, is predominantly Ukrainian; the Polish element comprises less than one-fifth of the total. The principal arguments in favor of the assignment of this area to Poland are economic rather than ethnic.

Line "F" divides Eastern Galicia into two parts of nearly equal size. The western part, the area between Line "A" and Line "F", which would fall to

Poland, had a total population, in 1931, of 2,301,000 of whom 927,000 (40 percent) were Polish and 1,155,000 (50 percent) were Ukrainian.

Line "J" runs through Eastern Galicia roughly along the western boundary of the province of Tarnopol, leaving that province to the Soviet Union, and leaving the provinces of Lwów and Stanislawów to Poland. This line is a poor boundary from the ethnic standpoint, since the province of Stanislawów, which would be left to Poland, has a three-to-one Ukrainian majority, whereas in the province of Tarnopol, which would be left to the Soviet Union, the Poles have a slight numerical advantage over the Ukrainians.

Under Line "J", the larger part of Eastern Galicia would fall to Poland. Its total population, in 1931, was 3,324,000 of whom 1,826,000 (55 percent) were Ukrainians and 1,178,000 (35 percent) were Poles. The Soviet share of Eastern Galicia, which would include the province of Tarnopol and a part of the district of Sokal in the province of Lwów, had a population of 1,643,000, of whom 801,000 (48 percent) were Poles, and 758,000 (46 percent) were Ukrainians.

Lines "G", "H" and "I" leave the whole of Eastern Galicia to Poland. Poland would acquire a Ukrainian population of over two and one-half millions. The Polish element numbers just under two million. Thus Poland has no good ethnic claim to the whole of Eastern Galicia. However, since some of the easternmost districts, on the former Polish-Soviet frontier, have Polish majorities, it is impossible to draw a line of partition which would not leave a considerable number of Poles outside Poland. Similarly, any line drawn far enough to the east to include within Poland the Poles of the Lwów and Tarnopol regions must include also a large number of Ukrainians.

IV. Economic Considerations

1. Agriculture

Eastern Poland is essentially an agricultural region. In the four provinces of Wilno, Nowogródek, Polesie and Wolyń, 86 percent of the population is rural; in Eastern Galicia the proportion is 78 percent. Throughout Eastern Poland the main crops are rye and potatoes, both of which are produced in abundance in other parts of Poland.

The soil of the northern provinces is poor, production per hectare is low, and the rate of increase of the rural population is high. The region of the Pripet marshes, comprising the province of Polesie and the northern part of Wolyń, is largely useless swampland; its agriculture is at a primitive level, which the Polish state did almost nothing to raise. In the Wilno area some flax was grown for the Polish textile industries, but otherwise the agricultural products of the eastern provinces were consumed locally and contributed little to the economic life of other parts of Poland. From the agricultural standpoint, the region would probably be a liability either to Poland or to the Soviet Union, although there are possibilities for a greater development of fruit culture, industrial fibre plants, and cattle-raising.

Eastern Galicia has more fertile soil than the northern provinces; it produced besides rye and potatoes, a large part of the wheat, maize, barley and hemp grown in pre-1939 Poland. It is very thickly settled and is faced with an acute problem of rural over-population. The economy of the Soviet Union could probably absorb the surplus population more easily than could the economy of Poland.

2. Forests

The area east of the Soviet-German line of 1939 (Line "A") has about 63 percent of the forest area of former Poland. All the eastern provinces, except Tarnopol, are more than 20 percent wooded. Polesie has the largest wooded area,

1,222,000 hectares, while the Carpathian region in the provinces of Lwów and Stanislawów is endowed with extensive pine and hardwood forests. Poland's forest wealth was rather recklessly exploited in the last twenty years but always remained an important item in the national economy.

About one-half of the Polish timber production was consumed locally as fuel, some went to Polish factories, and the remainder was exported. Timber alternated with coal as Poland's chief export product, averaging 17 percent of total exports in the period from 1924 to 1938. The loss of all the timber land in the eastern provinces would be felt severely by Poland. Any compromise line, however, which left at least the province of Bialystok and a part of Eastern Galicia to Poland, would give to Poland a substantial share of the forest area.

3. *Mineral Resources*

Poland's principal oil fields were situated in Eastern Galicia. The total crude oil output of these fields reached two million tons in 1909, but then gradually declined to 507,000 tons in 1938, a consequence of the exhaustion of the existing wells. The fields of the Krosno-Jaslo region, west of Line "A", registered steady gains, but those of the Drohobycz-Boryslaw and Stanislawów regions, east of Line "A", produced less each year. However, the eastern region remained the principal producing area; in 1938 it accounted for two-thirds of Poland's total production.

The opinion is generally held by geologists and technicians that the decline in production will continue, and that the Galician oil industry will not be of any great importance in the future either to Poland or to the Soviet Union. However, both Polish and Soviet sources can be quoted in support of the thesis that an increase in production can be effected by extensive exploration and drilling, the use of new equipment, and the wider application of new techniques. The Soviet authorities drew up ambitious plans for the expansion of the industry in 1939, but the period of Soviet control was not long enough to test them.

Without the oil wells of the disputed Drohobycz and Stanislawów regions, Poland would have to import most of its oil. In the late 1930's Poland exported only a fraction of its petroleum products; almost all were consumed domestically. The oil wells of Eastern Galicia sent nearly 80 percent of their oil products to central and western Poland. Poland was free from dependence on foreign sources of oil, but economically it gained little by possessing its own oil-fields. Galician oil, crude or refined, was not able to compete on an equal basis, even in Poland, with American or Rumanian oil. Its value to Poland lay in its favorable influence on the country's foreign exchange position and its possible use in time of war or economic isolation. From that standpoint it would be more essential to Poland than to the oil rich Soviet Union, although the latter country could make use of the Galician oil for mechanized farming operations in White Russia and Western Ukraine.

The other mineral resources of Eastern Poland are located almost entirely in Eastern Galicia. Natural gas, production of which has increased while that of petroleum has been falling, comes mainly from the Drohobycz and Daszawa regions; it has been used for the manufacture of gasoline, for heat and light in nearby cities, and as an industrial fuel. The reserves are not great and are not expected to be of great economic importance in the future. Ozokerite is also produced in the Drohobycz region; this is the world's only significant commercial source of ozokerite.

Important deposits of potassium salts, valuable for agriculture and for the chemical industry, are located near Kalusz, in the province of Stanislawów. Smaller deposits are found near Stryj and near Drohobycz. The total production from all these sources was only 54,000 tons in 1923 but rose rapidly to 560,000 tons in 1938. The Carpathian region also contains large quantities of rock salt, which enabled Poland to meet all domestic demands and to have a surplus for export.

There are little-worked deposits of phosphates and gypsum in the provinces of Stanislawów and Tarnopol, in the valley of the Dniester River. Pyrites are mined near Rudki in the province of Lwów. There is some lignite in the province of Tarnopol. Altogether, the mineral resources of Eastern Galicia are varied, and they are of some economic importance to Poland; a more intense exploitation of them would probably be a definite part of any plan for the improvement of agriculture and for the development of industry in the central and eastern parts of Poland.

The other eastern provinces have practically no mineral wealth, except for the granite and basalt in the province of Wolyń, the kaolin on the border between Wolyń and Polesie, which supplied raw material for the whole Polish porcelain industry, and scattered deposits of lignite and peat over the whole area.

4. *Industries*

The principal manufacturing industries are 1) the textile industries of Bialystok, which produced between five and ten percent of all Polish textile goods; 2) various finishing industries in the two largest cities, Wilno and Lwów; 3) the industries connected with the exploitation of the forest and mineral resources.

In 1938 there were twenty-three oil refineries in Eastern Poland, with only one cracking-plant. Almost all of them are located near the Drohobycz oil-fields or at Lwów. Saw-mills are located in the main forest areas, especially in the Carpathian region of Eastern Galicia. In the 1930's the saw-mills of the eastern provinces accounted for about one-half of Poland's production of lumber. Important cellulose, paper, and cardboard factories are located in the province of Wilno and in Eastern Galicia.

5. *Economic Aspects of the Alternative Boundaries*

Although no one economic factor, or combination of factors, seems to deserve decisive weight in the determination of a permanent boundary, the loss of the whole area east of Line "A" might be a serious blow to Poland's economy, since the Polish-Soviet frontier will probably be a real barrier to the exchange of goods. A compromise boundary which left at least some of the mineral resources of Eastern Galicia to Poland might soften the blow without greatly affecting the economic position of the Soviet Union, which has little need of the meager resources of Eastern Poland.

In the northern sector no economic factors are sufficiently important to affect boundary considerations, except perhaps the textile industries of Bialystok, which lie to the west of all the alternative lines save Line "A". When Bialystok was under Soviet occupation, in 1940, it was announced that it would be developed into one of the largest textile centers of the Soviet Union. Both Poland and the Soviet Union have other textile centers, of much greater importance.

In Eastern Galicia, the San River line (Lines "A", "C" and "E") is the least favorable economically to Poland, depriving it of two-thirds of its oil and natural gas wells, most of its oil refineries, and all its deposits of ozokerite, potash, phosphates, and gypsum. Line "B" would also deprive Poland of all those economic resources. Line "D", on the other hand, leaves to Poland the Drohobycz-Boryslaw oil fields, the natural gas wells in the same region, the ozokerite mines, and some of the larger Carpathian salt deposits. The phosphates, gypsum, granite, basalt, kaolin, and the major share of the potassium salts would be left within the Soviet Union. The city of Lwów, with its refineries and other industrial establishments, would fall to Poland.

Line "F" is somewhat more favorable to Poland than Line "D", since it runs to the east of the main potash deposits near Kalusz and Stryj; it also gives Poland a greater share of the petroleum and natural gas area and of the Carpathian forests. Poland would also regain the paper and cellulose factories located near Żydaczow.

Lines "G", "H" and "I" leave the whole of Eastern Galicia to Poland, giving that country the maximum opportunities for economic development and thus for absorbing the surplus rural population. Line "J" would have about the same consequences; it leaves only the province of Tarnopol, which has the fewest economic resources, to the Soviet Union. From an economic standpoint, Poland could afford to renounce its claim to all territory east of Line "J".

The territory which falls to the Soviet Union under all the alternative lines includes the greater part of the provinces of Wilno, Nowogródek, Polesie and Wolyń. It has considerable forest land, a low level of agricultural production, no important industries, and no minerals except stone, granite, basalt, kaolin, and some lignite and peat.

IV. [V] COMMUNICATIONS

1. Railway and Canal Systems

The railways of Eastern Poland form a western extension of the Soviet railway system, most of the lines having been built by the Imperial Russian regime. Although practically no new lines were constructed during the period of Polish administration, these railways are also closely linked to the network of Central Poland by the trunk lines to Warsaw, Lublin and Kraków.

The density of the railway network is 3.9 kilometers per hundred square kilometers, considerably less than in the other parts of pre-1939 Poland, although the density in relation to the population is about the same. The main east-west lines were little used in the 1919-1939 period because of the insignificant volume of Polish trade with the Soviet Union. The secondary lines are of some importance to the local economic life of the eastern provinces; their inadequacy and worn-out condition, however, have retarded the exploitation of the economic resources of the region.

The roads are also quite inadequate. The Polish government built some 200 miles of new highways in the eastern provinces, and the official statistics give the total length of the "public highways" as 19,000 kilometers; almost none of the roads have a paved surface or a stone substructure of any kind.

The rivers and canals, particularly in the region of the Pripet marshes, form the basis for an excellent waterway system, but they have suffered a marked decline in traffic, largely because they have been cut by political frontiers. The Dvina, Niemen, Pripet, Bug and Dniester Rivers are navigable by small boats and by timber rafts. Three important canals, the Augustów, the Oginski, and the Royal (Dnieper-Bug) Canals connect the Baltic with the Black Sea by joining the tributaries of the Dnieper with those of the Vistula and the Niemen. This system is capable of developing an expanded traffic.

2. Line "A"

Line "A" would give the Soviet Union two north-south railways connecting the main points on the east-west lines; one connects Wilno with Baranowicze, Luniniec, Sarny, Równe and Lwów; the other connects Wilno with Grodno, Bialystok, Brest-Litovsk, Kowel and Lwów. From all important frontier cities on the Soviet side of the line there are railway communications to the other main points of the region by north-south lines as well as by those running to the east. The most direct lines from Brest-Litovsk to Lwów and Przemyśl are cut by Line "A", but the available alternative routes are not much longer.

On the Polish side of the line, railway communications are less adequate, since there would be no north-south trunk railway nearer to the frontier than the Warsaw-Lublin-Przemyśl line. The lines in the eastern part of the province of Lublin would be cut off from the important junctions of Brest-Litovsk and Rawa Ruska.

Soviet possession of Eastern Galicia would cut the direct railway connection between Poland and Rumania, the line running through Lwów and Stanislawów to Cerñauți, in Bukovina. This line, one of the main routes between Central Europe and the Black Sea, would be of great economic importance to an East European federation.

The Soviet Union might put to fuller use the canals which link the Pripet, Bug and Niemen river systems. The timber traffic which flourished on the Niemen before 1914 might be revived.[19]

3. *Line "B"*

Line "B" and Line "J" would deprive the Soviet railway system of the important junction of Bialystok. Between Grodno and Brest-Litovsk there would be no direct connection within Soviet territory except the roundabout route *via* Baranowicze. A more direct connection could be provided by shifting the boundary a few kilometers to the west in the region north of Brest-Litovsk, so as to leave the whole length of the Brest-Hainowka-Wolkowysk railway on the Soviet side of the line.

Under line "B", Polish communications in Galicia would be improved by the inclusion within Poland of the railway junctions of Przemyśl and Chyrów, but would still be handicapped by the loss of Rawa Ruska, which provides the connection between the lines of Lwów province and those in the eastern part of Lublin. The Soviet Union would hold the most important communications center in Eastern Galicia, Lwów, whence railway lines run south to the oil-fields and to the Carpathian passes, southeast to Rumania, and east and northeast toward Kiev and Moscow.

Under Line "B" and Line "J", the Niemen River would form the Polish-Soviet frontier in the Grodno area and would not be likely to carry much traffic unless an international régime including all the riparian states were established.

4. *Lines "C" and "E"*

Lines "C" and "E" are identical with line "A" in the central and southern sectors. In the north, line "C" follows the eastern boundary of the province of Bialystok. The cities of Grodno, Wolkowysk and Bialystok would be tied into the Polish system of railway and canal communications. The Soviet Union would hold the frontier points of Wilno, Baranowicze and Brest-Litovsk, and the railways running eastward and southward from those points.

Line "E" leaves to Poland the Wilno region, which would be connected with the Polish railway network by lines running to Central Poland by way of Bialystok and by way of Lida and Wolkowysk. Both these lines would remain in Poland.

The Wilno area is an essential link in Poland's communications with Lithuania. If these two countries are expected to work in close economic cooperation, this area should be attached either to the one or to the other. The principal lines of transportation between them are the Niemen River and the three railway lines

---

[19] See T 221 : "The Niemen River". [Not printed.]

which connect central Lithuania with the main Warsaw-Leningrad railway, which they join in the Wilno region.

5. Line "D"

Line "D" is identical with Line "C" in the northern and central sectors. In the south it leaves a larger share of Eastern Galicia, including the city of Lwów, to Poland. Lwów is the junction of the trunk lines from Warsaw and from Kraków, and of the secondary lines from the oil-fields region and others points to the south and west. The principal line from the Drohobycz-Boryslaw oil region, however, runs by way of Stryj, which would lie on the Soviet side of the boundary.

Inclusion of Lwów in Poland would deprive the Soviet railways in the provinces of Tarnopol and Stanislawów of their key junction.

Poland would have direct contact by rail with Ruthenia by way of the Lwów-Užhorod line. The other two lines connecting Eastern Galicia with Ruthenia would be in Soviet hands. Soviet territory would form a wedge separating Poland from Rumania and cutting the main Lwów-Cernăuţi railway.

6. Line "F"

Line "F" leaves to Poland the Wilno area and good river and rail communications with Lithuania. In the central sector, it leaves to Poland the cities of Brest-Litovsk, Wlodzimierz and Sokal, which are located east of the Bug River. Although the main railway connecting these three points runs through Kowel, which would be in Soviet territory, their possession by Poland would greatly improve the Polish railway network.

The railway between Lwów and the Drohobycz oil-fields, by way of Stryj, would run entirely within Polish territory. Poland would have an additional direct rail link with Ruthenia, the Lwów-Mukačevo line. The Soviet Union would have access to only one line to Ruthenia, the line which runs through the Jablonica Pass. Since the Soviet Union would hold the eastern part of the province of Stanislawów all the way to the Carpathians, the Lwów-Cernăuţi railway would still run across Soviet territory.

7. Lines "G", "H", and "I"

In the northern sector, Lines "G" and "H" follow the eastern boundary of the province of Bialystok, leaving to Poland the railway junctions of Bialystok and Wolkowysk, and waterway communication with Lithuania and the Baltic Sea by way of the Augustów Canal and the Niemen River. Line "I" leaves to Poland, in addition, the city of Wilno and three railway connections with Lithuania.

In the central sector, Line "G" follows the Bug, while Lines "H" and "I" run further to the east, leaving to Poland the cities of Brest-Litovsk, Wlodzimierz and Sokal, thus facilitating Polish communications. Communication between Poland's share of Eastern Galicia and the Bialystok region would be difficult without use of railway lines crossing Soviet territory. The main route by the Polish railways, via Lublin and Warsaw, would involve a wide détour to the west. However, if there were a real economic demand for a Bialystok-Lwów railway, there would be no important physical obstacles to its construction.

These three lines leave the whole of Eastern Galicia to Poland. Poland would have three direct lines of rail communications with Ruthenia and two with Bukovina.

8. Line "J"

Line "J" is identical with Line "B" in the northern and central sectors, where, from the standpoint of communications, it is more favorable to the Soviet Union than to Poland, particularly if a slight rectification should be made, so as to leave the Brest-Hainowka-Wolkowysk railway in Soviet hands. In the south it cuts across Eastern Galicia, leaving the province of Tarnopol to the Soviet Union; it terminates at the border of Bukovina near Zaleszczyki. The whole length of the Lwów-Cernăuţi railway as far as the border of Bukovina, and the lines branching off from it and running to the Carpathian passes, would be in Polish hands. The loss of the province of Tarnopol would not adversely affect Polish communications in the rest of Eastern Galicia.

APPENDIX 18
May 19, 1943 [20]

Poland: Soviet Union: Territorial Problems Polish-Soviet Frontier

I. THE PROBLEM

The problem is the disposition of that area of Eastern Poland which was incorporated into the Soviet Union in 1939.

The problem arises from the fact that, whereas the Soviet Government regards these areas as parts of the White Russian, Lithuanian and Ukrainian Soviet Republics, the Polish Government considers them as part of the Polish Republic.

In September 1939 Soviet forces occupied all of eastern Poland up to a line fixed in agreement with Germany. This area subsequently was annexed to the White Russian and Ukrainian Soviet Socialist Republics, except for a small strip including Wilno, which was ceded to Lithuania by the Soviet Government and was later incorporated into the Soviet Union as part of the Lithuanian Soviet Republic. By a treaty of July 1941 between Poland and the Soviet Union the Soviet Government recognized that the Soviet-German treaties as to territorial changes in Poland had lost their validity. The Polish Government-in-exile claims the restoration of the frontier of September 1, 1939. This frontier was established in 1921 by the treaty of Riga between Poland and the R.S.F.S.R., and in its southern sector was confirmed by the award to Poland, in 1923, of Eastern Galicia, which Austria had ceded to the Allied and Associated Powers in 1919. The Soviet Government has denounced this Polish claim as untenable; although the Soviet press maintained in 1941 that neither the Riga line nor the 1939 line could be regarded as valid, more recently the Soviet Government has repeatedly indicated that it regards as Soviet territory the entire area annexed in 1939.

Neither the British nor the United States Government is committed to the establishment of any specific boundary between Poland and the Soviet Union.

The territory in dispute has an area of approximately 78,700 square miles, and its population, in 1939, was about thirteen million. In 1931, according to the Polish census of that year, the population was 50 percent Ukrainian, White Russian, or Russian, 40 percent Polish, and 9 percent Jewish.

Since the accuracy of the census of 1931 has been challenged, and since drastic changes in the composition of the population have taken place since that time, these figures will have to be corrected by a new census or investigation after the war.

---

[20] A policy summary paper or "H–document."

The area contains two-thirds of the producing oil-fields, over one-half of the forests, and the greater part of the natural gas reserves of pre-war Poland. These resources are of more importance to Poland than to the Soviet Union.

II. ALTERNATIVE SOLUTIONS

(Indicated on Map 13, Polish Series) [see appendix 19]

A. *A Boundary Following the Curzon Line from the Former Polish-Lithuanian Boundary to the Northern Border of Eastern Galicia, then Following the Bug River and the Western Boundary of the Province of Tarnopol to the Border of Bukovina* (Line "J" on Map 13)

This solution would leave to the Soviet Union most of the disputed territory, with an area of 56,630 square miles and a population of 7,557,000 (1931 census), of whom 52 percent were Ukrainians, White Russians or Russians, and 37 percent were Poles. It would leave to Poland most of the province of Bialystok, which is 70 percent Polish in population, and the provinces of Lwów and Stanislawów, where the Ukrainians account for 55 percent, and the Poles for 35 percent, of the population. Poland would regain the Galician oil-fields, the city of Lwów, and a common frontier and direct railway connection with Rumania, should the latter retain Bukovina.

1. *Discussion of the Political Subcommittee*

Several members of the Political Subcommittee regarded this solution as a logical compromise. . . . [One member] stated that the Curzon Line would probably be the minimum demand of the Soviet Government, and pointed out that such a revision of the boundary of September 1, 1939, might be based on the principle of making adjustments most likely to make for a permanently peaceful situation. It was thought by some members that this solution would have the support of American public opinion. It was agreed that an effort should be made to keep the greater part of Eastern Galicia, including the line of the Carpathians, within Poland, on the ground that the extension of Soviet territory to the Carpathians would represent an insuperable obstacle to the creation of an East European federation.

2. *Discussion of the Territorial Subcommittee*

The Territorial Subcommittee was of the opinion that, if a restoration of the pre-war boundary should prove impossible, this solution represented the maximum satisfaction that should be given to the Soviet claims. It was thought desirable to prevent the establishment of a common Soviet-Czechoslovakian frontier and to prevent the extension of Soviet control into the strategically vital Carpathian area. The subcommittee felt that there was nothing to be gained by the incorporation of the Ukrainians of Eastern Galicia into the Soviet Union. . . . it was agreed that the restoration of Polish sovereignty in Eastern Galicia was the most desirable solution, and that possible concessions in that area to the Soviet Union should be limited to the province of Tarnopol.

B. *Restoration of the Boundary of September 1, 1939*

This solution is in accord with the principle of non-recognition of territorial changes brought about by force, and with that of minimum boundary changes. Established by a Soviet-Polish treaty, this boundary was changed by military action on the part of the Soviet Union.

1. Discussion of the Political Subcommittee

The Political Subcommittee did not reject this solution outright, but placed emphasis on the difficulty of securing Soviet consent to it, even as a basis of negotiations.

2. Discussion of the Territorial Subcommittee

The Territorial Subcommittee recommended that the Riga Line be regarded as the eastern boundary of Poland as a starting-point for negotiation. . . . It was recommended that direct negotiations be encouraged initially between Poland and the Soviet Union. The subcommittee was ready to accept such modifications of the Riga boundary as might result from free negotiation between the two governments directly concerned.

C. *A Boundary Leaving the Wilno Region, the Province of Bialystok, a Strip of Territory East of the Bug River, and all of Eastern Galicia to Poland* (Line "I" on Map 13)

The area which would be left to the Soviet Union by this solution amounts to 37,275 square miles and had a population, in 1931, of 4,353,000, of whom 62 percent were Ukrainians, White Russians, and Russians, while 26 percent were Poles. Poland would obtain the Galician oil-fields and virtually all other important resources, as well as the strongly Polish cities of Wilno and Lwów, to which the Poles have great sentimental attachment. Poland's communications with Lithuania and with Rumania would be preserved.

1. Discussion of the Territorial Subcommittee

This solution was not discussed specifically in any of the subcommittees. The Territorial Subcommittee, however, expressed its preference for a compromise between the Riga and Curzon lines over the Curzon Line itself. The attribution of Eastern Galicia to Poland would be in accord with the subcommittee's recommendation that the Soviet frontier should not reach the Carpathians.

D. *A Line Following the Eastern Boundaries of the Provinces of Bialystok, Lublin and Lwów, from the Southern Border of Lithuania to the Northern Border of Czechoslovakia* (Line "D" on Map 13)

This solution was not discussed in any subcommittee.

This line, in its northern and central sectors, separates ethnically Polish from mixed territory. In its southern sector (Eastern Galicia) it cuts through a mixed Polish and Ukrainian area, leaving the city of Lwów to Poland. The Soviet Union would acquire the provinces of Wilno, Nowogródek, Polesie, Wolyń, Tarnopol and Stanislawów, with a total area of 61,375 square miles. Most of the disputed area would be included in the Soviet share, which had a population, in 1931, of 8,725,000, of whom 56 percent were Ukrainians, White Russians, or Russians, and 34 percent were Poles. A minority of slightly over one million Ukrainians and White Russians would be left in Poland by this solution, while about three million Poles would come under Soviet jurisdiction. Poland would obtain the most important oil-fields. The Soviet Union would have a common frontier with Czechoslovakia on the Carpathians, and a wedge of Soviet territory would separate Poland from Rumania.

E. *The Line Fixed by the Supreme Council of the Allied and Associated Powers in December 1919, later known as The Curzon Line, and its Continuation in Eastern Galicia* (Line "B" on Map 13)

This line separates ethnically Polish territory from territory of mixed population. It would leave to the Soviet Union an area of 68,400 square miles, or all but a fraction of the territory in dispute. The population of this area, in 1931, was 10,575,000, of whom 53 percent were Ukrainians, White Russians, or Russians, while 36 percent were Poles. Nearly four million Poles would come under Soviet jurisdiction, while less than one million Ukrainians and White Russians would be left in Poland. Poland would lose the cities of Wilno and Lwów and the greater part of the petroleum, natural gas, and other mineral resources of Galicia. The Soviet frontier would follow the Carpathians along the entire length of the border between Ruthenia and Eastern Galicia.

1. *Discussion of the Political Subcommittee*

The discussions of the Political Subcommittee showed a general willingness to accept the Curzon Line if it proved impossible to secure a boundary more favorable to Poland. The continuation of the Curzon Line in Eastern Galicia, though not definitely rejected, was not favored.

2. *Discussion of the Territorial Subcommittee*

The Territorial Subcommittee considered the Curzon Line to be the maximum concession that should be made to the Soviet Union after negotiations. It rejected the continuation of the Curzon Line in Eastern Galicia, recommending that the Soviet frontier should not reach the Carpathians.

F. *Establishment of the Soviet-German Partition Line of 1939 as the Polish-Soviet Frontier* (Line "A" on Map 13)

This solution is the least favorable to Poland. It would bring the Soviet frontier to within one hundred kilometers of Warsaw and to the crest of the Carpathians along the northern border of Ruthenia. It would leave to the Soviet Union solidly Polish-populated territory in the province of Bialystok as well as all the areas of mixed population. Nearly five million Poles (census of 1931) would be left on the Soviet side of the frontier.

1. *Discussion of the Political and Territorial Subcommittees*

Neither the Political nor the Territorial Subcommittee favored this solution, although it was mentioned in both that the situation in this area at the close of formal hostilities might be such that this line would have to be accepted.

III. DOCUMENTATION

A. *Available Memoranda* [research paper numbers omitted]

Polish-Soviet Frontier: Alternative Boundaries (Mar. 26, 1943).
An analysis of ten alternative boundaries in their strategic, ethnic and economic aspects. [Appendix 17]

Poland: Ethnic Composition of the Population East of the Soviet-German Demarcation Line of September 28, 1939 (Jan. 12, 1943).
Conclusions based on the mother tongue statistics of the Polish census of 1931. [Appendix 16]

A Note on the Eastern Provinces of Poland (June 26, 1942).
Statistics on the four provinces of Bialystok, Nowogródek, Polesie and Wolyn, with comments on the relationship of that area to Poland and to the Soviet Union.

The Curzon Line (undated).
An account of the negotiations of 1919 concerning Poland's frontier with Russia, emphasizing the part played by the American delegates.

An Historical Note on the Republic of the West Ukraine (June 26, 1942).
Résumé of events in Eastern Galicia in 1919 and 1920.

The Role of Eastern Galicia in Transportation and Defense (July 10, 1942).

Political Consciousness and Experience of the Ukrainians of Eastern Galicia, Bukovina, Ruthenia (June 27, 1942).

Official Russian Statements (July 1941–November 1942) (Nov. 11, 1942).

Soviet War Aims (Dec. 19, 1942).
A summary of opinions expressed in Soviet publications in 1941 and 1942.

Soviet Rule in Eastern Poland, 1939–1941 (Jan. 23, 1943).

The Niemen River (Jan. 23, 1943).

B. *Maps*

Polish Series [research paper numbers omitted]
Eastern Poland: Distribution of Population According to Mother Tongue; Curzon Line and its Continuation; Hypothetical Lines.
Poland: Eastern Frontier.
Poland: Distribution of Peoples.
Minorities in Poland, 1931.
Number of Persons in Main Language Groups, by Provinces.
Language Groups East and West of Curzon Line.
Sources of Livelihood, East and West of Curzon Line.
Employment in Industry, East and West of Curzon Line.
Estimated Mineral Resources and Production in 1937.
Poland separated from Russia by recommendation of "The Inquiry", Jan. 21, 1919.
Poland, as recommended by "The Inquiry" on basis a) of indisputably Polish population, and/or b) union with Lithuania.
Four Possible lines . . . as projected in Report of Inter-Allied Mission to Poland, April 8, 1919.
Boundary Recommendations of the Commission on Polish Affairs, April 22, 1919.
Final Line as approved by the Supreme Council, December 8, 1919.

C. *Committee Discussions*

Political Subcommittee: Nov. 28, 1942; Dec. 12, 1942.
Territorial Subcommittee: June 13, 1942; June 27, 1942; July 10, 1942; Oct. 9, 1942; Jan. 29, 1943.
Security Technical Committee: Jan. 20, 1943.

IV. PLANS FOR FURTHER RESEARCH

Population Changes in Eastern Poland since 1939.
Attitudes of Polish Political Groups on the Question of the Eastern Frontier.
Political Movements among the White Russians, 1918–1943.
Political Movements among the Ukrainians in Poland, 1918–1943.
Polish-Lithuanian Relations and the Wilno Question, 1918–1943.
Eastern Galicia as an International Problem, 1918–1943.
The Importance of the Mineral Resources of Eastern Galicia to Poland.
The Origin and History of the "Curzon Line" (to supplement Document [on Curzon Line, undated, above]).

[Letter From Chairman of Subcommittee on Territorial Problems (Bowman) to Executive Director of the Advisory Committee on Post-War Foreign Policy (Pasvolsky)]

On Monday, May 17, I was asked by telephone to Baltimore (General Watson) to call on President Roosevelt the following day at 12 : 30 to confer with him on a matter that "had arisen in connection with the conferences we are having with our distinguished visitors (Prime Minister Churchill and his party)."

As you now know, the question which the President raised with me in this private conference was Libya. . . . At the close the President asked me if it would be possible to prepare a memorandum on the subject for his personal use before his second conversation with Mr. Churchill on Sunday evening, May 23, and have it in his hands by Saturday afternoon, May 22. In making the request he asked for "the results of research on this question."

The assignment was given to a group of qualified men on the Research Staff of the Department of State on Tuesday afternoon with general instructions on contents and form as follows :

1) a main text with facts and an analysis of them ;
2) a summary not to exceed two pages ;
3) a set of interpretative maps.

Short conferences between me and the research specialists followed on Thursday, Friday, and Saturday morning. References were assembled from the Library of Congress and the American Geographical Society of New York, as well as the Department of State. The Geographer's Office of the Department handled the map construction. By four o'clock on Saturday, May 22, the final text was revised and final typing done. By seven-thirty Saturday afternoon I delivered the whole of the material, together with a covering letter from me, to the White House usher, Mr. Claunch. When I expressed anxiety over the delivery at such an hour on Saturday, Mr. Claunch replied : "The President has gone into the country. Before departing he left word that the memorandum which Dr. Bowman would deliver was to be given to two secret service men who are now waiting to receive it. They have been instructed to take it by motor car at once to its destination. I can assure you that within an hour it will actually be in the hands of the President."

Good organization, sound scholarship, and close teamwork are required to do a job like this. It is unnecessary for me to dwell on the importance to the President of an immediate and reliable response to a matter on which he himself can spend only a few hours at most and which involves consultation and agreement with the head of another government, and especially Mr. Churchill and Great Britain. The Research staff still lacks manpower but it has demonstrated in this instance as in so many others that it is an indispensable agency in the responsible discussion and decision of questions of policy before our government.

Draft of United Nations Agreement on Relief [as Developed and Approved by the Subcommittee on Economic Reconstruction]

The Governments whose duly-authorized representatives have subscribed hereto,

Having subscribed to a common program of purposes and principles embodied in the Declaration of January 1, 1942, known as the United Nations Declaration and the Joint Declaration of the President of the United States of America and the Prime Minister of the United Kingdom of Great Britain and Northern Ireland dated August 14, 1941, known as the Atlantic Charter,

To the end that victory shall bring relief as well as freedom from oppression and cruelty, being determined that immediately upon the liberation of any area by their armed forces the population thereof shall receive aid and relief from their sufferings, food, clothing and shelter, assistance in obtaining the means of again cultivating their fields and in sustaining and increasing flocks and herds, assistance in resuming the production of essential things and in restoring essential services, the return of exiles and prisoners to their homes, the prevention of pestilence and the recovery of the health of their people, and assistance in general in restoring the essential foundations upon which a liberated world may build anew,

Have agreed as follows:

Article I

There is hereby established the United Nations Relief and Rehabilitation Administration, which shall be a body corporate, the object and purpose of which shall be the planning and administration of international measures for relief and rehabilitation in all areas liberated by the forces of the United Nations or any of them. The Administration shall have power to take, hold and convey property, to enter into contracts and undertake obligations, to manage undertakings, and in general to perform any legal act appropriate to its object and purpose.

Article II

The Members of the United Nations Relief and Rehabilitation Administration

The members of the United Nations Relief and Rehabilitation Administration shall be the governments signatory hereto and such other governments as may upon application for membership be admitted thereto by action of the Council or the Executive Committee thereof.

Article III

The Council and the Executive Committee

Section 1. Each member shall name one representative upon the Council of the United Nations Relief [and] Rehabilitation Administration, which shall be the policy-making body of the Administration. The Council shall, for each of its sessions, select one of its members to preside at the session.

Section 2. The Council shall be convened on the first Tuesday in July by the Executive Committee. It may be convened in special session whenever the Executive Committee shall deem necessary, and shall be convened within sixty days after request therefor by a majority of the members.

Section 3. The Executive Committee of the Council, consisting of the representatives of China, the Union of Soviet Socialist Republics, the United Kingdom, the United States of America, and three representatives of other member countries chosen annually by the Council, shall between sessions of the Council exercise all the powers and functions thereof, and, during sessions, shall constitute the steering committee of the Council. The Director General shall preside at the sessions of the Executive Committee.

Section 4. The Executive Committee shall be convened at any time on the request of any of its members or of the Director General.

Article IV

The executive authority of the United Nations Relief and Rehabilitation Administration shall be in the Director General, who shall be appointed by the Executive Committee after consultation with the member governments. The Director General shall, after consultation with the Executive Committee, appoint the principal officers of the Administration, fix their compensation, and determine their duties; he may employ such personnel as may be necessary to perform the functions of the Administration.

Article V

Standing Committees of the Administration

1. The following permanent committees of the Administration are established:

Committee on Materials and Supplies
Committee on Finance
Committee on European Relief
Committee on Middle Eastern Relief
Committee on Far Eastern Relief
Committee on Repatriation
Committee on Agriculture
Committee on Nutrition
Committee on Health
Committee on Transport

The Director General with the advice and consent of the Executive Committee shall appoint the members of the foregoing committees and shall report such membership to the annual meeting of the Council. He shall provide the necessary technical assistance from the staff of the administration to assist the committees. The standing committees shall advise and participate in the making of plans and the formulation of policy and may report to the Director General, the Executive Committee or the Council matters in their judgment requiring decision or investigation.

2. The Director General may appoint such other committees including committees on the special problems of particular countries or areas as may be found necessary.

Article VI

1. In respect of any action which may be contemplated by the Executive Committee or the standing committees the government of any of the United Nations whose population is involved shall be entitled to participate in the deliberations in which such action is contemplated.

2. All activities of the Administration in respect of the population of any of the United Nations shall, so far as practicable, be conducted in collaboration with the member government of such population and with such established relief agencies as may be in a position to render assistance to such population.

Article VII

1. Each member government pledges full support, subject to the requirements of its constitutional procedure, through contributions of funds, materials, equipment, supplies and services, to the Administration in order to accomplish the purposes of this Agreement. To the fullest extent possible the local expenses in any area receiving relief or rehabilitation aid shall be borne in the currency and by the governmental authority of that area.

2. The Administration shall, in conducting operations, in any area under military occupation by the armed forces of the United Nations, take account of the military necessities.

3. All purchases, chartering of ships, and other procurement activities in aid of relief or rehabilitation by the Administration or by any of the member governments (beyond their own territories) shall be done only after consultation with the appropriate United Nations control authorities and (in the case of member governments) after consultation with the Director General. Wherever possible all such activities shall be conducted through the appropriate United Nations agency.

Article VIII

The provisions of this agreement may be amended by unanimous vote of the Executive Committee and two-thirds vote of the Council.

Article IX

The present agreement shall become provisionally effective upon signature hereof, and shall come definitely into force in respect of each member country upon compliance with its legal requirements.

APPENDIX 22 [21]
March 21, 1949

The Research Staff (February 3, 1941–January 14, 1944)

The term "research staff" refers to the officer personnel of the Division of Special Research and the succeeding Divisions of Political Studies and Economic Studies.

I. DIVISION OF SPECIAL RESEARCH, FEBRUARY 3, 1941–JANUARY 1, 1943
Establishment

"Departmental Order 917–A

"There is hereby established in the Department of State a Division of Special Research, charged with the conduct of special studies in the foreign relations field; the analysis and appraisal of developments and conditions arising out of

---

[21] Compiled for this volume.

present day disturbed international relations; collaboration in this field as necessary with other interested departments and agencies of the Government; and with such other duties as may be assigned by the Secretary of State.

"Dr. Leo Pasvolsky is designated as Chief of the new Division and in that capacity shall continue to act as Special Assistant to the Secretary.

"The symbol designation of the Division shall be SR. This order shall be effective immediately.

CORDELL HULL

Department of State,
February 3, 1941."

Personnel of Professional Status:

Chief (in his capacity as Special Assistant to the Secretary of State)—Leo Pasvolsky, February 3, 1941 [22]—

Assistant Chief (Political field including territorial, security and armament problems)—Harley A. Notter, (assistant, May 19, 1941–March 17, 1942), March 17, 1942–

Assistant Chief (Economic field)—H. Julian Wadleigh (assistant, February 3, 1941–June 1, 1942), June 1, 1942–

Assistant Chief (Administration)—Charles W. Yost, June 1–December 18, 1942.

Assistant Chief (Territorial field)—Philip E. Mosely (consultant, March 26–June 15, 1942; assistant June 15–November 16, 1942), November 16, 1942–

Assistant Chief (Security field)—Durward V. Sandifer (assistant, July 1–November 16, 1942), November 16, 1942–

Acomb, Evelyn M., June 15, 1942–
Anderson, Frances D., *see* Gulick.
Barnes, Maynard B., Foreign Service officer, consultant, August 8–December 7, 1942 (returned to Foreign Service post).
Bartimo, (Mrs.) Kathryn D., December 7, 1942–
Bartlett, Alice C., June 22, 1942–
Berdahl, Clarence A., consultant, November 9, 1942–
Blakeslee, George H., consultant, August 23, 1942–
Blue, George V., July 16, 1942–
Boggs, Marion W., April 20, 1942–
Bonnell, Allen T., August 1, 1942–January 1, 1943.
Borton, Hugh, October 19, 1942–
Burnett, S. Bertha, September 24, 1942–
Campbell, John C., July 17, 1942–
Carroll, Mitchell B., consultant, November 11, 1942–
Chamberlin, Waldo, June 18, 1942–
Chipman, Norris B., Foreign Service officer, July 20, 1942–
Clough, Shepard B., September 28, 1942–
Coville, Cabot, Foreign Service officer, September 30, 1942–
Diebold, William P., Jr., consultant, March 26, 1942–
Dulles, (Mrs.) Eleanor L., September 1, 1942–
Eichelberger, Clark M., consultant, August 6, 1942–
Eldridge, Richard, February 3, 1941–
Evans, John W., August 4, 1941–February 11, 1942.
Fearey, Robert A., October 7, 1942–
Fluegel, Edna R., July 9, 1942–

---

[22] Dates attached to names indicate periods of service with the division; open entries indicate service to or beyond the close of the period.

Fosdick, Dorothy, November 2, 1942–
Gerig, O. Benjamin, June 22, 1942–
Green, James F., June 20, 1942–
Green, Suzanne, August 13, 1942–
Gulick, (Mrs.) Frances D. (Anderson), August 1, 1942–
Halderman, John W., August 16, 1942–
Harris, David, June 26, 1942–
Hartley, (Mrs.) Virginia Fox, December 30, 1941–
Hoskins, Halford L., consultant, October 20, 1942–
Howard, Harry N., July 13, 1942–
Ireland, Philip W., July 15, 1942–
Jones, Joseph M., Jr., June, 1942–
Jones, S. Shepard, July 15, 1942–
Kennedy, Mary T., November 16, 1942–
Kirk, Grayson L., consultant, March 26, 1942, regular appointment September 29, 1942–
Knight, Melvin M., December 11, 1942–
Koren, William, Jr., June 22, 1942–
McDiarmid, (Mrs.) Alice M., June 29, 1942–
McKisson, Robert M., September 15, 1942–
Maddox, William P., consultant, March 26–July 1, 1942.
Masland, John W., Jr., June 29, 1942–
Myers, Denys P., June 16, 1942–
Padelford, Norman J., consultant, November 1, 1942–
Pfankuchen, Llewellyn, July 27, 1942–
Potter, (Mrs.) Margaret Hardy, December 19, 1941–October 16, 1942.
Power, Thomas F., Jr., July 17, 1942–
Preuss, Lawrence, July 27, 1942–
Radius, Walter A., June 29, 1942–
Reece, Lenore, July 6, 1942–
Reinsch, Pauline H., September 8, 1942–
Ridgeway, George L., August 1, 1942–
Ronhovde, Andreas G., September 28, 1942–
Rosenson, Alexander M., June 24, 1942–
Ross, James A., Jr., December 16, 1942–
Rothwell, C. Easton, June 28, 1941–
Russell, Ruth B., February 5, 1941–
Schairer, Julia E., July 15, 1942–
Schmitter, Lyle L., February 2–December 1, 1942.
Sharp, Walter R., consultant, March 26, 1942, regular appointment September 1, 1942–
Spiker, Clarence J., Foreign Service officer, September 23, 1942–
Sullivan, M. Carmel, August 3, 1942–
Taylor, Paul B., April 1, 1941–September 23, 1942 (furlough for military service)
Terrill, Robert P., July 1942–
Vandenbosch, Amry, September 8, 1942–
Van Wickel, Jesse F., Foreign Service officer, October 19, 1942–
Veatch, Roy, October 5–December 13, 1942.
Williamson, David, November 1, 1941–January 31, 1942.
Wood, Bryce, August 5, 1942–
Yale, William, December 1, 1942–

Chart of Research Staff as of December 31, 1942
(at termination of Division of Special Research)

POLITICAL: Notter ECONOMIC: Wadleigh

International organization and arrangements	Territorial problems		
Gerig		Mosely	Bonnell
Berdahl	*Western*	*Eastern*	Burnett
Eichelberger	*Europe*	*Europe*	Carroll
Fosdick	Sharp	Howard	Diebold
Myers	Acomb	Campbell	Dulles
Wood	Clough	Chipman	Eldridge
	Green, J. F.	Power	Fearey
Security and armaments and law	Koren	*Near East*	Knight
	Ridgeway	Ireland	Radius
Sandifer	Ronhovde	Hoskins	Rosenson
Kirk	*Central*	Yale	Ross
Boggs	*Europe*		Russell
Pfankuchen	Harris	*Far East*	Schairer
Reinsch	Padelford	Blakeslee	Terrill
(and)	Rothwell	Borton	Van Wickel
Preuss		Coville	
Halderman		Masland	
McDiarmid		Spiker	
		Vandenbosch	

Joint Services

Commitments Unit
   Hartley, in charge
   Blue
   Green, S.
Post-War Trends Unit
   Jones, J., in charge
   Fluegel
   Gulick
   Bartimo

Documents Unit
   Chamberlin, in charge
   Sullivan
   McKisson
Library Unit
   Chamberlin, in charge
   Bartlett
Public Relations Unit
   Jones, S., in charge
   Reece
   Kennedy

II. DIVISIONS OF POLITICAL STUDIES AND OF ECONOMIC STUDIES, JANUARY 1, 1943–JANUARY 14, 1944 [23]

Establishment:

"Departmental Order 1124

"There are hereby established in the Department of State a Division of Political Studies and a Division of Economic Studies, which shall function under the general supervision of Mr. Leo Pasvolsky in his capacity as Special Assistant to the Secretary of State.

---

[23] For subsequent reorganization, see appendix 32, p. 565.

"The Division of Political Studies shall have responsibility for the conduct of continuing and special research, for the preparation of studies required in the formulation of policies, the planning of integrated programs as a basis for action in the field of foreign political relations affecting the interests of the United States, with particular reference to the long-range implications of current policies, actions and developments in this field affecting post-war political reconstruction, and for the formulation of appropriate recommendations with respect to the foregoing. In carrying out these responsibilities, the Division of Political Studies shall cooperate fully and maintain effective liaison with other divisions and offices of the Department, in particular the Division of Economic Studies, with other departments and agencies, and with interdepartmental and intergovernmental agencies having joint interest or authority in the field of activity.

"Mr. Harley A. Notter is hereby designated Chief, and Mr. Durward V. Sandifer, Mr. Philip E. Mosely and Mr. S. Shepard Jones are hereby designated Assistant Chiefs of the Division of Political Studies, the symbol designation of which shall be PS.

"The Division of Economic Studies shall have responsibility for the conduct of continuing and special research and for the preparation of studies required in the formulation of policies and the planning of integrated programs as a basis for action in the field of foreign economic relations affecting the interests of the United States, with particular reference to the long-range implications of current policies, actions and developments in this field affecting post-war economic reconstruction, and for the formulation of appropriate recommendations with regard to the foregoing. In carrying out these responsibilities, the Division of Economic Studies shall cooperate fully and maintain effective liaison with other divisions and offices of the Department, in particular the Division of Political Studies, with other departments and agencies and with interdepartmental and intergovernmental agencies having joint interest or authority in the field of activity.

"Mr. Leroy D. Stinebower is hereby designated Chief, and Mr. H. Julian Wadleigh is hereby designated an Assistant Chief of the Division of Economic Studies, the symbol designation of which shall be ES.

"The various divisions and officers of the Department shall cooperate fully and maintain effective liaison with the Division of Political Studies and the Division of Economc Studies and, in particular, they shall keep those divisions fully informed of current policy decisions, activities and developments in their respective political and economic fields, inviting their participation whenever feasible and appropriate in the formulation of policy decisions having long-range implications, and shall route to them for their information or advice communications and other material of a policy character falling within the scope of their responsibilities or interests.

"There is hereby established a Committee on Special Studies, the purpose of which shall be to facilitate the carrying out of the responsibilities defined in this Order. Mr. Pasvolsky shall be the Chairman of the Committee on Special Studies, the other members of which shall be the Chiefs of the Divisions of Political Studies and Economic Studies, and such other officers as may be designated by the Secretary of State.

"The Division of Special Research is hereby abolished and its personnel, equipment and other facilities are hereby transferred to the new divisions.

"The provisions of this Order shall be effective as of January 1, 1943 and shall supersede and cancel the provisions of any existing Order in conflict therewith.

CORDELL HULL

Department of State,
January 14, 1943."

522 APPENDIX 22

Personnel of Professional Status

Special Assistant to the Secretary with general supervision of both Divisions—
Leo Pasvolsky *, January 1, 1943–

Division of Political Studies

Chief: Harley A. Notter *, January 1, 1943–

Asst. Chief (International Organization and Security): Durward V. Sandifer *, January 1, 1943–

Asst. Chief (Territorial Problems): Philip E. Mosely *, January 1, 1943–

Asst. Chief (Administration): S. Sheppard Jones *, January 1–August 31, 1943.

Asst. Chief (Central Services): C. Easton Rothwell *, (assistant January—August 16, 1943), August 16, 1943–

Asst. Chief (Central European Problems): David Harris* (assistant January 1–October 16, 1943), October 16, 1943–

Acomb*, Evelyn M., January 1–October 16, 1943.

Armstrong, Elizabeth H., October 22, 1943–

Ball, M. Margaret, March 3, 1943–

Bartimo*, (Mrs.) Kathryn, January 1, 1943–

Bartlett*, Alice C., January 1, 1943–

Berdahl*, Clarence A., consultant, January 1, 1943–

Black, Cyril E., January 12, 1943–

Blaisdell, Donald C., April 13, 1943–

Blakeslee*, George H., consultant, January 1–September 16, 1943; regular officer, September 16, 1943–

Blue*, George V., January 1, 1943–

Boggs*, Marion W., January 1–February 23, 1943 (furloughed for military service).

Borton*, Hugh, January 1, 1943–

Bradshaw, Mary E., February 1, 1943–

Bunche, Ralph J., January 4, 1944–

Campbell*, John C., January 1, 1943–

Cargo, William I., October 1, 1943–

Chamberlin*, Waldo, January 1, 1943–

Chase, Emily T., April–August, 1943.

Chase, Eugene P., November 15, 1943–

Division of Economic Studies

Chief: Leroy D. Stinebower, January 1, 1943–

Asst. Chief (Financial Problems): H. Julian Wadleigh*, January 1–August 11, 1943.

Asst. Chief (General Economic Problems): Bernard F. Haley, August 11, 1943.

Asst. Chief (Financial Problems): Paul T. Ellsworth, September 18, 1943–

Asst. Chief (Territorial Economic Problems): Melvin M. Knight *, (assistant, January 1–February 1, 1943), February 1, 1943–

Amos, Paul S., September 23, 1943–

Balabanis, Homer P., November 5, 1943–

Bowen, Ralph H., February 15, 1943–

Brown, William Adams, Jr., July 1, 1943–

Burnett*, S. Bertha, January 1, 1943–

Carroll*, Mitchell B., consultant, January 1, 1943–

Chapin, John S., September 17, 1943–

Clough*, Shepard B., January 1–September 30, 1943.

Crane, Joan S., October 15, 1943–

Diebold*, William P., Jr., consultant, January 1–May 15, 1943.

Dulles*, (Mrs.) Eleanor L., January 1, 1943–

Eldridge*, Richard, January 1, 1943–

Emerson, Charlotte M., February 25, 1943–

Fay, Harold V. V., February 11, 1943–

Gideonse, Max, March 1, 1943–

Loftus, John A., November 2, 1943–

MacLean, Henry Coit, October 3, 1943–

Merlin, Sidney D., December 13, 1943–

Phillips, William T., September 8, 1943–

Piquet, Howard S., August 16, 1943 [24]–

Plank, Ellsworth T., August 20, 1943–

Potter*, (Mrs.) Margaret Hardy, June 16–November 1, 1943.

Radius*, Walter A., January 1, 1943–

---

[24] Officer *pro tem* under administrative assignment to permit him to serve as Executive Secretary of the Interim Commission on Food and Agriculture.

*Was an officer in the preceding Division of Special Research.

Division of Political Studies

Chipman*, Norris B., Foreign Service officer, January 1, 1943–

Clement, (Mrs.) Nell F., June 1, 1943–

Coville*, Cabot, Foreign Service officer, January 1–February 5, 1943 (returned to Foreign Service post).

Denby, James O., Foreign Service officer, August 11, 1943–

Dickinson, Hazel M., August 11, 1943–

Doolittle, Hooker A., Foreign Service officer, October 1943–

Driscoll, Elizabeth C., March 16, 1943– (previously clerical assistant).

Eagleton, Clyde, consultant, October 12, 1943, regular officer, December 16, 1943–

Edgar, Donald D., December 1, 1943–

Eichelberger*, Clark M., consultant, January 1, 1943–

Exton, Thérèse, December 17, 1943–

Fearey*, Robert A., January 1, 1943–

Flather, Georgianna N., December 13, 1943–

Fluegel*, Edna R., January 1, 1943–

Fosdick*, Dorothy, January 1, 1943–

Fuller, Leon W., February 1, 1943–

Furber, Holden, June 28, 1943–

Gerig*, O. Benjamin, January 1, 1943–

Gooch, Robert K., August 3, 1943–

Green*, James F., January 1, 1943–

Green*, Suzanne, January 1, 1943–

Gulick*, (Mrs.) Frances Anderson, January 1–April 21, 1943.

Halderman*, John W., January 1–September 8, 1943 (furlough for military service).

Hale, Madeleine, January 1, 1943–

Harris*, David, January 1, 1943–

Hartley*, (Mrs.) Virginia F., January 1, 1943–

Hoskins*, Halford L., consultant, January 1–May 21, 1943.

Howard*, Harry N., January 1, 1943–

Ireland*, Philip W., January 1, 1943–

Jones*, Joseph M., Jr., January 1–June 29, 1943.

Kennedy*, Mary T., January 1–August 31, 1943.

Kirk*, Grayson L., January 1, 1943–

Koren*, William, Jr., January 1–July 31, 1943 (mil. service).

Division of Economic Studies

Ramsey, (Miss) Fredlyn, September 25, 1943–

Reeves, William H., July 27–October 22, 1943.

Rosenson*, Alexander M., January 1, 1943–

Ross*, James A., Jr., January 1, 1943–

Schairer*, Julia E., January 1, 1943–

Terrill*, Robert P., January 1, 1943–

Van Wickel*, Jesse, Foreign Service officer, January 1, 1943–

Wachenheimer, Caroline E., October 27, 1943–

Williams, Frank S., Foreign Service officer, September 1, 1943–

Young, John Parke, February 12, 1943–

---

*Was an officer in the preceding Division of Special Research.

Division of Political Studies

McDiarmid*, (Mrs.) Alice M., January 1, 1943–

McKaig, Catherine, December 1943–

McKisson*, Robert M., January 1, 1943–

McMahon, (Mrs.) Virginia M., March 16, 1943–

Maktos, John, March 16, 1943–

Masland*, John W., Jr., January 1, 1943–September 1, 1943.

Mecham, John L., October 30, 1943–

Myers*, Denys P., January 1, 1943–

Padelford*, Norman J., consultant, January 1–June 28, 1943, regular appointment June 28, 1943–

Patterson, John, February 1–December 15, 1943.

Perkins, Mahlon F., Foreign Service officer, September 1, 1943–

Pfankuchen*, Llewellyn M., January 1–September 28, 1943.

Power*, Thomas F., Jr., January 1, 1943–

Preuss*, Lawrence, January 1, 1943–

Reece*, Lenore M., January 1, 1943–

Reinsch, Pauline H., January 1, 1943–

Ridgeway*, George L., January 1–September 1, 1943

Division of Political Studies—Cont.

Ronhovde*, Andreas G., January 1, 1943–

Sharp*, Walter R., January 1–September 30, 1943.

Simering, Chauncey L., March 18–December 8, 1943.

Simpson, R. Smith, March 8, 1943–

Smyth, Howard M., November 5, 1943–

Spiker*, Clarence J., Foreign Service officer, January 1–March 8, 1943 (returned to Foreign Service post).

Stickney, Edith P., July 1, 1943–

Sullivan*, M. Carmel, January 1, 1943–

Summers, Lionel M., December 17, 1943–

Thompson, Jane H., September 23, 1943–

Tomlinson, John D., November 1, 1943–

Trivers, Howard, November 1943–

Vandenbosch*, Amry, January 1, 1943–

Vedeler, Harold C., November 1, 1943–

Wheeler, Jane G., September 21, 1943–

Whitaker, Arthur P., August 26, 1943–

White, Wilbur W., March 2–September 14, 1943.

Williams, Benjamin Harrison, August 1, 1943–

Wood*, Bryce, January 1–July 12, 1943.

Wright, Gordon J., January 3, 1944–

Yale*, William, January 1, 1943–

Chart of Research Staff as of January 14, 1944

(at termination of the Divisions of Political and Economic Studies)

Special Assistant to the Secretary

Leo Pasvolsky

DIVISION OF POLITICAL STUDIES [25]

Notter, Chief

International Organization Section

Sandifer, Asst. Chief

International Organization Unit
Gerig, in charge
Berdahl
Cargo
Eagleton
Edgar
Eichelberger
Fosdick
Myers
Padelford
Simpson

Security Unit
Kirk, in charge
Blaisdell
Reinsch
Williams

Legal Unit
Preuss, in charge
Maktos
McDiarmid
Summers

---

*Was an officer in the preceding Division of Special Research.

Territorial Section

Mosely, Asst. Chief

Harris, Asst. Chief

Eastern European Unit
Howard, in charge
Black
Bradshaw
Campbell
Chipman
Power

Western European Unit
Gooch, in charge
Armstrong
Chase, E. P.
Green, J.
Koren
Ronhovde
Vandenbosch
Wheeler
Wright

Near East and African Unit
Ireland, in charge
Bunche
Denby
Doolittle
Furber
Hoskins
Yale

Central European Unit
Harris, in charge
Fuller
Smyth
Trivers
Vedeler

Far Eastern Unit
Blakeslee, in charge
Bartimo
Borton
Fearey
Perkins

Latin American Unit
Whitaker, in charge
Ball
Mecham

Joint Services and Administration
Rothwell, Asst. Chief

Commitments Unit
Hartley, in charge
Blue
Green, S.
Thompson

Documents Unit
Chamberlin, in charge
Sullivan
McKisson
Driscoll
Clement

Biographical Analysis Unit
Fluegel, in charge
Stickney
McMahon
Hale
Dickinson
Flather
Exton

Library Unit
Bartlett, in charge

Administration Unit
Reece, in charge
McKaig

[25] Cumulative total of personnel in this Division—96; personnel at dissolution—77. Personnel leaving this Division in the course of the year for military service or other reasons: Wood, Halderman, Pfankuchen, and Boggs (International Organization); Acomb, Ridgeway, Sharp, White, Hoskins, Coville, Masland, and Spiker (Territorial); Simering (Administration); Gulick, J. Jones, S. Jones, Kennedy, Patterson, and E. T. Chase (of the Public Affairs Unit and Post-War Trends Unit transferred during the year.)

APPENDIX 23
August 14, 1943 [27]

The Charter of the United Nations

(Draft)

PREAMBLE

The United Nations, determined to banish the scourge of war, to establish the rule of law among states, and to promote the freedom, dignity and welfare of all peoples, do ordain and establish this Charter.

Article 1

THE UNITED NATIONS

1. The community of nations organized within the framework of this Charter shall be known as The United Nations.

2. The seat of The United Nations shall be at ——————.

Article 2

MEMBERSHIP

1. Membership in The United Nations shall be open to states signing and ratifying this Charter.

2. By a vote of three-fourths of the Members represented in the General Conference, any other independent state may be admitted to membership by adherence to this Charter.

---

[26] Cumulative total of personnel in this Division—38; personnel at dissolution—33. Personnel leaving this Division in the course of the year: Wadleigh (Asst. Chief), Reeves (Financial); Diebold, Potter (General); and Clough (Territorial Economic).

[27] As written by the Research Staff.

3. Admission to membership in The United Nations shall constitute acknowledgment by all Members of the international rights and privileges of the state so admitted.

Article 3

THE GENERAL CONFERENCE

1. The General Conference shall consist of representatives of the Members of The United Nations.

2. In matters of international concern affecting the community of nations, the General Conference shall determine the general policies of The United Nations and may initiate action where the initiative is not specifically reserved to the Council.

3. The General Conference shall review the work of the organs of The United Nations, shall vote the appropriations for their activities, and shall exercise such other specific powers as are conferred upon it by this Charter.

4. Each Member of The United Nations shall have one vote in the General Conference and shall have not more than six representatives, including representation from the national legislative body.

5. Except as otherwise provided in this instrument, decisions by the General Conference shall be by a three-fourths vote of the Members present and voting. Procedural questions, including the appointment of committees, shall be decided by a majority of the Members present and voting.

6. The General Conference shall meet annually at the seat of The United Nations. Special sessions may be convened upon the request of any five Members. The Conference shall elect a President and Vice-President, for annual terms, and otherwise perfect its organization. It shall adopt its own rules of procedure.

Article 4

THE COUNCIL

1. The Council shall consist of representatives of certain Members with indeterminate tenure whose special position devolves upon them exceptional responsibilities for the maintenance of international security, together with the representatives of an equal number less one of Members elected by the General Conference for annual terms and not immediately eligible for reelection. Upon nomination of the Council, the General Conference may name additional Members to the Council.

2. Initially, the United States of America, the United Kingdom of Great Britain and Northern Ireland, the Republic of China, and the Union of Soviet Socialist Republics shall be the Members of the Council with indeterminate tenure, and three other Members shall be elected by the General Conference for annual terms.

3. The Council shall have primary responsibility for the maintenance of international security, and general responsibility for giving executive effect to policies determined by the General Conference. Between sessions of the General Conference the Council may initiate any necessary action within the competence of The United Nations, subject to review by the General Conference. It shall exercise such specific powers as are conferred upon it by this Charter.

4. Any Member of The United Nations not represented on the Council shall be entitled, subject to approval by a majority of the Council, to attend and be heard during the consideration of matters specially affecting that Member.

5. If the Council, in giving executive effect to a decision of the General Conference, deems that certain modifications are desirable, it may request the General Conference to reconsider the matter.

6. The [Director General] of The United Nations shall preside over the Council. He may participate in its deliberations without the right to vote.

7. Each Member of the Council shall have one representative and one vote. Except as otherwise provided in this Charter, decisions by the Council shall be by a two-thirds majority of the Members present and voting, provided all the Members with indeterminate tenure present and voting concur. Procedural questions, including the appointment of committees, shall be decided by a majority of the Members present and voting. The Council shall adopt its own rules of procedure.

Article 5

THE ADMINISTRATIVE OFFICES

1. The General Administrative Office shall be established at the seat of The United Nations. Other administrative offices, wherever established, shall be subject to the staff regulations governing the General Administrative Office.

2. All administrative offices shall be under the direction of a [Director General] who shall be assisted by such directors and other officers as may be required. All general officers shall be appointed by the Council and confirmed by the General Conference. In making appointments the widest distribution, compatible with technical efficiency, shall be made among nationalities.

3. There shall be established such administrative offices as may be required for the various technical organizations and commissions, including offices in the fields of economics and finance, labor, food and agriculture, communications, health, social welfare, education and culture, and international territorial administration. Each office shall be in charge of a Director appointed by the Council upon the nomination of the highest executive authority of the technical organization concerned.

4. The Directors of the several offices, together with the [Director General], shall constitute an Administrative Committee to supervise and coordinate the administrative work of the various offices. This Administrative Committee shall sit with and advise the Council in coordinating the policies of the technical organizations. The Director of each technical office shall report and make recommendations directly to the Council on the work of the technical organization concerned.

5. The permanent officials of the administrative staffs shall agree to discharge their duties and regulate their conduct with the interests of The United Nations alone in view. The Members shall impose no obligations upon their nationals, officials of The United Nations, which are inconsistent with the performance of their duties.

6. Officials of The United Nations when engaged on the business of The United Nations, or when traveling to and from the seat of The United Nations, shall enjoy diplomatic privileges and immunities.

Article 6

THE JUDICIARY

1. The International Court of Justice is constituted in accordance with the terms of the Statute annexed to this Charter.

2. The General Conference is authorized to formulate and submit to the Members of The United Nations for adoption plans for the establishment of such other tribunals as may be required.

3. Any state, or any agency of The United Nations which is so authorized by the terms of the instrument by which it was created, may be a party to cases before the Court.

4. The Court shall be competent to hear and determine all cases involving disputes as to the respective rights of the parties, or as to the interpretation of this Charter, which are referred to it: (a) by agreement of the parties; (b) in accordance with the provisions of agreements, treaties or conventions in force; and (c) by the Council, in the event that a menace to the peace of nations exists. The Court may also give its opinion upon the legal aspects of any question within the competence of The United Nations, when so requested by a majority of the Members of the Council present and voting.

Article 7

PEACEFUL ADJUSTMENT

1. The Members of The United Nations agree to settle by peaceful means any of their disputes which may threaten the peace and security of nations.

2. Any dispute, the continuance of which may disturb the peace or the good understanding between nations, which is not settled by diplomacy, shall be submitted to conciliation, arbitration, judicial settlement or to the procedures of this Article.

3. In the event that any dispute has not been settled by other peaceful means, the Council, upon its own initiative or that of any party or any other state, shall endeavor to effect a settlement between the parties. The Council, by a majority of the Members present and voting, may undertake an investigation and make proposals for a settlement.

4. Should such a settlement not be effected the Council shall make recommendations which it deems just and equitable.

5. The Council may refer the dispute to the General Conference, which shall make such recommendations for settlement as it deems just and equitable.

6. In the event that any party to a dispute shall fail to observe or execute a recommendation by the Council or by the General Conference, the Council shall take steps to ensure compliance therewith.

7. In any decision taken by the Council or the General Conference under paragraphs 4, 5, or 6 of this Article, the votes of the parties shall be excluded.

Article 8

SECURITY AND ARMAMENTS

1. Any threat to international peace and security is declared to be a matter of concern to all Members of The United Nations, which hereby undertake effectively to support measures adopted by the Council and the General Conference for safeguarding or restoring peace.

2. In the event of a threat to, or a breach of, the peace between nations, the Chairman of the Council, after consultation with the Members of the Council, shall request the parties involved to desist from any action which might prejudice a peaceful settlement. States failing to comply with this request shall be regarded as intending a breach of the peace, and the Council shall forthwith institute such measures, including measures of force, as it deems appropriate for the maintenance or restoration of the peace. The Council shall apprise the General Conference of its action, and request the Members to take appropriate supporting action.

3. Members of The United Nations agree to prohibit all assistance to a state which is declared by the Council to have committed, or to be threatening, a breach of the peace.

4. In the event of Council action under paragraph 2, the Members of The United Nations agree to make available such of their national armaments, facilities and

installations, strategic areas, and contingents of armed forces as the Council, in consultation with the Member concerned, shall determine to be necessary. For this purpose, the Council shall be advised by a General Security and Armaments Commission whose composition and functions are set forth in a Protocol annexed to this Charter. In considering the contributions of a Member to a joint effort for the maintenance or restoration of peace, the Council shall take account of its geographical position, regional or special obligations, and relative resources. Freedom of passage shall be afforded by Members to all forces operating in behalf of The United Nations.

5. Members of The United Nations agree to cooperate in executing such economic, commercial or financial measures against a state threatening, or committing a breach of, the peace as the Council or the General Conference shall determine to be necessary. They further agree to support one another in resisting measures resulting from such action, and in equalizing excessive losses incurred thereby.

6. Members of The United Nations undertake to maintain their armaments at the lowest point consistent with their internal order and with the effective discharge of their respective obligations for maintaining international security. An appropriate system of armaments regulation shall be established by the Council, with the advice of the General Security and Armaments Commission, and in consultation with the Members of The United Nations. Account shall be taken of the special responsibilities for security assumed by Members of the Council with indeterminate tenure, and the collective responsibility assumed by all.

7. Limitations and regulations established under paragraph 6 shall be enforced by a system of inspection carried out by an Armaments Inspection Commission under the direction of the General Security and Armaments Commission. Members shall accord this Commission every facility for the effective discharge of its responsibility.

8. Any action by the Council under this Article shall require a two-thirds majority vote of the Members present and voting, including three-fourths of the Members with indeterminate tenure.

Article 9

HUMAN RIGHTS

The Members of The United Nations agree to give legislative effect to the Declaration of Human Rights annexed to this Charter. Measures of enforcement shall be applied by the administrative and judicial authorities of each Member without discrimination as to nationality, language, race, political opinion, or religious belief.

Article 10

ECONOMIC AND SOCIAL COOPERATION

1. The United Nations shall assist its Members in developing collaboration in economic and social matters. For this purpose the General Conference is authorized to establish or to bring within the framework of the United Nations appropriate technical organizations, including organizations in the fields of economics and finance, labor, food and agriculture, communications, health, social welfare, and education and culture.

2. The General Conference, taking into account the recommendations of each organization, shall determine the general policies of technical organizations of The United Nations.

3. The Council, with the advice and assistance of the Administrative Committee provided for in Article 5, shall coordinate the activities of the technical organizations.

4. Each technical organization shall have a statute which shall be consistent with this Charter.

Article 11

TERRITORIAL ADMINISTRATION

1. The Council shall establish a system of administration for territories which may be placed under the authority of The United Nations by treaty or other agreement.

2. The Council shall establish by separate instruments for each such territory the terms and conditions under which it shall be administered. All instruments shall include provisions to assure:

(a) the education and cultural advancement of the inhabitants;

(b) freedom of conscience and speech;

(c) protection of the inhabitants from exploitation;

(d) promotion of economic and social welfare;

(e) establishment and maintenance of non-discriminatory commercial treatment;

(f) promotion of equality of economic opportunity consistent with the safeguarding of the interests of the local inhabitants.

3. The Council, on behalf of The United Nations, shall administer these territories either directly or through such authorities as it may recognize or establish.

4. To assist the Council in exercising its powers of administration and supervision, commissions shall be established whose number, composition and powers shall be defined by the Council. Each commission shall have the right to conduct inspections in territories under its supervision to ensure that the policies of the Council are being carried out, and it shall make periodic reports and recommendations to the Council.

5. The Council shall be the final authority in all matters relating to modification or termination of the provisions of this Article. It shall also decide to what degree any of the provisions shall be modified for special reasons of international security.

6. Each Member of The United Nations undertakes to observe in the other non-self-governing territories under its control the same standards of administration as are required by the terms of this Article.

Article 12

REGIONAL ARRANGEMENTS

Nothing in this Charter shall affect regional arrangements, agreements, or associations, now existing or which may be entered into between Members, which are consistent with the obligations assumed under this Charter.

Article 13

FINANCIAL PROVISIONS

1. The expenses of The United Nations shall be borne by the Members on a basis of apportionment determined by the General Conference with the approval of the Council.

2. Regulations for the financial administration of The United Nations, including provision for the payment of the travel expenses of official representatives

to meetings of the General Conference and the Council, shall be approved by the General Conference.

3. A Treasurer, appointed by the Council and confirmed by the General Conference, shall receive and administer all funds of The United Nations.

Article 14

REGISTRATION OF TREATIES

Every treaty and agreement entered into by the Members of The United Nations shall be registered with the General Administrative Office for publication. The texts of the instruments so registered shall be regarded by The United Nations as authentic.

Article 15

RATIFICATION AND BINDING FORCE

1. This Charter shall be ratified, and shall come into force when ratifications have been deposited with the President of the United States of America by 25 states, including those Members of the Council with indeterminate tenure. It shall remain in force indefinitely.

2. The authorities of each Member shall take such measures as may be necessary to give full force and effect to the provisions of this Charter.

3. The Members agree to take such steps as may be required to obtain their release from any obligations inconsistent with the undertakings of this Charter; and they further agree that they will not hereafter enter into any treaty or agreement inconsistent with these undertakings.

Article 16

WITHDRAWAL FROM MEMBERSHIP

1. Membership in The United Nations shall be for a period of ten years, and shall continue for successive periods of ten years unless a Member shall, not less than two years before the expiration of a ten-year period, give notice to the President of the General Conference of its intention to withdraw.

2. Withdrawal from membership shall not release a state from any obligations whatsoever which it has incurred while a Member of The United Nations, nor shall it affect the binding force of this Charter for the remaining Members.

Article 17

AMENDMENTS

Amendments to this Charter shall be adopted by the General Conference and be submitted forthwith by the [Director General] to the Members of The United Nations. They shall come into force if ratified within five years by four-fifths of the number of Members of The United Nations at the time of the adoption of the amendment, including all Members of the Council with indeterminate tenure.

TRANSITORY ARTICLE

1. The first meetings of the General Conference and of the Council of The United Nations shall be called by the President of the United States of America, within six months after this Charter enters into force, at such time and place as he may designate.

2. The Council shall determine the time and manner in which provisional agencies shall be superseded by permanent organs of The United Nations.

[EXTRACT FROM THE ACCOMPANYING COMMENTARIES] [28]

INTRODUCTORY COMMENT

The Charter of the United Nations was drafted under a directive calling for a brief and simple instrument which, in the light of past experience, current discussions and political feasibility, would serve to establish the permanent international machinery necessary to perform the essential functions of international organization.

The minimum functions which it was agreed require action on an international plane, fall under seven heads: (1) security against aggression and war, (2) control of armaments, (3) political settlement of disputes, (4) judicial settlement of disputes, (5) promotion of economic and social cooperation, (6) administration of certain dependent areas, and (7) safeguarding of certain basic human rights.

Extensive studies were made of the experience of the League of Nations and of other international agencies which had the same or similar objects. Similarly the current official and unofficial views in the various countries were analyzed to find some least common denominators, and the discussions and views of the various Subcommittees were examined.

Within this frame of experience and current discussion the various views were subjected, as far as possible, to the test of practical and political feasibility.

The document which emerged is not a radical departure from national and international experience. Two, and perhaps only two, alternatives in the basic form of organization were open: (1) the cooperative form, or (2) the federal form. The latter, while urged by many prominent individuals and groups, was rejected by the drafting committee as politically not feasible. The various governments and peoples are not believed to be ready for an international federal government even if it were theoretically desirable. Yet the name of the organization and the provisions of the Charter itself provide a basis for steady growth toward closer relationships and even toward more unified forms of world cooperation.

The Charter of The United Nations is, however, based on the principle of free cooperation among states. But this cooperation must be given a reasonable chance to be effective, especially in matters of security. The projected organization, accordingly, differs from the League of Nations in several basic respects: (1) it gives the great powers exceptional and immediate responsibility for security, and for this purpose gives them a permanent preponderance in the membership and vote control of the Council, (2) it enables action both in the Conference and the Council to be instituted with less than complete unanimity, (3) it provides for more effective international control of armaments, and (4) it provides for a more effective system of administration and supervision of certain dependent territories.

Like the League, it is based on the conception of universal membership, although it may be established by the United Nations and the nations presently associated with them.

This Charter differs from the plan projected in the International Organization Subcommittee in differentiating the respective powers of the Conference and the Council, and making the full representative Conference an important policy-

---

[28] The commentaries on each paragraph of the draft Charter were extensive and are not printed here. They were completed by Sept. 7, 1943, which is the date of the Introductory Comment above.

making body while providing for the necessary control in the Council. It was considered preferable to vest all powers of an executive character in a single organ, the Council, including security powers and to organize it for effective action.

Another plan, whereby only machinery would be established, without commitments or undertakings, in order to make it possible to get early and quick acceptance, was examined but felt to be inadequate for this purpose.

The Charter envisages an organization on the universal pattern but does not preclude regional developments—existing or future—provided such development are consistent with the universal organization.

As to the functional organizations, the Charter is based on the principle of integrating the several technical and other bodies within its general policy and budgetary framework while leaving ample room for autonomous action by these constituent bodies. Since many of the technical bodies may be in existence before The United Nations itself it is assumed that their statutes will provide for the necessary relation with the universal body when established.

The Charter in its present form is designed for a permanent organization to be established sometime after the end of hostilities. However, with some adjustments, it could be used for an organization to begin at any time, with the wartime United Nations as a nucleus. If it were instituted before the end of hostilities, an additional transitory article would be necessary, giving priority to all war-time emergency agencies until such time as their functions were transferred to one of the organs of the permanent organization—The United Nations.

APPENDIX 24
October 25, 1943

[Research Staff Memorandum]

PS AND ES MEMBERS OF COUNTRY COMMITTEES

In the interest of escaping some minor confusions that have arisen the following should be carefully noted.

1. The name of the committees is in each case the Inter-Divisional Country Committee on ——————— (fill in the name of the country or the area concerned). Both PS and ES should be represented on all country committees.

2. The purposes of the committees are:

    a. Careful study of all current developments in the country area with special attention:

        (1) to the problems arising in sequence calling for policy decision by this Government,

        (2) to commitments of policy toward the country or area, and

        (3) to the objectives and commitments of the country or countries of an area.

    b. Critical examination of pertinent H documents in order to make them representative of the exact thought of the experts from the divisions represented on the country committees. (H stands for our policy summary handbook, and there should be such a handbook on each country or area. The handbooks of course contain many individual documents, corresponding to the different problems concerning the country or the area. Whether or not currently so organized, in due course the H documents on each country will be brought together as one book on its policy problems.)

The H documents may be presented to the country committee either before or after review in PS or ES or both, as the agenda of the committee may necessitate. Whether finally reviewed or not, the presentation of a document to a country committee should be approved by an Assistant Chief. When presented before Divisional review such studies should be labeled H-Preliminary #———. If an H document previously reviewed is revised during the committee examination, the revision should be returned to your Division for review and the earlier form attached with the notation that it has been superseded. Responsibility for carrying out this procedure rests with each Divisional member of a country committee.

c. The formulation of the views of the Inter-Divisional Country Committees. Such views should constitute a supplement to the H documents. Supplements should be headed "Views of the Inter-Divisional Country Committee on _____". The given views, together with any expression of preference (avoid use of "recommendation"), would then appear as a separate document but attached to the H document to which it relates. This may be illustrated as follows:

Austro-German Frontier H–35 (Supplement) Views of the Inter-Divisional Country Committee on Germany.

d. At the bottom of the supplement the ascription should read:

> Prepared and reviewed by: [e.g.]
> PS: Red (drafting officer)
> ES: White
> Eu: Gray, et al.

3. The supplement document, as it emanates from consultation in the country committee, should indicate the policy preferred together with a brief adduction of the reasons why the committee prefers it and disapproves of other alternatives. The statement should not attempt to recapitulate the factual information and the analyses contained in the basic H document.

4. When the supplement has been completed, it together with its H document should promptly be submitted by the appropriate Inter-Divisional Country Committee to the chiefs of each of the divisions represented on the Committee. It should be accompanied with an indication that it is being submitted by the Inter-Divisional Country Committee for simultaneous review by the interested divisions, and that any comments will be considered by the Committee as quickly as possible. It should also be stated that the Country Committee will keep abreast of further developments which may cause modification of the document and will re-submit it for review when appropriate. When the supplement with its related policy summary has been so reviewed, it with copies should be deposited in the PS–ES joint file for presentation at any time on request of the Chairman of the Country Committee. The responsibility for the procedure outlined in this paragraph is the responsibility of the Chairman of the Country Committee. This should be made clear to the Country Committee.

5. Submission of H documents and Supplements to Political and other Advisers will be undertaken by the Chiefs of PS and ES.

6. Documents other than H documents. The provisions of the second paragraph of 2b and those of 2d should be applied to all secret or confidential supporting memoranda.

7. While copies of working preliminary documents should be made available to the members, only one carbon copy of a finished document can be provided for file purposes to each Division represented on a Country Committee.

8. From time to time, if and as subject matter may require, the chairmen of Country Committees should invite other officers of the Department possessing special competence to attend particular meetings. However, great care should be taken to keep every committee small.

Please terminate procedures not in accord with the above. Such PG [Policy Group] documents as have been completed should bear the additional label, in ink: H-Supplement A.

HARLEY A. NOTTER
LEROY D. STINEBOWER

The Twelve Special Economic Committees of the (Interdepartmental) Committee on Post-War Foreign Economic Policy, 1943

SPECIAL COMMITTEE ON INTERNATIONAL AVIATION

Established: April 16, 1943, by conversion of preceding "Interdepartmental Committee on Aviation"

Membership:
  *Adolf A. Berle, Jr., Assistant Secretary of State, *Chairman*
  Stokeley W. Morgan, Chief, Aviation Division, Department of State
  *Artemus L. Gates, Assistant Secretary of Navy for Air (Adviser)
  *Robert A. Lovett, Assistant Secretary of War for Air (Adviser)
  *Wayne C. Taylor, Under Secretary of Commerce
  *L. Welch Pogue, Chairman, Civil Aeronautics Board
  Stephen Latchford, Aviation Division, Department of State
  Joseph C. Grew, Special Assistant to Secretary of State
  *Paul T. David, Chief Fiscal Analyst, Bureau of the Budget, *Secretary*
  Wayne Coy, Assistant Director, Bureau of the Budget (alternate)
  (Milo R. Perkins was a member originally).

Subcommittees [30]

Subcommittee 1: Joint Subcommittee with the Special Committee on Shipping
L. Welch Pogue, Civil Aeronautics Board, Chairman
Huntington T. Morse, Maritime Commission, Co-Chairman

---

[29] Compiled for this volume from information mainly derived from the Directory of the Executive Committee on Economic Foreign Policy under date of Apr. 15, 1944. Starred name or specific explanation denotes member at date of establishment of the Special Committee. Since membership was based on representation of interested agencies, there was some fluctuation among persons attending. It should be noted that approximately an equal number of other interdepartmental committees existed.

[30] While the subcommittees named throughout this appendix existed when the report of April, 1944 was prepared, certain others had been created, functioned, and disbanded during the following year. Membership is not shown since these working groups, normally containing a number of experts, fluctuated as their assignments of duty changed in their Departments or agencies.

*Starred name or specific explanation denotes member at date of establishment of the Special Committee.

SPECIAL COMMITTEE ON LABOR STANDARDS AND SOCIAL SECURITY

Established: April 19, 1943

Membership:
*Frances Perkins, Secretary of Labor, *Chairman*
*A. F. Hinrichs, Acting Commissioner, Bureau of Labor Statistics, Department of Labor, *Vice Chairman*
*Isador Lubin, Assistant to the President
*Katharine F. Lenroot, Chief, Children's Bureau, Department of Labor
*Verne A. Zimmer, Director, Division of Labor Standards, Department of Labor
*Mary Anderson, Director, Women's Bureau, Department of Labor
*Carter Goodrich, Columbia University (and Chairman of Governing Board, International Labor Organization)
*Herbert Feldman, Dartmouth College
*Professor J. Douglas Brown, Princeton University
*The Rt. Rev. Msgr. John A. Ryan, Director Social Action Department, National Catholic Welfare Conference
*Amy Hewes, Mount Holyoke College
*Adolf A. Berle, Jr., Assistant Secretary of State
  Otis E. Mulliken, Labor Division, Department of State (alternate)
*Emil Rieve, General President, Textile Workers Union of America
*Philip Murray, President, Congress of Industrial Organizations
*Raymond J. Walsh, Director, Education and Research, Congress of Industrial Organizations (alternate)
*David Dubinsky, President, International Ladies' Garment Workers Union
*William Green, President, American Federation of Labor
*Arthur J. Altmeyer, Chairman, Social Security Board
  Hugh S. Hanna, Department of Labor, *Secretary*

Subcommittees (7)

Subcommittee 1: Social Insurance and Public Assistance
Arthur J. Altmeyer, Social Security Board, Chairman
Subcommittee 2: Women
Mary Anderson, Labor, Chairman
Subcommittee 3: Wages and Hours
Isador Lubin, Chairman
Subcommittee 4: Working Conditions
Verne A. Zimmer, Labor, Chairman
Subcommittee 5: Child Labor
Katharine F. Lenroot and Verne A. Zimmer, Labor, Chairman not designated
Subcommittee 6: Marine Labor Standards
Carter Goodrich, Columbia University, Chairman
Subcommittee 7: Implementation of Labor Standards
Otis E. Mulliken, State, Chairman

SPECIAL COMMITTEE ON POWER

Established: April 23, 1943

Membership:
*Leland Olds, Chairman, Federal Power Commission, *Chairman*
*Major General Thomas M. Robins, Assistant Chief of Engineers, War Department

---

*Starred name or specific explanation denotes member at date of establishment of the Special Committee.

*Abe Fortas, Under Secretary of Interior
*Charles E. Carey, Bureau of the Budget
*Walter A. Radius, Department of State (originally *Secretary*)
William T. Phillips, Department of State, *Secretary*
(David E. Lilienthal was technically a member but did not attend)

SPECIAL COMMITTEE ON PRIVATE MONOPOLIES AND CARTELS

Established: May 28, 1943

Membership:

*Dean G. Acheson, Assistant Secretary of State, *Chairman*
*Edward S. Mason, Office of Strategic Services, *Deputy Chairman*
*Hugh B. Cox, Assistant Attorney General, Department of Justice (originally Vice-Chairman)
Theodore J. Kreps, (alternate for Department of Commerce)
*Emilio G. Collado, Division of Financial and Monetary Affairs, Department of State
*Lynn R. Edminster, Vice Chairman, Tariff Commission
Loyle A. Morrison, Chief, Economics Division, Tariff Commission (alternate)
Corwin Edwards, Department of Justice
Mordecai Ezekiel, Economic Adviser to the Secretary, Department of Agriculture
Walter C. Louchheim, Jr., Assistant Director, Trading and Exchange Division, Securities and Exchange Commission
Ben Lewis, Office of Foreign Economic Administration
*Homer Jones, Chief, Division of Investigation and Research, Office of Alien Property Custodian
Moses Abramowitz, Office of Strategic Services
*Donald H. Wallace, Special Economic Adviser to the Deputy Administrator, Office of Price Administration
Bernard F. Haley, Commodities Division, Department of State
Horace B. McCoy, Department of Commerce
*Robert P. Terrill, Commodities Division, Department of State, *Secretary*
(Louis Domeratzky, Creekmore Fath and Sigmund Timberg were originally members)

Subcommittee

Ad Hoc Joint Subcommittees with the Special Committee on Commodity Agreements and Methods of Trade

Corwin Edwards, Justice, Chairman
Lynn R. Edminster, Tariff Commission, alternate Chairman

SPECIAL COMMITTEEE ON RELAXATION OF TRADE BARRIERS

Established: June 11, 1943

Membership:

William A. Fowler, Division of Commercial Policy, Department of State, *Chairman;* Harry C. Hawkins, original *chairman*
* Walter Salant, Head Economist, Office of the Economic Adviser, Office of Price Administration
* Leslie A. Wheeler, Director, Division of Foreign Agricultural Relations, Department of Agriculture'

---

*Starred name or specific explanation denotes member at date of establishment of the Special Committee.

Harry D. White, Assistant to the Secretary, Treasury Department (N. T. Ness, original member)
* Oscar B. Ryder, Chairman, Tariff Commission
* Amos E. Taylor, Director, Bureau of Foreign and Domestic Commerce, Commerce Department
*H. P. MacGowan, Chief, Trade Agreements Unit, Department of Commerce (alternate)
* Raymond C. Miller, Assistant Director, Bureau of Foreign and Domestic Commerce, Department of Commerce
* George B. L. Arner, Foreign Trade Adviser, Office of Foreign Agricultural Relations, Department of Agriculture
Edward W. Kelly, Division of Commercial Policy, Department of State, *Secretary*
(Lynn R. Edminster of Tariff Commission, William P. Stone of War Production Board and Arthur Smithies of Budget Bureau were originally members)

Subcommittees (8)

Subcommittee A—Tariffs

Oscar B. Ryder, Tariff Commission, Chairman
Benjamin B. Wallace, Tariff Commission, alternate Chairman

Subcommittee B—Quantitative Restrictions (Import) and Export Taxes and Restrictions

Edgar B. Brossard, Tariff Commission, Chairman
Loyle A. Morrison, Tariff Commission, alternate Chairman

Subcommittee C—Preferences and Discriminations

E. Dana Durand, Tariff Commission, Chairman
Benjamin B. Wallace, Tariff Commission, alternate Chairman

Subcommittee D—State Trading

Amos E. Taylor, Commerce, Chairman

Subcommittee E—Subsidies and Dual-Price Systems

Leslie A. Wheeler, Agriculture, Chairman

Subcommittee F—International Commercial Organization and Commercial Principles

Lynn R. Edminster, Tariff Commission, Chairman
Earle M. Winslow, Tariff Commission, alternate Chairman

Subcommittee G—Integration of Domestic and International Economic Policies

John H. G. Pierson, Labor, Chairman

Subcommittee H—Exchange Discrimination

Amos E. Taylor, Commerce, Chairman

SPECIAL COMMITTEE ON COMMODITY AGREEMENTS AND METHODS OF TRADE

Established: June 15, 1943

Membership:
*Lynn R. Edminster, Vice Chairman, Tariff Commission, *Chairman*
Prentice N. Dean, Economic Division, Tariff Commission (alternate)

*Starred name or specific explanation denotes member at date of establishment of the Special Committee.

*Leslie A. Wheeler, Director, Office of Foreign Agricultural Relations, Department of Agriculture

*Oscar C. Stine, Head, Division of Historical Research, Department of Agriculture

David Lusher, Chief, Agricultural Section, Research Division, Office of Price Administration

*Robert M. Carr, Assistant Chief, Commodities Division, Department of State

John P. Young, Department of State

*Horace B. McCoy, Chief, Division of Industrial Economy, Department of Commerce

*Max Gideonse, Commodities Division, Department of State, *Secretary*

(Edward Cole, Emilio G. Collado, Margaret S. Gordon, Howard S. Piquet and H. Julian Wadleigh were members at date of establishment)

Subcommittees (5)

Subcommittee 1: Ad Hoc Joint Subcommittee with the Special Committee on Private Monopolies and Cartels

Corwin Edwards, Justice, Chairman

Lynn R. Edminster, Tariff Commission, alternate Chairman

Subcommittee 2: Buffer Stocks

Oscar C. Stine, Agriculture, Chairman

Subcommittee 3: International Commodity Organization

Robert M. Carr, State, Chairman

Subcommittee 4: Code of Principles

Robert M. Carr, State, Chairman

Subcommittee 5: Commodities Likely to be in Surplus Supply

Horace B. McCoy, Commerce, Chairman

SPECIAL COMMITTEE ON PETROLEUM

Established: June 15, 1943

Membership:

*Herbert Feis, Adviser on International Economic Affairs, Department of State, *Chairman*

*Hon. William C. Bullitt, Special Assistant to Secretary of Navy

*Brig. Gen. Boykin C. Wright, War Department

*J. Terry Duce, Office Petroleum Administrator for War

*Paul H. Alling, Chief, Near Eastern Division, Department of State

Commodore A. F. Carter, Navy Department

C. S. Snodgrass, Office Petroleum Administrator for War

E. L. DeGolyer, Office Petroleum Administrator for War

Alger Hiss, Special Assistant to Director, Office of Far Eastern Affairs, State Department

*James C. Sappington, Office of Petroleum Adviser, State Department

Howard J. Trueblood, Office of Adviser on International Economic Affairs, State Department, *Secretary*

---

*Starred name or specific explanation denotes member at date of establishment of the Special Committee.

NOTE: This Special Committee ceased to function in the Fall of 1943 and was succeeded by:

(1) An interdivisional Petroleum Committee, established in the Department of State in December 1943 with membership entirely from the interested geographic and other operating divisions of the Department: James C. Sappington of the Petroleum Division, Chairman.

(2) An interdepartmental group of oil technicians to review the technical aspects of the work, supply data, assist the American Technical Group in talks with the British:

Charles B. Rayner, Petroleum Adviser, *Chairman*
James C. Sappington, State Department
John A. Loftus, State Department
Walter Levy, Office of Strategic Services
Brandon Grove, Foreign Economic Administration

(3) A Cabinet Committee on the Anglo-American Petroleum Conversations, established at a Cabinet meeting February 15, 1944:

Secretary of State Hull, *Chairman*
Secretary of Interior Ickes, *Vice Chairman*
Secretary of the Navy Forrestal
Under Secretary of War Patterson
Charles E. Wilson, Vice Chairman of the War Production Board
Charles B. Rayner, *Executive Officer*

Subsequently Leo T. Crowley, Foreign Economic Administration, and Ralph K. Davies, War Department, were included.

(4) The Cabinet Committee on April 1, 1944, established an interdepartmental Petroleum Committee. Each member of the Cabinet Committee appointed a personal representative to this committee—to discuss and examine documentation (mainly from the State Department's interdivisional Committee) and to advise him:

Charles B. Rayner, Petroleum Adviser, State Department, *Chairman*
Harry C. Hawkins, Chief, Office of Economic Affairs, State Department (alternate)
Ralph K. Davies, Deputy Petroleum Administrator for War
Julius H. Amberg, Special Assistant to the Secretary of War
General Howard L. Peckham, War Department
Comdr. A. F. Carter, Navy Department
Dr. William Y. Elliott, War Production Board
James C. Sappington, *Executive Secretary*
John A. Loftus, *Recording Secretary*

(5) An American Technical Group for the exploratory Anglo-American conversations April 18–May 3, 1944:

Charles B. Rayner, State Department, *Chairman*
Ralph K. Davies, Petroleum Administrator for War, *Vice Chairman*
Paul H. Alling, State Department
Leroy D. Stinebower, State Department
George Walden, Special Assistant to Deputy Petroleum Administrator for War
C. S. Snodgrass, Petroleum Administrator for War
Brig. Gen. Howard L. Peckham, War Department
Commander A. F. Carter, Navy Department
James C. Sappington, *Recording Secretary*

The group met with ten representatives of American oil industry, three of whom (John A. Brown, N. S. S. Rodgers, A. Jacobsen) were designated advisers for the discussions.

SPECIAL COMMITTEE ON COMMUNICATIONS

Established: June 21, 1943

Membership:

Adolf A. Berle, Jr., Assistant Secretary of State, *Chairman*, succeeding Assistant Secretary Breckinridge Long after December 1, 1943
Honorable Claude Pepper, Senate
Honorable Alfred L. Bulwinkle, House of Representatives
Honorable Charles A. Wolverton, House of Representatives
Paul T. David, Bureau of the Budget
*Dr. John H. Dellinger, National Bureau of Standards
*Francis Colt de Wolf, Department of State
*James Lawrence Fly, Federal Communications Commission
*Joseph F. Gartland, Post Office Department
*Green H. Hackworth, Department of State
Commander Charles Horn, Navy Department
Major General H. C. Ingles, War Department; Major General Olmstead, original member
Ewell K. Jett, Federal Communications Commission
Colonel Fred G. Miller, Signal Corps
*Warren Lee Pierson, Export-Import Bank
Major B. R. Powell, Jr., War Department
*Rear Admiral Joseph R. Redman, Navy Department
Lloyd Simson, Department of Commerce
*C. I. Stanton, Department of Commerce
*Harvey B. Otterman, State Department, *Secretary*

Department of State Advisers:

Paul T. Culbertson
Philip W. Bonsal
Joseph E. Johnson (Louis T. Halle, Jr., original adviser)
Walter A. Radius

Subcommittees (6)

Subcommittee 1: Peace Terms
Colonel Fred G. Miller, War Department, Chairman
Subcommittee 2: Global Communications
James Lawrence Fly, Federal Communications Commission, Chairman
Subcommittee 3: Regional Communications
Warren Lee Pierson, Export-Import Bank, Chairman
Subcommittee 4: Technical Matters
John H. Dellinger, National Bureau of Standards, Chairman
Subcommittee 5: Communications Other Than Telecommunications
Joseph F. Gartland, Post Office, Chairman
Subcommittee 6: Short Wave Broadcasting
James Lawrence Fly, Federal Communications Commission, Chairman

---

*Starred name or specific explanation denotes member at date of establishment of the Special Committee.

SPECIAL COMMITTEE ON METALS AND HEAVY INDUSTRY

Established: June 22, 1943

Membership:
*Herbert Feis, Adviser on International Economic Affairs, State Department, *Chairman*
*E. W. Pehrson, Bureau of Mines, Department of Interior
*Charles W. Wright, Bureau of Mines, Department of Interior
*Donald H. Davenport, Labor Department
*William Y. Elliott, War Production Board
*G. Temple Bridgman, Metals Reserve Company
*Paul H. Nitze, Chief, Metals and Minerals Branch, Foreign Economic Administration
Rear Admiral Harold G. Bowen, Navy Department
*Brigadier General Hugh C. Minton, War Department
*John C. Russell, Tariff Commission
*Brooks Emeny, Director of the Council of Foreign Affairs of Cleveland, Ohio
*Howard J. Trueblood, *Secretary*
(Simon D. Strauss, John W. Evans, Commander Paul F. Linz were among the original members)

This special committee was abolished in October 1943 when, at the recommendation of the State Department on October 12, 1943, the Committee on Stockpiling was established as a separate interdepartmental committee but not a special committee.

SPECIAL COMMITTEE ON MIGRATION AND SETTLEMENT

Established: June 23, 1943

Membership:
*H. F. Arthur Schoenfeld, Department of State, *Acting Chairman*
*George L. Brandt, Department of State
*Major General John H. Hilldring, Chief, Civil Affairs Section, War Department
Colonel E. P. Allen, Civil Affairs Division, War Department (alternate)
*Captain H. L. Pence, Officer in Charge, Naval Office for Occupied Territories, Navy Department
Lt. John D. Rockefeller, III, U. S. N. (alternate)
*Dean Jay, American Red Cross
Sidney A. Mitchell, Department of State
*Laurence Duggan, Department of State
George L. Warren, Department of State, consultant
Samuel W. Boggs, Chief, Geographic Division, Department of State
Stephen A. Mitchell, Assistant Director Liberated Areas, Foreign Economic Administration, Adviser
*Bernard Gufler, Department of State, Adviser
*Thomas Parran, Surgeon General, Public Health Service
Dr. James A. Crabtree, Public Health Service (alternate)
Cyril E. Black, Department of State
*Hugh Jackson, UNRRA
*Eleanor L. Dulles, Department of State, *Secretary*
(Adolf A. Berle, Jr., Herbert H. Lehman, Breckinridge Long, Philip Young were originally members)

---

*Starred name or specific explanation denotes member at date of establishment of the Special Committee.

Subcommittees (3)

Subcommittee 1: European Areas
George L. Brandt, State, Chairman
Subcommittee 2: Communications
Dean Jay, American Red Cross, Chairman
Subcommittee 3: Far Eastern Areas
Prof. Joseph P. Chamberlain, Columbia University, Chairman

SPECIAL COMMITTEE ON SHIPPING

Established: July 5, 1943

Membership:
Adolf A. Berle, Jr., Assistant Secretary of State, *Chairman*, succeeding Assistant Secretary Breckinridge Long after December 1, 1943
*Vice Admiral Russell R. Waesche, United States Coast Guard
Rear Admiral Emory S. Land, Maritime Commission
*Dean G. Acheson, Assistant Secretary of State
South Trimble, Jr., Department of Commerce
*Green H. Hackworth, Department of State
*Huntington T. Morse, Assistant to the Chairman, Maritime Commission
*Herbert E. Gaston, Assistant Secretary of the Treasury
*Jesse E. Saugstad, Department of State
*Rear Admiral W. W. Smith, Navy Department
*Paul T. David, Chief Fiscal Analyst, Bureau of the Budget
*Brigadier General John M. Franklin, Assistant Chief of Transport, War Department
Hon. Scott W. Lucas, United States Senate
Hon. Schuyler Otis Bland, House of Representatives
Hon. J. Hardin Peterson, House of Representatives (alternate)
Hon. Richard J. Welch, House of Representatives
*Walter A. Radius, Department of State, *Secretary*
(William L. Clayton was originally a member, from the Commerce Department at that time)

Subcommittees (4)

Subcommittee 1: Section of Peace Terms Relating to Shipping
Rear Admiral Emory S. Land, Maritime Commission, Chairman

Subcommittee 2: Post-War Shipping Aims
Huntington T. Morse, Maritime Commission, Chairman

Subcommittee 3: Shipping Problems before the Cessation of Hostilities
Vice Admiral Russell R. Waesche, U. S. Coast Guard, Chairman

Subcommittee 4: Joint Subcommittee with the Special Committee on Aviation
L. Welch Pogue, Civil Aeronautics Board, Chairman
Huntington T. Morse, Maritime Commission, Joint Chairman

SPECIAL COMMITTEE ON INLAND TRANSPORT

Established: October 9, 1943

Membership:
*Paul T. Culbertson, Department of State, *Chairman*
*Robert G. Hooker, Jr., Office of Assistant Secretary Berle, Department of State

---

*Starred name or specific explanation denotes member at date of establishment of the Special Committee.

*Norman J. Padelford, Department of State
*Donald Hiss, Office of Economic Affairs, Department of State
Edgar S. Hoover, Assistant Chief, Division of Research, Office of Strategic
    Services, (Consultant)
Colonel F. A. Blair, General Staff Corps, Supply Division (G4), War Depart-
    ment, (Consultant)
John B. Crane, Chief, Transportation Unit, Department of Commerce,
    (Consultant)
*Ellsworth H. Plank, Department of State, *Secretary*
*Walter A. Radius, Department of State, *Acting Secretary*
(Eugene Staley was originally a member)

APPENDIX 26
April 15, 1943

[Research Staff Memorandum dated April 19, 1943 Accompanying Map]

EUROPE: PROBLEM AREAS

The accompanying map indicates the following problem areas of Europe, numbered correspondingly [map on following page]:

1. *The Northern Finnish Border*—Fisherman's (Rybachi) Peninsula was a part of Tsarist Russia until 1918; was claimed by independent Finland, and was divided by the Treaty of Tartu, October 1920, giving Finland the western portion of approximately 400 square kilometers. This portion was ceded to Soviet Russia by the Treaty of Moscow, March 12, 1940.

2. *Karelia, the Hanko Peninsula, and the Gulf of Finland Islands*—The Karelian Isthmus boundary and the status of the Gulf Islands were fixed by the Treaty of Tartu, October 14, 1920. In the negotiations of 1939 the Soviets proposed changes in the boundary on the Isthmus and a lease of the Gulf Islands and of Hanko Peninsula. The Finnish counterproposals were rejected. By the treaty of Moscow of March 12, 1940 the Isthmus boundary was moved north and west, the Gulf Islands were ceded to the Soviets and a 30-year lease of Hanko was granted.

The area in dispute is mainly that ceded to the Soviet Union in 1940, a total of 13,500 square miles, of which 9,549 square miles were in the Karelian Isthmus region. Forty-seven square miles at Hanko were leased to Russia. The population of this area was approximately 450,000 in 1939. Nearly 95 percent moved back into Finland after the Treaty of Moscow, and an indeterminate number may have moved back into the area since 1941. In the disputed area the population was approximately 97.6 percent Finnish-speaking, 1.3 percent Swedish-speaking, and 0.9 percent Russian-speaking. The ceded and leased areas are chiefly of strategic importance to Russia. They are of both strategic and economic importance to Finland, and Viipuri is of special sentimental significance to the Finns.

---

*Starred name or specific explanation denotes member at date of establishment of the Special Committee.

The Salla Sector—This area (7,770 square kilometers) was a part of Finland after 1595. It was ceded to the Soviets by the Treaty of Moscow in 1940.

3. *Estonia, Latvia* and *Lithuania*—These republics proclaimed their independence of Russia in 1918 and secured it in 1920. By treaties of October 1939 their military and naval bases were occupied by Soviet troops and by ultimata of June 1940 they were required to institute new governments. Legislatures subsequently elected under complete Soviet occupation established soviet socialist republics and petitioned for admission to the U. S. S. R., which was granted in August 1940.

Estonia: Area, 18,353 square miles; population (est. 1939), 1,134,000. Ethnic composition: Estonians, 87.8%; Russians, 8.2%; Germans, 1.7%; Swedes, 0.7%; Jews, 0.4%; others, 1.3%.

Latvia: Area, 25,402 square miles; population, 1,950,502. Ethnic composition: Latvians, 75.5%; Russians, 10.59%; Jews, 4.79%; Germans, 3.19%.

Lithuania: Area, 22,959 square miles; population 2,879,070. Ethnic composition: Lithuanians, 80.14%; Jews, 7.11%; Poles, 3.02%; Russians, 2.34%; Germans, 4.08%.

4. *Suwalki* area—This area was acquired by Poland under the Treaty of Riga, October 12, 1921. It was occupied by German troops following the Polish campaign of 1939, and would be involved in any adjustments of Poland's eastern boundary, following a German defeat.

This small area includes the former Polish administrative district of Suwalki and a part of that of Augustów. Its total population, according to the census of 1931, was 184,875, of whom 154,381 were Polish-speaking, 12,257 were Yiddish-speaking, 7,731 were Russian-speaking, 6,782 were Lithuanian-speaking, and 2,672 were German-speaking.

5. *Memelland*—The Memelland was renounced by Germany in the Treaty of Versailles, June 28, 1919. It was placed under Lithuanian administration by the convention signed on May 7, 1924 by the Principal Allied Powers and by Lithuania on May 17, 1924. It was ceded by Lithuania to Germany on March 22, 1939.

Memelland had an area of 1,099 square miles, and a total population of 152,000. In 1925 the ethnic-linguistic division was: 44 percent German-speaking, 27 percent Lithuanian, and 25 percent Memellander. Memel is the principal Baltic port of Lithuania and is the outlet for the important Niemen waterway system. In 1939 approximately three-fourths of Lithuanian foreign commerce passed through this port.

6. *East Prussia*—East Prussia remained under German sovereignty after the corridor was transferred to Poland by the Treaty of Versailles. The western and part of the southern boundaries between East Prussia and Poland were fixed by the Principal Allied and Associated Powers, August 16, 1920, following a plebiscite in the Marienwerder and Allenstein districts, held in accordance with the Treaty of Versailles. Under the final settlement, Poland received a narrow riparian strip along the east bank of the Vistula, varying in width from a few feet to a half mile.

The area of East Prussia under the 1920 boundaries was 14,283 square miles. According to the census of May 1939 the population was 2,496,017 persons. According to the census of 1925—the most reliable index of linguistic distribution—the Polish population of East Prussia was 40,502. This census, however, did not include the populous district of Koenigsberg. According to the census of 1933 the total number of Poles in East Prussia was reported as 4,522, while the 1939 census showed this number as having been decreased to 3,718. In the district of Allenstein there were reported to be 62,596 Masurians in 1925.

7. *Danzig*—The Danzig area was renounced by Germany in the Treaty of Versailles, June 28, 1919, and proclaimed a Free City with a High Commissioner appointed by the League of Nations on November 9, 1920, in accordance with the terms of the same treaty. It was re-incorporated in Germany on September 1, 1939.

The total area of the Free City of Danzig was 731 square miles. The population in 1936 numbered 412,000. According to the Danzig census of 1923, the Free City had a total population of 366,730, of whom 12,027 spoke Polish or Kashub.

Polish Corridor—This was a serious source of friction between Poland and Germany from 1919 to 1939.

8. *East Poland between the Riga Line and Moscow line*—This area includes former Austro-Hungarian and Russian territory. Eastern Galicia was renounced by Austria-Hungary in the treaty of St. Germain, September 10, 1919, and was awarded to Poland on March 15, 1923 by the Principal Allied Powers acting under Article 87 of the Versailles Treaty. The former Russian territory was acquired by Poland by the treaty of Riga, October 12, 1921. The entire area was occupied from September 1939 to June 22, 1941 by Russia under agreement with Germany.

This part of former Poland has an area of 77,703 square miles. Its total population, according to the Polish census of 1931, was 11,850,571, of whom 4,733,046 were Polish-speaking, 4,055,365 were Ukrainian-speaking, 986,605 were White Russian-speaking, 119,269 were Russian-speaking, 707,088 were listed as "local" inhabitants of the province of Polesia, 1,036,576 were Yiddish-speaking, 83,850 were German-speaking, and 75,949 were Lithuanian-speaking.

9. *Subcarpathian Ruthenia*—Formerly a part of the Kingdom of Hungary, this area was renounced in the treaty of Trianon, June 4, 1920, and awarded to Czechoslovakia as an autonomous province by the treaty of Sèvres, August 10, 1920. Subcarpathian Ruthenia lost 612 square miles to Hungary on November 2, 1938, being reduced to 4,259 square miles. On March 15, 1939, it was incorporated by force into Hungary.

The area of Subcarpathian Ruthenia is 4,871 square miles. The population in 1930 was 725,357, of whom 450,925 (62.17 percent) were Ruthenian; 34,511 (4.76 percent), Czechoslovak; 13,804 (1.90 percent), German; 115,805 (15.98 percent), Magyar; and 95,008 (13.10 percent), Jewish. A mountainous and agricultural region, the region had strategic significance for Czechoslovakia in that it separated Poland from Hungary and provided a connecting link with Rumania.

10. *Northern Bukovina to the line of Russian occupation*—Formerly belonging to Austria-Hungary, Bukovina was renounced in the treaty of St. Germain, September 10, 1919, and awarded to Rumania by the treaty of Sèvres, August 10, 1920. The northern area was occupied by Russian troops on June 28, 1940, and formally incorporated in the Ukrainian S. S. R., August 2, 1940.

The area of Northern Bukovina is approximately 2,240 square miles. Its total population, according to the Rumanian census of 1930, was 529,462, of whom 267,908 were Russians and Ukrainians by mother-tongue and 137,073 were Rumanians.

11. *Bessarabia*—Bessarabia was a province of pre–1917 Russia. It proclaimed its independence on December 17, 1917, and during Rumanian military occupation, voted its union with Rumania on April 8 and November 27, 1918. Rumania's sovereignty was recognized in the treaty of Paris, October 28, 1920, by Great Britain, France, Italy and Japan. The U. S. S. R. re-occupied Bessarabia on July 28, 1940, and on August 2 united the northern and southern

portions with the Ukrainian S. S. R. and formed the Moldavian S. S. R. of the remainder together with the former Moldavian A. S. R.

The area of Bessarabia is 17,143 square miles. Its total population, according to the Rumanian census of 1930, was 2,864,402, of whom 1,598,573 were Rumanian-speaking, 370,112 were Russian-speaking, 331,183 were Ukrainian-speaking, 201,278 were Yiddish-speaking, 164,551 were Bulgarian-speaking, and 101,356 were Turkish-speaking.

12. *Transylvania*—including the Grand Principality of Transylvania, Maramuresh, Crishana, and Rumanian Banat—Cession of this area by Hungary to Rumania was implicit in the Treaty of Trianon, June 4, 1920, which fixed the common boundary between the two states. The division of the Banat between Rumania and Yugoslavia was determined by the Allied Supreme Council and accepted by the two states in August 1919, and confirmed with slight modifications by a protocol signed at Belgrade on November 24, 1923, and an additional protocol signed in Bucharest, June 4, 1927. By the Vienna Award of August 30, 1940, all of Maramuresh, most of Crishana, and over half of Transylvania proper was ceded to Hungary.

The area of Transylvania is 39,686 square miles. Its total population, according to the Rumanian census of 1930, was 5,548,363, of whom 3,207,880 were Rumanians by declared nationality, 1,353,276 were Hungarians, 543,852 were Germans, and 43,342 were Yugoslavs.

13. *Southern Dobruja*—The Southern Dobruja was ceded by Bulgaria to Rumania in the Treaty of Bucharest, August 10, 1913, following the second Balkan war. It was retroceded in September 1940.

The area of Southern Dobruja is 2,983 square miles. Its total population, according to the Rumanian census of 1930, was 378,344, of whom 144,659 were Turkish-speaking, 142,403 were Bulgarian-speaking, and 79,739 were Rumanian-speaking.

14. *Yugoslav-Bulgarian frontier zone*—These areas were ceded by Bulgaria to Yugoslavia by the Treaty of Neuilly, November 27, 1919. Since the defeat of Yugoslavia in 1941, they have been occupied by Bulgarian troops.

This zone includes the districts of Timok, Tsaribrod, Bosilegrad, and Strumitsa, having together a total of 1,002 square miles and a population of 75–85,000. The inhabitants are predominantly Bulgarian although in the Timok district there are 4–5,000 Wallachians and in Strumitsa there is a disputed proportion of Serbs, Bulgars and Macedonians. Tsaribrod is important strategically by virtue of commanding the Sofia-Nish railway.

15. *Western Thrace*—This area was acquired by Greece from Bulgaria in the Treaty of Neuilly, November 27, 1919; its boundary with Turkey was fixed by the Treaty of Lausanne, June 24, 1923. Since the defeat of Greece in the spring of 1941 it has been occupied by Axis and Bulgarian troops.

Western Thrace has an area of approximately 3,300 square miles and has approximately 350,000 inhabitants. The large number of refugees from Anatolia, introduced in the population exchange with Turkey, has made the area predominantly Greek. The area is strategically important since it represents the only possible territorial outlet for Bulgaria on the Aegean.

16. *Southern Albania*—This area was claimed by Greece at the peace conference in 1919. The Conference of Ambassadors, however, decided on November 9, 1921 to confirm the Albanian boundaries as fixed by the Conference of Ambassadors in London in 1913, subject to certain specified modifications to be carried out by a Boundary Commission. The boundary was definitely fixed by the Conference of Ambassadors, Paris on July 30, 1926. This area, together with the rest of Albania, was incorporated in Italy in April 1939.

The area involved includes approximately 1,000 square miles and has a population of approximately 140,000 persons, predominantly Albanian.

17. *The Dodecanese Islands*—The Dodecanese Islands include the following: Rhodes, Kos, Patmos, Lipso, Kalymnos, Leros, Nisyros, Tilos, Khalki, Symi, Astypalai, Karpathos, Kasos and Kastellorizo. Italy came into "temporary" possession of the islands as a result of the Turco-Italian war of 1911–1912 (Treaty of Lausanne, October 18, 1912). The secret treaty of London, April 26, 1915, promised Italy full sovereignty over the islands. Italian sovereignty was recognized in the treaty of Sèvres, August 10, 1920 (Article 122) and in the treaty of Lausanne, July 24, 1923 (Article 15).

The total area of the Dodecanese Islands is 1,035 square miles. The total population (1936) is 140,848, eighty to eighty-five percent of which is Greek. Without great economic significance, the islands are of strategic importance as stepping stones to the Asiatic mainland, particularly Rhodes and Leros.

18. *Pantelleria*—This strongly fortified Italian island is of strategic significance in the control of the waist of the Mediterranean. It is an important air and submarine base.

The total area is 45 square miles and the population in 1931 was 9,679.

19. *Yugoslav Macedonia*—The territory indicated was lost by Turkey in the first Balkan war of 1912–1913 (Treaty of London, May 30, 1913). In spite of the Serbo-Bulgar Treaty, March 13, 1912, all but the Strumitsa wedge was claimed by Serbia and yielded to her by Bulgaria after the second Balkan war in the Treaty of Bucharest, August 10, 1913. The Strumitsa wedge was ceded by Bulgaria to Yugoslavia in the Treaty of Neuilly on November 27, 1919. Since the defeat of Yugoslavia in 1941, this area, together with certain other Yugoslav territories, is under Bulgarian occupation.

The district has an area of approximately 12,000 square miles and has a population of around 1,200,000 persons. This population is preponderately "Macedonian" who speak a language akin to both Serb and Bulgarian, and who are claimed by both Serb and Bulgarian nationalists.

20. *Regions of Djakovo and Dibra*—These areas [part of larger area] were awarded to Albania (under Italian sovereignty) after the defeat of Yugoslavia in May 1941.

These are small frontier regions with a total area of approximately 200 square miles. The population of some 25,000 is predominantly Albanian.

21. *Yugoslav-Hungarian border lands*, including Prekomurje, Medjumurje, Baranja, Bachka and Vojvodina (Banat) [*sic* and the Yugoslav Banat]—These areas were ceded to Yugoslavia by Hungary in the Treaty of Trianon, June 4, 1920. Since the defeat of Yugoslavia in 1941 they have been occupied mainly by Hungarian forces; Axis troops in Vojvodina are largely German.

The area involved includes 12,092 square miles and has a total population (1931) of 1,516,659 persons. According to the census of 1921, the area included 670,000 Serbo-Croats, 392,000 Magyars, 320,000 Germans, and 68,000 Rumanians.

22. *Zara*—Formerly a part of Austrian Dalmatia, Zara was ceded to Italy by the Treaty of St. Germain, September 10, 1919.

The Zara district includes only the city of Zara and its immediate vicinity, the total area being 42 square miles. The population, according to the census of 1921 (the latest census containing a breakdown of the population into language groups), was 17,065, of whom 12,075 were Italian-speaking, 1,255 Serbo-Croat-speaking, and 3,735 "foreigners" (chiefly Yugoslavs).

23. *Istria, Gorizia, Trieste, Fiume and the Italian Islands on the Dalmatian Coast*—With the exception of Fiume, these areas were ceded by Austria to Italy in the Treaty of St. Germain, September 10, 1919. The boundary between Yugoslavia and Italy was confirmed by the Treaty of Rapallo, November 12, 1920.

Fiume was renounced by Hungary in the Treaty of Trianon, June 4, 1920, and established as a Free City by the Treaty of Rapallo, November 12, 1920. It was incorporated in Italy by the Treaty of Rome, January 27, 1924.

The territory has an area of 3,415 square miles. Its total population, according to the census of 1921 (the last census in which the inhabitants were listed according to language) was 946,000, of whom 507,591 were Italian-speaking; 50,589 were Ladin-speaking, 258,944 were Slovene-speaking, and 103,613 were Serbo-Croat speaking.

24. *South Tyrol and Trentino*—These areas were ceded by Austria to Italy in the Treaty of St. Germain, September 10, 1919.

The territory has an area of 5,252 square miles. Its total population, according to the Italian census of 1921 (the last census in which the inhabitants were listed according to language) was 647,703, of whom 408,385 were Italian-speaking, 18,253 were Ladin-speaking, and 195,650 were German-speaking.

25. *Felsburg*—involving Austria and Czechoslovakia. . . . 70 square miles of Czechoslovakian territory, consisting of the county of Felsburg.

26. *Berchtesgaden, Passau, Ausserfern*—involving Austria and Germany. . . . the German areas of Berchtesgaden and Passau, and a connecting link between the Austrian enclave of Ausserfern and the Tyrol.

27. *Hungarian-Slovak frontier zone*—This area was ceded by Hungary to Czechoslovakia in the Treaty of Trianon, June 4, 1920. Some of the parts indicated were re-occupied by Hungary under the Vienna protocol, November 2, 1938; a further zone was ceded to Hungary under the agreement of April 3, 1939.

The area annexed involved about 4,000 square miles. According to the 1930 census the total population was 992,496, of whom 288,803 were Czechoslovaks, 587,692 Magyars and 51,000 Jews. The territory is important agriculturally. It borders the Danube River.

28. *Sudeten area*—As part of the lands of the crown of Bohemia, these areas were ceded to Czechoslovakia by Austria in the Treaty of St. Germain, September 10, 1919. They were incorporated into Germany as a consequence of the Munich agreement of September 30, 1938. This agreement was subsequently denounced by Great Britain and France, and was never recognized by the United States and the Soviet Union.

The area of the so-called Sudetenland, which was ceded to Germany in 1938, was 11,236 square miles. According to the 1930 census, the total population of this area was 3,756,719, of whom 2,822,899 were German and 738,502 Czechoslovak. The German census of 1938 indicated a population of 3,396,244, but did not give the ethnic distribution. The Sudetenland is not a continuous territory, but extends around the frontiers of Czechoslovakia. Cession of the territory destroyed the defenses, the communications system, and the economy of Czechoslovakia.

29. *Teschen*—The Duchy of Teschen was renounced by Austria in the Treaty of St. Germain, September 10, 1919. It was divided between Czechoslovakia and Poland by the Conference of Ambassadors on July 28, 1920, after a plebiscite which had been ordered by the Supreme Council on September 27, 1919. Part of the area awarded to Czechoslovakia was ceded to Poland on November 1, 1938. The remainder has been a part of the Protectorate of Bohemia-Moravia since March 15, 1939.

The area of Czech Teschen is 212 square miles. According to the census of 1930 the total population of the district was 85,334. The Poles numbered 44,184 (51.78 percent) ; the Czechoslovaks, 33,513 (29.27 percent) ; and the Germans 6,505 (7.62 percent). The area is especially important as an industrial region for steel manufacture.

30. *German Upper Silesia*—The area shown was awarded to Germany by the Conference of Ambassadors, October 19, 1921, following a plebiscite held in accordance with the terms of the Treaty of Versailles, June 28, 1919. It is claimed by Poland. Substantially this same area is now demanded by the Polish Government-in-Exile.

The territory claimed by the Polish Government has an area of 2,950 square miles (1.62 of the area of Germany in 1937) and had a population of 1,354,000 in 1939. The industrial district in the extreme east had one-tenth the area and one-third the population of the territory in question. In 1925 the exclusively German-speaking population was 57 percent of the whole, 72 percent of the population in the industrial district.

31. *Ems Estuary*—involving the Netherlands and Germany. The German-Dutch border through the Ems estuary is inadequately defined in a treaty of July 2, 1824, between Hanover and the Netherlands. The German Government claims, and has acted on the assumption, that the German frontier extends across the estuary and up to the low-tide mark on the Dutch shore. . . .

32. *Waterways Questions Involving Belgium and the Netherlands*—(a) *Wielingen Channel*. Though the Netherlands possesses sovereignty over both banks of the mouth of the Scheldt, it does not have undisputed control over the main channel connecting the Scheldt with the North Sea. The only serviceable channel for large vessels is the Wielingen, which, just before it joins the sea, bends toward the Belgian shore and passes through the Belgian maritime belt for a few miles. The Netherlands claims jurisdiction over the Wielingen Channel on historic rights while Belgium stresses the fact that the channel is within its three-mile limit. Treaty negotiations between the two countries in 1920 broke down when this issue was brought into the dispute. . . .

(b) *Waterways Connections between Antwerp and the Rhine*. By the Treaty of 1839, the Netherlands granted Belgium the right of passage on the Dutch inland waterways connecting Antwerp with the Rhine. Belgium claims that the Netherlands has not provided adequate canal connections in this area. Under the treaty initialled in 1925 Belgium would have received the right to construct a large canal along the most direct route between Antwerp and Moerdyke on the Hollandsch Diep. The proposed treaty also provided for a canal between Antwerp and Ruhrort across Dutch Limburg. These canals would have made Antwerp a strong competitor with Rotterdam for the transit traffic from the industrial Rhine hinterland. The proposed grant of these rights-of-way was bitterly attacked in Holland and was the chief cause for the defeat of the Treaty.

33. *Eupen, Malmédy, and Moresnet.*—These three districts form the entire Belgian-German frontier. Eupen and Malmédy, formerly part of Germany, were transferred to Belgium in 1920 by the Conference of Ambassadors, following an expression of public opinion held in accordance with the terms of the Treaty of Versailles; and Moresnet, formerly neutral territory, was awarded to Belgium by the same Treaty. These territories were claimed by Germany and on May 19, 1940, were re-incorporated into the Reich by Hitler.

The districts cover an area of 366.59 square miles and have a total population, according to the census of 1930, of 66,618, of whom 12,166 are French-speaking and 51,383 are German-speaking.

34. *Alsace-Lorraine*—This territory was lost by France in 1871 when it was ceded to Germany under the Treaty of Frankfort May 10, 1871. It was returned to France according to the Peace Treaty with Germany (June 28, 1919), as from the date of the Armistice November 11, 1918. In 1940 this region was annexed by Germany.

The territory covers an area of approximately 5,605 square miles, with a total population of 1,915,627 according to the census of 1936.

APPENDIX 27
August 11, 1943 [31]

Tentative Draft of a Joint Four-Power Declaration

The Governments of the United States, Great Britain, the Soviet Union and China:

united in their determination, in accordance with the Declaration by the United Nations of January 1, 1942, and subsequent declarations, to continue hostilities against those Axis powers with which they respectively are at war until such powers have laid down their arms on the basis of unconditional surrender;

conscious of their responsibility to secure the liberation of themselves and the peoples allied with them from the menace of aggression;

recognizing the necessity of ensuring a rapid and orderly transition from war to peace and of establishing and maintaining international peace and security with the least diversion of the world's human and economic resources for armaments;

jointly declare:

1. That their united action, pledged for the prosecution of the war, will be continued for the organization and maintenance of peace and security.

2. That those of them at war with a common enemy will act together in all matters relating to the surrender and disarmament of that enemy, and to any occupation of enemy territory and of territory of other states held by that enemy.

3. That they will take all measures deemed by them to be necessary to provide against any violation of the requirements imposed upon their present enemies.

4. That they recognize the necessity of establishing at the earliest practicable date a general international organization, based on the principle of the sovereign equality of all nations, and open to membership by all nations, large and small, for the maintenance of international peace and security.

5. That for the purpose of maintaining international peace and security pending the reestablishment of law and order and the inauguration of a general system of security, they will consult and act jointly in behalf of the community of nations.

6. That, in connection with the foregoing purpose, they will establish a technical commission to advise them on the military problems involved, including the composition and strength of the forces available in an emergency arising from a threat to the peace.

7. That they will not employ their military forces within the territories of other states except for the purposes envisaged in this declaration and after joint consultation and agreement.

8. That they will confer and cooperate to bring about a practicable general agreement with respect to the regulation of armaments in the post-war period.

---

[31] Document as taken by Secretary of State (Hull) to First Quebec Conference and the Moscow Conference, 1943.

Germany: Partition

I. The Problem

The problem is an assessment of the desirability of a partition of Germany in the interest of post-war security, and if desirable, its possible character.

The issue as developed here is not a choice between partition and no controls whatever, but whether there is utility in partition as a possible substitute for, or supplement to, certain other international controls of Germany.

II. Alternative Proposals

A. *Partition or Unity*

The basic argument advanced in favor of partition is that since world security demands that Germany should never again become a menace to peace, the means to that end is the destruction of the power concentrated in the Government of the Reich and the decentralization of German energies by a division that would split and cut across the political and moral forces of the land. If there is danger that security controls over a united Germany could not be maintained, successful partition would postpone if not obviate future aggression. Partition would not necessarily impair the efficiency of a military occupation of the whole of Germany, and it could simplify the task of treating the different areas with the necessary precautions i. e., could facilitate special controls over the militaristic portions of Prussia and the industrialized western areas.

The argument is also advanced that dividing Germany would be a powerful supplement to defeat and occupation as a demonstration of the necessity for a renunciation of military ambitions. It is argued that partition would allow the Germans, under the leadership of anti-Prussian and other peaceful groups, to find a happy and prosperous place in the new world order. While resentment and demagogic protests could be anticipated, religious differences, provincial loyalties and other centrifugal forces might provide the soil in which lasting partition could take root.

In opposition it is held that partition would make no useful contribution to the occupation of Germany and might complicate the task of administration. It might also encourage single power occupation of the different partite states. This argument further holds that partition would not be an economical substitute for military and economic controls; that uncertainties prevailing in a defeated Germany could not permit the victors to abandon the controls imposed directly on a potential war-machine until the long-run effects of partition were assessed. It is held that partition without an external force permanently to maintain it would constitute a threat to security; if on the other hand the victors did continue to wield enough power to enforce partition they could rigorously enforce the less offensive military and economic controls which would suffice for security.

The basic argument against partition is that it would not take root, but would, on the contrary, engender a bitter hostility among the German people that would jeopardize eventual German reconciliation with the peace settlement and the ultimate assimilation of Germany into the society of law-abiding nations. German acceptance of partition would mean a reversal of a century-old trend in which the dynamic forces have been working toward greater economic, politi-

---

[32] A policy memorandum based on an "H–document" for briefing Secretary Hull in connection with the First Quebec Conference.

cal and cultural integration. After 1871 political unity was enthusiastically accepted by the people and when the present war came there was no serious separatist sentiment. Internal debate on particularism had become a moderate contest over the degree of centralization. The attempts in 1919 and 1923 to establish an independent Rhineland had little popular support and French patronage of the movement robbed it of all prestige. Continuing loyalty to the ancient princely dynasties between 1871 and 1941 proved not incompatible with the allegiance to the Reich. Catholicism, even though it leaned toward federal decentralization, did not lag behind Protestantism in its national loyalty. Those political parties of the Weimar period which in general terms were the most nationalistic prior to the National Socialist Party, were most vigorously in favor of a federal structure. In turn, the remarkably uniform upsurge of the Nazi movement all over Germany after 1928 suggests no substantial geographic variation in the strength of the national sentiment.

There have been recently some indications of a recrudescence of centrifugal forces in Germany under the impact of the war and the Nazi tyranny, but past developments point to no marked geographic lines of cleavage that show promise of developing through internal momentum—short of a radical or Communist seizure perhaps of Berlin or of a collapse of the national economy—into deep and lasting fissures in German political life. The fate of French attempts to promote separatism in the Rhineland suggests a warning against external attempts to foster partition.

The argument against partition, therefore, holds that the most reasonable expectation is that an internal break-up of the unity of the Reich is hardly probable and that a break-up through external coercion would evoke an enduring opposition from the German people. Coercion, however, even if successful, would raise two serious problems: that of constantly forestalling the devices which German ingenuity could devise for circumventing partition, and that of maintaining the unanimity of the victorious powers when the dangers of German arms will not be felt so immediately and when German propaganda floods the world with protests and accusations.

A final argument against partition might be advanced on economic grounds. The problem of what to do with the highly integrated economy of Germany would present a serious dilemma. If the economy of each partite state were shut off from the others by some stipulation of complete independence, the result would be a period of confusion and distress followed by a lowered standard of living for Germany and for the rest of Europe. The division would raise up incessant problems of control which could create irritating bickerings and resentments both on the part of the Germans and of the enforcing powers. If, on the other hand, the partite states were allowed a customs union or indeed any basis of economic collaboration, such collaboration would provide a strong dynamic force working toward restoration of complete unity.

B. *Relations between the Partite States in Case of Partition*

Suggestions for political relations between the partite states have varied from the extreme of complete independence for each unit to the restoration of a federal structure. Of the several possible alternatives—permission for special treaty arrangements, a common council, a circumscribed federation—independence of the partite states would be most offensive to German nationalism and therefore most conducive to resistance and to the multiplication of evasive devices. On the other hand, admission of some degree of special relations between the states would legally set in motion a centripetal force hard to control, and might therefore defeat the objectives sought by partition.

Economic relations, as indicated above, pose the two main alternatives of (1) a break-up of a highly developed economy to the detriment of German economic stability along with extremely difficult problems of control or (2) the retention of some form of inter-state collaboration which in the long run might either make political partition meaningless or lead to reunification. It has thirdly been suggested that the partite states be incorporated in a European economic union. The doubtful prospects of a significant economic federation put in doubt the possibility of escaping in this manner the economic problem created by partition. Were such a federation set up, however, the advanced development of German industry might result in a German domination of the continent not unlike that aimed at in Nazi ambitions. On the other hand, argument has been advanced that a customs union and an internationalization of European transportation should meet the legitimate needs of German economy and would not prejudice the success of partition.

C. *The Number of States in Case of Partition*

Decision as to the desirability of partition depends to some degree on finding internal lines capable of becoming natural barriers. Arguments have been advanced to favor a division primarily based on economic self-sufficiency of the hypothetical states; counter-arguments have held that self-sufficient units within Germany are impossible and that it is useless to search for economic lines of cleavage. Another set of arguments have been directed at religious differences. In one view, Catholicism represents a decentralizing influence and it would be desirable to establish at least one state with a Catholic majority in the prospect that such a state might go its separate way. Contrary arguments question the divisiveness of religion in present day Germany and point to the close relations between the two confessions (although a Communist régime in Berlin might lead to a revolt of the Catholic South and West).

A tripartite division has appeared to some supporters of partition as a means of adequately dispersing a dangerous concentration of power and at the same time avoid the confusions of too extended a fragmentation. The "F" lines— indicated on maps 16, 23, 24 and 28 of the German series [33]—were drawn to secure a relatively even distribution of Germany's economic activity (according to the figures of 1939) between the three states. While East emerges comparatively weak and Northwest comparatively strong, the distribution of economic activity is roughly proportional to the distribution of population. This distribution, however, had grown up in a free-trade area of unified legislation and administration. Any modification of that basic arrangement would disturb the equilibrium established through the exploitation of natural advantages and specialization, and so does not describe the possible future economy of each partite state if the economic unity of Germany were broken.

Nor can the political outlook of each of the partite states of such a division be anticipated. During the Weimar period there were slight variations in the voting in these regions, but the differences were by no means as striking as the similarities. Party votes in the whole of Germany and in each of the tripartite divisions show virtually the same kind of curve for each major political party. This homogeneity of outlook is especially revealed in the rise of the National Socialist Party. Each of the partite regions consistently polled a percent of the total Nazi vote approximately equivalent to its percent of the total German population. Strong centers of Catholicism lagged behind the average, but South was not predominantly Catholic in voting behavior and was not significantly different from the other two areas. The argument against this tripartite division concludes with the contention that these hypothetical states have no distinctive regional characteristics that would develop, through their own processes, into separate homogeneous states.

---

[33] Not reproduced here.

A bipartite division has been suggested on the basis of traditional differences between East and West on the one hand and North and South on the other. The Elbe River has conventionally been accepted as a frontier between two different kinds of Germans, although critical examination hardly supports this distinction. The military spirit has been notoriously cultivated in the East, but it would be more cautious, and more in harmony with historic experience, to identify Prussianism with a state of mind than with a geographic region. A division following the Elbe would mean an Eastern state only slightly stronger than the East of the "F" lines and a great combination of power in the West. A North-South division anywhere approaching the traditional differences would establish a South comparable to the South of the "F" lines and combine the other two areas. The great concentration of population and resources in the Northwest has taken place since these historical poles were established in popular thought and it has robbed them of usefulness in seeking a balance between German regions.

A multiple division following historic state lines suggests the possibility of capitalizing old provincial loyalties which perhaps might revive their vitality in reaction to Nazi centralization. It is not impossible that the Germans, if left alone to form a moderate-liberal régime, would restore some mild form of federal state. Coercion or obvious Allied support or pressure might, however, place on the proposal a stigma in popular German opinion. A return to historic lines would mean restoration of a large Prussia and a whole congeries of petty states. Combinations into non-historical groupings, in turn, might fail to canalize the centrifugal forces presumably inherent in a revived traditionalism. The invocation of the principle of legitimacy involves the difficult question of finding a series of states that would stand the tests of acceptability to the victors and of the best claims to the mantle of the legitimate past. These latter tests are not readily susceptible of logical demonstration.

D. The Duration of Partition

If the Germans remain hostile to the peace settlement, the greatest menace to security may appear some years hence when Germany has recovered from present disasters and when the victors, immersed in other problems, are no longer vigilant. It is at such a time that partition, should it be adopted as a means for weakening Germany, would be of greatest utility. Hence the argument that if partition is embarked upon it should be permanent. From another point of view, one might contend that partition should be maintained only until the ultimate conversion of the Germans was clear; once they are honestly established in peaceful ways, unification could be safely allowed. A stipulated period of division would have the advantage of clarity of obligation, but its expiration might find the German attitude threatening and in the meanwhile it would focus German attention on the day of liberation and inspire agitations for earlier release. Should the duration, however, be indefinite, one could anticipate comparable agitation and also the possibility that the nationalistic groups would misinterpret concessions as victories won through their hostility and be encouraged in their chauvinism. There might further be the danger of mistaking a temporary lull, such as that following Locarno, as a lasting reorientation of German life.

III. Documentation

This memorandum is an abridgement of a previous document (H 24, pp. 49, July 27, 1943). At the conclusion of that document are appended references to pertinent studies and maps prepared in the Department of State.[34]

---

[34] Not printed.

APPENDIX 29
September 23, 1943 [35]

The Political Reorganization of Germany

I. PARTITION

The Departmental Committee on Germany unanimously recommends that the United States Government oppose the enforced break-up of Germany as a part of the peace settlement.

The Committee bases its recommendation on the following considerations:

1. The crucial means of attaining security against further German aggression for some time to come will be controls to insure military and economic disarmament. If these controls are effectively enforced Germany will be incapable of waging war.

2. These measures will have to be maintained whether Germany is partitioned or left intact. Partition would make no useful contribution either to occupation or to the administration of the basic controls; it might, on the contrary, complicate the administration and, by setting up separate zones, lead to friction between the victor powers over the character of the occupation and the treatment of the several regions.

3. Because of the high degree of economic, political and cultural integration in Germany it is to be anticipated that partition would have to be imposed and maintained by external force and that such action would evoke a greatly increased resentment on the part of the German people to the serious detriment of their ultimate reconciliation with the peace settlement.

4. An imposed partition would require the enforcement of sweeping measures, over and above the basic military and economic controls, to prevent surreptitious collaboration of the partite states and to restrain the nationalistic drive for reunification. The victor powers would consequently impose on themselves through partition a burden unnecessary for the attainment of security and would give to the Germans, equally without necessity, a ready-made program of national resurgence at the expense of the peace.

5. By the tests of effectiveness, enforceability and continued acceptability to both victors and vanquished, partition would make no contribution to security and would, on the contrary, create such bitterness and require such rigorous methods of enforcement that it would constitute a grave danger to future world order.

II. DEMOCRACY

The Departmental Committee on Germany believes that it would be unwise for the United Nations to disinterest themselves in the kind of government which will be established in Germany after the war. The potentialities for evil on the part of a revived aggressive state point to the desirability of every feasible effort to prevent the resurgence of a government and people dominated by excessive nationalism. The committee anticipates that there will be strong incentives for individual states to exercise influence and suggests that the best means of forestalling such a dangerous procedure would be an agreement among the principal United Nations for a common policy in so far as it can be achieved.

---

[35] An interdivisional country committee policy recommendation. Exact date of its preparation supplied.

The committee is of opinion that, in the long run, the most desirable form of government for Germany would be a broadly-based democracy operating under a bill of rights to protect the civil and political liberties of the individual.

The committee is under no illusions as to the difficulties in the way of creating an effective democracy in Germany. It suggests that there are three conditions under which a new democratic experiment might survive:

1. A tolerable standard of living.

2. A minimum of bitterness against the peace terms in order, in so far as possible, to avoid an appealing program for future nationalistic upheavals at home and disturbances abroad. The committee is aware that the occupation and the permanent security controls which it deems imperative will give offense to many Germans, but it recommends, because of the importance of ultimate German reconciliation with the peace settlement, that the measures be kept to the minimum in number and in severity which will be compatible with security.

3. A harmony of policy between the British and American Governments on the one hand and the Soviet Government on the other. In case of friction Germany would be in a position to hold the balance of power with disastrous results both for treaty limitations and for political stability at home. The Soviet Government, in turn, would be in a position to use the Communist strength in Germany to the great disadvantage of the internal political peace of Germany and to the comparably great advantage of Russian interests.

The committee therefore recommends that the United States Government adopt, in the interest of fostering moderate government in Germany, the principle of a program looking to the economic recovery of Germany, to the earliest possible reconciliation of the German people with the peace, and to the assimilation of Germany, as soon as would be compatible with security considerations, into the projected international order. The Committee further recommends that the Soviet Government be invited to give its support to a new democratic experiment and to the principle of the suggested program.

The committee believes that there is a marked disadvantage, both from the viewpoint of political warfare against National Socialism and from the viewpoint of preparing the democratic forces of Germany for action, in the failure of the United States and British Governments to announce their support of future German democracy. The committee likewise believes that the recent appearance of a democratic German program under tacit Russian patronage might serve to give the Communists control of the democratic movement, and therefore establish a Russian hegemony in Germany, unless Anglo-American support encourages the moderates to participate and make the movement genuinely democratic.

III. DECENTRALIZATION

The committee is of opinion that the potential threat of Germany might be reduced by a decentralization of political structure that would deprive the government of the means of conducting a strong policy internally and abroad. Such a weakening might be accomplished by assigning to the federal units such functions as police power, the major taxation powers, the right to ratify international commitments, control over education, etc.

The committee believes that the victorious powers should give all the support that is prudent and possible to any internal movement for decentralization that might arise from the living tradition of federalism and from a reaction to Nazi centralization. It has doubts, however, of the ultimate wisdom of coercing the Germans, as would be necessary if a sweeping devolution of political authority were desired. An imposed weakening of the governmental structure would place a premium, in the minds of the nationalistic groups, on flouting the constitution, a practice ultimately detrimental to any political stability. There would likewise exist, in the form of a political party, or parties, an extra-constitutional but unattackable means of integrating the various political agencies and of securing rapid decision and action. The co-ordination of Danzig with the Reich before the present war may be cited as an illustration, together with the military effectiveness of the Bismarckian empire in spite of its cumbersome constitution.

It would point out that the economic and social necessities of modern life have everywhere imposed a progressive abandonment of federal devolution and that an extensive decentralization of Germany would probably make it impossible for the German people adequately to meet the present-day need for governmental participation in social and economic activities. One of the factors contributing to the discredit of the Weimar Republic was its weakness in the face of the problems the German people expected it to solve.

The committee therefore feels that the major emphasis in political reorganization should be placed on securing a democracy that will be able to withstand the attacks of some new version of Pan-Germanism or National Socialism. The character of the political outlook of the German people and their elected leaders will be more important than the machinery of government.

APPENDIX 30
October 20, 1943 [36]

Bases of Our Program for International Economic Cooperation

The basic objective of our economic policy is to help create conditions which would enable each country after the war to restore its economic activity as rapidly and as effectively as possible, and thereafter to improve progressively its production, distribution, employment and living standards. All this requires a large measure of international cooperation in many directions.

The first obvious steps, some of which will need to be undertaken even before the attainment of complete victory, relate to international cooperation in providing relief and to cooperative arrangements for the handling of economic problems involved in the occupation of enemy territories and operations in liberated countries. Arrangements required for these purposes are now under way through the negotiations looking to the convocation of a United Nations Conference on Relief and Rehabilitation and through such measures as the creation of the Mediterranean Commission.

Beyond these steps, international cooperation in the economic field will be indispensable for the following purposes:

1. *Bringing about an expansion of international trade on a non-discriminatory basis.* To this end we believe that consideration needs to be given to the following:

The conclusion of a general convention to which all of the important countries of the world would be parties, which would lay down the rules and principles that should govern trade relations between nations. Such a conven-

---

[36] Submitted by Secretary Hull to the Moscow Conference. Starred footnote in this appendix as in original.

tion would contain provisions whereby each country would abstain from practices such as nations in the past have adopted in a futile attempt to benefit themselves at the expense of world trade and the welfare of other nations. It would make provision for concrete steps whereby the participating countries would abandon preferences and discriminations, reduce their trade barriers and refrain from export dumping practices. The agreement or agreements would be so drawn as to enable a state-trading country to adhere on an equitable basis.

2. *The orderly regulation and ultimately the elimination of arrangements, public or private, to restrict production and trade in individual commodities.* To this end we believe that consideration should be given the following:

a. The conclusion of special international agreements relating primarily to the marketing of commodities in chronic over-supply or subject to extreme variation in prices.

b. International arrangements for the regulation of cartel activities.

3. *The establishment of stable foreign exchange rates and of the interchangeability of currencies.* To this end discussions are now in progress among the United Nations looking to the creation of an International Stabilization Fund.

4. *Promotion of the development of resources and industries wherever international assistance is necessary for this purpose.* To this end consideration is being given to the possibility of creating appropriate international investment agencies and other improved facilities for international investment and for exchange of technical information and personnel.

5. *Improvement of facilities for shipping, air traffic and other means of transportation.* This will involve:

a. International consideration of the reestablishment of the merchant fleets of the world, the adjustment of ship-building activity, and related topics.

b. International agreement on all aspects of commercial aviation, including passenger and freight traffic arrangements, landing rights, rights of transit, exchange of technical information, questions of subsidization.

c. Similar international discussions regarding problems involved in the improvement of other transportation facilities.

6. *Improvement of means of telecommunication.* This will require the extension of international collaboration already existing in this sphere.

7. *Improvement of nutrition and consumption in general.* The United Nations Conference on Food and Agriculture, held at Hot Springs, Virginia, May 18 to June 3, 1943, laid the foundation for international collaboration in this field with regard to the consumption of agricultural products. This work is being carried forward by the Interim Commission on Food and Agriculture. It looks forward to the promotion of appropriate domestic policies for each country and to the establishment of a permanent international organization in this field.

8. *Improvement of labor standards and conditions.* This involves primarily development of the work which has been well carried on by the International Labor Organization.

It is clear that in connection with most of these subjects there will be need for organized discussions among the United Nations, both informal and in formal conferences. We believe that the time has come for the establishment of a Commission comprising representatives of the principal United Nations and possibly certain others of the United Nations for the joint planning of the best procedures to be followed in these matters. Such a Commission might consist of technical economic experts of the United States, the United Kingdom, Soviet

Union, China, and possibly certain other countries such as Canada, the Netherlands and Brazil.

Even before the establishment of such a Commission we believe it to be of the greatest importance that our government and the governments of each of the major United Nations should confer with each other on the technical level as freely and as promptly as possible with the view to exploring the problems which are bound to confront them and the world.

The Government of the United States has recently addressed an invitation to the Government of the Union of Soviet Socialist Republics to send to Washington a group of economic experts to engage in discussions with our experts of matters relating to Article VII of the Mutual Aid Agreement. Similar invitations were extended to the Governments of the United Kingdom and of China.

In response to this invitation, the British Government has sent such a group of experts to Washington, and as a result a most fruitful informal interchange of views has taken place between us on many topics of basic importance in the fields of monetary stabilization, international investment, commercial policy, commodity arrangements and related questions.* These conversations provided an opportunity to discover the extent to which there is common ground and the extent to which there are differences of importance in the points of view of those whose expert advice may frequently be utilized in the formulation of policy.

It is particularly important that similar conversations be arranged soon between Soviet and American experts. It is our earnest hope, therefore, that the Soviet Government, which participated in the Hot Springs Conference and is now participating in the work of the Interim Commission and in the discussions relating to relief, will find it possible to arrange for such an interchange of views in the near future.

[Attachment]

MEMORANDUM CONCERNING THE WASHINGTON MEETING BETWEEN BRITISH AND AMERICAN ECONOMIC EXPERTS WITH REFERENCE TO ARTICLE VII OF THE MUTUAL-AID AGREEMENT

In the informal discussions which ended on October 18 in Washington between United States and United Kingdom economic experts the following general topics were explored:

1. Commercial Policy.
2. International Commodity Arrangements.
3. Cartels.
4. Coordination of measures to promote employment.

Parallel with these discussions further exchanges of views took place at the Treasury with regard to monetary stabilization. There was also a preliminary exchange of views on the subject of promotion of international investment.

The following are brief summaries of the topics discussed under each of the four headings listed above. It will be noted that in each case no attempt was made to reach definite conclusions but rather to prepare an orderly agenda for further study by each of the respective governments and for possible further informal joint conversations.

---

*See attached Memorandum Concerning the Washington Meeting Between British and American Economic Experts With Reference to Article VII of the Mutual-Aid Agreement.

1. *Commercial policy.*

Consideration was given to the relative effectiveness and feasibility of the multilateral as compared with the bilateral method for bringing about a reduction of tariffs. In this connection a number of formulas were examined and compared without, however, at this stage attempting a selection. Consideration was also given to the substantial abolition of preferences and discriminations and the question of the relation of action in this field to the reduction of tariff barriers.

The need for and feasibility of the abolition on a multilateral basis of quantitative restrictions on trade were examined. The question of abolishing export taxes and restrictions was similarly considered as was the general question of subsidies.

The subject of state trading of various types and the need for harmonizing the interests of countries employing such a system with those of other countries was examined. Although no attempt was made to reach definitive conclusions it was apparent from the discussions that this problem should present no great difficulties.

Finally, provisional consideration was given to the need for creating some international body to facilitate the application of such basic principles of commercial policy as may be developed.

2. *International Commodity Arrangements.*

The problems discussed were:

(a) Short-term price fluctuations in primary products.

(b) Periodic slumps in demand and in prices as related to the business cycle.

(c) Excess capacity in relation to past stimulation of high-cost production and to special wartime measures affecting production.

Methods of dealing with these problems were considered, having regard to securing efficient production and, at the same time, to mitigating the hardship on producers in making adjustments to conform to demand.

The methods included:

(a) Buffer stocks.

(b) Quantitative regulation schemes.

The discussion included the possibility of stating principles which might govern arrangements for dealing with commodity problems and the possible relation of such arrangements to existing inter-governmental and private international commodity schemes and to other parts of the international economic system, including commercial policy agreements.

3. *Cartels.*

Consideration was given to problems likely to arise in the post-war world from the activities of international cartels. The interchange of views was not so extensive as in the case of the other topics discussed. It was agreed that much further discussion was needed. The officials recommended that each group separately should examine the problems arising from international cartels and appropriate measures, national and international, to solve them with a view to joint discussion at some future date.

Preliminary views were presented by the United States officials on the possible consequences of international cartels in obstructing production and trade and in endangering national and international security.

The United States officials proposed that further consideration should be given to the possibility of intergovernmental undertakings:

(a) To register all non-governmental international agreements for the establishment of enduring relationship between private business enterprises;

(b) To introduce measures to make information about registered agreements available to governments or to international institutions;

(c) To prohibit practices by international cartels inimical to the expansion of production, trade and consumption including, inter alia, price fixing and restrictions on the exploitation of inventions.

4. *Employment policies.*

The problems discussed under the foregoing three heads relate to a wide complex of policies which influence the level of employment in individual countries and in the world as a whole. Some of these policies are of a domestic nature, but facilities should be provided for consultation and for the exchange of information between governments on these matters as well as on matters of a more directly international nature with a view to the harmonization of policies.

The experts therefore discussed:

(a) The desirability of establishing an international advisory economic staff charged with the study of international economic questions with particular reference to the harmonization of measures, national and international, for the maintenance of high levels of productive employment.

(b) The functions and organization of such a staff.

(c) The character of the governing body to which it should be responsible.

APPENDIX 31
February 1, 1944 [37]

Fields of Work of the Committee on Post-War Programs

The work will be organized in such a way that for each problem involved in the topics indicated below, and in such other topics as may be added from time to time, there will be presented to the Committee in due course for its consideration and action the following documents:

1. A statement of alternative policy objectives and of alternative procedures for the attainment of these objectives; recommendations as to the most desirable alternative; and, where and as necessary,

2. Drafts of appropriate agreements, conventions, legislation, or other necessary documents.

The following list of topics does not suggest any order of priority. Each topic is being broken down into its component problems, and a more comprehensive list of the work done to date will be presented soon, together with a survey.

I.   Treatment of enemy countries, including terms of surrender, reparation, and controls.

II.   Treatment of liberated countries.

III.   Treatment of countries having special status, e. g. Italy, Austria, Thailand.

---

[37] Memorandum by the Executive Director of the Committee (Pasvolsky).

IV.   Dependent areas and trusteeship.

V.   Problems growing out of special war-time relations among the United Nations, including lend-lease liquidation.

VI.   Problems growing out of special war-time relations with neutral countries.

VII.   Federations and other groupings.

VIII.   Post-hostilities security arrangements pending the establishment of permanent arrangements.

IX.   Permanent international organizations and arrangements, general and regional, for the maintenance of peace and security.

X.   International arrangements for coordinating activities in economic, social, and related fields.

XI.   International agencies for education and cultural cooperation.

XII.   Rehabilitation and reconstruction financial arrangements.

XIII.   Pre-War debts.

XIV.   Monetary stabilization.

XV.   Long-range investment and development.

XVI.   Relaxation of trade barriers.

XVII.   Commodity problems.

XVIII.   Cartels and private international industrial agreements.

XIX.   Food and nutrition.

XX.   Labor and social problems.

XXI.   Migration, resettlement, and transfer of populations.

XXII.   Aviation.

XXIII.   Shipping.

XXIV.   Inland transport.

XXV.   Telecommunications.

XXVI.   Power.

APPENDIX 32

March 21, 1949[38]

The Research Staff, January 15, 1944–April 24, 1945

Under the general reorganization effected by Secretary Hull in Departmental Order 1218 of January 15, 1944, the Division of Political Studies was replaced by the Office of Special Political Affairs containing two divisions, International and Security Organization and Territorial Studies. A staff was created to assist the Executive Director (Mr. Leo Pasvolsky) of the new Committee on Post-War Programs. Personnel of the Division of Economic Studies, which was abolished, were assigned to various existing and newly created regular economic divisions, except for those entering the Division of Territorial Studies.

In the next general reorganization of the Department, effected by Secretary Stettinius in Departmental Order 1301 of December 20, 1944, the Office of Special Political Affairs was continued, but the Division of International Security and Organization was terminated and its main branches, without significant initial changes of personnel, were elevated into the three Divisions of International Organization Affairs, of International Security Affairs, and of Dependent Area Affairs. The Division of Territorial Studies was continued (but was abolished

[38] Compiled for this volume. For organization Feb. 3, 1941–Jan. 14, 1944, see appendix 22.

three months afterward, its personnel being distributed primarily to the geographic offices and divisions of the Department). The Post-War Programs Committee staff was transferred to a new Joint Secretariat of the Secretary's Staff Committee and the Coordinating Committee. The conversion of the remaining special staff for the postwar preparation into operational work in the Department occurred gradually during 1945, beginning with the San Francisco Conference.

—A—

THE RESEARCH STAFF

January 15–December 19, 1944

Departmental Order 1218 of January 15, 1944:

[Excerpts]

"Office of Special Political Affairs:

"There is hereby created an Office of Special Political Affairs which shall have responsibility under the general direction of the Secretary, and Under Secretary, for the initiation and coordination of policy and action in special matters of international political relations.

"The Division of Political Studies is hereby abolished and its functions and responsibilities transferred to the Office of Special Political Affairs.

"All other offices and divisions in the Department shall assure full participation by the Office of Special Political Affairs and its component divisions as hereinafter provided for in the formulation and execution of policy affecting the responsibilities of this Office.

"*Mr. James C. Dunn* is hereby designated Acting Director of the Office of Special Political Affairs . . . .

"The Office of Special Political Affairs shall be composed of the following divisions, with functions and responsibilities as indicated.

"1. *Division of International Security and Organization*

"The Division of International Security and Organization shall have responsibility for the initiation and coordination of policy and action in matters pertaining to: (a) general and regional international peace and security arrangements and other arrangements for organized international cooperation; (b) liaison with international organizations and agencies concerned with such matters; and (c) liaison within the scope of its responsibilities with the War and Navy Departments and such other departments and agencies of the Government as may be concerned.

"*Mr. Harley A. Notter* is hereby designated Chief, and *Mr. Durward V. Sandifer, Mr. C. Easton Rothwell* and *Mr. O. Benjamin Gerig* are hereby designated Assistant Chiefs of the Division of International Security and Organization. . . .

"2. *Division of Territorial Studies.* The Division of Territorial Studies shall have responsibility for: (a) analyzing and appraising developments and conditions in foreign countries arising out of the war and relating to post-war settlements of interest to the United States; (b) maintaining liaison in this field with other departments and agencies of the government; and (c) formulating policy recommendations in regard to these matters in collaboration with other divisions in the Department.

"*Mr. Philip E. Mosely* is hereby designated Chief, and *Mr. David Harris* and *Mr. Philip W. Ireland* are hereby designated Assistant Chiefs of the Division of Territorial Studies. . . ."

OFFICE OF EXECUTIVE DIRECTOR, COMMITTEE ON POST-WAR PROGRAMS [39]

Pasvolsky,* Leo—Special Assistant to the Secretary of State and Executive Director of the Committee on Post-War Programs.

Rothwell,* C. Easton—(from Division of Political Studies); Executive Secretary for Political Affairs; became Executive Secretary of the Joint Secretariat of the succeeding Staff and Coordination Committees.

Fuqua, John H.—Executive Secretary for Economic Affairs; became Special Assistant to the Chairman of the United States Section of the Anglo-American Caribbean Commission.

Brown,* William Adams, Jr.—(from Division of Economic Studies); economic analyst; became head of Policy Analysis Branch, Joint Secretariat.

Fluegel,* Edna R.—(from Division of Territorial Studies), political analyst, from October 6, 1944; became foreign affairs specialist, Policy Analysis Branch, Joint Secretariat.

Hartley, Robert W.—special assistant to Mr. Pasvolsky from June 16, 1944; became executive assistant to Mr. Pasvolsky.

Russell,* Ruth B.—(from Mr. Pasvolsky's Office); economic analyst, until July 12, 1944; entered Foreign Service Auxiliary.

Stabler, Wells—political analyst, July 1–October 6, 1944; returned to Foreign Service.

Bell, M. Kathleen—assistant, from March 20, 1944; transferred to Division of International Organization Affairs.

Sullivan,* M. Carmel—(from Division of International Organization and Security), head of reference unit, from July 1, 1944; continued in same capacity in Joint Secretariat.

Hill, A. Almeda—reference analyst, from October 16, 1944; continued in same capacity in the Joint Secretariat.

McMahon,* Virginia M.—(from Division of International Security and Organization), reference analyst, from July 1, 1944; continued in same capacity in the Joint Secretariat.

Walmsley, Mary S.—reference analyst, from October 16, 1944; continued in same capacity in the Joint Secretariat.

Exton,* Thérèse—(from Division of International Security and Organization), reference analyst, July 1–October 16, 1944 (resigned).

OFFICE OF SPECIAL POLITICAL AFFAIRS

Director

Dunn, James C., acting, January 15–May 7, 1944 (also Director of Office of European Affairs).

Wilson, Edwin C., from May 8, 1944.

Deputy Director

Hiss, Alger, from November 1, 1944. (Special assistant to Director since May 1, 1944).

Adviser

Notter,* Harley A., from November 1, 1944.

---

*The asterisk identifies officers with previous service on the research staff.

[39] Officers to whose names no dates are attached served throughout the period Jan. 15–Dec. 19, 1944.

Dates attached to names of officers indicate the beginning or ending of their service during the period Jan. 15–Dec. 19, 1944. Subsequent assignment is shown in instances in which officers transferred from position stated.

Administrative

White, Louise, from February 16, 1944.

Reece,* Lenore M., until May 1, 1944 (transferred to Division of Personnel).

Clement,* Mrs. Nell F., from March 24, 1945 (from Division of International Organization Affairs).

Division of International Security and Organization [40]

Chief

Notter,* Harley A., until November 1, 1944 (thereafter, Adviser of the Office of Special Political Affairs).

Sandifer,* Durward V., acting, from November 1, 1944.

Associate Chiefs

Sandifer,* Durward V., from November 1, 1944, for International Organization Legal Branch (Assistant Chief until October 31, 1944).

Gerig,* O. Benjamin, from November 1, 1944, for General and Regional International Organization Branch (Assistant Chief until October 31, 1944).

Assistant Chief

Blaisdell,* Donald C., from May 3, 1944 (head of International Security Branch until May 2, 1944).

Legal Branch [41]

Preuss,* Lawrence, senior in charge under Assistant Chief.

Maktos,* John, until June 1, 1944 (transferred to Mexican Claims Commission).

Maylott, Marcia V. N., from May 16, 1944.

McDiarmid,* Alice M., assistant to section chief.

Myers,* Denys P.

Summers,* Lionel M., until August 16, 1944 (transferred to Office of Legal Adviser).

Reiff, Henry A., from September 21, 1944.

General and Regional International Organization Branch

General International Organization Section

Fosdick,* Dorothy, assistant to Chief of Division.

Eagleton,* Clyde (from International Security Branch in October 1944).

Stone, Ivan M., from August 1, 1944.

Berdahl,* Clarence A., consultant, until June 30, 1944.

Padelford,* Norman J., consultant (also with Legal Branch).

Wright, Quincy, consultant during August 1944.

Local and Regional Arrangements Section

Green,* James F., from January 21, 1944, in charge (previously in Division of Territorial Studies).

Ball,* M. Margaret, until August 21, 1944 (returned to university).

Cargo,* William I., until April 27, 1944 (furloughed for military service).

Finkelstein, Lawrence S., from July 1, 1944.

Specialized Agencies Section

Kotschnig, Walter M., from June 6, 1944 (in Local and Regional Arrangements Section until October 1944), in charge.

Tomlinson,* John D.

Brunauer, Esther C., from March 8, 1944.

---

*The asterisk identifies officers with previous service on the research staff.

[40] Based upon chart for budget purposes dated Aug. 15, 1944.

[41] No sections in this branch.

Burnett, Philip M., from April 1, 1944.
Edgar,* Donald D., until May 1, 1944 (transferred to Office of the Secretary).
Simpson,* R. Smith, until May 1, 1944 (transferred to Division of Labor Relations).

International Security Branch

Regulation of Armaments and Maintenance of Security Section
Adams, J. Wesley, Jr., from July 18, 1944.
Buehrig, Edward H., from August 4, 1944.
Cordier, Andrew W., from September 16, 1944.
Preuss,* Mrs. Pauline (Reinsch), assistant to Chief.
Roberts, Warren A., from September 1, 1944.
Williams,* Benjamin Harrison, until May 15, 1944 (to War Department).
Earle, Edward M., consultant, from March 5, 1944.
Kirk,* Grayson L., consultant, from July 6, 1944.
Sprout, Harold H., consultant, from May 25, 1944.

Joint Services
(shared by entire staff)

Official Views Section
Hartley,* Mrs. Virginia Fox, in charge.
Blue,* George Verne
Green,* Suzanne
Thompson,* Jane H., until October 18, 1944 (resigned).

Documents Section
Chamberlin,* Waldo, in charge until June 4, 1944 (resigned).
Sullivan,* M. Carmel, until July 1, 1944 (to Committee on Post-War Programs)
Driscoll,* Elizabeth C., head from June 4, 1944.
McKisson,* Robert M., until August 1, 1944 (to Division of Southern European Affairs)
Gough, Betty C., from September 16, 1944 (previously clerical assistant on staff)
McMahon,* Virginia M., until July 1, 1944 (to Committee on Post-War Programs)
Exton, Thérèse, until July 1, 1944 (to Committee on Post-War Programs)

Library
Bartlett,* Alice C.

(NOTE: The Division of Territorial Studies is reported separately in part C of this appendix).

B.

THE RESEARCH STAFF
December 20, 1944–April 24, 1945 [42]

Departmental Order 1301, issued and effective December 20, 1944:

[Excerpts [43]]

Office of Special Political Affairs

"The Office of Special Political Affairs shall have responsibility, under the general direction of the Special Assistant to the Secretary in charge of inter-

---

*The asterisk identifies officers with previous service on the research staff.
[42] At the date of Apr. 25, most of the officers listed served on the United States Delegation to the San Francisco Conference, or on the Secretariat of that Conference.
[43] These excerpts are confined strictly to the special research staff for postwar problems and omit references to other allocations of duties concerning long-range policy in the Department, whether pertaining to long established fields of foreign relations or to new ones developed during the war period.

national organization and security affairs [Pasvolsky], for the formulation and coordination of policy and action relating to such affairs, with special emphasis on the maintenance of international peace and security through organized action.

"A The Division of International Security and Organization, established by Departmental Order 1218 of January 15, 1944, is hereby abolished, and its functions, personnel, records, and equipment shall be transferred to the several divisions of the Office of Special Political Affairs as determined by the Director of the Office in consultation with the appropriate divisions of the Office of Departmental Administration.

"B The Office shall consist of the Division of International Organization Affairs, the Division of International Security Affairs, the Division of Dependent Area Affairs, and the Division of Territorial Studies.

"1 *Division of International Organization Affairs.*

"(a) The Division of International Organization Affairs shall be responsible for the formulation and coordination of policy and action in all matters regarding:

> "(1) The establishment of the proposed United Nations Organization and relations with that Organization.
>
> "(2) All matters regarding the relations between the proposed United Nations Organization and specialized or regional agencies and organizations, already in existence or hereafter established, and the coordination of their policies and activities through the Organization.
>
>> "(i) In such matters the division shall collaborate with the appropriate geographic and functional divisions, on the functions, powers, and structure of specialized or regional agencies and organizations.
>>
>> "(ii) Where no functional division exercises primary substantive policy jurisdiction with respect to any specialized international agency, the division shall itself assume such substantive policy functions.
>
> "(3) Within the scope of its jurisdiction, liaison with international agencies and organizations and with other Federal departments and agencies.

"(b) The functions and responsibilities with respect to international organizations and agencies, formerly vested in the Division of International Conferences, are hereby transferred to the Division of International Organization Affairs.

"2 *Division of International Security Affairs.* (a) The Division of International Security Affairs shall have responsibility for the formulation and coordination of policy and action regarding all security phases of the proposed United Nations Organization, including the security aspects of relations between regional systems or arrangements and the Organization and, together with the Division of International Organization, relations with the Organization on security matters and relevant security aspects of United States foreign policy generally.

"(b) In performing this function the Division shall collaborate with the geographic and functional divisions which deal with other aspects of security policy and shall advise and consult with them for the purpose of bringing about a correlation and coordination of policy on security matters.

"(c) The Division shall maintain liaison, within the scope of its jurisdiction, with international organizations and agencies and with other Federal Departments and agencies.

"3 *Division of Dependent Area Affairs.* The Division of Dependent Area Affairs shall have responsibility for the formulation and coordination of policy and action regarding:

"(a) Activities of the proposed United Nations Organization affecting dependent areas and, together with the Division of International Organization, the conduct of relations with the Organization on such matters. In performing this function the Division shall collaborate with geographic and functional divisions charged with responsibility for other aspects of dependent area policy and relations and shall advise and consult with them for the purpose of bringing about a correlation and coordination of policy on dependent area matters.

"(b) Within the scope of its jurisdiction, liaison with international agencies and organizations and with other Federal departments and agencies.

"4 *Division of Territorial Studies.* The Division of Territorial Studies shall be responsible for:

"(a) Analysis and appraisal of conditions and developments in foreign countries that bear upon United States foreign policy, including post-war settlements of interest to the United States;

"(b) Collaboration with the various divisions of the Department, especially the geographic divisions, through background studies, trend analyses, and policy recommendations formulated jointly with such divisions in connection with their work."

OFFICE OF SPECIAL ASSISTANT TO THE SECRETARY FOR INTERNATIONAL ORGANIZATION AND SECURITY AFFAIRS [44]

Leo Pasvolsky,* Special Assistant
Robert W. Hartley,* Executive Assistant
M. Kathleen Bell *

OFFICE OF SPECIAL POLITICAL AFFAIRS

Director
Wilson,* Edwin C., until January 27, 1945 (appointed Ambassador Extraordinary and Plenipotentiary to Turkey)
Hiss,* Alger, acting from January 28, 1945; Director, March 19, 1945.
Adviser
Notter,* Harley A.
Administrative
White,* Louise, until April 3, 1945 (to Division of International Organization Affairs)
Distribution
Clement,* Mrs. Nell F., from March 24, 1945.

Division of International Organization Affairs

Chief
Sandifer,* Durward V.

Consultant
Padelford,* Norman J.

Assistant to Chief
White,* Louise, from April 4, 1945.

Associate Chiefs
Gerig,* O. Benjamin, from February 1, 1945; concurrently Chief, Division of Dependent Area Affairs.

---

[44] Absence of dates below indicates service throughout period Dec. 20, 1944–Apr. 25, 1945. The Office of Special Political Affairs and its divisions as here set forth continued until Jan. 21, 1948, when it was superseded by the Office of United Nations Affairs and its divisions.

*The asterisk identifies officers with previous service on the research staff.

Sanders, William, from April 1, 1945.
Kotschnig,* Walter M., April 4, 1945 (acting from February 1, 1945).
Preuss,* Lawrence, acting, February 1, 1945.

Assistant Chief

Gideonse,* Max, from April 1, 1945.

General Organization Branch

Fosdick,* Dorothy.
Stone,* Ivan M.

Regional Organization Branch

Sanders,* William.
Allen, Ward P., from March 22, 1945.
Armstrong,* Elizabeth H., from March 1, 1945.
Howard,* Harry N., from March 1, 1945.

Judicial Organization and Legal Branch

Preuss,* Lawrence.
Maylott,* Marcia V. N.
McDiarmid,* (Mrs.) Alice M.
Myers,* Denys P.
Eagleton,* Clyde.
Reiff,* Henry A.
Halderman,* John W. from February 23, 1945.

Specialized Organization Branch

Kotschnig,* Walter M.
Gideonse,* Max, from April 1, 1945, Assistant Chief.
Tomlinson,* John D.
Brunauer,* Esther C.
Burnett,* Philip M.

Joint Services

Official Views Section

Hartley,* Virginia F., head.
Blue,* George V.
Green,* Suzanne.
Muther,* Jeannette E., from February 8, 1945 (previously clerical assistant on staff).
Turnbull,* Jean F., from January 17, 1945 (previously clerical assistant on staff).

Documents Unit

Driscoll,* Elizabeth C., head.
Gough,* Betty C.

Library

Bartlett,* Alice C., head.

Distribution Unit

Clement, (Mrs.) Nell F., July 1, 1944–March 24, 1945 (to Office of Special Political Affairs).

Division of International Security Affairs

Chief

Johnson, Joseph E., acting from December 20, 1944.

---

*The asterisk identifies officers with previous service on the research staff.

Consultants
Earle,* Edward M.
Kirk,* Grayson L.
Sprout,* Harold H.

Associate Chief
Blaisdell,* Donald C., from December 20, 1944.

Maintenance of Security Branch

Blaisdell,* Donald C., Associate Chief.
Adams,* J. Wesley, Jr.
Roberts,* Warren A.
Preuss,* (Mrs.) Pauline Reinsch.

Regulation of Armaments Branch

Cordier,* Andrew W.
Buehrig,* Edward H.

Division of Dependent Area Affairs

Chief
Gerig,* O. Benjamin

Assistant to Chief
Chase,* Eugene P.

Associate Chief
Bunche,* Ralph J., April 16, 1945 (acting Associate Chief from February 1, 1945).

Assistant Chief
Green,* James F., April 1, 1945 (acting Assistant Chief from February 1, 1945).

Trusteeship Administration Branch

Green,* James F.
Finkelstein,* Lawrence S.

Regional Commissions Branch

Bunche,* Ralph J.
Power,* Thomas F., Jr.
Wheeler,* Jane G.

C.

THE TERRITORIAL RESEARCH STAFF
January 15, 1944–March 1, 1945

(Departmental Orders of January 15 and December 20, 1944, relevant to the territorial staff are cited above in Parts A and B)

Division of Territorial Studies
January 15, 1944–March 1, 1945 [45]

Chief
Mosely,* Philip E., until June 21, 1944 (detached to American staff of European Advisory Commission)
Harris,* David, acting, from June 22, 1944; Chief from December 20, 1944 (to Division of Central European Affairs)

---

[45] Owing to the fact that this Division was being absorbed into the geographic offices and divisions after Dec. 20, 1944, its composition in the period after that date until its abolition is not separately noted. Absence of date indicates service throughout the dates of this period.

*The asterisk identifies officers with previous service on the research staff.

Assistant Chiefs

Harris,* David, until June 21, 1944, for Central and Eastern European Branch (to Acting Chief)

Ireland,* Philip W., until March 1, 1945, for Near Eastern and African Branch (to Office of Near East and African Affairs)

Knight,* Melvin M., until June 26, 1944, for Special Economic Studies (returned to university)

Gooch,* Robert K., until May 22, 1944, for Western European, British Commonwealth and Latin American Branch (to Board of Appeals on Visa Cases)

Western European, British Commonwealth and Latin American Branch

Chase,* Eugene P., acting head from May 24, 1944 (to Division of Dependent Area Affairs)

Western and Northern European Section

Wright,* Gordon J., until November 28, 1944 (to Foreign Service Auxiliary)
Vandenbosch,* Amry, until July 1944 (returned to university)
Van Wickel,* Jesse, until February 7 1944 (returned to Foreign Service post)
Perkins,* Mahlon F. (to Office of Far Eastern Affairs)
Ronhovde,* Andreas G. (to Division of Northern European Affairs)
Power,* Thomas F., Jr. (to Division of Dependent Area Affairs)
Bowen,* Ralph H. (to Division of Commercial Policy Affairs)
Hale,* Madeleine, until January 11, 1945 (to Division of Cultural Cooperation)

British Commonwealth Section

Chase,* Eugene P., section head to May 24, 1944.
Green,* James F., until June 30, 1944 (to Division of International Organization and Security)
Armstrong,* Elizabeth H. (to Division of International Organization Affairs)
Denby,* James O., until December 28, 1944 (returned to Foreign Service post)

Latin American Section

Whitaker,* Arthur P., section head.
Burgin, Miron, from May 22, 1944.
Mecham,* John Lloyd, July 1–November 14, 1944 (returned to university).

Far Eastern Section

Blakeslee,* George H., consultant and section head (to Office of Far Eastern Affairs)
Borton,* Hugh (to Office of Far Eastern Affairs)
Williams,* Frank S., until April 30, 1944 (to Division of Japanese Affairs)
Fearey,* Robert A. (to Office of Far Eastern Affairs)
Josselyn, Paul R. (returned to Foreign Service post)
Bartimo,* Kathryn D. (to Office of Far Eastern Affairs)

Near Eastern and African Branch

Ireland,* Philip W., Assistant Chief.

Near Eastern and African Section

Bunche,* Ralph J., January 15–December 20, 1944, section head (to Division of Dependent Area Affairs)
Mecham,* John Lloyd, until July 1, 1944 (to Latin American Section)
Furber,* Holden (to Division of British Commonwealth Affairs)
Yale,* William (to Division of Near Eastern Affairs)

*The asterisk identifies officers with previous service on the research staff.

Grant, Christina P., February 7–August 7, 1944 (resigned)
Wheeler,* Jane G. (to Division of Dependent Area Affairs)

Central and Eastern European Branch

Harris,* David, until June 21, 1944 (to acting Chief of Division)

Central European Section

Chapin,* John S. (to Division of Central European Affairs)
MacLean,* Henry C., until August 26, 1944 (to office of United States Representative, Advisory Council for Italy)
Eldridge,* Richard, until September 7, 1944 (to Foreign Service Auxiliary)
Fuller,* Leon W. (to Division of Central European Affairs)
Smyth,* Howard M. (to Division of Southern European Affairs)
Trivers,* Howard (to Division of Central European Affairs)
Vedeler,* Harold C. (to Division of Central European Affairs)

Eastern European Section

Howard,* Harry N., section head (to Division of International Organization Affairs)
Campbell,* John C. (to Division of Southern European Affairs)
Black,* Cyril E. (to Foreign Service Auxiliary)
Bradshaw,* Mary E. (to Division of Research and Publications)
Chipman,* Norris B., until September 13, 1944 (returned to Foreign Service post)
Fisher, Raymond H., from September 1, 1944 (to Division of Eastern European Affairs)
Dolbey, Mary Joanna, until January 23, 1945 (to War Refugee Board)
Adams, George P., Jr., from July 25, 1944 (to Division of Foreign Economic Development)

Assisting Units

1. *Biographical Analysis* (transferred to Division of World Trade Intelligence)

Fluegel,* Edna R., unit head, until October 16, 1944 (to Committee on Post-War Programs)
Dickinson,* Hazel M., until October 16, 1944 (to Division of World Trade Intelligence)
Hale,* Madeleine, until July 1, 1944 (to Western and Northern European Section)
Otis, Margaret M., June 21–October 16, 1944 (to Division of World Trade Intelligence)
Rathbun,* (Mrs.) Georgianna N. (Flather), until October 16, 1944 (to Division of Foreign Activity Correlation)
Stickney,* Edith P., until April 1944 (to Library of Congress)

2. *Special Studies* (Economic, no staff separate from other sections)

Knight,* Melvin M., until June 26, 1944 (returned to university)

3. *Statistics*

Burnett,* S. Bertha, until August 1, 1944 (to Commodities Division)

Departmental Order 1309, issued February 27, 1944, effective March 1, 1945:

"Abolition of the Division of Territorial Studies (TS), Office of Special Political Affairs (SPA)

"*Purpose.* This order is issued to insure that the geographic Offices and divisions of the Department shall receive the full potential of service of its territorial research staff.

---

*The asterisk identifies officers with previous service on the research staff.

"*Background.* Several years ago a special staff was organized in the Department to analyze and conduct background studies on post-war territorial settlements. The time has now arrived when post-war-planning problems and policy have become current problems and policy; therefore the closest association in the staffs is advisable.

"1. *Abolition of the Division of Territorial Studies and transfer of its staff.* The Division of Territorial Studies of the Office of Special Political Affairs is hereby abolished, and its functions and staff transferred among the several geographic Offices and divisions, in accordance with the determination of the Director of the Office of Departmental Administration in collaboration with the Directors of the Offices concerned. The staff shall continue its research activities, organized in the Offices and divisions as the Directors of Office shall determine. Several members of the staff of the Division of Territorial Studies are hereby transferred to other divisions of the Office of Special Political Affairs.

"2. *Departmental Order Amended.* Departmental Order 1301 of December 20, 1944 . . . is accordingly amended."

APPENDIX 33
December 29, 1943 [46]

Memorandum for the President

I transmit herewith for your consideration a statement of the basic ideas which might be embodied in a constitution of an international organization for the maintenance of peace and security, to be established in accordance with the provisions of the Atlantic Charter, of Point 4 of the Moscow Declaration, and of the Congressional Resolutions. The statement was prepared by our group working on the problems of international organization. Attached to the statement is a memorandum on the principal obligations which would have to be assumed by the members of the projected international organization.

The drafters of the statement recommend

(1) That there should be a small Executive Council with adequate powers and adequate means to investigate conditions, situations and disputes likely to impair security or to lead to a breach of the peace; to recommend measures for the adjustment of such conditions, situations and disputes; to employ the processes of mediation, conciliation, arbitration, etc., for the settlement of disputes; to prescribe the terms of settlement where other procedures have failed; to enforce its decisions; and to repress acts or threats of aggression;

(2) That there should be a General Assembly, composed of all member states, whose principal functions and powers should relate to the setting up of a general framework of policy, the development of international law, and the promotion of international cooperation in general;

(3) That there should be an International Court of Justice; and

(4) That, as needed, there should be created or brought within the frame work of the international organization agencies for cooperation in economic and social activities, for trusteeship responsibilities, and for other appropriate purposes.

---

[46] Transmitting memorandum from Secretary of State (Hull).

The drafters have not been able to reach definitive conclusions on a number of crucial questions which are presented in the statement in the form of alternatives. These are indicated on pages 3, 4 and 5.

The entire plan is based on two central assumptions:

First, that the four major powers will pledge themselves and will consider themselves morally bound not to go to war against each other or against any other nation, and to cooperate with each other and with other peace-loving states in maintaining the peace; and

Second, that each of them will maintain adequate forces and will be willing to use such forces as circumstances require to prevent or suppress all cases of aggression.

I hope that at our meeting tomorrow you will find it possible to discuss these matters with us.

[Attachment]

December 23, 1943.

PLAN FOR THE ESTABLISHMENT OF AN INTERNATIONAL ORGANIZATION FOR THE MAINTENANCE OF INTERNATIONAL PEACE AND SECURITY [47]

I. FUNCTIONS AND PURPOSES

The primary functions of the international organization to be established in accordance with the provisions of the Atlantic Charter, of Point 4 of the Moscow Declaration, and of the Congressional Resolutions, should be, *first,* to establish and maintain peace and security, by force if necessary; and, *second,* to foster cooperative effort among the nations for the progressive improvement of the general welfare. The organization should provide means of cooperative action for the creation, operation, and coordination of agencies and procedures for the following purposes:

1. to prevent the use of force or of threats to use force in international relations except by authority of the international organization itself;
2. to settle disputes between nations likely to lead to a breach of the peace;
3. to strengthen and develop the rule of law in international relations;
4. to facilitate the adjustment of conditions likely to impair the security or undermine the general welfare of the peace-loving nations;
5. to promote through international cooperative effort the political, economic, and social advancement of nations and peoples.

II. STRUCTURE AND POWERS

For purposes of maintaining peace and security, the international organization should have the following organs:

1. An Executive Council
2. A General Assembly
3. An International Court of Justice

All members of the organization should be represented on the General Assembly. The representation on the Executive Council should be limited, as indicated below.

For purposes of fostering good international relations and promoting general welfare, the organization should have, in addition to the organs above indicated,

[47] Brackets within the text of this appendix as in original.

an agency for cooperation in economic and social activities, an agency for trusteeship responsibilities and such other agencies as may be found necessary.

The various component organs and agencies of the organization should have appropriate administrative staffs.

The organization should have powers as follows:

1. to examine and investigate any condition or situation the continuation of which is likely to impair the security or undermine the general welfare of the peace-loving nations;
2. to recommend measures for the adjustment of such conditions and situations;
3. to prescribe the terms of settlement of disputes referred to it when the parties to the disputes have failed to find other means of pacific settlement;
4. to take jurisdiction over disputes upon its own initiative;
5. to enforce its decisions with regard to the settlement of disputes;
6. to determine the existence of threats or acts of aggression and to take measures necessary to repress such threats or acts;
7. to establish a system of armaments regulation upon the basis of international agreement.

These powers should be exercised by the respective organs of the international organization in the manner indicated below.

III. THE EXECUTIVE COUNCIL

The composition of the Executive Council should be determined upon the principle that certain nations have exceptional responsibilities for the maintenance of international security and therefore should have indeterminate tenure; the responsibility of other states for the maintenance of security should be reflected by membership of a number of such states elected for limited periods.

The Executive Council should accordingly consist initially of:

The United States of America, the United Kingdom, the Union of Soviet Socialist Republics, and China (members with indeterminate tenure), together with

1. three other members, with the understanding that the Executive Council should always consist of members with indeterminate tenure and an equal number less one of elected members. *or*
2. not less than three nor more than eleven other members.

The elected members should be chosen annually by a two-thirds vote of the General Assembly, but should not be immediately eligible for re-election. The General Assembly may alter the total membership of the Executive Council, the membership with indeterminate tenure, the method of selecting other members and the length of their tenure. Such alterations should be effected by a two-thirds vote of the General Assembly, provided all the members having indeterminate tenure on the Executive Council vote in the affirmative.

Alternatively

[The Executive Council might initially be composed of the United States of America, the United Kingdom, the Union of Soviet Socialist Republics, and China solely.]

The Executive Council should be in continuous session and should have primary responsibility with respect to the security functions and security powers of the international organization. Except for procedural decisions, which should be taken by a majority vote, all other decisions should be by a two-thirds vote, with the qualifications indicated below. In no decision of the Executive Council should the vote of a party directly involved in a dispute and represented on the Executive Council be counted. A party deemed by the Executive Council to be directly involved in a dispute and not represented on the Council should be invited to participate in the consideration of the dispute in the Council, without right of vote.

The Executive Council should operate as follows:

1. Any member of the international organization may bring to the attention of the Executive Council any condition, situation, or dispute the continuation of which is likely to impair the security of itself or of any other member of the organization, or to lead to a breach of the peace. The Executive Council should have the right to institute an investigation of any such condition, situation, or dispute, and to make recommendations to the states concerned.

2. Any member of the international organization may refer to the Executive Council for settlement any dispute in which it may be involved. The Executive Council should have the right, upon its own initiative, to take jurisdiction over any dispute the continuation of which, in its judgment, may lead to a breach of the peace.

3. The Executive Council should have the right (a) to prescribe the terms of settlement of a dispute within its jurisdiction, (b) to institute measures for the enforcement of its decisions, (c) to determine the existence of a threat or act of aggression, and (d) to institute measures to repress such threat or act. The decision of the Executive Council in these matters should require:

unanimity of all members with indeterminate tenure

Alternatively

[three-fourths vote of the members with indeterminate tenure]

[a. any abstaining or dissenting member being obligated by the decision; or
[b. any abstaining member being obligated, but a dissenting member not being obligated by the decision though bound not to obstruct action; or
[c. any abstaining or dissenting member not being obligated by the decision but obligated not to obstruct action.]

4. The Executive Council should have the right to ask the assistance of the General Assembly in the settlement of any dispute pending before it, and it should inform the General Assembly of any decisions or recommendations made by it. Whenever feasible, the Executive Council should ask the General Assembly for its assistance in the enforcement of its decisions.

5. The Executive Council should have the right to request from the International Court of Justice an advisory opinion on the legal aspects of any question pending before it.

6. The Executive Council should have the right to set up any technical agencies it may deem necessary for the performance of its functions.

IV. THE GENERAL ASSEMBLY

The initial membership of the General Assembly should comprise all of the United Nations and nations associated with them. The General Assembly should meet annually, but it may be convened in special session on its own initiative or on the initiative of the Executive Council. Its decisions should be by a majority vote, except as indicated below.

Alternatively

[The International Organization should be instituted by the United and Associated Nations. But when the basic document secures the requisite ratifications to become effective, all duly recognized independent states should be considered member states. In case of doubt, the Executive Council should determine whether a state is a duly recognized independent state.

[A state which in the judgment of the Executive Council has violated the peace of nations may be debarred by the Executive Council from exercising any or all of the rights given to member states under this Constitution for a stated period of time.]

The General Assembly should operate as follows:

1. Any member may bring to the attention of the General Assembly any condition, situation, or dispute the continuation of which is likely to impair the security or the general welfare of itself or of any other member of the organization, or to lead to a breach of the peace. The General Assembly should refer to the Executive Council, for the institution of measures, any condition, situation, or dispute related to security which it deems of sufficient gravity to require immediate consideration. It should refer to the Executive Council or to the appropriate agencies of the international organization any condition or situation not directly related to security which it deems to merit their consideration.

2. The General Assembly should receive from the Executive Council, from the agency for cooperation in economic and social activities, from the agency for trusteeship responsibilities, and from other agencies, reports of their decisions and recommendations.

3. The General Assembly should initiate studies and make recommendations concerning (a) the interpretation and revision of rules of international law and (b) the promotion of international cooperation.

4. The General Assembly should, by a two-thirds vote, admit other nations to membership in the international organization.

Alternatively

[All duly recognized independent states shall be considered member states. In case of doubt the Executive Council shall determine whether a state is a duly recognized independent state.]

5. The General Assembly may alter the total membership of the Executive Council, the membership with indeterminate tenure, the method of selecting other members and the length of their tenure. Such alterations should be effected by a two-thirds vote of the General Assembly, provided all members having indeterminate tenure on the Executive Council vote in the affirmative.

6. The General Assembly should, by a two-thirds vote, select judges of the International Court of Justice.

7. Except for such agencies as may be created by the Executive Council, the approval of the General Assembly should be required for the creation or modification of permanent technical agencies included within the framework of the international organization.

8. All administrative and budgetary arrangements should require approval of the General Assembly, except such arrangements as the General Assembly may empower agencies of the organization to make on their own initiative.

[Attachment]

December 29, 1943

PRINCIPAL OBLIGATIONS OF A MEMBER STATE

1. To refrain from use of force or threat to use force in its relations with other states and from any intervention in the internal affairs of other states, except in performance of its obligation to contribute to the enforcement procedures instituted by the Executive Council.

2. To settle all disputes with other states by pacific means, and failing such settlement, to submit any such dispute likely to endanger the peace to the Executive Council or to such agencies or procedures as the Council may designate.

3. To recognize the right of the Executive Council, on its own initiative or on the initiative of any member state, to examine, investigate, and act upon any dispute, condition, or situation deemed by it as likely to endanger the peace.

4. To accept as binding the decisions of the Executive Council in the settlement of a dispute of which the Council takes jurisdiction and to carry out in good faith the recommendations of the Council with respect to conditions or situations deemed by it as likely to endanger the peace.

5. To submit all justiciable disputes in which it may be engaged to the International Court of Justice and to accept as binding the decisions of the Court.

6. To make such contribution to the facilities and means which the Council may require for the enforcement of its decisions or for the prevention or repression of aggression as may be agreed upon in advance or, in the absence of such agreement, as the Executive Council may deem appropriate.

7. To enter into an eventual general agreement with other member states for the regulation of national armaments.

APPENDIX 34
February 17, 1944

Topical Outline

A. *General Character of An International Organization*

What should be the general structure, functions and powers of an international organization for the maintenance of peace and security established in accordance with the provisions of the Moscow Four-Nation Declaration?

B. *A General Assembly*

1. What should be the functions and powers of a representative general assembly with respect to:

    a. general policy of the organization?
    b. promotion of international cooperation?
    c. settlement of disputes and security action in relation to a council?

C. *An Executive Council*

1. What should be the composition of an executive council?
2. What should be its functions and powers with respect to:

    a. settlement of disputes?
    b. restraint or suppression of threats to or breaches of the peace?
    c. a system of regulation of armaments?
    d. economic and social cooperation?

3. By what vote should decisions be reached?

D. *A Court of Justice*

1. How should an international court of justice be constituted and what should be its position and its functional relation to the other organs of the international organization?
2. What should be the jurisdiction of the court in the settlement of disputes?
3. Should the court be empowered to render advisory opinions?

E. *Arrangements for Security*

What arrangements and procedures should be provided:

1. for the pacific adjustment of conditions or settlement of disputes likely to lead to a breach of the peace?
2. for the establishment of a system of regulation of armaments and for its enforcement?
3. for the determination of threats to or breaches of the peace?
4. for the application of non-military measures?
5. for the availability and use of armed forces and facilities in the prevention or suppression of threats to or breaches of the peace?

F. *Economic and Social Cooperation*

What functions and powers should the organization have with respect to development of international cooperation in economic and social activities and the coordination of international agencies and action in these fields?

G. *Territorial Trusteeships*

What provisions should be made for the performance of such territorial trusteeship responsibilities as may devolve upon the international organization?

H. *Administration and Secretariat*

What should be the nature and functions of the administrative and secretariat services that may be necessary for the central and related organs and agencies of the organization?

I. *Establishment*

When and by what procedures should the organization be established?

APPENDIX 35
April 29, 1944

Possible Plan for a General International Organization [48]

I

GENERAL CHARACTER OF AN INTERNATIONAL ORGANIZATION

A. *Nature of the Organization*

1. The general international organization to establish and to maintain security and peace, as projected in the Four-Nation Declaration, signed at Moscow, October 30, 1943, should be based on the principle of cooperation freely agreed upon among sovereign and peace-loving states. The organization should be open to membership by all such states, large and small, and should be world-wide in character.

2. The United Nations and the nations associated with them, and such other nations as the United Nations may determine, should comprise the initial membership of the organization.

---

[48] The "Table of Contents" in the original document is omitted here.

3. The organization should be empowered to make effective the principle that no nation shall be permitted to maintain or use armed force in international relations in any manner inconsistent with the purposes envisaged in the basic instrument of the international organization or to give assistance to any state contrary to preventive or enforcement action undertaken by the international organization.

4. The organization should be so constituted as to make possible the existence of regional organizations or other arrangements not inconsistent with its purposes, and to enable such organizations and arrangements to function on their own initiation or by reference from the general organization on matters of security and peace which are appropriate for regional adjustment. The general organization should at all times be kept informed of the activities in matters of security and peace undertaken by regional organizations or under regional or other arrangements.

5. The organization should comprise arrangements for cooperation in the fields of economic and other specialized activities.

B. *Purposes*

1. The primary purposes of the organization should be, *first*, to maintain international security and peace, and *second*, to foster cooperative effort among the nations for the development of conditions essential to the maintenance of security and peace.

C. *Methods*

As methods to be used for achieving these purposes, the international organization should:

a. encourage peaceful adjustment by the parties;
b. initiate cooperative action by member states for the settlement of disputes;
c. recommend political or diplomatic action to adjust differences;
d. provide and encourage resort to procedures of mediation, conciliation and arbitration;
e. encourage reference of justiciable matters to the international court of justice;
f. refer to the court justiciable questions pending before the organization;
g. settle disputes referred to it by the parties or over which it assumes jurisdiction on its own initiative;
h. determine the existence of threats to the peace or breaches of the peace;
i. arrange, when necessary, for economic, commercial, financial and other measures of enforcement not involving use of armed force;
j. provide for the institution of other enforcement measures, including, when necessary, arrangements for the use of armed forces and facilities.

D. *Principal Organs and Agencies*

1. The international organization should have as its principal organs:

a. A general assembly.
b. An executive council.
c. An international court of justice.
d. A general secretariat.

2. The international organization should have additional organs, councils, commissions, or other agencies for cooperation in international economic and social activities, for territorial trusteeship responsibilities, and for such other functions as may be found necessary.

II

A General Assembly

A. *Composition*

The general assembly should be composed of representatives of the states members of the international organization.

B. *Powers*

1. It should be empowered to receive and to examine representations addressed to the international organization on matters deemed to be of concern to the organization, and to take action in matters of concern to the international organization which are not allocated to other organs by the basic instrument.

2. The principal powers of the general assembly should be as follows:

a. to make, on its own initiative or on request of a member state, reports on and recommendations for the peaceful adjustment of any situation or controversy the continuation of which it deems likely to impair the general welfare;

b. to assist the executive council, upon its request, in enlisting the cooperation of all states toward giving effect to action under consideration in or decided upon by the council with respect to:

    (1) the settlement of a dispute the continuance of which is likely to endanger security or to lead to a breach of the peace;

    (2) the maintenance or restoration of peace; and

    (3) any other matters within the jurisdiction of the council;

c. to initiate studies and make recommendations for:

    (1) the promotion of international cooperation;

    (2) the development and revision of rules of international law; and

    (3) the promotion of the observance of basic human rights in accordance with principles or undertakings agreed upon by the states members of the international organization;

d. to admit to membership in the organization independent states not initial members of the organization;

e. to elect the members of the executive council not having continuing tenure, the judges of the international court of justice, and the president of the general international organization;

f. to determine the basis of apportionment of expenses of the international organization among the member states, and to approve all administrative and budgetary arangements for the organs and agencies of the organization;

g. to receive reports of all decisions and recommendations of the executive council and of all bodies or agencies brought into relationship with the international organization;

h. to provide for harmonizing the general policies of the permanent or temporary agencies brought into relationship with the international organization, except such agencies as may be created for purposes of security by the executive council;

i. to set up any bodies or agencies it may deem necessary for the performance of its functions; and

j. to propose amendments of the basic instrument, which should come into force when approved by two-thirds of the member states through their constitutional processes, including the members having continuing tenure on the executive council.

C. *Representation and Voting*

1. The delegation of each member state should consist of not more than six representatives.

2. Each member state should have one vote in the general assembly.

3. Decisions involving the admission to membership in the organization, the election of the non-continuing members of the executive council, and the election of judges of the international court of justice should be taken by a two-thirds vote. Other decisions should be taken by a majority vote.

D. *Organization and Sessions*

1. The general assembly should meet annually, but it may be convened in special session on the initiative of the executive council or under any procedure the assembly may adopt.

2. It should elect its president, vice-presidents, and other principal officers who should serve for annual terms or until their successors assume office. It should perfect its organization and adopt its own rules of procedure.

3. It should maintain headquarters at the seat of the international organization but may hold its sessions in whatever places would best facilitate the accomplishment of its work.

III

AN EXECUTIVE COUNCIL

A. *Composition and Representation*

1. The executive council should consist of the United States of America, the United Kingdom of Great Britain and Northern Ireland, the Union of Soviet Socialist Republics, and the Republic of China as member states with continuing tenure, together with an equal number of member states elected for annual terms by the general assembly, which states should not be immediately eligible for re-election.

2. Each state member of the executive council should have one representative.

3. Any state member of the organization not having a seat on the executive council should be entitled to attend and be heard on matters specially affecting that member.

B. *Powers*

1. The executive council should have primary responsibility for the maintenance of international security and peace and should in such matters represent and act on behalf of, all the members of the international organization.

2. The principal powers of the executive council are enumerated below in sections IV *Pacific Settlement of Disputes*, VI *Determination of Threats to the Peace or Breaches of the Peace and Action with Respect Thereto*, VII *Regulation of Armaments and Armed Forces*, and X *General Administration and Secretariat*.

C. *Voting*

1. Each state member of the executive council should have one vote.

2. Decisions with respect to the following matters should be taken by a majority vote including the concurring votes of all member states having continuing tenure:

    a. the assumption on its own initiative or on reference to it of jurisdiction over a dispute;

    b. the terms of settlement of disputes;

    c. the negotiations for a general agreement on the regulation of armaments and armed forces;

d. the determination of threats to the peace, of breaches of the peace, and of acts obstructing measures for the maintenance of security and peace; and

e. the institution and application of measures of enforcement.

3. Other decisions should be taken by a majority vote.

4. In all decisions any state member of the executive council should have the right to abstain from voting, but in such case the abstaining member should be bound by the decision.

D. *Organization and sessions*

1. The executive council should be in continuous session. Its headquarters should be maintained at the seat of the organization, but its meetings may be held at any places best facilitating its work.

2. The president of the organization should be the chairman of the executive council.

3. The executive council should be empowered (a) to set up any bodies or agencies it may deem necessary for the performance of its functions, (b) to perfect its own organization, and (c) to adopt its own rules of procedure.

IV

Pacific Settlement of Disputes

1. All states, whether members of the international organization or not, should be required (a) to settle disputes by none but peaceful means, and (b) to refrain from the threat or use of force in their international relations in any manner inconsistent with the purposes envisaged in the basic instrument of the international organization.

2. The parties to any dispute the continuance of which is likely to endanger international security or peace should be obligated, first of all, to seek a settlement by negotiation, mediation, conciliation, arbitration or other peaceful means of their own choice.

3. Where feasible regional or other arrangements should be employed to bring about adjustment or settlement of local or regional controversies.

4. If the parties fail to effect a settlement of such a dispute, by the means above indicated, they should be obligated to refer it to the executive council for a just and equitable settlement.

5. Any member state should have the right to bring to the attention of the general assembly or the executive council any condition, situation, or controversy the continuance of which the member deems likely to endanger international security or peace.

6. The general assembly should refer to the executive council any such condition, situation, or controversy which it deems to require action to prevent an immediate threat to the peace or breach of the peace.

7. The executive council, at the instance of any member state, or upon reference from the general assembly, or upon its own initiative, should investigate any such condition, situation, or controversy and should recommend appropriate procedures or measures of adjustment.

8. The executive council, when it determines upon its own initiative that there exists between member states a dispute which constitutes a threat to security or peace, should assume jurisdiction to effect a just and equitable settlement.

9. In case of a dispute involving a member and a non-member state, or non-member states only, and which is likely to lead to a breach of the peace, the executive council should be authorized to take jurisdiction either upon its own initiative or at the request of any party.

10. In discharging these responsibilities the executive council should be authorized to seek the advice and assistance of the general assembly, to appoint commissions of inquiry or conciliation, to refer to the international court of justice justiciable disputes or legal aspects of disputes not wholly justiciable, to employ regional or group procedures, or to take any other appropriate measures to effect a settlement.

11. The executive council should be empowered with respect to any dispute referred to in the preceding paragraphs to take necessary measures to assure compliance with the terms of any settlement determined under the authority of the international organization.

V

An International Court of Justice

The Permanent Court of International Justice should be reconstituted in accordance with a revision of its present Statute. The revised Statute should be made a part of the basic instrument of the international organization.

VI

Determination of Threats to the Peace or Breaches of the Peace and Action With Respect Thereto

A. *Determination of Threats to the Peace or Breaches of the Peace*

1. The executive council should be empowered to determine the existence of any threat to the peace or breach of the peace, and to decide upon the action to be recommended or taken to maintain or restore peace. It should be empowered to seek the advice and assistance of the general assembly in any matter in this connection, and of the international court of justice in any matter within the competence of the court.

2. The executive council should be empowered to determine whether any condition, situation, or act involving an alleged threat to the peace or breach of the peace is of sufficient gravity to require action.

Note: The conditions, situations, and acts envisaged above include, for example:

a. employment of military forces by a state within the jurisdiction of another state not authorized by the international organization;

b. failure to comply with a request of the executive council to accept procedures of pacific settlement in any dispute;

c. failure to accept terms of settlement of a dispute as prescribed under the authority of the international organization;

d. failure to comply with a request of the executive council to maintain the existing position or to return to a prior position as determined by the executive council;

e. failure to observe obligations with respect to the regulation of armaments and armed forces and the manufacture of and international traffic in arms; and

f. obstruction of measures for the enforcement of security and peace through failure to comply with a call from the council (1) to carry out agreed undertakings regarding measures of enforcement, and (2) to make available, upon the basis of agreed obligations, forces and facilities for enforcement action.

B. *Initiation of Action*

1. When the executive council determines that a threat to the peace or breach of the peace exists, it should immediately (a) require the parties to refrain from any action likely to aggravate the situation and (b) decide upon the measures to be recommended or taken.

2. In the event that a threat to the peace or breach of the peace occurs at a time when the executive council is in recess, the council should immediately be convened by the chairman who should be empowered also to initiate such emergency measures as may be necessary, subject to review by the council when it resumes session.

3. All states, whether members of the international organization or not, should be required to refrain from giving assistance to any state contrary to preventive or enforcement action undertaken by the international organization.

C. *Non-Military Measures*

1. The executive council should be empowered to call upon member states to institute measures not requiring the use of armed force in support of its decisions and to determine, in any instance necessitating action, what measures should be employed and the extent to which the respective member states should be called upon to apply them.

2. In any case in which such enforcement action has been decided upon by the executive council, member states should be obligated:

a. to cooperate with the executive council and the general assembly in obtaining the information necessary for action and in appropriate measures of publicity;

b. to take part in concerted diplomatic measures;

c. to take part in collective economic, commercial, and financial measures; and

d. to join in mutual efforts to afford relief and aid to states assuming undue burdens through participation in non-military measures of enforcement of security and peace instituted by the executive council.

D. *Provision and Use of Armed Forces and Facilities*

1. In order to assure the maintenance of security and peace, the member states should undertake to furnish forces and facilities when needed for this purpose, at the call of the executive council, and in accordance with a general agreement governing the number and kind of forces and facilities to be provided. Such an agreement should be concluded among the member states at the earliest possible moment after the organization comes into existence. It should be a duty of the executive council to formulate as rapidly as possible plans and procedures for the negotiation of such agreement. In formulating plans for the agreement and in carrying out operations under the agreement, the council should take account of the geographical position of the member states, their regional or special obligations, their population, and their relative resources.

2. The general agreement should provide that member states should be obligated to maintain in condition of effective readiness the armaments and armed forces which by the agreement they respectively undertake to make available for international cooperative action.

3. Pending the conclusion of the general agreement, the states parties to the Four-Nation Declaration, signed at Moscow, October 30, 1943, and other states in position to do so should provide, on the basis of their various capacities and of undertakings among themselves, such forces and facilities as may be needed for establishing and maintaining security and peace.

4. The executive council should be empowered to call upon the member states for economic, financial, and commercial assistance necessary to support and to supplement forcible international action as and when undertaken. Member states should undertake:

    a. to afford such assistance, the terms to be determined in consultation between the executive council and member states;

    b. to deny economic or other assistance to a state against which enforcement action is undertaken, the nature of such assistance to be defined by the executive council at the time of the action; and

    c. to join in mutual efforts to afford relief and aid to states assuming undue burdens through participation in military measures of enforcement of security and peace instituted by the executive council.

5. The executive council should be empowered to call upon member states to grant rights of passage and to furnish facilities, including bases, necessary to the effective action of forces operating under authority of the council. The conditions of the exercise of these rights and of the furnishing of facilities, including bases, should be determined, in advance or at the time of action, by agreement between the executive council and the member states in whose territories these rights and facilities are required.

6. The executive council, advised and assisted by the permanent security and armaments commission described in part E below, should be responsible for the planning of, and should exercise general supervision over, any use of force determined to be necessary under the provisions of the basic instrument of the international organization.

E. *Security and Armaments Commission*

1. The executive council should establish a permanent security and armaments commission to provide necessary expert advice and assistance to the council.

2. The principal duties to be performed by the security and armaments commission, responsible to and under authority of the executive council, should be:

    a. to report on the strategical, tactical, and logistical aspects of situations which might threaten the peace;

    b. to study, plan for, and make recommendations concerning the composition, organization, command, supply, utilization, and maintenance of forces and facilities, and the application of enforcement measures;

    c. to recommend plans and procedures for the regulation of armaments and armed forces.

3. The security and armaments commission should have authority, with the approval of the executive council, to establish subordinate agencies and otherwise perfect its organization.

4. The executive council should have authority to appoint *ad hoc* commissions to perform special security missions.

VII

REGULATION OF ARMAMENTS AND ARMED FORCES

1. In order to promote the establishment and maintenance of international security and peace with the least diversion of the world's human and economic resources for armaments, the executive council should be made responsible for initiating negotiations for the conclusion of a general international agreement, envisaged in the Four-Nation Declaration signed at Moscow, October 30, 1943,

for the establishment of a system of regulation of armaments and armed forces and for the control of, manufacture of, and international traffic in arms.

2. The armaments and armed forces of the Axis states [to be named later] should be governed by the terms of their surrender and by the authority established thereunder.

X [49]

GENERAL ADMINISTRATION AND SECRETARIAT

A. *Office of President*

1. A person of widely recognized eminence should be elected by the general assembly, on the nomination of the executive council, as president of the international organization. He should serve for a period of two years, and should be eligible for re-election.

2. The president of the organization should act as chairman of the executive council, and when presiding should be free to participate in the deliberations as representing the general interests and purposes of the organization, without right of vote. He should open each new session of the general assembly and preside until the election of its president. He should perform other duties of a general political character as entrusted to him by the general assembly or by the executive council.

3. The president should be empowered to nominate for election by the council one or more deputies to serve in his absence as chairman of the council and to assist him in the discharge of his other duties.

4. The president and his deputies should not during their terms of office hold any other public office.

B. *Office of Director-General and the Central Administrative Staff*

1. A director-general of the international organization should be elected by the general assembly with the concurrence of the executive council. He should serve for a period of five years and should be eligible for re-election.

2. The director-general should have the responsibilities of the chief administrative officer of the organization. He should serve as the secretary-general of the general assembly, of the executive council, and of such other agencies of the international organization as the assembly or the council may direct. He should direct, within the general policies appertaining to administration established by the general assembly, administrative procedures and regulations of the specialized agencies brought into relationship with the international organization. He should report to the general assembly on the work of the various commissions, agencies, and other bodies of concern to the international organization.

3. The director-general should appoint (a) such deputies and other officers of the central administrative staff as may be required, subject to confirmation by the general assembly, (b) directors of commissions and agencies created by the executive council or the general assembly subject to confirmation by the creating organ, and (c) other personnel of secretariats for which he is responsible.

4. The director-general and his deputies should not during their terms of office hold any other public office.

5. Officers appointed to the central administrative staff should be selected on the basis of technical or administrative competence and experience, and of the

---

[49] Missing sections VIII, IX, and XI on Economic and Social Cooperation, Arrangements for Territorial Trusteeships, and Establishment were still in preparation.

widest practicable distribution among nationalities. These officials should be constituted as a continuing international civil service, and they should undertake to perform the duties entrusted to them in the impartial manner and spirit necessary to advance the interests and purposes of the international organization.

C. *Obligations of Member States With Respect to Officials of the Organization*

1. Member states should impose no obligations upon their nationals who are officials of the international organization that are inconsistent with the performance of their duties.

2. Member states should grant the customary diplomatic immunities to officials of the international organization when engaged on business of the international organization or when traveling to and from their offices.

APPENDIX 36
May 4, 1944[50]

Japan: The Post-War Objectives of the United States in Regard to Japan

I. *Fundamental Objectives*

(*a*) Japan must be prevented from being a menace to the United States and the other countries of the Pacific area.

(*b*) American interests require that there be in Japan a government which will respect the rights of other states and Japan's international obligations.

In order to achieve these fundamental purposes the policies of the United States should be considered separately for three distinct periods of Japan's post-war development.

The first of these periods will be that during which the immediate terms of surrender for Japan will be enforced, and Japan will undergo the stern discipline of occupation as the inevitable retribution for military aggression.

The second period will be one of close surveillance; restrictions will be progressively relaxed as Japan demonstrates its willingness and ability to live at peace with other nations.

The third period will be one which will look toward the ultimate aim of the United States, namely, *a Japan properly discharging its responsibilities in the family of peaceful nations.*

II. *The First Period*

In accordance with the Cairo Declaration Japan is to withdraw from Manchuria, the Mandated Islands and all areas under Japanese military occupation and is to be deprived of Korea, Formosa and all islands obtained since the beginning of the first world war.

Japan's military and naval forces are to be disarmed and disbanded, its military and naval installations destroyed and the country placed under military occupation and government.

---

[50] Original bears following notation : Document of Interdivisional Area Committee on the Far East as approved with changes by the Post-War Programs Committee. Changes from the original document are underscored.

III. *The Second Period*

(*a*) There will be developed such national or international bases as may be necessary to prevent Japanese aggression and to facilitate military policing.

(*b*) Measures designed to eradicate militarism would include:

(1) Military inspection to prevent rearmament;

(2) Economic controls to prevent the development of a war potential;

(3) *Encouragement of democratic* thought through the press, radio, cinema, and schools;

(4) Impressing upon the moderate elements in Japan their responsibility for convincing the Japanese people that militarism is disastrous to their real interests;

(5) Adoption of such other measures as will most effectively strengthen liberal political elements and liberal thought in Japan and assist the development of a civil government actually responsible to the people;

(6) Rooting out of ultra-nationalistic societies.

(*c*) Japan is to be permitted, within the framework of the restrictions necessary for international security, and having due regard for the matter of reparations, to begin to share in the world economy on a reasonable basis.

IV. *The Third Period*

The precise measures, whether political or economic, to be taken during the third period cannot be determined at this time. There is, however, to be borne in mind the fact that the break-up of the Japanese Empire, through the loss of dependencies, will call for permanent adjustments of fundamental importance.

APPENDIX 37
July 28, 1944[51]

Policy Toward the Settlement of Territorial Disputes in Europe

I. *Summary Recommendations*

1. Participation by the United States in the making of territorial settlements in Europe should in each case be in association with other nations, either within the framework of the present wartime relationships or within that of the projected international organization. This Government might withhold express approval of a given territorial settlement which, in its opinion, is contrary to the requirements of a durable peace.

2. The United States should maintain its declared policy that individual territorial questions should be settled preferably within the framework of the general structure of peace. While this policy implies the postponement of decisions until after the cessation of hostilities, we should recognize that it may be possible and desirable to settle certain territorial disputes before that time. In such cases the solution adopted should, if possible, be based on the same permanent factors which we expect to govern the territorial settlements reached after the war.

3. The Government should examine each territorial dispute on its merits and should seek a solution which would contribute to peace and orderly development

---

[51] A Post-War Programs Committee document.

in Europe. The freely expressed wishes of the peoples concerned and the political and economic aspects of proposed solutions should be given more weight than historic or strategic claims. Consideration should be given to the advisability of transferring minority populations as a means of making the boundary settlements more stable. The relationship of the various claimant states to the Allies is a factor to be considered but should not unduly influence the American position on any given territorial problem.

II. *American Interest and Participation in the Settlement of Territorial Disputes in Europe*

From an examination of possible American policies in respect of European territorial questions, ranging from abstention to the exertion of a strong and direct influence, it emerges that the American interest in promoting long-range peace and stability will be served most effectively by this Government's undertaking a degree of participation in territorial decisions and of responsibility for them consonant with its position as a great power, with its contribution to the victory of the United Nations, and with its relatively impartial outlook on such questions. The United States should not disclaim an interest in the territorial arrangements of Europe, any more than it should disclaim a concern in the arrangements made by European states concerning trade, cartels, aviation or other matters in which this Government has already indicated its direct interest. Nor would it rule out the consideration of territorial grievances on mere grounds of expediency or legalism. It would attempt to measure the degree of its participation in the settlement of European boundary problems on the rough basis of their importance to its over-riding aim—the assuring of enduring peace and orderly development.

Success in creating and maintaining a system of international security will depend in no small measure on the achievement, in so far as is possible, of durable solutions to the more than thirty territorial disputes in Europe. Wholehearted American participation in the international organization, which implies our co-operating in maintaining the new frontiers against the attempt to alter them by the use or threat of force, can hardly be expected unless the post-war territorial settlement is reasonably well adjusted to the needs and desires of the peoples of Europe and commands the general approval of the American people.

American participation in territorial settlements should in every case be a matter of joint action with other governments. Having once arrived at a decision as to its own policy on a given territorial question, the United States should advocate in international councils a settlement consistent with that policy, but should be prepared to accept a different settlement in case the American view should be clearly in the minority. However, this Government might refuse to give its express approval of settlements which it is convinced are not just or durable but which are insisted upon by states with a more direct interest. In the case of settlements made before the cessation of hostilities and in the immediate post-hostilities period, presumably this Government would act within the framework of its present war-time association with allied states; in the case of settlements made at a later date it would act as a member of the international organization. Whatever the final settlements, they should be made upon the responsibility of all the United Nations, and the United States should undertake no individual responsibility for making or maintaining them.

III. *The Time of Making Territorial Settlements*

One basic question which arises in connection with territorial problems in Europe is whether they should be settled chiefly by the three principal United Nations during the war or should be deferred for subsequent settlement by international agencies after the war. If boundary problems are not settled within a reasonable time after the close of hostilities, the serious political, social and economic confusion which will, in any case, prevail over large parts of Europe may be considerably intensified and prolonged. The longer the settlement is delayed after the cessation of hostilities, the more bitter both local and national feelings will become and the more serious will be the danger that the United Nations will be divided over territorial questions. A subsidiary disadvantage of a long postponement of territorial settlements is found in those cases in which the boundary settlements may be accompanied or followed by transfers of populations; since a substantial part of the peoples of Europe will have to start rebuilding almost from the ground up, it would be better in the long run for resettled populations to begin rebuilding at once in the area in which they are to live permanently.

Against settling territorial disputes during the war there are several weighty arguments. As the experience of the secret treaties in the first World War has shown, the equity and permanence of boundaries agreed upon primarily in order to attain temporary war-time objectives would generally be open to serious doubt. Even if permanent factors form the basis for the decision, it would be difficult to measure during the war the effect of a given territorial arrangement on the general settlement. Until the shape of post-war international political and security arrangements is visible to the peoples of Europe, they will continue to place great emphasis upon the strategic factor in drawing frontiers; this emphasis may lead to the sacrifice of ethnic and other considerations in territorial settlements made under the impact of war-time invasion and suffering and prior to the establishment of an effective security organization. Moreover, members of the United Nations are naturally reluctant to suggest or consider, during hostilities, definitive territorial settlements which, in some cases, might involve adjustments to the advantage of Axis satellites, more particularly since it is uncertain whether and how soon those states can be assimilated into orderly political and economic international arrangements. Furthermore, the competence of some of the governments concerned to enter into new territorial arrangements will be open to serious dispute until they have returned to their homelands or until new governments have emerged capable of speaking for their peoples. Finally, there can be no opportunity to consult the wishes of the populations concerned until after the close of hostilities, if such consultation should be invoked.

The general policy of the United States Government is that the settlement of boundary questions should be considered as part of "the general peace settlement". The basic reasoning which underlies this policy is that, whether or not there is any general peace conference, there should be a general settlement designed to promote peace and stability, within the framework of which all territorial settlements should be considered, and that they should not be made in piecemeal fashion under the pressure of war-time exigencies. In assuring the invaded members of the United Nations, together with Austria and Albania, of its desire to see their independence restored, this Government has refrained from making any specific commitments with respect to their future frontiers. It has, however, declared that Germany and its allies shall not benefit from seizures of territory effected by force or the threat of force.

The British Government has adopted a similar policy, although it has shown a disposition to favor the settlement during the war of territorial disputes involving members of the United Nations. The Soviet Government, the only one of the principal Allies which has territorial claims in Europe, has naturally shown more inclination to enter into detailed discussions and to seek and offer, during the war, commitments with respect to territorial settlements, more particularly in Eastern Europe.

The United States need not adhere rigidly to its declared formula of postponing decisions on boundary questions until after the war. It should be willing to proceed to the settlement of some territorial disputes as soon as it is possible to do so with the assurance that no harm will thereby be done to the successful prosecution of the war and that full weight will be given to the permanent factors on which we believe durable settlements should be based. In certain cases involving Soviet claims this Government is not disposed to object to settlements arrived at during hostilities by mutual agreement. In addition, in working out plans for the post-surrender treatment of Germany, the pressure of events may oblige this Government to take part in settling the territorial status of certain parts of Germany, which can hardly be held open for later settlement.

IV. *Principles for the Settlement of Territorial Disputes*

This Government should seek a settlement of each dispute based on the merits of the specific problem and on the relation of that problem to the whole settlement. Each proposed solution should be judged, above all, in the light of its contribution to peace and orderly development in Europe. The chief criteria would appear to be the wishes of the populations involved, the economic effects on the area in dispute, on the claimant states and on other countries, and the political effects on the states directly concerned and on the international organization. Claims based on historic possession and on strategic considerations should be given less weight, if any.

In view of the fact that American participation in European territorial settlements may be affected by the relationship of the various claimant states to the Allies, the following section contains recommendations based on a classification of these disputes into six principal categories (See Appendices I and II and Map 4, European Series). These relationships will be a factor to be considered in each case, although the American position should in no instance be determined automatically by them. [Remaining Section and Appendixes not printed.]

APPENDIX 38
July 18, 1944

[United States] Tentative Proposals for a General International Organization [52]

I

GENERAL CHARACTER OF AN INTERNATIONAL ORGANIZATION

A. *Nature of the Organization*

1. The general international organization to establish and to maintain security and peace, as projected in the Four-Nation Declaration, signed at Moscow, October 30, 1943, should be based on the principle of cooperation freely agreed upon among sovereign and peace-loving states. The organization should be open to membership by all such states, large and small, and should be world-wide in character.

---

[52] The "Table of Contents" in the original document is omitted here.

2. The United Nations and the nations associated with them, and such other nations as the United Nations may determine, should comprise the initial membership of the organization.

3. The organization should be empowered to make effective the principle that no nation shall be permitted to maintain or use armed force in international relations in any manner inconsistent with the purposes envisaged in the basic instrument of the international organization or to give assistance to any state contrary to preventive or enforcement action undertaken by the international organization.

4. The organization should be so constituted as to make possible the existence of regional organizations or other arrangements or policies not inconsistent with its purposes, and to enable such organizations and arrangements to function on their own initiation or by reference from the general organization on matters of security and peace which are appropriate for regional adjustment. The general organization should at all times be kept informed of the activities in matters of security and peace undertaken by regional organizations or under regional or other arrangements.

5. The organization should comprise arrangements for cooperation in the fields of economic and other specialized activities.

B. *Purposes*

1. The primary purposes of the organization should be, *first*, to maintain international security and peace, and *second*, to foster through international cooperation the creation of conditions of stability and well-being necessary for peaceful and friendly relations among nations and essential to the maintenance of security and peace.

C. *Methods*

As methods to be used for the maintenance of security and peace, the international organization should:

a. encourage peaceful adjustment of controversies by the parties themselves;
b. initiate cooperative action by member states for the settlement of disputes;
c. encourage the use of local or regional procedures for the settlement of disputes capable of adjustment by such procedures;
d. recommend political or diplomatic action to adjust differences;
e. provide for, and encourage resort to, processes of mediation, conciliation, and arbitration;
f. encourage reference of justiciable matters to the international court of justice;
g. refer to the court justiciable questions pending before the organization;
h. settle disputes referred to it by the parties or over which it assumes jurisdiction on its own initiative;
i. determine the existence of threats to the peace or breaches of the peace;
j. arrange, when necessary, for economic, commercial, financial, and other measures of enforcement not involving use of armed force;
k. provide for the use of armed force, when necessary in support of security and peace, if other methods and arrangements are inadequate.

D. *Principal Organs and Agencies*

1. The international organization should have as its principal organs:

a. A general assembly;
b. An executive council;
c. An international court of justice; and
d. A general secretariat.

2. The international organization should have additional organs, councils, commissions, or other agencies for cooperation in international economic and social activities, for territorial trusteeship responsibilities, and for such other functions as may be found necessary.

II

A GENERAL ASSEMBLY

A. *Composition*

The general assembly should be composed of representatives of the states members of the international organization.

B. *Powers*

1. It should be empowered to receive and to examine representations addressed to the international organization on matters deemed to be of concern to the organization, and to take action in matters of concern to the international organization which are not allocated to other organs by the basic instrument.

2. The principal powers of the general assembly should be as follows:

a. to make, on its own initiative or on request of a member state, reports on and recommendations for the peaceful adjustment of any situation or controversy the continuation of which it deems likely to impair the general welfare;

b. to assist the executive council, upon its request, in enlisting the cooperation of all states toward giving effect to action under consideration in or decided upon by the council with respect to:

(1) the settlement of a dispute the continuance of which is likely to endanger security or to lead to a breach of the peace;

(2) the maintenance or restoration of peace; and

(3) any other matters within the jurisdiction of the council;

c. to initiate studies and make recommendations for:

(1) the promotion of international cooperation;

(2) the development and revision of rules of international law; and

(3) the promotion of the observance of basic human rights in accordance with principles or undertakings agreed upon by the states members of the international organization;

d. to admit to membership in the organization independent states not initial members of the organization;

e. to elect the members of the executive council not having continuing tenure and the judges of the international court of justice;

f. to approve the budget of the organs and agencies of the organization, to determine a provisional and a continuing basis of apportionment of expenses of the organization among the member states together with the procedure of apportionment, and to review, make recommendations on, and take other action concerning the budgets of specialized agencies brought into relationship with the international organization in accordance with the terms agreed upon between such agencies and the international organization;

g. to receive reports from the executive council and other organs and agencies of the organization and from all specialized bodies or agencies brought into relationship with the international organization;

h. to exercise the powers with respect to economic and social activities and territorial trusteeship stipulated in Sections VIII and IX;

i. to provide for the coordination of the general policies of all organs and agencies of the international organization and organizations and agencies brought into relationship with it;

j. to set up any bodies or agencies it may deem necessary for the performance of its functions; and

k. to propose amendments of the basic instrument, which should come into force when approved by two thirds of the member states through their constitutional processes, including the members having continuing tenure on the executive council.

C. *Representation and Voting*

1. The delegation of each member state should consist of not more than six representatives.

2. Each member state should have one vote in the general assembly, except as provided for in paragraph 3 below.

3. In taking decisions with respect to the budget of the organs and agencies of the organization, the continuing basis of apportionment of expenses of the organization, and the budgets of specialized agencies brought into relationship with the organization each member state should have voting power in proportion to its contribution to the expenses of the organization.

4. Decisions with respect to the admission to membership in the organization, the election of the members of the executive council, the election of judges of the international court of justice, and the provisional basis of apportionment of expenses, should be taken by a two-thirds vote.   Other decisions should be taken by a majority vote.

D. *Organization and Sessions*

1. The general assembly should meet annually, but it may be convened in special session on the initiative of the executive council or under any procedure the assembly may adopt.

2. It should elect its president, vice-presidents, and other principal officers who should serve for annual terms or until their successors assume office.   It should perfect its organization and adopt its own rules of procedure.

3. It should maintain headquarters at the seat of the international organization but may hold its sessions in whatever places would best facilitate the accomplishment of its work.

III

AN EXECUTIVE COUNCIL

A. *Composition and Representation*

1. The executive council should consist of eleven states members of the international organization.   These states should be elected annually by the general assembly and should not be immediately eligible for re-election except that the United States of America, the United Kingdom of Great Britain and Northern Ireland, the Union of Soviet Socialist Republics, and the Republic of China should have continuing tenure.

2. There should be a provision in the basic instrument that whenever the executive council finds that a government freely chosen by the French people has been established and is in effective control of the territory of the French Republic, France should be added to the list of states members having continuing tenure on the council.

3. Each state member of the executive council should have one representative.

4. Any state member of the organization not having a seat on the executive council should be entitled to attend and to be heard on matters specially affecting that member.

B. *Powers*

1. The executive council should have primary responsibility for the peaceful settlement of international disputes, for the prevention of threats to the peace and breaches of the peace, and for such other activities as may be necessary for the maintenance of international security and peace. It should in such matters represent, and act on behalf of, all the members of the international organization and should in every case seek a just and equitable settlement of international disputes.

2. The principal powers of the executive council are enumerated below in Section V, *Pacific Settlement of Disputes*, Section VI, *Determination of Threats to the Peace or Breaches of the Peace and Action with Respect Thereto*, Section VII, *Regulation of Armaments and Armed Forces*, and Section X, *General Administration and Secretariat*.

C. *Voting*

1. Each state member of the executive council should have one vote.

2. Decisions with respect to the following matters should be taken by a majority vote including the concurring votes of all member states having continuing tenure, except as provided for in paragraphs 4 and 5 below:

    a. the assumption on its own initiative or on reference to it of jurisdiction over a dispute;

    b. the terms of settlement of disputes;

    c. the negotiations for a general agreement on the regulation of armaments and armed forces;

    d. the determination of threats to the peace, of breaches of the peace, and of acts obstructing measures for the maintenance of security and peace; and

    e. the institution and application of measures of enforcement.

3. Other decisions should be taken by a simple majority vote.

4. In all decisions any state member of the executive council should have the right to abstain from voting, but in such case the abstaining member should be bound by the decision.

5. Provisions will need to be worked out with respect to the voting procedure in the event of a dispute in which one or more of the members of the council having continuing tenure are directly involved.

D. *Organization and Sessions*

1. The executive council should be in continuous session. Its headquarters should be maintained at the seat of the organization, but its meetings may be held at any places best facilitating its work.

2. It should elect its chairman.

3. It should be empowered (a) to set up any bodies or agencies it may deem necessary for the performance of its functions, (b) to perfect its own organization, and (c) to adopt its own rules of procedure.

IV

An International Court of Justice

1. The Permanent Court of International Justice should be reconstituted in accordance with a revision of its present Statute.

2. The revised Statute should be made a part of the basic instrument of the international organization.

V

PACIFIC SETTLEMENT OF DISPUTES

1. All states, whether members of the international organization or not, should be required (a) to settle disputes by none but peaceful means, and (b) to refrain from the threat or use of force in their international relations in any manner inconsistent with the purposes envisaged in the basic instrument of the international organization.

2. The parties to any dispute the continuance of which is likely to endanger international security or peace should be obligated, first of all, to seek a settlement by negotiation, mediation, conciliation, arbitration, reference to the international court of justice, or other peaceful means of their own choice.

3. Where feasible, regional or other arrangements should be employed to bring about adjustment or settlement of local or regional controversies.

4. If the parties fail to effect a settlement of such a dispute by the means above indicated, they should be obligated to refer it to the executive council.

5. Any member state should have the right to bring to the attention of the general assembly or the executive council any condition, situation, or controversy the continuance of which the member deems likely to endanger international security or peace.

6. The general assembly should refer to the executive council any such condition, situation, or controversy which it deems to require action to prevent an immediate threat to the peace or breach of the peace.

7. The executive council should be empowered to investigate any such condition, situation, or controversy and should recommend appropriate procedures or measures of adjustment. It should be empowered to do this upon its own initiative, or upon reference from the general assembly, or at the instance of a member state.

8. The executive council, when it determines upon its own initiative that there exists between member states a dispute which constitutes a threat to security or peace, and which is not being adequately dealt with by other procedures, should be authorized to assume jurisdiction to effect a settlement.

9. In case of a dispute involving a member and a non-member state, or non-member states only, and which is likely to lead to a breach of the peace, the executive council should be authorized to take jurisdiction either upon its own initiative or at the request of any party.

10. In discharging its responsibilities with respect to pacific settlement the executive council should be authorized to seek the advice and assistance of the general assembly, to appoint commissions of inquiry or conciliation, to refer to the international court of justice justiciable disputes or legal aspects of disputes not wholly justiciable. to employ regional or local procedures, or to take any other appropriate measures to effect a settlement.

11. The executive council should be empowered with respect to any dispute referred to in the preceding paragraphs to encourage and facilitate the execution of the terms of any settlement determined under the authority of the international organization.

VI

DETERMINATION OF THREATS TO THE PEACE OR BREACHES OF THE PEACE AND ACTION WITH RESPECT THERETO

A. *Determination of Threats to the Peace or Breaches of the Peace*

1. The executive council should be empowered to determine the existence of any threat to the peace or breach of the peace, and to decide upon the action to

be recommended or taken to maintain or restore peace. It should be empowered to seek the advice and assistance of the general assembly in any matter in this connection, and of the international court of justice in any matter within the competence of the court.

2. The executive council should be empowered to determine whether any condition, situation, or act involving an alleged threat to the peace or breach of the peace is of sufficient gravity to require action.

Note: The conditions, situations, and acts envisaged above include, for example:

a. employment of military forces by a state within the jurisdiction of another state not authorized by the international organization;

b. failure to comply with a request of the executive council to accept procedures of pacific settlement in any dispute;

c. failure to accept terms of settlement of a dispute as prescribed under the authority of the international organization;

d. failure to comply with a request of the executive council to maintain the existing position or to return to a prior position as determined by the executive council;

e. failure to observe obligations with respect to the regulation of armaments and armed forces and the manufacture of and international traffic in arms; and

f. obstruction of measures for the enforcement of security and peace through failure to comply with a call from the council (1) to carry out agreed undertakings regarding measures of enforcement, and (2) to make available, upon the basis of agreed obligations, forces and facilities for enforcement action.

B. *Initiation of Action*

1. When the executive council determines that a threat to the peace or breach of the peace exists, it should immediately (a) require the parties to refrain from any action likely to aggravate the situation and (b) decide upon the measures to be recommended or taken.

2. All states, whether members of the international organization or not, should be required to refrain from giving assistance to any state contrary to preventive or enforcement action undertaken by the international organization or with its authorization.

C. *Measures Not Involving the Use of Armed Force*

1. The executive council should be empowered to call upon member states to institute measures not requiring the use of armed force in support of its decisions and to determine, in any instance necessitating such action, what measures should be employed and the extent to which the respective member states should be called upon to apply them.

2. In any case in which such action has been decided upon by the executive council, member states should be obligated:

a. to cooperate with the executive council and the general assembly in obtaining the information necessary for action and in appropriate measures of publicity;

b. to take part in concerted diplomatic measures;

c. to take part in collective economic, commercial, and financial measures; and

d. to join in mutual efforts to afford relief and aid to states assuming undue burdens through participation in such measures instituted by the executive council.

D. *Measures Involving the Use of Armed Force*

1. In the event that other measures prove to be inadequate, the executive council should be authorized to provide for the use of armed force to assure the maintenance of security and peace.

2. The member states should undertake to furnish forces and facilities when needed for this purpose at the call of the executive council and in accordance with a general agreement governing the number and type of forces and the kind and extent of facilities to be provided. Such an agreement should be concluded among the member states at the earliest possible moment after the organization comes into existence. It should be a duty of the executive council to formulate as rapidly as possible plans and procedure for the negotiation of such agreement. In formulating plans for the agreement and in carrying out operations under the agreement, the council should take account of the geographical position of the member states, their regional or special obligations, their population, and their relative resources.

3. The general agreement should provide that member states should be obligated to maintain in condition of effective readiness the armaments and armed forces which by the agreement they respectively undertake to make available for international cooperative action.

4. Pending the conclusion of the general agreement, the states parties to the Four-Nation Declaration, signed at Moscow, October 30, 1943, and other states in position to do so should provide, on the basis of their various capacities and of undertakings among themselves, such forces and facilities as may be needed for establishing and maintaining security and peace.

5. The executive council should be empowered to call upon the member states for economic, financial, and commercial and other assistance necessary to support and to supplement international action involving the use of armed force as and when undertaken. Member states should undertake:

   a. to afford such assistance, the terms to be determined in consultation between the executive council and member states;

   b. to deny economic or other assistance to a state against which enforcement action is undertaken, the nature of such assistance to be defined by the executive council at the time of the action; and

   c. to join in mutual efforts to afford relief and aid to states assuming undue burdens through participation in security measures involving the use of armed force instituted by the executive council.

6. The executive council should be empowered to call upon member states to grant rights of passage and to furnish facilities, including bases, necessary to the effective action of forces operating under authority of the council. The conditions of the exercise of these rights and of the furnishing of facilities, including bases, should be determined, in advance or at the time of action, by agreement between the executive council and the member states in whose territories these rights and facilities are required.

7. The executive council, advised and assisted by the permanent security and armaments commission described in part E below, should be responsible for the planning of, and should exercise general supervision over, any use of force determined to be necessary under the provisions of the basic instrument of the international organization.

E. *Security and Armaments Commission*

1. The executive council should establish a permanent security and armaments commission.

2. The permanent security and armaments commission should provide the executive council with the expert military advice and assistance necessary for the discharge of the responsibilities of the council concerning the employment of force and the regulation of armaments and armed forces, and should perform such duties of study, recommendation, administration, and execution as the council may assign to it.

3. The security and armaments commission should have authority, with the approval of the executive council, to establish subordinate agencies and otherwise perfect its organization.

VII

REGULATION OF ARMAMENTS AND ARMED FORCES

1. In order to promote the establishment and maintenance of international security and peace with the least diversion of the world's human and economic resources for armaments, the executive council should be made responsible for initiating negotiations for the conclusion of a general international agreement, envisaged in the Four-Nation Declaration signed at Moscow, October 30, 1943, for the establishment of a system of regulation of armaments and armed forces and for the regulation of the manufacture of and international traffic in arms.

2. The executive council should be authorized to exercise such powers for the execution of obligations stipulated in the general international agreement as may be assigned to it by the agreement.

3. The armaments and armed forces of the Axis states [to be named later] should be governed by the terms of their surrender and by the authority established thereunder. The executive council should be empowered to take responsibility for assuring the execution of stipulations governing the armaments and armed forces of the Axis states, to the extent that such responsibility may be assigned to it in succession to the authority established under the surrender terms.

VIII

ARRANGEMENTS FOR ECONOMIC AND SOCIAL COOPERATION

A. *Purpose and Relationships*

1. With a view to the creation of conditions of stability and well-being which are necessary for peaceful and friendly relations among nations, the general international organization should facilitate and promote solutions of international economic and social problems, including educational and cultural problems. Responsibility for the discharge of this function should be vested in the general assembly, and under the authority of the general assembly, in an economic and social council, established in the basic instrument of the organization.

2. The various specialized economic and social organizations and agencies would have responsibilities in their respective fields as defined in their statutes. Each specialized economic or social organization or agency should be brought into relationship with the general international organization. The terms under which each specialized organization or agency should be related to the general international organization should be determined by agreement between the economic and social council and the appropriate authorities of the specialized organization or agency, subject to approval by the general assembly.

B. *Powers*

1. The economic and social council should be empowered:

a. to carry out, within the scope of its functions, recommendations of the general assembly in regard to economic or social matters;

b. to make recommendations, on its own initiative, to the various specialized organizations or agencies, to governments, or to the general assembly, with respect to economic or social problems, including those beyond the scope of the specialized organizations, with a view to promoting the fullest and most effective use of the world's economic resources, to achieving high and stable levels of employment, and in general to advancing the well-being of all peoples;

c. to coordinate the activities of the specialized economic and social organizations or agencies through advisory consultations with, and recommendations to, such organizations;

d. to receive and consider reports of the activities, decisions and recommendations of the specialized organizations or agencies, and to submit annually an analysis of such reports to the general assembly;

e. to examine the administrative budgets of the specialized organizations or agencies with a view to recommending to the organizations or agencies concerned, and in appropriate cases to the general assembly, as to the most effective utilization of resources; and

f. to perform such other functions within the general scope of its competence as may be assigned to it by the general assembly, or as may be provided for in future agreements among member states.

C. *Composition and voting*

1. The economic and social council should consist of qualified representatives of a specified number [24] of member states. The states designated for this purpose should be selected by the general assembly for terms of three years, and each such state should have one representative.

2. Each representative of a state designated as a member of the economic and social council should have one vote. Decisions of the council should be taken by majority vote.

3. The economic and social council should make suitable arrangements for representatives of the specialized organizations or agencies to participate without vote in its deliberations and in those of the commissions established by it.

D. *Organization*

1. The economic and social council should establish an economic commission, a social commission, and such other commissions as may be required to facilitate the consideration of problems within the scope of its functions. Such commissions should consist of experts specially qualified in their respective fields, who may be nationals of any member state of the general international organization. The members of the commissions should be appointed for periods of three years.

2. The economic and social council should elect a chairman from among its members. A director and a staff of competent experts should serve as the permanent secretariat of the economic and social council and of the commissions, and should constitute a part of the central administrative staff of the general international organization.

3. The council should adopt its own rules of procedure and otherwise perfect its organization.

IX

ARRANGEMENTS FOR TERRITORIAL TRUSTEESHIPS

Note: Documents on this subject will be available later [53]

---

[53] Notation as in original document. See, however, appendix 39, p. 606.

X

General Administration and Secretariat

A. *Office of Director-General and the Central Administrative Staff*

1. A director-general of the international organization should be elected by the general assembly with the concurrence of the executive council. He should serve for a period of five years and should be eligible for re-election.

2. The director-general should have the responsibilities of the chief administrative officer of the organization. He should serve as the secretary-general of the general assembly, of the executive council, and of such other organs and agencies of the international organization as the assembly or the council may direct. He should also provide for coordination, within the general policies appertaining to administration established by the general assembly, of the administrative procedures and regulations of the specialized agencies brought into relationship with the international organization. He should report to the general assembly on the work of all the organs and agencies of the organization and of commissions, agencies, and other bodies of concern to the international organization.

3. The director-general should appoint such deputies and principal officers of the central administrative staff as may be required, subject to confirmation by the general assembly, and such other personnel of secretariats for which he is responsible. He should recommend for appointment by the general assembly or the executive council respectively the directors of commissions and agencies responsible respectively to these two organs.

4. The director-general and his deputies should not during their terms of office hold any other public office.

5. Officers appointed to the central administrative staff should be selected on the basis of technical or administrative competence and experience, and of the widest practicable distribution among nationalities. These officials should be constituted as a continuing international civil service, and they should upon their appointment pledge themselves to perform the duties entrusted to them in the impartial manner and spirit necessary to advance the interests and purposes of the international organization.

B. *Obligations of Member States With Respect to Officials of the Organization*

1. Member states should impose no obligations upon their nationals who are officials of the international organization that are inconsistent with the performance of their duties.

2. Member states should grant the customary diplomatic immunities to officials of the international organization when engaged on business of the international organization or when traveling to and from their offices.

XI

Procedure of Establishment and Inauguration

1. The general international organization for the maintenance of peace and security projected in the Four-Nation Declaration signed at Moscow, October 30, 1943, should be established at the earliest practicable date—if feasible, prior to the termination of hostilities.

2. The United States of America, the United Kingdom of Great Britain and Northern Ireland, the Union of Soviet Socialist Republics, and the Republic of China, the signatories of the Four-Nation Declaration, should take immediate

steps to reach agreement in principle on the fundamental features of a plan of the organization.

3. An agreed statement of the fundamental features of the plan of the organization should then be transmitted to the governments of the other United Nations and the nations associated with them, together with an invitation to communicate comments and suggestions for the purpose of arriving at a substantial consensus of views on the fundamental features of the plan.

4. As soon as practicable, the signatories of the Four-Nation Declaration should convene a conference of the United Nations and the nations associated with them for the formulation and signature of an agreement which would constitute the basic instrument of the organization. The agreement should be submitted to the participating governments for ratification in accordance with their respective constitutional procedures.

5. Provision should be made in the agreement for its coming into force when ratified by fifteen states including the signatories of the Four-Nation Declaration.

6. The signatories of the Four-Nation Declaration should be empowered by the agreement to call the first meeting of the general assembly of the organization under the agreement upon its coming into force.

7. The general assembly should elect at its first meeting the non-continuing members of the executive council, and the council should thereupon immediately come into existence and proceed to organize itself.

APPENDIX 39
July 6, 1944 [54]

IX. Arrangements for Territorial Trusteeships

A. *Scope and Purposes*

1. Subject to such exceptions as may be made by common agreement in the interests of international peace and security, the international organization should establish a system of international trusteeship by which it would (a) succeed to the rights, titles, and interests of the Principal Allied and Associated Powers under the Treaty of Versailles and the Treaty of Lausanne and to the rights and responsibilities of the League of Nations under the Covenant with respect to the non-self-governing territories detached from previous sovereigns in 1919, and (b) acquire authority over certain territories which may be detached from the present enemy states. By action of the general assembly the system might be extended to any territories for which assistance is requested by member states having control over such territories. Italy and Japan should be required by the terms of the peace settlement to relinquish all their rights, titles, and interests in the present mandated territories.

2. The basic objectives of the trusteeship system should be: (a) to promote, in accordance with the provisions of any declaration or code that may be agreed upon, the political, economic, and social advancement of the trust territories and their. inhabitants and their progressive development toward self-government;

---

[54] Projected Chapter IX on Trusteeship as prepared prior to the Dumbarton Oaks Conversations.

(b) to provide non-discriminatory treatment in trust territories for appropriate activities of the nationals of all member states; and (c) to further international peace and security.

B. *Structure and Composition*

1. The responsibilities of trusteeship should be vested in the general assembly and should be exercised through a trusteeship council and through administering authorities in the trust territories.

2. The trusteeship council should be composed of persons of special competence designated (a) one each by the states administering trust territories as continuing members and (b) one each by an equal number of other states named periodically for that purpose by the general assembly.

3. The administering authority in each trust territory should be a state or a specially constituted international administration. Each territory now administered under a mandate, except those so administered by Japan, should be administered under the trusteeship arrangements by the state which now administers it, unless in a particular case or cases some other disposal is made by the international organization.

4. Each territory should be governed in accordance with a territorial charter, which should constitute the fundamental law of the territory, defining the rights and obligations of the parties concerned. Each charter should be so drawn as to take into account the special circumstances of each territory.

C. *Powers*

. 1. The general assembly should be empowered: (a) to call for, receive, and consider the reports, recommendations, and decisions of the trusteeship council; (b) to take action upon the recommendations of the trusteeship council concerning the initial territorial charters, alterations in such charters, designation of administering authorities, removal of such authorities for cause, and the conditions of termination and the act of termination of trusteeship in any territory; (c) to establish advisory commissions of a regional or technical character with respect to trust territories situated in a given region; and (d) to encourage and facilitate cooperation between the administering authorities and the specialized agencies brought into relationship with the international organization.

2. The trusteeship council exercising general supervision over trust territories, should be empowered: (a) to advise the administering authorities; (b) to examine reports from the administering authorities; (c) to interrogate representatives of those authorities; (d) at its discretion, to receive petitions and to hear petitioners in person; (e) to recommend or pass upon economic projects of more than a minor local character and to conduct investigations relevant to such projects; (f) to conduct periodic inspections in the trust territories; and (g) to make recommendations to the general assembly regarding the territorial charters, the administering authorities, and other aspects of the trusteeship system.

D. *Procedures*

1. The financial position of each trust territory should be reviewed periodically by the trusteeship council. The costs of administration should in general be met from the regular revenues of the trust territory, and the costs of supervision should be provided in the budget of the international organization.

2. The administering authorities should cooperate fully in the application of any international security measures specified by the executive council.

Memorandum [from Secretary Hull] for the President

We have developed the following plans for handling the forthcoming discussions with the British, Russians, and Chinese on the subject of international organization and security:

Plan for discussions

The discussions, which are scheduled to begin on August 2, are envisaged as an informal interchange of views at a high diplomatic level, relating both to basic policies and to technical questions. It is contemplated that the order of the discussions will follow three phases: (1) consideration of basic policies; (2) detailed technical discussions in separate groups, based on the discussion of basic policies; and (3) further consideration of basic policies in the light of the detailed technical discussions.

The topics to be discussed fall naturally into three broad categories: (1) the structure and establishment of the proposed international organization, (2) arrangements for pacific settlement of disputes, and (3) security arrangements. The detailed discussions would be conducted in three separate sections corresponding to these categories, as indicated in the attached tentative agenda.

Assignments of American group

The Secretary of State would be the senior American representative. He would have general direction of the proceedings and would preside over the first and third phases of the discussions.

The Under Secretary of State would head the American group responsible for the detailed technical discussions and would be chairman of the third section, to which the detailed technical discussions of security arrangements is assigned.

It is contemplated that, in the American-British-Soviet phase of the discussions, a British official would be chairman of the first section and a Soviet official would be chairman of the second section. In the American-British-Chinese phase, a Chinese official would be chairman of the second group.

The American group would be assigned to the three sections as follows:

First section: Messrs. Bowman, Grew, and Pasvolsky.
Second section: Messrs. Hackworth, Hornbeck and Cohen.
Third section: Messrs. Stettinius, Dunn and Wilson, Admirals Hepburn, Willson and Train, and Generals Embick, Strong and Fairchild.

Members of all sections and Assistant Secretary of State Long would be present at the first and third phases of the discussions.

Advisers and Secretariat

The American group would have advisers and a secretariat to assist them in preparation for and in the conduct of the discussions. Arrangements would be made for the assignment of Army and Navy officers to the secretariat. This secretariat would also function as the secretariat for the discussions. The advisers would be Mr. Notter and officers of the four geographic offices of the Department. Mr. Alger Hiss would act as executive secretary.

Arrangements

Tentative arrangements have been made for using Dumbarton Oaks in Georgetown, the former estate of Mr. Robert Woods Bliss, now the property of Harvard University, as headquarters for the discussions.

Meetings might be held there for a few hours in the latter part of each morning and afternoon, with luncheon and perhaps tea being served. There would be a few offices available for consultation and immediate drafting needs, but the groups representing the other nations would presumably do the major part of their separate drafting in their own embassies before and after the daily meetings.

Preparatory period

The members of the American group would immediately organize themselves in three committees, corresponding to the three sections. Mr. Stettinius would take general charge of the necessary preparations for the discussions and would look to Mr. Pasvolsky as responsible for the activities of the first committee; Mr. Hackworth for the second; and Mr. Dunn for the third. We are planning to have the entire group meet once a week with the Secretary of State. There would also be a small informal steering committee, both for the period of preparation and of actual discussions. It would be under the chairmanship of the Secretary with Mr. Stettinius as vice chairman. Its members would be Messrs. Dunn, Hackworth, Pasvolsky, Admiral Willson and General Strong.

I hope that these arrangements meet with your approval.

TENTATIVE AGENDA

I. The structure and establishment of the proposed international organization.

1. General structure and scope of the organization.
2. Membership, functions, powers, and voting procedures of a general assembly.
3. Membership, functions, powers, and voting procedures of a smaller executive body (executive council).
4. Administration and secretariat of the organization.
5. Arrangements for coordination of economic and other functional activities and agencies, and the relation of such agencies and of any regional arrangements to the general organization.
6. Procedure of establishment and inauguration of the Organization.

II. Arrangements for pacific settlement of disputes.

1. Methods of pacific settlement.
2. Procedures, regional and otherwise, outside the central organization.
3. Procedures in the council and in the assembly.
4. The structure and functions of the Court of Justice.

III. Security arrangements.

1. Scope and character of joint action with respect to
   a. Determination of threats to or breaches of the peace;
   b. Prevention or suppression of such threats or breaches;
   c. Enforcement of decisions.
2. Methods of joint action.
   a. Not involving use of armed forces.
   b. Involving use of armed forces.
3. Arrangements for provision of armed forces and facilities.
4. Relationship to mutual defense and regional systems.

5. Arrangements for the regulation of armaments and the manufacture of and traffic in arms.

6. Structure and functions of an armaments and security commission.

7. Interim arrangements pending the effective functioning in the field of security of the general organization.

APPENDIX 41
March 10, 1949[55]

Example of Bracketing

An example of bracketing is shown below by tracing the development during the Conversations of three sentences of paragraph 9, Section B, Chapter VIII of the Dumbarton Oaks Proposals.

September 4 draft:

"There should be a military committee the functions of which should be to advise and assist the council on all questions relating to the employment [and command] of forces placed at the disposal of the council [and relating to the regulation of armaments and armed forces]. [It should be responsible under the council for the strategic direction of any armed forces placed at the disposal of the council.] The committee should be composed [initially] of the Chiefs of Staff of the permanent members of the council or their representatives. . . ."

September 10 draft:

"There should be a military committee the functions of which should be to advise and assist the council on all questions relating to the council's military requirements for the maintenance of peace and security, to the employment [and command] of forces placed at its disposal, to disarmament and to the regulation of armaments. [It should be responsible under the council for the strategic direction of any armed forces placed at the disposal of the council.] The Committee should be composed of the Chiefs of Staff of the permanent members of the council or their representatives. . . ."

September 20 draft:

"There should be a Military Staff Committee the functions of which should be to advise and assist the Security Council on all questions relating to the Security Council's military requirements for the maintenance of peace and security, to the employment and command of forces placed at its disposal, [to disarmament] and to the regulation of armaments. It should be responsible under the Security Council for the strategic direction of any armed forces placed at the disposal of the Security Council. The Committee should be composed of the Chiefs of Staff of the permanent members of the Security Council or their representatives. . . ."

Final draft as it appeared in the Proposals:

"There should be established a Military Staff Committee the functions of which should be to advise and assist the Security Council on all questions relating to the Security Council's military requirements for the maintenance of international peace and security, to the employment and command of forces placed at its

---

[55] Compilation prepared for this book.

disposal, to the regulation of armaments, and to possible disarmament. It should be responsible under the Security Council for the strategic direction of any armed forces placed at the disposal of the Security Council. The Committee should be composed of the Chiefs of Staff of the permanent members of the Security Council or their representatives. . . ."

APPENDIX 42
September 13, 1944 [56]

Compromise Proposal

C. VOTING

1. Each member of the Security Council should have one vote.

2. Decisions with respect to the following matters should be taken by _____ _____ majority vote including the concurring votes of the permanent members of the Security Council:

a. All decisions coming under Section VIII–B, entitled "Determination of Threats to the Peace, Acts of Aggression, or any Breaches of the Peace, and Action with Respect Thereto", and under Section VIII–C, entitled "Regional Arrangements."

b. All matters relating to [disarmament] and regulation of armaments.

c. Recommendations to the General Assembly with regard to admission of new members, suspension and restoration of rights of membership, and expulsion of members.

d. Establishment by the Security Council of its subsidiary bodies or agencies.

3. Decisions under Section VIII–A, entitled "Pacific Settlement of Disputes", should be taken by _____ majority including the concurring votes of the permanent members of the Council, but excluding the votes of such member or members of the council as are parties to the dispute.

4. All other decisions should be taken by _____ majority vote.

APPENDIX 43
October 7, 1944

[The Dumbarton Oaks] Proposals for the Establishment of a General International Organization

There should be established an international organization under the title of the United Nations, the Charter of which should contain provisions necessary to give effect to the proposals which follow.

CHAPTER I. Purposes

The purposes of the Organization should be:

1. To maintain international peace and security; and to that end to take effective collective measures for the prevention and removal of threats to the

---

[56] Informal paper developed during Dumbarton Oaks Conversations.

peace and the suppression of acts of aggression or other breaches of the peace, and to bring about by peaceful means adjustment or settlement of international disputes which may lead to a breach of the peace;

2. To develop friendly relations among nations and to take other appropriate measures to strengthen universal peace;

3. To achieve international cooperation in the solution of international economic, social and other humanitarian problems; and

4. To afford a center for harmonizing the actions of nations in the achievement of these common ends.

CHAPTER II. Principles

In pursuit of the purposes mentioned in Chapter I the Organization and its members should act in accordance with the following principles:

1. The Organization is based on the principle of the sovereign equality of all peace-loving states.

2. All members of the Organization undertake, in order to ensure to all of them the rights and benefits resulting from membership in the Organization, to fulfill the obligations assumed by them in accordance with the Charter.

3. All members of the Organization shall settle their disputes by peaceful means in such a manner that international peace and security are not endangered.

4. All members of the Organization shall refrain in their international relations from the threat or use of force in any manner inconsistent with the purposes of the Organization.

5. All members of the Organization shall give every assistance to the Organization in any action undertaken by it in accordance with the provisions of the Charter.

6. All members of the Organization shall refrain from giving assistance to any state against which preventive or enforcement action is being undertaken by the Organization.

The Organization should ensure that states not members of the Organization act in accordance with these principles so far as may be necessary for the maintenance of international peace and security.

CHAPTER III. Membership

1. Membership of the Organization should be open to all peace-loving states.

CHAPTER IV. Principal Organs

1. The Organization should have as its principal organs:

    a. A General Assembly;

    b. A Security Council;

    c. An international court of justice; and

    d. A Secretariat.

2. The Organization should have such subsidiary agencies as may be found necessary.

CHAPTER V. The General Assembly

Section A. Composition

All members of the Organization should be members of the General Assembly and should have a number of representatives to be specified in the Charter.

Section B. Functions and Powers

1. The General Assembly should have the right to consider the general principles of cooperation in the maintenance of international peace and security,

including the principles governing disarmament and the regulation of armaments; to discuss any questions relating to the maintenance of international peace and security brought before it by any member or members of the Organization or by the Security Council; and to make recommendations with regard to any such principles or questions. Any such questions on which action is necessary should be referred to the Security Council by the General Assembly either before or after discussion. The General Assembly should not on its own initiative make recommendations on any matter relating to the maintenance of international peace and security which is being dealt with by the Security Council.

2. The General Assembly should be empowered to admit new members to the Organization upon recommendation of the Security Council.

3. The General Assembly should, upon recommendation of the Security Council, be empowered to suspend from the exercise of any rights or privileges of membership any member of the Organization against which preventive or enforcement action shall have been taken by the Security Council. The exercise of the rights and privileges thus suspended may be restored by decision of the Security Council. The General Assembly should be empowered, upon recommendation of the Security Council, to expel from the Organization any member of the Organization which persistently violates the principles contained in the Charter.

4. The General Assembly should elect the non-permanent members of the Security Council and the members of the Economic and Social Council provided for in Chapter IX. It should be empowered to elect, upon recommendation of the Security Council, the Secretary-General of the Organization. It should perform such functions in relation to the election of the judges of the international court of justice as may be conferred upon it by the statute of the court.

5. The General Assembly should apportion the expenses among the members of the Organization and should be empowered to approve the budgets of the Organization.

6. The General Assembly should initiate studies and make recommendations for the purpose of promoting international cooperation in political, economic and social fields and of adjusting situations likely to impair the general welfare.

7. The General Assembly should make recommendations for the coordination of the policies of international economic, social, and other specialized agencies brought into relation with the Organization in accordance with agreements between such agencies and the Organization.

8. The General Assembly should receive and consider annual and special reports from the Security Council and reports from other bodies of the Organization.

Section C. Voting

1. Each member of the Organization should have one vote in the General Assembly.

2. Important decisions of the General Assembly, including recommendations with respect to the maintenance of international peace and security; election of members of the Security Council; election of members of the Economic and Social Council; admission of members, suspension of the exercise of the rights and privileges of members, and expulsion of members; and budgetary questions, should be made by a two-thirds majority of those present and voting. On other questions, including the determination of additional categories of questions to be decided by a two-thirds majority, the decisions of the General Assembly should be made by a simple majority vote.

Section D. Procedure

1. The General Assembly should meet in regular annual sessions and in such special sessions as occasion may require.

2. The General Assembly should adopt its own rules of procedure and elect its President for each session.

3. The General Assembly should be empowered to set up such bodies and agencies as it may deem necessary for the performance of its functions.

CHAPTER VI. The Security Council

Section A. Composition

The Security Council should consist of one representative of each of eleven members of the Organization. Representatives of the United States of America, the United Kingdom of Great Britain and Northern Ireland, the Union of Soviet Socialist Republics, the Republic of China, and, in due course, France, should have permanent seats. The General Assembly should elect six states to fill the non-permanent seats. These six states should be elected for a term of two years, three retiring each year. They should not be immediately eligible for reelection. In the first election of the non-permanent members three should be chosen by the General Assembly for one-year terms and three for two-year terms.

Section B. Principal Functions and Powers

1. In order to ensure prompt and effective action by the Organization, members of the Organization should by the Charter confer on the Security Council primary responsibility for the maintenance of international peace and security and should agree that in carrying out these duties under this responsibility it should act on their behalf.

2. In discharging these duties the Security Council should act in accordance with the purposes and principles of the Organization.

3. The specific powers conferred on the Security Council in order to carry out these duties are laid down in Chapter VIII.

4. All members of the Organization should obligate themselves to accept the decisions of the Security Council and to carry them out in accordance with the provisions of the Charter.

5. In order to promote the establishment and maintenance of international peace and security with the least diversion of the world's human and economic resources for armaments, the Security Council, with the assistance of the Military Staff Committee referred to in Chapter VIII, Section B, paragraph 9, should have the responsibility for formulating plans for the establishment of a system of regulation of armaments for submission to the members of the Organization.

Section C. Voting

(NOTE.—The question of voting procedure in the Security Council is still under consideration.)

Section D. Procedure

1. The Security Council should be so organized as to be able to function continuously and each state member of the Security Council should be permanently represented at the headquarters of the Organization. It may hold meetings at such other places as in its judgment may best facilitate its work. There should be periodic meetings at which each state member of the Security Council could if it so desired be represented by a member of the government or some other special representative.

2. The Security Council should be empowered to set up such bodies or agencies as it may deem necessary for the performance of its functions including regional subcommittees of the Military Staff Committee.

3. The Security Council should adopt its own rules of procedure, including the method of selecting its President.

4. Any member of the Organization should participate in the discussion of any question brought before the Security Council whenever the Security Council considers that the interests of that member of the Organization are specially affected.

5. Any member of the Organization not having a seat on the Security Council and any state not a member of the Organization, if it is a party to a dispute under consideration by the Security Council, should be invited to participate in the discussion relating to the dispute.

CHAPTER VII. An International Court of Justice

1. There should be an international court of justice which should constitute the principal judicial organ of the Organization.

2. The court should be constituted and should function in accordance with a statute which should be annexed to and be a part of the Charter of the Organization.

3. The statute of the court of international justice should be either (a) the Statute of the Permanent Court of International Justice, continued in force with such modifications as may be desirable or (b) a new statute in the preparation of which the Statute of the Permanent Court of International Justice should be used as a basis.

4. All members of the Organization should ipso facto be parties to the statute of the international court of justice.

5. Conditions under which states not members of the Organization may become parties to the statute of the international court of justice should be determined in each case by the General Assembly upon recommendation of the Security Council.

CHAPTER VIII. Arrangements for the Maintenance of International Peace and Security Including Prevention and Suppression of Aggression.

Section A. Pacific Settlement of Disputes

1. The Security Council should be empowered to investigate any dispute, or any situation which may lead to international friction or give rise to a dispute, in order to determine whether its continuance is likely to endanger the maintenance of international peace and security.

2. Any state, whether member of the Organization or not, may bring any such dispute or situation to the attention of the General Assembly or of the Security Council.

3. The parties to any dispute the continuance of which is likely to endanger the maintenance of international peace and security should obligate themselves, first of all, to seek a solution by negotiation, mediation, conciliation, arbitration or judicial settlement, or other peaceful means of their own choice. The Security Council should call upon the parties to settle their dispute by such means.

4. If, nevertheless, parties to a dispute of the nature referred to in paragraph 3 above fail to settle it by the means indicated in that paragraph, they should obligate themselves to refer it to the Security Council. The Security Council should in each case decide whether or not the continuance of the particular

dispute is in fact likely to endanger the maintenance of international peace and security, and, accordingly, whether the Security Council should deal with the dispute, and, if so, whether it should take action under paragraph 5.

5. The Security Council should be empowered, at any stage of a dispute of the nature referred to in paragraph 3 above, to recommend appropriate procedures or methods of adjustment.

6. Justiciable disputes should normally be referred to the international court of justice. The Security Council should be empowered to refer to the court, for advice, legal questions connected with other disputes.

7. The provisions of paragraph 1 to 6 of Section A should not apply to situations or disputes arising out of matters which by international law are solely within the domestic jurisdiction of the state concerned.

Section B. Determination of Threats to the Peace or Acts of Aggression and Action With Respect Thereto

1. Should the Security Council deem that a failure to settle a dispute in accordance with procedures indicated in paragraph 3 of Section A, or in accordance with its recommendations made under paragraph 5 of Section A, constitutes a threat to the maintenance of international peace and security, it should take any measures necessary for the maintenance of international peace and security in accordance with the purposes and principles of the Organization.

2. In general the Security Council should determine the existence of any threat to the peace, breach of the peace or act of aggression and should make recommendations or decide upon the measures to be taken to maintain or restore peace and security.

3. The Security Council should be empowered to determine what diplomatic, economic, or other measures not involving the use of armed force should be employed to give effect to its decisions, and to call upon members of the Organization to apply such measures. Such measures may include complete or partial interruption of rail, sea, air, postal, telegraphic, radio and other means of communication and the severance of diplomatic and economic relations.

4. Should the Security Council consider such measures to be inadequate, it should be empowered to take such action by air, naval or land forces as may be necessary to maintain or restore international peace and security. Such action may include demonstrations, blockade and other operations by air, sea or land forces of members of the Organization.

5. In order that all members of the Organization should contribute to the maintenance of international peace and security, they should undertake to make available to the Security Council, on its call and in accordance with a special agreement or agreements concluded among themselves, armed forces, facilities and assistance necessary for the purpose of maintaining international peace and security. Such agreement or agreements should govern the numbers and types of forces and the nature of the facilities and assistance to be provided. The special agreement or agreements should be negotiated as soon as possible and should in each case be subject to approval by the Security Council and to ratification by the signatory states in accordance with their constitutional processes.

6. In order to enable urgent military measures to be taken by the Organization there should be held immediately available by the members of the Organization national air force contingents for combined international enforcement action. The strength and degree of readiness of these contingents and plans for their combined action should be determined by the Security Council with the assistance of the Military Staff Committee within the limits laid down in the special agreement or agreements referred to in paragraph 5 above.

7. The action required to carry out the decisions of the Security Council for the maintenance of international peace and security should be taken by all the members of the Organization in cooperation or by some of them as the Security Council may determine. This undertaking should be carried out by the members of the Organization by their own action and through action of the appropriate specialized organizations and agencies of which they are members.

8. Plans for the application of armed force should be made by the Security Council with the assistance of the Military Staff Committee referred to in paragraph 9 below.

9. There should be established a Military Staff Committee the functions of which should be to advise and assist the Security Council on all questions relating to the Security Council's military requirements for the maintenance of international peace and security, to the employment and command of forces placed at its disposal, to the regulation of armaments, and to possible disarmament. It should be responsible under the Security Council for the strategic direction of any armed forces placed at the disposal of the Security Council. The Committee should be composed of the Chiefs of Staff of the permanent members of the Security Council or their representatives. Any member of the Organization not permanently represented on the Committee should be invited by the Committee to be associated with it when the efficient discharge of the Committee's responsibilities requires that such a state should participate in its work. Questions of command of forces should be worked out subsequently.

10. The members of the Organization should join in affording mutual assistance in carrying out the measures decided upon by the Security Council.

11. Any state, whether a member of the Organization or not, which finds itself confronted with special economic problems arising from the carrying out of measures which have been decided upon by the Security Council should have the right to consult the Security Council in regard to a solution of those problems.

Section C. Regional Arrangements.

1. Nothing in the Charter should preclude the existence of regional arrangements or agencies for dealing with such matters relating to the maintenance of international peace and security as are appropriate for regional action, provided such arrangements or agencies and their activities are consistent with the purposes and principles of the Organization. The Security Council should encourage settlement of local disputes through such regional arrangements or by such regional agencies, either on the initiative of the states concerned or by reference from the Security Council.

2. The Security Council should, where appropriate, utilize such arrangements or agencies for enforcement action under its authority, but no enforcement action should be taken under regional arrangements or by regional agencies without the authorization of the Security Council.

3. The Security Council should at all times be kept fully informed of activities undertaken or in contemplation under regional arrangements or by regional agencies for the maintenance of international peace and security.

CHAPTER IX. Arrangements for International Economic and Social Cooperation

Section A. Purpose and Relationships

1. With a view to the creation of conditions of stability and well-being which are necessary for peaceful and friendly relations among nations, the Organization should facilitate solutions of international economic, social and other humanitarian problems and promote respect for human rights and fundamental free-

doms. Responsibility for the discharge of this function should be vested in the General Assembly and, under the authority of the General Assembly, in an Economic and Social Council.

2. The various specialized economic, social and other organizations and agencies would have responsibilities in their respective fields as defined in their statutes. Each such organization or agency should be brought into relationship with the Organization on terms to be determined by agreement between the Economic and Social Council and the appropriate authorities of the specialized organization or agency, subject to approval by the General Assembly.

Section B. Composition and Voting

The Economic and Social Council should consist of representatives of eighteen members of the Organization. The states to be represented for this purpose should be elected by the General Assembly for terms of three years. Each such state should have one representative, who should have one vote. Decisions of the Economic and Social Council should be taken by simple majority vote of those present and voting.

Section C. Functions and Powers of the Economic and Social Council

1. The Economic and Social Council should be empowered:

   a. to carry out, within the scope of its functions, recommendations of the General Assembly;
   b. to make recommendations, on its own initiative, with respect to international economic, social and other humanitarian matters;
   c. to receive and consider reports from the economic, social and other organizations or agencies brought into relationship with the Organization, and to coordinate their activities through consultations with, and recommendations to, such organizations or agencies;
   d. to examine the administrative budgets of such specialized organizations or agencies with a view to making recommendations to the organizations or agencies concerned;
   e. to enable the Secretary-General to provide information to the Security Council;
   f. to assist the Security Council upon its request; and
   g. to perform such other functions within the general scope of its competence as may be assigned to it by the General Assembly.

Section D. Organization and Procedure

1. The Economic and Social Council should set up an economic commission, a social commission, and such other commissions as may be required. These commissions should consist of experts. There should be a permanent staff which should constitute a part of the Secretariat of the Organization.

2. The Economic and Social Council should make suitable arrangements for representatives of the specialized organizations or agencies to participate without vote in its deliberations and in those of the commissions established by it.

3. The Economic and Social Council should adopt its own rules of procedure and the method of selecting its President.

CHAPTER X. The Secretariat

1. There should be a Secretariat comprising a Secretary-General and such staff as may be required. The Secretary-General should be the chief administrative officer of the Organization. He should be elected by the General Assembly, on recommendation of the Security Council, for such term and under such conditions as are specified in the Charter.

2. The Secretary-General should act in that capacity in all meetings of the General Assembly, of the Security Council, and of the Economic and Social Council and should make an annual report to the General Assembly on the work of the Organization.

3. The Secretary-General should have the right to bring to the attention of the Security Council any matter which in his opinion may threaten international peace and security.

CHAPTER XI. Amendments

Amendments should come into force for all members of the Organization, when they have been adopted by a vote of two-thirds of the members of the General Assembly and ratified in accordance with their respective constitutional processes by the members of the Organization having permanent membership on the Security Council and by a majority of the other members of the Organization.

CHAPTER XII. Transitional Arrangements

1. Pending the coming into force of the special agreement or agreements referred to in Chapter VIII, Section B, paragraph 5, and in accordance with the provisions of paragraph 5 of the Four-Nation Declaration, signed at Moscow, October 30, 1943, the states parties to that Declaration should consult with one another and as occasion arises with other members of the Organization with a view to such joint action on behalf of the Organization as may be necessary for the purpose of maintaining international peace and security.

2. No provision of the Charter should preclude action taken or authorized in relation to enemy states as a result of the present war by the Governments having responsibility for such action.

NOTE: In addition to the question of voting procedure in the Security Council referred to in Chapter VI, several other questions are still under consideration.

Washington, D. C.

APPENDIX 44
April 4, 1944 [57]

Statement of the Problem and Summary of the Issues and Recommendations on International Commodity Policy

1. *Statement of the Problem.* The case for a jointly agreed international commodity policy rests upon four sets of conditions, namely, (a) the effects of the present war in promoting a lop-sided development of raw material production, and the subsequent likelihood of serious maladjustment in the conditions of supply and demand of a number of primary commodities during the post-war period; (b) the distress conditions existing, or likely to exist, in a number of branches of primary production, due to the rapidity of peace-time changes in the basic conditions of supply and demand; (c) the relative price instability

---

[57] Paper from the Special Committee on Commodity Agreements and Methods of Trade, considered by the Post-War Programs Committee on Apr. 12, 1944. The footnote that follows in this appendix is in the original document.

of primary products, as compared to manufactured products, particularly in the course of cyclical business fluctuations; (d) the dangers inherent in allowing the further growth of unilateral national policies in support of producers of internationally-traded commodities, such as crop loans, guaranteed prices, benefit payments to producers, export subsidies, import restrictions and trade preferences.

2. *Possible Methods for Dealing with the Problem.* It has been suggested that a vigorous policy of reducing international trade barriers would be an effective means of remedying international commodity problems. In the case of commodities whose difficulties can be traced back to the growth of economic protectionism, the relationship between a liberal commercial policy and international commodity problems is obvious without further explanation, but there is reason to suppose that whatever success might be achieved along this line would not in all cases be sufficient to cope with the specific problems confronting particular branches of primary production. The basic causes of imbalance in such industries may include such factors as the opening up of new sources of supply, the development of substitutes, an unusually rapid rate of technological change in the methods of production and marketing, inadequate opportunities for high-cost factors of production to shift to alternative employments, changes in consumption habits and the dislocations attributable to major wars, as well as the pursuit of national economic policies to protect or stimulate domestic production. Where such other factors play a part, it may be necessary to supplement a liberal commercial policy with other measures of a special character, such as international commodity agreements to regulate international trade and production and designed to promote an orderly and internationally agreed adjustment of the factors of production to the changes in the market over a period of time. Properly conceived, such agreements might in periods of deflation relieve balance of payments difficulties of raw material exporting countries, and thus facilitate the progress of a general program for the relaxation of trade barriers.

Past experience with international commodity agreements tends to demonstrate, however, that such agreements may become mere instruments for maintaining the precarious position of high and low cost producers alike without adequate regard to the interests of the consuming public or the possible need for transferring the high cost elements in the industry to other fields of activity. It is desirable, therefore, to guard more systematically against the abuse of international commodity agreements in any future use which may be made of them, so as to make them conform with the broad objectives of an economy of expansion and the requirements of a liberal commercial policy.

It has also been suggested, particularly by the representatives of the United Kingdom at the Hot Springs Food Conference and in the informal joint conversations between the United States and the United Kingdom last fall, that international commodity policy ought to center around a program for international buffer stocks. Such a program would focus primarily upon the possibility of mitigating excessive price fluctuations of primary commodities with a twofold objective, namely, (a) to stabilize the conditions prevailing in the markets of particular commodities and (b) to contribute to the solution of the problem of general business fluctuations by extending the scope of buffer stocks operations to a large number of commodities. However, there are a number of difficult problems connected with international buffer stocks, which need fuller investigation before the probable effects of such a program can be measured with reasonable accuracy. Moreover, international buffer stocks do not appear to be well adapted for dealing with commodities in surplus supplies, and such commodities are likely to be most urgently in need of concerted international action.

3. *Recommended Action.* The Special Committee on Commodity Agreements believes that an adequate program for dealing with international commodity problems will require, in addition to the vigorous pursuit of a commercial policy to reduce trade barriers, other special measures to deal with particular problems. It recommends the following:

a. The establishment of an international code of principles for governing intergovernmental regulation of international trade or production in order to

i. provide opportunities for full participation in such regulation by countries representing consumer interests as well as exporting countries, and
ii. provide that increasing opportunities will be afforded under such regulation for supplying world needs from the most efficient sources of production.

b. The establishment of an intergovernmental commodity organization to

i. facilitate international cooperation in the solution of world commodity problems,
ii. participate in and supervise international commodity arrangements, whenever such arrangements are found to be necessary, and to review the operations of such arrangements in the light of the general code of principles, and
iii. investigate the possibilities of international buffer stocks operations.

The particular conditions under which intergovernmental agreements to regulate the international trade and production of particular commodities may be desirable are listed as follows:

i. to enable countries to find solutions to particular commodity problems without resorting to unilateral action having the effect of shifting the burden of their problems to other countries and thus tending to provoke retaliatory measures and international trade warfare.
ii. to prevent, or to diminish the severity of, extreme economic and political dislocations which may occur when, owing to difficulties of finding alternative employment, production adjustments cannot be effected as rapidly as required by the free play of market forces,
iii. to provide a period of transition during which, with the assistance of such national or international measures as may be appropriate, the fundamental conditions of supply and demand become readjusted to a basis conforming to the requirements of an expanding world economy.[58]

The recommendations of the Committee with respect to international buffer stocks are based upon the report of its subcommittee on buffer stocks and the discussions of this report in its meetings.

---

[58] There is at present some difference of view between the Special Committees on Cartels and Commodity Agreements as to the area of jurisdiction to which cartel policy and commodity policy respectively would apply, particularly with respect to minerals and commodities with manufactured substitutes, and the conditions under which recourse to intergovernmental agreements would be justified in this area. A joint subcommittee of the two Committees is now considering these problems.

Summary of the Interim Report of the Special Committee on Relaxation of Trade Barriers

The attached report sets forth the preliminary conclusions of the Special Committee on Relaxation of Trade Barriers, which may be summarized as follows:

I. BASIC CONSIDERATIONS

A. *Basic objectives of the United States*

A great expansion in the volume of international trade after the war will be essential to the attainment of full and effective employment in the United States and elsewhere, to the preservation of private enterprise, and to the success of an international security system to prevent future wars.

In order to create conditions favorable to the fullest possible expansion of international trade, on a nondiscriminatory basis, it will be necessary for nations to turn away from the trade-restricting and trade-diverting practices of the inter-war period and to cooperate in bringing about a reduction of the barriers to trade erected by governments during that period. International trade cannot be developed to an adequate extent unless excessive tariffs, quantitative restrictions on imports and exports, exchange controls, and other governmental devices to limit trade are substantially reduced or eliminated. Moreover, if this is not done, there may be a further strengthening of the tendency, already strong in many countries before the war, to eliminate private enterprise from international trade in favor of rigid control by the state.

B. *Influence of the United States on International Trade Policies*

The only nation capable of taking the initiative in promoting a world-wide movement toward the relaxation of trade barriers is the United States. Because of its relatively great economic strength, its favorable balance-of-payments position, and the importance of its market to the economic well-being of the rest of the world, the influence of the United States on world commercial policies far surpasses that of any other nation. While the cooperation of the United Kingdom will be essential to the success of any broad program to reduce trade barriers, the prospective postwar economic position of the United Kingdom is such that its cooperation can be obtained only if it is assured that strong leadership will be furnished by the United States.

C. *The Time Element*

The most propitious time for inaugurating a program of trade-barrier reduction would appear to be as soon as possible—preferably before the end of the war. Economic and political conditions, both national and international, are more favorable to such a program now than they have ever been in the past. It would seem desirable to take advantage of the present spirit of close international cooperation engendered by the war to reach agreement on such a program. If agreement is too long delayed, economic problems in the immediate post-war period may be handled in a way which would intensify the difficulties and postpone agreement on ultimate objectives indefinitely.

---

[59] Considered by the Post-War Programs Committee on Mar. 15, 1944.

II. MEASURES FOR THE RELAXATION OF TRADE BARRIERS—PROPOSED MULTILATERAL CONVENTION

Barriers to the expansion of world trade on a sound economic basis consist broadly of tariffs, prohibitions and quantitative restrictions on imports, export taxes and restrictions, governmental subsidization of production or exports, certain types of state trading, exchange discrimination, and the discriminatory application of trade controls generally. The Committee believes that the most promising means of reducing, eliminating or regulating these various types of trade restrictions, on a world-wide basis, is the negotiation among as many countries as possible of a multilateral convention on commercial policy. The Committee's tentative conclusions regarding the desirable scope of the provisions of such a convention are briefly as follows:

A. *Tariffs*

It is essential that the proposed convention provide for a substantial reduction of protective tariffs in all countries. Such a reduction might be accomplished at one step or by stages. The report describes a number of multilateral tariff-reduction formulas which the Committee has considered and which it is continuing to study from the viewpoint of their equity and technical soundness. The Committee is also considering, either as a necessary substitute for a multilateral tariff reduction formula or as a supplement to it, provisions whereby each nation would agree to negotiate bilateral tariff-reduction agreements with the countries supplying its imports.

B. *Prohibitions and quantitative restrictions on imports*

Prohibitions and quantitative restrictions on imports (quotas) are among the devices most destructive of international trade and least conformable to a system of private enterprise. It is believed that the proposed convention should provide for the abolition of such measures, with appropriate exceptions for quantitative restrictions on imports imposed to prevent the aggravation of a seriously adverse balance-of-payment position or to give effect to a recognized international agreement regulating the trade in particular commodities.

C. *Export taxes and restrictions*

Although export taxes and restrictions have been used only to a minor extent in the past, they are potentially of great importance, particularly for the purposes of giving indirect protection to domestic industries or semi-monopolized raw materials. It is contemplated that the convention would provide for the abolition of export taxes and restrictions with certain carefully-safeguarded exceptions (e. g. export taxes imposed for revenue purposes only and restrictions on trade in implements of war).

D. *Preferences and Discriminations*

A basic objective of the proposed convention should be the elimination of all forms of discriminatory treatment in international trade, the most important examples of which are the widespread Imperial preferential arrangements. The extent to which this can be achieved will depend in important part on how far the United States will be willing to go with regard to 1) the reduction of its tariffs; and 2) the abolition of its own preferential trade arrangements with the Philippines, the Virgin Islands and Cuba. The Committee is giving first attention to these points with a view to formulating definite recommendations.

E. *State Trading*

The objective with regard to state trading should be to establish principles for international trade between private enterprise and state-trading organizations (including complete state monopolies of foreign trade, state monopolies of trade in specific products, and nonmonopolized trading by the state), which will harmonize the commercial interests of both, prevent discrimination and increase international trade. The report tentatively recommends certain desirable principles for possible inclusion in the proposed convention.

F. *Subsidies*

Export subsidies tend to engender international ill-will and lead to retaliation, and it is contemplated that the proposed convention would contain provisions looking toward their elimination. An exception would probably be necessary for export subsidies imposed pursuant to recognized international commodity agreements. With regard to domestic subsidies, which do not result in consumer price disparities between the domestic and foreign markets, it is believed that while these are generally preferable to tariffs and other import restrictions as a means of assisting producers, they should be kept to a minimum. The Committee is considering in particular the question of setting limits to the subsidization of production of goods, especially agricultural products, of which world surpluses exist.

G. *Exchange Discrimination*

While proposals for an international currency stabilization agreement are not within its purview, the Committee has assumed that such an agreement will be concluded which will permit the substantial abolition of exchange control. The tentative recommendations in the report regarding exchange control, therefore, relate to provisions in the proposed convention designed to eliminate the discriminatory and protective aspects of such exchange controls as may be permitted by a currency stabilization agreement or imposed by countries which are not members of such an agreement.

H. *International Commercial-Policy Organization*

An international commercial-policy organization will be essential to the successful operation of the proposed convention, particularly of certain relatively important provisions requiring the assistance of an internationally representative body of experts. The general purposes of such an organization would be to 1) provide information to member countries, 2) afford a source of consistent interpretation of the convention, 3) carry out investigative and fact-finding functions, 4) adjust differences among members, and 5) recommend amendments to the convention. If international organizations are also established in the fields of commodity policy and cartel policy, some means should be found of assuring decisions by these bodies which are consistent with those of any commercial-policy organization. Moreover, it seems essential that there be close cooperation between the proposed commercial-policy organization and any organizations set up to administer international currency stabilization and international investment.

III. INTEGRATION OF DOMESTIC AND INTERNATIONAL ECONOMIC POLICIES

Domestic policies, for example to promote full employment, may have an important influence on international trade and are, therefore, a matter for international concern. Any organization set up to demobilize war industry and to promote employment should develop policies which encourage and do not obstruct the reduction of trade barriers and the expansion of international trade.

APPENDIX 46
May 29, 1944[60]

Summary: Tentative Program for Dealing With International Cartels

1. The United States should advocate, in discussions with other nations, the adoption of a co-ordinated program by which each nation undertakes to prohibit the most restrictive cartel practices which burden international trade.

2. International conventions and national laws about patents, trade marks, and company organizations should be amended or supplemented to make such restrictive cartel practices more difficult.

3. Restrictive programs undertaken for such purposes as the furtherance of international security, the conservation of natural resources, the protection of public health and morals, or the relief of insupportable distress during the application of constructive measures to shift resources from over-developed industries into more productive uses should be agreed upon between governments rather than between private interests.

4. To facilitate the development and administration of this program, there should be established an International Office for Business Practices as outlined in appendix A.[61]

Comment

These proposals are based upon conclusions that the typical effects of cartels are to reduce output, raise and stabilize selling prices, increase profit margins, reduce employment, and protect high cost members; and that through such activities cartels reduce employment and investment opportunities, hinder the development of liberal policies in international trade, delay the readjustment of dislocated industries, and sometimes thwart national policies or serve as the instrument of aggressive governments. The claims that cartels help preserve balance in international payments and that they can help solve problems of economic readjustment are regarded as unfounded.

It is recognized that pressures to organize cartels arise in large part from depressions, trade barriers, and unbalanced over-expansion of particular industries, and that the success of a program directed against cartel restrictions must depend in large part upon successful policies for coping with such matters.

---

[60] Paper from the Special Committee on Private Monopolies and Cartels, considered by the Post-War Programs Committee on June 2, 1944.
[61] Not printed.

Proposals for Consideration by an International Conference on Trade and Employment

A. NEED FOR INTERNATIONAL ECONOMIC COOPERATION

1. Collective measures to safeguard the peoples of the world against threats to peace and to reach just settlements of disputes among nations must be based not only on international machinery to deal directly with disputes and to prevent aggression, but also on economic cooperation among nations with the object of preventing and removing economic and social maladjustments, of achieving fairness and equity in economic relations between states, and of raising the level of economic well-being among all peoples.

2. Important contributions have already been made toward the attainment of these objectives. The Food and Agriculture Organization of the United Nations has been established. An International Monetary Fund to maintain reasonable exchange stability and facilitate adjustment in the balance of payments of member countries, and an International Bank for Reconstruction and Development to provide financial resources on a cooperative basis for those purposes are awaiting the action of governments required for their establishment.

3. In order to reach the objectives of the Atlantic Charter and Article VII of the mutual-aid agreements, it is essential that the cooperative economic measures already taken or recommended be supplemented by further measures dealing directly with trade barriers and discriminations which stand in the way of an expansion of multilateral trade and by an undertaking on the part of nations to seek full employment.

4. Cooperative action with respect to trade and employment is indispensable to the success of such other measures as those dealing with monetary and exchange stability and the flow of investment capital. Effective action in regard to employment and to trade barriers and discriminations must, therefore, be taken or the whole program of international economic cooperation will fail, and an economic environment conducive to the maintenance of peaceful international relations will not be created.

B. PROPOSALS CONCERNING EMPLOYMENT

Since high and stable levels of employment are a necessary condition for an enlarged volume of trade, and since problems of trade and employment are to be considered jointly at an international conference, the following propositions are advanced.

Governing Principles

1. It is recognized that:

a. In all countries high and stable employment is a main condition for the attainment of satisfactory levels of living.

b. The attainment of approximately full employment by the major industrial and trading nations, and its maintenance on a reasonably assured basis, are essential to the expansion of international trade on which the full

---

[62] Made public by the Secretary of State, Dec. 6, 1945.

prosperity of these and other nations depends; to the full realization of the objectives of all liberal international agreements in such fields as commercial policy, commodity problems, restrictive business practices, monetary stabilization, and investment; and, therefore, to the preservation of world peace and security.

2. Domestic programs to expand employment should be consistent with realization of the purposes of liberal international agreements and compatible with the economic well-being of other nations.

3. It is recognized that the adoption of the Bretton Woods Agreements and of measures to reduce restrictions on trade will contribute substantially to the maintenance of productive employment.

4. The United Nations have pledged, in the Charter of the United Nations Organization, to take joint and separate action in cooperation with the Organization to achieve the economic and social purposes of the United Nations, including higher standards of living, full employment, and conditions of economic and social progress and development.

Effectuation of Aims

There should be an undertaking that:

1. Each of the signatory nations will take action designed to achieve and maintain full employment within its own jurisdiction, through measures appropriate to its political and economic institutions.

2. No nation will seek to maintain employment through measures which are likely to create unemployment in other countries or which are incompatible with international undertakings designed to promote an expanding volume of international trade and investment in accordance with comparative efficiencies of production.

3. Signatory nations will make arrangements, both individually and collaboratively under the general sponsorship of the Economic and Social Council of the United Nations Organization, for the collection, analysis, and exchange of information on employment problems, trends, and policies.

4. Signatory nations will, under the general sponsorship of the Economic and Social Council, consult regularly on employment problems and hold special conferences in case of threat of widespread unemployment.

C. PROPOSALS CONCERNING AN INTERNATIONAL TRADE ORGANIZATION

Need for an International Trade Organization

1. Measures designed to effect an expansion of trade are essential because of their direct contribution to maximum levels of employment, production and consumption. Since such expansion can only be attained by collective measures, in continuous operation and adaptable to economic changes, it is necessary to establish permanent machinery for international collaboration in matters affecting international commerce, with a view to continuous consultation, the provision of expert advice, the formulation of agreed policies, procedures and plans, and to the development of agreed rules of conduct in regard to matters affecting international trade.

2. It is accordingly proposed that there be created an International Trade Organization of the United Nations, the members of which would undertake to

conduct their international commercial policies and relations in accordance with agreed principles to be set forth in the articles of the Organization. These principles, in order to make possible an effective expansion of world production, employment, exchange, and consumption, should:

>   *a.* Provide an equitable basis for dealing with the problems of governmental measures affecting international trade;
>   *b.* Provide for the curbing of restrictive trade practices resulting from private international business arrangements; and
>   *c.* Govern the institution and operation of intergovernmental commodity arrangements.

Proposed International Trade Organization

There follows an outline of the principles which it is proposed should be incorporated in the articles of the Organization.

Chapter I

Purposes

The purposes of the Organization should be:

1. To promote international commercial cooperation by establishing machinery for consultation and collaboration among member governments regarding the solution of problems in the field of international commercial policies and relations.

2. To enable members to avoid recourse to measures destructive of world commerce by providing, on a reciprocal and mutually advantageous basis, expanding opportunities for their trade and economic development.

3. To facilitate access by all members, on equal terms, to the trade and to the raw materials of the world which are needed for their economic prosperity.

4. In general, to promote national and international action for the expansion of the production, exchange and consumption of goods, for the reduction of tariffs and other trade barriers, and for the elimination of all forms of discriminatory treatment in international commerce; thus contributing to an expanding world economy, to the establishment and maintenance in all countries of high levels of employment and real income, and to the creation of economic conditions conducive to the maintenance of world peace.

Chapter II

Membership

The original members of the Organization should be those countries participating in the Conference on Trade and Employment which accept membership.

Chapter III

General Commercial Policy

Section A. General Commercial Provisions

Members should undertake:

1. To accord to products imported from other members treatment no less favorable than that accorded to domestic products with regard to matters affecting the internal taxation and regulation of the trade in goods.

2. To provide, for products in transit through their territories, coming from or going to other members, freedom from customs and transit duties, from unreasonable transit charges, and from discriminatory treatment of all kinds.

3. To subscribe to a general definition of the circumstances under which anti-dumping and countervailing duties may properly be applied to products imported from other members.

4. To give effect, as soon as practicable, to agreed principles of tariff valuation designed to assure the use of true commercial values as a basis for assessing duties, and to cooperate with other members and with the Organization in working out internationally acceptable valuation procedures of a standardized character.

5. To give effect, as soon as practicable, to agreed principles looking toward the simplification of customs formalities with a view to eliminating unnecessary requirements which afford an indirect protection to domestic products.

6. To eliminate excessive requirements regarding marks of origin in so far as they affect products imported from other members.

7. To refrain from governmentally financed or organized boycotts or campaigns designed to discourage, directly or indirectly, importation or consumption of products of other members.

8. To provide for adequate publicity regarding laws and regulations affecting foreign trade, and to maintain or establish national tribunals of an independent character to review and correct administrative customs action.

9. To transmit to the Organization appropriate trade information and statistics.

10. To cooperate with the Organization and with other members in carrying out or implementing the articles of the Organization.

Section B. Tariffs and Preferences

1. *Import tariffs and preferences.* In the light of the principles set forth in Article VII of the mutual aid agreements, members should enter into arrangements for the substantial reduction of tariffs and for the elimination of tariff preferences, action for the elimination of tariff preferences being taken in conjunction with adequate measures for the substantial reduction of barriers to world trade, as part of the mutually advantageous arrangements contemplated in this document.

As an initial step in the process of eliminating tariff preferences it should be agreed that:

    a. Existing international commitments will not be permitted to stand in the way of action agreed upon with respect to tariff preferences.

    b. All negotiated reductions in most-favored-nation tariffs will operate automatically to reduce or eliminate margins of preference.

    c. Margins of preference on any product will in no case be increased and no new preferences will be introduced.

2. *Export tariffs and preferences.* Export duties should be open to negotiation in the same way as import duties. Members should undertake not to impose or maintain export duties which differentiate by reference to the destinations to which the goods are exported.

3. *Emergency action.* Commitments with regard to tariffs should permit countries to take temporary action to prevent sudden and widespread injury to the producers concerned. Undertakings for reducing tariffs should therefore contain an escape clause to cover such contingencies.

Section C. Quantitative Trade Restrictions

1. *General elimination of quantitative restrictions.* Except as provided for elsewhere in this Chapter, members should undertake not to maintain any

quotas, embargoes, or other quantitative restrictions on their export or import trade with other members. This undertaking should not, however, apply to the following:

a. Import and export prohibitions or restrictions, imposed during the early postwar transitional period, which are essential to (a) the efficient use of shipping space in short supply, (b) the equitable international distribution of products in short supply, or (c) the orderly liquidation of temporary surpluses of government stocks accumulated as a result of the war. Such prohibitions and restrictions should be removed not later than three years after the close of hostilities, but provision should be made whereby this period may be extended with the concurrence of the Organization.

b. Export prohibitions or restrictions temporarily imposed to relieve conditions of distress in the exporting country caused by severe shortages of foodstuffs or other essential products.

c. Export prohibitions or restrictions necessary to the application of suitable standards for the classification and grading of commodities in international commerce.

d. Export or import quotas imposed under intergovernmental commodity agreements conforming to the principles set forth in Chapter V.

e. Import quotas on agricultural products, imported in any form, necessary to the enforcement of governmental measures which operate (a) to restrict the quantities of like domestic products which may be marketed or produced, or (b) to remove a temporary surplus of like domestic products by making such surpluses available to certain groups of domestic consumers free of charge or at prices below the current market level. Such quotas should not be more restrictive than necessary, should be removed as soon as they cease to be necessary for the purposes of this subparagraph, and should be made the subject of periodic consultation with the Organization. If such quotas are allocated among sources of supply, they should be allocated fairly, on the basis of imports during a previous representative period, account being taken in so far as practicable of any special factors which may have affected or which may be affecting the trade in the product concerned. Import quotas imposed under (a) of this subparagraph should not be such as would reduce imports relatively to domestic production as compared with the proportion prevailing in a previous representative period, account being taken in so far as practicable of any special factors which may have affected or which may be affecting the trade in the product concerned.

2. *Restrictions to safeguard the balance of payments.* Members confronted with an adverse balance of payments should be entitled to impose quantitative import restrictions as an aid to the restoration of equilibrium in the balance of payments. This provision should be operative under conditions and procedures to be agreed upon. These conditions and procedures

a. should set forth criteria and requirements in the light of which balance-of-payments restrictions might be imposed;

b. should, as regards the use of such restrictions in the post-war transitional period, be framed on principles which would be designed to promote the maximum development of multilateral trade during that period and which in no event would be more restrictive of such trade than the principles applicable, under Article XIV of the International Monetary Fund Agreement, to the use of exchange restrictions in the transitional period;

c. should provide for the determination of the transitional period for the purposes of subparagraph b, above, by a procedure analogous to that contained in Article XIV of the International Monetary Fund Agreement;

d. should provide for the full application of nondiscrimination in the use of such restrictions after the transitional period; and

e. should make appropriate provision for international consultation regarding balance-of-payments restrictions, whether imposed during the transitional period or thereafter.

3. *Equality of treatment.* Quantitative restrictions imposed on balance-of-payments grounds should be deemed nondiscriminatory if they are administered on a basis which does not discriminate among sources of supply in respect of any imported product.

a. In the case of restrictions imposed in the form of quotas, members imposing such quotas should publish the global amounts or values of the various products which will be permitted to be imported during a specified future period. Any allocation of such quotas among sources of supply should be based in so far as practicable upon the proportion of the total imports of the product in question supplied by the various member countries in a previous representative period, account being taken of any special factors which may have affected or which may be affecting the trade in that product.

b. In the case of restrictions not imposed in the form of quotas, the member imposing the restrictions should undertake to provide, upon the request of any other member having an interest in the product concerned, all relevant information as to the administration of the restriction, including information as to the import licenses granted over a past period and the distribution of such licenses among sources of supply.

c. Any member should be entitled to raise with the Organization the question as to whether another member was imposing balance-of-payments restrictions, whether in the form of quotas or otherwise, in a manner not in harmony with the guiding principles stated above or in a manner which unnecessarily injured its commerce, and the member imposing the restrictions should undertake in these circumstances to discuss the grounds on which it had acted.

4. *Inconvertible currencies.* The undertakings set forth in paragraph 3, above, should not apply in cases in which their application would have the effect of preventing a member from utilizing inconvertible currencies for buying needed imports.

5. *Scarce currencies and currencies of territories having a common quota in the Monetary Fund.* Members should not be precluded by this Section from applying quantitative restrictions a) in pursuance of action which they may take under Article VII of the International Monetary Fund Agreement, relating to scarce currencies, or b) in a manner designed to maintain the par value of the currencies of territories having a common quota in the Monetary Fund, in accordance with Article XX, Section 4 (g) of that Agreement.

|6. *Application of quantitative restrictions by state-trading organizations.*| The provisions of this Section relating to quantitative restrictions on imports for balance-of-payments reasons should apply equally to the restriction of imports by state-trading organizations for the same reasons.

Section D. Subsidies

1. *Subsidies in general.* Subject to the provisions of paragraphs 2 and 3, below, members granting any subsidy which operates to increase exports or reduce imports should undertake to keep the Organization informed as to the extent and nature of the subsidy, as to the reason therefor and as to the probable effects on trade. They should also be prepared, in cases where, under procedures approved by the Organization, it is agreed that serious injury to international trade threatens to result from the operation of the subsidy, to discuss with other members or with the Organization possible limitations on the quantity of the domestic product subsidized. In this paragraph, the term "subsidy" includes any form of internal income or price support.

2. *Export subsidies.* Subject to the provisions of paragraph 3, below, members should undertake not to take any action which would result in the sale of a product in export markets at a price lower than the comparable price charged for the like product to buyers in the home market, due allowance being made for differences in conditions and terms of sale, for differences in taxation, and for other differences affecting price comparability. This undertaking should take effect, at latest within 3 years of the establishment of the Organization. If at the end of that time any member considers itself unable to comply with the undertaking in respect of any particular commodity or commodities, it should inform the Organization, with an explanation of the reasons. It should then be decided by consultation among the interested members under procedures approved by the Organization whether there should be some further extension of time for the member desiring it in respect of the commodity or commodities concerned.

3. *Commodities in surplus supply.*

a. When it is determined, in accordance with procedures approved by the Organization, that a commodity is, or is likely to become in burdensome world surplus, the members which are important producers or consumers of the commodity should agree to consult together with a view to promoting consumption increases, to promoting the reduction of production through the diversion of resources from uneconomic production, and to seeking, if necessary, the conclusion of an intergovernmental commodity arrangement in accordance with the principles of Chapter V.

b. If, however, within a reasonable time to be agreed upon, such steps should fail of their object, the provisions of paragraphs 1 and 2, above, should cease to apply to such product until such time as it has been agreed under procedures approved by the Organization that those provisions should be reapplied to it.

c. With regard to any export subsidies whch may be imposed under subparagraph (b), no member should employ such subsidies so as to enlarge its share of the world market, as compared with the share prevailing in a previous representative period. The question as to what period would be representative in respect of the particular product concerned should be a subject for international consultation through the Organization.

Section E. State Trading

1. *Equality of treatment.* Members engaging in state trading in any form should accord equality of treatment to all other members. To this end, members should undertake that the foreign purchases and sales of their state-trading

enterprises shall be influenced solely by commercial considerations, such as price, quality, marketability, transportation and terms of purchase or sale.

2. *State monopolies of individual products.* Members maintaining a state monopoly in respect of any product should undertake to negotiate, in the manner contemplated for tariffs, the maximum protective margin between the landed price of the product and the price at which the product (of whatever origin, domestic or foreign) is sold in the home market. Members newly establishing such monopolies should agree not to create protective margins greater than the tariffs which may have been negotiated in regard to those products. Unless the product is subject to rationing, the monopoly should offer for sale such quantities of the product as will be sufficient to satisfy the full domestic demand.

3. *Complete state monopolies of foreign trade.* As the counterpart of tariff reductions and other actions to encourage an expansion of multilateral trade by other members, members having a complete state monopoly of foreign trade should undertake to purchase annually from members, on the nondiscriminatory basis referred to in paragraph 1, above, products valued at not less than an aggregate amount to be agreed upon. This global purchase arrangement should be subject to periodic adjustment in consultation with the Organization.

Section F. Exchange Control

1. *Relation to the International Monetary Fund.* In order to avoid the imposition of trade restrictions and discriminations through exchange techniques, the members of the International Trade Organization should abide by the exchange principles established pursuant to the Articles of Agreement of the International Monetary Fund and for this reason it should be required that the Organization and the Fund have a common membership.

2. *Equality of exchange treatment.* Members maintaining or establishing exchange restrictions should undertake to accord to the trade of other members the equality of treatment with respect to all aspects of such restrictions required under the provisions of the Articles of Agreement of the International Monetary Fund or, in cases where the approval of the Fund is required, the equality of treatment prescribed by the Fund after consultation with the International Trade Organization.

Section G. General Exceptions

The undertakings in this Chapter should not be construed to prevent members from adopting or enforcing measures:

1. necessary to protect public morals;
2. necessary to protect human, animal or plant life or health;
3. relating to the traffic in arms, ammunition and implements of war, and, in exceptional circumstances, all other military supplies;
4. relating to the importation or exportation of gold or silver;
5. necessary to induce compliance with laws or regulations, such as those relating to customs enforcement, deceptive practices, and the protection of patents, trademarks and copyrights, which are not inconsistent with the purposes of the Organization;
6. relating to prison-made goods;
7. imposed for the protection of national treasures of artistic, historic or archaeological value;
8. undertaken in pursuance of obligations for the maintenance of peace and security; or
9. imposed, in exceptional cases, in accordance with a recommendation of the Organization formulated in accordance with criteria and procedures to be agreed upon.

Section H. Territorial Application of Chapter III

1. *Customs territories.* The provisions of Chapter III should apply to the customs territories of the members. If any member has more than one customs territory under its jurisdiction, each customs territory should be considered a separate member for the purpose of applying the provisions of Chapter III.

2. *Frontier traffic and customs unions.* The provisions of Chapter III should not prevent any member *a*) from according advantages to adjacent countries in order to facilitate frontier traffic or *b*) from joining a customs union, provided that such customs union meets certain agreed criteria. Members proposing to join a customs union should consult with the Organization and should make available to it such information as would enable it to make appropriate reports and recommendations.

CHAPTER IV

Restrictive Business Practices

1. *Curbing of restrictive business practices.* There should be individual and concerted efforts by members of the Organization to curb those restrictive business practices in international trade (such as combinations or agreements to fix prices and terms of sale, divide markets or territories, limit production or exports, suppress technology or invention, exclude enterprises from particular fields, or boycott or discriminate against particular firms) which have the effect of frustrating the objectives of the Organization to promote expansion of production and trade, equal access to markets and raw materials, and the maintenance in all countries of high levels of employment and real income.

2. *Cooperation among members.* In order to achieve the purposes of paragraph 1, the Organization should be charged with the furtherance of this objective. The Organization should receive complaints from any member (or, with the permission of the member, from commercial enterprises within its jurisdiction who allege that their interests are affected), that the objectives of the Organization are being frustrated by a private international combination or agreement. The Organization should be empowered to call upon any member to provide information relevant to such a complaint; it should consider such data and, if warranted, make recommendations to the appropriate members for action in accordance with their respective laws and procedures; it should be empowered to request reports from members as to their actions in implementing such recommendations, and to report thereon. The Organization should also be authorized, within the scope of its subject matter, to conduct studies, to make recommendations concerning uniform national standards, and to call conferences of member states for purposes of general consultation.

3. *Continued effectiveness of national laws and regulations directed against restrictive business practices.* Any act or failure to act on the part of the Organization should not preclude any member from enforcing within its own jurisdiction any national statute or decree directed toward the elimination or prevention of restrictive business practices in international trade.

4. *Special enforcement arrangements.* It should be provided that members may, by mutual accord, cooperate in measures for the purpose of making more effective any remedial order which has been issued by a duly authorized agency of another member.

CHAPTER V

Intergovernmental Commodity Arrangements

The production of, and trade in, primary commodities is exposed to certain difficulties different in character from those which generally exist in the case of manufactured goods; and these difficulties, if serious, may have such widespread repercussions as to prejudice the prospect of the general policy of economic expansion. Members should therefore agree upon the procedure which should be adopted to deal with such difficulties.

1. *Special commodity studies.*

a. Special studies should be made in accordance with the procedure set forth in b, below, of the position of particular commodities of which excess supplies exist or are threatened, to the end that, if possible, consumption may be increased and the anticipated difficulties may thereby be averted.

b. Members substantially interested in the production or consumption of a particular commodity should be entitled, if they consider that special difficulties exist or are expected to arise regarding that commodity, to ask that a special study of that commodity be made, and the Organization, if it finds that these representations are well founded, should invite the members principally concerned in the production or consumption of that commodity to appoint representatives to a Study Group to make a special study of that commodity.

2. *Intergovernmental commodity conferences.* If it is concluded, in the light of an investigation of the root causes of the problem, that measures for increasing the consumption of a commodity are unlikely to operate quickly enough to prevent excess supplies of the commodity from accumulating, the members may ask the Organization to convene an intergovernmental conference for the purpose of framing an intergovernmental commodity agreement for the commodity concerned.

3. *Objectives of intergovernmental commodity agreements.* It should be recognized that intergovernmental commodity agreements involving restrictions on production or trade would be justified in the circumstances stated in paragraph 2 above to achieve the following objectives:

a. To enable member countries to find solutions to particular commodity problems without resorting to unilateral action that tends to shift the burden of their problems to other countries.

b. To prevent or alleviate the serious economic problems which may arise when, owing to the difficulties of finding alternative employment, production adjustments cannot be effected by the free play of market forces as rapidly as the circumstances require.

c. To provide a period of transition which will afford opportunities for the orderly solution of particular commodity problems by agreement between member governments upon a program of over-all economic adjustments designed to promote a shift of resources and manpower out of over-expanded industries into new and productive occupations.

4. *Principles of intergovernmental commodity agreements.* Members should undertake to adhere to the following principles governing the institution of intergovernmental commodity agreements:

a. Members having an interest in the production or consumption of any commodity for which an intergovernmental commodity agreement is proposed, should be entitled to participate in the consideration of the proposed agreement.

b. Members should undertake not to enter into intergovernmental commodity agreements involving the limitation of production or exports or the allocation of markets, except after:

1) Investigation by the Study Group of the root causes of the problem which gave rise to the proposal;

2) Determination, in accordance with procedures approved by the Organization, either:

a) that a burdensome surplus of the product concerned has developed or is developing in international trade and is accompanied by widespread distress to small producers accounting for a substantial proportion of the total output and that these conditions cannot be corrected by the normal play of competitive forces because, in the case of the product concerned, a substantial reduction of price leads neither to a significant increase in consumption nor to a significant decrease in production; or

b) that widespread unemployment, unrelated to general business conditions, has developed or is developing in respect of the industry concerned and that such unemployment cannot be corrected by the normal play of competitive forces rapidly enough to prevent widespread and undue hardship to workers because, in the case of the industry concerned, i) a substantial reduction of prices does not lead to a significant increase in consumption but leads, instead, to the reduction of employment, and ii) the resulting unemployment cannot be remedied by normal processes of reallocation;

3) Formulation and adoption by members of a program of economic adjustment believed to be adequate to insure substantial progress toward solution of the problem within the time limits of the agreement.

c. Intergovernmental agreements involving the limitation of production or exports or the allocation of markets in respect of fabricated products should not be resorted to unless the Organization finds that exceptional circumstances justify such action. Such agreements should be subject to the principles set forth in this Chapter, and, in addition, to any other requirements which the Organization may establish.

5. *Operation of commodity agreements.* Members should undertake to adhere to the following principles governing the operation of intergovernmental commodity agreements:

a. The agreements should be open to accession by any member on terms not less favorable than those accorded to members parties thereto.

b. The members adhering to such agreements which are largely dependent for consumption on imports of the commodity involved should, in any determinations made relating to the regulation of prices, trade, stocks, or production, have together a voice equal to those largely interested in obtaining export markets for their production.

c. The agreements should, when necessary, contain provisions for assuring the availability of supplies adequate at all times for world consumption requirements at reasonable prices.

d. The agreements should, with due regard to the transitional need for preventing serious economic and social dislocation, make appropriate provision to afford increasing opportunities for satisfying world requirements from sources from which such requirements can be supplied most effectively.

6. *Termination and renewal of commodity agreements.* Intergovernmental commodity agreements should not remain initially in effect for more than five years. The renewal of an agreement should be subject to the principles governing new agreements set forth in paragraph 4, above, and to the additional principle that either *a*) substantial progress toward a solution of the underlying problem shall have been accomplished during the initial period of the agreement or that *b*) the renewed agreement is so revised as to be effective for this purpose.

7. *Review of commodity agreements.* Members should undertake to transmit to the Organization, for review, intergovernmental commodity agreements in which they now participate or in which they propose to participate in the future. Members should also transmit to the Organization appropriate information regarding the formulation, provisions and operation of such agreements.

8. *Publicity.* Full publicity should be given to any commodity agreement proposed or concluded, to the statements of considerations and objectives advanced by the proposing members, to the operation of the agreements, and to the nature and development of measures adopted to correct the underlying situation which gave rise to the agreement.

9. *Exceptions.* The provisions of Chapter V are not designed to cover international agreements relating to the protection of public morals; the protection of human, animal or plant life or health; the conservation of reserves of exhaustible natural resources; the control of international monopoly situations; or the equitable distribution of commodities in short supply. However, such agreements should not be used to accomplish results inconsistent with the objectives of Chapter IV or Chapter V. If any such agreement involves the restriction of production or of international trade, it should not be adopted unless authorized or provided for by a multilateral convention subscribed to by a substantial number of nations, or unless operated under the Organization.

CHAPTER VI

Organization

Section A. Functions

The functions of the Organization should include the following:

1. To collect, analyze and publish information, regarding the operation of Chapter III, relating to general commercial policy, Chapter IV, relating to the prevention of restrictive business practices, and Chapter V, relating to intergovernmental commodity arrangements, or in general regarding international trade and commercial policy.

2. To provide technical assistance to members as may be required or appropriate under the provisions of Chapters III, IV and V.

3. To make recommendations to members regarding the operation of Chapters III, IV and V, including the following:

   a. Recommendations regarding the relaxation or removal of trade control measures permitted under Chapter III.

   b. Recommendations as to measures for implementing the objectives with regard to restrictive private business practices, set forth in Chapter IV.

   c. Recommendations regarding the application to commodity arrangements under consideration by members of the principles governing commodity arrangements set forth in Chapter V; and recommendations initiating proposals for new commodity arrangements, or proposing such modifications, including termination, of commodity arrangements already concluded, as may be deemed appropriate under the commodity principles or in the general interest.

d. Recommendations designed to promote the maximum obtainable consistency in the operation of Chapters III, IV and V and in other arrangements in the fields of general commercial policy, commodity arrangements and private business practices.

4. To interpret the provisions of Chapters III, IV and V, to consult with members regarding disputes growing out of the provisions of those Chapters, and to provide a mechanism for the settlement of such disputes.

5. In accordance with criteria and procedures to be agreed upon, to waive particular obligations of members, in exceptional circumstances.

6. To make recommendations for international agreements designed to improve the bases of trade and to assure just and equitable treatment for the enterprises, skills and capital brought from one country to another, including agreements on the treatment of foreign nationals and enterprises, on the treatment of commercial travelers, on commercial arbitration, and on the avoidance of double taxation.

7. Generally to perform any function appropriate to the purposes of the Organization.

Section B. *Organs*

The Organization should have as its principal organs: A Conference, an Executive Board, a Commercial Policy Commission, a Commission on Business Practices, a Commodity Commission, and a Secretariat.

Section C. *The Conference*

The Conference should have final authority to determine the policies of the Organization and to exercise the powers conferred upon the Organization.

1. *Membership.* All states members of the Organization should be members of the Conference.

2. *Voting.* Each member of the Conference should have one vote. Except as may be otherwise specifically provided for, decisions of the Conference should be reached by a simple majority vote. It may be desirable to provide for special voting arrangements with regard to the exercise of certain functions of the organization.

3. *Sessions.* The Conference should meet at least once a year.

Section D. *The Executive Board*

The Executive Board should be authorized to take provisional decisions between meetings of the Conference and to exercise such powers as may be delegated to it by the Conference. The Conference should in general be authorized to delegate its powers to the Executive Board.

1. *Membership.* The Executive Board should consist of not more than eighteen member states, each of which should have one representative. Member states of chief economic importance should have permanent seats. The Conference should elect the states to fill the nonpermanent seats for 3-year terms, one-third of the nonpermanent members retiring every year. The number of nonpermanent seats should exceed the number of permanent seats, but the latter should not be fewer than one-third of the total number of seats.

2. *Voting and sessions.* The Executive Board should regulate its own procedure.

Section E. *The Commissions*

The Commission on Commercial Policy, the Commission on Business Practices and the Commodity Commission should be responsible to the Executive Board. Each Commission should be given as much initiative and independence of action as may be necessary for the effective discharge of its functions.

1. *Membership.* The Commissions should be composed of experts appointed by the Executive Board. The terms and other conditions of office of the members of the Commissions should be determined in accordance with regulations prescribed by the Conference. Such terms and conditions need not be uniform, but may vary from Commission to Commission. Pursuant to the reciprocal arrangements with other specialized international organizations contemplated in Section H, paragraph 2, of this Chapter, provision should be made for appropriate representation on the Commodity Commission of the Food and Agriculture Organization of the United Nations and of other specialized international organizations having an important interest in the commodity operations discussed in Chapter V.

2. *Chairmen.* The Chairmen of the Commissions should be nonvoting members of the Executive Board and should be permitted to participate, without vote, in the deliberations of the Conference.

3. *Voting and sessions.* Each Commission should regulate its own procedure, subject to any decisions made by the Executive Board.

4. *Functions.* The functions of the Commissions should include the following:

a. *The Commercial Policy Commission.* The Commercial Policy Commission should:

1) Review, and advise the Executive Board regarding, the operation of treaties, agreements, practices and policies affecting international trade.

2) Investigate, and advise the Executive Board regarding, the economic aspects of proposals to waive certain obligations of members in accordance with the provisions of paragraph 5, Section A, of this Chapter.

3) Investigate, and advise the Executive Board regarding, the economic aspects of proposed customs unions.

4) Develop and recommend to the Executive Board, for adoption by members of the Organization, cooperative projects of a technical nature in the field of commercial policy (e. g. standard bases and methods of determining dutiable value, uniform customs nomenclature, and standardization of statistical methods and nomenclature in foreign trade statistics).

5) Develop and recommend to the Executive Board additional programs designed to further the objectives of the Organization in the general field of commercial policy.

b. *The Commission on Business Practices.* The Commission on Business Practices should:

1) Inquire into activities on the part of private commercial enterprises which have the effect or purpose of restraining international trade, restricting access to international markets, or of fostering monopolistic controls in international trade.

2) Advise the Executive Board with regard to the recommendations which should be made to members in respect of business divestitures, reorganizations, dissolutions or other remedial actions.

3) Conduct investigations and make recommendations to the Executive Board looking to the promotion and adoption in all countries of codes of fair business practices designed to facilitate and enlarge the flow of international trade.

4) Advise the Executive Board as to the types of information which members should file with the Organization.

5) Facilitate appropriate intergovernmental arrangements for the international exchange of technological information, on a nondiscriminatory basis.

c. *The Commodity Commission.* The Commodity Commission should:

1) Investigate commodity problems, including the problem of an international buffer stocks organization or other arrangements which are proposed as a means of promoting solutions to commodity problems.

2) Make recommendations to the Executive Board on appropriate courses of action, including recommendations for the establishment of Study Groups for particular commodities. Such Study Groups should be established by the Executive Board, upon the recommendations of the Commodity Commission, for the purpose of investigating problems with respect to particular commodities. The Study Groups should be composed of representatives of member governments invited to participate by the Executive Board and one or more representatives designated by the Commodity Commission.

3) Make recommendations to the Executive Board as to whether or not a particular commodity is in world surplus.

4) Make recommendations to the Executive Board as to whether an application made by a member for the convening of an intergovernmental conference should be granted.

5) Designate members of the Commission to participate in an advisory capacity in the formulation of intergovernmental commodity agreements.

6) Make recommendations to the Executive Board regarding the application of commodity agreements under consideration by members.

7) Designate the Chairman and Secretary for any Commodity Council established to administer an intergovernmental commodity agreement.

8) Maintain continuous review of the conduct of the operations of intergovernmental commodity agreements in the light of the terms of the agreements, the commodity principles in Chapter V, and the general welfare; and make recommendations to the Executive Board with regard thereto.

Section F.   Industrial and Mineral Unit

The Conference should create an Industrial and Mineral Unit responsible to the Executive Board. The Industrial and Mineral Unit should promote by technical assistance and other appropriate means the expansion of production and trade with regard to fabricated products and with regard to minerals and other primary commodities in respect of which such promotional activities are not under the jurisdiction of the Food and Agriculture Organization.

Section G.   The Secretariat

The Secretariat, which should be divided into three or more offices, should serve all the organs of the Organization and the Commodity Councils established to administer specific commodity arrangements. It should be headed by a Director-General. Under his authority there should be three or more Deputy Directors-General each of whom should be in charge of an office. The Director-General, and on the advice of the Director-General, the Deputy Directors-General, should be appointed by the Conference upon the nomination of the Executive Board. The Director-General should be the chief administrative officer of the Organization and should be an *ex officio* member, without vote, of the Executive Board. Three Deputy Directors-General should be *ex officio* members of the three Commissions. The Director-General and the Deputy Directors-General should have the authority to initiate proposals for the consideration of any organ of the Organization.

Section H. Relations with Other Organizations

1. *Relations with the United Nations Organization.* The Organization should be brought into relationship with the United Nations Organization on terms to be determined by agreement between the Executive Board and the appropriate authorities of the United Nations Organization, subject to approval by the Conference.

2. *Relations with other specialized international organizations.* In order to provide for close cooperation between the Organization and other specialized international organizations with related responsibilities, the Executive Board, subject to the approval of the Conference, should be authorized to enter into agreements with the appropriate authorities of such organizations defining the distribution of responsibilities and methods of cooperation.

3. *Administrative arrangements.* The Director-General should be authorized, subject to the authority of the Conference or of the Executive Board, to enter into agreements with other international organizations for the maintenance of common services, for common arrangements in regard to recruitment, training, conditions of service, and other related matters, and for interchanges of staff.

APPENDIX 48
June 16, 1944 [63]

Summary: Displaced Persons—Europe

I. HISTORICAL BACKGROUND

More than twenty million displaced persons in continental Europe, exclusive of the areas of the Soviet Union, which have recently been occupied by Germany, confront the military with grave problems affecting post-surrender order, security, control, health of the European population, and reconstruction. Approximately one half of the total displaced persons are displaced within their own countries. There are between seven and nine million United Nations nationals in Germany who will want to return to their countries in western and eastern Europe immediately after the war. Some two and one half million Germans in countries contiguous to Germany will desire to return to Germany at the same time.

The largest single group is that of forced laborers in Germany. Other important categories are Allied prisoners of war, evacuees from bombed areas, refugees from military action, racial, religious, and political refugees, and occupants removed from whole areas by the Germans in pursuit of German colonization schemes. The center of the problem of displaced persons is in Germany. The dispersal of people in Poland is also serious.

---

[63] Paper from Special Committee on Migration and Resettlement, accepted by Post-War Programs Committee on June 21, 1944. Through common usage, the term "resettlement" had been substituted for "settlement" in the title of this committee.

II. Basic Objectives

The Special Committee on Migration and Resettlement has prepared two sets of documents giving background material and policy recommendations with respect to displaced persons in eighteen European countries. It has also prepared documents with respect to registration and communication. These latter are now being revised.

The policy recommendations are developed separately for each country. They are addressed to the United States military authorities and apply only to early phases of direct military government.

The recommendations in the documents have to do with five different categories, namely:

1. Allied prisoners of war.
2. Allied and neutral civilian internees.
3. Allied nationals and neutrals having status of forced laborers.
4. Displaced nationals of the country under discussion.
5. Axis nationals.

Variations in the problems and the administration by categories are indicated in each paper.

The basic program outlined in the recommendations provides for the return of displaced persons to their home countries in an orderly manner at the earliest possible date. It is recognized that there will be great impatience to return, transportation facilities will be inadequate, and many displaced persons will start for home on foot. The return movement must, however, be controlled for reasons of order, to avoid the spread of disease and to insure that home areas will be prepared to receive the displaced persons. While a complete standstill order may be necessary initially because of military necessity, the policy suggested for the treatment of displaced persons lies between the two extremes of a standstill order on the one hand and complete freedom of movement on the other. To halt by rigorous restraints attempts by individuals or groups to return home by their own means is not likely to prove effective. Equally, a policy of complete freedom of movement would result in serious disorder, great disturbance at borders, and danger in the spread of epidemic diseases.

III. Particular Recommendations

More particularly the programs are concerned with the following main considerations subject to security aims and military necessity:

1) *Registration and Identification*

It is not anticipated that all displaced persons will need to be registered. Those displaced within their own countries will not require registration. It is assumed that the great majority of the nationals of the western European countries who are in Germany as forced laborers will have identifying documents in their possession sufficient to satisfy the officials of their governments, who will pass upon their acceptability for return. It is expected that groups of displaced persons who have to be held in camps for varying periods of time pending repatriation will need to be registered. Axis nationals who do not succeed in returning to Germany from United Nations countries in advance of the retreating German armies will probably need to be registered. Allied prisoners of war who have lost their prisoner-of-war status by action of the Germans will need to be identified. The Committee has recommended careful preparation of plans for registration in advance and has included a draft registration form suitable for persons to be held in camps in its recommendations.

2) *Notification to foreign governments of the presence of their nationals in the territories covered*

The recommendations provide that Allied and neutral governments are to be notified of the presence of their nationals in a given country other than their own, in a manner and at a time to be determined by the military authorities.

3) *Examination of political prisoners for the purpose of identification and the determination of the cause of detention*

The Committee recognizes that the type of offense, or the alleged offense, for which the individuals are confined may vary from the holding of particular views to the commission of high crimes. The need for distinguishing the different situations before release of all or some is presumed to call for investigation.

4) *Health and medical supervision including epidemic control*

The importance of preliminary plans and prompt action to isolate those with contagious diseases, to provide for treatment and care and to take other precautions against the spread of diseases has been recognized.

5) *Surveys of areas from which displaced persons have been removed, to determine the advisability and the time of return of the displaced groups*

In certain areas bomb damage, military operations, health conditions, or lack of economic capacity to absorb returning nationals may delay repatriation and require inquiry on the spot to determine the feasibility of returning residents to the area.

6) *Temporary shelter and feeding, including feeding on the road*

The importance of adequate provision for displaced persons both in their places of temporary residence and on the homeward journey is recognized. The Committee did not make any specific recommendations as to the administration or financing of feeding and care.

7) *Direction and supervision of homeward movements*

The programs indicate the desirability of control and direction of homeward movements.

8) *Provision of transport facilities if and when practicable*

In providing facilities for repatriation the pressures for transport of military and other supplies will make it difficult to meet the demands for repatriation. While some can return without depending on the use of railways or trucks others will have to wait until facilities can be made available. A system of priorities may be needed.

9) *Identification and registration of all Axis nationals and their detention when necessary*

This recommendation has application particularly in territories of the United Nations, liberated from the Germans, in which Axis nationals may remain. It is assumed that comprehensive measures in the interest of security and military necessity will be applied to enemy nationals.

10) *Employment*

Persons not subject to immediate repatriation and physically able to work should be given the opportunity to engage in suitable employment.

IV. ADMINISTRATION

1. The Committee assumes that on the request of the theater commander appropriate agencies will assist with personnel in the carrying out of the above recommendations.

a) The Department of State will assist with such appropriate personnel as are available on the request from the military authorities.

b) UNRRA will presumably assist in those territories where it has been invited to function by the government or authorities in control.

The Committee does not undertake to prescribe the extent or the manner of such assistance since the nature of the request for aid will be determined by the military, and ability to meet these requirements will depend on circumstances not now evident.

V. Communication and Registration

1. The Committee has recommended the preparation of forms and the outlining of a system of registration to be applicable where and when needed.

a) The Committee recommends registration of groups whose identification is doubtful, whose early repatriation is unlikely, and in other special circumstances.

The earlier report of the Committee covering these matters is being revised in the light of experience to date in areas occupied by the Allies.

Tentative [United States] Draft for a United Nations Organization for Educational and Cultural Reconstruction

1. Preamble

The cold blooded and considered destruction by the fascist governments of the cultural resources of great parts of the continents of Europe and Asia; the murder of teachers, artists, scientists and intellectual leaders; the burning of books; the pillaging and mutilation of works of art; the rifling of archives and the theft of scientific apparatus, have created conditions dangerous to civilization, and therefore to peace, not only in the countries and continents ravaged by the fascist powers, but throughout the entire world. To deprive any part of the inter-dependent modern world of the cultural resources, human and material, through which its children are trained and its people informed, is to destroy to that extent the common knowledge and the mutual understanding upon which the peace of the world and its security must rest.

To restore, insofar as they can be restored, the cultural resources destroyed by the fascist governments, is the simple duty of the freedom loving nations of the world, in their own interest and in the interest of the world's peace. Cooperative activity in education and in the furtherance of cultural interchange among the peoples of the world will promote the freedom, the dignity, and the well-being of all, and therefore assist in the attainment of security and peace.

The governments and authorities of the United Nations and of the nations associated with them in the war, therefore, join in an Organization for Educational and Cultural Reconstruction to repair, insofar as is possible, the injury done to the common cultural inheritance of the world by the fascist powers, and to lay the foundations for the establishment as soon as practicable of a continuing international organization dedicated to the proposition that the free and unrestricted education of the peoples of the world, and the free and unrestricted interchange between them of ideas and knowledge are essential to the preservation of security and peace.

II. Functions

The functions of the United Nations Organization for Educational and Cultural Reconstruction shall be:

1. to investigate the character and extent of the destruction of cultural and educational facilities, materials and personnel; to determine what remedial action is most urgently necessary to reestablish essential educational and cultural services upon an emergency basis, particularly for the reopening of schools for the children and youth of the war-torn countries; and to develop a program to deal with these emergency needs;

2. to determine what assistance in materials and personnel will be required in the liberated areas to restore their educational systems and institutions, and to develop programs to meet these needs by international action, insofar as they can not be met by the liberated nations themselves;

3. to investigate the looting and destruction of basic cultural resources including books, archival materials, works of art and scientific apparatus in the liberated areas and to develop programs for the restoration insofar as possible of these resources through international action and particularly through the cooperation and assistance of the libraries, archives, sources of supply of scientific equipment, educational institutions and similar agencies of those nations able and willing to assist and to seek the cooperation of other bodies having similar purposes;

4. to investigate and to provide for the interchange between nations of information concerning educational and cultural matters including scientific research;

5. to assist in the exchange between governments, through bilateral arrangements and otherwise, of such direct educational and cultural aid from one country to another as may appear mutually desirable;

6. to determine, upon the basis of the work of reconstruction and rehabilitation, the nature of the continuing cultural and educational matters which may warrant international consideration and activity; to recommend to the member governments for their action at the appropriate time the responsibilities and functions which a continuing international organization should undertake; and meanwhile to provide for such development of its own activities in the direction determined and within the limits suggested by experience as may seem to its members advisable.

III. Membership

Membership shall be open to all of the governments and authorities of the United Nations and the nations associated with them in the war. Other nations may be admitted to membership on application to the Executive Board and approval by the Conference.

IV. Structure

1. *The Conference*

   a. There shall be a Conference of the Organization in which each member shall have not more than five delegates representative of the government and of the educational and cultural interests of the nation, selected in such manner as each member shall determine.

b. Each member shall have one vote.

c. The Conference shall meet at least once each year.

d. The Conference shall elect annually a Chairman, a Vice-Chairman and such other officers as it may determine, shall regulate its own procedure, authorize necessary committees and other subordinate bodies, and make rules governing the convocation of sessions and the adoption of agenda.

e. Functions

(1) The Conference shall determine the general policies of the Organization, make necessary regulations governing its operation, approve the budget and exercise the other powers conferred upon it by this instrument.

(2) The Conference may adopt recommendations concerning educational and cultural matters to be submitted to the governments of the members for consideration with a view to national action.

(3) The conference may establish such committees and other subordinate bodies as may be necessary to achieve the purposes of the Organization.

(4) The Conference shall elect an Executive Board and delegate to it such powers as it may determine with the exception of the appointment of the Director, the definition of the functions of the Conference and amendment of this instrument, which powers are reserved to the Conference.

The Conference in selecting the Executive Board shall give due consideration to the desirability of having personnel with varied experience in educational and cultural fields, taking account also of geographic distribution.

The Chairman and Vice-Chairman of the Conference shall serve as Chairman and Vice-Chairman, respectively, of the Executive Board. Additional personnel shall be elected from among the delegates in the Conference to constitute a Board of not more than fifteen. Not more than one delegate from any member shall serve as an officer or member of the Board.

(5) The Conference shall elect a Director of the Organization by such procedure and on such terms as it may determine.

2. *The Executive Board*

a. Acting under the general policies determined by the Conference the Executive Board shall:

(1) establish regulations governing appointments to the staff of the Secretariat by the Director;

(2) prepare the agenda for the meetings of the Conference;

(3) exercise the powers delegated to them by the Conference on behalf of the whole Conference and not as representatives of their respective governments;

b. Between the meetings of the Conference the Executive Board may appoint standing committees subject to subsequent approval by the Conference.

3. *The Director and the Staff*

a. The Director, subject to the supervision of the Executive Board, shall administer the work of the Organization.

b. The Director, or a deputy designated by him, shall participate, without the right to vote, in all meetings of the Conference and of the Board and shall formulate for consideration by the Conference and the Board proposals for appropriate action.

c. The staff of the Organization shall be appointed by the Director under regulations established by the Executive Board.

d. The staff of the Organization shall be responsible to the Director who himself shall be responsible to the Executive Board. The Director and the staff in the performance of these duties shall be responsible exclusively to the Organization and they shall not seek or receive instructions in regard to the discharge thereof from any authority external to the Organization.

V. FINANCE

1. *Administrative*

a. The administrative expenses of the Organization shall be borne by the members in proportions to be determined by the Conference.

b. Each member shall, upon its acceptance of this instrument, undertake in accordance with its constitutional procedures to contribute its proportion of the annual administrative budget for the remainder of the current financial year.

2. *Emergency Restoration Fund*

For the reconstruction of the educational and cultural facilities of war-devastated countries which are unable with their own resources to provide the minimum requirements there shall be created an Emergency Restoration Fund provided by the nations able to contribute to it. The total amount of this fund and the proportion of it to be recommended as the contribution of each nation deemed able to contribute shall be determined by the Conference on the basis of a report prepared by an Emergency Restoration Fund Committee, subject to any such contribution being approved and provided for pursuant to the constitutional processes of the respective members. The Committee shall be composed of one representative from each of the three members which make the largest contributions to the administrative budget of the Organization and three additional members selected by the Executive Board. The Committee shall also be responsible for allocating this fund for use in the respective war-devastated countries which are unable to meet their minimum requirements for restoration.

VI. ADOPTION, AMENDMENT AND INTERPRETATION OF THE INSTRUMENT

1. *Adoption of the Instrument*

When twenty of the governments and authorities of the United Nations and the nations associated with them in the war file with the Secretary of the Conference of Allied Ministers of Education official notice of their acceptance of this instrument, the Conference of the Organization shall be convened by call of the Chairman of the Conference of Allied Ministers of Education for the purpose of taking such action with respect to policies and plans as may seem desirable under the provisions of the instrument.

2. *Amendment of the Instrument*

a. Amendments to this instrument involving new obligations for members shall require the approval of the Conference by a vote concurred in by a two-thirds majority of the members of the Conference present and voting and shall take effect on acceptance by two-thirds of the members for each member accepting the amendment and thereafter for each remaining member on acceptance by it.

b. Other amendments shall take effect on adoption by the Conference by a two-thirds majority of the members present and voting.

3. *Interpretation of the Instrument*

Any question or dispute concerning the interpretation of this instrument shall be referred for determination to an international court or arbitral tribunal in the manner prescribed by rules to be adopted by the Conference.

VII. MISCELLANEOUS PROVISIONS

1. *Reports by Members*

a. Each member shall report periodically to the Organization in a manner to be determined by the Conference, on activities and developments related to the functions of the Organization and on the action taken on the recommendations by the Conference.

b. The Director shall submit these reports, together with analyses thereof, to the Conference and shall publish such reports and analyses as may be approved for publication by the Executive Board.

c. Each member shall upon publication communicate to the Organization laws, regulations, official reports and statistics concerning its educational and cultural institutions.

2. *Cooperation with International Organizations and Agencies*

a. The Organization shall wherever feasible cooperate with other international organizations and agencies with related interests.

b. The Conference may enter into agreements with the competent authorities of such organizations and agencies defining the distribution of responsibilities and methods of cooperation and may maintain such joint committees with such organizations and agencies as may be necessary to assure effective cooperation.

3. *Relation to the General International Organization*

This Organization or any permanent organization established in continuance, transformation, or supersession of the present Organization shall be brought into relationship with the general international organization by action of the appropriate organs of both bodies.

4. *Legal Status*

a. The Organization shall have legal capacity to conclude contracts, to acquire, to hold, and to convey property, to accept endowments or gifts and in general to assume and discharge obligations and perform any legal act appropriate to its purpose within this instrument. The acquisition of real property by the Organization within the territory of any member shall be governed by the law of that nation.

b. The Government of each member undertakes, insofar as may be possible under its constitutional procedures, to accord to Delegates to the Conference, to the Director and senior staff diplomatic privileges and immunities and to accord the other members of the staff all facilities and immunities accorded to non-diplomatic personnel attached to diplomatic missions.

APPENDIX 50
March 8, 1945 [64]

International Organization for Education and Cultural Cooperation

THE HIGH CONTRACTING PARTIES,

Determined that all possible steps shall be taken to further the attainment of international security and peace and to advance the welfare of the peoples of the world,

Recognizing that cooperation in education and the furtherance of cultural interchange among the peoples of the world will promote the freedom, the dignity and the well-being of all and therefore assist in the attainment of security and peace, and

Dedicated to the proposition that the free and unrestricted education of the peoples of the world, and the free and unrestricted exchange among them of ideas and knowledge are essential to the preservation of security and peace,

Hereby establish the International Organization for Education and Cultural Cooperation and agree to support its broad purposes and functions as expressed in this constitution through their participation in the activities of this international agency and through their respective national educational and cultural programs.

ARTICLE I

Purposes

The purposes of the International Organization for Education and Cultural Cooperation shall be:

1. To develop and maintain mutual understanding and appreciation of the life and culture of the peoples of the world as a basis for effective international organization and world peace.

2. To cooperate in making available to all peoples for the service of common human needs, the world's full body of knowledge, and in assuring the constructive contribution of educational, cultural, and scientific interchange to the economic stability, political security, and the general well-being of the peoples of the world.

ARTICLE II

Principal Functions

To achieve these purposes the Organization shall:

1. Facilitate consultation among leaders in the educational and cultural life of all peace-loving countries.

2. Assist the free flow of ideas and information among the peoples of the world through schools, universities, libraries, publications, the press, the radio and motion picture, international conferences, and exchange of students, teachers, scientists, and other representatives of educational and cultural life; with special attention to exchange of information on major educational and cultural developments.

---

[64] Final United States draft, communicated to Conference of Allied Ministers of Education in London. The two annexes to which this document refers were not presented with it and are not printed here.

3. Encourage the growth, within each country and in its relations with other countries, of educational and cultural programs which give support to international peace and security and discourage the member states from engaging in any educational and cultural activities which threaten harmonious relations among nations.

4. Develop and make available educational and cultural plans and materials for such consideration and use as each country may deem appropriate.

5. Conduct and encourage research and studies on educational and cultural problems related to the maintenance of peace and the advancement of human welfare.

6. Assist countries that need and request help in developing their educational and cultural activities.

Article III

Membership

1. Members of the general international organization shall automatically be granted the right of membership. Other nations may be admitted by the Conference, acting by a two-thirds vote, upon recommendation of the Executive Board.

2. Any member may withdraw from the Organization after two years' notice of intention to do so, provided that its financial obligations shall have been fulfilled at the time of withdrawal.

3. Each member nation undertakes, subject to the requirements of its constitutional procedure, to contribute to the organization promptly its share of the expenses. The right of a member to vote in the Conference and the eligibility of its nationals to be elected to the Executive Board may be suspended by the Conference on recommendation of the Executive Board for any member that fails for two successive years to meet its financial obligations to this Organization.

4. Members of the Organization which are suspended from the exercise of the rights and privileges of membership in the general international organization shall automatically be suspended from the rights and privileges of this Organization.

Article IV

Organs

1. The organs of the Organization shall be a Conference, an Executive Board, and a Secretariat.

2. Within each member state, there shall be established a National Commission for Education and Cultural Cooperation to cooperate with the international organization as provided for in Article VIII.

Article V

The Conference

A. *Composition*

The Conference shall consist of the representatives of the members of the Organization. Each member shall designate not more than five delegates, who shall be selected in agreement with the National Commission on Education and Cultural Cooperation.

B. *Functions and Powers*

1. The Conference shall determine the general policies and the program of the Organization.

2. The Conference is empowered to make recommendations to the members, and to adopt for submission to the members agreements on educational and cultural programs designed to accomplish the purposes of the Organization.

3. The Conference shall advise the general international organization on the educational and cultural aspects of matters of concern to the latter in accordance with terms and procedures agreed upon between the appropriate authorities of the two organizations.

4. The Conference shall receive and consider reports submitted periodically by the members on educational and cultural developments within their respective territories and on the effect given to the recommendations of the Organization.

5. The Conference shall elect the members of the Executive Board. It shall admit new members to the Organization and elect the Director-General on recommendation of the Executive Board.

6. The Conference shall approve the budget of the Organization and the allocation of financial responsibility to the members.

7. Gifts and bequests may be accepted by the Conference and utilized under its direction provided the conditions of the gift or bequest are consistent with the purposes and policies of the Organization.

C. *Voting*

Each member shall have one vote in the Conference. Decisions shall be made by a simple majority of those present and voting, except where otherwise specified in this instrument.

D. *Procedure*

1. The Conference shall meet annually in regular session; it may meet in extraordinary session on the call of the Executive Board. Normally the sessions shall be held at the seat of the Organization.

2. The Conference shall set up such committees and other subordinate bodies as may be necessary for the performance of its functions.

3. The Conference shall elect its own officers and adopt its own rules of procedure.

ARTICLE VI

The Executive Board

A. *Composition*

The Executive Board shall consist of fifteen persons elected by the Conference from among the delegates. Not more than one delegate from any member state shall serve on the Board at any one time. The members of the Board shall serve for a term of three years and shall not be immediately eligible for reelection. At the first election, five persons shall be elected for a three-year term, five for two years, and five for one year. Thereafter, five persons shall be elected each year.

B. *Functions and Powers*

1. The Executive Board shall be responsible within the competence of the Organization for giving effect to the program for the Organization adopted by the Conference.

2. The Executive Board shall supervise the administration of the Organization and prepare the agenda for meetings of the Conference.

3. The Executive Board shall recommend to the Conference the admission of new members to the Organization.

4. It shall be empowered to make appointments to fill vacancies in its membership, which appointments shall terminate at the next meeting of the Conference, when an election shall be held for the unexpired term.

C. *Procedure*

The Executive Board shall elect its own officers and determine its own rules of procedure.

ARTICLE VII

The Secretariat

1. The Secretariat shall consist of a Director-General and such staff as may be required.

2. The Director-General shall be nominated by the Executive Board and elected by the Conference under such conditions of tenure and compensation as the Conference may approve. He shall be the chief administrative officer of the Organization, immediately responsible to the Executive Board. He, or a deputy designated by him, shall participate, without the right to vote, in all meetings of the Conference, the Board, and all committees of the Organization. He shall formulate proposals for appropriate action by the Conference and the Board.

3. The Director-General shall appoint the staff of the Secretariat under regulations adopted by the Executive Board. Subject to the requirements of efficiency and technical competence, the staff shall be recruited on as wide a geographical basis as possible.

4. In the performance of their duties, the Director-General and the staff shall be responsible only to the Organization. Their responsibilities shall be exclusively international in character, and they shall not seek or receive instructions in regard to the discharge thereof from any authority external to the Organization. The members undertake to respect fully the international character of the responsibilities of the Secretariat and not to seek to influence any of their nationals in the discharge of such responsibilities.

ARTICLE VIII

National Commissions

A. *Composition*

Each member of the International Organization for Education and Cultural Cooperation shall establish a National Commission on Education and Cultural Cooperation, broadly representative of the government and the groups devoted to and interested in educational and cultural matters. Delegates to the Conference shall, during their period of service, be included in the National Commission. Each member shall be free to adapt the size and scope of the National Commission to its own special conditions.

B. *Functions and Powers*

1. The National Commission shall act in an advisory capacity to the government and to the national delegation to the Conference.

2. The national delegation to the Conference shall be appointed by the government in agreement with the National Commission.

3. The National Commission shall consider recommendations and reports made by the International Organization for Education and Cultural Cooperation and take such steps as it considers desirable to secure action on these matters within its own country and to further the general objectives of the Organization.

4. Each member may assign to the National Commission such additional functions as are consistent with the purposes of the Organization.

ARTICLE IX

Reports by Members

1. Each member shall report periodically to the Organization, in a manner to be determined by the Conference, on activities and developments related to the functions of the Organization and on the action taken on the recommendations by the Conference.

2. Each member shall upon publication communicate to the Organization laws, regulations, official reports and statistics concerning its educational and cultural institutions and organizations.

ARTICLE X

Juridical Status of the Organization and Its Personnel

1. The Organization shall possess international personality and legal capacity. The members of the Organization shall accord to the Organization the privileges, immunities, exemptions and facilities which they accord to each other, including, in particular (a) immunity from every form of legal process; (b) exemption from taxation and customs duties; and (c) inviolability of premises occupied by, and of the archives and communications of, the Organization.

2. The members of the Organization shall accord diplomatic privileges and immunities to persons appointed by other members as their representatives in or to the Organization, and to the higher officials of the Organization not being their own nationals. They shall accord to all officials and employees of the Organization (a) immunity from suit and legal process relating to acts performed by them in their official capacity; (b) exemption from taxation of their official salaries and emoluments; and, in general, (c) such privileges, exemptions and facilities as they accord under similar circumstances to officials and employees of foreign governments.

ARTICLE XI

Amendments

1. Proposals for amendments to this instrument shall require the approval of the Conference by a two-thirds majority, and amendments shall take effect on ratification by two-thirds of the member states. The draft texts of proposed amendments shall be communicated by the Director-General to the members at least six months in advance of their consideration by the Conference.

2. The Conference shall have power to adopt by a two-thirds majority rules prescribing the times within which proposed amendments must be accepted in order to become effective and other rules of procedure to carry out the provisions of this Article.

ARTICLE XII

Interpretation

Any question or dispute concerning the interpretation of this instrument shall be referred for determination to the international court of justice or to an arbitral tribunal as the Conference may determine.

Article XIII

Relations with the General International Organization

1. The Organization shall be brought into relationship with the general international organization, this relationship to be defined in an agreement approved by the appropriate organs of both bodies.

2. Notwithstanding the provisions of Article XI, such agreement may, if approved by the Conference by a two-thirds majority, involve modification of the provisions of this Constitution, provided that no such agreement shall modify the purposes and limitations of the Organization.

Article XIV

Relations with Other Specialized International Organizations

1. The Organization shall cooperate with other specialized international organizations, both public and private, whose interests and activities are related to and in harmony with its purposes.

2. The Executive Board, with the approval of the Conference, may enter into agreements with the component authorities of such organizations defining the distribution of responsibilities and methods of cooperation, and maintain such joint committees with them as may be necessary to assure effective cooperation.

3. Whenever the Conference of this Organization and the competent authorities of any other organization whose purposes are similar deem it desirable to effect transfer of the resources and functions of the latter to this Organization, the Executive Board, subject to the approval of the Conference, may enter into mutually acceptable arrangements for this purpose.

Article XV

Establishment of the Organization

This instrument shall come into effect when fifteen of the governments of the United Nations shall have filed with the Secretary of the Conference of Allied Ministers of Education or its successor official notice of their acceptance of it and adherence to the Organization. Thereupon, the Chairman of the Conference of Allied Ministers of Education or its successor shall convene the first Conference of the Organization, which shall proceed with the election of the Executive Board and the Director-General and shall make whatever other arrangements may be necessary to put the Organization into operation.

Transitory Provisions

1. For the first meeting of the Conference, the provision in Article IV, Section A, that the delegates designated by any member shall be selected in agreement with the National Commission on Educational and Cultural Cooperation, shall not apply, but in naming delegates to this meeting each member shall endeavor to provide for representation of the educational and cultural interests of the nation.

2. The following exceptional arrangements shall apply in respect of the financial year in which this constitution comes into force; the budget shall be the provisional budget set forth in Annex I to this constitution; and the amounts to be contributed by the member nations shall be in the proportions set forth in Annex II to this constitution.

Memorandum for the President
Establishment of An Emergency High Commission
for Liberated Europe

I recommend that at your meeting with Marshal Stalin and Prime Minister Churchill you propose the immediate establishment of an Emergency High Commission for Liberated Europe, the initial membership to consist of the Governments of the United States, the United Kingdom, and the Soviet Union, and the Provisional Government of France. A proposed draft declaration and protocol are attached for your consideration.

The proposed Emergency High Commission would be set up as a joint, temporary agency of the four governments through which they would act together to assist in establishing popular governments and in facilitating the solution of emergency economic problems in the former occupied and satellite states of Europe. It would *not* have responsibilities in regard to the conduct of the war or the post-war control of Germany. Questions regarding Germany would remain solely in the province of the European Advisory Commission, and of such agencies as may be established for control of Germany.

Announcement from your meeting of agreement on the establishment of such a commission would reassure public opinion in the United States and elsewhere that these four nations will work together in the solution of pressing problems while further steps are being taken toward the establishment of the General International Organization.

There is urgent need for these four nations to achieve unity of policy, and joint action, with respect to:

1. Political problems emerging in the former occupied and satellite states of Europe, such as the return of certain exiled governments, the setting up of provisional regimes, the maintenance of order within countries, and the arranging of early elections where necessary to establish popular and stable governments;
2. Immediate economic problems such as the care for destitute populations and the restoration of functioning economic life of particular countries.

The proposed Emergency High Commission would constitute the agency for providing for the necessary regular consultation and cooperative action in these matters. Also it would greatly help to remove the difficulties being encountered by United Nations' agencies in related fields.

[Attachment 1]

DECLARATION ON LIBERATED EUROPE

The President of the United States of America, the Prime Minister of the United Kingdom, the Premier of the Union of Soviet Socialist Republics, and the President of the Provisional Government of the French Republic, having consulted with each other in the common interests of the peoples of their countries and

---

[65] Date supplied. Handed same date to Secretary of State Stettinius and transmitted by him to the President with additional papers for his use at the Crimea Conference. Brackets in text as in original.

those of liberated Europe, jointly declare their mutual agreement to concert the action of their four governments in assisting the peoples liberated from the domination of Nazi Germany and its satellites to solve by democratic means their pressing political and economic problems.

The retreat of the Nazi war machine and the collapse of its puppet regimes, under the relentless blows of the victorious armies and resistance forces of the United Nations, are leaving behind confusion and disorder, and incalculable distress and suffering. The agony of the liberated peoples must be relieved. Swift steps must be taken to help them in the orderly reconstruction of their daily living.

The establishment of order in Europe and the rebuilding of national economic life must be achieved by processes which will enable the liberated peoples to destroy the last vestiges of Nazism and Fascism and to create democratic institutions of their own choice. This is a promise of the Atlantic Charter—the right of all peoples to choose the form of government under which they will live— the restoration of sovereign rights and self-government to those peoples who have been forcibly deprived of them.

To foster the conditions in which the liberated peoples may exercise these rights, the Governments of the United States of America, the United Kingdom, and the Union of Soviet Socialist Republics, and the Provisional Government of the French Republic have agreed to establish, for such joint action as may be necessary, an Emergency High Commission for Liberated Europe, as set forth by the protocol of this date.

By this declaration we reaffirm our faith in the principles of the Atlantic Charter, our pledge in the Declaration by United Nations, and our determination to build in cooperation with other peace-loving nations a world order under law, dedicated to the peace and security and the general well-being of all mankind.

[Attachment 2]

EMERGENCY HIGH COMMISSION FOR LIBERATED EUROPE

Pursuant to the Declaration on Liberated Europe and with a view to concerting their policies with respect to the objectives set forth therein, the Governments of the United States of America, the United Kingdom, and the Soviet Union, and the Provisional Government of the French Republic hereby establish an Emergency High Commission for Liberated Europe.

A. *Functions and Scope*

1. The Emergency High Commission for Liberated Europe shall have responsibility in such former occupied states of Europe and in such former enemy states as in the judgment of the four governments conditions may make necessary:

   a. To assist where circumstances require in the maintenance of internal order;

   b. To assist as may be required in the taking of emergency measures for care of the population and for solution of pressing economic problems;

   c. To assist where circumstances require in setting up governmental authorities broadly representative of all democratic elements in the population and pledged to the earliest possible establishment through free elections of governments responsible to the will of the people;

   d. To assist as may be appropriate in making arrangements for, and in conducting free elections to determine the type and composition of governments;

   e. To perform such other duties as may be assigned to it by agreement of the governments represented on the Emergency High Commission.

2. The Emergency High Commission shall have no authority, functions, or responsibilities with regard to the conduct of military operations in the prosecution of the present war against Germany, or the occupation and control of Germany.

3. The Emergency High Commission shall consult with other international agencies as necessary on problems which are of mutual concern.

B. *Membership*

1. The membership of the Emergency High Commission shall consist of the Governments of the United States, the United Kingdom, and the Soviet Union, and the Provisional Government of the French Republic, each of which shall appoint one representative. As may be necessary the Emergency High Commission may enlarge its membership.

2. Representatives of other United Nations and of provisional authorities or of governments in Europe shall be invited by the Emergency High Commission to sit with it when matters of direct interest to them are under consideration.

C. *Location and Organization*

1. The headquarters of the Emergency High Commission shall be in [Paris]. It may meet in other places as occasion requires.

2. It may designate officials of member governments to represent it in individual countries or areas.

3. The Governments which are members of the Emergency High Commission shall provide such military or other special advisers as may be required to assist it in performing its functions.

4. It shall organize its technical staff and otherwise establish and perfect its organization and procedure. Its chairmanship shall be held successively by representatives of the member governments.

D. *Termination*

The Emergency High Commission for Liberated Europe shall terminate when the functioning of popular and stable governments and the operations of appropriate organs or agencies of the general international organization shall have removed the need for its activities.

APPENDIX 52
November 15, 1944[66]

Memorandum for the President
Voting Procedure in the Security Council

Background

There are three issues involved in this connection, as follows:

1. Size of majority
2. Unanimity of permanent members
3. Procedure in the event that one of the permanent members is a party to a dispute

The Russians took the position that the Council should make decisions by a simple majority vote; that unanimity of the permanent members should be re-

---

[66] Considered by Acting Secretary Stettinius and some of his associates with the President on the same date.

quired, except on procedural questions; and that the unanimity rule should prevail even when one of the permanent members is a party to a dispute.

The British took the position that the Council's decisions should be by a two-thirds majority vote, except that procedural questions might be settled by a simple majority vote; that unanimity of the permanent members should be required on all substantive matters; and that parties to a dispute should not vote.

The Chinese position was similar to the British.

In accordance with your instructions, our delegation took a position similar to the British, except that we expressed our willingness to accept either a simple majority or a two-thirds majority.

In the course of the Dumbarton discussions, in order to meet the conflicting views, proposals were tentatively made that decisions should require the affirmative votes of seven members, rather than of six members as would be the case under a simple majority rule, or of eight members as would be the case under a two-thirds rule; and that unanimity of the permanent members should be required on all substantive matters, except that in decisions of the Council relating to pacific settlement of disputes (Section A of Chapter VIII) parties to a dispute should not vote. These proposals were not accepted, although they were favorably regarded by Sir Alexander Cadogan and his associates and by Dr. Koo and his associates.

Recommendation

It is recommended that

This government accept the formula embodied in the attached draft of a proposal on this subject and seek to obtain the acceptance of that formula by Soviet Russia and the United Kingdom.

The proposed formula is essentially along the lines of the compromise solution discussed at Dumbarton Oaks. It provides that parties to a dispute should abstain from voting in those decisions of the Council which relate to the investigation of disputes, to appeals by the Council for peaceful settlement of disputes, and to recommendations by the Council as to methods and procedures of settlement. It retains the unanimity rule for decisions relating to the determination of the existence of threats to the peace or breaches of the peace and to the suppression of such threats or breaches.

This proposal should be acceptable to this country, since no party to a dispute would sit as a judge in its own case so long as judicial or quasi-judicial procedures are involved, but would participate fully in procedures involving political rather than judicial determination. It should be acceptable to Soviet Russia because it meets her desire that no action be taken against her without her consent.

PROPOSAL FOR SECTION C OF THE CHAPTER ON THE
SECURITY COUNCIL

C. VOTING

1. Each member of the Security Council should have one vote.

2. Decisions of the Security Council on procedural matters should be made by an affirmative vote of seven members.

3. Decisions of the Security Council on all other matters should be made by an affirmative vote of seven members including the concurring votes of the permanent members; provided that, in decisions under Section VIII A and under paragraph 1 of Section VIII C, a party to a dispute should abstain from voting.

APPENDIX 53
January 15, 1945[67]

Principal Substantive Decisions on Which the Security Council Would Have to Vote

Under the voting formula proposed by the President, all of the decisions listed below would require the affirmative votes of 7 members of the Security Council, including the votes of the permanent members. The only exception would be that, in the event that a permanent member is a party to a dispute or a situation before the Council, that member would not cast its vote in decisions listed under "Promotion of Peaceful Settlement of Disputes" (Category III below).

I. Recommendations to the General Assembly on

1. Admission of new members;
2. Suspension of a member;
3. Expulsion of a member;
4. Election of the Secretary General.

II. Restoration of the rights and privileges of a suspended member.

III. Promotion of peaceful settlement of disputes, including the following questions:

1. Whether a dispute or a situation brought to the Council's attention is of such a nature that its continuation is likely to threaten the peace;
2. Whether the Council should call on the parties to settle or adjust the dispute or situation by means of their own choice;
3. Whether the Council should make a recommendation to the parties as to methods and procedures of settlement;
4. Whether the legal aspects of the matter before it should be referred by the Council for advice to the international court of justice;
5. Whether, if there exists a regional agency for peaceful settlement of local disputes, such an agency should be asked to concern itself with the controversy.

IV. Removal of threats to the peace and suppression of breaches of the peace, including the following questions:

1. Whether failure on the part of the parties to a dispute to settle it by means of their own choice or in accordance with the recommendations of the Security Council in fact constitutes a threat to the peace;
2. Whether any other actions on the part of any country constitute a threat to the peace or a breach of the peace;
3. What measures should be taken by the Council to maintain or restore the peace and the manner in which such measures should be carried out;
4. Whether a regional agency should be authorized to take measures of enforcement.

V. Approval of special agreement or agreements for the provision of armed forces and facilities.

---

[67] This document bears the following notation: Copies of this document were given informally to the Soviet and British Ambassadors in Washington shortly after January 15, 1945.

VI. Formulation of plans for a general system of regulation of armaments and submission of such plans to the member states.

VII. Determination of whether the nature and the activities of a regional agency or arrangement for the maintenance of peace and security are consistent with the purposes and principles of the general organization.

APPENDIX 54
December 30, 1944

[Letter, Secretary of State (Stettinius) to Secretary of the Navy (Forrestal)]

MY DEAR MR. SECRETARY: I refer to a letter to me of August 3, 1944 from General Marshall and to my reply of August 5, 1944 on the subject of international trusteeships.[68]

In deference to the wishes of the Joint Chiefs of Staff, we were glad to eliminate this topic from the Dumbarton Oaks conversations. However, the topic was raised at Dumbarton Oaks on a number of occasions by the other participants. Briefly summarized, those occasions were substantially as follows:

The Soviet delegation asked why the subject was not being discussed, expressed their desire to discuss it, and, when informed that we considered it wiser to leave the subject for future consideration, asked whether it would be discussed at the general conference or made the subject of a prior exchange of views. They expressed a desire for the latter procedure. The British delegation raised the question and were told that we had under consideration the possibility of exchanging papers on the subject. They said that they were prepared to participate in such an exchange. The Chinese delegation also raised the question, and they, too, expressed a desire to exchange papers on the subject. In none of the above instances was any question raised as to the particular territories which might be involved. The emphasis was exclusively upon general principles and particularly upon the kind of machinery which might effectively and appropriately be established in conjunction with the international organization.

The question has also been raised many times in public discussion about the Dumbarton Oaks proposals both here and abroad. There has been a considerable amount of criticism that the subject of international trusteeships was omitted from the proposals.

It is clear, therefore, that we are confronted with the need of re-examining the whole matter from the viewpoint of further procedure. In such consideration as we have so far given it, we have come to the following conclusions:

1. It is inescapable that the question of international trusteeships will have to be discussed at least at the general conference, and that in all likelihood a chapter on general principles and machinery will have to be included in the final charter of the United Nations.

2. It is entirely possible, in dealing with this subject, to separate the formulation of general principles and of provisions for machinery from consideration of specific territories, the latter subject to be left for future determination.

---

[68] Not printed.

We are now working on a draft proposal for incorporation in the final charter of the United Nations which will be drawn up at the general conference to be called for that purpose. This proposal will be limited to expressions of general principles and to provision of appropriate machinery of an international nature. We are giving consideration to the possibility of discussing our proposal with the British, Soviet and Chinese Governments prior to the general conference.

We would very much like to have the Joint Chiefs of Staff and the War and Navy Departments participate with us in the preparation of this proposal, and we hope that you will designate representatives of the Joint Chiefs of Staff for that purpose. As we are hopeful that the general conference can be held sometime this winter we naturally wish to formulate the proposal as promptly as possible.

I am sending a similar letter to Secretary Stimson.

Sincerely yours,

E. R. STETTINIUS, JR.

APPENDIX 55
January 23, 1945 [69]

Memorandum for the Secretary

SUBJECT: *Recommended Action on Points Which Must Be Decided at The Three-Power Meeting*

1. *Text of the voting provisions:* Adoption of the President's formula with slight modification as to Chapter VIII, Section C. (Text attached) [70]

2. *International Trusteeships:* Decision that provisions for the establishment of trusteeship machinery within the framework of the proposed organization will be included in the Charter and that the sponsoring Governments will consult with each other before the Conference as to detailed proposals on this subject. (Memorandum attached)

3. *Position of France:* Decision that France should become the fifth sponsoring power.

4. *Nations to be Invited:* Decision that invitations be issued to the same 44 nations which had been invited to the Hot Springs, Atlantic City and Bretton Woods Conferences. (List attached) [71]

5. *Time and Place of Conference:* Decision that the Conference be held in the United States (exact location to be left for future determination). Tentative decision as to time, subject to later consultation with China and France and possibly other countries.

6. *Form of Invitation:* Decision that invitations be issued by the United States on behalf of the five sponsoring Powers in the form of the attached draft. [71]

7. *Consultation with China and France:* Authorization for the United States to consult with China and France on behalf of Britain and the Soviet Union to obtain Chinese and French agreement to the above points.

8. *Public Announcements:* Statement at the meeting along the lines of the attached draft. [71] No further publicity until final decision has been reached on the

---

[69] Memorandum transmitted by Mr. Pasvolsky to Secretary Stettinius for use in connection with the Crimea Conference.

[70] Not printed. The text of the formula was identical with that quoted below in appendix 57, and the accompanying analysis was identical in substance with that in appendix 53.

[71] Not printed.

form of invitation, at which time the texts of the invitation and of the completed proposals would be made public upon their transmission to the governments invited.

[Attachment]

INTERNATIONAL TRUSTEESHIP

I

BACKGROUND

1. A chapter on trusteeship should be included in the Charter of the International Organization for the following reasons:

   a. The liquidation of the League will require some disposition of the mandated territories which were placed under its supervision as a "sacred trust of civilization".

   b. At the end of this war there may possibly be other territories detached from enemy states for which international supervision may be considered desirable.

   c. There may also be other territories which it might be advisable to place under trusteeship by mutual agreement.

   d. There is a strong feeling in this country that dependent territories should not be the subject of barter but should be the concern of the whole world community.

It was the understanding at Dumbarton Oaks that the question of trusteeship, although not taken up at that time, was a proper subject for discussion among the governments represented there, and that in due course the sponsoring governments would consult with each other and perhaps exchange papers on the subject in order to save time at the Conference itself. Other governments have subsequently suggested the inclusion of arrangements for dependent territories.

2. The view was expressed informally to us by Colonel Stanley that other colonial powers might at this stage be brought into the consultations on international arrangements affecting dependent territories. It is our view, however, that such consultations at this stage should be confined to the states participating in the Dumbarton Oaks Conversations. The British position is clearly designed to win support from other states with colonies in order to offset the support which, they anticipate, the United States will receive from the Soviet Union and China.

3. Our desire that only general principles and procedures relating to international trusteeship be discussed at present is based upon the view that territorial dispositions should be left for consideration until the end of hostilities. We consider it of the utmost importance, nevertheless, to get an agreement on the principle of trusteeship, in order that our basic distinction between trust territories and all other dependencies may be maintained. Colonel Stanley made it clear that the British wish to eliminate this distinction, a procedure which we would regard as retrogressive.

4. We have long felt that, as indispensable parts of an over-all program, a complete system for dependencies would provide for:

   a. Creation of a trusteeship mechanism by which the International Organization would assume direct responsibility for the administration of certain dependent territories, in order to promote the social, economic, and political advancement of the peoples of trust territories and to enable these territories to contribute to international peace and security;

b. Establishment of regional advisory commissions for dependent territories generally, on the model of the Anglo-American Caribbean Commission, which would include the states administering dependencies in the particular region and other states having major strategic or economic interests therein; and

c. Adoption of a general declaration of principles designed to establish minimum political, economic, and social standards for all non-self-governing territories, whether colonies, protectorates, or trust territories.

5. The British probably will propose regional advisory commissions as the sole device for expressing international responsibility with respect to dependent territories. Regional commissions, in their view, could be employed to discharge, through consultation, a limited international accountability for the administration of dependent territories. In our view, regional commissions are desirable, but only as one part of an over-all international system.

II

RECOMMENDATIONS

We recommend that at the forthcoming talks decisions be reached that:

1. There should be included in the Charter of the General International Organization a chapter on Trusteeship Arrangements;

2. The sponsoring governments consult with each other before the Conference as to the detailed proposals which should be made on this subject, and prepare a draft text.

These proposals should deal only with the principles and the mechanism which should govern these trusteeship arrangements. They should not be concerned at this stage with specific territories to be placed under trusteeship or with the disposition or allocation of particular territories.

A general Declaration of Standards and Regional Advisory Commissions should be regarded as additions to and not substitutions for the Trusteeship Arrangement. These, however, may also need to be discussed at the Conference and decisions taken as to how they might be related to each other, and perhaps to the General Organization.

APPENDIX 56
February 9, 1945

[United States Draft] Declaration on Liberated Europe [as Submitted at Sixth Formal Meeting of the Crimea Conference]

The Premier of the Union of Soviet Socialist Republics, the Prime Minister of the United Kingdom and the President of the United States of America have consulted with each other in the common interests of the peoples of their countries and those of liberated Europe. They jointly declare their mutual agreement to concert during the temporary period of instability in liberated Europe the policies of their three governments in assisting the peoples liberated from the domination of Nazi Germany and the peoples of the former Axis satellite states of Europe to solve by democratic means their pressing political and economic problems.

The establishment of order in Europe and the rebuilding of national economic life must be achieved by processes which will enable the liberated peoples to destroy the last vestiges of Nazism and Fascism and to create democratic institutions of their own choice. This is a principle of the Atlantic Charter—the right of all peoples to choose the form of government under which they will live—the restoration of sovereign rights and self-government to those peoples who have been forcibly deprived of them by the aggressor nations.

To foster the conditions in which the liberated peoples may exercise these rights, the three governments will jointly assist the people in any European liberated state or former Axis satellite state in Europe where in their judgment conditions require, (*a*) to establish conditions of internal peace; (*b*) to carry out emergency measures for the relief of distressed peoples; (*c*) to form interim governmental authorities broadly representative of all democratic elements in the population and pledged to the earliest possible establishment through free elections of governments responsive to the will of the people; and (*d*) to facilitate where necessary the holding of such elections.

The three governments will consult the other United Nations and provisional authorities or other governments in Europe when matters of direct interest to them are under consideration.

When, in the opinion of the three governments, conditions in any European liberated state or any former Axis satellite state in Europe make such action necessary, they will immediately establish appropriate machinery for the carrying out of the joint responsibilities set forth in this declaration.

By this declaration we reaffirm our faith in the principles of the Atlantic Charter, our pledge in the Declaration by the United Nations, and our determination to build in cooperation with other peace-loving nations a world order under law, dedicated to peace, security, freedom and general well-being of all mankind.

APPENDIX 57
February 6, 1945

[Statement of the American Position on Voting in the Security Council of the United Nations as Read by Secretary of State Stettinius at Third Formal Meeting of the Crimea Conference]

1. *Review of Status of this Question.*

It was agreed at Dumbarton Oaks that certain matters would remain under consideration for future settlement. Of these, the principal one was that of voting procedure to be followed in the Security Council.

At Dumbarton Oaks, the three Delegations thoroughly explored the whole question. Since that time the matter has received continuing intensive study by each of the three Governments.

On December 5, 1944, the President sent to Marshal Stalin and to Prime Minister Churchill a proposal that this matter be settled by making Section C, Chapter VI of the Dumbarton Oaks proposals read substantially as follows:

"C. VOTING

"1. Each member of the Security Council should have one vote.

"2. Decisions of the Security Council on procedural matters should be made by an affirmative vote of seven members.

"3. Decisions of the Security Council on all other matters should be made by an affirmative vote of seven members including the concurring votes of the permanent members; provided that, in decisions under Chapter VIII, Section A and under the second sentence of paragraph 1 of Chapter VIII, Section C, a party to a dispute should abstain from voting."

2. *Analysis of the American Proposal.*

(*a*) We believe that our proposal is entirely consistent with the special responsibilities of the great powers for the preservation of the peace of the world. In this respect our proposal calls for unqualified unanimity of the permanent members of the Council on all major decisions relating to the preservation of peace, including all economic and military enforcement measures.

(*b*) At the same time our proposal recognizes the desirability of the permanent members frankly stating that the peaceful adjustment of any controversy which may arise is a matter of general world interest in which any sovereign member state involved should have a right to present its case.

We believe that unless this freedom of discussion in the Council is permitted, the establishment of the World Organization which we all so earnestly desire in order to save the world from the tragedy of another war would be seriously jeopardized. Without full and free discussion in the Council, the Organization, even if it could be established, would be vastly different from the one we have contemplated.

The paper which we have placed before the other two delegations sets forth the text of the provisions which I have read and lists specifically those decisions of the Council which, under our proposals, would require unqualified unanimity and, separately, those matters in the area of discussion and peaceful settlement in which any party to a dispute would abstain from casting a vote.

3. *Reasons for the American Position.*

From the point of view of the United States Government there are two important elements in the matter of voting procedure.

First, there is the necessity for unanimity among the permanent members for the preservation of the peace of the world.

Second, it is of particular importance to the people of the United States that there be provision for a fair hearing for all members of the organization, large and small.

We believe that the proposals submitted by the President to Marshal Stalin and Prime Minister Churchill on December 5 of last year provide a reasonable and just solution and satisfactorily combine these two main considerations.

It is our earnest hope that our two great Allies will find it possible to accept the President's proposal.

[United States Draft] Statute of the Permanent Court of International Justice With the Revisions Proposed.

(The barred words [shown in this text in canceled type] are omitted, and the underscored words [in this text italicized] are added, by the proposed revisions.)

Article 1

A *The* Permanent Court of International Justice is hereby established, in accordance with Articles 14 of the Covenant of the League of Nations, *established by the Protocol of Signature of December 16, 1920 and the Protocol for the Revision of the Statute of September 14, 1929 shall be, as adapted to the purposes of the general international organization, the chief judicial organ of the general international organization.* This Court shall be in addition to the Court of Arbitration organized by the Conventions of The Hague of 1899 and 1907, and to the special Tribunals of Arbitration to which States are always at liberty to submit their disputes for settlement.

CHAPTER I

ORGANIZATION OF THE COURT

Article 2

The Permanent Court of International Justice shall be composed of a body of independent judges, elected regardless of their nationality from amongst persons of high moral character, who possess the qualifications required in their respective countries for appointment to the highest judicial offices, or are jurisconsults of recognized competence in international law.

Article 3

The Court shall consist of fifteen members.

Article 4

The members of the Court shall be elected by the *general* assembly and by the *executive* council of the *general international organization* from a list of persons nominated by the national groups in the *Permanent* Court of Arbitration, in accordance with the following provisions.

In the case of Members of the League of Nations *general international organization* not represented in the Permanent Court of Arbitration, the lists of candidates shall be drawn up by national groups appointed for this purpose by their Governments under the same conditions as those prescribed for members of the Permanent Court of Arbitration by Article 44 of the Convention of The Hague of 1907 for the pacific settlement of international disputes.

The conditions under which a State which has accepted the Statute of the Court but is not a Member of the League of Nations *general international organization*, may participate in electing the members of the Court shall, in the absence of a special agreement, be laid down by the *general* assembly on the proposal of the *executive* council.

Article 5

At least three months before the date of the election, the ~~Secretary-General~~ *director-general* of the ~~League of Nations~~ *general international organization* shall address a written request to the members of the *Permanent* Court of Arbitration ~~belonging to the States mentioned in the Annex to the Covenant or to the States which join the League subsequently,~~ and to the ~~persons~~ *members of the national groups* appointed under paragraph 2 of Article 4, inviting them to undertake, within a given time, by national groups, the nomination of persons in a position to accept the duties of a member of the Court.

No group may nominate more than four persons, not more than two of whom shall be of their own nationality. In no case must the number of candidates nominated be more than double the number of seats to be filled.

Article 6

Before making these nominations, each national group is recommended to consult its Highest Court of Justice, its Legal Faculties and Schools of Law, and its National Academies and national sections of International Academies devoted to the study of Law.

Article 7

The ~~Secretary-General~~ *director-general* of the ~~League of Nations~~ *general international organization* shall prepare a list in alphabetical order of all the persons thus nominated. Save as provided in Article 12, paragraph 2, these shall be the only persons eligible for appointment.

The ~~Secretary-General~~ *director-general* shall submit this list to the *general* assembly and to the *executive* council.

Article 8

The *general* assembly and the *executive* council shall proceed independently of one another to elect the members of the Court.

Article 9

At every election, the electors shall bear in mind that not only should all the persons appointed as members of the Court possess the qualifications required, but the whole body also should represent the main forms of civilization and the principal legal systems of the world.

Article 10

Those candidates who obtain an absolute majority of votes in the *general* assembly and in the *executive* council shall be considered as elected.

In the event of more than one national of the same *State or* Member of the ~~League~~ *general international organization* being elected by the votes of both the *general* assembly and the *executive* council, the eldest of these only shall be considered as elected.

Article 11

If, after the first meeting held for the purpose of the election, one or more seats remain to be filled, a second and, if necessary, a third meeting shall take place.

Article 12

If, after the third meeting, one or more seats still remain unfilled, a joint conference consisting of six members, three appointed by the *general* assembly and three by the *executive* council, may be formed, at any time, at the request of either the *general* assembly or the *executive* council, for the purpose of choosing one name for each seat still vacant, to submit to the *general* assembly and the *executive* council for their respective acceptance.

If the Conference is unanimously agreed upon any person who fulfils the required conditions, he may be included in its list, even though he was not included in the list of nominations referred to in Articles 4 and 5.

If the joint conference is satisfied that it will not be successful in procuring an election, those members of the Court who have already been appointed shall, within a period to be fixed by the Council, proceed to fill the vacant seats by selection from amongst those candidates who have obtained votes either in the *general* assembly or in the *executive* council.

In the event of an equality of votes amongst the judges, the eldest judge shall have a casting vote.

Article 13

The members of the Court shall be elected for nine years.

They may be re-elected.

They shall continue to discharge their duties until their places have been filled. Though replaced, they shall finish any cases which they may have begun.

In the case of the resignation of a member of the Court, the resignation will be addressed to the President of the Court for transmission to the ~~Secretary-General~~ *director-general* of the ~~League of Nations~~ *general international organization.* This last notification makes the place vacant.

Article 14

Vacancies which may occur shall be filled by the same method as that laid down for the first election, subject to the following provision: the ~~Secretary-General~~ *director-general* of the ~~League of Nations~~ *general international organization* shall, within one month of the occurrence of the vacancy, proceed to issue the invitations provided for in Article 5, and the date of the election shall be fixed by the *executive* council at its next session.

Article 15

~~A member of the Court elected to replace a member whose period of appointment has not expired, will hold the appointment for the remainder of his predecessor's term.~~ *The term of a member of the Court shall expire upon his attaining the age of seventy-five years, and no person may be elected a member of the Court after he has attained the age of seventy-two years.*

Article 16

The members of the Court may not exercise any political or administrative function, nor engage in any other occupation of a professional nature.

Any doubt on this point is settled by the decision of the Court.

Article 17

No member of the Court may act as agent, counsel or advocate in any case.

No member may participate in the decision of any case in which he has previously taken an active part as agent, counsel or advocate for one of the contesting parties, or as a member of a national or international Court, or of a commission of enquiry, or in any other capacity.

Any doubt on this point is settled by the decision of the Court.

Article 18

A member of the Court can not be dismissed unless, in the unanimous opinion of the other members, he has ceased to fulfil the required conditions.

Formal notification thereof shall be made to the ~~Secretary-General~~ *director-general* of the ~~League of Nations~~ *general international organization*, by the Registrar.

This notification makes the place vacant.

Article 19

The members of the Court, when engaged on the business of the Court, shall enjoy diplomatic privileges and immunities.

Article 20

Every member of the Court shall, before taking up his duties, make a solemn declaration in open Court that he will exercise his powers impartially and conscientiously.

Article 21

The Court shall elect its President and Vice-President for three years; they may be re-elected.

It shall appoint its Registrar.

The duties of Registrar of the Court shall not be deemed incompatible with those of Secretary-General of the Permanent Court of Arbitration.

Article 22

The seat of the Court shall be established at The Hague.

The President and Registrar shall reside at the seat of the Court.

Article 23

The Court shall remain permanently in session, except during the judicial vacations, the dates and duration of which shall be fixed by the Court.

Members of the Court whose homes are situated at more than five days' normal journey from The Hague shall be entitled, apart from the judicial vacations, to six months' leave every three years, not including the time spent in traveling.

Members of the Court shall be bound, unless they are on regular leave or prevented from attending by illness or other serious reasons duly explained to the President, to hold themselves permanently at the disposal of the Court.

Article 24

If, for some special reason, a member of the Court considers that he should not take part in the decision of a particular case, he shall so inform the President.

If the President considers that for some special reason one of the members of the Court should not sit on a particular case, he shall give him notice accordingly.

If in any such case the member of the Court and the President disagree, the matter shall be settled by the decision of the Court.

Article 25

The full Court shall sit except when it is expressly provided otherwise.

Subject to the condition that the number of judges available to constitute the Court is not thereby reduced below eleven, the Rules of Court may provide for allowing one or more judges, according to circumstances and in rotation, to be dispensed from sitting.

Provided always that a quorum of nine judges shall suffice to constitute the Court.

Article 26

~~Labor cases, particularly cases referred to in Part XIII (Labor) of the Treaty of Versailles and the corresponding portions of the other Treaties of Peace, shall be heard and determined by the Court under the following conditions:~~

~~The Court will appoint every three years a special Chamber of five judges, selected so far as possible with due regard to the provisions of Article 9. In addition, two judges shall be selected for the purpose of replacing a judge who finds it impossible to sit. If the parties so demand, cases will be heard and determined by this Chamber. In the absence of any such demand, the full Court will sit. In both cases, the judges will be assisted by four technical assessors sitting with them, but without the right to vote, and chosen with a view to insuring a just representation of the competing interests.~~

~~The technical assessors shall be chosen for each particular case in accordance with rules of procedure under Article 30 from a list of "Assessors for Labor Cases" composed of two persons nominated by each Member of the League of Nations and an equivalent number nominated by the Governing Body of the Labor Office. The Governing Body will nominate, as to one-half representatives of the workers, and as to one-half representatives of employers from the list referred to in Article 412 of the Treaty of Versailles and the corresponding Articles of the other Treaties of Peace.~~

~~Recourse may always be had to the summary procedure provided for in Article 29, in the cases referred to in the first paragraph of the present Article, if the parties so request.~~

~~In Labor cases, the International Office shall be at liberty to furnish the Court with all relevant information, and for this purpose the Director of that Office shall receive copies of all the written proceedings.~~

The Court may from time to time form one or more chambers for dealing with particular cases or with particular categories of cases. The Court's rules may provide for assessors to sit with such chambers, without the right to vote.

If the parties so request, cases will be heard and determined by such chambers.

Article 27

~~Cases relating to transit and communications, particularly cases referred to in Part XII (Ports, Waterways and Railways) of the Treaty of Versailles and the corresponding portions of the other Treaties of Peace, shall be heard and determined by the Court under the following conditions:~~

~~The Court will appoint every three years a special Chamber of five judges, selected so far as possible with due regard to the provisions of Article 9. In addition, two judges shall be selected for the purpose of replacing a judge who finds it impossible to sit. If the parties so demand, cases will be heard and determined by this Chamber. In the absence of any such demand, the full Court will sit. When desired by the parties or decided by the Court, the judges will be assisted by four technical assessors sitting with them, but without the right to vote.~~

~~The technical assessors shall be chosen for each particular case in accordance with rules of procedure under Article 30 from a list of "Assessors for Transit and Communications Cases" composed of two persons nominated by each Member of the League of Nations.~~

~~Recourse may always be had to the summary procedure provided for in Article 29, in the cases referred to in the first paragraph of the present Article, if the parties so request.~~

A judgment given by any of the chambers provided for in Articles 26 and 29 shall be a judgment rendered by the Court.

Article 28

The ~~special~~ chambers provided for in Articles 26 and ~~27~~ *29* may, with the consent of the parties to the dispute, sit elsewhere than at The Hague.

Article 29

With a view to the speedy dispatch of business, the Court shall form annually a Chamber composed of five judges who, at the request of the contesting parties, may hear and determine cases by summary procedure. In addition, two judges shall be selected for the purpose of replacing a judge who finds it impossible to sit.

Article 30

The Court shall frame rules for regulating its procedure. In particular, it shall lay down rules for summary procedure.

Article 31

Judges of the nationality of each of the contesting parties shall retain their right to sit in the case before the Court.

If the Court includes upon the Bench a judge of the nationality of one of the parties, the other party may choose a person to sit as judge. Such a person shall be chosen preferably from among those persons who have been nominated as candidates as provided in Articles 4 and 5.

If the Court includes upon the Bench no judge of the nationality of the contesting parties, each of these parties may proceed to select a judge as provided in the preceding paragraph.

The present provision shall apply to the case of Articles 26, ~~27,~~ and 29. In such cases, the President shall request one or, if necessary, two of the members of the Court forming the Chamber to give place to the members of the Court of the nationality of the parties concerned, and, failing such or if they are unable to be present, to the judges specially appointed by the parties.

Should there be several parties in the same interest, they shall, for the purpose of the preceding provisions, be reckoned as one party only. Any doubt upon this point is settled by the decision of the Court.

Judges selected as laid down in paragraphs 2, 3 and 4 of this Article shall fulfil the conditions required by Articles 2, 17 (paragraph 2), 20 and 24 of this Statute. They shall take part in the decision on terms of complete equality with their colleagues.

Article 32

The members of the Court shall receive an annual salary.

The President shall receive a special annual allowance.

The Vice-President shall receive a special allowance for every day on which he acts as President.

The judges appointed under Article 31, other than members of the Court, shall receive an indemnity for each day on which they sit.

These salaries, allowances and indemnities shall be fixed by the *general* assembly of the ~~League of Nations~~ *general international organization*, ~~on the proposal of the Council.~~ They may not be decreased during the term of office.

The salary of the Registrar shall be fixed by the *general* assembly on the proposal of the Court.

Regulations made by the *general* assembly shall fix the conditions under which retiring pensions may be given to members of the Court and to the Registrar, and the conditions under which members of the Court and the Registrar shall have their traveling expenses refunded.

The above salaries, indemnities and allowances shall be free of all taxation.

Article 33

The expenses of the Court shall be borne by the ~~League of Nations~~ *general international organization,* in such a manner as shall be decided by the *general* assembly, ~~upon the proposal of the Council.~~

CHAPTER II

COMPETENCE OF THE COURT

Article 34

Only States or Members of the ~~League of Nations~~ *general international organization* can be parties in cases before the Court.

The Court may, subject to and in conformity with its own rules, request of public international organizations information r.levant to cases before it, and it shall receive such information voluntarily presented by such organizations.

Article 35

The Court shall be open to the Members of the ~~League~~ *general international organization* and also to States ~~mentioned in the Annex to the Covenant~~ *parties to the Statute.*

The conditions under which the Court shall be open to other States shall, subject to the special provisions contained in treaties in force, be laid down by the Council, but in no case shall such provisions place the parties in a position of inequality before the Court.

When a State which is not a Member of the ~~League of Nations~~ *general international organization* is a party to a dispute, the Court will fix the amount which that party is to contribute towards the expenses of the Court. This provision shall not apply if such State is bearing a share of the expenses of the Court.

Article 36

The jurisdiction of the Court comprises all cases which the parties refer to it and all matters specially provided for *in the basic instrument creating the general international organization and* conventions in force.

The Members of the ~~League of Nations~~ *general international organization* and the States ~~mentioned in the Annex to the Covenant~~ *parties to the Statute* may, ~~either when signing or ratifying the Protocol to which the present Statute is adjoined, or at a later moment,~~ *at any time* declare that they recognize as compulsory ipso facto and without special agreement, in relation to any other Member or State accepting the same obligation, the jurisdiction of the Court in all or any of the classes of legal disputes concerning:

(a) the interpretation of a treaty;

(b) any question of international law;

(c) the existence of any fact which, if established, would constitute a breach of an international obligation;

(d) the nature or extent of the reparation to be made for the breach of an international obligation.

The declaration referred to above may be made unconditionally or on condition of reciprocity on the part of several or certain Members or States, or for a certain time.

In the event of a dispute as to whether the Court has jurisdiction, the matter shall be settled by the decision of the Court.

Article 37

When a treaty or convention in force provides for the reference of a matter to a tribunal to be instituted by the League of Nations or the *general international organization,* the Court will be such tribunal.

Article 38

The Court shall apply:

1. International conventions, whether general or particular, establishing rules expressly recognized by the contesting States;
2. International custom, as evidence of a general practice accepted as law;
3. The general principles of law recognized by civilized nations;
4. Subject to the provisions of Article 59, judicial decisions and the teachings of the most highly qualified publicists of the various nations, as subsidiary means for the determination of rules of law.

This provision shall not prejudice the power of the Court to decide a case ex aequo et bono, if the parties agree thereto.

CHAPTER III

PROCEDURE

Article 39

The official languages of the Court shall be French and English. If the parties agree that the case shall be conducted in French, the judgment will be delivered in French. If the parties agree that the case shall be conducted in English, the judgment will be delivered in English.

In the absence of an agreement as to which language shall be employed, each party may, in the pleadings, use the language which it prefers; the decision of the Court will be given in French and English. In this case the Court will at the same time determine which of the two texts shall be considered as authoritative.

The Court may, at the request of any party, authorize a language other than French or English to be used.

Article 40

Cases are brought before the Court, as the case may be, either by the notification of the special agreement or by a written application addressed to the Registrar. In either case the subject of the dispute and the contesting parties must be indicated.

The Registrar shall forthwith communicate the application to all concerned.

He shall also notify the Members of the ~~League of Nations~~ *general international organization* through the ~~Secretary General~~ *director-general* and also any States entitled to appear before the Court.

Article 41

The Court shall have the power to indicate, if it considers that circumstances so require, any provisional measures which ought to be taken to reserve the respective rights of either party.

Pending the final decision, notice of the measures suggested shall forthwith be given to the parties and the *executive* council.

Article 42

The Parties shall be represented by agents.

They may have the assistance of counsel or advocates before the Court.

Article 43

The procedure shall consist of two parts: written and oral.

The written proceedings shall consist of the communication to the judges and to the parties of Cases, Counter-Cases, and, if necessary, Replies; also all papers and documents in support.

These communications shall be made through the Registrar, in the order and within the time fixed by the Court.

A certified copy of every document produced by one party shall be communicated to the other party.

The oral proceedings shall consist of the hearing by the Court of witnesses, experts, agents, counsel and advocates.

Article 44

For the service of all notices upon persons other than the agents, counsel and advocates, the Court shall apply direct to the government of the State upon whose territory the notice has to be served.

The same provision shall apply whenever steps are to be taken to procure evidence on the spot.

Article 45

The hearing shall be under the control of the President or, if he is unable to preside, of the Vice-President; if neither is able to preside, the senior judge present shall preside.

Article 46

The hearing in Court shall be public, unless the Court shall decide otherwise, or unless the parties demand that the public be not admitted.

Article 47

Minutes shall be made at each hearing, and signed by the Registrar and the President.

These minutes shall be the only authentic record.

Article 48

The Court shall make orders for the conduct of the case, shall decide the form and time in which each party must conclude its arguments, and make all arrangements connected with the taking of evidence.

Article 49

The Court may, even before the hearing begins, call upon the agents to produce any document, or to supply any explanations. Formal note shall be taken of any refusal.

Article 50

The Court may, at any time, entrust any individual, body, bureau, commission or other organization that it may select, with the task of carrying out an enquiry or giving an expert opinion.

Article 51

During the hearing any relevant questions are to be put to the witnesses and experts under the conditions laid down by the Court in the rules of procedure referred to in Article 30.

Article 52

After the Court has received the proofs and evidence within the time specified for the purpose, it may refuse to accept any further oral or written evidence that one party may desire to present unless the other side consents.

Article 53

Whenever one of the parties shall not appear before the Court, or shall fail to defend his case, the other party may call upon the Court to decide in favor of his claim.

The Court must, before doing so, satisfy itself, not only that it has jurisdiction in accordance with Articles 36 and 37, but also that the claim is well founded in fact and law.

Article 54

When, subject to the control of the Court, the agents, advocates and counsel have completed their presentation of the case, the President shall declare the hearing closed.

The Court shall withdraw to consider the judgment.

The deliberations of the Court shall take place in private and remain secret.

Article 55

All questions shall be decided by a majority of the judges present at the hearing.

In the event of an equality of votes, the President or his deputy shall have a casting vote.

Article 56

The judgment shall state the reasons on which it is based.

It shall contain the names of the judges who have taken part in the decision.

Article 57

If the judgment does not represent in whole or in part the unanimous opinion of the judges, dissenting judges are entitled to deliver a separate opinion.

Article 58

The judgment shall be signed by the President and by the Registrar. It shall be read in open Court, due notice having been given to the agents.

Article 59

The decision of the Court has no binding force except between the parties and in respect of that particular case.

Article 60

The judgment is final and without appeal. In the event of dispute as to the meaning or scope of the judgment, the Court shall construe it upon the request of any party.

Article 61

An application for revision of a judgment can be made only when it is based upon the discovery of some fact of such a nature as to be a decisive factor, which fact was, when the judgment was given, unknown to the Court and also to the party claiming revision, always provided that such ignorance was not due to negligence.

The proceedings for revision will be opened by a judgment of the Court expressly recording the existence of the new fact, recognizing that it has such a character as to lay the case open to revision, and declaring the application admissible on this ground.

The Court may require previous compliance with the terms of the judgment before it admits proceedings in revision.

The application for revision must be made at latest within six months of the discovery of the new fact.

No application for revision may be made after the lapse of ten years from the date of the sentence.

Article 62

Should a State consider that it has an interest of a legal nature which may be affected by the decision in the case, it may submit a request to the Court to be permitted to intervene as a third party.

It shall be for the Court to decide upon this request.

Article 63

Whenever the construction of a convention to which States other than those concerned in the case are parties is in question, the Registrar shall notify all such States forthwith.

Every State so notified has the right to intervene in the proceedings: but if it uses this right, the construction given by the judgment will be equally binding upon it.

Article 64

Unless otherwise decided by the Court, each party shall bear its own costs.

CHAPTER IV

ADVISORY OPINIONS

Article 65

Questions upon which the advisory opinion of the Court is asked shall be laid before the Court by means of a written request, signed ~~either~~ by the ~~President~~ *chairman* ~~of the Assembly or the President~~ of the *executive* council of the ~~League of Nations~~ *general international organization*, or by the ~~Secretary General~~ *director-general* of the ~~League~~ *general international organization* under instructions from ~~the Assembly or~~ the *executive* council.

The request shall contain an exact statement of the question upon which an opinion is required, and shall be accompanied by all documents likely to throw light upon the question.

Article 66

1. The Registrar shall forthwith give notice of the request for an advisory opinion to the Members of the ~~League of Nations~~ *general international organization*, through the ~~Secretary General~~ *director-general* of the ~~League~~ *general international organization*, and to any States entitled to appear before the Court.

The Registrar shall also, by means of a special and direct communication, notify any Member of the ~~League~~ *general international organization* or State admitted to appear before the Court or international organization considered by the Court (or, should it not be sitting, by the President) as likely to be able to furnish information on the question, that the Court will be prepared to receive, within a time-limit to be fixed by the President, written statements, or to hear, at a public sitting to be held for the purpose, oral statements relating to the question.

Should any Member or State referred to in the first paragraph have failed to receive the communication specified above, such Member or State may express a desire to submit a written statement, or to be heard; and the Court will decide.

2. Members, States, and organizations having presented written or oral statements or both shall be admitted to comment on the statements made by other Members, States, or organizations in the form, to the extent and within the time-limits which the Court, or, should it not be sitting, the President, shall decide in each particular case. Accordingly, the Registrar shall in due time communicate any such written statements to Members, States, and organizations having submitted similar statements.

Article 67

The Court shall deliver its advisory opinions in open Court, notice having been given to the ~~Secretary General~~ *director-general* of the ~~League of Nations~~ *general international organization* and to the representatives of Members of the ~~League~~ *general international organization,* of States and of international organizations immediately concerned.

Article 68

In the exercise of its advisory functions, the Court shall further be guided by the provisions of the Statute which apply in contentious cases to the extent to which it recognizes them to be applicable.

Chapter V

Amendment

Article 69

Amendments to this Statute, proposed by the general assembly of the general international organization acting by majority vote, shall become effective when ratified in accordance with their constitutional processes by two-thirds of the members of the organization, including all of the states having continuing tenure on the executive council.

APPENDIX 59
April 19, 1945

Memorandum for the President
Charter for the International Organization

The American Delegation to the United Nations Conference on International Organization is unanimously agreed that we should propose a few alterations in the Dumbarton Oaks Proposals during the San Francisco Conference. We will reserve our final positions on all of these, of course, until we learn the views of other governments. I am listing below for your information the most important points involved:

Purposes

1. Inclusion of a statement that the organization should act in accordance with the principles of justice and equity in adjusting or settling disputes, and that the organization should foster the development of international law.

2. Inclusion of a statement on the promotion of respect for human rights and fundamental freedoms (in the Dumbarton Oaks Proposals this is stated in the chapter on economic and social cooperation only).

Principles

1. Change the expression "sovereign equality of peace-loving states" to "the sovereign equality of all member states".

2. Make clearer that members must refrain from using any but peaceful means in settling their disputes and must use such means pursuant to the provisions of the Charter.

The General Assembly

1. Clarify to show that the General Assembly can at all times *discuss* any question bearing on the maintenance of peace and security, and that the limitation on its power to make recommendations concerning matters which are being dealt with by the Security Council should be confined to *specific* recommendations.

2. Give the General Assembly power to determine the qualifications of membership, and to admit new members by its own action unless the Security Council interposes objections for reasons of security.

3. Apportionment by the General Assembly of expenses among the members should be on the basis of an appropriate pro-ration.

4. Add to recommendatory powers, so can make recommendations relative to the promotion of measures to establish justice, to foster the observance of human rights and fundamental freedoms, and to encourage the development of rules of international law.

5. Extend power to recommend measures for peaceful adjustment to include situations likely to violate the principles enunciated in the Atlantic Charter and situations arising out of any treaties or international engagements.

The Security Council

1. Eliminate provision that regional subcommittees of the Military Staff Committee can be established.

Maintenance of Peace and Security

1. Propose that the exclusion from the scope of the Security Council in peaceful settlement of matters within the domestic jurisdiction of a state should be stated without the present qualification that those matters must be ones which "by international law" are "solely" within domestic jurisdiction.

Amendments

We should hold to the present proposals, but serious consideration is being given to proposing or supporting a possible additional provision to the following effect:

"A general conference of the members of the United Nations may be held at a date and place to be fixed by a two-thirds vote of the General Assembly with the concurrence of the Security Council, for the purpose of reviewing the Charter. Each member shall have one vote in the Conference. Any alterations of the Charter recommended by a two-thirds vote of the Conference shall take effect when ratified in accordance with their respective constitutional processes by the members of the organization having permanent membership on the Security Council and by a majority of the other members of the Organization".

Questions deferred

We have been considering, but have deferred, making decisions on the following questions:

1. Wording of the Preamble.

2. Defining the right of self-defense.

3. Possible changes in the wording in the chapter on economic and social cooperation.

4. Possible withdrawal provision.

E. R. STETTINIUS, Jr.

APPENDIX 60
March 28, 1945 [72]

Memorandum

It is recommended that at the San Francisco Conference the four inviting powers should retain their character as sponsoring governments in the presentation of suggestions and recommendations which they may individually or severally have to bring before the Conference. This will make for a more orderly procedure and avoid the appearance of lack of support by the sponsoring governments of the agreements already reached.

Such a procedure would be in keeping with the spirit which has enabled the principal United Nations to act in agreement on the many basic and fundamental questions represented by the Dumbarton Oaks Proposals.

In order to implement this procedure it is proposed that the four sponsoring governments should agree among themselves that any substantial changes which any of them may have to suggest to the Conference should only be brought forward after consultation among the four governments.

This should not be construed, however, in a restrictive sense. Each government should be free, in the course of commission or committee discussions, to make recommendations and suggestions designed to improve the charter so long as they are within the framework of the Dumbarton Oaks Proposals. Moreover, each government would obviously have the right, in the course of such discussions, to comment without prior consultation on proposals or suggestions which may be advanced by other participating governments.

Department of State,
Washington.

APPENDIX 61
May 2, 1945 [73]

Changes in Dumbarton Oaks Proposals as Suggested by the United States Delegation

[NOTE: Amendments are shown by italicizing added passages and using canceled type for deleted passages.]

CHAPTER I: PURPOSES

1. To maintain international peace and security; and to that end to take effective collective measures for the prevention and removal of threats to the peace and the suppression of acts of aggression or other breaches of the peace, and to bring about by peaceful means, *and with due regard for principles of justice and international law,* adjustment or settlement of international disputes which may lead to a breach of the peace.

---

[72] Transmitted by the Department of State to the British, Soviet and Chinese Embassies on the same date.

[73] Communicated on same date to British, Soviet, and Chinese Delegations at the San Francisco Conference.

3. To achieve international cooperation in the solution of international economic, social, *cultural* and other humanitarian problems, and *to promote respect for human rights and fundamental freedoms.*

CHAPTER II: PRINCIPLES

1. The Organization is based on the principle of the sovereign equality of all ~~peace loving states~~ *its members.*

3. All members of the Organization shall ~~settle their disputes by~~ *in the settlement of their international disputes* use peaceful means in such a manner that international peace and security are not endangered.

CHAPTER V: THE GENERAL ASSEMBLY

Section B. Functions and Powers

6. The General Assembly should initiate studies, and make recommendations for the purpose of promoting international cooperation in political, economic, ~~and~~ social *and cultural* fields, *and in measures to establish justice; fostering the observance of human rights and fundamental freedoms; and encouraging the development of rules of international law.* ~~and of adjusting~~ *The General Assembly should recommend measures for the peaceful adjustment of* situations likely to impair the general welfare *or to violate the principles accepted by them in the Preamble of the Declaration by United Nations of January 1, 1942 including situations arising out of any treaties or international engagements.*

CHAPTER VI: THE SECURITY COUNCIL

Section D. Procedure

2. The Security Council should be empowered to set up such bodies or agencies as it may deem necessary for the performance of its functions. ~~including regional subcommittees of the Military Staff Committee.~~

CHAPTER VIII: ARRANGEMENTS FOR THE MAINTENANCE OF INTERNATIONAL PEACE AND SECURITY INCLUDING PREVENTION AND SUPPRESSION OF AGGRESSION

Section A. Pacific Settlement of Disputes

7. The provisions of paragraphs 1 to 6 of Section A should not apply to situations or disputes arising out of matters which ~~by international law~~ are ~~solely~~ within the domestic jurisdiction of the state concerned.

Section B. Determination of Threats to the Peace or Acts of Aggression and Action With Respect Thereto

1. Should the Security Council deem that a failure to settle a dispute in accordance with procedures indicated in paragraph 3 of Section A, or in accordance with its recommendations made under paragraph 5 of Section A, constitutes a threat to the maintenance of international peace and security, it should take any measures *set forth in paragraphs 3 and 4 of this Section* necessary for the maintenance of international peace and security in accordance with the purposes and principles of the Organization.

2. In general the Security Council should determine the existence of any threat to the peace, breach of the peace or act of aggression and should make recommendations or decide upon the measures *set forth in paragraphs 3 and 4 of this Section* to be taken to maintain or restore peace and security.

CHAPTER IX: ARRANGEMENTS FOR INTERNATIONAL ECONOMIC AND SOCIAL COOPERATION

Section A. Purpose and Relationships

1. With a view to the creation of conditions of stability and well-being which are necessary for peaceful and friendly relations among nations, the Organization should facilitate solutions of international economic, social, *cultural,* and other humanitarian problems and promote respect for human rights and fundamental freedoms. Responsibility for the discharge of this function should be vested in the General Assembly and, under the authority of the General Assembly, in an Economic and Social Council.

Section D. Organization and Procedure

1. The Economic and Social Council should set up an economic commission, a social commission, *a human rights commission,* and such other commissions as may be required. These commissions should consist of experts. There should be a permanent staff which should constitute a part of the Secretariat of the Organization.

CHAPTER X: THE SECRETARIAT

4. *In the performance of their duties, the Secretary-General and the staff should be responsible only to the Organization. Their responsibilities should be exclusively international in character, and they should not seek or receive instructions in regard to the discharge thereof from any authority external to the Organization. The members should undertake fully to respect the international character of the responsibilities of the Secretariat and not to seek to influence any of their nationals in the discharge of such responsibilities.*

CHAPTER XI: AMENDMENTS

2. *A general conference of the members of the United Nations may be held at a date and place to be fixed by a three-fourths vote of the General Assembly with the concurrence of the Security Council voting in accordance with the provisions of Chapter VI, Section C, paragraph 2, for the purpose of reviewing the Charter. Each member shall have one vote in the Conference. Any alterations of the Charter recommended by a two-thirds vote of the Conference shall take effect when ratified in accordance with their respective constitutional processes by the members of the Organization having permanent membership on the Security Council and by a majority of the other members of the Organization.*

APPENDIX 62
May 4, 1945 [74]

Amendments Proposed by the Governments of the United States, United Kingdom, Soviet Union, and China

The Delegations of the four Governments which participated in the Dumbarton Oaks conversations, the United States, the United Kingdom, the Soviet Union, and China, have consulted together concerning amendments to the Dumbarton

[74] As submitted to the San Francisco Conference by midnight this date.

Oaks Proposals which each of them desired to submit. The proposed amendments on which the four find themselves in agreement are submitted to the Conference as joint proposals. Such further amendments as each of these Governments may wish to propose will be presented separately.

[NOTE: Amendments are indicated by italicizing added passages and using canceled type for deleted passages.]

CHAPTER I. PURPOSES

1. To maintain international peace and security; and to that end to take effective collective measures for the prevention and removal of threats to the peace and the suppression of acts of aggression or other breaches of the peace, and to bring about by peaceful means, *and with due regard for principles of justice and international law,* adjustment or settlement of international disputes which may lead to a breach of the peace;

3. To achieve international cooperation in the solution of international economic, social, *cultural* and other humanitarian problems *and promotion and encouragement of respect for human rights and for fundamental freedoms for all without distinction as to race, language, religion or sex;* and

CHAPTER II. PRINCIPLES

1. The Organization is based on the principle of the sovereign equality of all ~~peace-loving states~~ *its members.*

3. All members of the Organization shall settle their *international* disputes by peaceful means in such a manner that international peace and security are not endangered.

New paragraph to be added following paragraph 6, to take the place of paragraph 7 of Chapter VIII, Section A, which would be deleted:

Nothing contained in this Charter shall authorize the Organization to intervene in matters which are essentially within the domestic jurisdiction of the State concerned or shall require the members to submit such matters to settlement under this Charter; but this principle shall not prejudice the application of Chapter VIII, Section B.

CHAPTER V. THE GENERAL ASSEMBLY

Section B. Functions and Powers

6. The General Assembly should initiate studies and make recommendations for the purpose of promoting international cooperation in political, economic, ~~and~~ social *and cultural* fields *and to assist in the realization of human rights and basic freedoms for all, without distinction as to race, language, religion or sex and also for the encouragement of the development of international law* ~~and of adjusting situations likely to impair the general welfare.~~

New paragraph to follow paragraph 7:

The General Assembly should examine the administrative budgets of such specialized agencies with a view to making recommendations to the agencies concerned.

CHAPTER VI. THE SECURITY COUNCIL

Section A. Composition

The Security Council should consist of one representative of each of eleven members of the Organization. Representatives of the United States of America, the United Kingdom of Great Britain and Northern Ireland, the Union of Soviet Socialist Republics, the Republic of China, and, in due course, France, should have permanent seats. The General Assembly should elect six states to fill the non-permanent seats, *due regard being specially paid in the first instance*

*to the contribution of members of the Organization towards the maintenance of
international peace and security and towards the other purposes of the Organization,
and also to equitable geographical distribution.* These six states should be elected
for a term of two years, three retiring each year. They should not be immediately
eligible for reelection. In the first election of the non-permanent members three
should be chosen by the General Assembly for one-year terms and three for two-
year terms.

Section D. Procedure

2. The Security Council should be empowered to set up such bodies or agencies
as it may deem necessary for the performance of its functions, ~~including regional
subcommittees of the Military Staff Committee.~~

5. Any member of the Organization not having a seat on the Security Council
and any state not a member of the Organization, if it is a party to a dispute under
consideration by the Security Council, should be invited to participate in the discussion relating to the dispute. *In the case of a non-member, the Security Council
should lay down such conditions as it may deem just for the participation of such a
non-member.*

CHAPTER VII. AN INTERNATIONAL COURT OF JUSTICE

The provisions of Chapter VII of the Dumbarton Oaks Proposals should be
adjusted to bring it into conformity with the recommendations of Commission
IV in light of the report of the Jurist's Committee.

CHAPTER VIII. ARRANGEMENTS FOR THE MAINTENANCE OF INTERNATIONAL PEACE AND SECURITY INCLUDING PREVENTION AND SUPPRESSION OF AGGRESSION

Section A. Pacific Settlement of Disputes

The following new paragraph should be inserted before Paragraph 1 of Section A
of Chapter VIII:

*Without prejudice to the provisions of paragraphs 1–5 below, the Security Council
should be empowered, if all the parties so request, to make recommendations to the
parties to any dispute with a view to its settlement in accordance with the principles
laid down in Chapter II, Paragraph 3.*

2. Any state, whether member of the Organization or not, may bring any such
dispute or situation to the attention of the General Assembly or of the Security
Council. *In the case of a non-member, it should be required to accept, for the purposes
of such dispute, the obligations of pacific settlement provided in the Charter.*

4. If, nevertheless, parties to a dispute of the nature referred to in paragraph 3
above fail to settle it by the means indicated in that paragraph, they should obligate
themselves to refer it to the Security Council. ~~The~~ *If the* Security Council
~~should in each case decide whether or not~~ *deems that* the continuance of the
particular dispute is in fact likely to endanger the maintenance of international
peace and security, ~~and, accordingly, whether the Security Council should deal
with the dispute; and, if so, whether it should take action under paragraph 5~~ *it
shall decide whether to take action under paragraph 5 or whether itself to recommend
such terms of settlement as it may consider appropriate.*

7. ~~The provisions of paragraph 1 to 6 of Section A should not apply to situations
or disputes arising out of matters which by international law are solely within the
domestic jurisdiction of the state concerned.~~

(*Note:* This paragraph would be replaced by the new paragraph proposed for
addition following paragraph 6, Chapter II, Principles.)

Section B. Determination of Threats to the Peace or Acts of Aggression and Action with Respect Thereto

1. Should the Security Council deem that a failure to settle a dispute in accordance with procedures indicated in paragraph 3 of Section A, or in accordance with its recommendations made under paragraphs *4 or* 5 of Section A, constitutes a threat to the maintenance of international peace and security, it should take any measures necessary for the maintenance of international peace and security in accordance with the purposes and principles of the Organization.

2. In general the Security Council should determine the existence of any threat to the peace, breach of the peace or act of aggression and should make recommendations or decide upon the measures *set forth in paragraphs 3 and 4 of this Section* to be taken to maintain or restore peace and security.

Insert the following paragraph between paragraphs 2 and 3:

Before making the recommendations or deciding upon the measures for the maintenance or restoration of peace and security in accordance with the provisions of paragraph 2, the Security Council may call upon the parties concerned to comply with such provisional measures as it may deem necessary or desirable in order to prevent an aggravation of the situation. Such provisional measures should be without prejudice to the rights, claims or position of the parties concerned. Failure to comply with such provisional measures should be duly taken account of by the Security Council.

9. There should be established a Military Staff Committee the functions of which should be to advise and assist the Security Council on all questions relating to the Security Council's military requirements for the maintenance of international peace and security, to the employment and command of forces placed at its disposal, to the regulation of armaments, and to possible disarmament. It should be responsible under the Security Council for the strategic direction of any armed forces placed at the disposal of the Security Council. The Committee should be composed of the Chiefs of Staff of the permanent members of the Security Council or their representatives. Any member of the Organization not permanently represented on the Committee should be invited by the Committee to be associated with it when the efficient discharge of the Committee's responsibilities requires that such a state should participate in its work. Questions of command of forces should be worked out subsequently. *The Military Staff Committee, with the authorization of the Security Council, may establish regional subcommittees of the Military Staff Committee.*

CHAPTER IX. ARRANGEMENTS FOR INTERNATIONAL
ECONOMIC AND SOCIAL COOPERATION

Section A. Purpose and Relationships

1. With a view to the creation of conditions of stability and well-being which are necessary for peaceful and friendly relations among nations *based on respect for the principle of equal rights and self-determination of peoples,* the Organization should facilitate solutions of international economic, social, *cultural,* and other humanitarian problems and promote respect for human rights and *for* fundamental freedoms *for all without distinction as to race, language, religion or sex.* Responsibility for the discharge of this function should be vested in the General Assembly, and under the authority of the General Assembly, in an Economic and Social Council.

Section C. Functions and Powers of the Economic and Social Council

1. The Economic and Social Council should be empowered:

Insert after paragraph a new paragraph as follows:

To make recommendations for promoting respect for human rights and fundamental freedoms;

b. To make recommendations, on its own initiative with respect to international economic, social, *cultural* and other humanitarian matters;

c. To receive and consider reports from the economic, social, *cultural* and other organizations or agencies brought into relationship with the Organization, and to coordinate their activities through consultations with, and recommendations to, such organizations or agencies;

Section D. Organization and Procedure

1. The Economic and Social Council should set up ~~an economic commission, a social commission and such other commissions as may be required~~ *commissions in the fields of economic activity, social activity, cultural activity, promotion of human rights and any other field within the competence of the Council.* These commissions should consist of experts. There should be a permanent staff which should constitute a part of the Secretariat of the Organization.

Chapter X. The Secretariat

1. There should be a Secretariat comprising a Secretary-General, *four deputies* and such staff as may be required. ~~The Secretary-General should be the chief administrative officer of the Organization. He should be elected by the General Assembly, on recommendation of the Security Council, for such term and under such conditions as are specified in the Charter.~~ *The Secretary-General and his deputies should be elected by the General Assembly on recommendation of the Security Council for a period of three years, and the Secretary-General should be eligible for re-election. The Secretary-General should be the chief administrative officer of the Organization.*

4. *In the performance of their duties, the Secretary-General and the staff should be responsible only to the Organization. Their responsibilities should be exclusively international in character, and they should not seek or receive instructions in regard to the discharge thereof from any authority external to the Organization. The members should undertake fully to respect the international character of the responsibilities of the Secretariat and not to seek to influence any of their nationals in the discharge of such responsibilities.*

Chapter XI. Amendments

1. *The present Charter comes into force after its ratification in accordance with their respective constitutional processes by the members of the Organization having permanent seats on the Security Council and by a majority of the other members of the Organization.*

Note: The existing text of Chapter XI becomes paragraph 2.

2. *A general conference of the members of the United Nations may be held at a date and place to be fixed by a three-fourths vote of the General Assembly with the concurrence of the Security Council voting in accordance with the provisions of Chapter VI, Section C, paragraph 2, for the purpose of reviewing the Charter. Each member shall have one vote in the Conference. Any alterations of the Charter recommended by a two-thirds vote of the Conference shall take effect when ratified in accordance with their respective constitutional processes by the members of the Organization having permanent membership on the Security Council and by a majority of the other members of the Organization.*

APPENDIX 63
May 4, 1945 [75]

Additional Amendments to the Dumbarton Oaks Proposals Proposed by the United States

(NOTE: Amendments are indicated by underscoring [italicizing] added passages and striking out [using canceled type for] deleted passages.)

CHAPTER V. THE GENERAL ASSEMBLY

Section B—Functions and Powers

New paragraph to follow paragraph 6:

Subject to the provisions of paragraph 1 of this Section, the General Assembly should be empowered to recommend measures for the peaceful adjustment of any situations, regardless of origin, which it deems likely to impair the general welfare or friendly relations among nations, including situations resulting from a violation of the Purposes and Principles set forth in this Charter.

CHAPTER VIII. ARRANGEMENTS FOR THE MAINTENANCE OF INTERNATIONAL PEACE AND SECURITY INCLUDING PREVENTION AND SUPPRESSION OF AGGRESSION

Section C—Regional Arrangements

2. The Security Council should, where appropriate, utilize such arrangements or agencies for enforcement action under its authority. But no enforcement action should be taken under regional arrangements or by regional agencies without the authorization of the Security Council *with the exception of measures against enemy states in this war provided for pursuant to Chapter XII, paragraph 2, or, in regional arrangements directed against renewal of aggressive policy on the part of such states, until such time as the Organization may, by consent of the Governments concerned, be charged with the responsibility for preventing further aggression by a State now at war with the United Nations.*

ARRANGEMENTS FOR INTERNATIONAL TRUSTEESHIP

Additional Chapter Proposed by the United States

(NOTE: This draft deals with principles and mechanism only and makes no assumption about the inclusion of any specific territory.) [76]

(NOTE 2: If this draft is to be included as a chapter of the Charter of the Organization, the relevant paragraphs and clauses of the Charter would require revision in order that they might be brought into harmony with the trusteeship provisions.)

1. The Organization should establish under its authority a system of international trusteeship for the administration and supervision of such territories as may be placed thereunder by subsequent agreement.

---

[75] As submitted to the San Francisco Conference at midnight same date. The first two of the three amendments became joint sponsors' proposals on May 7, and were issued as such on May 11 by the United Nations Conference on International Organization in General Series Document 2 (English) G/29a.

[76] With the addition of the second parenthesized note, this document is the same as the United States proposal completed and dated Apr. 26, 1945.

2. The basic objectives of the trusteeship system should be: (a) to further international peace and security; (b) to promote the political, economic, and social advancement of the trust territories and their inhabitants and their progressive development toward self-government; and (c) to provide for non-discriminatory treatment in trust territories with respect to the economic and other appropriate civil activities of the nationals of all member states.

3. The trusteeship system should apply only to such territories in the following categories as may be placed thereunder by means of trusteeship arrangements: (a) territories now held under mandate; (b) territories which may be detached from enemy states as a result of this war; and (c) territories voluntarily placed under the system by states responsible for their administration. It would be a matter for subsequent agreement as to which territories would be brought under a trusteeship system and upon what terms.

4. The trusteeship arrangement for each territory to be placed under trusteeship should be agreed upon by the states directly concerned and should be approved as provided for in paragraphs 7 and 8 below.

5. The trusteeship arrangements in each case should include the terms under which the territory will be administered.

6. There may be designated, in the trusteeship arrangement, a strategic area or areas which may include part or all of the territory to which the arrangement applies.

7. All functions of the Organization relating to strategic areas, including the approval of the trusteeship arrangements and their alteration or amendment, should be exercised by the Security Council.

8. The functions of the Organization with regard to trusteeship arrangements for all other areas should be exercised by the General Assembly.

9. In order to assist the General Assembly to carry out those functions under the trusteeship system not reserved to the Security Council, there should be established a Trusteeship Council which would operate under its authority. The Trusteeship Council should consist of specially qualified representatives, designated (a) one each by the states administering trust territories; and (b) one each by an equal number of other states named for three-year periods by the General Assembly.

10. The General Assembly, and under its authority, the Trusteeship Council, in carrying out their functions, should be empowered to consider reports submitted by the administering authorities, to accept petitions, to institute investigations, and to take other action within their competence as defined by the trusteeship arrangements.

11. The administering authority in each trust territory within the competence of the General Assembly should make an annual report to the General Assembly upon the basis of a questionnaire formulated by the Trusteeship Council.

APPENDIX 64
May 15, 1945 [77]

Proposed Working Paper for Chapter on Dependent Territories and Arrangements for International Trusteeship

．　　　．　　　．　　　．　　　．　　　．　　　．

Underlined [italicized] portions indicate new matter added to United States draft for reference and convenience in consideration of proposed working paper for chapter on dependent territories and arrangements for international trusteeship.

(This paper is not proposed by any government at this time and does not constitute a withdrawal of the proposals put forward by any government.)

(NOTE: This draft deals with principles and mechanism only and makes no assumption about the inclusion of any specific territory.)

(NOTE: Section A might be considered for inclusion in the Chapter on Principles.)

A. *General Policy*

1. *States members of the United Nations which have responsibilities for the administration of territories inhabited by peoples not yet able to stand by themselves under the strenuous conditions of the modern world accept the general principle that it is a sacred trust of civilization to promote to the utmost the well-being of the inhabitants of these territories within the world community, and to this end:*

　(i) *to insure the economic and social advancement of the peoples concerned;*

　(ii) *to develop self-government in forms appropriate to the varying circumstances of each territory; and*

　(iii) *to further international peace and security.*

2. *States members also agree that their policy in respect of such territories, no less than in respect to their metropolitan areas, must be based on the general principle of good-neighborliness, due account being taken of the interests and well-being of other members of the world community, in social, economic, and commercial matters.*

B. *Territorial Trusteeship System*

1. The Organization should establish under its authority an international system of trusteeship for the administration and supervision of such territories as may be placed thereunder by subsequent individual agreements *and set up suitable machinery for these purposes.*

2. The basic objectives of the trusteeship system should be: (a) to further international peace and security; (b) to promote the political, economic, and social advancement of the trust territories and their inhabitants and their progressive development toward self-government *in forms appropriate to the varying circumstances of each territory; and* (c) to ensure equal treatment in *social, economic, and commercial matters for all members of the United Nations without prejudice to the attainment of (a) and (b) above, and subject to the provisions of paragraph 5, below.*

3. The trusteeship system should apply only to such territories in the following

---

[77] The United Nations Conference on International Organization, Commission II, General Assembly, Committee 4, Trusteeship System, Doc. 323 (English), May 15, 1945. This document as issued presented practically identical texts of the Working Paper in two forms; the second only is reproduced here.

categories as may be placed thereunder by means of trusteeship arrangements: (a) territories now held under mandate; (b) territories which may be detached from enemy states as a result of this war; and (c) territories voluntarily placed under the system by states responsible for their administration. It would be a matter for subsequent agreement as to which territories would be brought under a trusteeship system and upon what terms. *The trusteeship system should not apply to territories which have become members of the United Nations.*

4. The trusteeship arrangement for each territory to be placed under trusteeship should be agreed upon by the states directly concerned and should be approved as provided for in paragraphs 8 and 10 below.

5. *Except as may be agreed upon in individual trusteeship arrangements placing each territory under the trusteeship system, nothing in this chapter should be construed in and of itself to alter in any manner the rights of any state or any peoples in any territory.*

6. The trusteeship arrangements in each case should include the terms under which the territory will be administered *and designate the state which should exercise the administration of the territory or designate the United Nations Organization itself to exercise the administration of the territory.*

7. There may be designated, in the trusteeship arrangement, a strategic area or areas which may include part or all of the territory to which the arrangement applies.

8. All functions of the Organization relating to such strategic areas, including the approval of the trusteeship arrangements and their alteration or amendment, should be exercised by the Security Council. *The basic objectives as provided for in paragraph B. 2 above should be applicable to the people of each strategic area. The Security Council may avail itself of the assistance of the Trusteeship Council provided for in paragraph 11 below to perform those functions of the Organization under the trusteeship system relating to political, economic, and social matters in the strategic areas, subject to the provisions of the trusteeship arrangements.*

9. *It shall be the duty of the state administering any trust territory to insure that the territory shall play its part in the maintenance of international peace and security. To this end the state shall be empowered to make use of volunteer forces, facilities, and assistance from the territory in carrying out the obligations undertaken by the state for the Security Council in this regard and for local defense and the maintenance of law and order within the territory.*

10. The functions of the Organization with regard to trusteeship arrangements for all areas *not designated as strategic* should be exercised by the General Assembly.

11. In order to assist the General Assembly to carry out those functions under the trusteeship system not reserved to the Security Council, there should be established a Trusteeship Council which would operate under its authority. The Trusteeship Council should consist of specially qualified representatives, designated (a) one each by the states administering trust territories, and (b) one each by an equal number of other states named for three-year periods by the General Assembly.

12. The General Assembly, and under its authority, the Trusteeship Council, in carrying out their functions, should be empowered to consider reports submitted by the administering state, to accept petitions and examine them in consultation with the administering state, *to make periodic visits to the respective territories at times agreed upon with the administering state,* and to take other action, *in conformity with* the trusteeship arrangements.

13. The administering authority in each trust territory within the competence of the General Assembly should make an annual report to the General Assembly upon the basis of a questionnaire formulated by the Trusteeship Council.

Indexes

Index

[Index of persons follows this index]

Foreign Policy, Post-War, Advisory Council on, 213–215

Foreign Relations, Council on, 19, 56, 80, 82–83, 106, 131, 152

Foreign Relations, Problems of, Advisory Committee on, creation, duties, and membership, 3, 20–22, 23, 42, 47; tapering off of duties, 29, 30–31; reconstitution, 42, 45, 57, 462; Subcommittee on Economic Problems, membership, 22; general program, 23–24, 454–455; preparations for a conference of neutrals, 24–28; outline of memorandum on bases of an economic settlement, 456–457; ceases functioning as a separate body, 29; *see also* Post-War International Economic Problems and Policies, Interdepartmental Group to Consider Subcommittee on Limitation and Reduction of Armaments, 22 Subcommittee on Political Problems, membership, 22; preparations for a conference of neutrals, 24–28; study of regional organization for Europe 28, 458–460; consideration of results of possible German victory, 30; ceases functioning as a group, 30–31

Four Freedoms address of President Roosevelt, 42–43, 50

Four Nation Declaration (1943), 188, 189, 194, 197, 198, 199, 200, 201, 204, 246, 247, 264, 265, 274, 276, 282, 553

France, 8, 9, 10; World War II, 7, 15, 17, 26, 27, 31, 32, 36, 44, 59, 60, 301; Atlantic Charter, 52; postwar treatment, 128, 198, 228, 234; French Committee of National Liberation, 187, 188, 231, 244; Provisional Government, 344; Declaration by United Nations, 344; member, European Advisory Commission, 228, 344; Declaration on Liberated Europe, 372–373, 655–656; establishment of European Central Inland Transport Organization, 363; quadripartite Caribbean Commission (1946), 231n international organization: member of Security Council, 299, 385n; U. S. consultation with on decisions of Crimea Conference, 395, 397–398, 408–409, 410, 661; question of sponsorship of San Francisco Conference,

France—Continued.
385, 409, 410, 661 (*see also* United Nations Conference on International Organization); five-power consultations on trusteeship, 430, 431, 433, 445–446, 449, 688–689; five-power review of amendments of other participants at San Francisco Conference, 448, 449

France, Interdivisional Country Committee on, 177

Free French. *See* France

Fulbright resolution, 195, 197

Fund, International Monetary, 141–142, 184, 186, 192, 224, 240–242, 272, 354, 355, 360

General Advisory Committee, 53

General Assembly of the United Nations. *See* United Nations Charter, structure and functions

General Conference of United Nations. *See* General Assembly

Geneva Disarmament Conference, 10

German Atrocities, Declaration on (1942), 198

German War Crimes, Allied Declaration on (1942), 116

Germany, 9, 10, 13; World War II, 7, 14, 15, 17, 26, 27, 31–32, 36, 37, 43, 44, 47, 48, 54, 59–60, 61, 160, 167, 207, 301, 343, 344, 391–392, 448; subject of postwar study groups, 39, 223, 271, 367, 368–371, 393; postwar treatment, 71, 104, 116, 187, 189, 194, 198, 201, 232, 272, 287, 337, 365, 368–371, 423; partitioning, 127, 130, 138, 188, 244, 554–557; surrender policy, 127, 228, 229; political reorganization, 558–560

Germany, Cabinet Committee on, 369

Germany, Informal Policy Committee on, 370, 371

Germany, Interdivisional Country Committee on, 177, 194, 198, 221, 273, 369

Good-neighbor policy, 11

Great Britain, 8, 9, 10; prosecution of World War II, 7, 15, 17, 26, 27, 30, 31, 32, 36, 43, 44, 48, 59, 160, 161, 162, 234, 344, 345; Atlantic Charter (*see* Atlantic Charter); United Nations Declaration, 62; Eden mission to Moscow, 62–63, 71, 102; Treaty of Alliance with Soviet Union, 71, 102; First Quebec

Index of Persons

[Of the Americans mentioned in this book, only those directly participating in postwar preparation are herein listed.]

Acheson, Dean G., 1, 54n, 182n; member, Advisory Committee on Post-War Foreign Policy, 64, 75, 78, 81, 88, 92, 135, 136, 143; international conference and organization work, 137, 144, 145, 184, 205, 242n, 243, 384, 403, 408, 412, 421n, 437; member, Taylor Committee and Committee on Coordination of Economic Policy Work, 139, 140, 144, 180, 181; meetings of Cabinet Committee, 142; member, Policy Committee and Post-War Programs Committee, 209n, 210; Chairman, Executive Committee on Economic Foreign Policy and Liberated Areas Committee, 219, 224; increased responsibilities, 348, 349, 350, 350n; statement on trade policy, 359–360

Adams, J. Wesley, Jr., 419

Allen, Edgar, 225

Allen, George V., 210

Alling, Paul H., 97, 119n, 209n, 210, 296, 419n

Appleby, Paul H., 77, 78, 81, 135, 136, 139, 144, 145, 184, 191

Arends, Leslie C., 267, 324, 381, 413

Armour, Norman, 209n, 210, 279n, 399, 400

Armstrong, Elizabeth H., 147n, 415n

Armstrong, Hamilton Fish, 4, 19; member, Advisory Committee on Post-War Foreign Policy, 64, 73, 78, 82, 92, 97, 98, 108, 114, 117, 125, 146, 147; Special Assistant with rank of Minister in London, 229; Special Adviser to Secretary of State, 350; San Francisco Conference, 417, 432, 437, 442

Atherton, Ray, 75, 92, 97, 117, 125, 147, 188

Auchincloss, James C., 260

Austin, Warren R., 74, 97, 124, 259, 263, 264, 380, 384, 404, 412

Bailey, Josiah, W., 356

Balabanis, Homer P., 147

Ball, Joseph H., 267, 319, 324, 381, 413

Ball, M. Margaret, 119n, 249, 415n

Ballantine, Joseph W., 119n, 209n, 210, 296, 329, 419

Bard, Ralph A., 292, 370

Barkley, Alben W., 259, 263, 323, 380, 384, 412

Barrett, Frank A., 260

Bartlett, Alice C., 155, 420n

Batt, William L., 354

Bean, Louis, H., 77, 81, 92, 135, 136, 139n, 142

Bell, Daniel W., 141

Bell, M. Kathleen, 402n

Belt, Guillermo, 405

Berdahl, Clarence A., 415n

Berezhkov, Valentin M., 304, 305, 307

Berle, Adolf A., Jr., member, Advisory Committee on Problems of Foreign Relations and Interdepartmental Group to Consider Post-War Economic Problems and Policies, 20, 22, 29; international conferences, 33n, 185, 240, 356, 403, 404; member, Advisory Committee on Post-War Foreign Policy, 64, 75, 78, 81, 82, 86, 90, 92, 96, 97, 98, 99, 114, 117, 135, 136, 147; member, Taylor Committee and Committee on Coordination of Economic Policy Work, 131, 139, 140, 179, 181, 224, 243, 357; meetings of Cabinet Committee, 142; member, Policy Committee and Post-War Programs Committee, 208, 209n, 210; resignation from Department, 348

Bernstein, Bernard. 141

715

Norden, Carl F., 147

Notter, Harley A., 4, 17n, 19, 44, 53n, 176, 182, 222, 373, 386n; Advisory Committee on Post-War Foreign Policy, 78, 82, 83, 92, 97, 99, 108, 114, 117, 118, 125, 139, 147n, 467; Assistant Chief, Division of Special Research, 154, 155; Chief, Division of Political Studies, 157; Committee on Special Studies, 158; Informal Political Agenda Group and International Organization Group, 170, 171, 248; Policy Committee and Post-War Programs Committee, 209n, 210; Chief, Division of International Security and Organization, 216; Working Security Committee, 225; Dumbarton Oaks Conversations, 293, 295, 307, 314, 315, 316, 329, 332; adviser, Office of Special Political Affairs, 351; Mexico City Conference, 404, 404n; work on trusteeship, 387, 429, 432, 434; San Francisco Conference, 417, 436, 437

O'Konski, Alvin E., 260
Olds, Leland, 78, 180
Olive, James F., Jr., 77, 125, 132
Orekhov, Feodor T., 304

Padelford, Norman J., 176, 303, 415n, 424, 426
Parra Pérez, Caracciolo, 405
Parran, Thomas, 144, 145, 205n
Pasvolsky, Leo, 4, 40, 54n; Special Assistant to Secretary of State, 19; proposal for and direction of research in postwar field, 19, 41–42, 53, 152, 154, 156, 157, 158; member, Advisory Committee on Problems of Foreign Relations, 20, 22, 45, 462; Chairman, Interdepartmental Group to Consider Post-War Economic Problems and Policies, 29; international conferences, 33n, 143, 184, 195, 242n, 403, 405; member and Executive Director, Advisory Committee on Post-War Foreign Policy, 58–59, 65, 75, 78, 80, 81, 82, 83, 92, 97, 107, 108, 114, 117, 124, 131, 132, 135, 136, 157, 464n; member, Taylor Committee and Committee on Coordination of Economic Foreign Policy, 139, 140, 181, 191; meetings of Cabi-

net Committee, 141, 142; member, Political Planning Committee, 156n, 158; member, Informal Political Agenda Group and International Organization Group, 169, 170, 188, 248, 249, 268; Chairman, Interdivisional Committee on Finance, 184; member, Policy Committee and Post-War Programs Committee, 209n, 210, 211, 216–217; Director, Advisory Council on Post-War Foreign Policy, 214n; international organization and security preparation, 216, 222, 253, 256, 274, 275, 349, 350, 352, 373, 381, 386, 412; Dumbarton Oaks Conversations, 291, 292, 293, 295, 297, 298, 299, 302n, 305, 307, 308, 309, 311, 312, 316, 326, 331, 332; handling of "open questions," 375, 376, 377, 384, 424; work on trusteeship problems, 387, 388, 389, 390, 429; San Francisco Conference, 414, 415, 417, 432, 434, 435, 436, 437, 439n, 442, 443, 449n

Paul, Arthur, 224
Pence, H. L., 77, 125, 132
Pepper, Claude, 75, 180
Perkins, Frances, 78, 139, 180, 224, 240
Perkins, Milo, 29n, 77, 139
Peterson, J. Hardin, 75, 180
Pfankuchen, Llewellyn, 125, 415n
Phelps, Vernon L., 147
Pierson, Warren Lee, 29n, 143n, 405
Pius XII, Pope, 19, 20, 28
Potter, Margaret H., 53
Poulson, Norris, 260
Power, Thomas F., Jr., 415n
Poynton, A. H., 303
Pratt, John L., 232
Preuss, Lawrence, 115, 155, 176, 249, 295, 419, 424, 426
Preuss, Pauline Reinsch, 125, 249, 275, 303, 415n
Pu Hsueh-feng, 330, 332

Rabaut, Louis C., 418
Radius, Walter A., 135, 136n, 139
Ramspeck, Robert, 267, 324, 381, 413
Rayburn, Sam, 267, 324, 381, 413
Raynor, G. Hayden, 297, 312, 375, 381, 412, 415, 420, 432, 437, 439n, 440n, 442
Reber, James Q., 219
Reber, Samuel, 97, 125